Urban Geography

Urban Geography

A First Approach

DAVID T. HERBERT

Professor of Geography
University College of Swansea

and

COLIN J. THOMAS

Lecturer in Geography
University College of Swansea

1807 (JW) 1982

175 YEARS OF PUBLISHING

JOHN WILEY & SONS

Chichester · New York · Brisbane · Toronto · Singapore

Library of Congress Cataloging in Publication Data:

Herbert, David T.
  Urban geography.

  Includes index.
  1.   Cities and towns.   2.   Anthropo-geography.
  I. Thomas, Colin J.   II.   Title.
  GF125.H47   307.7′6   81-16041
                          AACR2
  ISBN 0 471 10137 0 (cloth)
  ISBN 0 471 10138 9 (paper)

British Library Cataloguing in Publication Data:

Herbert, David T.
  Urban geography
  1.   Cities and towns
  2.   Anthropogeography
  I. Title   II. Thomas, Colin J.
  910′.091732   GF125

  ISBN 0 471 10137 0 (cloth)
  ISBN 0 471 10138 9 (paper)

Photosetting by Thomson Press (India) Ltd., New Delhi, and printed in the United States of America by Vail-Ballou Press, Inc., Binghamton, N. Y.

For

Tonwen and Megan

Contents

Preface

The teaching of urban geography has become an important component of degree schemes in Geography and has also found a place at earlier stages of the educational system as both schools and examination boards accept the value of achieving a better understanding of the urban environments in which most of us live. This book is designed to provide an introduction to the sub-discipline as part of the wider geographical curriculum and also to demonstrate ways in which geographers are contributing to the more general, interdisciplinary field of urban studies. As with all texts, this book will reveal the biases and predispositions of its authors and these will be elaborated and discussed in greater detail in the first chapter. The text contains, however, those topics which are judged to be the most significant at this point in time and it seeks to analyse and discuss these in greater depth than is perhaps common in introductory books of this kind. If the choice lies between a wide-ranging 'omnibus' approach which aims to be fully comprehensive but sacrifices detail at the expense of coverage and a more selective approach which focuses in depth on a smaller number of themes, then we have opted consciously for the latter. The book does not seek to be dismissive of any of the tried and trusted urban geographical topics of study but it does recognize that there are some traditional concerns which no longer warrant the kind of prominence which they have previously been given.

Chapter 1 has the roles of setting the context for the book as a whole and also of dealing fairly briefly with some of the older concepts, theories, and modes of analysis. Following this introduction, Chapter 2 takes a wide-ranging look at some of the conceptual bases of urban geography and is written in the belief that urban geography must now be set firmly in the context of the philosophies of the social sciences. Although this survey cannot be comprehensive and must necessarily oversimplify some complex methodological issues, some of the main influences upon an emerging subdiscipline can be recognized. It is likely that such philosophical frames of reference will be of increasing importance and the 'blueprint' for the future development of urban geography is becoming apparent.

This book was conceived of as a joint authorship and has, in its writing, fulfilled these purposes. Colin Thomas had the primary tasks of contributing on interurban and urban system themes and he is the author of Chapters 4, 5, and 6. David Herbert has written the remaining chapters which both establish the methodological and historical bases of urban geography and consider the city as a territory with a particular focus on the social perspective. At Swansea, Geinor B. Lewis undertook the considerable cartographic task of preparing the illustrations and added his own interpretations as well as his technical skills to that part of the exercise. Mrs Mary Owens typed the manuscript with great efficiency and Alan Cutliffe provided photographic assistance. Our families have had to put up with the byproducts of our commitment to a major piece of writing and we are grateful, as always, to them for their forbearance.

DAVID HERBERT
COLIN THOMAS
June 1981

List of Figures

Chapter 1

An Introduction to Modern Urban Geography

The student contemplating a first approach to urban geography faces questions of definition and content of a kind common to all new fields of study. There is the question of how *urban* is defined and of what constitutes a *city*. There is the question of stating the precise nature of *urban geography*, its objectives, methodologies and place in relation to the wider discipline of which it is part. Urban geography may be easily distinguished *within* geography by the phenomenon it studies—the town or city—but a further question is then raised on its distinctiveness *vis-à-vis* other social science disciplines which are also concerned with this same phenomenon. Increasingly, there are also questions on the relevance of a field of study to issues in modern society, does it have a concern with matters which are of significance in the real world? Although the proper answers to these questions can only emerge by detailed discussion and example, one purpose of this introductory chapter is to provide at least some guidelines and working definitions on issues of this kind. A further aim is to provide an indication of the strategy which has been adopted in the compilation of this book. Urban geography is still a relatively young branch of geography but it has experienced a considerable amount of change since the early 1960s. The type of urban geography studied before this point in time can almost be classed as 'traditional' and was certainly far narrower in its scope than the subject as it is now practised. The main emphasis in this book is upon modern urban geography and the directions which it is now taking but some of the main concerns of the 'traditional' approach need to be identified and summarized. Where earlier modes of analysis have continuing significance in modern urban geography, this will be reflected in the chapters which follow.

Any text will, through its organization, emphases and sins of omission, betray the values of its authors and their ideas on what the content of a subject should be. This book is no exception to this rule and a number of initial statements can be made which both indicate and justify some of the emphases.

Firstly, although some evidence of urban studies by geographers can be traced to the early origins of the discipline, there is little written before the 1950s which has any serious impact on the present-day practice of urban geography. Notable exceptions to this generalization, such as central place theory, are few and far between, and there is no serious attempt in this text to trace the development of urban geography over time.

1

Secondly, although the traditional division of urban geography into those studies which are concerned with the city as a *point* or *location* and those concerned with the city as *area*, has continuing value and is used in the organization of this text, the fact that recent urban geography research has tended to emphasize the internal structure of the city is reflected in the overall balance of chapters. The more established focal concerns of urban geographers with city as location, such as population-size distributions, functional classifications, and central place systems are discussed although these have received limited research attention in the 1970s. Other important themes concerned with systems of cities and city–regional interaction have been most vigorously developed in the closely related 'branches' of regional science and economic geography. In short, then, the text does not attempt an equal balance between interurban and intraurban studies, though the former are well represented in several major chapters.

Thirdly, although Smith (1977, p. 13) is technically correct when he suggests that 'urban geography' is, in a sense, regional geography at the urban scale, its content has in fact been far more selective and this again is reflected in this text. Although early, descriptive town studies included sections on physical geography, urban geography is now a branch of human geography. Further, the focus of interest *within* a human geography of the city has shifted from one which was initially historical, to an economic dominance and subsequently to the social and political emphasis which tends to dominate modern studies. Shifts of this kind have not generally involved the discarding of former concerns but urban geography has always been a more specialized field of study than the term 'regional geography at an urban scale' implies.

A fourth assertion has more of the nature of an apology. This text, like so many of its predecessors, has a strong ethnocentric bias and draws most of its examples from the Anglo-American literature. Third World case studies are developed in some chapters and there are also attempts to demonstrate the comparative qualities, at a global scale, of general processes such as urbanization, but the emphasis is upon the Western city. There are collections of essays (Jones, 1975) which are centrally concerned with global patterns of urbanization but these serve an essentially different purpose.

These are all limiting assertions in the sense that they indicate themes which the text will develop in somewhat greater detail than others. In summary the emphases are upon modern urban geography as it has been developed in relation to Western societies in general, and Britain and North America in particular. The emphases selected represent the interests of the authors and, to a large extent, the consensus evident within the academic community upon what is the proper content and concern of urban geography.

ON DEFINING URBAN GEOGRAPHY

Some definitional issues can now be discussed. Firstly, the question of defining urban geography as a branch of human geography can be considered in rather more detail. This idea of a branch or subdiscipline is important as it is indicative of the fact that the methodology which gives urban geography its distinctiveness in relation to other social sciences which study the same phenomenon—the city—is drawn from a wider disciplinary context:

Geography is generally accepted by its practitioners as 'that discipline that seeks to describe and interpret the variable character from place to place of the earth as the world of man'; urban geography attempts such description and interpretation for those parts of the earth's surface classified as urban places (Johnston, 1980, p. 13).

The sentiment involved in this definition is undoubtedly correct. Human geography has the prime responsibility of defining purposes and methodologies; its subdisciplines or branches apply these to the specific phenomena which form their focus of interest. As already recognized, urban geography has some particular problems in so far as its phenomenon is an *area* rather than a *systematic theme*. Figure 1.1 demonstrates its position between the specialized systematic branches of geography on the one hand and regional geography or area studies on the other. As indicated earlier, the danger of a catholicity of interest associated with an area is present, but urban geography, by narrowing down its mainstream research interests to a smaller number of themes, has tended to assume more of the character of a systematic study. Of relevance to

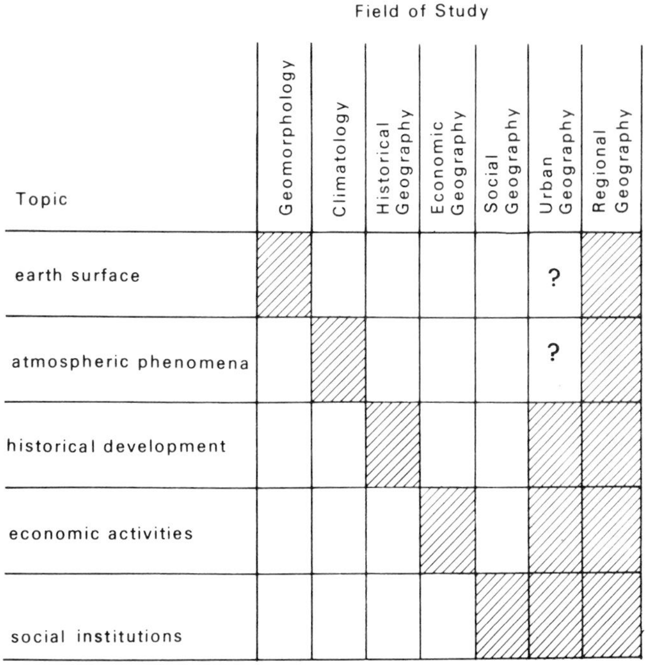

Field of Study

Topic	Geomorphology	Climatology	Historical Geography	Economic Geography	Social Geography	Urban Geography	Regional Geography
earth surface	///					?	///
atmospheric phenomena		///				?	///
historical development			///			///	///
economic activities				///		///	///
social institutions					///	///	///

Figure 1.1   Urban geography as a subdiscipline. The focus upon an *area* allows a number of systematic or topical approaches

this issue is Frey's (1973) discussion of the nature of study divisions within geography and his comparison of regional and systematic approaches. He suggests that the raw material of geography is formed of both single elements and assemblages and that these may be studied *systematically* by topic or *regionally* by area. As all data have initially to be collected from particular areas and all hypotheses have to be tested in specific areas, it follows that all geographical studies have both areal and systematic qualities and are:

located along a line which at one end is labelled 'area' and where the dominant purpose of study is to illuminate the region, and the other end labelled 'topic' where the study is very largely systematic and draws on one or a variety of regional examples merely for illustration (Frey, 1973, p. 121).

Within this framework and along this 'continuum', something of the position of urban geography can be understood. Its focus of study, the city, is an 'assemblage' which is also an 'area'; on both these considerations it holds affinities with regional geography. Its methodology, however, is typically focused on a small number of topical themes and could be more accurately described as systematic in character. Those urban studies which approximate regional geographies of specific cities (Jones, 1960; Kerr and Spelt, 1965) have become increasingly exceptional and the dominant focus is clearly upon the city *in* and *as* a socioeconomic–political system.

Given this focus, a number of definitions of social geography provide strong guidelines towards the nature and content of modern urban geography:

(1) the processes and patterns involved in an understanding of socially-defined populations in their spatial setting .... The social geographer is thus concerned with 'the lesser divisions of cities, town and country', which ... are likely to become more and more sharply differentiated according to *social* criteria (Pahl, 1965, p. 81).

(2) the study of the areal (spatial) patterns and functional relations of social groups in the context of their social environment; the internal structure and external relations of the nodes of social activity, and the articulation of various channels of social communication (Buttimer, 1968, p. 142).

(3) Social geography involves the understanding of the patterns which arise from the use social groups make of space as they see it, and of the processes involved in making and changing such patterns (Jones, 1975, p. 7).

These three definitions are too emphatically social to suit our purposes but still reflect the real content more accurately than the catholic type of perspective evident, for example, in Johnston's definition. For this text, a compromise position is preferred:

(4) Urban geography studies the patterns and processes which occur among and within urban places; the objective form which these take, the subjective manner in which they are interpreted, and their mode of origin at both local and societal scales. The roles of urban geography are *descriptive*, in the sense that they seek to depict accurately the spatial expressions of urban conditions, *explanatory*, in that they need to investigate cause and effect relationships, and *evaluative* in that they need both to recognize the inequities arising from the spatial allocation of scarce resources and to identify those

alternative states which might more closely satisfy the criteria of efficiency and/or social justice.

Two further points need to be made in respect of this definition. The first of these involves contexts. As a branch of human geography, urban geography must be defined within the context of a wider discipline and here Pattison's (1964) classification of the four traditions of geography—spatial, area, man–land, and earth science—is useful. Of these the spatial tradition is firmly involved with interest in patterns, locations and spatial interaction; the area tradition is also dominant with the focus on territory, regionalizations, and the essence of place; and man–land has some relevance if it is translated into man–urban environment interaction. Only the earth science tradition has no effective role as urban studies have been contained within the development of human geography. A second context is shown by Figure 1.2 which relates urban geography to other social sciences interested in the analysis of cities. The common philosophical bases which urban geography shares with other social sciences are only presently being properly recognized and serve to emphasize the strong bonds which exist among different perspectives upon the city. The special qualities of urban geographical interest and the methodology employed to study these provide the subject with its distinctiveness but as geographers examine the origins of patterns and processes at greater depth and see the city as the spatial manifestation of deeper-lying social forces, they are drawn into further contact with other disciplines and—for some purposes—towards the goal of a unified social science.

The definition offered for urban geography begs one further definitional question: What is urban? (or) What constitutes an urban place? Whereas many people have intuitive and reasonably accurate answers to these questions, 'urban' remains an elusive concept to pin down with any degree of detail. Sizes and densities of settlements form two of the more common 'rule of thumb' criteria and the former has been widely used in official statistical returns, such

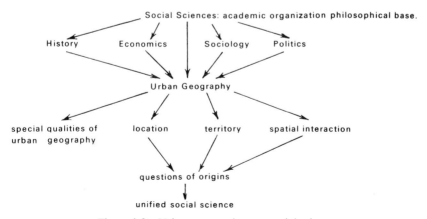

Figure 1.2   Urban geography as a social science

as national censuses, to designate particular places as urban. Some examples
of this usage and of other attempts to define urban will be reviewed.

WHAT IS URBAN?

Population size

Undeniably, urban places are *larger*, so the point at which the rural village
becomes a town or city should be identifiable at some point along the
population-size continuum of settlements. Difficulties arise because this *point*
seems to vary over both time and space. For several Scandinavian countries,
including Denmark and Sweden, any settlement which has more than 200
inhabitants is classed as urban in the national census; at least 1000 inhabitants
forms the required threshold in Canada, but 2500 is the minimum for the United
States. Many countries impose much higher thresholds on resident population
before a classification of urban can be obtained; Greece, for example, stipulates
10,000 inhabitants, whilst Japan requires 30,000. From examples such as these,
the diversity is initially confusing, but on a global scale there is some measure
of logic and comprehensibility. We are reminded that population-size and
indeed 'urban' may well be relative criteria which are best judged within their
societal contexts. Given the physical geography of Scandinavia, for example,
and the ways in which its settlement patterns have evolved over time, a settlement with over 200 permanent inhabitants may well be regarded as urban.
In a country like Japan, on the other hand, with a relatively limited land area
and considerable population pressure, virtually all settlements may exceed
such a low threshold and a high figure such as 30,000 may provide the only
realistic line of demarcation. By no means all of the inconsistencies in
population-size thresholds for urban can be explained in these ways, but there
are grounds for recognizing some order in the apparent diversity.

Urban functions

Most official censuses adopt a population-size definition of urban, largely in
response to the fact that it is simple and that an information base of statistics
is readily available. It is widely acknowledged, however, that there are more
telling criteria and that the unit area for which population or any other attribute
is measured is itself a critical definitional consideration. Urban places have
functions which distinguish them from rural settlements, functions that are
various but have at least two significant qualities. Firstly, they are non-
agricultural in character and, secondly, they may well be primarily concerned
with the exchange rather than with the production of goods. On the first of
these qualities, arguments revolve around notions of the 'economic base' of
a settlement or the dominant activities which are conducted within its environs.
Rural settlements possess activities but these are exclusively concerned with
land as a resource and with agricultural production. A simple definition of

urban, based upon activities, is therefore one which expresses dominance of non-agricultural functions. Such a criterion, combined with a population-size criterion, is employed in Israel, where a settlement must have in excess of two-thirds of its labour force engaged in non-agricultural work to be classed as urban. Similarly, in India, a qualification of over 75 per cent of the adult male population in non-agricultural work is used.

Reference to an 'economic-base' approach, based upon dominant activities opens up a considerable range of possible definitions of urban. It is clear that over time a large number of settlements has emerged with specialized functions which are certainly not rural and to which the term urban could properly be applied. The administrative function, often with political connotations, has one of the longest historical tenures and was frequently designated to settlements which were established to control or administer regions of a country. Greek and Roman cities are early examples of administrative/political centres in a tradition which has been carried through to modern capital cities such as Canberra, Ottawa, and Brasilia. Early urban places were often multifunctional and religion, with defence and culture amongst their primary roles. Religion has provided a key specialist function for many urban places from the religious centres of the Middle East and Southern Asia to the cathedral cities of medieval Europe. Although there were crafts and mining-dominated urban settlements in the ancient and medieval worlds (see Jacobs, 1969), the manufacturing centre only really dominated settlement evolution with the progress of the industrialization in Europe in the later eighteenth and nineteenth century. Industrialization has undoubtedly created a large number of settlements which were urban. Distinguished by size, density and dominance of industrial employment they were, in Britain at least, the new towns of the nineteenth century.

Single-function settlements, whether they are religious or cultural centres or manufacturing towns, may persist in their original roles over long periods of time. As cities develop, however, they are more likely to add to these original roles or even to replace them. These are changes which may well have the effect of consolidating urban status.

The activities conducted in a settlement are clearly of importance in defining its character and the economic-base approach has a valid contribution to make in this context. A stronger line of enquiry relating to a definition of urban, in terms of economic functions, however, has focused upon the functions of distribution and exchange and the marketing role of urban places. Pirenne (1925) in his well-known study of the emergence of urban settlement in medieval Europe, placed great emphasis upon the town as a market place; his central thesis, as Jones (1966) suggests, was that the city is a 'community of merchants'. This emphasis upon the economic functions of marketing and exchange, became explicit in the ways in which urban geographers defined central places and the urban 'hierarchy'. Dickinson (1964) emphasized the roles of urban places as institutional centres for a surrounding territory or hinterland; the demand for services calls the urban settlement into being and once established it extends a network of functional relationships over the region. Work stimulated by Christäller's (1933) central place theory, made this nodality or centrality status of urban places explicit. Most of the empirical work on central place studies has focused upon economic services, particularly retail and wholesale trade, which are the most tangible and easily measured. Urban geographers and others, however, have retained an awareness of the significance of non-economic institutions and services in affording urban status to settlements; as Mumford (1938) has suggested, the city should not be over-regarded as an aggregate of economic functions; it is above all a seat of institutions in the service of the region, it is art, culture, and political purposes. It was in these latter roles that early cities could be most clearly identified.

Urbanism

A further strand in the definitional debate has developed in the context of sociology and is often associated with Louis Wirth's (1938) statement on urbanism as a way of life; a statement which continues to attract discussion and elaboration. Wirth argued that urban places can be distinguished by the lifestyles of their inhabitants. Affected by qualities of population size, density and heterogeneity which typify 'urban' settlements, the 'urbanite' becomes distinguishable from the 'ruralite'. Relative anonymity and a paucity of face-to-face relationships were seen as the hallmarks of an urban lifestyle, and this type of hypothesis found support in the theories of contrast which were developed in anthropological studies. Tonnies, Weber, and Redfield (see Reissman, 1964) were amongst those who postulated rural–urban contrasts such as sacred–secular, traditional–rational, and personal–impersonal. Such contrasts cannot be sustained in empirical studies and the general concept now has limited credibility. Lewis (1966) made a detailed re-examination of Redfield's work in Tepoztlan and found that factors other than place were of central relevance in understanding societal differences. There is, suggests Lewis, a 'culture of poverty' which unites poor urbanites and rural peasants throughout the Third World. Other studies have confirmed this and Abu-Lughod (1961) has shown that particular districts of Cairo were populated by migrants from specific rural areas, whose values and lifestyles, derived from those areas, were perpetuated in an urban setting. Differences were less between urban and rural than between rich and poor.

These studies are frequently quoted in the literature, but the evidence from Third World countries on this issue remains somewhat ambiguous. Clearly there are no consistent, measurable, abrupt changes of attitudes and values between 'urban' and 'rural' populations, and in many ways the vast 'armies' of poor urban dwellers have more in common with their rural counterparts than with the professional and business elites who occupy the same cities. The more telling question, however, is whether poor urbanites in, for example, one Latin American city begin to resemble poor urbanites in another more closely than the rural peasants of the same region. There is some sense in believing that this may be so. The whole rhythm and content of life in urban places is different from that in rural areas and this difference may well deepen with length of urban residence. Key factors in this process include the mechanisms of urban–rural relationships, the efficacy of transport and communication networks and the form of spatial diffusion processes; in many third world situations these factors may well operate to the effect that urban places are places apart and their populations, over time, become distinctive.

Critiques of Wirth's urbanism and of the theories of contrast have followed rather different paths in studies of Europe and North America. Numerous studies (Gans, 1962; Young and Willmott, 1957) have demonstrated that social cohesiveness and face-to-face relationships exist within localities of cities; urban neighbourhoods or communities serve as the territories for such interaction. As general features, therefore, anonymity and impersonality do not serve to distinguish urban places. It is now also evident that the progress of Western urbanization has reduced urban–rural differences to a point at which they become almost meaningless. Transport and communication networks have become so efficient that a place of residence loses some of its significance as a formulative influence upon attitudes, values and behaviour. Certainly some traditional differences remain and there continue to be residual and distinctive rural enclaves, but urbanization has generally become a pervasive societal process. A related and more general point, which will be pursued in a different context, is that all settlements are merely outcomes of more general societal forces; the form of the outcome is less important that the nature of the forces.

Evidence of lifestyle differences between urban and rural places is particularly ambiguous. There are qualifications to be made over both space and time which suggest that contrasts may be more real at some stages of societal development than at others. Urban–rural differences are blurred and almost meaningless in some advanced Western societies; a similar position seems to exist, though for different reasons, in some Third World societies which have experienced recent and large-scale rural-to-urban migration. There are points along the continuum of urban development, however, at which urban places, in some generalized ways, do exhibit distinctive lifestyle characteristics.

Urban places

These various approaches to urban definition have not brought us to a consensus view; with hindsight it was almost inevitable that the result would be inconclusive. The meaning and reality of urban and urban places will vary considerably over both time and space; a town or city is a physical concentration of people and buildings, but it also has economic, social and political qualities which are specific to the cultural context within which it emerges. Perhaps the strongest contemporary focus in definitional terms is less concerned with defining 'urban' as a quality than with defining 'urban place' as an entity. Two central objectives of this approach are, firstly, to recognize the reality of urban *regions*, comprising city and hinterland, as meaningful functional units and, secondly, to provide a framework of standardized urban units which will make the tasks of comparative analysis easier, Simmons and Bourne (1978) demonstrate that by the mid-1970s, most countries had adopted some notion of an 'extended' city to measure urbanization. This, defined normally on the bases of minimum population size, density and journey-to-work area, is labelled a standard metropolitan statistical area (SMSA) in the United States; a census metropolitan area (CMA) in Canada; and a labour-market area in Sweden.

The concept of the extended urban area has been pioneered by the United States Bureau of Census since 1910 and its modern definition as SMSA (see Berry, Goheen, and Goldstein, 1968) summarizes the key features of recent research and comprises:

1. Either one central city with a total population of 50,000 or more, or two contiguous cities constituting a single community with a combined population of 50,000 and a minimum population of 15,000 for the smaller of the two.
2. The remainder of the county to which the central city belongs.
3. Adjacent counties, if

   (a) 75 per cent or more of the labour force is non-agricultural;
   (b) at least 15 per cent of workers in the outlying county work in the central county, or 25 per cent of workers in that county live in the central county, i.e. there are significant journey-to-work links between areas;
   (c) at least 50 per cent of residents in a county meet density requirements *or* non-agricultural employment thresholds.

This definition (see Simmons and Bourne, 1978) has been stated in some detail because it does include measures of population size, centrality and economic functions. It is standardized across the United States so comparative analysis is possible and it forms a useful study-base because it does approximate the services and labour catchment area of the central city.

The British equivalent of the SMSA, the Standard Metropolitan Labour Area (SMLA) (see Drewett, Goddard, and Spence, 1974) has no official standing or usage. It consists of a 'core' together with a 'metropolitan ring' and is classified as an SMLA if the combined population exceeds 70,000. Cores are primarily defined as areas with job densities over 5 per acre (13.75 per hectare) and total numbers of jobs in excess of 20,000; they may be individual or contiguous local authority areas with a set of rules to cover exceptional cases. A metropolitan ring consists of contiguous local authorities from which at least 15 per cent of the labour force travel to work in the core. Although the criteria differ, the SMSA principle of defining an 'extended city' remains. Global surveys exist, and the International Population and Urban Research Units has adopted an SMA definition of at least 100,000 population in an urban region which comprises core and hinterland, with at least 65 per cent of the labour force engaged in non-agricultural activities. This definition allows international comparisons on degree of urbanization and urban population growth and also defines metropolitan regions within each country.

These recent researches are concerned with defining urban places rather than what is urban. They are furthermore concerned with larger urban places and the thresholds adopted exclude many small towns and cities. It is, however, a line of research which has witnessed high levels of cooperation between academic researchers and various departments of government which have a common interest in monitoring urban change and in providing standardized recording units for comparative analysis. Whereas the question of defining urban can remain a topic for academic debate with no pressing need for resolution, the question of defining urban places, despite the fact that it contains similar imponderables, has practical implications and of necessity *some* answer must be found.

THE DEVELOPMENT OF URBAN GEOGRAPHY

The student of urban geography need not go back very far in time to establish the basis of the subject. Whereas it is true that Strabo had something to say about cities, he also had something to say about most other things. For James (1972), von Humboldt, who died in 1859, was the last of the 'universal scholars', actors on an academic stage at a time when it was pointless to distinguish between those who were geographers and those who were not. Several reviews of the early development of urban geography (Berry and Horton, 1970; Carter, 1972) have identified more specific examples of early urban studies. These initial works were strongly descriptive and amounted to little more than observations on the general characteristics of urban places. They have the character of town-guides rather than theory-related pieces of academic work.

From these tenuous beginnings, urban geography has become in the third quarter of the twentieth century, one of the most popular elements of geographical study. Whereas in the early 1950s a separate course on urban geography at an English-speaking university was quite exceptional, today the *absence* of such a course would be equally remarkable. Although the real momentum for this change can be placed in the 1950s and 1960s, the first steps towards the establishment of an academic subdiscipline can be discerned much earlier in the twentieth century. For Carter (1972) it was the replacement of description by *interpretation* of location which laid the foundations for urban geography to develop as a special study. From the early pioneering works, a form of urban geographical study which centred around the *analysis* of site and situation became established. Although this basic format was soon subject to advance and modification, it provided a schema for elementary town study by geographers which was to persist over several decades. Indeed the style and methodology of this form of analysis remains a basic building block in preliminary stages of the teaching of urban geography. The more general concept of environmentalism, with its emphasis on man–land relationships, is strongly mirrored in this type of approach.

This mode of analysis had its critics, however; Crowe (1938) used town studies as examples of geographers concentrating upon inanimate objects of landscape rather than upon people and movement. This type of criticism was to gather force and become overwhelming in the 1960s. Site-situation studies had an associated emphasis upon the evolutionary form of urban growth and became encapsulated in the development of urban morphology as an approach to urban analysis. Urban morphology, perhaps the only truly 'indigenous' line of evolution within urban geography, developed as an analysis of the built fabric of the city and of the ways in which it had evolved over time.

Urban morphology

More traditional studies of the sites and situations of urban settlements were also typically concerned with the historical growth phases and ways in which these could be related to urban form and morphology. Regular street lines of early Roman settlement, for example, could sometimes be discerned as nuclei to which less well-ordered medieval quarters were subsequently added. During the late 1940s and 1950s some British geographers moulded this type of perspective into what can be termed the urban morphological approach. Their first task during this period was to introduce a more specifically geographical methodology into a type of study which had been dominated by essentially historical approaches. Smailes (1955) developed the concept of 'townscape' which in its simplest terms is the urban equivalent of landscape and comprises those visible forms of environment which may be recorded and classified. The three main components of townscape are street-plan or layout, architectural style of buildings and their design, and land-use; of these, plan and land-use have been the most generally studied by geographers, and the relationship between town plan and building design on the one hand and land-use on the other–the form–function relationship–has prompted useful research. Many cities display considerable internal variety of building-types, often dating from specific historical periods, and it is this diversity of townscapes within individual cities which formed the focus of most morphological analyses. There are cities, however, which because their urban development was contained within or dominated by a particular time-period, have an overall plan or grand design. The planned towns of early medieval Europe, the *bastides* with their regular grid form, offer one example of these, the more ornate and aesthetically designed Baroque towns of the later Renaissance period form another. There are more recent examples of uniform city plans affecting wide areas. Stanislawski (1946) traces the origin and spread of the grid-iron town in the United States with its regular rectangular forms and right-angled intersections. Modern 'new towns' in various parts of the world are not unified by a single design but are all products of preconceived blueprints which specify the locations in space of various land-uses and the design forms which they assume.

All these examples of an overall plan involve a high level of central control and an 'authority' able to specify design characteristics to a high level of detail. Planning of this kind has often affected quarters within cities, such as the colonial districts of some Indian cities and the Baroque areas of larger European capitals. In other instances, uniform historical imprints upon townscape emerge less from the imposition of some overall plan than from less organized common practices and shared values of like individuals. The Georgian squares of London and Dublin and their equivalents elsewhere are of this type of genesis.

During the most active period of urban morphology, much of the emphasis was upon the classification of subregions within individual cities and the relating of urban growth phases to these. Most of the townscape studies took this form and Carter (1965) provided a large number of case studies as part of his more general survey of Welsh towns. Smailes (1955) was particularly interested in identifying broad classes of morphological divisions which could have more general application to British cities, and did in fact suggest a model. His categories of morphology, however, such as 'terrace-ribbing' and 'villa-studding' were broad and imprecise and had no more than a general descriptive value. Conzen (1960, 1962) developed the technique of town-plan analysis which involved a much higher order of detail and greater focus upon the need to relate form to process and to seek generalizations.

Conzen argued that of the three components of townscape—plan, archi-tectural style, and land use—the former is the most resistant to change whereas the latter is the most dynamic. Discord between form and function will occur as changing land-uses produce the need for functions to adapt to built-forms which were originally designed for different purposes. In the original case study of Alnwick (Conzen, 1960), a central thrust of town-plan analysis was that of matching plan-elements, with their associated architectural features, to specific time-periods of urban growth. Town plan analysis included concepts which were explicitly process rather than pattern-oriented and which provided bases for generalizations. The burgage cycle concept had reference to a specific form of land-holding system and traced the development of a parcel of land through institutive, repletive, climax and recessive stages. Each stage described the extent to which urban building occupance affected the parcel of land. The fixation line concept recognizes the limits to the urban built-up area which can be identified during a still-stand period in the urban growth process. Fringe-belts are zones of land, beyond fixation lines, which become locations for those urban functions which require large amounts of space and peripherality rather than centrality. Typical fringe-belt functions in the modern city are cemeteries, golf-courses and public utilities, but each historical growth-phase tends to be marked by its own fringe-belt with a typical cluster of functional uses. As urban growth proceeds, following a period of still-stand, former fringe-belts are engulfed within the larger city and remain as recogniz-able, though fossilized, components of urban land-use. Conzen's work undoub-tedly added an extra dimension to urban morphological analysis by the early 1960s which was characterized both by its depth of detail and its search for recurrent phenomena. Along with the rest of urban morphology, town-plan analysis became subject to severe criticism and disregard by the 'new' geographers of the 1960s who were more interested in functional classifications and the economic bases of urban systems. In the best-known critique of this time, Garrison (1962) characterized urban morphology as mainly descriptive, lacking in good measurement techniques and failing to develop a general theory. It was a critique which contemporaneously at least did not produce convincing counter-arguments.

Since the early 1960s there has been continued interest in urban morphology along a limited number of fronts. The more significant developments have been those which reduce the 'isolation' of the urban morphological approach and seek to integrate its concepts with other dimensions of the urban system. Whitehand (1967) has continued to develop some of Conzen's ideas and focuses on the nature of urban fringe-belts. He has investigated the competition for fringe-belt sites and the way in which the outcomes of this competition have to be seen in the context of building cycles and the activities of house-builders. Institutional land-uses are likely to be most successful in obtaining sites during times of housing slump, and a cycle of booms and slumps in house-building will be reflected by zones of varying admixtures of residential and institutional land-use. Davies (1968) has developed analysis of the form–function relationship in which he shows that morphological adaptations can be used as indicators of functional changes in commercial streets. Watson's (1959) study of Halifax, Nova Scotia provides a clearly argued example of the influence of relict morphologies and their associated land-uses, upon the subsequent development of an urban area. Bourne (1967), from a different contextual background, argues for the need to recognize the effect of physical structures, real-estate and inherited urban fabric upon modern functional change in Toronto's inner city.

Recent interest in 'fabric effects' or the way in which inherited morphology can affect modern land-use has given greater focus to the architectural or building style component of the morphological approach. Social geographers have found the availability of older housing of a particular form to be an important influence upon the founding and expansion of immigrant areas in British cities. The impact of gentrification is similarly affected by the location of housing-types most amenable to renovation and upgrading. House-type studies in the older morphological tradition were often guilty of adopting gross classifications and paying too little regard to architectural detail. Some later studies moved some way towards correcting these deficiencies. Forster (1968) used thirteen measures of house-style, including information of building material, roof material, windows and entrance styles to characterize house-types constructed in Hull between 1854 and 1914. The cul-de-sac court was identified as a dominant and recurrent type of architecture in the city during this period. This approach has been little developed and has value in identifying key features of buildings or house-types which are indicative of a particular region or time-period.

Urban morphology had an important role in the development of urban geography, especially in Britain, and provided an important impetus for the identification of a separate branch of geography during the immediate postwar period. Morphological research usefully continues and there is a more general awareness, expressed through concepts such as the fabric effect, of the need to consider the involvement of morphology in more general urban processes. Criticisms of urban morphology during the early 1960s in part explain its demise but more telling may have been the fact that urban geographers found more interesting themes to attract their research activities. Urban morphology, an indigenous geographical perspective, focused on the observable and the inanimate. Other derivative perspectives demonstrated that this was merely the framework and that the people and their activities who occupied urban space provided it with its dynamism.

Derivative sources: land economics

Ideas from land economics strongly influenced urban geographers during the 1960s, though there were often considerable time-lags between the original exposition of these ideas and their general adoption in urban geographical study. Among the more influential sets of ideas were early theories on city location, such as those of Cooley (1894) and Weber (1899) who attached central importance for urban development to the nature of routeways and nodal points in the transportation system. Again, the work on urban land-values, rents and costs within cities (Hurd, 1903) focused on accessibility and became very influential. Haig (1926) saw rent as a charge for accessibility or a saving in transport costs which involved a bidding process to determine the occupancy and use of land. Ratcliff (1949) developed the argument, and the eventual model involved the concept of bid-rent curves and their influence upon land-use patterns within the city. Under model conditions, the assumption is that the central point within the city has greatest accessibility and that from this location centrality-value will decrease in a regular manner towards the urban peripheries. An efficient land-use pattern emerges within the city as various activities compete for locations by 'bidding' at various rent levels; their bids are calculated by weighing their need for centrality against their ability to pay higher rents and the fact that increased transport costs may be incurred with distance removed from the central city.

The use that can extract the greatest return from a given site will be the successful bidder . . . from this emerges an orderly pattern of land-use spatially organized to perform most efficiently the economic functions that characterize urban life (Ratcliff, 1949, p. 369).

Figure 1.3 illustrates the bid-rent model and the way in which it can be translated into broad concentric bands of land-use within the city. Those retailing functions which have the greatest need for accessibility in order to maximize profits pay the highest rents for the most central locations. Land in such locations is normally intensively used and involves vertical building

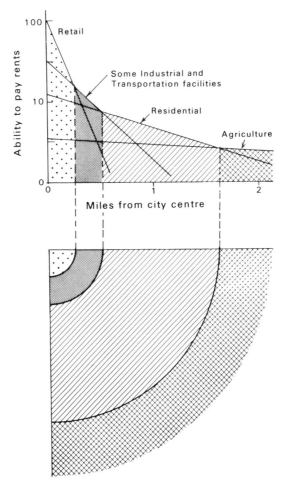

Figure 1.3 The bid-rent model and urban land-
use zones

development. Outside the retailing zone is a broader industrial/commercial zone containing functions which need centrality but cannot match the higher levels of rents and are content to settle for lower accessibility in slightly less central locations. Many activities in this zone, such as warehouses and offices, may in fact need less public accessibility and for them an optimum location has been achieved. Residential land-use occupies a large amount of urban space and involves a number of tradeoffs between land-costs, transport-costs and density. Closer to the centre, higher valued land will be occupied at high densities by groups who incur low transport costs. On the urban periphery where land is cheaper, large amounts of space may be involved per dwelling, giving lower densities, but high transport costs will be incurred. This type of model does make a number of assumptions which depart from reality, and recent empirical research has modified its interpretation in significant ways. Knos (1962) showed that the actual land-value surface of a city is more variegated than the model suggests with lesser peaks outside the central city; Yeates (1965) showed the diminishing importance of access to the central city. Land economics provided some insight into the dynamics of the urban system and were bases for spatial generalizations of an aggregate kind. These generalizations and the rules upon which they are predicated have some continuing value for urban geography.

Derivative sources: urban ecology

The Chicago school of social ecology, most closely associated with Robert Park, provided a second derivative source of concepts and ideas for urban geography. The book by Park, Burgess, and McKenzie (1925) collected some of the early work of the Chicago ecologists and had a profound and lasting influence on contemporary social sciences, though again the full impact upon urban geography was delayed significantly.

A great quality of Park and his contemporary ecologists was their first-hand knowledge about the city of Chicago. This intimate knowledge of the city and its people, based upon intensive field-work and involvement, was reflected in their many papers on the subject. Park has been described as an undisciplined empiricist, excited by the patterns and apparent explanations which he saw in city life, but his adoption of a general framework within which to study his patterns led him into a methodology which was committed to theory-building. This framework Park derived from an analogy with the biological world, and the belief that the patterns and relationships evident there could be paralleled by land-use and people within cities. This enthusiasm for a biological analogy can only really be understood in the context of the early part of this century when the appeal of Social Darwinism in particular, and the guidelines of classical economics, prompted lines of thought which found expression in many disciplines. A major attraction of the biological analogy was its totality: if offered a *gestalt* model which was simple and logical, the similarities to the biological world could everywhere be observed, measured and recorded, and each segment could be seen in its relevant place within the overall broad framework and explained by the same guiding principles.

Beyond the overall framework, biology also provided a source of other concepts and a terminology for the urban ecologists. *Symbiosis* described the most basic set of relationships and the mutual interdependence of the elements of the city. Park showed how symbiosis operated in the biological world, his best-known example being that of the humble bee and its place in the 'web of life'. McKenzie sought direct analogies within the city: 'In the struggle for existence in human groups, social organisation accommodates itself to the spatial and sustenance relationships existing among the occupants of any geographical area'. Closely allied to symbiosis was the concept of *competition*, translated into economic terms, whereby space would be allocated among alternative uses on a competitive basis. The essence of this kind of competition was that it operated at an impersonal level in a way reminiscent of the biological world. The concept of *community*, borrowed directly from biology, was applied to the city as a population group inhabiting a distinguishable geographical space and coexisting through a set of symbiotic relationships. Such a population group within the city was territorially organized and interdependent in the 'natural order' of the community. Within such a community, further symbiotic relationships and ecological processes could be identified. The *dominance* of one particular group within a community could be ascribed to its superior competitive power. *Segregation* of distinctive groups would occur within communities: 'Every area of segregation is the result of the operation of a combination of the forces of selection'. Other crucial ecological processes were those of *invasion* and *succession* which described the gradual incursion of one group into the territory of another and the eventual displacement as succession took place. Invasion and succession could be viewed as elements of a cycle which proceeded through a number of stages with, ideally, a complete change in land-use or in population type between first and last stages.

The analogy provided the framework and most of its conceptual ingredients, but there is ample evidence in the literature of urban ecology that differences between biological and human society were appreciated. It was never denied that human society had an extra dimension of cultural and traditional values not apparent in the biological world. Robert Park suggested that social organization could be studied at two levels, the *biotic* in which competition was the guiding process, and the *cultural* in which consensus and communication among members of society were the main factors. Park's notion here was that the biotic level could be studied separately as an analysis of aggregate behaviour and structure, ignoring the myriad of cultural or non-rational values which might be measurable on an individual basis. Despite this acknowledgement of non-biotic factors, however, the paucity of their treatment was to prove one of the major points of criticism of urban ecology. It is clear that Park, Burgess and the others consistently understated and often omitted to include the distinctively human qualities of the city in their conceptual framework which was essentially mechanistic and generalized.

The critics of urban ecology seized on this neglect of human and cultural factors as a basic deficiency and questioned the validity of using analogies. Perhaps the best-known example of this line of criticism is the work of Walter Firey (1947) in his study *Land Use in Central Boston*. Firey found ecological laws were not satisfactory explanations of the patterns which he observed. Cultural factors, which he described variously as non-rational values, sentiment and symbolism, were the dominant influences in some parts of the city: thus the motivations of the families who acted to preserve Beacon Hill, an old and prestigious residential district, against the encroachment of commercial functions and lower-status groups, were not economic. Others have found similar evidence, for example, Emrys Jones's study of the social geography of Belfast (1960). Milla Alihan (1938) rejected the biological analogy on the same grounds but had wider-ranging criticisms of the urban ecologists. She suggested that the Chicago monographs, although of lasting value as studies of urban-social structure, had not followed ecological rules, and used terminology inconsistently thus affecting the interpretation of key concepts such as community and society. This obsession with words was later to evoke cynical rejoinders: 'Human ecology has already inspired a generation of critics too easily irritated by figures of speech'; but contemporaneously the the defences were few. McKenzie died in 1940 and Park acquired a reputation as an undisciplined empiricist. Louis Wirth (1945), always a less committed ecologist, attempted to redefine a position for urban ecology as a perspective which focused attention upon localized or territorially defined social structures and phenomena. With this focus, he suggested, community has a central position in the conceptual framework but the term is inevitably ambiguous because all communities are also societies and all societies bear some characteristics of communities. Ecology provides a perspective but behaviour in the human world can only be understood in the light of habit, custom, institutions, morals, ethics and laws. Wirth's statement was a careful reappraisal of ecology in which the biological analogy had no necessary part.

Urban geographers did not take serious interest in the urban ecology approach until the 1960s, by which time its misconceptions were well understood. At this time it held several attractions. Firstly, although the biological analogy basis of its approach had been largely discredited, there were still reviewers such as Reissman (1964) prepared to describe ecology as the closest we have come to a systematic theory of the city. Secondly, urban ecology had a strong empirical and field-work content which had direct appeal to geographical method. For many of its concepts such as invasion, succession and segregation, which had empirical reality, the symbiosis line of explanation was not necessary. Thirdly, there were important land-use models and territorial concepts which had developed as part of the work of urban ecologists and these had very direct appeal.

Of the so-called 'classical' models of urban land-use, that proposed by Burgess (1925), Park's principal collaborator, is undoubtedly the best known. The concentric–zonal model (Figure 1.4(a)) offers a descriptive framework in which to view both the spatial organization of land use in the city and its change over time. Burgess was aware of the work on urban land values and bid-rents and his model was partly founded upon the kind of economic base which this proposed. The model made a number of assumptions which included a uniform land surface, universal accessibility to a single centred city and free competition for space. These assumptions were a mixture of those usually made for a pure model, such as an isotropic surface, and those typical of contemporary American society. In line with the latter, for example, assumptions included a heterogeneous population, a mixed industrial-commercial base, cheap transit and a capitalist system. Under conditions of this kind,

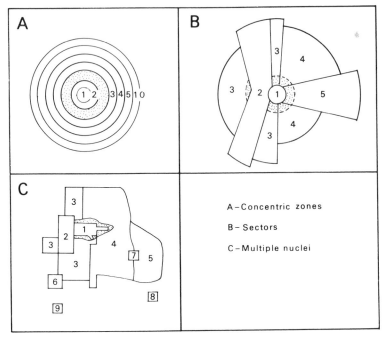

Figure 1.4 Spatial models of the city: these models, largely intended to provide descriptive generalizations of residential structure, are often described as the classical models. 1. CBD; 2. wholesale, light industry; 3. low-status residential; 4. medium-status residential; 5. high-status residential; 6. heavy industry; 7. outlying business; 8. residential suburb; 9. industrial suburb; 10. commuters' zone. Dot-shading marks the zone-in-transition

Burgess suggested that the zonal arrangement of land-uses from centre to periphery would be:

1. central business district;
2. transition zone;
3. zone of workingmen's homes;
4. zone of better residences;
5. commuters' zone.

Whilst clearly acknowledging that this model would not hold for each and every city, Burgess nevertheless thought that it might have some generality within North America, and its outlines could be recognized in Chicago and some other cities in the United States. The Burgess model was a description of urban structure but was also intended to serve as a mechanistic framework for urban growth and change. The main ecological processes involved in the dynamic aspects of the model were those of invasion and succession by which population groups gradually filtered outwards from the centre as their status and level of assimilation improved.

Later empirical tests of the zonal model offered a variety of criticisms. Some of these questioned the generality of the model, but as already suggested it was based upon existing conditions in interwar United States and was never intended to have universality. Empirically, researchers have argued that gradients are more easily demonstrated than zones and that related concepts such as 'natural areas' tend to emphasize the heterogeneity that can exist within zones. Much of the criticism arises from expectations of the zonal model which were never part of its original formulation. It is a *model* and its persistence can in many ways be attributed to its simplicity and breadth of generalization. The real world is more complicated and the search for concentric zones in many empirical studies was one of the less enlightened practices of the 1960s.

The sector model of urban land use formulated by Hoyt (1939) (Figure 1.4(b)) is normally regarded as the second of the classic models of urban spatial form. The Hoyt formulation was constrained by its narrow focus on housing and rent. He obtained rental and other data which he mapped by blocks for 142 American cities and from this empirical research suggested his sector model. The model took the form of a central business district with a series of sectors emanating from it. The high-grade residential areas pre-empted the most desirable space and were powerful forces in the pattern of urban growth. Other grades of residential area were aligned around the high-grade areas, with the lowest-grade areas occupying the least desirable land, often adjacent to manufacturing districts. The various residential areas took the spatial form of sectors, extending from the central city towards the periphery, and were thus in apparent contrast with the concentric zones suggested by Burgess. The common elements were the focal nature of the central business district and the presence of a transition-zone which was clearly identifiable in American cities. The sector model was also a growth framework and Hoyt's formulations on neighbourhood change were mainly aimed at describing the dynamic characteristics of the high-grade residential areas which he regarded as key elements. The high-grade areas would move, he suggested, towards amenity land, along transport routes, and towards the homes of leaders of the community.

The third classic model was that by Harris and Ullman (1945) which they termed the multiple nuclei model (Figure 1.4(c)). Its main distinctive quality was its abandonment of the central business district as a sole focal point, replacing it by a number of discrete nuclei around which individual land-uses were geared. As the conditions for the location of these nuclei may vary, there was no one generalized spatial form which could be suggested.

The merits of these three spatial models have been extensively discussed and although further general assessment is not necessary, a number of more specific points may be made. First, although the models appear to take different spatial forms, they are not necessarily contradictory. They may, for example, measure different aspects of urban structure and this idea of complementarity will be developed in a later chapter. Second, it is clear that the zonal form in particular has considerable generality and has been used to offer comparisons between preindustrial and industrial cities as well as modern regional variations, where the aim is to show broad similarities or differences. In this former context it also offers some guidelines for examining change over time. Lastly, the classical models, especially of zones and sectors, continue to have useful roles in urban geographical teaching as means of organizing study of the city and testing some of its more general theories.

CHANGING EMPHASES WITHIN URBAN GEOGRAPHY

Although these two main derivative sources for urban geography—land economics and social ecology—were well established by the 1930s, they had nothing like immediate effect. The barriers to the diffusion of new ideas into urban geographical research and practice proved extremely absorbent. Despite the seminal paper by Harris and Ullman (1945), which made clear the stimuli to geographical research that were available from economics and sociology, but whose publication during the war years undoubtedly delayed its impact, it was only really from the late 1950s that their general applications and possibilities became fully realized. Then, whereas the economics source was to strengthen and change drastically the geographical study of the city as a point or location, so the social ecology source was to have considerable repercussions upon the analysis of the town as area. Reviews of the state of urban geography in the 1950s, such as that by Mayer (1954) and a collection of readings (Mayer and Kohn, 1959), illustrated some diversity of types of study and an awareness of both new derivative sources and the major neglected indigenous source of central place theory, but still tended to reflect traditional emphases. It was during the 1960s and 1970s that a major reshaping of urban geography became apparent. Urban geography texts of this period reflect this change and in particular the influence of the two derivative sources. British texts such as Carter (1972) continued to give prominence to the morphological tradition but American texts (Yeates and Garner, 1971) had virtually no place for morphology and were dominated by the spatial analysis paradigm and the new foci of urban economics and central place theory in particular. There were contemporaneously more specialized books on urban-social geography (Herbert, 1972) which reflected the particular impact of social ecology and the burgeoning work on the social geography of the city.

As urban geography began to diversify in the 1960s and 1970s into a concern with a wider range of phenomena and greater variety of perspectives, its focus remained largely upon *patterns* of cities and within cities, the traditional geographical concern. Spatial analysis, modelling and quantification, with their essentially descriptive qualities, for some time served to perpetuate this emphasis. The realization that pattern description of point locations or areas, even accommodating temporal change in relatively sophisticated ways, contained its own limitations, gradually broadened the nature of urban geographical enquiry. The many threads can be summarized into three main categories in which pattern remains a pivotal point of interest but which require both its subsequent and consequent features to be included in a form of analysis which had an ever increasing content.

$$\text{process} \longrightarrow \text{pattern} \longrightarrow \text{response}$$

Studies of *patterns* represent a continuation and development of a traditional concern in urban geography, sustained by the legitimate argument that pattern identification is a basic starting-point for much geographical research. The pattern element is constant in urban geography whether it is concerned with the mapping of morphological units, house-types, land-values, or sociodemographic characteristics. Patterns, once identified, may raise issues or questions and reveal problems; between the extremes of localized clusters and complete dispersal there is an infinite variety of types of pattern which may help to identify research questions.

An awareness of the fact that patterns were the product of ongoing contemporary *processes* had always been implicit in the research literature. A strong link had always been forged, for example, between historical growth processes and morphological outcomes. The initial resurgence of research interest in processes of the later 1960s, however, had closer links with the social sciences and with behaviouralism in particular. In its more direct form this involved a stronger reference to the decision-making processes which underlay spatial patterns, a push towards individual rather than aggregate scale data, and the direct transfer of concepts such as place utility, stressors, stimuli and awareness space from the behavioural sciences. At the intraurban scale, the analysis of residential mobility provided a focal point. Perhaps *the* major outcome of pattern studies had been the characterization of the residential mosaic; the task now was to understand the processes which had produced this mosaic.

Response studies had innovative qualities but again there were precedents. Response studies are those which use patterns as bases for more detailed investigation, which respond to the questions and issues which patterns may raise. The application of territorial social indicators, for example, identified problem *areas* which urban geographers have subsequently studied in greater detail in research which often had policy implications. Patterns of 'social areas' identified within the residential mosaic were selected for detailed analysis as 'communities' or 'neighbourhoods' or might be used as sampling frameworks to study a range of forms of spatial behaviour. The research into urban environment and behaviour can be classified as a response study as can analysis of the roles of residential location in the competition for the externalities or 'goods' which households consume but do not produce themselves.

Studies which can be summarized into the categories of process, pattern and response have considerably diversified and continue to dominate the work of the urban geographer. There is now a greater diversity of pattern studies and a vastly improved 'technology' to enable this analysis; there is a strong focus on processes of many kinds and scales, and response studies are adding new dimensions and advancing the applied tradition. The focus of all of these studies in the 1960s and 1970s, however, remained the local interface or the urban environment *per se*. As the radical critique developed during the 1970s, its most valuable contribution has been its questioning of the primacy of this focus. Although urban geographers have always tried to place their research efforts in a broader context, preferably one which allows comparisons, the need to give the 'antecedents' of pattern, process and response as spatial outcomes greater primacy in research attention was gradually accepted. New *levels of analysis* had to be identified as context for continuing work at the local scale.

These levels can be summarized:

production	=	social formation
distribution	=	allocative systems
consumption	=	spatial outcomes

Under this scheme, the large majority of studies so far described under the heading of pattern, process and response can be located within the consumption level. It is no part of this argument that such studies are redundant. If, as will be shown, the research emphasis is shifting to other 'levels', it is to redress a balance rather than to discard or replace. Analyses at production and distribution levels can contribute significantly to the understanding of those forces which underpin urban environment and to which, ultimately, key features of pattern, process and response can be retraced.

Briefly to define terms. Research at the *production* level incorporates those studies concerned with 'institutions' at the macro-scale within society which give that society its particular form and character at a given point in time. The concept of social formation as a historically determinate, 'real' society composed of economic, political, and ideological levels finding expression as a complex whole, most adequately expresses the scale of this level of analysis. By *distribution*-level research is meant the study of allocative systems, with their roles in relationship with the means of production, and with the agencies— managers or gatekeepers—which filter policies and resources down to the *consumption* level. At this last level of *consumption* the scale is the urban environment, the local interface between societal forces and their spatial outcomes, within the context of which the major research effort in process, pattern and response during the 1960s and 1970s has been contained.

CONCLUSIONS

After a long period of slow change and a typical conservatism, urban geography has diversified considerably since the early 1960s. Each major new perspective has involved a critique but has also offered positive qualities which have been accommodated without serious threat to the unity and perspective of the 'subdiscipline'. Herbert and Johnston (1978) suggested a 'branching' model as the most appropriate description for the framework which had evolved. Both urban geography itself and its major components have developed distinctive features but have retained links with the wider discipline. The geographer's contribution to urban studies will continue to be distinguished by the attention which it focuses on the spatial dimension—on place, space, and person—environment interaction—but as most geographers would admit that spatial processes *per se* are rarely explanatory processes, the need to probe deeply into social, political and economic forces at a variety of levels of analysis will increasingly be recognized. The urban geography described in this text has its roots in the early traditions, sources and modes of analysis already described, but has its emphases in the broadening vistas of the past two decades. The urban geography of the future will surely be more firmly embedded in the wider philosophies of the social sciences than has hitherto been the case and it is towards this end that the following chapter seeks, in a broad and preliminary way, to identify these main methodological contexts.

Chapter 2

Paradigms and Theories: the Conceptual Bases of Urban Geography

Within what James (1972) has described as the contemporary period of the post 1950s, urban geography has experienced a number of 'paradigmatic shocks' which have both reoriented its perspectives and have left the sub-discipline with a number of unresolved internal tensions. One central feature of this period has been the decreasing isolation of human geography at large within the social sciences, a trend which has found both external and internal expression. Externally, there is a much greater awareness in other social sciences, especially in economics, sociology and political science, of a need to at least recognize and accommodate the roles of space in the comprehension of human behaviour. Internally, there is an enlarged willingness to adopt derivative concepts and theories and perhaps more significantly, to pay a much greater regard to the philosophies of the social sciences. The tensions arise from the speed with which new paradigms appear and the dominance which they threaten to assume. As the advance of quantitative methods and a much more scientific urban geography subsumed more traditional research activities and some of their established practitioners in the 1960s, so the radical critique of the 1970s is seen in a similar light; reactions are inevitable and by no means particular to urban geography.

The purposes of this chapter are to identify and evaluate these trends in the contemporary period. As a framework within which to context this period, however, the more traditional 'paradigms' within which the discipline as a whole has functioned need to be recognized. The term *paradigm* has been used widely in social science research (Kuhn, 1962) but without uniform consistency. It is used here in its more general form as comprising a body of ideas or a broad model which may be used to guide the development of theory and explanatory research; a paradigm constitutes an important reference point for practitioners within a particular discipline. Under this definition, a number of paradigms can be recognized in the development of human geography which, although associated principally with particular periods of time and 'stages' in the more general evolution of methodology, have shown considerable temporal stability. There are in a sense, no 'paradigms lost'; whereas new have been added, the old have rarely been totally discarded, if only because of the natural conservatism of scholars whose lifespans are generally

26

longer than the periods of intense activity in the paradigm within which they were socialized as academic geographers.

TRADITIONAL PARADIGMS

The question of which group of ideas or models for theory construction qualifies for description as a paradigm remains contentious. Three themes suggest themselves as having the influence of paradigms even if they have not all stimulated a strong theoretical context; these may be labelled as exploration, environmentalism, and regionalism.

The *exploration* paradigm belongs most clearly to the early and classical phases in the development of geographical thought. Its characteristic features were the charting of unknown places and the gathering of basic facts on spatial phenomena. This activity motivated the early observers and the map-making tradition in geography; it also inspired the explorers themselves who actually discovered new lands. Some of the explorers, such as von Humboldt, developed systematic methodologies for specimen collection and the maintenance of records which served as models for later workers. Although exploration in the sense of finding new lands has virtually disappeared, organizations such as the Royal Geographical Society maintain the ethos of this early geography and the business of data collection goes on though in more mundane ways. Although the theme of exploration has long been associated with geography, and is the quality by which the subject is most easily recognized, it has limited claims to be described as a paradigm. Its roles have essentially been those of classification and description and its limits at the theoretical level are clear.

Environmentalism as a paradigm has a long and somewhat chequered history in geographical study. It can be found within the 'classical' period (James, 1972) when there was an awareness of the need to investigate the ways in which the physical environment affects the functioning and development of societies; it moved into a central position with the advocacy of geographical determinism in its most strident form in the last part of the nineteenth century. Environmentalism, with its strong theoretical and problem-solution underpinning relating to the physical environmental controls on human activity, has clear claims to the status of a paradigm. In the context of the environmentalism debate, which remained active until the 1950s, a number of competing stances emerged. Determinism advocated the highest level of physical controls and was cast in a mould of positivist natural science; possibilism, in some ways so far removed from determinism in its advocacy for the primacy of human control over human activity as to fall outside the paradigm of environmentalism, belongs to the humanism of the early twentieth century. The determinist side of the environmentalist debate has limited relevance for modern geographical study (see, however, the continued use of some of its precepts in ecosystem studies—Moss and Morgan, 1967) but related issues of cause and effect (Harvey, 1969) and scientific positivism versus humanism (Ley, 1977) have continuing significance. Quite recent studies of environment and behaviour (Michelson, 1970) show a maintained interest in man–environment interaction, though the considered environments are manmade rather than natural.

Regionalism represents many faces to modern geography. It inherits some aspect of the fact-finding tradition of exploration, and in this aspect has a strong descriptive role, but also offers a synthesis of man and environment which has more theoretical connotations. Regional studies may involve the identification of uniform regions, the description of segments of the earth's surface, and specialized regional monographs. The 'style' of regional geographers has varied considerably since the humanistic approach of Vidal de la Blache and his view of the region as a 'medal cast in the likeness of its people'. Ley (1977) argues that this humanistic insight was diluted even within the early French school by the more formal representations of Brunhes and the quantitative coding of Demangeon. There have been many variants of the regional concept. The idea of '*landschaft*' has always been difficult to interpret but demanded, in essence, study of those phenomena which could be observed on the earth surface. Its focus was on human artifacts—farms and fields, hedges and houses—rather than on people; landscape is taken as a palimpsest of human activity, the study of which is virtually ignored. Interestingly, as the idea of 'townscape' was developed in urban morphology, it had exactly the same features and limitations. The regional concept has claims to be regarded as a paradigm. Whereas the regional study as the ultimate synthesis of systematic geographical specialisms now has little academic credibility, the teaching of regional geography remains an important part of the discipline. Regionalization, an important tool in urban and economic geography, has an objective, statistical methodology but is conceptually inherited from regionalism.

To varying degrees these three themes of exploration, environmentalism, and regionalism constitute the more traditional 'paradigms' of geographical study. In the United States a fourth theme which might be summarized as cultural ecology found particularly strong expression. Initiated in Chicago by Barrows (1923) and developed at Berkeley by Sauer (1925) it took the form of landscape morphology and although set in the tradition of man–land relationships, its humanistic approach gave it a distinctive character. For this type of cultural ecology, the focus was the historical antecedents of *place* rather than any search for general laws.

CONTEMPORARY PARADIGMS

The traditional paradigms dominated research and teaching in human geography over a long period of time and remain influential. Since the late 1950s, however, the pace of methodological change has quickened considerably and nowhere has the impact of this change been felt more immediately than in urban geography. Within this contemporary period, one major new paradigm became established and other significant trends which may yet acquire that status have appeared.

The case for a *spatial analysis* paradigm, strongly linked with quantitative methodologies and model-building, was made in the 1960s: 'In general we feel that geometrical analysis offers a logical, consistent and geographically more relevant alternative to the "element-oriented" approach with its inevitable tendency to subdivide geography and force it outwards towards the relevant external systematic disciplines' (Chorley and Haggett, 1967, p. 34).

This quotation evokes several comments. Firstly, it provides a significant thrust towards the formulation of geography as a more positive science; a thrust which was amply supplemented by the output of research papers in this mould. Secondly, its expressed aversion towards any fusion with external disciplines was to provide a sharp contrast with the objectives of later radical geographers and suggests a traditional isolationist character. Thirdly, the statement that *geometrical* analysis could provide the sufficient basis for advancing geographical analysis has been firmly refuted (Sack, 1972). These observations have the advantage of hindsight, and there can be no doubt that the move towards laws, models, and spatial analyses gave geography a new and valuable paradigm.

As a paradigm, with an associated set of methodologies and techniques, spatial analysis has recently dominated contemporary geography, generating a voluminous research literature. In comparison to its development stage, other new methodological positions of the contemporary period remain in an embryo state. They have nevertheless already had a telling impact within the discipline and can be closely related to more general trends affecting the social sciences as a whole. One of these trends has been more typified by a multiplicity of strands rather than by a cohesive whole, but can be summarized as the *subjective* approaches. Another strand which is commonly, though perhaps not accurately (see Stoddart, 1975) thought to have begun at the Association of American Geographers' conference in 1971, is that of *relevance*. Again, from being an initially diffuse reaction against the abstractions of spatial analysis, this trend has developed into a more radical critique which encompasses an essentially Marxist approach but has also spawned a more welfare-oriented interest in spatial justice and a more general research interest in underprivilege and disadvantage.

In discussing the evolution and present status of these methodological changes in the contemporary period, the emphasis now will be upon their impact upon urban geography. Some of the earlier characteristics of urban geography have already been noted in Chapter 1. During the period since the 1960s some of these, such as urban morphology, have been relegated to comparative insignificance in research interests; others, such as social ecology, have been elevated and modified. All, however, are carried forward in some form or another into the contemporary period and contribute to the basis from which urban geographical study has subsequently been developed.

Urban geography and spatial analysis

After the Second World War, a number of changes occurred in the geographical discipline, several of them reaching their apogee in the United States between 1955 and 1960 and in Great Britain a few years later. The origins of these changes are many and varied. Important among them was probably the war itself, the organization of which involved geographers working in teams with members of other disciplines (Ackerman; 1945; 1958) and thereby becoming aware of the current methods, interests and issues beyond the narrow horizons of the few other subjects–anthropology, geology, and history—with which they had maintained some contact. This was indeed a period of major change in many social science disciplines. Economics, for example, had passed through the Keynesian revolution and obtained both public (political) and scientific recognition for its role in ameliorating the ills of the 1920s and 1930s. Psychologists had been deeply involved in the American war effort, as studies by Stouffer *et al.* (1950) and others indicate, and they, plus associates in sociology, had begun to launch large programmes of survey research into human behaviour (notably the studies of communications and influence organized by Lazarsfeld, Berelson, and Gaudet, 1944). All of this work had the following characteristics.

1. It was nomothetic rather than idiographic, focusing on general trends and patterns and interpreting specifics within a theoretical matrix rather than stressing the unique and the exceptional.
2. It used numerical methods to analyse its data and so was 'scientifically' respectable.
3 It apparently had predictive power and so could be used in the development of public policy.

Two statements can be made about the conditions under which these characteristics became translated into urban geography as spatial analysis. Firstly, many of the ideas were derived from other disciplines and reflected the more general impact of normative, scientific approaches on the social sciences. Secondly, although one can find examples of generalizations in human geography from much earlier periods (James, 1972), the discipline in practice was centrally concerned with exceptionalism and stood in sharp contrast, for example, with the search for general laws in several branches of physical geography. From the isolated examples, such as Christäller (1933), Weber (1899), and Lösch (1954), a much more general shift towards a nomothetic discipline, in which the search for laws and models was a central concern, was one highly significant change in the contemporary period and one which, in Taylor's (1976) account, struck traditional geography at its very core. Associated with this shift was a much greater emphasis on quantitative analysis and statistics, an emphasis which both added a 'degree of difficulty' to the new paradigm and better equipped geographers for the development of a new methodology.

A number of scholars had key roles in relaying both developments in other disciplines and general shifts in the body of knowledge as a whole into human geography. Schaefer (1953) has a special place in what might already be described as the 'mythology' of this transition by virtue of a single essay in which he attacked the uniqueness or idiographic qualities of Hartshorne's (1939) areal differentiation philosophy. As an alternative he proposed the need for geographers to develop morphological laws of patterns, both of single phenomena and of several related phenomena, from which process laws might be developed in combination with the work of other social scientists. Hartshorne's (1955, p. 242) closely argued reply to the Schaefer article, made accusations of defective scholarship and of an almost complete misrepresentation of both the German sources used and of *The Nature of Geography* itself. Despite this severe criticism, which could not be answered because of Schaefer's untimely death in 1953, the germs of the ideas launched by Schaefer were acknowledged by the new theoreticians of the early 1960s as fundamental influences upon their way of thinking (Bunge, 1962) and, either contemporaneously or subsequently, Schaefer's colleagues at Iowa (McCarty, Hook, and Knos, 1956) were adapting statistical methods to forms of geographical analysis and had moved some way to the establishment of laws and generalizations.

If Schaefer's plea for a move away from exceptionalism was a significant single event, more important in the longer term was the systematic development of spatial analysis by other American-based geographers, notably Garrison and Berry. Based initially at Seattle, the interests of this group were very much with spatial laws of two main kinds. The first were concerned with the patterns of points on the earth's surface, of which the main examples were clearly urban places; the second were of flows of goods and people, based upon a view of humans as exceptionally rational beings who reacted to the various costs of moving from one place to another by keeping them at a minimum. Their main stimuli were clearly from economics, both those provided by Christäller's central place theory and those from regional scientist-economists such as Isard, Lösch, Dunn, Greenhut and Ponsard (see Berry, 1959; Garrison, 1959, 1960). Their work was strongly mathematical, focusing, for example, upon operational models developed in linear programming, though they also adopted statistical procedures to present their morphological and associational laws and to test their notions about the economic rationality of men (Garrison, 1956; Garrison and Marble, 1967).

The impact of this group of influential scholars was both rapid and enormous, and was made effective by their energetic research and by a capacity to write and publish their new insights. Statistical training became an essential element of university courses in both North America and in Britain where similar ideas had been developed (see Gregory, 1976). Urban geography proved especially amenable to the impact of this move towards increased quantification, and the role of Brian Berry, who promoted the analysis of settlement patterns and sought spatial order in size and location of towns and cities, villages and hamlets, neighbourhood and regional centres, was considerable. Urban geography had some additional advantage in that the rediscovery of central place theory, a process helped by Baskin's (1966) translation of Christäller provided a comprehensive spatial model, which, both as a whole and in its many individual facets, provided a rich testing ground for many elements of an emerging quantitative methodology with all the assumptions of normative behaviour and a positivist-scientific approach. Dacey's (1962) use of nearest-neighbour analysis in Wisconsin to test distributions of central places, and Berry and Garrison's (1958a; 1958b) calculation of threshold populations were two of the best-known early studies.

The new methods of spatial analysis were by no means confined to central place studies. They were applied to classifications of settlements (R. H. T. Smith, 1965a); to examination of urban population sizes (Berry and Garrison, 1958b); and to the analysis of population densities within cities (Berry, Simmons, and Tennant, 1963). On internal urban structure, a considerable amount of research was aimed at the comprehension of land-use and associated land-value gradients (Yeates, 1965). Of the various texts, that by Haggett (1965) was amongst the most influential, and the application of models as a general panacea reached its height in Chorley and Haggett's work (1967). During the early 1960s interest in urban geography had shifted significantly towards social aspects of city life. This shift became associated with the increasing influence of spatial analysis and gave quantification and model-building a new and vigorous platform.

Renewed awareness of the social ecology of Park and Burgess was promoted by texts by geographers (E. Jones, 1960) and others (Theodorson, 1962). Geographers focused on the spatial order in residential patterns and the simple models which were already available (Burgess, 1925; Harris and Ullman, 1945; and Hoyt, 1939) became themes for testing, examination, and debate. From the enormously influential empirical work of the Chicago school came other concepts, notably those of the natural area (Zorbaugh, 1929) and of residential and land-use change processes (Burgess, 1925), which were to provide stimuli for closely allied lines of research. Not only were there, at one level of spatial resolution, operational models of the city which could be tested, but there was also at another level the idea that the city was a mosaic and the problem was one of the identification of the bases of residential differentiation of parts of the mosaic and their characterization. As the social geography of the city developed, the move was away from the more limited perspectives of traditional morphology towards a focus upon people as social beings. Social area analysis (Shevky and Bell, 1955) aided this new emphasis and also, through its dependence upon small area statistics, stimulated the application of quantitative methodologies. The factorial ecologists applied sophisticated statistical procedures to a basic problem of regionalization within cities to identify 'social areas' (Herbert, 1972; Johnston, 1971). Census data were ransacked to provide indices of differences between the various parts of urban areas; the availability of computers allowed mass manipulation of these data sets and, very rapidly, the study of intraurban residential patterns ousted central place investigations from their primacy within the interests of urban geographers.

Throughout the 1960s the methodology of these investigations was both extended and sharpened. The aim was to be scientific—as are physics and chemistry—and to provide quantifiable theories and laws; models became more sophisticated, their language became more symbolic, and mathematics rather than the now-accepted statistics became the expressed *desiderata* (Wilson, 1972). Some doubts on this trend emerged as many quantitative methods failed to 'deliver the goods' in terms of new insights and certainly in terms of practicalities. Spatial analysis had grown in geography as part of a general move towards positive science and this thrust towards laws and theories is well exemplified in Harvey's (1969) treatise on *Explanation in Geography*. These theories had a basis, often perhaps only implicit, in mechanistic assumptions of human decision-making; the concept of economic or perfectly rational man who made decisions on the basis of complete knowledge and omniscience and who was translated by geographers into spatial man (Nystuen, 1963), whose choice of locations was based upon a minimization of movement costs. Later there were models adopted from Parsonian functionalism, which accepted a view of society as composed of individuals allocated to particular places within the economic and social order from which, by dint of personal effort, they might escape to a higher level. The members of these various groups then compete for territory, with the resulting spatial order representing a consensus acceptance of a certain pattern. These derivative sources and the ways in which they were translated into geographical models and theories, ensured an essentially positivist and functionalist suite of postures. As quantification itself and the question of 'scientific' bases for the discipline were the natural handmaidens of these philosophies, urban geography by the later 1960s had assumed in its overall practice what was essentially a conservative, stereotyped and rather abstracted character.

From this position, the spatial analysis paradigm has suffered criticism on several counts. Firstly, its attempt to mould human geography as a 'science' with laws and models was questioned by the re-emergence of subjective approaches. Secondly, its relevance to the problems and realities of urban life was questioned by an emerging radical geography. Thirdly, the dominance of conservative political views arising from its functionalist qualities was attacked, though as Ryan (1973) argues functionalism has often been criticized on ideological rather than intellectual grounds because of its accidental alignment with conservatism. Fourthly, the intellectual shortcomings of a geometry of space paradigm claiming to have explanatory power were exposed by Sack (1972; 1978). In Sack's argument spatial analysis had developed a concern with points and lines which held little regard to what those symbols represent; geographical explanations cannot be found in geometry, they must be sought in more general laws.

The spatial analysis paradigm with its thrust towards laws and quantification gave urban geography an important new dimension and retains a valuable role, albeit modified and more limited. This role will be considered but firstly the key reactions to its dominance, which promised alternative approaches, will be elaborated.

The 'subjective' approach

'Subjectivism' has a long heritage in the literature of human geography. At various times it has become either manifest as a reaction to the overzealous advocacy of a scientific, 'objective' methodology; or it has itself been accused of the sins of formlessness, intuition and exceptionalism and has stimulated a move towards models and generalizations. Ley (1977) views the contribution of Vidal de la Blache to French regional geography as a balanced 'humanism' with all the virtues of a subjective interpretation and would put some of the early work of Robert Park in Chicago who showed that 'land-use unit becomes neighbourhood when it is stained with the particular sentiments of its population' in a similar category. As Vidal's regionalism became submerged by the more formal approaches of Brunhes and Demangeon, so Park's 'urbanism' was translated into social ecology and the biological metaphor. In the latter case it was, ironically, Firey's (1947) re-emphasis of sentiment and symbolism which provided one of the most telling critiques of the Chicago school. Again, as Ley (1977) has shown, these claims and counterclaims were matched elsewhere in the social sciences with subjectivism being advocated, for example, by Dilthey's work on historical consciousness and that of Weber on *verstehen* or imaginative understanding. In the contemporary period of human geography the 'return' to the subjective has several, only loosely coordinated strands, most of which began as a concern with the nomothetic, rationalistic methodology of the spatial analysis paradigm during the early 1960s. Kirk's (1951; 1963) characterization of the behavioural environment, for example, raised important questions; statements by Lowenthal (1961) and Tuan (1968) advocated a humanistic concern for the study of landscapes, and Wolpert (1965) stressed the role of the decision-maker in the processes which underlay spatial patterns.

In general terms the 'subjective' approach can initially at least be more clearly stated as a critique rather than as a precise methodology with a cohesive structure. There are signs, particularly with attempts to provide a philosophical underpinning or 'cement' to the diverse contents of the critique, that this situation may change but the attainment of that goal is not yet apparent. As a critique subjective perspectives have in common a reaction against the mechanistic, aggregative and 'dehumanizing' qualities of spatial analysis. As Ley (1977) argues, spatial analysts in their zest to construct models fail to separate fact from value and reduce place and space to abstract geometries in which man is a 'pallid entrepreneurial figure'. Because of its continuous thrust to generalize and to abstract from reality, spatial analysis forms only a superficial view of human behaviour with no real attempt to understand internal motives and the real nature of processes which are at work. Ley (1977, p. 501) states: 'the emergence of behavioural geography witnessed the explicit commitment to delve beneath the distribution maps and spatial facts to an examination of social and cognitive processes in their everyday context'.

As the spatial analysts threatened to transform geography into a geometry of space and to characterize place as an isotropic surface, subjectivists sought to reassert the role of human values in the way in which space is regarded and to study the meanings which underlay a sense of place. Location theory is not to be regarded as a series of equations which weigh cost and distance but as a complex and subtle process of decision-making in which the 'black box' itself—why and how a decision is made—is a central focus for research. Subjectivism has led to a number of important strands of study in urban geography concerned with decision-making, with perception and with spatial cognition. Before developing some discussion of these, however, some brief reference to the broader underpinnings of these approaches, in the philosophies of the social sciences, is needed.

Most geographers working within the broad framework of a subjective approach would now recognize the role of phenomenology, as developed by Husserl (1970) as a mainspring of their methodology. Husserl's later work (see Gregory, 1978) was an explicit critique of the logical positivism of the Vienna Circle and provides an early example of a 'rallying point' for dissidents from the nomothetic approach. Husserl's argument was that the world could only be understood through a knowledge of the attitudes and intentions which motivated human behaviour. For Husserl, the cognitive experiences which make up the 'life world' possess *intentional* structures through which the 'objects' of reality are endowed with personal meaning. This interpretation can imply a highly individualized level of experience and the taking of a subjective approach to its infinitely fragmented extreme. Husserl sought to avoid this 'atomization' by proposing a procedure through which empirical experience was translated into an *epoché*—or an act of pure philosophical reflection—from which reconstitution took place. A similarity of reflective procedures would allow identical reconstitutions of the world and possibilities of generalization. Husserl's characterization of this transition process from empirical through transcendental to reconstitution has never been clear and has been given little place in geographical uses of phenomenology. As Gregory (1978) argues, the main significance of Husserl was his vigorous rejection of the assumptions and aspirations of positivism and his provision of a benchmark for 'humanistic' geographers reacting against the mechanistics of spatial analysis.

Husserl's phenomenology provides an important backcloth for subjective studies in urban geography but there were others. Dilthey (see Gregory, 1978) distinguished between the natural sciences which *explain* phenomena by abstracting regularities from raw data, and the social sciences which seek to *understand* phenomena in a more direct way. Understanding in this sense (*verstehen*) is always subjective since the investigator must experience the phenomena being studied. Weber developed the concept of *verstehen* or imaginative understanding but did not accept the total separation of explanation and understanding in

Dilthey's terms. Individual behaviour could be studied as a 'science' of man in which the criterion of verification or empirical validation was, in contrast to the views of Husserl, an essential component. Whereas Weber's brand of sociological investigation provides an important bridge for the introduction of phenomenological perspectives to the study of human behaviour, Gregory (1978) and others acknowledge the important place of Schutz as a 'broker' between the Husserlian and Weberian schools. Schutz's 'subjective' philosophy has a number of closely related components (see Schutz, 1973). He argues that only experience already encountered is meaningful, that social actions are founded on past experiences and that individuals hold frames of reference for attitudes and behaviour which are negotiated with respect to past experiences. Schutz rejects the always imprecise *epoché* component of Husserlian phenomenology in favour of Weber's emphasis upon the need for empirical validation. Schutz did not accept the 'reductionist' or 'individualized' critique of phenomenology; for him *verstehen* could encompass the facts of typicality and the associated possibilities of generalization. Again, for Schutz, life-worlds are not individualized to the extent that they are discrete, life-worlds are intersubjective with shared meanings and relationships (see Ley, 1977).

Whereas most humanistic geographers are now prepared to allow the broader concepts of phenomenology to embrace their studies, Guelke (1974, 1978) has proposed the narrower concept of idealism as an appropriate context for research in human geography. Idealism focuses upon the ideas and beliefs that lie behind human action and argues that behaviour must be understood through the mind of the 'actor' at the point in time and space in which it occurs. A decision to migrate, for example, must be understood in the very particular context of a particular migrant and the circumstances in which that decision is made. At this literal level of interpretation, idealism is clearly reductionist and seems to propose highly individualized approaches, but it does admit the relevance of 'common' aspirations and motives and in this sense allows generalization. The question of empirical validation poses problems for the idealist. Guelke argues that idealism is verifiable through a form of procedure which resembles a 'court of law' rather than a scientific laboratory: 'A well-verified idealist explanation will be one in which a pattern of behaviour can be shown to be consistent with certain underlying ideas' (Guelke, 1978, p. 55). Interpretations of 'evidence' in this form, however, are likely to be tentative and critics (see Harrison and Livingstone, 1979) have argued that in interpreting the motives and attitudes of the 'actor', the observer will be unable to disassociate his own values and judgements. The point of debate is reminiscent of Dilthey's distinction between scientific investigation and *verstehen*—the idealist cannot *explain* but he may be able to *understand*. Idealism can be portrayed as a separate strand within the subjective perspective but in general the common bonds are more significant than the points of difference. The idealist, for example, shares the phenomenologist's concern with the understanding of different meanings which people attach to their surroundings; there is common ground between idealist and behaviouralist.

As a further example of a direct attempt to qualify the methodological context of phenomenology within which humanistic geographers work, Entrikin's (1977) essay on existentialism is of interest. Entrikin acknowledges the debt to Husserl but suggests that there are many other phenomenological strands outside those which he developed. Existentialism with its emphasis upon man's individuality and freedom of choice is a reaction against both positivism and idealism which 'abstract thought from action, knowledge from emotion and man from his existentialist situation', and in this sense is strongly reminiscent of early possibilism. In its unwillingness to accept transcendentalism, existentialism rejects Husserl's concept of *epoché*; in emphasizing individuality, subjectivity, and freedom of choice, it is opposed to a search for regularities in human behaviour. Entrikin argues that modern humanistic geography with its definition of *place* as a centre of meaning and focus of human emotional attachment, is applying an existentialist phenomenological perspective, but the humanistic approach is nevertheless best understood as a critique of spatial analysis, rather than as a self-contained alternative approach.

Summary of the ways in which subjectivism has impinged upon actual practice in urban geography is complicated by the fact that there is often an absence of any closely specified links between a set of philosophical concepts and empirical investigations. There are exceptions to this, such as Guelke who develops an idealist perspective from earlier writers such as Collingwood's (1956) and Entrikin's (1977) use of existentialism but generally, as Hay (1979) comments, geographers who subscribe to subjectivist positions are extremely eclectic in their citations and it is difficult to place them squarely in any phenomenological position.

Some direct outcomes of the broad influence of subjectivism can be identified in urban geography. Firstly, there is a general emphasis or re-emphasis on the subjective meanings of place and space. More particularly in urban geography, writers such as Buttimer (1976) and Ley (1977) have been sensitive to the needs of making subjective values central to the comprehension of urban environments and sociospatial behaviour. As in Firey's (1947) essay on the sentiments and symbolisms attached to a Boston neighbourhood and Emrys Jones's persistent emphasis of the social values attached to place, so Buttimer's (1976) emphasis upon the 'anchoring points' in urban space which are 'stamped by human intention, value and memory' retains and reinforces the need to understand the subjective qualities of the urban life-world. Ley has been particularly forceful in advocating the role of the 'social dynamic' with which place is endowed, as exemplified by his study of the Black inner city (Ley, 1974) and of graffiti (Ley and Cybriwsky, 1974). For the growing band of humanistic geographers, land-value gradients and morphological unities are of less significance than the sociocultural values with which place and space are invested. These are sentiments which are very little removed from the longer-developing social geography of the city (Herbert, 1972; Jones and Eyles, 1978).

A second expression of the influence of subjectivism in urban geography can be found in studies of behaviour and decision-making. In this context there are contrasted perspectives to be disentangled. The strand of behaviourism *per se* has strong links with the biological sciences and with work in environmental psychology; it rests substantially upon the notions of stimulus and response developed by psychologists in intensive experimental research, often under laboratory conditions. This type of behaviourist approach is quantifiable, has the goal of generalization, and belongs squarely in the tradition of positivist science. Applications of behaviouralism in urban geography have borne traces of this type of systematic study and range from Stea's (1973) qualified but very explicit use of the behaviourist analogy to other less explicit but still essentially 'scientific' analyses of human behaviour.

If experimental psychology provided an example of the study of behaviour in the tradition of positivist science, another psychologist introduced concepts which led to an emphasis upon the subjective limitations which are imposed upon social activity. H. A. Simon (1957) argued that two concepts were needed to qualify the assumption of *economic man*, a 'being' endowed with perfect knowledge, the wish to optimize, and the ability to calculate which course of action would achieve the desired optimum, which had formed the reference point for positive science and—in urban geography—for the models of spatial analysis. The concept of bounded rationality suggests that although man may strive to be rational, he is hampered by an incomplete knowledge and limited ability to calculate. That of 'satisficing' suggests that man may work towards a level of attainment which is satisfactory even though it may well fall far short of optimal. These are generalized concepts but they have led urban geographers into closer studies of individual behaviour and decision-making which are far removed from the abstractions of spatial analysis. 'Satisficer' man is a figure much closer to reality than economic man; behavioural studies maintain some modes of analysis which are in the positivist tradition but have added to these in the ways in which they collect their data and research in this field has developed towards the subjective position.

Geographers working within the behaviouralist perspective have become progressively less interested in the stimulus–response heritage of scientific behaviourism and more interested in qualitative studies of decision-making at an individual rather than at an aggregate level. Pred (1967) was concerned with the goals and information levels of decision-makers considering alternative locations; Wolpert (1965) introduced concepts such as place utility to the study of migration and pointed to the uncertainty with which men encounter the real world and to the importance of individual goals, levels of knowledge, and personal preferences (see Eyles and Smith, 1979). Such studies took urban geographers away from depiction of spatial patterns in the city and a mechanistic view of macro-processes to detailed studies of the individual decision-makers and the micro-processes which produced these patterns. This new emphasis with its early assumption of choice in movement had its own *caveats*, but the immediate benefits were the concerns with process and the decreasing dependence on aggregate statistics and models.

A further development within urban geography of the move towards subjectivism was the interest in spatial imagery and cognitive mapping. Boulding's (1956) work on the image was a key reference and his concept became central to much geographical work concerned with behaviour. In its simplest terms, Boulding's concept of image was the picture of the world carried around in the mind of the 'actor' which became the reference point for his behaviour. The form which the image takes is moulded by external conditions of socialization, experience and context and also by internal factors such as values and prejudices. For many urban geographers, image formed the link between phenomenal and behavioural environments (see; Doherty, 1969 Kirk, 1963). Again, psychology provided a fertile source of concepts and practices (see Lee, 1976) and highly influential empirical work was completed outside the discipline (Lynch, 1960). One strong research line proceeding from the concept of image is that associated with the construction of mental maps or spatial cognition. Here a variety of techniques has been employed to tease out one type of image of particular interest to geographers; the mental maps which people hold as reference points for spatial awareness and behaviour. Research into mental maps at a variety of scales has looked for generalizations and has often used quantitative techniques (Gould and White, 1974; Herbert and Raine, 1976) but has been strongly influenced by the concepts of subjectivism. Whilst the technical procedures have as yet had limited success in representing the problem and doubts continue to be expressed on the significance as well as the accuracy of cognitive mapping (Boyle and Robinson, 1979), work on spatial images has served to qualify concepts such as urban neighbourhood and urban environmental awareness. Downs (1970) suggests three approaches to the study of mental maps or geographical space perception which he terms structural, evaluative, and preference (see also Jones and Eyles, 1978). Lynch's work on Boston, in which he identifies five structural elements—paths, edges, districts, nodes, and landmarks—exemplifies the first type of approach. Levels of awareness of these elements indicate how individuals structure space and relate it to their behaviour. The second, evaluative, approach seeks to identify the accuracy with which individuals recognize the qualities of place and space— safe, dangerous, urban, rural—and the types of evaluations which they place upon it. The spatial preference approach, which has been strongly developed (Gould and White, 1974), seeks to assess the levels of desirability, attractiveness or preference held for place and space and to define the reasons for these. Research experience has revealed problems in identifying space preferences, not least of which are the very limited spatial awarenesses which people hold and their inability to rank, score, or even recognize places. More detailed studies of preference (Eyles, 1971; Rushton, 1969) have also shown the need to differentiate amongst types of preferences—absolute or relative, manifest or latent—and the need to link these to opportunities in more realistic ways. The concept of preference is subjective but research has often followed the analytical path of positive science in dealing with derived sets of data.

As part of the more detailed discussion of particular topics in later chapters of this book, examples of the application of behaviouralism, perception studies, and other strands of subjectivism can be developed. Whereas some of the broader methodological foundations of such studies are acknowledged in such examples, it is only in recent years that consistent attempts to link the applications to a coherent philosophical base have emerged. Some of the difficulties involved in reaching such coherence are now evident. Identifying scientific geography as an approach resting upon empirical observation, public verifiability and the isolation of fact from value, Entrikin (1977, p. 616) argues,

> ... humanist geography does not offer a viable alternative to, nor a presuppositionless basis for, scientific geography ... (it) is best understood as a form of criticism ... (which) helps to counter the overly objective and abstractive tendencies of some scientific geographers.

Others are more directly critical of subjectivist approaches. Hay (1979) sees the main problems as those of inability to verify, a dismissive attitude towards scientific procedures, and an unwillingness to admit the place of the real world in 'latent' structures. All of these attributes are typical of the more extreme protagonists of subjectivism, however, and are not evident in either the practice or restated methodological positions of recent interpretations. Gregory (1978) focuses on the problems of thinking of validation in other than individual terms but again subjectivists have responded positively to the critique of reductionism both in theory and in practice. On a broader front, Sack (1978) argues that it is unlikely that a general relationship exists between perceived and actual properties of space.

As subjectivism 'matures' in a geographical context it is achieving both clarity and cohesion. Schutz's thrust towards verifiability has important implications; Buttimer's (1976) strategy for a geography of life-world which 'conjoins' humanistic and scientific enquiry is consistent with Schutz's ideas. Similarly in Ley's (1977) objectives for a geography of phenomenology, there is a strong line of compromise and recognition of the need to use humanism to modify and validify more scientific postures. Ley's objectives are description which recognizes the pervasive presence of the subjective as well as the objective in all areas of behaviour, adoption of a philosophical base which embraces both fact and value, recognition of the 'intersubjectivity' of the life-world, and a view of place as an amalgam of fact and value. These objectives are not dismissive of normal science, nor are they an advocacy of the primacy of the individual. They go some way towards meeting Gregory's plea for a hermeneutic approach to help specify consensus and clarify the conditions under which understanding can take place. From the evidence available at this point in time, Entrikin (1977) may be right and humanism is best seen as a form of criticism, but the criticism is considerable and the modifications of a spatial analysis perspective which humanism requires are pervasive and far-reaching. A distinctive humanist paradigm may yet emerge.

Structural imperatives

By the early 1970s, both the quantitative–theoretical and the subjective–humanist approaches were being questioned on new grounds. This development, variously termed as a shift towards 'structuralism', 'radicalism', or 'political economy' (Robson, 1976) was to find strong methodological roots in the social sciences, but its entrance into human geography was initiated at a more pragmatic level with civil rights and the anti-Vietnam movements in the United States in the later 1960s. There were several fronts to this radical critique in geography (see also Peet, 1977a; 1977b). One reaction was against the assumption of a society in which there was 'fair' competition between buyers and sellers; another sought to establish an understanding that an economy based on 'accumulation for its own sake' would be crisis-ridden; whilst a third focused upon the contradiction of participatory democracy through electoral procedures in the political sphere and its absence in the workplace—the production sphere. Established science had mistakenly claimed an objective, value-free, politically neutral role and in so doing was working to serve the existing social system and enable its survival. A second criticism concerned the assumption of consensus arrangements among social groups. From a radical viewpoint, capitalist society comprises socioeconomic groups among which the real processes are conflict and dissensus rather than merely competition and consensus (Cox, 1973). Geographical patterns could, it was argued, only be interpreted through this conflict among unequal groups in terms of their control of resources. A third criticism suggested that spatial analysis had only a limited descriptive role and could predict only in a mechanical way within the prescriptions of existing orders. Finally, subjective approaches were dismissed as reductionism and a return to the idiographic and exceptional stances which had proved so inhibiting in the past. The mainsprings of this critique are undoubtedly derived from Marxism but many geographers are prepared to accept the validity of much of the critique without embracing the overall philosophy upon which it is founded.

Out of these critical postures, loosely gathered under the umbrella of radical geography, has emerged a further distinctive methodological base to the study of urban problems which can be usefully described as structuralist. Structuralism in itself does not present a coherent strategy, it has been described as a diffuse tendency rather than a neatly consistent doctrine. Structuralism in its most straightforward definition is a method of enquiry based on concepts of totality, self-regulation, and transformation. Hay (1979) distinguishes between functionalism and structuralism in terms of the latter's concern to grasp the meaning of underlying structures; Eisenstadt and Curelaru (1976) classify structural-functionalism as a sociological paradigm; Runciman (1973) is not convinced of any innovative qualities which structuralism offers. For the purposes of this limited discussion, the focus is placed on 'structuralism' as a holistic scheme which views patterns and processes as outcomes of 'structural imperatives'; it is the total nature of the encompassing system which contains clues both to the forms of behaviour and the sources of inequality.

Gregory (1978) demonstrates the several routes by which structuralism has evolved. Durkheim's social morphology, Mauss's exchange theory, the linguistic structuralism of Lévi-Strauss, Piaget's operational structuralism and the structural Marxism of Althusser all stand as separate perspectives, albeit with links both developmentally and conceptually. The tendency of some geographers to regard structuralism as synonymous with Marxism is clearly wrong. As with early moves towards subjectivism, geographers have sometimes worked in structuralist terms without any consistent explicit awareness of the evolving philosophical traditions which precede them. This despite the fact that some forms of structuralism have long geographical heritages, and Durkheim, for example, had considerable influence on French regional geography. The objective here is to consider some of the main subdivisions and debates under the broad heading of 'structuralism'. Three main subdivisions of structural-functionalism, structural-symbolism, and structural-historical materialism are discussed with the emphasis upon basic features and points of distinctiveness; fuller accounts are available elsewhere (see, for example, Eisenstadt and Curelaru, 1976).

Structural functionalism has provided one of the main sociological paradigms which has both served as a model for research in its own right and, through its ability to stimulate criticism, has inadvertently aided the development of other paradigms. Structural-functionalism has three main components which place it within the framework of a positivist science. These are a strong emphasis on values and consensus as major mechanisms for the acceptance of social order; a social-structural point of analytical departure; and a strong systemic, presumably an historical, conception of society. Jessop (1972, pp. 16–18) has summarized the features of structural-functionalism:

Every social system is confronted with four functional problems . . . of pattern mainten-ance, integration, goal attainment and adaptation. Pattern maintenance refers to the need to maintain and reinforce the basic values of the social system and to resolve tensions that emerge from continuing commitment to these values. Integration refers to the alloca-tion of rights and obligations, rewards and facilities, to ensure the harmony of relations between members of the social system. Goal attainment involves the necessity of mobilizing actors and resources in organized ways for the attainment of specific goals. And adaptation refers to the need for the production or acquisition of generalised facilities or resources that can be employed in the attainment of various specific goals . . . . Social order depends on the continuing fulfillment of the four functional problems and also on the maintenance of balanced relations between the social system, the other systems of action, and the physical environment.

The concept of consensus which underpins structural-functionalism appear-ed, initially at least, to specify roles as given. Normative patterns of behaviour were fixed in the institutional structure of society to which individuals—reduced to role performers—adjusted through socialization and interaction with other people. The holistic or systemic component led to the assumption that institutional arrangements were given, upheld by the value consensus and the needs of the social system. This form of structuralism, therefore, postulated a controlling social system, resting on the consensus needs of its society, in which individuals were socialized to fulfil roles or functions. The organized, consensus social structure was the reference point for comprehension of behaviour and other surface manifestations. As a positivist model, structural-functionalism has strong links with spatial analysis. Its tenets allow for the existence of economic man and the whole concept of models. Its mechanistic features and consensus base have stimulated many criticisms. It is accused of providing a structural referent which does not allow for notions of conflict and dissent, which ignores the historical and individualized dimensions, and which serves as a theory to sustain existing hegemonies and sociopolitical systems. The radical critique is heavily censorious of the: 'attempt of the structural-functional model to identify general abstract categories of social systems common to all societies', and the failure to 'stress the importance of the specific systemic characteristics of different historical situations which are determined by historically unique characteristic of the "focus of production", or of systems of domination prevailing in a given situation' (Eisenstadt and Curelaru, 1975, p. 203).

Structural-symbolism

Lévi-Strauss (see Rossi, 1974) is commonly regarded as the main exponent of a theory which stresses the autonomy of a cultural-symbolic dimension to human life. A key difference with the structural-functionalist school is the refusal to accept its assumption: ' ... that the symbolic realm, as manifested for example, in myth and ritual, is a function or reflection of the organizational integrative needs of the social system' (Eisenstadt and Curelaru, 1976, p. 204). In his exchange theory, Mauss (1970) provides important bases from which a form of structuralism that places far greater emphasis on the symbolic content of society can develop, Mauss studied gift exchanges and demonstrated that these could provide critical insights into a 'hidden structure' of values, traditions, and mores, which underpin society. Mauss influenced Lévi-Strauss whose goal became that of reassembling the 'instances' or manifest experiences which may disclose the 'hidden structure' and allow its comprehension. Eisenstadt and Curelaru (1976, p. 205) summarize the structural-symbolism position:

1. First, that there is in any society or culture some 'hidden structure' which is more real and pervasive than the overt social organization or behavioural patterns.
2. The rules which govern such a structure are not concrete rules of organization, and are not derived from organizational or institutional needs or problems, but are crystallized as codes in the rules of the human mind.
3. It is these rules which are the essential constitutive elements of culture and society, providing deeper ordering principles of the social and cultural realms.

In its extreme form, the structural symbolism approach maintained that the special properties of the symbolic sphere, the rules of the human mind, determined the basic rules and characteristics of social reality. This emphasis upon the autonomy of the symbolic realm and its influence upon hidden structure has tended to disregard the dimensions of power and the organizational needs of society. Its advocates were called upon by critics to: ' . . . specify the nature of the exact institutional loci and mechanisms through which the symbolic dimensions of human activities impinged on institutional life and on the working of social systems' (Eisenstadt and Curelaru, 1976, p. 280). As structural-symbolism has matured through the medium of criticism and debate, its ability to adapt to the need to accommodate power and organization in society has increased. Its basic reference point of a 'hidden structure' gives it a collectivist characteristic but its emphasis on the subjective and flexibility to allow individualistic differences, gives points of contact for humanistic interpretations in geography.

Structural–historical materialism

Marxism as a form of structuralism has distinctive features and a multi-dimensional character which as Gregory (1978) suggests should not be regarded as a preformed and pregiven science but as one which requires constant and critical examination. Although there are considerable contrasts between structural-symbolism and Marxist models, both emphasize the principle of a 'hidden structure' which explains the dynamic of a society. The classical Marxist approach also contains elements of a strong functionalist-systemic perspective, even though these are combined with awareness of conflict and change. Amongst the key component of a structural-historical materialism perspective are the concepts of social formation and of mode of production, though their precise meaning continues to be subject to debate. Boddy (1976, p. 58) defines social formation as a theoretical construct which conceptualizes

. . . particular real societies in terms of economic, political and ideological levels articulated in a specific way to form a complex whole. The structure of a particular social formation implies a particular distribution of class power and of the social product of the formation, and the social formation will tend to maintain this structure and continuously to reproduce itself.

Following Castells and Althusser, Pickvance (1974) sees every social formation as a 'structural whole' in which three fundamental 'instances' or 'levels'—the economic, political-legal, and the ideological—are articulated. The term *mode of production* refers to a specific combination of these instances; in the capitalist mode of production the economic instance is always dominant. Harloe (1974) argues, however, that any given social formation may contain a combination of different modes of production which are complexly related to each other. The social formation is said to exercise 'structural causality' and in this sense is comparable to the 'hidden structure' of the structural-symbolists. In the traditional Marxist scheme (see Burgess, 1976) the *base* consists of the prevailing forces of production and the economic level, whereas the *superstructure* comprises the network of political, legal, social and cultural institutions, together with the ideology which they emit to all other aspects of society. The superstructure is determined by the base in general character:

The sum total of these relations of production constitutes the economic structure of society, the real foundation, on which rises a legal and political superstructure and to which correspond definite forms of social consciousness. The mode of production of material life conditions the general process of social, political and intellectual life. It is not the consciousness of men that determines their existence but their social existence that determines their consciousness (Marx, quoted in Gregory, 1978, p. 110).

Many have seen this kind of statement on the influence of the *base* as an indication of the economic determinism of Marxist thought, but recent writers on Marxism in geography and elsewhere deny this type of interpretation. Lee (1979) argues that structural analysis in a Marxist sense is based upon the notion of mode of production with its philosophical bases of historical materialism—or science of social formations—and is not deterministic. It is rather an attempt to approach the totality of social existence by providing a set of concepts through which the societal process may be grasped as a whole. Similarly, Pickvance (1974) stresses that determination by the capitalist mode of production does not imply an absence of relative autonomy at other levels. Burgess (1976) argues that *base* is a conscious organization and *superstructure* is a rationalization through consciousness, so Marx is not applying strict determinism. In Althusser's (1969) interpretation, the economic level is both dominant and determinant in the capitalist mode of production, whereas in other modes of production other levels may be dominant but are still affected by conditions of the economic level. A further useful 'opening' in this context is provided by Pickvance (1974) who suggests that mode of production exercises a general rather than a specific effect upon the social content of spatial forms. Study of particular settlements or urban areas allows the effect of the prevailing mode of production to be understood but also enables specific local effects to be recognized. These can include 'symbolic' or social values and the impacts of more localized organization and institutions. Such an indication of flexibility is noted by Eisenstadt and Curelaru (1976, p. 254):

Some Marxists have attempted to specify the institutional loci of the principles of a society's hidden structure in the combination of structuralist and Marxist (mode of production) terms. This specification has often led them, through the confrontation of the two approaches and through the analysis of their data, to abandon the 'simplifications' and 'closures' of either camp—the rigid Marxist distinction between 'base' and 'superstructure' and the structuralist emphasis on the general rules of the mind without specification of this institutional anchorage. As a result they have sought the mechanisms through which the symbolic realm becomes part of the working of the social system and provides some of its principles.

These are 'openings' or moves towards more flexible positions but geographers working in a Marxist framework consistently stress the primacy of economic factors and relations as underpinnings to social relationships and residential patterns. Harvey (1978) for example, argues that capitalist society creates physical landscapes in its own image and its structural imperatives closely circumscribe its solutions to urban problems.

Structuralism and urban geography

The brief outlines of three forms of structuralism which have been provided touch upon some of their main qualities. Each of these has relevance to the practice of urban geography. Structural-functionalism stands apart from the other two but its main role has been contained in its link through positive science to the spatial analysis paradigm and the concept of models. As stated, both structural-symbolism and structural-historical materialism, emphasize a 'hidden structure' which is the basic point of reference for patterns and processes of behaviour. That hidden structure is very differently defined by each approach but its 'power' is similarly stressed. Both these structural approaches have value in the sense that they point geographers towards the broader context within which urban-spatial structures and social problems must be studied. They also introduce critical concepts such as symbolism and culture, conflict, and power, and historical specificity, to the realm of urban geography. The structural imperatives in these senses have been largely accepted by many urban geographers; the points of departure occur where the contribution to understanding which 'hidden structure' can make becomes exhausted and the finer details and nuances need to be added at a more 'individualistic' level. This need not be extreme or literal individualism but occurs at the point where to understand place and people in space, local factors and traditions have to be considered. Discussion of the subjective approach has already explored some of these possibilities but somewhat closer to 'hidden structure', analysis of the 'managers' in the societal system has valuable insights to offer.

MANAGERIALISM

On no account does the study of managerialism constitute a theory comparable to any of those developed under the broad heading of structuralism. It has numerous links with theories but in itself constitutes a *framework* for study rather than a cohesive conceptual argument. The basic thesis of managerialism can be simply stated. It suggests that whatever the social formation, there is an intermediate level of decision-makers between the central 'government' or central institutions concerned with the allocation of resources, working in accordance with agreed general principles, but capable of exercising some discretion. These allocative decisions affect social and spatial distributions, and the fact that discretion exists means that the managers are key figures to be studied in their own right. This interpretation of managerialism can be developed from Weber's belief that a clear distinction exists between *base* and *superstructure* and that the political-legal elements of the superstructure

can achieve a level of autonomy. Given this autonomous position, the decision-makers or managers in the superstructure hold *relatively* independent roles and make decisions not necessarily conditioned by the base. Structuralists are both sceptical of the idea of autonomy and of the amount of discretion which must be allowed to make managerialism a distinctive perspective. From a Marxist viewpoint managerialism is an ideology; managers exist within the system but are heavily conditioned by the 'rules' of the social formation and have very little discretion or independence. (See Duncan, 1976, and also Becker, 1976, though the latter is very largely concerned with managers in industry.)

In its earlier forms, managerialism was premised on a definite model of the large-scale society as a corporate state and it was the bureaucratic management which served as the focus of study: 'Increasingly . . . in the welter of directives and circulars from central government, the execution of social welfare and public services must fall into the hands of functionaries, professional servants of the public interest' (Mellor, 1977, p. 244). Given these origins, it is not surprising that the managerialist thesis has been most strongly developed in the context of government and has focused on those managers concerned with finance and housing supply. Norman (1975) also distinguishes between early managerialism which focused on the specific nature of management exercised and more recent forms which are more interested in power relations and their expression in an urban context.

Managerialism has been the subject of considerable criticism both from structuralists who tend to be dismissive of the whole thesis and from others who find inconsistencies in the argument (see Harloe, 1974). One criticism is that a focus on the roles of managers may be diversionary. If, for example, social disadvantage can be recognized in particular areas, a managerialist approach which attributes too much of its explanation to the decision-makers or 'middlemen', may contain the danger of an uncritical accommodation of the national élite and of society's 'master' institutions. A second problem is that of attributing the right amount of weight and autonomy to different gatekeepers in a diversity of circumstances. Some managers and bureaucrats may exaggerate their independent roles, others may portray them in a heavily constrained way; elucidation of the nature of the role is a careful evaluative task. The 'hidden mechanisms' through which distributions are achieved are complex even when they can be revealed. Managers in government are placed in intermediate positions between centrally and locally elected representatives and, increasingly, are faced by pressure groups at both these levels, national and local. A third criticism of managerialism is that it has overemphasized the public sector and has paid less attention to the large institutions of the private sector. With this wider brief, however, the question of 'Who are the managers?' becomes more difficult to answer. Are estate agents, for example, mediators or capitalists? Norman (1975) suggests that private managers as mediators should be employees rather than owners; this has some appeal but is unlikely to be a consistently useful criterion.

Despite the criticisms of the managerialist thesis, Pahl (1979a, 1979b) and others (see, for example, Williams, 1978) remain convinced of its value. Pahl argues that whatever form society takes, resources will always be scarce and procedures to effect their distribution will always be necessary. As societies increase in their complexity, so an increasing number of rules and procedures which *cannot* cover all contingencies will be needed. What is essential is the understanding that:

specific agents ultimately control and allocate resources. States may attempt to centralise in the interests of equality or efficiency, but discretion must remain at all levels. Administrative complexity has reached such a level that information overload is in danger of smothering the centre. This puts more discretion to the local level (Pahl, 1979a, p. 43).

Pahl supports his case by reference to evidence which, though not detailed, suggests that similar problems of unequal distributions of resources and similar reliance upon the discretionary roles of managers, exists in contrasted types of society. Musil's (1971) study of Czechoslovakia, for example, shows that in the absence of price mechanisms to regulate land-use, non-economic allocations occur which are largely sociopolitical processes, negotiated by political bodies with economic and interest organizations.

Managerialism offers a useful level of analysis in the study of urban geography. To understand distributions, knowledge of the decision-makers is a valuable framework for study. Although there are arguments for an extension of managerialist study to decision-makers in the macro-economy (Leonard, 1979), most research has focused on the local interface between need and provision. Whereas decision-makers have to be viewed in structural contexts, influenced by the policies of institutions that they serve, the refusal to treat them merely as 'pale, entrepreneurial figures' with mechanistic functions, brings a humanistic approach into perspective. Managerialism provides a useful way of penetrating the complex relationships that structure urban areas at the points of contact between consumer and allocators of scarce resources; it may help both to expose the allocative processes and the rationalities on which they are based.

CONCLUSIONS

After a long period of very slow change and an essential conservatism, human geography has acquired several new dimensions since the early 1960s. Very considerable changes have affected the practice of the subdiscipline of urban geography and have changed its character almost completely. Where practices and types of study-problem reminiscent of the previous time-period survive, they have been modified almost beyond recognition; even more 'traditional' approaches such as urban morphology have responded to criticisms of the early 1960s in ways which provide them with a more rational place in an evolving discipline (see Conzen, 1978). Urban geographers are now more sophisticated in the quantitative methodologies which they employ and a basic statistical competence is almost universal though the parallel of a healthy, informed and mature scepticism of the proper role of quantification is now evident.

On a broader front, urban geographers have also become more aware of the existence of alternative methodologies and philosophies and have shown a willingness to delve into the literature of the evolution of thought in the social sciences. New concepts rarely have an internal relevance only, and the waves of innovations which have repercussions throughout the literature are now more easily identified and incorporated into urban geography. It is unlikely that time-lags of the scale which preceded the arrival of innovations from the earlier part of this century will be replicated. There is also a greater acceptance of the fact that an investigation of the human condition cannot be ideologically neutral; geographers may agree completely on basic facts and even diagnoses, but the prescriptions for change may spring from a fundamental belief system and still produce alternative, if not opposed, strategies. To this end, there is among geographers a debate over whether these changes involve a series of revolutions in method, approach, and philosophy, or whether—as some would argue (Chisholm, 1975)—they are merely variations on the same theme and represent a steady evolutionary course.

The revolutionary model of science argues that change is brought about by recognition of the need for a revolution in method, by the adoption of a new paradigm of how work should proceed (Kuhn, 1962). According to this view of scientific disciplines, periods of what are termed 'normal science', in which the conservative model holds sway and researchers concentrate on adding further knowledge to the accepted model, retesting, verifying and extending its laws, are punctuated by revolutions or paradigmatic shocks, when the accepted model is overthrown because of its inability to answer the current questions. There are strong alternatives to Kuhn's interpretation of normative science, Popper (1960), for example, argues that changes in science are not revolutionary but a logical progression towards truth, that there is an *evolutionary* model in which scientists, as openminded individuals, push back the frontier of knowledge on the bases of their own ideas. This model also has conservative qualities in that it has rules and procedures but it may contain several paradigms.

Both these models have deficiencies, and a third view of scientific progress, the branching model (Herbert and Johnston, 1978) allows for evolution of ideas along the mainstream of disciplinary development but recognizes that large reorientations may evolve as *branches* which may develop their own normal science but will retain an attachment to the discipline. To break away might place the participants in the new branch in a vulnerable status position and could also weaken the main discipline. Branches may flourish and provide long-term extra dimensions to a discipline or they may have only a short-term existence as temporary diversions. This type of model fits the experience of urban geography most easily, new branches have been added but overall cohesion has not been significantly weakened. Although major changes have occurred along with 'revolutions' in method and philosophy, these have been added to more established approaches rather than replaced them; methodological, philosophical and ideological debates continue to be intense.

Support for the branching model is based on an interpretation of trends in urban geography over the past two decades and is also an 'article of faith' for the continuance of the subdiscipline as a separate field of study. This latter sentiment is predicated on the belief that a distinctive 'geography' of urban areas and urban processes has a manageable and valuable role to play. Both these attitudes need to be defended as trends are open to different interpretations and the subdiscipline can be extrapolated to various eventual goals. It could be argued, for example, that there are trends towards real fragmentation within urban geography, greater than a branching model could encompass, which may lead to independent paradigms. On the other hand, it can also be argued that as urban and social geography become more enmeshed within the social sciences, their separate identities will become blurred as they become an integral part of a broader social science perspective. A branching model needs to recognize and counter these possibilities.

Some parallels can be identified in modern sociological analyses. Eisenstadt and Curelaru (1976, p. 311) identify as 'crises' the trends towards increasing fragmentation of modes of enquiry into separate schools of thought which become mutually exclusive and antagonistic.

As a result of these tendencies, sociology could be presented as consisting of completely closed, 'totalistic' paradigms which differed not only in their analytic premises but also in their philosophical, ideological, and political assumptions, minimizing the possibility of scholarly discourse on problems of common interest.

A main thrust of one argument from Eisenstadt and Curelaru is the search for 'openings' or more flexible attitudes on the part of exponents of the various schools of thought from which some level of convergence on central issues of common concern might be achieved. In a similar vein, Butzer (1978) argues that disciplines would be better served if they encouraged a healthier mix of specialization and generalization, and of objectivity and subjectivity. Although there is less evidence of polarizations in urban geography, the trends are nevertheless discernible, and an early willingness to provide 'openings' could avoid eventual 'closed systems'. Hay (1979), in reaching out for reconciliations between positivism and its alternatives, turned to some arguments from Habermas (1972). These suggest that the sciences fall into three categories of *empirical* or nomological analysis, mainly positivist; *hermeneutic* analysis, mainly idealism and phenomenology; and *critical* analysis, mainly structural-Marxism. For Habermas, these were not mutually exclusive. Hay (1979, p. 22) recognizes some deficiencies in the argument but suggests that it could be extended to recognize:

... a *nomological* geography which seeks, for example to understand the workings of urban rent theory as positivistically observed, a *hermeneutic* geography which seeks to identify the meaning of the urban rent system for those who are participants ... and a *critical* geography which points to the extent to which present urban rent systems are themselves transformations of the capitalistic system.

This type of reconciliation accords with a branching model which recognizes different 'branches', each of which has a particular mode of analysis, but also acknowledges a common ground towards which convergences are necessary. There is, in fact, very little evidence in the recent development of urban geography that allegiances to particular paradigms or methodological viewpoints have led to any significant departures from the subdiscipline. Regional science, which was primarily a breakaway from economics, attracted some geographers to separate departments but many of its aspects are now incorporated into geographical syllabuses as spatial analysis. Advocacy of subjective approaches such as idealism (Guelke, 1974; 1978) and phenomenology (Ley, 1977) has been conducted very much within the context of geography and has often identified 'roots' in more traditional paradigms such as Vidal de la Blache's concept of regionalism. The structural/radical perspectives of the 1970s, more especially those based on Marxism, have greatest potential for 'separatism'. In practice, however, this perspective has been most strongly developed in relation to urban problems and in urban areas where the inequalities implicit in the capitalist system find most overt expression. These separate 'paradigms' or modes of interpretation can be accommodated within a branching model of an essentially evolutionary character.

Particularly from the structural/radical perspective, the main drive is not to create a separate paradigm *within* urban geography, but to recognize the futility of disciplinary boundaries and to merge the work of geographers into the general ethos of the social sciences. Trends in this direction can be recognized, both in the incorporation of geography into multidisciplinary studies which is now reasonably well-established and, more problematically, in occasional calls for the abandonment of independent disciplinary identities. Whereas the former of these trends is seen as highly desirable, the latter has less appeal. As has been already argued, a discrete urban geography has the advantages of developing an established methodological focus, of maintaining a field of enquiry of manageable propositions, and of providing a testing ground in the regional and local environment for theories developed in the wide spectrum of the social sciences. A discrete urban geography as a teaching and research subdiscipline does not imply an unthinking preoccupation with the 'fetishism of space' but does imply a focus on spatial qualities of urban phenomena in the context of their other characteristics, be they patterns, processes or policies. Any single discipline has only a partial contribution to offer and as its initial analyses must be conditioned by an awareness of broader points of reference and constraint within the social system, so its findings must eventually be fitted into those of other perspectives and disciplines. The branching model can accommodate innovations and alternatives in the development or urban geography within what is primarily an evolutionary ethos. Hay's (1979) tripartite scheme of reconciliations is one representation of the coexistence of different positions within urban geography. It leaves unanswered questions of how, when and in which way the approaches converge to provide some more total understanding of a basic issue, but the willingness of different branches to present 'openings' is critical in this process. It is likely that synthesis or convergence will be most consistently achieved in teaching rather than in research. The teacher of urban geography needs to present his subject in an interrelated way and to look for the point of convergence in both conceptual and practical ways; the researcher on his particular branch sees the primary task as one of developing the strength of a specific mode of analysis rather than of looking for linkages.

Urban geography will continue to accommodate a diversity of interests and approaches, pursued at differing 'scales of analysis' and 'levels of spatial resolution', and will be the richer for that characteristic. The geographers' contribution to urban studies will continue to be distinguished by the attention which it focuses on the spatial dimension—on place, space and people–environment interaction. Spatial processes in themselves however are rarely explanatory processes and need to be taken in conjunction with social, political and economic forces. Viewed from the branching model, urban geography will continue to develop in diverse ways but will retain both its essential unity and identity. This text has the task of giving some indication of the breadth of urban geography, and the wide range of applications which typifies it, and also of demonstrating the common methodological concerns which provide its unity. In this chapter the broader philosophical bases have been discussed in the belief that they provide an essential frame of reference for what urban geographers do. As will be evident, the relationship of empirical urban geography to philosophical bases has rarely been explicit in past studies but is likely to assume greater importance in the future development of this subdiscipline.

Chapter 3

The Emergence of the Urban System

URBAN ORIGINS

There are problems in the definition of what is urban, and similarly there are considerable difficulties in establishing the beginnings in time and place of the first urban settlements. The two issues are not unconnected and scholars from a variety of disciplines continue to find them questions for debate and new research. Much of the available evidence for very early forms of settlement is archaeological and goes back several millennia in time. In most of the detailed site investigations the scale and sophistication of the built environment, with its accumulation of artifacts, leaves little margin for doubt of the existence of an urban centre. Other evidence, particularly of smaller settlements, is contentious, however, and uncertainty remains. Archaeological evidence is often characterized by its unevenness. Some parts of the world have revealed little or no evidence of early cities but a number of reasons could explain this. Lack of evidence may confirm that cities did not exist, but it also possible that insufficient proof has survived in recognizable form. Detailed archaeological investigation is extremely expensive and time-consuming, and many of the major investigations were completed before the advent of major technological advances such as remote sensing and dating techniques. Without such studies only generalized statements are possible on parts of the world thought to have experienced early urbanization. McGee (1967) for example, can only suggest that the origins of south-east Asian cities are obscure and seem related to the diffusion of Chinese and Indian forms of political organizations in the first century AD. Again, even where very detailed evidence is available, as for Catal Huyuk in Anatolia (Jacobs, 1969; Mellaart, 1967), it is typically restricted to one site and cannot easily be generalized to encompass regional systems of settlements.

As with most urban topics, and particularly those which have been a focus of attention from other disciplines, the literature is voluminous. Though primarily a 'historical' question in a narrow disciplinary sense it is one which has received close and scholarly attention by some geographers. In what inevitably must be a summary which does scant justice to the debate at large, some prominence will be given to their views. Carter (1977) has offered a detailed and perceptive review of the theories of urban origins, whilst contrasted analytical insights have been suggested by Wheatley (1971) and Harvey (1973).

The 'traditional' theory of urban origins

There is an established theory of the origins of cities, mostly associated with Childe (1950), to which most scholars would subscribe in part at least, though its details have come to be regarded as tenuous and not fully substantiated. This might be termed the ecological or environmental theory—though the terms do less than justice to the breadth of Childe's thesis. One basic tenet is that the emergence of cities was consequential to a process of agricultural change. A neolithic revolution (Jones, 1966) which advanced society from a stage of primitive hunting and gathering to one of food producing was the necessary precondition for the emergence of towns. Domestication and cultivation led first to more permanent settlements, the neolithic villages. An increase in carrying capacity of the land and a rise in population gave more villages but also freed some of the community from the rhythm of agriculture and the new seasonality allowed for some periods of lower activity. There is evidence according to Jones (1966) that the standard Mayan plot could produce twice as much corn as was necessary to support an average family unit. The freedom from agriculture gave conditions under which specializations could develop, producing initially perhaps only priests, leaders and craftsmen but eventually a class of merchants.

The ecological or environmental thesis of urban origins requires favourable conditions of the natural environment or physical geography. The projected sequence of events is most likely to occur in those parts of the world favoured with topography, soils, water supply, and climate which make agricultural 'revolution' more possible. Some would argue that these natural conditions have to be matched by an advanced level of human endeavour through which critical changes in agriculture may be achieved. Such questions of 'circularity' of argument inevitably occur, however, and can seldom be adequately resolved (Carter, 1977).

Most writers would accept, in general terms at least, that part of the Childe thesis which suggests that agricultural surplus is the catalyst for change which leads to urban development. Mumford (1961) extends the notion of surplus back in time to the cave painters of the Upper Paleolithic Period. These specialists, perhaps with some religious roles, were released from the primary function of hunting and gathering by an abundance of game and thus exhibit some of the first strands of an urban tradition. A key question has been not the fact of surplus but the way in which it became the basis of city civilizations. Before considering that and other questions relating to surplus, however, it is useful to note that one viewpoint exists which disputes the basic tenet of agricultural change leading via surplus to cities. Jacobs (1969) has argued that transition from rural to urban does not bear close investigation either in terms of some archaeological evidence, or from modern interpretations of the relative roles of cities and countryside. Using the evidence of Catal Huyuk (Mellaart, 1967), an early Anatolian city, she argues that the city was the first form of settlement in the region and that change in rural areas was subsequent to it. Catal Huyuk was a mining centre in a previously unsettled area; it was in response to demand generated from the city and to innovations originating in the city that any significant changes in the rural area occurred. Jacobs extends the thesis by arguing that rural areas have rarely been sources of invention, innovation, and change; cities much more typically fill those roles. The argument has some force but doubtful generality. Modern examples may be found of mining centres in uninhabited areas which provide a stimulus, though often temporary, to local agricultural change; they tend to be exceptions rather than rules, however. Again, although cities have stronger records as centres of innovation rural areas have not been devoid of such roles. It is reasonable to assume that changes that only affect rural areas and that are part of a long process of evolution in settlement and economy, will originate within those areas. The case of Catal Huyuk then is valid but exceptional.

There are other more general criticisms of the Childe thesis. Friedmann and Wulff (1976) for example discount the term urban 'revolution'. The development of urban civilizations occupied a very long period of time, counted in hundreds of centuries, and took various and distinctive forms in different parts of the world. A more considerable debate surrounds the issue of *where* the nuclear areas of cities really were. The issue has two parts. Firstly, there is the basic question of the locations of the earliest urban civilizations; secondly, there is the related question of whether some areas were primary and others were derived—whether there was independent development or diffusion. Listings of the early urban civilizations do vary but have, nevertheless, a significant common core. Sjoberg (1973) included Egypt, Mesopotamia, and the Indus valley with later nuclear areas in North China and Middle America. Braidwood and Willey (1962) concluded that south-west Asia, Meso-America, Peru, India and China had urban civilizations by the beginning of the Christian period. Wheatley (1971) suggests seven areas of independent or primary urbanization: Mesopotamia, the Indus valley, the Nile valley, the North China plain, Meso-America, the central Andes, and south west Nigeria. (Figure 3.1) Both Braidwood and Willey, and also Wheatley, would argue that these are independent developments of urban civilizations, a scale of independence which discards most of the earlier notions of diffusion from single centres or from a very small number of centres. The concept of a single centre of diffusion in the Near East has always been difficult to maintain and, in particular, the appearance of urbanisms in central and South America has never successfully been accommodated. Most writers must accept that there were 'secondary' or 'derived' urban civilizations, as in Crete, south-east Asia and Etruria; there are well-documented examples of 'transplanted' cities which appear as part of a political process of imperial or colonial extensions. Towns in Roman Britain (Rivet, 1964) are of this type and McGee (1967) has attributed the earliest cities in south east Asia to a similar process. In summary then, a number

56

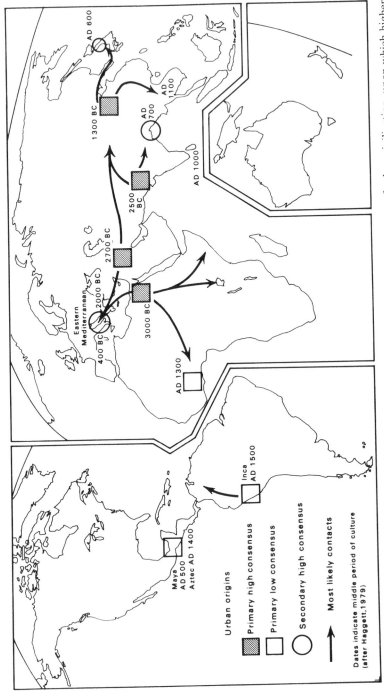

Figure 3.1 Urban origins: global patterns, some conjecture remains but those *primary* sources of urban civilization, upon which higher and lower levels of consensus have been reached, are shown together with most commonly agreed secondary sources and lines of contact (dates are extracted from Haggett (1979) Table 12.1, p. 278)

of independent centres of early urbanization may be recognized in both the Old World and the New World. They certainly did not coincide in time and their features often differed; Meso-American cities, for example, were created without animal husbandry, the wheel or an extensive alluvial setting (Sjoberg, 1965). Diffusion may have been less important in these very early periods than in late stages when imperialist and colonialist expansions used towns as instruments of control and administration. Both Childe (1950) and Sjoberg (1965) have stated that urbanization spread much more rapidly during the first five centuries of the Iron Age, with growth of empires, such as those of Persia China, India, Greece and Rome, than during the preceding fifteen centuries of the Bronze Age.

The concept of surplus

To return to questions surrounding the origins of cities and the concept of surplus; Harvey (1973, p. 216) has produced a succinct statement of the issue: 'There is general agreement that an agricultural surplus product was necessary for the emergence of city forms. Much controversy, however, surrounds the manner in which we should conceive of surplus and the way in which surpluses arise, are acquired and are put to use.' Part of the controversy refers to the concept of surplus and whether it is to be seen as an absolute or as a relative entity. It is clear that surplus belongs to a large group of concepts, which includes poverty and deprivation, which can only be viewed in relative terms. A threshold of need, beyond which a surplus exists, may vary from one society to another and ultimately among individuals. As Wheatley (1971, p. 268) has suggested: 'No primitive people have ever spent all their waking hours in eating, breeding and cultivating: even the most debilitated, by squandering some of their resources in non-utilitarian ways, have demonstrated the existence of a surplus'. Pearson (1957) has similarly argued that there are always potential surpluses available, and they must be measured not merely against biological needs, but also in relation to the social conditions in which they occur. Harvey (1973) warns against a 'formless relativism' in the context of surplus and argues the need for a general context from which to assess surplus, such as that offered by Marxism as a view of 'the universal human requirements of man's existence as a species' (1973, p. 219).

A great deal of research attention has focused on the way in which surplus, where identified, becomes translated into the chain of events which leads to the emergence of cities (see Figure 3.2). Here the search is for those key individuals, institutions, or groups whose role is to initiate and perpetuate the processes of change once the conditions for it are sufficient. In this search, the likelihood of a multistranded rather than a single-stranded causation process is now broadly acknowledged. Several recent pronouncements reflect this view: 'It is doubtful if a single, autonomous, causative factor will ever be identified in the nexus of social, economic, and political transformation which resulted in the emergence of urban forms' (Wheatley, 1971, p. 318); and 'The catalyst was probably the

58

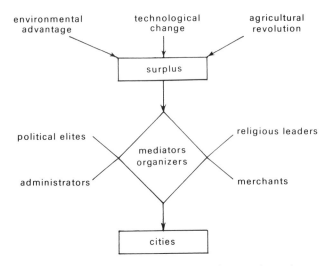

Figure 3.2   Urban origins: surplus to city, a schematic representation of ways in which surplus occurs and may lead to cities

intricately related role of temple, fortress and market place (Carter, 1977, p. 26).

Individual writers nevertheless have their own ideas on key institutions. Adams (1966), rather generally concluded that *social* institutions precipitated changes in technology and in other cultural realms. Hassan (1972), more specifically, emphasizes the role of religion in meeting the need for authority and organization. Wheatley (1971) would also afford critical roles to religion and sees the earliest cities as ceremonial complexes or centres of ritual. At the moment of transition, religious movements dominate but almost immediately secular forces intervene to help sustain a new form of social organization. Sjoberg (1960, p. 67) emphasizes political rather than religious leaders, though at key points the two may have been synonymous:

We must, if we are to explain the growth, spread, and decline of cities, comment upon the city as a mechanism by which a society's rulers can consolidate and maintain their power and, more important, the essentiality of a well-developed power structure for the formation and perpetuation of urban centres.

A belief that there are important *economic* bases to urbanism has many adherents. Perhaps the best-known of these is Pirenne (1925) who regarded commerce as the creator of the medieval towns. The concept of the town as a point of exchange through the medium of the market-place has earlier applicability and is generally acknowledged as at least *one* relevant factor by most writers. Carter (1977) is sceptical of the extent to which this concept of city as market-place has general applicability and points out that many markets and fairs are itinerant and have not necessarily engendered permanent urban forms of settlement. Defensive functions are similarly regarded as having urban associations; most early cities were fortified in some manner, but are also likely to be expressions of social and political organizations which led to cities rather than initiators in their own right.

For Harvey (1973) even the social institutions of religion and politics are 'superstructures' rather than primary forces in their own right. Each 'mode of production' and social organization has ideological content and political meaning and surplus has to be defined in ways which are internal to the workings of that particular mode of production. Surplus may be expropriated for welfare in an 'unalienated' society or for profit or redistribution in an 'alienated' society. The unalienated, reciprocal mode of production is typically pre-urban. Both redistributive and market exchange modes of production may lead to a permanent concentration of surplus value and the urban transition, but the market economy mode is most likely to do so. The extraction of surplus labour power does not necessarily give rise to urbanism; the latter relies upon the concentration of a significant quantity of social surplus product at one point in space—it is quite possible for social surplus to be extracted and yet remain dispersed. By this line of argument (Harvey, 1973), the 'social institutions' are themselves underlain by fundamental changes in the economic bases of society. Surplus becomes 'primitive accumulation' (Luxemburg, 1973) and as economic change leads to a transition from reciprocal to redistributive to market economies, the investment of expropriated surplus into permanent 'forms' gives rise to cities. These 'forms' are the monuments of urban culture, be they palaces, temples, market-places, gildhalls or overall city plans.

Clearly then, there is still considerable room from debate, discussion, and further research on several issues surrounding the origins of cities. On questions of where and when, the basic investigative procedure of archaeological research goes on and new evidence will appear to modify prevailing theories. Such evidence will probably not change our views on the locations of early cities dramatically but will help to refine and perhaps qualify our interpretations. On questions of how and why, room for conjecture and contention will remain. There are varying emphases among scholars on the critical factors and some opposed views, but there is also evidence of common ground. As support of a multi-stranded explanation grows, so the various theories may increasingly be seen as complementary rather than alternative. Cities reflect the societies of which they are part, and as those societies vary, so will their cities. There can be exceptional features affecting urban developments in some parts of the world and at some points in time, but there are also likely to be common features and comparable combinations of circumstances.

CITIES IN TRADITIONAL SOCIETIES

Although urban geography has focused its attention squarely upon modern cities and particularly upon those in Western societies, there is a relatively small but significant literature upon the nature of cities prior to this modern

60

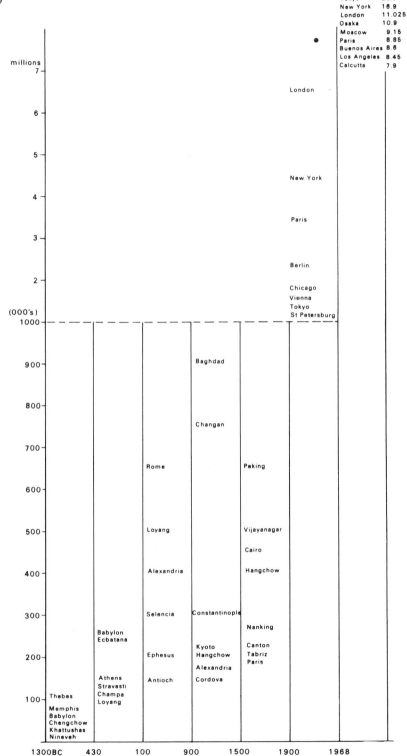

					Tokyo	20.5
---	---	---	---	---	New York	16.9
					London	11.025
					Osaka	10.9
					Moscow	9.15
					Paris	8.85
					Buenos Aires	8.6
					Los Angeles	8.45
					Calcutta	7.9

period. If the later eighteenth century with the Industrial Revolution and its enormous influence on people and settlements is taken as a divide, there is something of the order of 5000 years during which time cities existed in one or more parts of the world. Over this period urban civilizations grew and declined, periods of urban dominance were followed by times during which cities were abandoned or destroyed and rural forms of society gained ascendancy. These phases have been well documented (Chandler and Fox, 1974; Mumford, 1961) and for some authors, writing in a more popular idiom (Morgan, 1978), they suggest that a cyclic 'inevitability' may be associated with urban development. A time-period of these dimensions is clearly capable of detailed subdivision, but for our present purposes a simple two-fold division into cities in 'modern' and 'traditional' societies is sufficient; this section focuses on those cities of the preindustrial period which emerged as parts of 'traditional' societies.

Compared with the cities of the modern world, these preindustrial cities were generally small in population size and were relatively few in numbers. Chandler and Fox (1974) have compiled statistical estimates for much of this period and some of their results have been incorporated in Figure 3.3. In 1360 BC, for example, Thebes was the largest city in the world with a population of about 100,000 and there were only twenty cities with populations in excess of 20,000. By 100 AD, Rome had a population of 650,000 and the number of cities with more than 40,000 was just over 60. Not until the period 1750–1800 did any city reach 1 million in population size, and this was Peking. Throughout this period the capital cities, or what Jefferson (1939) called the 'primate' cities, were disproportionately larger than any other within their urban system. Langton (1978) records that in 1730 the vast majority of English towns had less than 5000 people, with larger regional centres of up to 25,000; London at this time, however, was already approaching a population of 600,000.

The concept of the preindustrial city

Sjoberg's (1960) concept of the preindustrial city is in many ways a pacesetter for theorizing in this field. It has proved controversial and has certainly been vulnerable to detailed criticism, but in the debate many positive advances have been made (see Radford, 1979 for a recent view). Sjoberg, correctly, saw cities as products of their societies. He also, perhaps less correctly, saw technology as the central force for differentiation and change and his main distinction, between preindustrial and industrial cities, rested upon the time divide of the Industrial Revolution and the ability to use inanimate sources of energy to power tools. In the long time-period prior to this 'divide', Sjoberg hypothesized that a single *broad type* of city was found. Society in this time-period was classified as feudal with a social stratification system which could be divided into a small elite and a much larger lower class. Radford (1979) argues that a vital component of Sjoberg's concept is control of the city by an elite

Figure 3.3 Cities over time. Data have been extracted from Chandler and Fox (1974) and, although estimates, they give some indication of the rise and fall of urban civilizations.

whose dominance was derived from non-economic, extraurban sources. In Charleston South Carolina, for example, low-country planters built town-houses in which they spent only part of the year. Sjoberg contended that this two-part stratification of preindustrial society had generality and could accommodate even apparently multistratified societies such as India with its caste system.

These cities were multifunctional and were not principally centres of economic activity. Religious, administrative, political, and cultural functions were dominant, and this was reflected in the power structure of the preindustrial city, in its institutions, and in its built fabric and land-use. Those economic activities which were contained within cities, such as trades and crafts, were of lesser status. Sjoberg also generalized upon the morphology of the preindustrial city and upon the spatial arrangement of land-uses within it. Key morphological features of preindustrial cities were the walls, which served as defences, as means of segmenting within the urban area, and as mechanisms for controlling the inflow of migrants and traders. Otherwise the internal morphology was typified by narrow streets, congested routeways, and an absence of order, 'houses, jumbled together, forming an irregular mass broken at intervals by open spaces in front of a temple or governmental building' (Sjoberg, 1960, p. 35).

Sjoberg's statements on the internal arrangement of land-uses and on socio-spatial differentiation in the preindustrial city have attracted the attention of urban geographers. Here, there are three broad generalizations. First, the elite groups of preindustrial cities are typically located close to the central area in near proximity to prestigious buildings and sources of power. This residential location may have had the additional advantage of placing the rich well within the defensive walls and away from the more noxious elements of urban life. Their choice of a place to live was also affected, however, by the non-material factors which helped produce an exclusive, high-status core. As Langton (1975, p. 2) has suggested,

Tight segregation was further encouraged by primitive transport technology, bad road surfaces, a street system designed more for house access than intra-city travel, the physical repulsiveness of the garbage-strewn, poorly built and crowded non-central area, and the tightly-knit structure of elite society, which was often reinforced by bonds of kinship and inter-marriage.

As a first and dominant characteristic, therefore, the social geography of the preindustrial city is typified by a prestigious central area occupied by the elite, and from centre to periphery in a general zonal form are found progressively less prestigious areas and less prosperous people (Figure 3.4).

As a second generalization, Sjoberg recognized that outside the central core of the city there were other differences in residential pattern of a more detailed kind, but these were in his view of minor significance in the overall structure. There were ethnic, occupational and kinship bases to these finer levels of segregation; spatially they took the form of quarters or precincts within the urban area. Thirdly, Sjoberg argued that over much of the preindustrial city there was a lack of functional differentiation of land-use patterns. Plots were

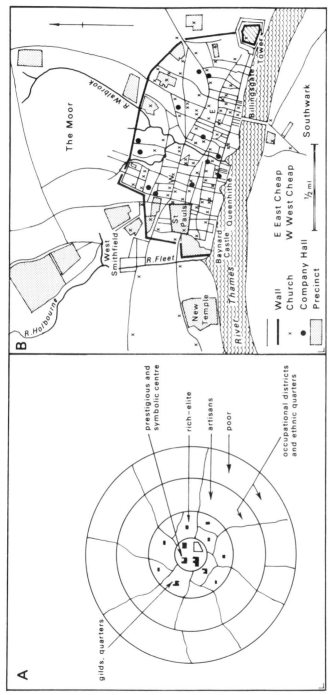

Figure 3.4   (a) A schematic representation of the preindustrial city with zonal 'class' areas and segmented occupational and ethnic quarters.
(b) Pre-industrial London (redrawn from Figure 3.4 in Dennis and Clout (1980) with permission). N. B. An earlier version of this map appeared in R. Clayton (Ed.) *The Geography of Greater London*, G. Philip. London

put to multiple uses, the separation of workplace and residence was uncommon, and nothing which resembled compartmentalized land-use zones or sectors could be seen to exist in any detail or uniformity.

Sjoberg presents an attractively simple and graphic account of the nature and form of the preindustrial city but there are questions on the accuracy of his interpretation. Some are obvious and general. How acceptable, for example, is the idea that one basic type of city existed in different parts of the world for varying phases of time within a time-span of about 5000 years? As Sjoberg himself argues, cities are part of the societies within which they are contained and will therefore reflect contrasts among those societies. As Egyptian society in the Ancient World differed from medieval society in western Europe, so the cities of those societies will mirror those differences. Similar overgeneralization, and some misuse of nomenclature, is revealed by Sjoberg's use of the term 'feudal' to describe all societies before the Industrial Revolution, when in the proper sense of the word some were clearly feudal and others were not (Wheatley, 1963). It is in his general use of historical data that Sjoberg has been most severely criticized. For Wheatley (1963, p. 183) he had treated the evidence of the past in a 'cavalier' fashion and had grossly understated the significance of cultural and religious factors. Burke (1975) was of the view that Sjoberg had based his concept upon secondary sources of information from limited parts of the world and that the quality of these secondary sources was not high.

A further example of overgeneralization is provided by Sjoberg's two-fold division of preindustrial society into an elite and a lower class. As Jones and Eyles (1977) have pointed out, feudal stratification in medieval Europe had intermediate classes such as clergy and bourgeoisie and some societies were further complicated by intricate caste systems. Although these latter could be reduced to the four major castes of priests, warriors, commoners and slaves, there were also other elements such as migrant and ethnic groups who played a large part in forming the residential mosaic. Langton (1975), in his study of seventeenth-century Newcastle-upon-Tyne, recognized a sharp stratification *within* the merchant community; again, below the merchants, the craft gilds were similarly differentiated in wealth and power.

Several authors have taken issue with Sjoberg over his depiction of the pre-industrial city as an essentially unplanned and disorganized collection of streets and dwellings. Wheatley (1963) argued that early Chinese cities had straight broad roads radiating from a nexus, along which lived the well-to-do with the poor in the interstices. Murphey (1974) described the remarkable uniformity of plan in Chinese cities with a square or rectangular form and walls surrounding a great cross with gates at the end of each of four arms. There are many other examples of planning in preindustrial cities; Roman towns and, later, Renaissance or Baroque cities in Europe, had walls, processional ways and a grid-iron plan. Mabogunje (1974) writing on the precolonial development of Yoruba towns, described the palace and market as forming a 'hub' from which roads radiated; these roads had importance as processional ways.

That part of Sjoberg's thesis which has had most corroboration is also the part which is of most direct interest to urban geographers. From many parts of the world and from many points in time there is evidence that cities in traditional societies possess a spatial arrangement of residential areas which can be generalized to the form of prestigious central areas and low-status urban peripheries separated by zones of decreasing status. De Planhof (1959) recorded Marco Polo's description of Lut, an Iranian city, as comprising a series of seven concentric walled circles, protecting various quarters, each of which was occupied by members of a single social class. The status of these classes increased towards the central citadel, progressing from peasants, through artisans, to tradesmen, warriors, and doctors of law. At a different place and time, Zweig (1942) described preindustrial Vienna as a clearly ordered city. Nobility and their palaces occupied the heart of the city, diplomats the next districts followed successively by industry and merchants, petty bourgeoisie and workers. More recently, Langton (1975) has scrutinized studies of British cities in the seventeenth century and concluded that three of the five largest English cities, together with Dublin, exhibited spatial patterns of wealth distribution similar to those postulated by Sjoberg. Again, in a more general survey of seventeenth-century English towns, Langton (1978) states that information from hearth tax returns makes it clear that the rich lived near the centre and that wealth declined towards the periphery (Figure 3.5). Radford (1979) identifies in Charleston, South Carolina a social organization of space with prestigious centre, gradient towards the periphery, and segmented slave

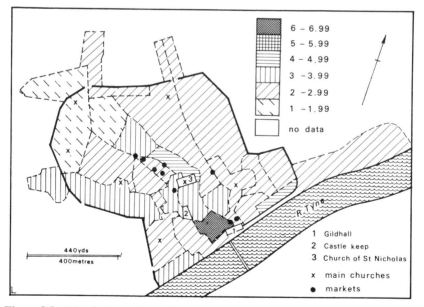

Figure 3.5 Distribution of wealth in Newcastle-upon-Tyne, 1665. Key shows the average numbers of hearths taxed per household (after Langton, 1975). Reproduced by permission of The Institute of British Geographers

quarters, broadly confirming the generalizations of Sjoberg's model. These examples could be replicated and the burden of evidence is such as to validate the Sjoberg hypothesis on the internal arrangement of land uses within the preindustrial city. The key to its validity is of course the level of generalization and the fact that it purports to be a model; in very general terms these arrangements of land-use can be discerned, and once details are scrutinized and the level of spatial generalization is reduced, divergences and distortions become evident. Two topics can be identified for further discussion. Firstly, the nature and symbolism of the functional centre of the preindustrial city; secondly, the extent to which the 'finer details' of differentiation distort the broader zonal pattern.

Institutions and symbolism

Whilst the pre-eminence of the central areas of cities in traditional societies can reasonably be conceded; the institutions with which that pre-eminence was associated did vary (Wheatley, 1963). For the medieval Muslim, the key features of his city were the mosque, market and public baths; for the early Dynastic Mesopotamian it was the temple; for the Carolingian, the keep, church and market; in Mauryan India, the palace and market, and so on. These institutions gave cities their definitive urban content and from them the strong symbolic value of the central area ensued. This symbolism came through most strongly in societies where religious institutions were paramount. McGee (1967) has described the south-east Asian city of Angkor Thom, built between 1181 and 1219 AD. At the centre of the city was the Bayon, the largest temple, a huge mountain of stone designed to symbolize the magical mountain which is the axis of the universe and abode of the gods.

Surrounding the Bayon there was an enclosure in which the palace of the king was located and surrounding this were the walls and a wide moat, some eight miles in circumference, which represented the mountain, walls, and the sea of the cosmological universe (McGee, 1967, p. 37).

Both McGee and Wheatley have stressed this *cosmological* significance of the centre and indeed of the whole plan and ethos of the city in traditional societies.

No account of the spatial relations of pre-industrial cities in East and South Asia can afford to ignore the cosmogonic significance of the ritual orientation of urban space (Wheatley, 1963, p. 182).

Besides the prestige and wealth of the central areas, therefore, there was an additional and pre-eminent ritual or religious symbolism attached to such areas. Jones and Eyles (1977) suggested that the ceremonial cores of the Mayan cities with their grouped pyramids, courts and plazas had similar attributes.

Districts and sectors

Outside the central areas of preindustrial cities, the evidence for simple patterns of zoning is by no means always present or unambiguous. In some societies, broader and vaguely sectoral divisions seem to exist. Tuan (1968) described the ninth-century city of Ch'ang-an as being divided into two parts by a long and very broad street. On one side of this street was the imperial court and its associated entourage; on the other were the merchants and other citizens. Jones and Eyles (1977) saw an analogy between this pattern and that which led to the development of the West End and East End in London. Regent Street acted as a boundary between what was later christened as the West End, housing a complex of government and power around Westminster and St James, occupied by nobility and gentry, and the narrower streets and meaner houses of the later East End, occupied by mechanics and traders.

From many other parts of the world there is evidence that at a more detailed level, the structure of cities in traditional societies possessed a segmented or compartmentalized form. Mabogunje (1974) suggested that in Yoruba towns each street formed a quarter consisting of a number of compounds housing members of one or more extended families. The compounds were enclosed spaces with single entrances but many internal subdivisions; individual families occupied each subdivision but the compound as a whole was united on a kinship basis. These square or rectangular compounds were thus the most distinctive components of the residential area structure, but they varied in size and form in ways which reflected the status of their occupants. Whereas compounds of poor families would cover no more than one-fifth of a hectare, those of chiefs would have an area in excess of 1 hectare. Davis (1974) also identified compounds in the preindustrial colonial cities of South America. Typically a 'monumental' centre, often fortified, was dominant but throughout the urban area native compounds occurred within which the Indian population was housed.

Vance (1971) has provided a closely argued thesis for the development of a segmented or compartmentalized city in medieval Europe during what he prefers to call the 'precapitalist' period. This is a more general thesis and Vance was primarily interested in land assignment as a formulative process in urban growth. For him the critical stage in the transformation from precapitalist to capitalist city was that at which men began to own rather than merely to hold land. This notion of transition is contentious (Langton, 1975) and will be discussed below; for the moment, however, Vance's portrayal of the internal structure of the medieval west European city is the relevant context of discussion. In the medieval city, Vance argues, land ownership was mainly functional in that it afforded a workman the place to practise his trade and shelter his family, apprentices and journeymen. The burgages which existed to provide for the land needs of city men were not intended to enhance personal wealth, but rather to provide an urban location suitable for their needs. Central to Vance's explanation for the emergence of a 'quartered' and many-centred medieval city was the role and status of the gild. Gild membership was the standard means of entry to established urban life, individual gildhalls were foci of interest and members tended to live within their precincts creating occupational districts. The gild offered a place of security, entertainment, social contact, surveillance of business and a religious orthodoxy—all effective bonds which cemented the territorial districts into cohesive communities. This 'factionalizing' role of the gild had a strong effect upon the social geography of the medieval west European city; it was paralleled by other social divides. For example, early ghettos can be dated from the twelfth century when Jews began to be excluded from Christian quarters, and political rivalry within cities led to physically identifiable quarters such as the *societá della torri* in Florence. For Vance the medieval city in western Europe was segregated, and multi-centred and the gild system underlay most of this compartmentalization.

The supervision of the quality of products, the conditions of manufacture, the ways the goods were sold, became important offices of the gild, and roles that encouraged the clustering together, in gild districts within the city, of the individual practitioners of the various 'mysterious arts' (Vance, 1971, p. 105).

Although portraying a segmented city with foci around many gilds, Vance also recognized some more general zonal order which served as an encompassing framework. 'Patrician' gilds, those which were pre-eminent in status, occupied the more central parts of the city. The notion of gradation from the centre is little developed by Vance and there is indeed scant reference to the place of the poor in urban society and city structure. Vance does, however, stress the vertical arrangement of land-uses and social classes which typified his pre-capitalist city. Ground floors of buildings may have been used to transact business, with the first floor as the family home and upper floors reserved for employees and others. Separation of workplace and home was not the rule.

Langton (1975) was critical of both Sjoberg and Vance and his detailed study of seventeenth-century Newcastle-upon-Tyne goes some way towards revealing the complexity of the city in traditional societies and the danger of overgeneralization. From an analysis based upon the taxed population of 1665, Langton showed that occupational groups were, to a significant degree, segregated into distinctive concentrations in Newcastle. There were four groups of activities—mercantile, victualling, shipping, and manufacturing—which corresponded with a degree of clustering around strategic facilities. This segmented pattern was reminiscent of Vance's conception of the internal structure of the city, and there was also some evidence for spatial grouping of craft activities, though others were dispersed. This pattern in Newcastle was complicated by the fact that emergent 'class' zones could be identified within which were contained a heterogeneity of occupational groups who were united by comparable levels of wealth.

Newcastle was not a feudal pre-industrial city, nor was it a pre-capitalist or capitalist city. A merchant clique was pre-eminent in wealth and municipal power. Its social domi-nance was expressed geographically in the existence of a mercantile quarter in that part of the city where its economic purposes were best served and where the institutions through which it dominated the city were located. In addition, the city possessed other regularly patterned occupational districts which were in some areas re-inforced by 'class-zoning' and in others countervailed by it (Langton, 1975, p. 21).

From this 'hybrid' situation revealed by a detailed investigation, there is some temptation to deduce that Newcastle in the seventeenth century was in a transitional stage between a residential structure dominated by occupational clusters to one based on zoning by socioeconomic status; Langton, however, rejects such a proposition as premature on the grounds that insufficient confirmatory evidence is available. Some related evidence on a decentralization process dating from the eighteenth century is provided by Tunbridge's (1977) study of Bristol. Using directories from 1794, Tunbridge showed that many professional groups, such as gentry, clergy, and doctors, had generally moved out of inner city residential locations. Other groups, however, were less decentralized and confirmed Vance's (1977) suggestion that those with close vocational connections with the commercial hub experienced the greatest locational inertia. Ships' captains occupied quality areas close to the harbour; lawyers were tightly clustered in the old city; and merchants retained central quarters. The preindustrial norm of combined workplace and residence prevailed for most of the groups studied, and Bristol displayed both inner-city quarters and an emerging peripheral zone of high-status residences.

Summary

There is ample evidence for the belief that whilst models of the type proposed by Sjoberg have some very general validity, any more detailed and systematic study of the city in traditional societies will reveal divergences, contrasts and exceptional features. Whereas technology may well have been a relatively blunt instrument to monitor differentiation and change over the very long pre-industrial period, culture, tradition and social values were not and are much more telling sources of diversity. Factors of this type, as Wheatley (1963; 1971) so persuasively argues, underpin the nature of early cities. Vance (1977, p. 223) identified strong contrasts within medieval Europe between 'mercantile towns' and the Renaissance cities:

No more revealing picture of the distinction between the city as the workshop of man and as the monument to enshrined and narrowly-held power could be furnished than by comparing Bristol in the West Country of England with the several dozen princely towns in Germany and Italy possessed of similar regional status.

Any view of the internal structure of the city in traditional societies may include broad generalizations, principally the existence of a prestigious central area with progressive zoning and a more detailed system of quarters, compounds and precincts, but it must also allow for diversity and indeed for change. Cities have rarely been static and the concept of urban change is as important as those of form, composition or ethos.

As stated earlier, it is sufficient for present purposes in this text to divide cities into the broad categories of cities in traditional and modern societies. Discussion so far has already recognized the diversity within traditional societies and will later similarly examine the variations within modern societies.

A further qualification is that the transition between these two broad types can never be abrupt. The urban landscape is a palimpsest, the process of change is slow and variegated; the city in *transitional* society may well be a 'category' in its own right.

URBANIZATION AS A PROCESS

The title of the preceding section 'the city in traditional societies' carries with it the implication that stages or at least phases of urban development—with which particular forms of city are associated—can be distinguished. The best-known attempts to identify and label such stages have been simple and are based upon a broad dichotomy. Preindustrial (Sjoberg, 1960) and precapitalist (Vance, 1971) are attempts to categorize forms of society and urbanization which existed before the modern era. In this section, the aim is to look more closely at the whole notion of classification and of 'types' or 'stages' of urban development and to consider the nature of the underlying processes under the broad heading of urbanization. A number of initial statements will serve as guidelines for the discussion which follows. Firstly, in seeking to examine urbanization, we are drawn into consideration of the whole question of societal changes; cities are but one expression of a larger process. Secondly, the notion that some kind of all-embracing force or set of forces is guiding all forms of urbanization has only marginal credibility at the broadest level of generality. Thirdly, classifications which suggest stages or points in some transition may have some utility in a general pedagogic sense, but should not be allowed to obscure the details and differences which are typical of reality.

Classifications, stages and models

Sjoberg's (1960) designation of the preindustrial city is the best-known attempt to classify a type of city and the 'stage' of development to which it belongs. Some detail of this attempt has already been provided and it is, in its level of generality and assumptions, fairly typical of others. As the labels preindustrial and industrial imply, technology and industrialization are the bases of the division though many other distinguishing attributes were subsequently recognized in both types. The significance of this divide has been frequently described. Berry (1973a, p. 36) suggests that the industrial city developed because 'Proximity meant lower transportation and communication costs for those interdependent specialists who had to interact with each other frequently or intensively'. Wellisz (1971, p. 39) stated that, 'Cities provide concentrations of population from which industrial labour may be drawn'; and Roberts (1978, p. 9) is of the view that 'Specialization and interdependence are thus the products of industrialization and it is this pattern of urbanization that distinguishes the modern period from earlier ones'.

The significance which Sjoberg attaches to industrialization and technological change has other adherents, therefore, and on roughly parallel lines, Hoselitz

(1960) spoke of orthogenetic and heterogenetic cities. The other classification already discussed, that of Vance (1971), adopts a different criterion to identify the divide in an admittedly narrower context. Precapitalist cities emerged in societies with different concepts of property, based on holding rather than owning land. The distinction is contentious but it again provides a single criterion from which stages in urbanization could be recognized and demarcated.

Other approaches to the problem of classifying 'stages' of urban development have used broader bases of differentiation. Reissman (1964) listed four main components of the urban process: urban status, industrial status, prevalence of a middle class, and prevalence of nationalism. In order to derive measures which could be systematically applied to individual countries, Reissman selected a number of key single variables. Urban status was measured by the percentage of population in cities of over 100,000; industrial status by the percentage of net domestic product contributed by manufacturing; prevalence of middle classes by *per capita* income; and prevalence of nationalism by rate of literacy. There is clearly a considerable gap between the conceptual objectives suggested by Reissman's components and the empirical variables which he uses to measure them. In combination, the indices add up to a general measure of economic development and this is reflected in the typology (Figure 3.6). The classification extends from Stage One underdeveloped countries such as Indonesia to Stage Four metropolitan countries such as the United States and the Netherlands (data are from 1950 sources).

Another four-fold basis of classification was proposed by Schnore (1965), though the main intention of this was to place spatial structures of cities in a comparative framework. This was an 'ecological complex' with four broad categories. Population included measures of size, growth rate, and composition; organization of economic base and social structure; environment of physical setting; and technology of development stage in technological change, especially

Stage 1				Stage 2			Stage 3				Stage 4	
underdeveloped	nationalizing	industrializing	urbanizing	transitional	industrializing	unbalanced urban	urban–transitional	rural balanced	urban–industrial	industrial–balanced	unbalanced metropolitan	metropolitan
Zaire				Mexico								
Indonesia					Greece			Norway			Chile	
	Turkey					Panama				Italy	Argentina	
		India								Canada		United Kingdom
			Egypt									United States
												Netherlands

Continuum monitored by measures of urban status, industrial status, prevalence of middle class and prevalence of nationalism

Figure 3.6   A staged typology of modern urbanization. Based upon information extracted from Reissman (1964)

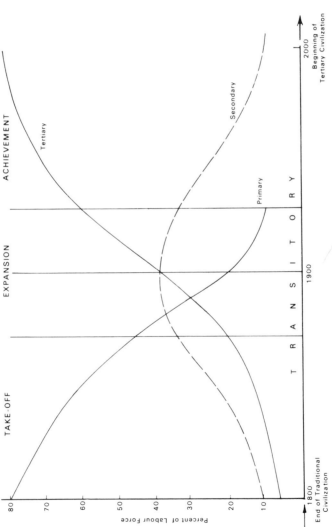

Figure 3.7 Urbanization and a three-sector theory of economic development (after Jakobson and Prakash, 1971: Fourastie, 1963)

of transport and communication. A variety of qualities, both local and societal, could therefore be used to classify cities and urban systems, though once again the prime 'change' variable was technology.

A more recent attempt to form a classification of urban development along these lines has been provided by Jakobson and Prakash (1971); their scheme has familiar terms and concepts to those of earlier proposals but has some advantages of flexibility and a tendency to view the process of urbanization as a continuum rather than as a series of sharply demarcated stages. Jakobson and Prakash draw support from Fourastié's (1963) three-sector theory of urban-economic development. Fourastié identifies three periods which he labels as those of primary or agriculturally based civilization, secondary or industrially based civilization, and tertiary or service-occupation based civilization. Moreover, the secondary period is regarded primarily as transitory between primary and tertiary phases. Between the end of the traditional or primary civilization and the beginning of the tertiary civilization, Fourastié subdivides the secondary period into three parts which he labels as takeoff, expansion, and achievement (see Figure 3.7). Jakobson and Prakash view the 'tertiary curve' as the S-curve of urbanization as it progresses from 10 to 80 per cent urbanized levels of population. They also add distinguishing locational characteristics to each of the main periods. Whereas the primary period is location-bound by resource and the tertiary period by market, the transitory secondary period is less space or location-bound. During the takeoff phase, Jakobson and Prakash associate urban growth with discrete nodes; during the expansion phase with metro-politanized (aggregative) areas; and during the achievement phase with megalo-politan (diffusive) spatial forms. Again, this theory is closely tied to economic and technological development but in their depiction of preindustrial, industrial, and postindustrial society (Figure 3.8) Jakobson and Prakash itemize a large number of attributes which they associate with each period or stage.

This line of argument led Jakobson and Prakash to a series of hypotheses relating to the manner in which societies progressed through the transitory period during which time industrialization and urbanization were key features. Their first hypothesis was that industrialism, modernization, and urbanization were integral features of this stage. Their second, that a country's relative position in this process of transformation from preindustrial to postindustrial society and the rate of this transformation is affected by four sets of factors which they labelled as physiographic (natural resource base), ecological (area and population-size), geopolitical (insularity and relation to world markets) and sociocultural (ethnic homogeneity, norms and values). At this stage, the framework begins to resemble those of Reissman and of Schnore and the key problems of fitting empirical measures remain. As with the other schemes the practicalities of reducing broad concepts to measures which are computable, accurate, and representative of the complexity of the urbanization process seem intractable.

Allied to Jakobson and Prakash's notion of a postindustrial society with distinctive urban forms, are Berry's (1976) developing ideas on counter-

	Pre-industrial	Industrial	Post-industrial
Population	Early demographic transition	Middle demographic transition	Advanced demographic transition
Education	Low	Middle	High
Resources	Natural resources underdeveloped	Natural resources overdeveloped	Natural resources conserved
Economy	Dominantly agricultural employment	Mixed employment with strong manufacturing sector	Dominantly service employment
Politics	Colonialism to independence Centrifugal tendencies	Empire to commonwealth Integration–nationalism	Trans-national linkages Less integration more trans–national
Linkages	Weak communication/transport network	Developing communication and transport	Highly developed communications and transport
Values	Localism	Nationalism–cosmopolitanism– activism	Trans-nationalism– megalopolitanism – Humanism
Power	Restricted elites	Multiple elites National planning system	Dispersed elites Trans–national planning systems

Figure 3.8 Attributes of the three-stage model: pre-industrial, industrial and post-industrial. (Based upon information contained in Jakobson and Prakash, 1971, p. 28)

urbanization. Here he suggests that a turning point has already been reached in American urban experience with counterurbanization as the new dominant force. The essence of this new trend is deconcentration of metropolitan areas which become typified by decreasing size, density and heterogeneity. Since 1970 in the United States, metropolitan areas—particularly the larger north-eastern seaboard agglomerations—have shown slower growth and a reversal of migration trends. Many factors are involved which include economic and technological change, demographic shifts and the state of the housing market, but they all seem to point to the diffuse form of a postindustrial, tertiary society, and accord with Bell's (1974) more general thesis.

Holistic theories and models clearly have their limitations. Generally they are very broadly based and cannot take sufficient account of the detailed facts of history and temporal change. Technological and economic development are often stressed at the expense of sociocultural factors, in part because the latter are much more difficult to measure and evaluate. This is particularly true of classificatory systems which rest largely on economic indicators. Even where other processes are recognized in a conceptual sense, the quality of the indices chosen to represent them are often of dubious merit. The better-known general models in the social sciences have typically paid little regard to spatial contexts of development. Urbanization takes place in a complexity involving the interaction of time, space, and regional cultures in addition to global imperatives towards economic change and 'modernization'. Whereas former excesses of generalization which regarded events in the Third World as reruns of western experience are now either avoided or heavily qualified, the 'convergence' view retains its adherents. Sjoberg (1965), for example, argued that industrial cities all over the world are becoming alike in many aspects of their social structure. The similarities, however, are only superficial and whilst models and classifications have value, they must be kept in perspective.

The nature of the process

Any examination of models and classifications of urbanization inevitably touches upon the nature of the process itself. One view of what urbanization means is that associated with the so-called theories of contrast and particularly with the views of Wirth (1938). Essentially, this is a sociological or perhaps social-anthropological perspective with an emphasis on lifestyle and rural–urban differences. This concept, which we have discussed, probably had little relevance for the twentieth-century city: 'He offered a theory upon which to build future research. In actuality, his theory was a peroration on a city that had passed' (Berry, 1973, p. 36). A related view of urbanization is that which recognized its links with demographic processes, with migration and with increasing concentration of population (see Lampard, 1965, for a review). The strongest and most consistent line of argument in explanation of the urbanization process, particularly in western experience, has been that which proposes close links with industrialization and economic development. Starting with

Weber's (1899) analysis of urban growth in the nineteenth century, a large number of studies have demonstrated the close correlation between industrialization in general and between specific indices, such as *per capita* income or percentages of labour force in manufacturing employment, and level of urbanization.

Increased division of labour and increased specialization, the necessary concomitants of increased productivity, inevitably became forces promoting population concentration in cities. Associated with this population shift . . . was a shift in *the* occupational structure of economies (Berry, 1973, p. 4).

As western societies industrialized and became technologically more advanced, so they became urbanized and emerged as nations of large cities.

The general theories of urbanization are well known and documented; a more recent trend has been to introduce a more explicit spatial dimension to the urbanization process. Friedmann and Wulff (1975, p. 11) specified a core (dominance) and periphery (dependency) model which is designed to accommodate the interactive relationship of city and region: 'Urbanization is thus perceived as a complex of spatial processes and their associated patterns, although the spatial relations of power (decision-making and control) are identified as the critical process to which all others are ultimately related'.

Decision-making and control—the distribution of effective political and economic power—is viewed as a major determinant of the spatial organization of an urban system and its evolution and is the first of four major spatial processes which Friedmann and Wulff consider to be part of the urbanization process. A second spatial process was identified as *capital flows*, or ways in which capital is mobilized and invested; a third is the process of *spatial diffusion* by which innovations, entrepreneurship, and modernization reach both down the urban system and outwards from core to periphery. For their fourth major spatial process, Friedmann and Wulff return to the familiar sphere of demographic change and specify the *migration process* as one of continuing significance in the forming of urbanized societies. This emphasis upon migration and indeed upon the whole spatial quality of urbanization, is reflected in Jakobson and Prakash's (1971) view of urbanization as a phenomenon which describes a process of change in the location of population due to changing conditions in society at large. People are arranged in space both as a consequence of initial urbanization and as a necessity for its continuance; as the industrial city grew it had need for a large pool of available labour irrespective of the sociopolitical system from which it emerged.

For many writers the city is a focus of change. Friedmann (1973) argued that cities are organizers of economic, cultural, and political space; centres of innovation; environments of opportunity and seedbeds of democratic change. Hoselitz (1960) likened his heterogenetic or industrial city to a 'generative' city, sponsoring change and Fujii (see Jakobson and Prakash, 1971, p. 22) argued that industrialization led inevitably to large cities which became autonomous 'power engines' in their own right; their dependency links with hinterland increase and the growth of large cities from capital accumulation stimulates the growth of the nation. This view of the city as a catalyst of change is by no means universally accepted (Morse, 1971) and may well be an instance of a general model formed from an oversimplified interpretation of western experience. McGee (1971, p. 31) explicitly argues that, 'In the context of the majority of Third World countries, it seems that a theoretical framework which regards the city as a prime catalyst of change must be disregarded'. His general thesis is that in order to understand the role of cities properly, one must investigate the conditions of underdevelopment which characterize the societies of which they are part. In a closely similar vein, Hauser (1957, p. 88) argues that in large measure the problems of Asian cities reflect the problems of the nation at large, problems which arise from low productivity and mass poverty. Whether cities become beneficial or destructive (McGee's catalysts or cancers), depends on the success of Asian countries in their efforts at social and economic development. These are national trends in which the city plays an important but not necessarily central role.

These observations are important in at least two respects. Firstly, they put cities in their place as manifestations of wide-reaching forces of societal change rather than separate phenomena, independent of the social systems of which they form part. The integrated role of the city in society has to be the first consideration, although there is force in the view that cities act as sources of change and modification—these are products of the city as well as of society. Secondly, the observations on Third World experience once more undermine the likelihood of universalities in discussing the urbanization process. Berry (1973, p. xii) is a powerful advocate of the need to disavow any view that urbanization is a universal process; it is clear, he argues,

Not only that we are dealing with several fundamentally different processes that have arisen out of differences in culture or time, but also that these processes are producing different results in different world regions, transcending only superficial similarities.

Berry resolves these different world regions into four broad groups within each of which urbanization, reflecting societal contrasts, has found differing expressions. At one extreme he recognizes the free enterprise, decentralized, *market-directed system* in which instruments of collective or governmental action are used only to support central institutions of the market and to maintain the required disposition of power. In a second group are the *Third World countries*, constituting a diverse mosaic in which traditional societies coexist with, or are being changed by, modernization. Typically countries in this group have low industrialization, continued dominance of agriculture, low *per capita* production and a dependence on external support. A third group is formed by the redistributive *welfare states* of western Europe in which free enterprise systems are modified along lines aimed at reducing inequalities through differential taxation and welfare policies. Fourthly are the *command economies* in which urban development has been bureaucratized and standardized under socialism.

This is one attempt to recognize the differences between contemporary societal systems and through these to obtain some basis for understanding the differing outcomes in terms of urbanization. As a general scheme it has utility, though the optimality of a four-fold classification can be argued. From a Marxist viewpoint some might argue that a two-fold division is sufficient with the various forms of capitalism producing only modestly dissimilar outcomes. In a comparable vein, Roberts (1978, p. 11) argues that, 'urbanization is essentially a product of capitalist development and expansion', though he does stress the important differences which occur even among advanced capitalist countries. A more likely objection to Berry's typology, however is that a four-fold division does less than justice to the differences in societal structure, not merely those produced by modern forces which can be identified but also by the inherited traditional mores which continue to mould their form.

This statement on the nature of the process of urbanization has focused on those theories linked with economic development. There are other theories based upon social and demographic change which have considerable significance but for the *modern* process of urbanization which is becoming global in its impact, the primary process appears to be related to economic development forces which have social and demographic effects. This generalization does not deter from the regional significance of other factors or from the likelihood of diverse outcomes, but it does recognize the most easily identified contemporary feature of world urbanization.

THIRD WORLD CITIES: SOME GENERAL CHARACTERISTICS

This text has a primary focus upon the western experience of urbanization. At the risk of brevity and superficiality, however, this section draws out some of the main characteristics of urbanization and cities in the Third World. Urbanization is now a global characteristic and processes of change and interaction at this scale are intricately interwoven. Cities in various parts of the Third World have many distinctive features but the likelihood of no western impact is remote.

Urbanization as a global process

The industrial city, initially in western Europe and later in other parts of the western world, was the product of the first major phase of modern urbanization. Taken as the process of changeover from a predominantly rural-based to a predominantly urban-based population, this process gathered force in the United Kingdom from the late eighteenth century. The so-called 'logistic curve' can be used to demonstrate the process of change (Figure 3.9). From a low level of urbanization, western societies have moved, through a stage of rapid acceleration and a later stabilizing stage, to a point at which around 80 per cent of their population could be classed as living in urban settlements. The United Kingdom was the initiator in this process but other western countries have since moved in similar ways. This kind of urbanization involved significant

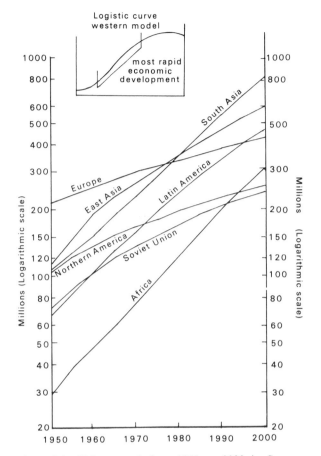

Figure 3.9 Urban population; 1950 to 2000 in Seven Major Areas. Inset shows the model 'logistic curve' as experienced in western society. (Part of diagram from Abu-Lughod and Hay, 1979, Figure 2, p. 91)

social change but its main underpinning forces were economic development and rural-to-urban migration. As western societies industrialized and experienced economic development, so the great cities emerged; as these cities and the smaller industrial towns came into existence, so rural areas began to export migrants and eventually to depopulate. This massive transfer of people was the major source of urban population growth. Western urbanization coincided with the expansionary phase of the demographic transition process but it was some time before natural population growth became the dominant contributing factor in urban growth.

In Third World countries the 'modern' process of urbanization is still unfolding. It has some characteristics which relate to the 'stage' already experienced by western societies in the nineteenth century but is substantially modified

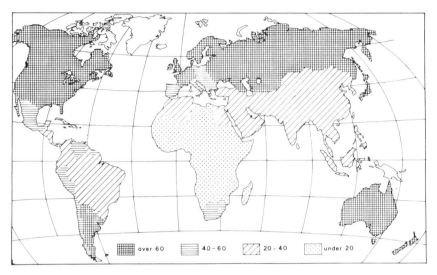

Figure 3.10   Levels of world urbanization. The distribution of urban populations as proportions of total population is shown for major political units. (Data are for 1975 and have been extracted from Abu-Lughod and Hay, 1979, Table 1)

by its own cultural contexts and by the fact that it is occurring in a radically different global framework. Figure 3.10 shows that many Third World countries remain relatively un-urbanized and that there are great differences among those countries. Whilst all countries show some trend towards increasing urbanization, it is important to remember that the process has no global inevitability. A highly urbanized future world is a credible scenario but possibly a large number of Third World countries will never approach the high levels of urbanization now evident in some western societies and some may remain predominantly rural societies. Whatever the longer term outcomes, however, it is clear that major changes, expressed more dramatically in absolute urban growth rather than in relative urban–rural ratios, are affecting Third World countries in modern times (Table 3.1(a).)

As the process of urbanization is unfolding in the Third World it does reveal special features. Most writers would agree with the view that some level of overurbanization or pseudo-urbanization is present. By this is meant the fact that urban growth is not being matched by sufficient economic development, industrialization and technological change to make it viable. The cities are structurally weak and because of their inadequate economic bases are merely 'formal' rather than 'functional' entities, even parasitic upon the rural societies within which they are placed. Whereas the great bulk of statistical evidence, demonstrating high unemployment and low economic growth on a variety of indices, supports this contention, some Third World writers have been less willing to accept the overurbanization thesis. Bose (1971) argues that Third World countries in the later twentieth century are comparable to western

Table 3.1   Some trends in Third World cities

A. Absolute population change in selected Third World cities

	1960		1977	
	City	Urbanized area	City	Urbanized area
Bombay	4,941,000	—	5,970,575	—
Buenos Aires	2,966,816	7,000,000	2,982,000	9,749,000
Cairo	2,852,000	2,993,000	5,084,463	—
Calcutta	3,040,000	5,919,000	3,148,746	7,031,382
Karachi	1,912,598	2,060,000	3,498,634	—
Mexico City	2,832,133	4,666,000	8,988,230	13,993,866
Peking	4,010,000	—	7,570,000	—
Shanghai	6,900,000	—	10,820,000	—
São Paulo	3,164,804	—	7,198,608	—

Sources: *UN Demographic Yearbooks*, 1962 and 1978.

B. Migrants as a percentage of population growth

City	Period	Inc. (000s)	Migrants as % of total
Bombay	1951–61	1207	52
Caracas	1960–66	501	50
Djakarta	1961–68	1528	59
Istanbul	1960–65	428	65
Lagos	1952–62	393	75
São Paulo	1960–67	2543	68

Source: extracted from Berry (1973).

NB Qualitative evidence suggests that during the 1970s, higher proportions of total
   population growth in cities is accounted for by natural increase.

C. Squatter settlement in some Third World cities

City	Total population	Squatter
Hong Kong (1979)	5,010,000	500,000
São Paulo (1980)	8,000,000	870,000
Rio de Janeiro (1979)	5,100,000	1,700,000
Manila (1973)	4,510,000	1,356,000
Mexico City (1977)	8,988,230	*ca.* 4,000,000

societies at similar stages of development and sees urbanization as an essential
element in the process of economic growth and social change in south and
south-east Asia; a change which involves the transformation of traditional,
rural, agricultural economies into modern, urban, industrial economies.
The universality and indeed desirability of this scenario is open to debate.

Demographic change is the second variable which underlies urbanization in
the Third World and again there are important points of difference with western
experience. Firstly, it can be said that as urbanization occurs many of these
countries are experiencing unprecedented rates of general population expansion.
Death rates have fallen, birth rates have remained high and, with a very few

exceptions, have declined only slowly giving very fast rises in population. This 'explosion' has affected all kinds of areas, both urban and rural, and the continuing increase of rural populations has masked the relative impact of urban growth. Secondly, there are no sharp contrasts between natural rates of increase in urban and rural areas. In the United Kingdom case, for example, urban populations, because of demographic imbalance and bad living conditions, were not self-propagating for part of the nineteenth century and only the inflow of migrants caused growth. In Third World countries this situation does not exist and there is some evidence that cities, as places from which medical and other innovations are diffused, are healthier than rural areas. Thirdly, the role of rural-to-urban migration is different. In all Third World countries there are very large migrations from rural areas to cities (Table 3.1(b)) and these have very significant impact upon those cities in demographic and social terms. These migrant streams, however, are by no means the sole source of urban population growth, neither have they led to large-scale depopulation of rural areas. Urbanization in the Third World needs to be viewed in the whole demographic context within which it occurs.

This highly selective overview will now focus on a limited number of characteristics of Third World cities. Firstly, some attention will be paid to the phenomenon of the colonial city as a direct and early imprint of western urban values in the Third World. Secondly, some overview of the general features of Third World cities will be attempted and, finally, the issue of housing and of squatter settlements in particular will be examined.

Colonial cities

McGee (1971) has shown the most consistent awareness of the significance of the colonial city in any system of urban classifications which purports to demonstrate an evolution of urban forms.

Perhaps the greatest fault of Sjoberg's twofold division of cities is that he has failed to take account of cities that have grown as links in the interaction of two civilizations. Such towns were flourishing even in the pre-industrial society; for example, as a result of the contact of the Roman Empire and the North African cultures (McGee, 1971, p. 50).

In similar terms Horvath (1969) proposed that the colonial city is a discrete subtype of urbanization, having characteristics that distinguish it both from the industrial and the preindustrial models. Others have recognized that the technological variable, which tends to distinguish preindustrial and industrial, is not centrally relevant to the colonial city case. On the basis of a detailed study of Oaxaca, Mexico, in the seventeenth and eighteenth centuries and a belief that its emergence could best be understood within the framework of a colonial variety of commerical capitalism, Chance (1975, p. 225) argues,

It is his failure to acknowledge commercial capitalism as a socio-economic system prior to the industrial revolution of the 19th century which constitutes a major flaw in Sjoberg's argument and the chief reason why his model does not apply to the Latin American case.

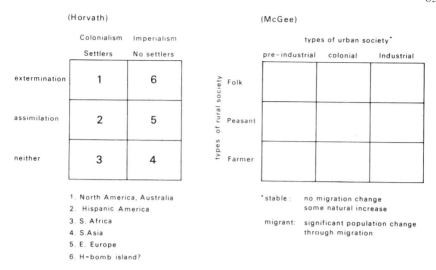

Figure 3.11   Frameworks for the colonial city (after Horvath, 1969, and McGee, 1971 a)

McGee has proposed one framework within which the colonial city may be fitted (Figure 3.11). As a type of urban society, intermediate to preindustrial and industrial, it could be characterized by 'stable' or 'migrant' in terms of population change, the latter involving significant levels of migration. Rural societies within which these urban forms occur could range from 'folk' to commercial farmer. Colonial cities are more likely to have limited rural-to-urban migration, at least in earlier phases, because of their tendency to be separate from the indigenous societies. Horvath (1969, p. 73), perhaps more realistically, views the colonial city as one component of a broader theory of colonialism which he defines in a general sense as ' . . . a form of domination where one group controls a part of the affairs of the other group'. The presence of permanent, colonizing settlers distinguishes colonialism from imperialism and the relationship of colonizers to colonized may be summarized as 'assimilation' or 'extermination'. These variables can be formed into a matrix (Figure 3.11). McGee (1971) recognizes some of these distinctions with his use of the term 'replica' towns in the North American and Australasian context but Horvath's more detailed typology is a better guide to the fact that colonial cities will reflect the particular nature of the *colonial* society within which they are placed.

Colonial cities were of several types. Some were literally new towns, others were grafted onto pre-existing nuclei, but typically the most important were major ports which acted as receiving and exporting centres for the colonial empires. These often became 'primate' cities in which colonial power and interest were concentrated. In its fullest expression, the colonial city was the microcosm of colonial society and served as a political, military, economic, religious, social and intellectual entrepôt between colonizers and colonized. Not all European countries founded urban settlements in their colonies; Davis (1974) notes, for example, that whereas the founding and maintenance of towns was a deliberate part of Spanish colonial policy, this was not true of the Portuguese.

Many features set colonial cities apart from the rural societies in which they were placed. They were transplants of an alien culture and the gulf, always considerable, has tended to diminish only slowly over time. Bromley (1979) writing on small colonial towns in the Central Highlands of Ecuador, suggests that their colonial characteristics have persisted into the modern era and have allowed them to remain ethnically and culturally distinct from rural areas. Main distinguishing marks of colonial towns were their predominantly white populations, agro-administrative functions, and a thriving commercial tradition. Studies of larger colonial cities have similarly stressed their distinctiveness, and continuity but have also suggested more plural features of population composition *within* the cities. Redfield and Singer (1954) characterized the colonial city as a grouping of communities, each of which carried on its pattern of life in a different way. Horvath (1969) recognized a stratification system of three major components in Latin American colonial cities. Top of the hierarchy was the Spanish-speaking elite, followed by a mixed-blood group and supported by the indigenous population. In a similar context, Davis (1974) classified the *peninsulares* or Spanish colonists who had little knowledge or interest in industry; the *creoles* who, though permanent settlers, imitated the elite and were parasitic; and the native Indians and negro slaves, deficient in skills and afflicted by disease, who formed the labouring classes. Where demand for urban labour necessitated the transfer of Indians into towns, they were maintained in compounds at high levels of segregation. For Friedmann and Wulff (1976) this kind of social stratification reflects the nature of dependent capitalism.

Several generalizations emerge from this summary of the main features of colonial cities. As a type, they merit some special designation though the prime determinants of their form are as extensions of political change and commercial capitalism rather than any criterion of technological change. In these roles they were parasitic and remained separate from the rural societies in which they were placed. Key features were this separation and 'dualism' which signify the failure of western urbanization to integrate with more slowly evolving Third World societies. The continuity of colonial cities and the dualism over time is more surprising. It can be argued that integration was never intended or encouraged. Roberts (1978) views many forms of backwardness and uneven development in Third World countries as a product of the way in which dependent capitalism has expanded. There are variations on these themes. Smaller towns (Bromley, 1979) may have been most persistent in retaining distinctive forms and traditional roles; larger cities with their plural populations and adjusting forms of overseas investment have both become more integrated into international urban systems and have also developed more real relationships with their regional hinterlands. As 'implants', colonial cities await the general development of the countries in which they are placed before assuming fuller urban roles.

Characteristics of Third World cities

Colonial cities provide a useful bridge with Western civilization but by no means all Third World cities were colonial in origin. Urban forms in the third world are a rich diversity inherited from different traditions and cultures and mediated by variable contemporary forces. Friedmann and Wulff (1976), in a summary which can usefully be followed, have classified knowledge of Third World cities under four headings of morphology, ecology, social organization and economy.

Urban morphology

Land-use patterns in the third world often reflect a dual city in which western capitalism has been intruded into traditional culture and the two forms co-exist in a weakly integrated way. The *traditional*, precolonial city has a mixture of land uses and few clear functional areas. Open spaces only occur around institutions such as mosque or temple and many transactions occur in streets. Morphological elements of walls and narrow streets make for congestion and difficulty of movement; older prestige residences faced inwards towards interior courts in order to achieve a privacy denied by their densely built-up environs. The *modern* city, in sharp contrast, has more spacious layout and geometry and features reminiscent of the western city. Where no urban nucleus predates the colonial city, as in Lagos, the dualism is not evident but in other situations, such as Delhi/New Delhi, where two urban forms have been grafted together, it is the dominant feature.

Social ecology

The relatively unambiguous bases of spatial segregation which can be identified for western cities, are less evident in the Third World. Ethnicity, caste, religion, language and similar cultural variables overlie the more basic variables of economic and demographic nature to provide complex discrimination of sociospatial structure. With the weight of rural-to-urban migration evident everywhere and the accompanying struggle for an urban foothold, 'migrant status' is an important population variable in its own right. Districts in the city into which rural values have been imported and persist are distinguishable in many parts of the Third World. In the evolving social geography of the city there are signs for both convergence and divergence when measured against western experience. Whereas the elites aspire to western modes of urbanism and are adjusting their styles of living in those directions, the differences inspired by sociocultural values and inertia are likely to remain. The aspirations of the elite,

... may simply come to nothing under the impact of accelerating migration and the growing inability of the urban economy to absorb the incoming workers in productive occupations. The Third World city under dependent capitalism is predominantly a poor city, and the poor are growing in both absolute and relative numbers. The resultant ecology of poverty may be a very different one from the essentially middle-class cities of North America and Western Europe (Friedmann and Wulff, 1976, p. 45).

Social organization

Urbanites in the Third World can be placed both in a *horizontal* social dimension of kinship and informal social networks and in a *vertical* system of class structures. The persistent strength of kinship alliances has been reported from many parts of the Third World; they are critical amongst recent rural migrants and have strong locality-bases which rest on communal ties, shared services and mutual support. Whereas this 'haven' allows the migrant to find a place within the city and to fit into a familiar network, it also inhibits his eventual assimilation into urban living in a fuller, more innovative sense.

Throughout the Third World, the proto-proletariat is encapsulated in a kind of ghetto, blocked from participation in wider social realms, only marginally absorbed by the urban economy, exploited by the elites, ignored by the middle strata and viewed with deep suspicion, if not hostility, by the blue-collar workers (Friedmann and Wulff, 1976, p. 47).

Class structures possess an inert inflexibility in the Third World with enormous gulfs between elite and poor. Some writers (Adams, 1970) have identified voluntary associations which may serve to link classes and inject some fluidity into the social barriers. Awareness of the political overtones of poverty and the plight of the poor is a constant element of social organization and control.

Urban economy

Many writers are unimpressed with the quality of research into the economy of Third World cities. Friedmann and Wulff (1976, p. 51) suggest that economic models are either descriptive or 'structuralist' and used mainly for grand historical speculations about dependency, immiseration and revolutionary potential. It is in relation to the impact of industrialization and economic development that variations within the Third World become most striking. Most societies have some level of industrialization and a 'modern' sector of the economy which seems to point the way to progress. Such sectors are diverse in type, dimensions and potential and seem to have achieved limited success in stimulating economic growth. Whereas reliable statistics are rarely available, unemployment remains very high and only bureaucracy appears to proliferate. Recent research emphases have focused upon tertiary employment and in particular upon the 'informal sector' which by some estimates occupies 60 to 80 per cent of urban populations. McGee (1971 p. 165) has suggested that the cities of South Asia can be divided into two economic sectors. A *modern* sector which is capital-intensive and a *bazaar* sector which is labour-intensive: 'The persistence of this dualistic structure, basically a symptom of economic under-development, is the most important variable affecting the function of contemporary Asian cities'.

A central feature of the traditional bazaar economy is its capacity to absorb labour. This is drawn from both its intensive use of labour and its self-inflationary qualities—as more participants enter, more activities and transactions are generated. Kinship allegiances underpin the system and assist entry, it has strong links with the peasant economy. Roberts (1978) who studied Latin American cities also detects a dualistic economic structure but not one which is directly analogous to McGee's South Asian case. Roberts identifies a large-scale sector on which modern economic growth is concentrated and a small-scale sector which operates on low wages and low profits, provides cheap services, and absorbs workers into a large reserve of unskilled and casual labour. Unlike the bazaar economy, however the small-scale sector does not cater for a special segment of the population and has no 'neighbourhood' base. The integration of Latin American countries into world markets over a long time period, reinforced by foreign investment, has created patterns of consumer preference similar to those of advanced capitalist countries. The state, with its ever-increasing role in economic development enables the persistence of the small-scale sector but at the expense of investment in social infrastructure.

Housing and squatter settlements

As in most western societies, the richer groups exercise considerable choice in terms of housing. Their traditional locations are generally adjacent to prestigious institutions in the central city with an emphasis on dwelling design to counteract the congested immediate environs. Whilst these locations may persist, there is also a good deal of evidence that the elite is abandoning the the older core areas and moving to more peripheral locations. These trends vary cross-culturally and by size of city; pressures for change may be greater in large urban areas. There are also significant cross-cultural variations in the 'form' in which new prestige housing is being constructed; whilst preference for low-rise and space remains, much new construction in Third World cities is typically of high-rise apartments. Below the elite in the social stratification system, Johnston (1972) isolated two middle-class groups in Latin America which he labelled as 'upper-class mimickers' and 'satisfied suburbanites'. Whereas the former are upwardly mobile and seek to occupy housing adjacent to the upper class in a type of 'filtering' system, the latter are less status-conscious and their priority in housing is security of tenure which they normally find on the urban periphery.

Central questions on housing involve the conditions under which the poor live; several large-scale surveys have served to demonstrate their situations of extreme hardship. Abrams (1964) in one of the best-known of these surveys suggested that in terms of housing three classes of poor urbanites could be discerned. First is the large class of homeless or the street sleepers who in some third world cities can be numbered in hundreds of thousands. Often more recent migrants or refugees, or those who from some kind of disability have failed to assimilate, these people live in abject poverty. Second are the slum or tenement dwellers, especially in South Asia, who occupy densely built-up areas of the old cities. Their problems are of overcrowding in multi-occupied buildings with severe shortages of basic facilities; 'home' could be a small, windowless cubicle, shared by between 6 to 10 people, in the centre of a tenement building. Third, are the squatters or occupants of the shantytowns, ubiquitous throughout the Third World. Squatters are by definition illegal occupants of urban space though many, through length of tenure, have achieved a kind of *de facto* legality. Turner (1967) first focused attention on the squatter settlements as *acceptable* facets of urban growth with his argument that they should be encouraged to improve in quality. General opposition of city government to squatters had made for many sources of urban conflict over space in the cities.

Dwyer (1974) and others have documented the emergence of shantytowns, particularly since the 1940s. As Third World cities have increased rapidly in population, so the formal housing market has proved unable to cope and squatter settlements have provided the only form of shelter. Araud *et al.* (1975) estimated a deficiency of five million dwelling units in Mexico City by 1980; everywhere rates of house construction fail to approach the demand for shelter. Hong Kong is in many ways an exceptional case and there Dwyer (1974) shows that one million squatters have been rehoused in multistorey settlement schemes; special circumstances in Hong Kong, particularly its high rate of economic growth, make this possible. In Latin America, Roberts (1978) suggests that between 10 and 20 per cent of the large city populations are squatters; the figures for South Asia are more typically between 20 and 30 per cent (Table 3.1 (c)). The quality of shanty dwellings is normally rudimentary; initial squatter settlements in particular will use thatch, cardboard, wood, zinc sheets or any constructional material which happens to be locally available. In areas of general poverty or with a refugee problem, shanties persist in these forms; in other parts of the world where some foothold in employment or security of tenure is possible, space may be added, materials replaced, and there is improvement *in situ*. Severe absence of public services is often a problem. Unpaved roads, crude systems of sanitation, inadequate water supplies, educational and medical services, are all features. Such deficiencies have often led, particularly in Latin America, to shanties emerging literally overnight, clustered around high-status residential projects to which they are attracted by the possibilities of tapping supply lines for water or electricity.

Who occupies the shanties may seem an unnecessary question, and for the most part it is the urban poor. Laquian (1971, p. 190) suggests that 'Almost all the studies of slum and squatter areas in the cities of South and South-east Asia to date show that these settlements are peopled mainly by migrants from the countryside.' Several Latin American studies, however, have made it clear that not only the poor occupy shanties. Roberts (1978) argues that shanties cater for diverse needs. They attract families from inner-city tenements who have outgrown their cramped conditions, they suit specific groups—such as single women with children—and are not infrequently occupied by small businessmen or professional people who are trying to accumulate capital. Squatter settlements often have real attractions—a strong sense of community, a spirit of self-help and protection, and often some organized cooperative endeavours. Settlement of these qualities have the capacity to improve but many others have different qualities; Dwyer (1974) describes many squatter areas as static or consolidating but with no progressive upgrading.

It is in relation to the potential for improvement that Turner (1967) argues for more positive attitudes towards squatter settlements but attitudes of city government have varied considerably. Dwyer (1974) suggests that most official policies have the character of 'benign neglect', but incidents such as that in Manila where 3000 shanties were destroyed in three weeks are by no means untypical. Turner is critical of the instant, official development projects in comparison with self-built shanties. The latter offer much more space, scope for initiative, and the possibility of making an investment—the great need is for better services and security of tenure. Turner argues for improvement schemes to provide materials, legalize the position of squatter settlements, and erect an infrastructure to serve them. Not all would agree. At one extreme are those who view squatter settlements as 'infestations' which mar Third World cities; at another are those who see shanty improvement as a diversionary exercise. Roberts (1978) argues that although squatter settlements show what can be achieved by people with few resources and are not a social problem, neither should they be regarded as a solution to resource-scarcity. If token improvement schemes are introduced, squatter settlements may be used by governments as a means of patronizing low-income population at little cost. Between these two extreme viewpoints, are involved the politics of the Third World.

The activism of the poor, however, is a factor in urban politics since their behaviour constitutes an unknown element which is alternatively feared and sought after depending on the strength and political complexion of the government of the day (Roberts, 1978, pp. 157–8).

CONCLUSIONS

This chapter has covered several major themes which are important components of any study of the city. It has been concerned with urban origins and the nature of the city in traditional or preindustrial societies on the one hand and the modern global process of urbanization and its impact in the Third World on the other. In attempting to provide a broad framework of this kind, there are inevitably losses in terms of depth of discussion and this is particularly evident in the context of Third World cities. Several of the themes which have been established in this chapter, however, will be developed in chapters which follow, and the concept of urbanization as a temporal process and the types of urban expressions which it involves will be discussed, with particular reference to western cities, in Chapter 7.

Chapter 4

Theories of the Urban System

In Chapter 3 we considered the question of urban origins and traced the patterns and processes involved in the development of early cities. This perspective has focused upon urban settlements as discrete elements in geographical and societal space. However, as individual cities became less localized in their impact and acquired functions of trade, commerce and industry, *urban* interdependence increased and networks of towns forming an urban *system* became functional realities. Throughout the nineteenth century, the urban system of western societies became functionally and formally more complex; population in general, and urban population in particular, was increasing dramatically. Individual cities became functionally more integrated into the wider urban system and through increased physical extension created an integrated and larger economic and social system at the intraurban scale; both 'systems of cities' and the 'city as a system' became accurate descriptions of urban development (Berry, 1967a).

This process was evolutionary and Bourne (1975, p. 12) has offered a schematic representation (Figure 4.1) which is currently applicable to western industrial countries:

(1) a *national system* dominated by metropolitan centres and characterised by a step-like 'size' hierarchy, with the number of centres in each level increasing with decreasing population size in a regular fashion;

(2) nested within the national system are *regional sub-systems* of cities displaying a similar, but less clearly differentiated hierarchical arrangement, usually organized about a single metropolitan centre, and in which city sizes are smaller overall and drop off more quickly than in (1) above as one moves down the hierarchy;

(3) contained within these are *local sub-systems* or *daily urban systems* representing the life space of urban residents which develop as the influence of each centre reaches out, absorbs and reorganises the adjacent territory. In small countries levels (2) and (3) may be difficult to differentiate, whereas in larger countries both of these levels may show further subdivision.

This simple notion of national, regional and local urban systems gives us one broad framework to which we will return. The earlier literature of urban

90

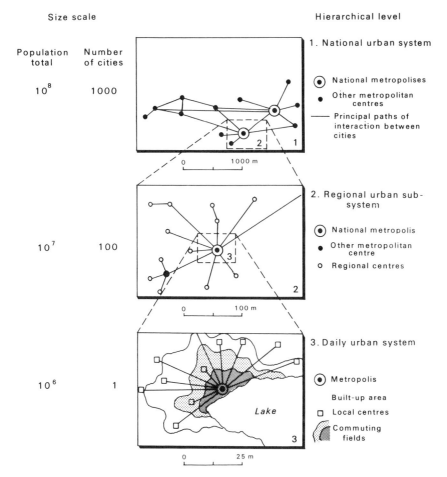

Figure 4.1   The urban system at the intra-urban, regional, and national scales.
Source: Bourne, 1975; reproduced by permission of Oxford University Press

geography, however, has been dominated by more narrowly conceived approaches to classification of urban settlements, which have focused on functions
and population sizes. A review of this work forms the basis of this chapter.

REGULARITIES IN THE CITY–SIZE DISTRIBUTION OF URBAN SYSTEMS

The law of the primate city

One of the earliest generalizations concerning the size–distribution of cities in
a country was the 'law of the primate city' propounded by Jefferson (1939).
This was based upon the observation that a country's leading city is usually

disproportionately larger than any others in the system; London for example was seven times the size of Liverpool, Copenhagen nine times larger than Aarhus, and Mexico City five times the size of Guadalahara. Based upon such observations the law stated that: 'A country's leading city is always disproportionately large and exceptionally expressive of national capacity and feeling' (Jefferson, 1939, p. 227). Jefferson argues that in the early stages of a country's urban development the city which emerges as larger than the rest for whatever reason develops an impetus for self-sustaining growth. It emerges as the centre of economic opportunity and attracts to it the most energetic individuals and active minds from other parts of the country. Usually it becomes an expression of the national identity of the state in relation to other states and for this reason tends to attract political functions and become the capital city. This ultimately results in the gravitation of all the 'superlatives' of a nation's life towards it: the opportunities, services and personalities which ensure self-sustaining growth.

At a very general level the idea has some foundation since 'primate cities' can be recognized in most countries. In fact, it is interesting to note the significant concentration of the leaders of British life in London and the south-east of England illustrated by mapping a sample of the addresses of entries in *Who's Who*, which is generally considered as indicative of the 'British Establishment' (Coates, Rawstron 1971). Whilst such a distribution persists, regional imbalances in economic opportunity can never be entirely redressed.

Whereas Jefferson admits that extreme primacy is by no means universal, he does seek to explain deviations from his model. Some states incorporate more than one national identity, often coinciding with regional concentrations of identifiable ethnic minority groups. This may result in one or more cities of comparable size rather than a single primate city. In Spain, for example, Madrid is the centre of Castilian nationalism, but Barcelona, central to the Catalan group, has comparable size and influence. On a smaller scale, Bilbao acts as the centre for the Basques. Similarly, in Italy, provincial nationalism which predates the unification of the Italian state is reflected in the tendency towards multiple primacy associated with Naples, Rome and Venice, while the prodigious industrial growth of Milan in the twentieth century has created a fourth element.

There are, therefore, historical reasons for non-primate situations where present-day states are amalgams of formerly separate regions. Similar patterns may also arise from the contemporary effects of size and distance. In the United States, for example, New York dominates the north-eastern seaboard, but there are several other regional clusters of settlement, each with their dominant urban centre. Both the USSR and China demonstrate some evidence for the emergence of more than one very large city as a result of both historical and modern forces, while in Canada the traditional duality of Toronto and Montreal, as centre for the English-speaking and French-speaking communities respectively, has been added to by the more recent emergence of Vancouver in the western part of the country.

Despite these deviations, the concept of the primate city has some limited significance if applied selectively to distinct regions defined in terms of cultural identity or geographical distinctiveness. With population growth and economic development, however, other cities emerge as alternative major growth points and erode the position of the primate city by creating a far more complex city-size distribution. For this reason it has been suggested, notably by Berry (1961), that the law of the primate city is most relevant to countries in the very early stages of economic development; this contention was developed further by Linsky (1965) who suggests that the concept of primacy is more appropriate to countries which have a relatively simple economic and spatial structure, a small area and population, low *per capita* incomes, economic dependence upon agricultural exports and a colonial history. Primacy is a simple concept and has some credibility but it takes us no further than a single city and its general relationship with the urban system; other concepts have been more comprehensive.

The rank–size rule

The rank–size rule (Stewart, 1947; Zipf, 1949), is the best known alternative proposition. Zipf suggests that the city–size distribution in integrated systems of cities in economically advanced countries is expressed by the simple formula:

$$Pr = \frac{Pi}{r}$$

where Pr is the population of a city ranked r, Pi is the population of the largest city, and r is the rank of city Pr.

Thus, the second ranking city of a country has one-half of the population of the largest city, the third ranking city one-third of the largest, and so on down the scale. The graphical plot of the rank–size distribution approximates to the lognormal statistical distribution. When represented on a double logarithmic graph this becomes transformed into a straight line (Figure 4.2). This is useful for comparative purposes since by plotting a country's city–size distribution on double logarithmic graph paper, the degree to which the distribution conforms to the rank–size rule is visually expressed by the degree to which it deviates from a straight line. In addition, if the city–size distribution of a country which has a strong degree of primacy is plotted on such a graph the resulting curve deviates considerably from the rank–size norm, indicating the domination of one very large city, the absence of cities of intermediate size and a relative profusion of small cities. This is graphically represented by an initial steep incline away from the rank–size distribution, but flattening out in the later stages to an approximation of the rank–size norm.

The association of primacy with the early stages of economic development and the rank–size with advanced, economically integrated countries, leads to the hypothesis that a country's actual city–size distribution is a direct

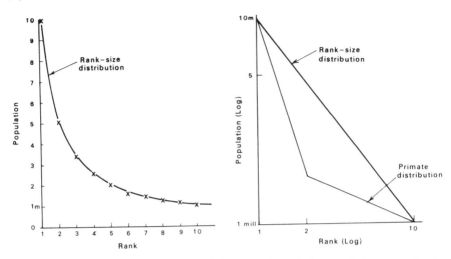

Figure 4.2   Schematic representations of the rank–size rule by population sizes of cities on arithmetic and logarithmic scales

function of its level of economic development. Underdeveloped countries in the early stages of urbanization are expected to demonstrate a near primate distribution and highly urbanized, economically advanced countries a rank–size distribution.

This contention was tested by Berry (1961) in relation to the city–size distribution of 38 countries at varying levels of development. However, these distributions were not presented in the form of double logarithmic graphs. Berry considered it more convenient to represent the distributions as cumulative frequencies on lognormal probability paper. Despite the use of a different graphical method, however, if the city–size distribution of a country is lognormal, it again assumes the form of a straight line. Thirteen countries were found to have rank–size (lognormal) distributions (Figure 4.3), and these ranged from highly developed western economies such as the United States and West Germany to countries in the developing world with a relatively long urban tradition such as India and China. At the other extreme fifteen countries demonstrated strong tendencies towards primacy, and these ranged from the smaller developed countries such as Denmark and Sweden to developing countries such as Thailand and Mexico. The remaining ten countries demonstrated intermediate distributions whereby it appeared that a relatively small number of primate cities were grafted onto a lower level rank–size distribution. Again, considerable variation in the levels of economic development was found in these countries, which ranged from England and Wales, Australia, Canada and New Zealand at the one extreme to Pakistan and Malaya at the other.

Clearly, the evidence of this study completely refutes the hypothesis that the degree to which the city–size distribution of a country progresses from a state of primacy to that described by the rank–size rule bears a direct relationship to its level of economic development and urbanization. Instead, Berry introduces

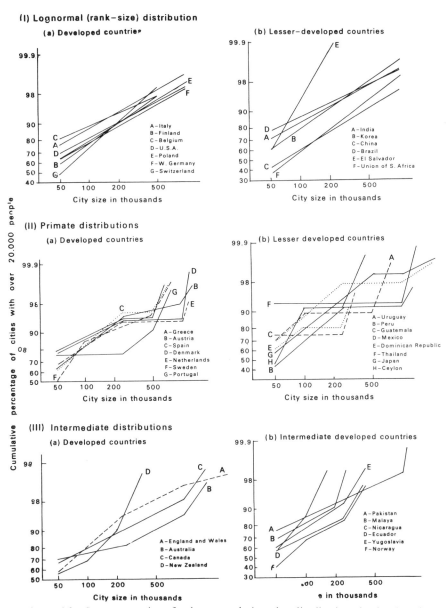

Figure 4.3   Some examples of urban population size distributions in developed, intermediate, and less developed countries. Reprinted from B. J. L. Berry, City size distributions and economic development, *Economic Development and Cultural Change*, **9**, 1961, by permission of the University of Chicago Press.
© 1961 University of Chicago Press

the earlier work of Simon (1955) to provide an alternative explanation. Simon suggested that lognormal distributions are produced by stochastic growth processes which result in a steady-state condition (entropy). Or, expressed more simply, the rank–size distribution of cities is the result of the operation of a large number of forces over a long period of time so that once the rank–size distribution has been obtained the operation of any one of these forces is only likely to produce a random and relatively minor deviation from the norm. This forms the basis of Berry's alternative explanation. Thus, rank–size distributions are expected to result from the complexity of economic and political life usually associated with advanced industrial economies; but may also be found in Third World countries with a long history of urban development such as India and China; or in large developing nations such as Brazil which have a proliferation of large resource-based cities. On the other hand, primacy is expected to be associated with a few simple strong forces. This may typify the urban system of newly developing countries where the primate city may be associated with an emerging capital; but such a condition can also be found in small countries such as Denmark where the forces of economic centralization create a tendency towards primacy; or in countries which have been developed under colonial influences and which have a relatively short urban history such as Australia and New Zealand. Thus, the progression from a primate to a rank–size distribution can be used as a framework within which generalizations relating to the urban system of a country may be made, not simply in relation to levels of economic development and urbanization, but by consideration of the length and degree of complexity of the urban development forces which has considerable empirical validity as well as intuitive appeal. This basic conclusion remains valid and the progression from primacy to the rank–size distribution provides a neat framework within which to view variations in the city–size distribution of countries, albeit of descriptive rather than explanatory or predictive value.

A relatively recent study of New Zealand (Johnston, 1971) serves to underline the last point. The rank–size model is used to describe the city–size distribution of the country and its various regions. This demonstrates a tendency towards primacy at the national and regional levels which is associated with the colonial history of 140 years duration and a strong economic dependence upon external trade. However, the expectation that increasing urbanization, economic development and a 'closure' of the economy will be automatically accompanied by a progression from primacy to a rank–size relationship has not been fulfilled. The primacy of Auckland has increased, and in 1966 with a population of 548,000 it was well over twice the size of the next largest city of Christchurch (247,000). Similarly, the regional primate cities had also maintained their dominance over their hinterlands. Johnston associates this deviation from expectations with the small size of the country and the peculiarities of its location and economy. Economic development has been concentrated upon import-replacement industries. Such industries require imported raw material so the advantages of a port location are clear. In addition, access to a local market and a location which facilitates distribution to a wider market are also advantageous. In a country of less than three million people, only one such developmental site is really feasible, in this case Auckland, which has emerged economically as an increasingly primate city. As a result, while the regional centres have maintained their primate relationship over their hinterlands, their less advantageous locations have precluded their economic advance relative to the enhanced status of Auckland. Clearly, the explanatory and predictive aspects of the primacy–rank–size model have to be approached with a degree of caution.

CLASSIFICATION AND THE FUNCTIONAL BASES OF CITIES

In addition to statements concerning the size–distribution of cities, a body of information has been developed which illustrates their functional bases. Historically, cities have developed to serve a variety of functions. Some have grown in association with the development of primary extractive industries such as the coalmining towns of the north and western parts of Britain or the iron and steel-making centres of Scunthorpe and Corby. Many others have grown initially as centres of secondary manufacturing industries such as the textile spinning and weaving towns of Lancashire or the metal-fabricating centres of the West Midlands. The initial development of others has been associated with the tertiary marketing function, particularly in areas which depend to a significant degree upon agriculture for their livelihood. Particular historical or geographical site advantages have also resulted in the development of other specific types of market town. The defensive function of the Norman castle towns of Britain is related to both factors, while towns which developed at nodal points on the railway network, at trans-shipment ports and in recreational areas are all related to the geographical advantages of their locations. In addition, some cities have been based upon decision-making, transactional functions, and quaternary activities. Centres of government established specifically for this purpose such as Canberra, Ottawa and Brasilia are cases in point.

Whatever the primary reason for the existence of a town, as it grows it will usually accumulate a range of the other functions. Thus, at any one point in time the economic structure of a town will consist of a complex amalgam of functions of varying strength. Whereas this consideration tends to preclude the development of an unambiguous classification of towns based upon function, most towns tend to display significant imbalances in their functional bases which are related to past and contemporary economic circumstances. A knowledge of such functional imbalances is clearly of useful value to the analyst of urban systems and many attempts have been made to classify cities in terms of their functional bases. These vary considerably in their degree of sophistication but all provide useful insights into the economic bases of urban systems, albeit of mainly pedagogic significance.

The earliest attempts at classification were mainly concerned with *qualitative methods* involving empirical observations and largely intuitive typologies. Aurousseau's (1921) scheme was based upon functional specialization and suggested six major categories, each of which was subdivided into a variable number of subgroups. Cities were divided into administrative, defensive, cultural, productive, communication and recreational types. A similar approach was adopted by Harris and Ullman (1945). Cities were divided into three main categories according to their predominant functions, although a more explicitly spatial component was incorporated into the scheme:

1. A clustered pattern of cities consisting of places performing specialized functions such as mining and recreation was identified. Their location was related to the localization of particular resources not found elsewhere in the region.
2. A linear pattern of centres performing transport-orientated functions such as railway centres, break of bulk points and ports was also suggested. Their location was directly related to the disposition of transport routes.
3. A regular pattern of centres termed central place cities was recognized whose primary function was the provision of retail and administrative services for a dispersed hinterland population.

Clearly, such systems suffer from imprecision and awareness of this led to the search for more precise *quantitative methods* of classification.

Initially, employment or occupational data was most commonly used, on the assumption that this would most accurately describe the functional structure of a city. Such an assumption is, of course, subject to the limitations associated with the classification of occupations used in national censuses, a point which is well made by Carter's (1972) discussion of the methods of functional classification of cities.

One of the earliest methods measured the economic base of cities by utilizing the *basic–non basic* division of urban economic functions (Alexander, 1954; Hoyt, 1954). The economic base theory suggests that the urban economy is composed of two distinct classes of productive effort: the basic activities which produce and distribute goods and services to a market outside the defined local economic area; and the non-basic or service activities whose goods and services are consumed by the local population. The former are considered to be the city-forming functions and the latter the city-serving. For this reason, it is considered that the functional classification of cities should concentrate on the basic activities since they are the elements most important to an understanding of the functional basis of city growth. However, the practical difficulty of defining basic and non-basic employment figures for a large number of towns and cities in a region or country have precluded its use as a classificatory device. There is no clear division between basic and non-basic employment in published data on occupation groups since most manufacturing or retail establishments serve a local as well as a wider hinterland population; the problem can only be overcome, therefore, by various imprecise rule-of-thumb procedures. Similarly, the ratio of basic to non-basic employment is very sensitive to the 'local economic area' for which it is computed. Therefore, comparative figures for different cities are liable to errors associated with a lack of comparability of their assumed economic areas (Roterus and Calef, 1955). Thus, this method has been used in a more limited way to investigate the economic base characteristics of single or small group of cities for practical economic planning purposes. This involves the determination of the importance of *basic* output for the operations of a range of large employers, using a combination of direct interviewing and inference, for areas defined by some proxy measure of the local economic area such as the primary retail trade area or the circulation area of local newspapers. The detailed basic–non-basic ratios are used as indicators of the relative and potential economic strength of cities by assessing the growth potential of basic employment and the likely multiplier effect that this would have upon non-basic employment; this type of research question has been tackled most systematically, by urban economists and regional scientists.

There are other approaches to the functional classification of cities. Harris (1943) used employment statistics from the 1930 United States census. The classification was based upon the function considered to be of greatest *importance*, not necessarily of greatest numerical significance, to the city. Guidelines were established by examining the employment structure of sample cities considered to be of well-defined functional types. Manufacturing cities were defined as those with more than 60 per cent of employees in manufacturing, retail centres as those with more than 50 per cent in retail trades. Centres which did not exceed any of these threshold levels were designated 'diversified'. Additional empirical rules were derived to designate transport cities, mining settlements, university towns and resorts and retirement centres. The spatial distribution of these categories demonstrates interesting regional patterns and provides insights into the functional and spatial structure of the urban system of the United States.

This method of classification has to be treated with caution since it has a number of limitations. Clearly, the threshold levels are arbitrarily defined, while the classification of each city into a single type obscures the considerable functional diversity of many cities. In fact, 80 per cent of the largest cities fall into the 'diversified' category.

Later attempts to circumvent these problems have involved using *arithmetic means* derived directly from employment data as the basis of classification. Examples exist for New Zealand (Pownall, 1953) and the Netherlands (Steigenga, 1955). Mean employment in a range of occupational categories was calculated for a variety of size-groupings of cities, and the positive deviations from the mean were taken as indicative of a degree of functional specialization. Clearly, the means are not arbitrarily defined and a city can exhibit a significant degree of specialization in more than one diagnostic function. A slightly more sophisticated application of this method is associated with Nelson's (1955) study in the United States. In this instance significant deviations from the mean were measured in terms of *standard deviations*. Any function which demonstrated an employment percentage of greater than one standard deviation from the mean was taken to show functional specialization in that city.

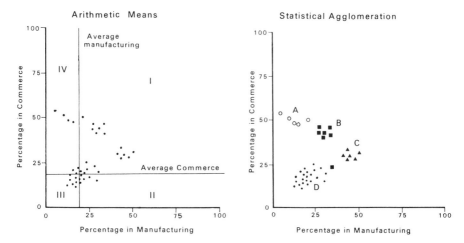

Figure 4.4 The subjectivity of classifications of towns: different criteria can produce sharply contrasted classifications of the same set of urban places. Source: R. H. T. Smith, 1965a; reproduced by permission of the Association of American Geographers

The advantages of this scheme are that the number of standard deviations from the mean for any single function indicates very precisely the degree of specialization in that function, whereas if specialization occurs on more than one function this can still be easily accommodated.

The disadvantages of basing a classification upon the arithmetic mean are, however, considerable. The mean of a set of values is not representative of the distribution from which it is calculated; it is sensitive to a small number of extremely high values so that in some instances no single figure is even approximately represented by the mean. This point is convincingly made by R. H. T. Smith (1965a) in his review of the literature relating to the functional classification of towns. Two graphs are presented illustrating classifications of a hypothetical set of towns. The first is based upon arithmetic means, and the second upon the statistical agglomeration of like units (Figure 4.4). It is immediately apparent that the four-fold classification (groups I–IV) based upon mean values is a much inferior representation of functional distinctiveness than that (groups A–D) derived from the agglomerative procedure and use of the latter involves a move in the direction of the development of more sophisticated methods of numerical taxonomy in the classification of towns based upon large numbers of variables (R. H. T. Smith, 1965b).

The *minimum requirements approach* is most closely associated with Alexandersson (1956). For American cities of greater than 10,000 population, the minimum percentage of employed population in the overall range of occupational categories was determined from a cumulative distribution graph and the point below which 5 per cent of the cities were represented was taken to be the required figure. (Figure, 4.5). The point 'K' was considered appropriate to eliminate highly atypical cities, and the value at this point was considered

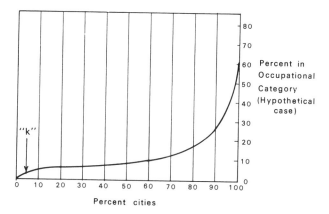

Cumulative Distribution Graph of Employment for
Selected Occupations in U.S.A. cities (based on
Alexandersson, 1956)

Figure 4.5   A hypothetical example of the application of
the minimum requirements approach to the classification
of towns. Based upon examples provided by Alexandersson
1956

to represent the minimum requirement of employed population in each occupational category for all cities except the most highly atypical. Employment above that figure for each occupational category was considered to represent the 'city-forming' or basic employment. Economic specialization was subsequently measured by the percentage employment above the K value for each occupational class. This method was subsequently used by Morrissett (1958) and developed further by Ullman and Dacey (1960) who used a sample from a number of size groupings of American cities and calculated the percentages employed in each of fourteen occupations. After determining the minimum percentage requirements, the sum of the minima for each of the city–size groupings was taken to determine the city-serving, or non basic employment. The remaining percentage and its occupational variation was taken to illustrate the functional characteristics of the city-forming or basic employment structure.

   In more recent years the aim has changed from an attempt to distinguish cities in terms of their particular specialized functions to one of grouping together cities with the greatest functional similarity. This involves a much more comprehensive use of the available employment data and the application of *multivariate* analytical techniques. An early example of such an approach was that adopted by Smith (1965b) in his analysis of 422 Australian towns with populations of greater than 500. He obtained data from the 1954 census relating to employment in twelve industry groups. A simple correlation coefficient was used as an index of the functional similarity of each town with every other, and linkage analysis was used to derive an optimal grouping in which each group member was functionally more similar to another town in the group than to one outside. In all, seventeen groups of towns were distinguished and these comprised three groups of manufacturing towns, six service groups, two types of resort towns, and towns which had significant employment concentrations in transport, communications, mining, public utilities, administration and primary production. Clearly this study provided both a useful description and some valuable insights into the functional and spatial characteristics of the Australian urban system.

Although this procedure provides a neat classification of the towns, the distinguishing functional characteristics of each group are not determined until a second stage of analysis in which the functional identity of groups is discovered by comparing the average percentages of employed persons in each of the twelve categories of each group with the average figure for all towns. This introduces a slightly arbitrary element into the functional labels attached to the seventeen groups, although *not* into the classification procedure.

Other multivariate analyses have adopted alternative procedures and have included data relating to a wider range of variables than those merely concerned with economic functions. Moser and Scott's early study (1961) of British towns is a case in point. They assembled data from the 1951 census and other published material for 157 towns of over 50,000 population; in all, 57 variables relating to population size and structure, population change, household characteristics, economic characteristics, social class, voting behaviour, health and education were obtained. This was analysed using the principal component variant of factor analytical procedures, which derives the most significant dimensions of variation in the original data matrix in descending order of importance. The most meaningful elements of variation are normally expressed by a small number of the early extracted *components*. In fact, in this example 60 per cent of the covariance was summarized by the first four components and these were by far the most diagnostic elements of variation in the original data. These were interpreted as follows:

Component 1   Social class
Component 2   Population growth 1931–51
Component 3   Population growth 1951–58
Component 4   Overcrowded housing conditions

The third stage of the analysis gives each town an index value (component weighting or score) for each of the derived components which expresses its characteristics in terms of each of the dimensions of variation. For example, a town with a *high positive* component weighting for Component 1 would tend to have an imbalance of its population in the higher social classes, while the converse would be the case for a town with a *high negative* component weighting. Clearly, used in this way, Component 1 could provide the basis for a classification of British towns in terms of their social class characteristics, while the other three components could provide alternative classifications based upon their particular diagnostic characteristics.

However, Moser and Scott proceeded to a fourth stage where the component weightings for each of the 157 towns for the four extracted components were plotted on scatter graphs using the four components, in sequence, as axes and the towns as points. Fourteen groups of towns were identified by visual inspection and this provided a combined classification in terms of the original input data:

1 Resorts, administrative and commercial centres
   (a) Seaside resorts
   (b) Spas, professional and administrative centres
   (c) Commercial centres.

2 Industrial towns
   (a) Railway centres
   (b) Ports
   (c) Textile centres of Yorkshire and Lancashire
   (d) Industrial towns of the North–east and Welsh mining towns
   (e) Metal manufacturing centres

3 Suburbs and suburban-type towns
   (a) Exclusive residential suburbs
   (b) Older mixed residential suburbs
   (c) Newer mixed residential suburbs
   (d) Light industrial suburbs, national defence centres, and towns within the influence of larger metropolitan conurbations
   (e) Older working-class industrial suburbs
   (f) Newer industrial suburbs.

This classification has considerable descriptive interest and, unlike the method used by Smith (1965b), it incorporates an interpretation of the central characteristics.

Other more recent studies have adopted similar procedures with the same kinds of result. Ahmad (1965) undertook a principal components analysis of 102 Indian cities with population exceeding 100,000 using 62 variables. He found the eight components accounted for 70 per cent of the original variation and these encompassed a diverse set of characteristics:

1. A north–south regionalism based on female labour force and sex ratio;
2. generalized accessibility;
3. compactness;
4. occupational structure (commercial versus industrial);
5. rural orientation;
6. city-size;
7. population change;
8. east–west regionalism based on occupation and migration characteristics, sex ratio and degree of clustering.

Clearly, some of these dimensions are similar to those in Moser and Scott's study and this prompted Ahmad to suggest that his method could be adopted to investigate the occurrence of variation of dimensions across international and cross-cultural examples. However, due principally to the lack of internationally comparable data of a suitable kind, this has not been accomplished and the obvious truism that the input conditions the output is now more properly appreciated. Nevertheless, in this particular example the weightings of eight components were used as the basis of a linkage analysis similar to that used by Smith (1965b) to provide a more precise classification of Indian cities. Five major groups were recognised:

1. the national metropoli of Bombay, Delhi, and Calcutta;
2. Calcutta suburbs, eight of more than 100,000 population;
3. northern cities;
4. southern cities;
5. centrally located cities.

The strong regional component in this classification suggests that outside the 'primate' cities, regional sociocultural variations are more important differentiating factors than the elements of functional specialization noted in the studies in the western developed countries.

An additional variant of these studies is provided by King (1966). He adopted a similar methodology to that of Ahmad to study 106 Canadian cities of over 10,000 population using 50 variables. However, in this case the analysis was undertaken for two periods of time, 1951 and 1961, to determine whether the dimensions of the urban system and the resulting classification of cities were stable over time. A considerable amount of detailed information relating to the dimensions of the urban system and a classification of towns was provided for both time-periods and two interesting conclusions were suggested. Firstly, the urban dimensions were not stable over time, and this led King to suggest that a more detailed examination of the changes might provide additional insight into the changing nature of urban society. Secondly, despite this instability the city-groupings which resulted from the classification process were far more consistent, particularly for those exhibiting strong regional contiguities. This suggested an important element of spatial order in the process of development and change in the urban system, a point which was also considered worthy of further investigation.

The preceding section has reviewed a range of methods applied to the classification of towns and cities by function. These range from the early observational empirical descriptions, through the development of simple quantitative procedures, usually based upon employment and occupational data, to the statistically more sophisticated and more broadly based methods of multivariate analysis. The general aim of these approaches has not varied a great deal. Principally, they have all attempted to provide a descriptive framework and some exploratory insight into the functional characteristics of the urban system as a first stage in the development of a more comprehensive understanding of its characteristics and of the development process on which it is based. However, in practice few have proceeded to an analytical investigation of specific aspects of the nature and growth of the system. This point was strongly made by Smith (1965a) who suggested that while early studies had considerable pedagogic and descriptive value, a change in direction was necessary. He suggested that future classification should be undertaken as a prelude to a more detailed analytical investigation of some *particular* aspect of the urban system. In effect, classification should not be an end in itself and the nature of the data used should be matched to a particular research design. Urban geographers have in more recent years shown little specific interest in the classification of cities, though interest has been retained in the rapidly growing field of regional analysis. This trend will be re-examined in the relevant part of the next chapter.

CENTRAL PLACE THEORY

Whereas spatial analysis *per se* has been of secondary interest in the studies of city–size distributions and of functional classification, it is of central interest to those studies which have been developed in the context of central place theory. Much of this work has been based upon the seminal study of Walter Christäller (1933) in southern Germany and focuses on the attempt to develop a deductive theory to explain the distribution and sizes of towns in terms of the services they performed for surrounding hinterlands, in other words, their centrality. Thus, the theory is most applicable to an understanding of urban systems which have developed principally as centres of *tertiary* activity, although it should be noted at the outset that the current relevance of the theory is not restricted to such systems. Most towns, even if based initially upon some of the specialized primary, secondary or quaternary functions noted in the previous section, tend to accumulate a tertiary function, and the concepts and methodologies developed within the context of central place theory can be extensively used to provide insights into the nature of urban systems in general.

Christäller's central place theory

Christäller observed an element of order in the spacing and sizes of service centres in southern Germany. A relatively few large centres, spaced at relatively long distances apart, provided specialized goods and services to large complementary regions (hinterlands). These were termed *high-order* central places. Conversely, more numerous smaller centres were found at a number of different levels. These were located closer together, provided less specialized goods and services to geographically more localized populations, and were termed *low-order* central places. Christäller's theory sought to explain the principles which determined the nature of such a system.

At the outset it should be noted that the theory was based upon an *idealized* landscape. The characteristics of this landscape were such that each point had an equal chance of receiving a central place, and the relative accessibility of one point to any other was a direct function of distance, irrespective of direction—in other words there was a uniform transportation surface. This degree of abstraction is not, however, as comprehensive as that included in the concept of the *isotropic* surface which many subsequent commentaries have assumed was associated with Christäller's theory (see, for examples Carter, 1972; Haggett 1972; Yeates and Garner, 1971). In addition, isotropism assumes the existence of a homogeneous plane surface and an even distribution of population and consumer purchasing power and, as has been suggested by Beavon (1977), Christäller's scheme does not depend upon the existence of the latter elements of isotropism; variations in these factors in space would merely result in minor variations in the deductively derived idealized settlement system. This consideration will be examined further following the discussion of the derivation of Christäller's theory.

At the next stage of theory derivation, Christäller considered that every good or service provided from a central place has a range with an upper and a lower limit. The upper limit of the range is the maximum distance a consumer will travel to a centre to obtain the goods, beyond which he is more likely to travel to an alternative nearer centre or, if there is no nearer centre, will go without the good altogether. This notion can be measured in terms of the distance (r) over which the good with the strongest degree of attraction (highest-order good) provided in a centre can be provided from that centre. Consequently, the maximum area to be served from a centre will be a circular complementary region around the centre of radius (r), given the uniform transportation surface of the idealized landscape. The lower limit of the range (r') is the minimum distance necessary to circumscribe a service area with sufficient population to generate enough consumer demand to make the offering of the good just economically viable from a centre. The relationship between the upper and lower limit of the range of a good is significant to the later stages of the analysis. If the lower limit of the range (r') is greater than the upper limit (r), then clearly such a good cannot be economically provided in the area. If the upper limit (r) of the good is equal to the lower limit (r'), then that good can just be provided profitably. In addition, if the upper limit of the range (r) is greater than the lower limit (r'), then the good can be provided and the trader can potentially earn excess profits by serving the population in the area between the two circles (Figure 4.6).

The goods and services required by the population of the idealized landscape will comprise an array from high order to low order. High-order goods were considered to be those, such as large items of furniture or fashion clothing, which are relatively costly and tend to be required at infrequent intervals. Thus, consumers are usually willing to travel relatively long distances to high-order centres, which are likely to offer the greatest range of choice, to obtain them. Clearly, the upper and lower limits of the range of such goods are likely to be

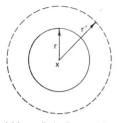

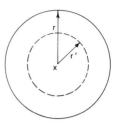

(a) lower limit of range (r')
> upper limit (r)
The good will not be
provided from x

(b) upper limit of range (r)
= lower limit (r')
The good will be provided
from x with no excess
profit

(c) upper limit of range (r)
> lower limit (r')
The good will be provided
from x with excess profits

Figure 4.6   Relationships between threshold and range in central place theory

relatively distant. Conversely, low-order goods are those such as groceries which may be perishable or required in relatively large amounts at frequent intervals. Thus, consumers will tend to be unwilling to travel far to obtain them and a wide range of product choice will not normally be demanded. The ranges of such goods are consequently likely to be small. An array of goods and services with consumer characteristics intermediate to these two extremes can also be envisaged.

From these initial observations Christäller deduced a model of settlement distribution for the idealized landscape. However, since he was initially concerned to develop a theory to explain the characteristics of a settlement system which was based upon the evolution of rural-market service centres over a long period of time, he suggested two organizing constraints on his system which comprised the *marketing principle.* These were that (1) there should be a minimum number of points of supply of all sizes so that trader profits could be maximized; and (2) the whole population of the area should be supplied with each good and service. The relevance of these constraints will become clear in the ensuing discussion.

To satisfy the first constraint, the most important element in the generation of the settlement model is the upper limit of the range of a good supplied from a centre. This is necessary if the number of centres of any size is to be minimized. Accordingly, as a first step, Christäller assumed the existence of a series of settlements ranked 'B'. The upper limit of the range of the highest order good provided in such a centre is designated (r) and, notionally, the area can be covered with B-centres spaced at distances of $2r$ and arranged on a regular equilateral triangle lattice (Figure 4.7). However, such a system does not satisfy the second constraint, since there are limited areas between any three circular hinterlands which cannot be served with the highest-order good offered at the B-centres. Thus, a slightly modified structure of overlapping circles becomes necessary to conform to the marketing principle, although the fundamental spatial geometry of the system is largely maintained (Figure 4.8). The B-centres are still arranged according to a regular equilateral triangular lattice spaced slightly more closely together at distance (d), which is a direct function

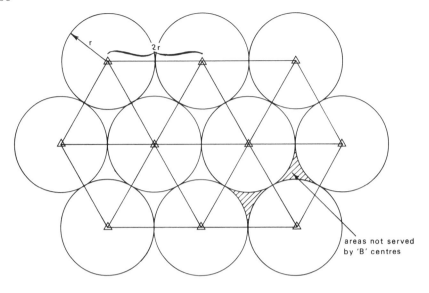

△ 'B' centres (First Order)

Figure 4.7   Relationships among *B*-centres in central place theory; the derivation of regular equilateral triangular lattices of centres

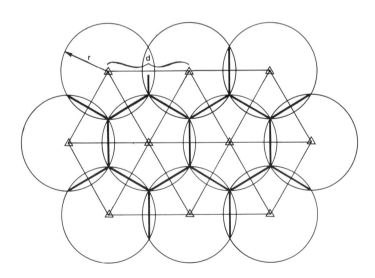

△ 'B' centres (First Order)

Figure 4.8   Relationships between ideal circular hinterlands of centres in central place theory and their generalization into hexagons

of the upper range of the *B*-centres. In addition, the hinterlands of the B centres can be generalized to give exclusive regular hexagonal areas rather than the overlapping circles, the rationale for which is that consumers will tend to use the nearest centre to them if each offers the same goods and services.

Since, by definition, sufficient consumers can be attracted to each B centre to make its highest-order function economically viable; in other words, the lower limit of the range of that function has been superseded; it follows that all goods and services with less extensive lower limits to their ranges can also be provided at B centres, since sufficient people visit them to make such functions economically viable.

Proceeding to the next stage, the outer limits of the ranges of successively lower-order functions can be diagrammatically represented as having radii of $r - 1$, $r - 2$, $r - 3$, etc. (Figure 4.9). Any function supplied from a *B*-place which has an outer range of less than (r) cannot be supplied to all parts of its complementary area without some consumers undertaking excessively long journeys, or by obtaining the lower order functions while visiting the *B*-place for its highest order functions. This consideration provides the logical basis for the formation of a lower grade of central places, designated *K* by Christäller, which

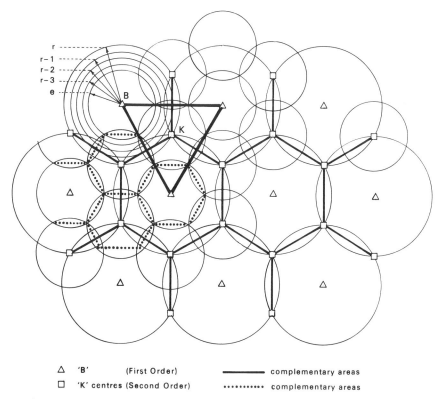

△	'B' (First Order)	——— complementary areas
□	'K' centres (Second Order)	·········· complementary areas

Figure 4.9   The derivation of a 2nd lower order of centres in central place theory

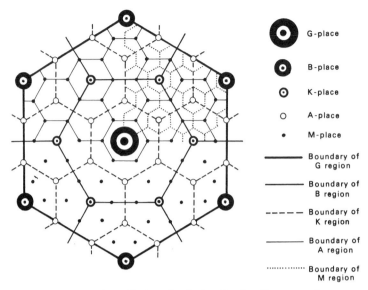

G-place
B-place
K-place
A-place
M-place
Boundary of G region
Boundary of B region
Boundary of K region
Boundary of A region
Boundary of M region

Figure 4.10   Christäller's   classical $K = 3$ diagram.   Source: Christäller, 1966; reproduced by permission of Carlisle W. Baskin

will be located at some distance from the B-centres, in the centre of the peripheral parts of their complementary areas. To be most competitive with the B-grade centres, and at the same time central to the peripheral areas, the K-centres will be located in the centre of the equilateral triangles subtended by three B-grade centres. This coincides with the point at which the hexagons defining the hinterlands of the B-centres intersect. The highest order function which can be provided by the K-centres is geometrically determined by radius (e) which defines the outer limit of its range. Consumers requiring functions which have outer limits to their ranges of greater than radius (e) but less than radius (r) will, therefore, have to obtain them when travelling to the B-centres for their highest-order functions.

For the same reasons as noted for B-centres, the K-centres can provide all the functions with less extensive lower limits to their ranges than the outer range of the highest-order function provided in the K-centres. In addition, in a similar manner to that described in the previous paragraph, successively lower order A and M-grade centres can be generated. The resulting system of central places derived by Christäller according to the marketing principle is represented in hexagonal form in Figure 4.10. At the centre of this system is the G-centre. This is considered to result from the upgrading of a centrally accessible B-location, if over time an element of demand for functions of a higher order than those provided at typical B-centres develops in the region.

The settlement system derived in this manner according to the marketing principle by Christäller was termed the $K = 3$ framework. This expresses the number of hexagonal trade areas of one order which are contained within a hexagon of the next highest order. (Figure 4.11). In this illustration the

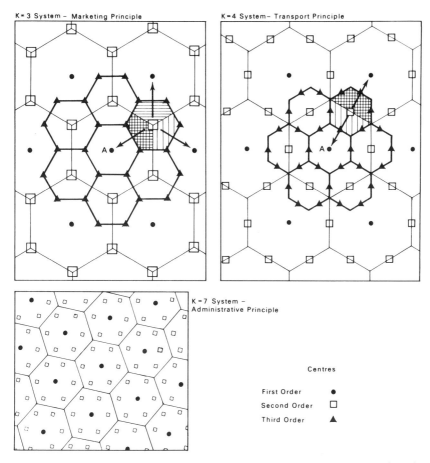

Figure 4.11 $K = 3$, $K = 4$, and $K = 7$; the marketing, transport, and administrative
principles

centrally located first-order centre marked 'A' is taken to transact the whole
of the first-order trade for the second-order hexagonal trade area immediately
adjacent to it, as well as a third of the first-order trade of the six second-order
hexagons surrounding it. In addition, there will be three times as many centres
at each successively lower order. Note also that according to the system the
first-order centre 'A' will also transact the second-order trade for the second-
order hexagonal area adjacent to it.

However, Christäller recognized the fact that systems of settlements did
not all necessarily develop based upon the evolution of rural market centres
over a long period of time. Two major variants were noted: the *transportation*
principle and the *administrative* principle. These represent inductive modifications to the original theory. In the first case, he considered that many settlement
systems do not develop in areas which have a uniform transportation surface.
Historically, early established routeways are very persistent in their effect

upon the development of settlement nodes, while the relatively rapid colonization of new territory in the nineteenth and twentieth centuries has been markedly influenced by the development of railways and roads. In these circumstances the development of 'B'-grade centres will develop in an area in much the same manner as that already described, although the centres will be orientated along lines of transportation rather than placed initially at random in a more idealized landscape. In addition, the development of a next lower order of centres is not expected to gravitate to a median position between three higher-order centres to maximize competitive impact as is expected to occur in the $K = 3$ system. Such a location would clearly be off the main transportation links between the higher-order centres and, for this reason, would not have the competitive advantage of accessibility associated with a routeway location. Thus, the K-grade centres would be expected to develop on the routeway, at a midpoint between any two B-centres, and successively lower-order centres would be expected to develop in a similar manner. This results in the development of the $K = 4$ framework illustrated in Figure 4.11. In this case the hexagonal trade area of any one order contains within it the equivalent of four trade areas of the next lower-order centre. Also, the relationship between the number of centres of successively lower orders tends to be represented by a factor of four.

The derivation of the framework associated with the administrative principle tends even more strongly towards empiricism. Again in this instance the development of the B-centres is expected in the manner already described. However, the settlement pattern of the area is now assumed to have been developed primarily within the context of stronger administrative or political control. Thus, the complementary regions of the successively lower-order centres have to be completely contained within the boundaries of a higher-order centre in order to eradicate the administrative ambiguity which might be associated with the 'border' locations of centres of successively lower order in the $K = 3$ and $K = 4$ arrangements. The resulting system is termed the $K = 7$ framework since the complementary region of any one order of centres contains within it the equivalent of seven regions of the next lower order, although for geometrical reasons these cannot now be regular hexagonal arrangements. This underlines Christäller's attempt to move away from the initial deductive theory towards real-world settlement systems (Figure 4.11). It also is interesting to note that the number of centres of successively lower orders tends towards the much higher factor of seven, while the much smaller complementary regions of successively lower orders suggests that the actual size of the settlements declines precipitously. The resulting arrangement of few high-order centres exerting an element of control over relatively numerous small low-order centres suggests that this system incorporates a much stronger element of primacy than that associated with the alternative frameworks. Thus, it is anticipated that this system is most likely to be found in the very early stages of development or in areas which have been developed based upon a strong element of administrative or political control.

Christäller's central place system

Structural and behavioural characteristics

Whatever framework is considered most appropriate to explain the nature of the urban system of a region or a country, it is apparent from Christäller's work that it will incorporate a number of *explicit* structural and *implicit* behavioural characteristics. These are considered to be the essence of Christäller's derived systems so it is appropriate that they should be emphasized at this point.

Firstly, while Christäller did not initially use the term hierarchy (Buursink, 1975), the derived systems are organized functionally and spatially into hierarchies. These have the following characteristics:

1. There are a relatively small number of the highest-order largest centres.
2. There are larger numbers of smaller centres at the successively lower orders. These orders will be distinguished from each other by marked discontinuities in the population size and range of functions offered in each order. It is this aspect of Christäller's system which has been subject to the closest scrutiny by subsequent empirical investigation. This point will be reintroduced later.
3. The highest-order centres will serve the widest complementary regions with the highest-order goods and services. In addition, they will serve their own local hinterlands with all the lower-order functions.
4. Successively lower-order centres will provide a smaller range of goods and services to increasingly localized trade areas. The population living in or near such centres will, conversely, depend upon the higher-order centres for more specialized goods and services. The spatial and functional aspects of the dependence of the lower-order centres on the higher has subsequently been termed the 'nesting' relationships.

In addition, there are a number of implicit behavioural assumptions:

5. It is assumed that consumers will use the nearest centre offering goods and services which they require. This has more recently been termed the *nearest centre assumption*.
6. The entry of suppliers of goods and services into the system is organized so that the number of establishments and centres is minimized. This has been termed the *profit maximization assumption*, which implies that suppliers have perfect information relating to the nature of the system and that they are capable of making economically optimal location decisions. In effect, a system of perfect competition appears to be assumed.

Variations relating to societal characteristics of regions

A further important consideration should also be introduced at this point. It was noted earlier that the most important element in the derivation of the settlement systems of Christäller was the upper limit of the range of the highest-order good supplied from a centre. If considered in detail it is apparent that the degree of specialization of functions which can be provided and the specific values for such ranges are likely to vary considerably from area to area depending upon the characteristics of the particular societies under review, Berry (1967b):

1. Of particular note in this respect is the density distribution of the population. Clearly, the denser the distribution of the population, the greater the potential consumer expenditure contained within an area of unit distance from any location. Hence, the greater the potential number of levels in the hierarchy and the greater the degree of functional specialization of the highest-order centres.
2. Of similar note is the effect of variations in the amount of consumer expenditure available, usually in association with variations in the degree of sophistication of consumer demand. In a peasant society, barely above subsistence level, expenditure will be low and demand will only exist for very basic requirements. Thus, a hierarchy of few levels with a low level of specialization of functions available in even the highest level is likely. In contrast, the opposite hierarchical characteristics are likely to typify a prosperous society with highly sophisticated consumer demands.
3. The transportation technology available to the society will also be of considerable importance. Slow or high-cost transport facilities will increase the friction of distance and promote a large number of levels in the hierarchy because of the importance attached to the demand for local offerings of goods and services. Conversely, convenient, rapid, low-cost forms of transport reduce the importance of local low-order centres relative to the enhanced significance of relatively more distance, highly specialized centres.

These points are important to an appreciation of central place theory for a number of reasons. They suggest that the detailed characteristics of the central place system which develops in an area is strongly dependent on the specific combination of these factors which existed at the time when the system began to emerge. Since all three factors vary considerably in societies over time and space, it should be expected that central place systems vary in their detailed characteristics from place to place, although the basic elements of such a system will remain whatever the area. It was probably for this reason that Christäller attached specific figures derived from his fieldwork area in southern Germany to the upper limits of the ranges of his system of centres. For example, the range of G centres was taken to be 36 km, B centres 21 km, and K centres 12 km. Since this was done to test the empirical validity of his deductive system, perhaps the observation by Carter (1972) and Beavon (1977) that specific figures should form no part of a deductive theory is too harsh?

In addition, the fact that the central place system which develops in an area tends to be in a state of adjustment with the societal characteristics which existed during its initial development might be considered to have certain dynamic-predictive connotations. Traditionally, this has not been the case since many writers have formerly considered central place theory to provide only a static model of settlement systems. However, whatever the basic characteristics of a system which develops in an area these will change over time in a reasonably predictable manner. For example, changes in the density of population, change in relative levels of affluence and associated consumer demand, as well as changes in the personal mobility of the population are all likely to precipitate changes in various levels of the central place hierarchy. The problem of prediction is, of course, that all three factors may be changing at the same time and may be interrelated. Nevertheless, the theory has predictive value, even if only at a conceptual level and has been used in this manner in recent years. However, it is also worthy of note that even though the detailed characteristics of the central place system of an area are likely to change over time strong elements of inertia are likely to be retained in its geographical expression which can be traced *back* to the early stages of the evolution of the system.

EARLY EMPIRICAL TESTS OF CHRISTÄLLER'S CENTRAL PLACE THEORY

Early studies undertaken in response to central place theory in south-west England (Bracey, 1953) and in south-western Wisconsin (Brush, 1953) empirically demonstrated the existence of a hierarchical system of rural service centres despite differences in population density and settlement history. Both study areas approximated the conditions of the idealized landscape hypothesized by Christäller, and these studies were subsequently supplemented by a comparative analysis of the same areas (Brush and Bracey, 1955). However, the implicit acceptance of the tenets of central place theory in these papers was not without criticism. Vining (1955), for example, strongly criticized the recognition of a hierarchical system of central places in Brush's initial study. Vining considered that the service centres formed a continuum from small to large with no distinct breaks into hierarchical classes. This criticism was considered of fundamental importance since the alternative of a *continuum* of central places rather than a stepped *hierarchy* was contrary to the whole concept of Christäller's theory. Thus, Berry and Garrison (1958a and b) set out in a more precise manner to test the empirical validity of the existence of a hierarchical system of service centres in Snohomish County, Washington by graphically plotting the population of 33 centres against the number of functions they offered (Figure 4.12). From this data three hierarchical classes with fundamentally different population sizes and ranges of functions were suggested. However, in detail it might be suggested that the limits differentiating the three hierarchical classes were arbitrary and little account was taken of those deviant cases—represented towards the top of the graph—which, for their populations, had abnormally few functions. In south-western Iowa, Berry, Barnum, and Tennant (1962) used more sophisticated methods of multivariate analysis to investigate data relating to the potential existence of a central

116

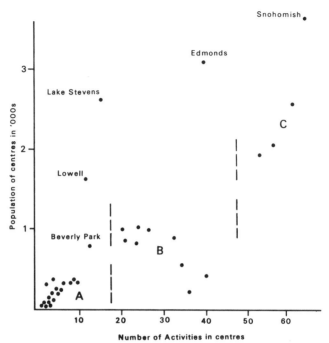

Figure 4.12 Classes of central places in Snohomish County:
relationships between population size and functional status.
Source: Berry and Garrison, 1958; reproduced by permission of
Economic Geography

place system. They examined the size and spacing of centres, patterns of
consumer travel behaviour for high and low-order goods, and systems of
trade areas and their interrelationships. A hierarchy of centres was proposed
which consisted of cities, towns and villages, with over 55 functions, 28–54
functions and 10–27 functions, respectively, and comparable differences in
population size. Under scrutiny, however, the breaks in the hierarchy are too
slight to rule out a continuous relationship between population size and numbers
of functions; in a large number of subsequent studies, evidence for the continuous relationship appears to be the rule rather than the exception (Barnum,
1966; Stafford, 1963).

Deviations from a stepped hierarchy

It must be stressed that the demonstration of a definite hierarchical functional
structure of urban centres is not absolutely critical to the validity and subsequent utility of the theory. There are many reasons why an idealized hierarchy
might, in practice, be transformed into a continuum of centres; though some
of these suggest further limitations of the original theory. It is opportune
at this point to examine these issues.

The original work of Christäller does, in fact, draw attention to a number of considerations which are likely to create deviations, albeit minor, from a strictly hierarchical structure. Of these, the most important is that associated with potential spatial variations in population density or purchasing power in the idealized landscape. Saey (1973) was the first to draw particular attention to this point which is expressed by Christäller (1933) in the following terms:

if population density or purchasing power vary, the spacing of the central places (the hexagonal pattern) does not change but the number of functions may vary, even to such an extent that the centres in some subareas attain a higher order than normal, whereas centres in other subareas fall in a lower order.

It is not altogether clear from this statement why the spacing of central places does not change. In fact, variations in population density and purchasing power clearly influence the upper and lower limits of the range of a function and, given the nature of the theory, this must create variations in the spacing of centres. However, the latter part of the statement provides flexibility and a rationale for deviations from a strict hierarchical structure, and for minor variations in the range of functions offered by centres of the same hierarchical status.

In addition, Christäller recognized two situations in which the consumer behaviour assumption of the theory might deviate from the norm. These are highlighted by Pred (1967) and they rest on the assumption that a shopper will sometimes attempt to maximize total travel effort, often by combining shopping for high and low-order goods or by combining shopping with some other activity (multipurpose trips), rather than merely minimizing the travel cost for an individual good. Thus, a consumer may obtain both low and high-order goods from a high-order centre which is more distant than the closest low-order centre, or may travel to a distant centre if sales-price savings exceed additional transport costs. Such behavioural variations, if systematically relevant to consumer behaviour, would tend to result in the enhancement of the status of relatively distant high-order centres and the diminution of the functions of low-order centres which may be bypassed. Christäller merely noted this consideration as a minor deviation from the norm which was unlikely to alter fundamentally the nature of the hierarchical structure. However, Saey (1973) suggests that this consideration is likely to result in the boundaries of market areas being systematically closer to smaller centres than to larger centres and illustrates the possible nature of a central place system 'corrected' for multipurpose trips (Figure 4.13). This diagram indicates that centres of similar hierarchical status may have trade-areas of variable size. Thus some may have a relatively wide range of functions and others a relatively narrow range of functions. This would transform an idealized stepped hierarchical structure of centres into a continuum.

Other real-world deviations from the idealized landscape assumed by Christäller are also likely to modify a stepped hierarchical system of centres. Physiographic irregularities make it unlikely that each part has an equal chance of

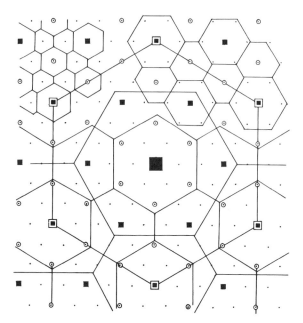

Figure 4.13   The $K = 3$ system modified to accommodate
multipurpose trips (adapted from Saey, 1973). Reproduced
by permission of KNAG

receiving a central place, while deviations from a uniform transportation surface, which is the more usual real-world situation, is likely to result in considerable deviations from the expected norm of regular hexagonal trade-areas. Also, as noted by Berry, Barnum, and Tennant (1962) the larger the area studied the greater the likelihood of encountering such random variations, and these again are likely to result in the modification of a distinctly stepped hierarchical structure towards a continuous distribution of centre sizes.

The measurement of centrality

Problems of measurement of the hierarchical status of centres are also of considerable importance. Central place theory was postulated to explain variations in the size and spacing of centres in terms of the functions provided for the population of surrounding complementary regions, in other words in terms of their centrality. Clearly, the population of a town cannot be used as a measure of centrality since most towns, and particularly the larger ones, tend increasingly to be multifunctional, even if their original development was related to the service function. Thus, population tends to measure the overall importance of a town rather than its centrality alone. Christäller attempted to solve this problem by devising a measure of centrality based upon the relative concentration of the telephones of a region into particular central places:

$$\text{Centrality} = Tz - Ez.\frac{Tg}{Eg}$$

where

Tz is the number of telephones in the particular central place
Ez is the population of the central place
Tg is the number of telephones in the region
Eg is the population of the region

This measure was reasonably appropriate to the period that Christäller was working in southern Germany since telephones were by no means as common a piece of household equipment as they are today. Nevertheless, the measure was still a rather imprecise surrogate of relative centrality since it was merely inferred that telephone concentration was an indicator of service status.

Subsequently, a great variety of measures of centrality have been devised, usually based upon the number and degree of specialization of retail facilities and other services provided in a centre. The earliest were often based upon the *key criteria* method. A pioneering example was provided by Smailes (1944) for the whole of England and Wales. Relative status in the urban hierarchy was determined with reference to the number of banks in a centre, the presence of a Woolworth's store, grammar school, hospital, the number of cinemas and the presence of a local newspaper. Clearly, the choice of criteria and the numerical limits adopted introduces an arbitrary element into such classifications, but they can be used to some descriptive advantage as is demonstrated by a more comprehensive recent study of similar type (R. D. P. Smith, 1968). Smith designates 35 significant retail and service criteria, and on the basis of the number of some and the presence or absence of others, suggests a hierarchy of central places for England comprising eleven different levels for 1965 (Figure 4.14). The same method has been adopted at a variety of different scales; Smailes and Hartley (1961) devised a nine-level classification for the shopping centres of Greater London based upon 21 key functions, while Carruthers (1962) developed a classification of centres for the same area based upon only six key functions, supplemented by indices of the rateable values of the shops and the accessibility of the centres to bus routes. Similarly, Lomas (1964) graded 133 retail centres in the English Midlands according to the numbers of six key retail functions, while Thorpe and Rhodes (1966) used a variant of this technique to define a four-fold hierarchy of shopping centres in the Tyneside urban region. Their 'centrality index' was subjectively defined as the square root of the number of non-food shops multiplied by a score comprising the number of non-food multiple shops, the number of banks and the number of grocery shops.

Subsequent to these early studies a more quantitatively refined measure of centrality was provided by the *functional index* derived by Davies (1967). This

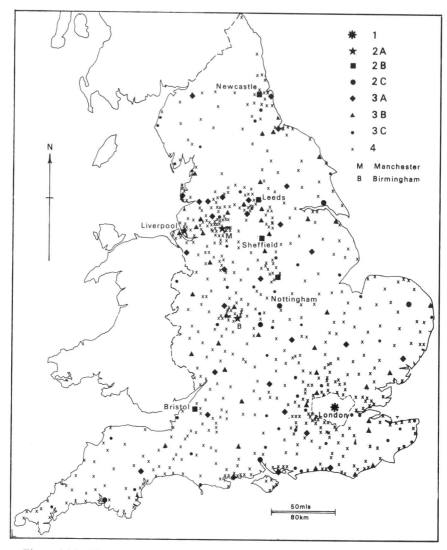

Figure 4.14   The urban hierarchy of England, 1965. Source: R. D. P. Smith, 1968

was based upon the location coefficient of a single establishment of each defined functional type in a specified area:

$$c = \frac{t}{T} \times 100$$

where c was the location coefficient of function t, t was one outlet of function t, and T was the total number of outlets of t in the whole system.

The multiplication of the location coefficient of a particular function by the number of establishments of that function in a centre gave the centrality value of that function for the centre. The addition of the centrality values of each function used in the study then gave the functional index of the centre. A comparison of the functional indices of different centres was considered to provide a measure of their relative service status. In addition, a weighting for numbers of employees or floorspace can be used to allow for variations in size of outlet. This provided a less subjective measure of hierarchical status than those previously mentioned since it was a function of the system under investigation rather than an arbitrary artifact. However, the degree of objectivity of this measure should not be overstated since the functional index is affected by the areal extent of the assumed closed system for which it is derived, as well as by the number of arbitrarily defined functions used in a particular investigation.

Indices of centrality have also been derived from census sources. In Britain, the Census of Distribution and Other Services is most important since it provides statistics relating to shopping turnover, number of establishments and numbers of employees, subdivided in each case into a number of functional types, for both the larger central shopping centres and for all local authority areas. These figures have been used to considerable advantage at both national (Thorpe, 1968) and regional scales of analysis (Davies, 1970). Similar data was derived from the US Census of Business by Preston (1971) in his investigation of the structure of the central place system of the Pacific north-west.

Any one of these methods is capable of providing an empirical classification of the service status of centres for most general practical purposes. However, all are surrogate measures of centrality, in most instances strongly based upon retail criteria, and the range of indices attests to the lack of consensus on an objective measure of centrality. In fact, a number of comprehensive reviews of the range of ranking procedures, notably by Davies (1970), indicate a lack of detailed comparability of alternative indices despite a degree of interchangeability of some of the measures.

More recently the debate on the precise measurement of centrality has been taken a step further by Preston (1971; 1975). He suggests that Christäller's concept of centrality had not been properly applied, that is, a measure of the service functions of a centre, *strictly limited* to that element relating to its surrounding complementary region. All the measures previously noted incorporate an element of centrality which relates to the services provided in the centre for its own population. These measure a centre's nodality rather than its own centrality—its absolute, not-relative importance. While this is a valid consideration, it clearly complicates the measurement of centrality. Preston (1971; 1975) overcomes this problem by adopting a specific definition of centrality:

$$C = N - L$$

where

C = the surplus of importance, that is, the relative importance of a place or *centrality*;

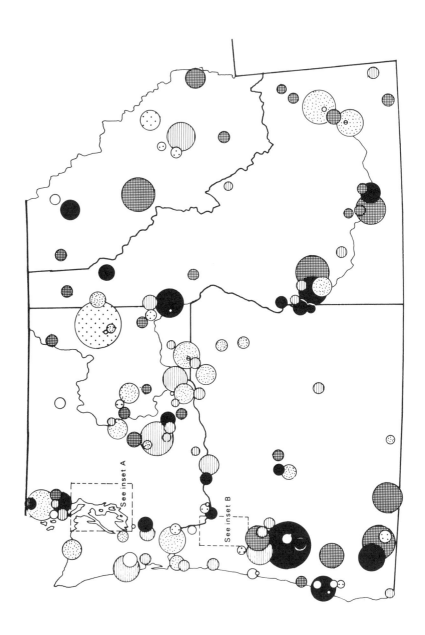

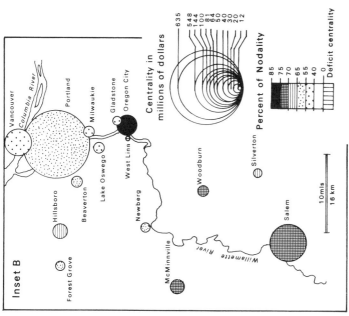

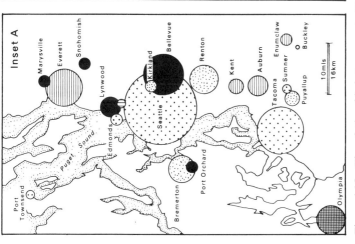

Figure 4.15 The relationship between centrality and nodality in the Pacific north-west. Source: Preston, 1971: reproduced by permission of *Economic Geography*

N = the importance of a place plus its complementary region, that is, absolute importance or *nodality*;

L = the importance of a town as a unit consuming central goods and services, or local consumption.

Using information from the 1963 Census of Business, the 1960 Census of population, and average annual expenditure patterns for urban families in 1960–61 reported by the Bureau of Labor Statistics for cities with populations greater than 2500 in the Pacific north-west, a map of centrality was produced. This also expressed centrality as a percentage of nodality (Figure 4.15). The relationship between the centrality and the nodality of centres varied considerably. There was a strong tendency for the centrality of the larger multifunctional centres such as Seattle, Portland and Tacoma to form a relatively low percentage of their nodality measure, since a major part of their service function was orientated towards their local industrial population. The converse tended to be demonstrated by the smaller, essentially service centres, but not invariably since some of the smaller centres had significant elements of non-service-orientated employment. The variable relationships between centrality and nodality are intrinsically interesting but also demonstrate the fact that if the theory is to be applied in its classical form, more precise measures of centrality are appropriate rather than the conceptually broader measures of nodality. The latter are more likely to transform hierarchical tendencies into a continuous distribution.

Attempts to measure centrality have been of considerable value in urban geography, since their practical application has provided vast amounts of information relating to the hierarchical and spatial aspects of the service function of urban systems. However, with regard to the measurement of *centrality*, the difficulties involved in deriving a precise and objective measure, combined with the ambiguity in the literature between the concepts of centrality and nodality and their apparently variable relationship over space, make it unlikely that a distinctly stepped hierarchical central place system will be demonstrated in practice. A continuous distribution of centre sizes is more likely in real-world situations.

The behavioural axioms of central place theory

Deviations from the behavioural axioms of central place theory might also transform an idealized hierarchy into a settlement continuum. Consumer behaviour in classical central place theory is determined by the *nearest centre assumption* by which the time-cost budgets of journeys for particular goods and services are minimized. Until comparatively recently, empirical tests of the theory were largely confined to determining whether the structural facets of the central place system could be approximately demonstrated in practice. If this proved to be the case, it was inferred that consumer behaviour conformed to the theoretical norm. However, more recent work indicates that the simple inference of behaviour from structure considerably overstates behavioural realities. Golledge, Rushton, and Clark (1966) working in rural Iowa collected information relating to the distance travelled to the towns where the maximum purchase and the nearest purchase of 33 different goods and services were obtained. From this information the goods were categorized according to the spatial characteristics of the trips generated. 'Spatially flexible' goods, such as clothing, were described as those for which consumers were willing to travel to alternative centres whereas 'spatially inflexible' goods such as groceries, were those for which consumers usually used the nearest centre. Considerable doubt was cast upon the nearest centre axiom, which appeared only to be relevant to the low-order goods. A more exhaustive investigation of the grocery shopping patterns of the same population (Rushton, Golledge, and Clark 1967) demonstrated that the nearest centre assumption accounted for only 52 per cent of the journeys undertaken. Consumer behaviour is in fact a complex, and as yet unexplained, tradeoff of the attractions (advantages) of increasing centre size and the disincentives associated with longer journeys. Lentnek, Lieber, and Sheskin (1975) investigated interurban food shopping behaviour in four areas at varying levels of economic development. Food shopping behaviour was found to conform to a 'dual assignment rule': households living relatively close to a limited range of opportunities typically used the nearest centre, whereas households living some distance from the nearest opportunity preferred shopping in larger, more distant places. If, therefore, a reasonably convenient opportunity exists it tends to be used, but if a journey is necessary at all it might as well continue until a higher-order centre, providing a greater range of food and other shopping opportunities, is reached. Also of interest is the fact that the change from using the nearest centre to a more distant larger centre, increased from 3 km (2 miles) in Mexico, progressively, to 19 to 21 km (12 to 13 miles) for respondents in Michigan (Figure 4.16). This reflected a combination of increases in income, personal mobility and the degree of specialization of food shopping requirements associated with increases in the level of economic development of the sample populations. There are more complex patterns of consumer behaviour as levels of economic development and personal affluence increase, and whereas the nearest centre assumption may have approximated the behavioural realities of southern Germany prior to 1933, its extrapolation to areas with higher levels of economic development in more recent times is extremely doubtful.

An additional axiom is that the entry of suppliers of goods and services into the system is determined by the *profit maximization assumption*. Pred (1967) has suggested that this dependence upon the 'economic man', concept is a significant weakness of the theory. Instead, suppliers (and consumers) are considered more likely to be 'boundedly rational satisficers' a concept derived from the earlier work of H. A. Simon. They are considered unlikely to have perfect information relating to spatial economic opportunities and, rather than optimizing their behaviour, they are likely to be satisfied with something rather less.

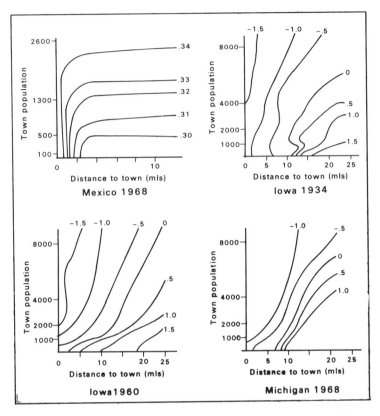

Figure 4.16   The nearest centre hypothesis investigated in four different societal circumstances by indifference curves. Source: Lentnek *et al.*, 1975; reproduced by permission of the Association of American Geographers

These considerations represent significant deviations from the behavioural assumptions of central place theory, which together are easily capable of introducing an element of random variation into the development of an idealized central place hierarchy. This is likely to create sufficient variability in the detailed hierarchical status of centres of the same order to transform a stepped hierarchy into a continuum.

In a similar manner, a comparable random element might be introduced into an idealized system with change over time. It was suggested earlier that, logically, the details of a central place system are responsive to changes in the population density distribution, the level of consumer expenditure, and the level of personal mobility of consumers. Such features might change consistently throughout an area or differentially faster in some areas rather than others. In the latter situation it is likely that some centres in each hierarchical grade will either rise or fall in status so transforming a stepped hierarchy into a continuous relationship.

As a result of the combined modifying influences of all these factors, it is unlikely that an idealized stepped hierarchy of service centres will be found in real-world situations. Instead only hierarchical *tendencies* should be expected, of a form which could also be interpreted as a continuum. However, this need not necessarily invalidate the utility of the theory. It is still an approximate explanation for the development of a hierarchical system of service centres, for the functional interrelationship both between consumers and centres, and between centres of varying sizes, and for the prediction of changes in a system associated with changing societal characteristics. Thus, central place theory as originally proposed by Christäller represents an approximate idealized explanation for the sizes and spacings of service centres in an area. As such it still has considerable conceptual and organizational value for the analysis of systems of cities in a region.

In this context a recent paper by Parr (1978) suggests an additional modification to the theory to make it more consistent with reality. He considers that the assumption of the fixed K value (for example, 3, 4 or 7) relationship between each successive market area size to be unreal. Instead, he suggests that during

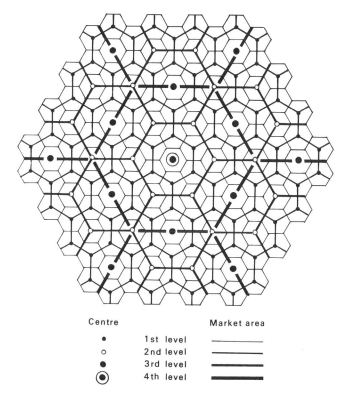

Centre		Market area
•	1st level	
○	2nd level	
●	3rd level	
◉	4th level	

Figure 4.17 The general hierarchical model of a central place system. $K_1 = 3$; $K_2 = 3$; $K_3 = 4$. Source: Parr, 1978; reproduced by permission of *Urban Studies*

the evolution of a central place system, from a proliferation of low-order centres to the subsequent development of high-order centres, the characteristics of a society are likely to change so that the organizing principle associated with the development of each successive level of centres is not constant. Thus, a 'general hierarchical model' is proposed which allows the K value to vary for each level of the hierarchy, and an example of a resulting spatial framework is shown in Figure 4.17. From applications of this model to published studies of central place systems in Scandinavia, the United States, Canada and the Philippines, a number of interesting conclusions emerge. The general hierarchical model is a more appropriate description of the central place systems than that of Christäller in each case other than that of Denmark, but most systems are still *approximately* described by the principles derived by Christäller. In fact, in only one case ($K2 = 16$ in the Philippines) is there evidence for a framework other than that proposed by Christäller, and there is strong support for the conceptual utility of Christäller's central place theory, albeit in a modified form.

BERRY AND GARRISON'S REINTERPRETATION OF CENTRAL PLACE THEORY: THE THEORY OF TERTIARY ACTIVITY

The preceding discussion of central place theory has been developed from the perspective of Christäller's (1933) original work. However, much of the work undertaken under the heading of central place theory was stimulated by Berry and Garrison's (1958a and b) reinterpretation of the theory in the form of the theory of tertiary activity. This is related to the fact that the English translation of Christäller's work did not become easily available until 1966. Unfortunately, recent re-evaluations of the theory of tertiary activity, notably by Saey (1973) and Beavon (1977) suggest that Berry and Garrison misinterpreted some of Christäller's ideas and that these misinterpretations have become irretrievably entrenched in the literature. Since this creates confusion in the minds of students introduced to the notions of central place theory, a number of points of clarification are perhaps necessary at this stage of the discussion.

In the first instance, Berry and Garrison (1958a and b) assumed that Christäller's theory depended upon a homogeneous distribution of consumer expenditure in an area. As indicated earlier, this implied a degree of isotropism which Christäller did not envisage for the idealized landscape. Thus, the theory was not dependent upon this assumption. In addition, Berry and Garrison considered that the idealized spatial frameworks were derived from the lower limit of the range of a centre (redesignated the 'threshold') rather than the upper limit (redesignated the 'range'). This was also considered to provide a strong reason why most suppliers of goods and services could earn excess profits in the system, a consideration which was assumed (erroneously) to be excluded from Christäller's version. It is assumed that the population of an area has to be supplied with n central functions and that these can be ranked from 1 to n in ascending order of threshold expenditure requirements. The highest-order centres in the area offering function n will be spaced in much the same manner as that described for the B-grade centres in Christäller's scheme, but in this instance with reference to the threshold of the highest-order function rather than its range. Functions with lower threshold requirements such as $n - 1$, $n - 2$, etc., will now earn excess profits since their effective ranges will extend beyond their particular threshold distances. Again, as in the case of the Christäller scheme, a second order of centres can be envisaged developing in the centre of equilateral triangles subtended by three first-order centres. The highest-order function to be supplied from these centres can be designated $n - i$, the threshold of which is defined by the geometry of equal hexagonal trade areas centred on a first-order centre and on the six nearest second-order centres. By definition function $n - i$ will not be able to earn excess profits since its hexagonal trade areas only circumscribe a bare threshold population. Functions n and $n - i$ were termed hierarchically marginal functions since they introduce new levels into the hierarchy where only normal profits are possible. In the same manner, lower-order centres with thresholds $n - j$, $n - k$, etc., can be postulated. Again, by definition functions $n - j$ and $n - k$ can only earn normal profits but it is clear that suppliers of all other functions can obtain excess profits.

This interpretation of central place theory is geometrically valid, but it does not provide any clear reason why the economically precise threshold rather than the more nebulous range of central functions should be the 'preferred' generative force. The use of the threshold implies that excess profits in the resulting system are minimized. It may well be that this is considered the normal tendency in a competitive free market economy as more and more suppliers freely enter the market.

In contrast, Christäller assumed that in a free market economy there should be a minimum number of points of supply of all sizes. It is only if the range of a central function is the basic generating force of the systems that this assumption can be satisfied. This implies the development of a stronger element of excess trader profits than is allowed in the Berry and Garrison version. For this reason Christäller's theory has subsequently been associated with a 'profit maximization assumption'.

Whether the threshold concept and the minimization of excess profits, or the range and the minimization of points of supply, are the basic generative tendencies associated with the development of systems of central places remains obscure in the subsequent literature. Clearly, further attention will have to be given to the behavioural tendencies of *suppliers* of central functions if this issue is to be resolved. Nevertheless, the spatial and hierarchical characteristics of the central place systems derived from the work of Christäller and Berry and Garrison have strong similarities despite their detailed theoretical differences.

Thus, while the literature on central place theory owes much to the pioneering work of Berry and Garrison and their subsequent writings, note should be taken of these qualifications if an appreciation of potential points of confusion in the literature on central place theory is to be obtained.

LÖSCH'S CENTRAL PLACE THEORY

An additional major contribution to central place theory is that of August Lösch, originally published in German in 1940 but translated as *The Economics of Location* in 1954. Like Christäller, Lösch developed a deductive system to explain the size and spacing of settlements in a region, although it differed from that of Christäller in a number of fundamental ways. It was derived for a hypothetical area with the degree of homogeneity associated with the isotropic surface rather than Christäller's less regular idealized landscape. Lösch assumed a vast flat plain with an equal distribution of raw materials, an equality of transportation costs and a regular and continuous distribution of population and associated consumer demand. Also, unlike Christäller, he did not initially assume a hierarchy of centres and develop a theory to explain its spatial organization, proceeding from the location of the highest order to the lowest-order centres. Instead, he deduced an optimal pattern of centres of production and their associated hinterlands for each of the commodities required by the population of the plain, proceeding from a consideration of the lowest-order commodity to the highest. The last sentence also indicates another difference between the theories of Christäller and Lösch. Lösch initially developed his theory with respect to centres of *production* and their associated hinterlands. Thus, interest focused on the market-orientated manufacture, or the secondary sector of the economy, rather than the tertiary service function. However, this difference has not subsequently been considered since many authors agree (for example, Beavon, 1977) that Lösch's theory is as appropriate to tertiary activity as it is to secondary activity. This standpoint has been adopted here.

The derivation of Lösch's economic landscape

The derivation of Lösch's central place system is based initially upon the threshold requirement of the lowest-order function which it is possible to supply to the population of the plain. Given a uniform transportation surface and a uniform distribution of population, this threshold value can be translated into a radius necessary to circumscribe sufficient consumer demand to allow this function to be offered from any point on the plain. A second point from which this function could be offered would have to be a distance of at least twice this radius from the first. A third centre could emerge at the vertex of an equilateral triangle subtended from the first two centres. Such a system can be generalized to cover the whole plain. However, in this system there are limited areas between any three circular hinterlands which are beyond the threshold distance of the function. If, as is *required* by Lösch, the whole area is to be within the threshold area of a centre, a modified system of slightly overlapping circles is necessary which can be generalized to give a system of exclusive hexagonal trade areas based upon the threshold requirement of the lowest-order function. This defines the basic lattice upon which Lösch's theory is based and it is apparent that it comprised a hypothetical set of centres arranged on an equilateral triangular framework with regular hexagonal hinterlands. This framework is strikingly similar in form to the $K = 3$ framework of Christäller, although it should be noted that it is conceptually different since it is based upon the threshold requirement rather than the range of the function. The whole of the population of the place can be supplied with the lowest-order function from this arrangement of centres, and because it is based upon the threshold each supplier is only just economically viable, in other words, there are no excess profits in the system. Thus, like the theory of tertiary activity of Berry and Garrison, the *minimization of excess profits* is a basic organizing principle.

However, so far an ideal pattern of centres and their associated hinterlands for the provision of only *one* function has been considered. Hypothetically, as many similar networks can be constructed as there are functions required by the population of the plain, the details of each being directly related to its threshold requirement. In fact, an infinite number of such networks could be envisaged. However, Lösch constrained his consideration of such networks to those which are a derivative of the basic $K = 3$ lattice. The constraint *implied* by Lösch, but made explicit by Beavon and Mabin (1975), is that the centre of each hexagon in a network of hexagons must be located at a point on the basic lattice. Thus, lattices of successively larger size must have K values of 3, 4, 7, 9, 12, 13, 16, 19, 21, 25, 27 . . . etc. The nine smallest lattices are illustrated in Figure 4.18.

Lösch further hypothesizes that these networks can be laid over the plain at random. Despite the resulting disorder and multiplicity of centres, every person on the plain would have access to every product and, since each network is based upon the threshold of each function of successively higher order, excess profits will not be obtained by suppliers. However, this arrangement will be uneconomic due to the multiplicity of points of supply, many of which will be relatively close to one another and yet supply only one function. Thus, Lösch proposes a more economic arrangement of the networks. Each can be laid out in such a way that all have one point in common, the pivotal point. By definition, at this point all the functions required by the population of the plain can be provided so that here would develop the highest-order centre, the metropolis. Lösch further suggests that the nets can be rotated about the pivot point in order to produce six 'city-rich' and six 'city-poor' sectors in which the greatest number of points coincide. It is interesting to note that Beavon (1977) demonstrates that the production of city-rich and city-poor sectors is the result of a geometrical *constraint* on the rotation process rather than a *consequence* of it, as seems to have been implied in Lösch's original work.

This process results in the 'economic landscape', which Lösch considers

132

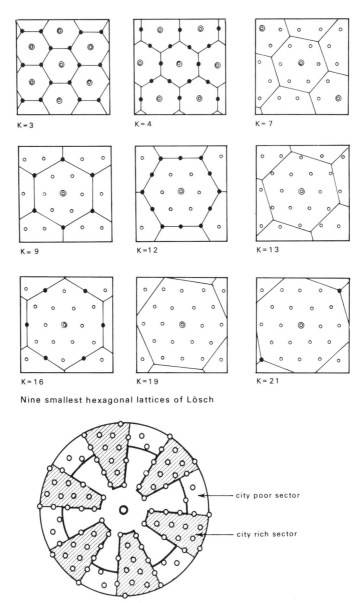

Figure 4.18   The nine smallest hexagonal lattices of Lösch and the
Löschian economic landscape. Source: Lösch, 1954; reproduced by
permission of Gustav Fischer Verlag

provides the most economically efficient system of centres of supply of goods
and services. It consists of a central metropolis which is the highest-order centre
providing the full range of goods and services required by the population of
the plain; six city-rich sectors which have relatively numerous, higher-order

centres; six city-poor sectors which have fewer centres of generally lower order (Figure 4.18). Because of the complexity of the rotation process a complex combination of functions will coincide at particular points so that each larger centre will not necessarily offer all the functions of a lower-order centre. This is an important deviation from the theories developed by either Christäller or Berry and Garrison. For the same reason the size–distribution of centres is likely to be a continuum rather than a distinctly stepped hierarchy, while the K value for the whole landscape is likely to vary from area to area depending upon the variety and threshold requirements of the functions demanded, rather than approximate to a 3, 4 or 7 relationship.

In the current context, interest in this system lies in the provision of a theoretical rationale for the continuum of centre-sizes so commonly found by empirical investigations of city systems. Similarly, it suggests an expectation of a degree of variability of function between centres of similar size, a feature which is not allowed for in the alternative schemes. Perhaps its greatest value, therefore, lies in the suggestion that, in contrast with hierarchical systems, a greater degree of flexibility might be expected in the size and spacing of settlements in a region.

Whether Lösch's model, in fact, provides a more comprehensive explanation is far more problematic. The principles upon which the model is based have even less behavioural validation. Like Berry and Garrison's interpretation, Lösch's scheme is strongly related to the principle of the minimization of excess profits. It may well be that this is an important generative principle governing the development of a system of service centres in competitive market economies, but until this is specifically examined within the context of central place theory it remains unproved. Even more important, the derivation of the economic landscape is based upon the geometry of regular hexagonal trade areas, the constraints associated with their successive relationship to each other, and the geometric constraints imposed upon the rotation process necessary to create the six city-rich and six city-poor sectors. The justification for the procedures seems to that they minimize the total number of central places in the system and this might be considered a natural extension of the need to minimize excess profits. If these procedures are behaviourally valid, they clearly form a significant element in the derivation of a deductive theory designed to provide an idealized explanation for the development of a central place system. However, the degree of homogeneity assumed to be necessary for the development of the economic landscape has not been found in reality. In fact, variations capable of modifying the idealized system of Lösch are likely to be associated with all the structural and behavioural factors which were considered in the context of Christäller theory. Thus, it seems highly unlikely that Lösch's economic landscape will ever be validated with reference to a real-world situation. As a result, while central place theory in general might be considered to provide an approximate explanation for the development and change of systems of service centres in specific geographical contexts, it is not yet possible to distinguish whether they are most closely associated with the theoretical details proposed by Christäller, Berry and Garrison, or Lösch.

THE CONCEPTUAL VALUE OF CENTRAL PLACE THEORY

The preceding discussion indicates that central place theory provides an approximate rather than a comprehensive explanation of the sizes and spacing of centres in systems of central places. There are considerable outstanding problems concerning the relative explanatory value of the basic generative principles suggested by Christäller, Berry and Garrison and Lösch, and it is unlikely that any of the idealized systems will be recognized in reality. Nevertheless, the body of literature generated by central place theory has provided many concepts and methodologies which have been extensively used in the study of urban systems, irrespective of whether they clarify aspects of the original theoretical formulations; several of these are worthy of reiteration.

Centrality and nodality: the search for order

The search for hierarchical and spatial order in systems of cities has resulted in the derivation of a large number of indices of centrality of varying degrees of statistical sophistication. These can be used to measure Christäller's strict theoretical concept of centrality which Preston (1975) suggested is most appropriate for studies attempting to test the empirical validity of the theory; or they can be used to measure the broader concept of the nodality of a centre. In either case the resulting measures can be used to provide a classification of centres which neatly *describes* the relative service status of centres in a region, whether the city system has developed principally to provide a service function for surrounding hinterlands (centrality) or whether the service status of the settlements partly reflects other functions which have contributed to their growth (nodality). This might be considered an essential prerequisite for a more detailed analysis of some specific aspect of the urban system.

Similarly, attempts to determine whether central place hierarchies can be recognized empirically have involved the development of questionnaire survey techniques and secondary data collection designed to investigate the functional relationships between centres of particular hierarchical orders, their complementary regions, and expected consumer behaviour patterns. An early example of a study employing a questionnaire survey was that of Berry, Barnum, and Tennant undertaken in south-western Iowa (1962). They demonstrated the expected relatively localized hinterlands of centres for the provision of low-order functions such as food shopping, banking and dry cleaning for a sample of the rural population living south-west of Omaha (Figure 4.19). In contrast, shopping for higher-order goods such as clothing and furniture was much more highly concentrated on the higher-order centres, as anticipated

135

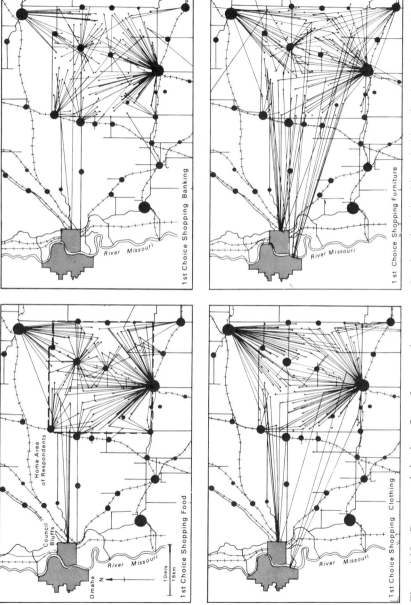

Figure 4.19 Consumer behaviour flows from rural areas near Omaha—food, banking, clothing, furniture. Source: Berry, Barnum and Tennant, 1962; reproduced by permission of the Chairman, Regional Science Association

by central place theory. However, this information provided only approximate support for the existence of an idealized central place hierarchy. The hinterlands of the centres for the different functions overlapped to a significant degree since consumer behaviour patterns only roughly approximated the nearest centre assumption. A more recent analysis employing secondary interaction data is provided by Preston's (1971) study of the central place system of the Pacific north-west. In this case a range of data obtained from local censuses and directories was used to describe the functional interrelationships among centres of differing hierarchical status. The dependence of hamlets and small settlements upon local small towns for the provision of banking services, the circulation hinterlands of centres providing daily and Sunday newspapers, the commuting areas of the higher-order centres, and the relationships between branch firms and their parent companies were all used to illustrate the hierarchical status of centres and their functional interrelationships. Again, a general approximation to the expected central place relationships was demonstrated.

A further development in methodology was provided by the use of graph theory techniques—developed by Nystuen and Dacey (1961)—which are based upon data indicating the functional association between centres in a region. Their initial study used numbers of intercity telephone calls as an index of interaction. The first stage in the analysis involved the construction of an interaction matrix indicating the number of telephone calls between each centre in the system (see Table 4.1). The columns indicate the number of calls received by a city and their sum provides an indication of the relative centrality or hierarchical status of each city. In this example centre C is the highest order city and G the lowest order. The rows indicate the number of calls transmitted from each centre and these are used to illustrate the extent

Table 4.1 Hypothetical interaction matrix figures indicate telephone calls between centres

		To centre:						
		A	B	C	D	E	F	G
	A	0	30	100	80	50	40	10
	B	20	0	200	100	150	70	10
	C	40	80	0	200	250	80	20
From	D	20	40	300	0	70	50	20
centre:	E	80	40	200	60	0	60	30
	F	40	30	100	150	40	0	20
	G	60	60	300	20	30	70	0
Column total		260	280	1200	610	590	370	110
Rank order		6	5	1	2	3	4	7

and strength of the functional relationship between a centre and its complementary region. The most important linkages are indicated by the largest number of outgoing calls from each centre (underlined in Table 4.1). In this example centre C emerges as a strong nodal point of interaction since it is the focus of the largest number of outflows from five of the other six centres. Using this type of data Nystuen and Dacey (1961) describe the hierarchical structure of centres and their associated nodal regions in Washington State.

Subsequently, variants of this technique have been used to describe the hierarchical and nodal structure of urban systems using a variety of interaction data. Davies and Robinson (1968), for example, use journey-to-shop data obtained from a household questionnaire survey to define the nodal structure of the Solent region, and, Davies and Lewis (1970) use telephone linkage data between 99 units in Wales and the borderland, for similar purposes.

The various approaches provide insights into validity of the functional interrelationship within urban systems as anticipated by central place theory, and also add to an understanding of the functional characteristics of urban systems and the manner in which these might be further investigated.

Central place theory has also developed concepts which have predictive significance for the analysis of urban systems. As indicated earlier, the hierarchical and spatial characteristics of systems of cities tend to be in a state of adjustment with the density distribution of the population, the amount of consumer expenditure, and the level of transport technology. Changes in any one of these factors will result in changes in the relative importance of centres at different levels of the hierarchical structure of a region. Thus, an analysis of changes in these factors over time and their effects on the settlement system of a region is likely to provide predictive insight into the nature of change in central place systems.

The time dimension and periodic markets

This perspective has been adopted by a number of studies, which have provided consistent conclusions. Most noteworthy is the classic study by Hodge (1965) based on Saskatchewan for the period 1941–61, but with conclusions which were considered relevant to Alberta, North Dakota, Kansas and Missouri. During this period fundamental changes occurred which affected all three factors mentioned above. Increases in the mechanization of agriculture and the associated amalgamation of farms into fewer, larger units resulted in a decline in the rural population, but for the remaining farmers, a concomitant increase in their income. This created a decline in demand for low-order convenience goods, but an increase in demand for the more specialized, expensive goods and services normally found in higher-order service centres. At the same time, the growth in car ownership resulted in a greater personal mobility which made the rural population less dependent upon their local low-order service centres for the provision of goods and services. The combined influences of these changes pointed in the same direction: towards the decline of the lower-order service centres and the increased status of the larger centres.

This was reflected in changes in the number and status of the service centres over the 20-year period, with centres classified according to a seven-fold hierarchical structure. The lowest three orders were subject to a drastic decline. An apparent buoyancy of the hamlets was illusory since it resulted from the decline in status of convenience centres rather than the growth of new hamlets. In addition, smaller centres located within 16 km (10 miles) of a high-order centre were particularly susceptible to decline and the four higher-order centres demonstrated a significant enhancement in status.

Assuming that the changes noted were likely to continue, Hodge suggested a number of implications from his study. The number of hamlets would continue to decline, while the two types of convenience centre would disappear altogether. In contrast, the partial and complete shopping centres would increase by 20 to 30 per cent, while the higher-order centres would continue to increase their hierarchical status, particularly at the expense of lower-order centres located less than 24 km (15 miles) away. As a result, the rural population would have to travel approximately a third further, on average, to obtain the services they required. There were also implications for planning. With the further decline in population and in the number of service centres, there would be an associated decline in the availability of local services such as schools, health care, local government and public transport. It was considered that in certain areas this would result in intolerable levels of local services which planning would need to redress by the stimulation of growth nodes at locations which could be designated from the analysis.

A similar sequence of events has been documented for south-western Iowa between 1930 and 1960 by Berry (1967b) resulting from similar societal changes:

Changes of central-place populations in Iowa, 1930–60

Levels of centre	Average annual growth rate (%)
Hamlet	−2.69
Village	−0.58
Town	−0.15
Country seat	+0.44
Regional city	+0.94

An additional study which adopted a much longer time perspective also reached comparable conclusions. Lewis (1975) analysed the changes in urban status of 21 centres in a rural area in mid-Wales, and the middle Welsh border-land within the regional spheres of influence of Shrewsbury and Hereford, for the period 1791 to 1964–65. Their commercial importance was measured and studied for a number of selected dates in a comparative framework. The analysis revealed a progressive widening of status differences with increasing concentration in the two major centres of Shrewsbury and Hereford, while the status of the low-order towns was gradually eroded. The only deviations from this general pattern were associated with the sudden enhancement of status of particular towns which acquired additional special functions such as the woollen industry, spa activities and livestock marketing, for limited periods.

These findings were interpreted with reference to Carter's (1969) conceptual framework relating to the growth of systems of centres which suggests that the principal influences on the development of systems of centres are:

1. the economic, technological and organizational changes which progressively bring new pressures to bear;
2. the series of minor exogenous influences which, except in very unusual cases, continually affect the system.

Studies by Hodge (1965) and others show clearly that the incorporation of a time element and the notion of change over time are of fundamental importance for the understanding of a central place system. These facts have been brought out most strongly, however, by modern research into the periodic markets which continue to be a major component of the retailing and wholesaling system of third world countries, and which had similar roles at earlier points in time in western societies. Whereas central place theory is founded on the assumption that goods and services are provided from permanent establishments in fixed places, this assumption is not met where periodic markets have key roles. Such markets because of their *periodicity*, the fact that they only occur on specific days of the week in a given location and their traders will migrate in well-defined ways from one market location to another, must be analysed in a temporal as well as a spatial setting. Such markets continue to exist in the developed world; between 1 and 2 per cent of British retailing and between 20 and 50 per cent of its wholesaling, for example, is still transacted through periodic markets. In less developed countries, such as Mexico, depending upon the commodity, between 20 and 80 per cent of trade is conducted in this type of institution. In terms of the settlement hierarchy within less-developed countries, periodic markets are most dominant in rural areas and small towns but are still found in large cities though it is there that they are most subject to pressures of modernization.

In a typical market situation, a basic daily market will function on the site each day of the week but will be augmented considerably on one or two days of the week. Evidence suggests that as a city develops or 'modernizes', the differences between the peaks and lows of activity will gradually diminish as the transformation towards a permanently established market takes place. The length of weeks is a critical feature in the periodicity of markets and will vary with cultural norms from one society to another. Whereas the most common Christian and Muslim week is of a seven-day duration, in China it is ten or twelve days, in Java five, and in various parts of West Africa ranges from two to eight days. The length of a week will determine the *cycle* as the market, or more accurately the market traders, moves around. Skinner (1965) in a study of rural China, identified a ten-day cycle which was subdivided

140

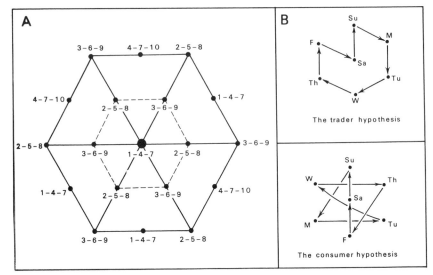

Figure 4.20   Periodic markets: Consumer and trader hypotheses

into three units of three days each, with no business on the tenth day. There are three levels of markets from the central or highest order to intermediate to standard or lowest order. An individual trader may spend days one, four, and seven in the central market and follow regular routes among *various* lower order markets on the intervening days. Figure 4.20(A) idealizes the distribution of market locations and the main days of activity; in this system central goods can be circulated around several markets on a regular schedule and traders can accumulate enough trade to remain profitable. There is a time–space system of rotating rather than fixed central place functions.

Skinner's study and others (Hodder, 1961) have been interpreted in terms of traditional central theory, as suggested by Figure 4.20(A), in which periodicity is incorporated with spatial location to suggest a hierarchy and an ordered distribution of centres. Bromley, Symanski, and Good (1975) argue for a more complex system influenced by the lack of divorce between producing and selling and an inertia factor which relates to non-economic considerations. The market in the Third World is normally much more than a commercial activity; it has religious connotations and provides the opportunities for recreation, social and business contacts.

Some of the attempts to measure amounts of spatio-temporal integration in systems of periodic markets have used Smith's trader and consumer hypotheses (see Figure 4.20(B)) (Bromley, 1980). Whereas the *trader hypothesis* suggests that markets are synchronized to enable traders to follow routes which minimize their weekly travel costs, the *consumer hypothesis* suggests that the synchronization is designed to enable dispersed rural populations to have easy access to markets through the week. Neither of these has been shown to have general validity and the *commodity hypothesis* (D. M. Smith, 1974) which suggests that market schedules will be attuned so that adjacent market-places that supply different types of goods would meet on different days and that these will normally be at different levels of the market-place hierarchy, may well provide a more appropriate concept.

Such theoretical concepts have been reviewed extensively elsewhere (Bromley, 1980) and cannot be adequately discussed here. It is clear that periodic markets raise time–space relationships into central focus in the study of central place systems, it is also clear that such markets are still of considerable economic and social significance in many parts of the world despite the evidence that 'modernization' is diminishing their roles.

CONCLUSIONS

Despite the fact that they have been under close scrutiny for several decades, some of the detailed theoretical elements of central place theory are still controversial. Nevertheless, the research generated by central place theory has provided much of conceptual and methodological value to assist in the investigation of the characteristics of urban systems in general. Of particular note are the methods developed which are capable of providing useful hierarchical descriptions of systems of cities. Similarly, techniques have been developed by which it is possible to illustrate the functional interrelationships of centres, while concepts have also been introduced which are capable of providing additional insights into the process of development of urban systems. In more general terms, central place theory has provided one of the main platforms from which the 'spatial analysis' paradigm in human geography, which has been so influential throughout the 1960s and early 1970s in particular, has developed.

Chapter 5

Urban Systems in the Modern World

Whereas urban geographers have frequently made the distinction between *city as area* and *city as a location* within a wider urban system, many theories continue to overemphasize the idea that the city is a distinct and separate unit. There are important functional linkages among cities and between cities and their hinterlands which have increased dramatically in the twentieth century as transport and communications have been revolutionized. For many types of analysis, the city has to be viewed within the context of both the wider urban system and the more localized 'urbanized region' of which it is part. This chapter is concerned with attempts which have been made to characterize these urbanized regions, to classify them and to give them labels. Classifications need to be placed in some sort of evolutionary context; certainly the history of the urbanization process cannot be ignored (see Chapter 3). The simplest evolutionary framework is that of three *stages* in the development of urbanized regions, each of which has a typical population size, spatial form, and level of interconnectedness. Whereas, as already shown, the universality of these stages is questionable, in advanced societies at least they tend to reflect particular levels of technological development in transport and communication (Friedmann, 1978; Robson, 1973). The three-stage model used as a framework is briefly summarized (see also Figure 3.8); of central interest here is its implications for city–hinterland relationships.

STAGES OF URBAN SYSTEMS DEVELOPMENT

The preindustrial stage: an urban nucleus

The great majority of preindustrial cities were small. Most had populations of less than 50,000 and a rudimentary form of economic, social and political organization which was reasonably typical of the period prior to large-scale industrialization. Only in primate cities, usually capitals of more powerful states, did populations exceed 10,000. The transport technology associated with the development of these cities was equally rudimentary. Communications depended upon the pedestrian or on draught animals. Thus, the urban fabric tended to be arranged so that journeys within the city could be kept relatively

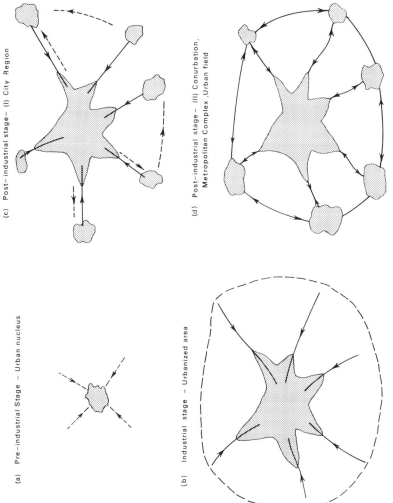

(a) Pre-industrial Stage – Urban nucleus

(b) Industrial stage – Urbanized area

(c) Post–industrial stage– (I) City Region

(d) Post–industrial stage – (II) Conurbation, Metropolitan Complex , Urban field

Figure 5.1   Types of urban regions with stylized functional inter-relationships

short. Consequently, despite the continuing debate relating to the variety of reasons for the development of preindustrial cities and their internal patterns of sociospatial differentiation, most authorities are agreed upon their characteristically compact form (Langton, 1975; Sjoberg, 1960; Vance, 1971). Similarly, because of the limitations of transport facilities, the spheres of influence of such cities were either: restricted to the provision of urban services for a relatively localized population living within the area of a day's 'round trip'; or if the city also provided commercial, religious, social or political functions for a wider hinterland, then the frequency of visits by long-distance travellers and the associated functional interrelationships between the city and the outer limits of its hinterland tended to be relatively low. In either case, the city tended to be a distinct urban nucleus loosely related to a wider rural area and to other cities (Figure 5.1(a)).

The industrial stage: urbanized area

In the early stages of industrialization, town growth was usually associated with the localization of particular resources, and many towns increased considerably in size in relation to the natural advantages which they possessed. Canals and railways provided more efficient means of intercity transport, principally for the conveyance of industrial materials and finished products, and this increased the economic interlinkages between towns with complementary industrial structures and also between industrial towns and major market areas. However, since a town's prosperity tended to be related to the processing of raw materials, the early relationship between neighbours was as often competitive as it was complementary and economic linkages were frequently stronger between relatively distant markets than between near neighbours. In effect, despite the steady increase in economic linkages over space, individual towns still tended to retain a distinct and separate functional identity to a significant degree. Nevertheless, towns became much larger than their preindustrial counterparts, although they retained their relatively compact form. Intracity mobility for the most part depended upon public transport. However, the relatively long hours and low wages of the industrial workers necessitated the avoidance of the time and cost associated with a significant journey to work and this gradually became linked with increasing residential differentiation on social class lines. Thus, low-status housing gravitated markedly to areas of industrial employment, while new industrial areas and higher status residential suburbs tended to develop along the public transport routes of the major arterial roads radiating outward from the city centres, creating a distinctly tentacular urban form (Robson, 1973). This process of development resulted in the 'urbanized area' of the industrial period, characterized by larger, but still relatively compact, cities than those of the preindustrial period and increasing, but still relatively weak, functional linkages extending beyond the city boundaries (Figure 5.1(b)).

The postindustrial stage

The postindustrial period is characterized by a considerable increase in the speed and efficiency of communications. Of particular note was the development in the late nineteenth century of the telephone which initiated the growth of improved forms of electronic communication. Similarly, the rapid growth in importance of motor vehicles from the early years of the twentieth century, and particularly in the period since 1945, has changed the emphasis of inter-urban transport from canal and rail to road, while intracity personal mobility has shifted from public transport to the private car. These changes have reduced the constraint of distance on the development of economic and social linkages both between and within cities. Thus, spatial dispersal has become an increasingly important element of the urban system, a point which was forcefully made by Webber (1963) in the early 1960s. The distinction between urban and rural, and the functional separateness of individual cities, has been drastically reduced as communicative efficiency has increased. Also, ease of communication has allowed additional factors to influence the locational characteristics of urban systems. Of particular note in this respect has been the influence of amenity. A significant section of the more mobile labour force—mobility being closely associated with the ability to pay—has been able to seek out attractive areas for their homes in wider areas than was formerly the case. This has resulted in the suburbanization of vast tracts of land around most major cities. Similarly, industries which have high inputs of skill and labour relative to raw materials have been able to gravitate to formerly smaller urban concentrations in the particularly attractive regions of a country, as exemplified by postwar development in California. In terms of Webber's (1963) thesis, economic and social propinquity ceased to be as dependent upon spatial pro-pinquity as was formely the case. However, this has never implied that distance no longer exerts any influence upon the locational characteristics of urban systems. Most dispersed development has remained an associated feature of metropolitan centres partly because of the forces of inertia and partly because the costs of developing and maintaining the complex system of physical and electronic communications in such areas are usually less than those involved in developing new systems in completely new areas. Spatial dispersal in the form of suburbanization is an increasingly significant element of the post-industrial urban system; and the 'urbanized region' has emerged as an important form of urban system (Figure 5.1(c) and (d)).

It is from evidence of a further progressive increase in the efficiency of communications in the western world since 1970 that the process of 'counter-urbanization' has been suggested (Berry, 1976). This began as a reaction against the urban environmental and social problems associated with the concentrated forms of nineteenth-century, *laissez-faire* industrial urbanization and is strongly affected by macro-societal processes involving employment, transport and housing. In particular, preferences have increased for living in smaller settlements at lower densities offering improved environmental amenities. In detail, this process has taken a variety of different forms, depending upon the nature of the society in which it is developed. In the United States 'individualistic decentralization' or suburbanization of a relatively unconstrained kind has emerged. In the welfare states of western Europe a more systematically planned form of decentralization, with the development of various satellite settlements or new towns, is the most common response. In the socialist states there has been a search for new settlement forms designed to reconcile the traditional conflict between the city and the country, while in the Third World a strong reaction against the concentrated urban primacy of colonialism has tended to promote a decentralization or even ruralization of urban development.

A TYPOLOGY OF 'URBANIZED' REGIONS

There have been a number of attempts to characterize these 'urbanized regions' and there are some grounds for suggesting that a typology now exists. Whereas the types which are discussed can be taken broadly to represent evolutionary stages, they are not necessarily mutually exclusive and there are 'transitions' from one stage to the next rather than sharp discontinuities. Furthermore, irrespective of the sophistication of communications technology developed in a country, the more spatially extensive types of urbanized region tend to be confined to the larger, more populous areas.

The city region

The term 'city region' has generally been applied to an area including the major employment centre of a region and the surrounding areas for which it acts as a strong focus for employment and the provision of major services. Its development represents the first stage in the functional integration of urbanized regions. Mackinder (1902) was one of the first writers to use the term in this manner to convey the view that the city region of London already encompassed the greater part of the whole of south-eastern England. The essential functional relationship between city and region is considered to be one of dependence and for this reason functional relationships are nodal, focusing on the major city (Figure 5.1(c)). The delimitation of the city and its complementary region has subsequently been an important theme in urban geographical investigation. It was an important element of Christäller's (1933) work, which stimulated the development of a number of methods designed to define the spheres of influence of cities. Similarly, the concept of the city region has been extensively investigated by Dickinson (1947), and within the context of the 'urban field' by Smailes (1947), in what were early major studies in urban geography.

More recently, Davies (1972) used the concept to define the city region of Greater Swansea based upon an investigation of high-order shopping trips. A variant of the graph theory technique developed by Nystuen and Dacey (1961) was used to analyse the data obtained from a survey of trips and a particularly significant map was produced which indicated the percentage of

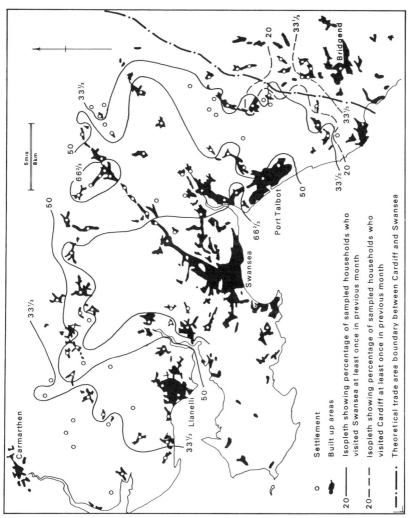

Figure 5.2   An example of a city-region: Greater Swansea—showing generalized consumer behaviour and trade area boundary. Source: Davies, 1972; reproduced by permission of W. K. D. Davies and Regional Studies

persons interviewed at different sites who travelled to either Swansea or Cardiff to shop in the month prior to the survey. In the east the 33 per cent line was considered approximately to demarcate the breakpoint between the spheres of influence of Swansea and Cardiff for the highest-order shopping functions (Figure 5.2). Similarly, it was suggested that the 33 per cent line provided a reasonable indication of the limits of the Greater Swansea city region and encompassed an area of just in excess of 500,000 population. This is significantly larger than the administrative county of West Glamorgan (1971 population 370,000) defined in the local government revision of 1974. Arguably, the city region defined by Davies represents a closer approximation to the functional unit of Greater Swansea. West Glamorgan, like the other counties produced in the local government reform of 1974, was defined with greater emphasis on the location of pre-existing administrative boundaries, combined with an attempt to locate sufficient residential and industrial development within the boundaries of the adjacent 'rural' counties to generate adequate rate revenues.

Evidence of this kind suggests that the city region remains an appropriate concept to describe unicentred urban regions of less than 500,000 population found in the less populous parts of even the most highly urbanized countries. In fact, it is interesting to note that investigations of the structure of large urban concentrations frequently use variants of the city-region concept based upon employment nodes and associated commuter fields as the basic statistical building block for the purposes of comparative analysis. For example, in the United States the Standard Metropolitan Statistical Area (United States Bureau of the Budget, 1964) and the Daily Urban System (Berry, 1973a) have been used, while in Europe the extensive surveys of Hall and Hay (1980) and Drewett (1980) relate their comparative investigations to nodal regions comprising an urban centre or core and contiguous areas comprising a bounded hinterland or ring.

The 'dispersed city' variant of the city-region concept is also worthy of mention (Burton, 1963). The concept was originally developed to explain the urban centres found in the counties of Perry, Franklin, Jackson and Williamson of southern Illinois. These comprised thirteen closely related but physically and politically separate towns, the total population of which was 157,000. They were economically based upon the localization of natural resources, in this instance a coalfield and intensive mixed farming activities. No town was more than twice the size of its neighbour, while several were of the same size class. It was hypothesized that in this kind of situation each town would not function as a discrete unit. Instead, physical proximity would promote the specialization of each unit in particular functions and together they would function as a single urban unit in which the hierarchical status of the services provided would be related to the total population rather than to their individual sizes. Burton (1963) considered that if the concept of the dispersed city was valid, each centre would demonstrate an unexpectedly high degree of service specialization for particular functions, while abnormally high degrees of service interaction might be expected among the centres. A limited amount of functional specialization in particular towns was demonstrated for activities such as furniture shopping, clothing shopping, newspaper publication and the location of university facilities. However, a nearby larger city outside the local urban system captured most of the high-order retail trade. Thus, while the validity of the concept could not be absolutely refuted, the supportive evidence was extremely weak. Subsequently, the functional characteristics considered essential to the concept have not been empirically demonstrated in any of the cities suggested by Burton (1963) such as the lower Rio Grande valley of Texas, the upper Grand Rivers of southern Ontario, the Salzgitter area of Germany, the Okayama region of Japan and the Nottingham–Derby coalfield of England, as places which might comprise dispersed cities. In fact, a recent re-examination of the situation in southern Illinois by Clements (1977) rejected the existence of its hypothesized functional characteristics. Thus, the utility of the concept is confined to descriptions of closely spread collections of similarly sized settlements associated with natural advantages. As such it probably represents no more than a physical variant of the city-region unit.

Conurbation, metropolitan complex or urban field

In the more populous, rapidly growing parts of a country, urban development rarely produces a single urban centre. Instead, from the fortuitous circumstances which promote growth, a number of important cities may develop in relatively close proximity. Such a situation developed in Britain during the industrialization of the nineteenth century. Largely based upon the location of coal reserves and associated port facilities, a multicentred form of development emerged which initiated the development of large urban agglomerations centred on Birmingham and the Black Country, Liverpool and Manchester, Clydeside, Tyneside and the West Riding of Yorkshire. The growth of these initially separate, but close-packed centres, resulted in the physical coalescence of the urban units of these areas, although each major centre tended to retain a partially separate identity despite the strong functional linkages which often developed. The resulting urban form was described by Geddes (1915) as a *conurbation*, a term which stressed the characteristic feature of physical agglomeration. Subsequently, with the improvement of communication and transport the functional influence of the conurbations has spread throughout a wider surrounding hinterland, well beyond the limits of their built-up areas, so that the term is now widely used in the British literature to describe not merely physical spread but also multinodal *functional* units (House, 1973). Usually the most advantageously located centre in the conurbation grows larger than its neighbours and exerts a degree of economic, social and cultural dominance over the whole unit. However, the functional relationships *within* the conurbation have some special features and are essentially different from those of the city region. There is, for example, an element of dominance by the largest unit, but the other relatively large specialized cities have many functional linkages; there is no exclusive focus on the major city.

Elsewhere, in areas of population growth which have developed in relation to the locational advantages of centrality rather than the localization of natural resources, a similar type of urban form has tended to develop. Maximum initial growth tends to take place in the most advantageous location so that, initially, the urban form is similar to the city region. However, as the forces promoting growth gather momentum, increased land costs, congestion and the associated deterioration of the urban environment stimulate an element of decentralization of development to the immediately surrounding region. Many of the small towns in such areas accumulate increased economic significance and develop into moderately sized cities which usually have close functional linkages with the major centre but again develop significant degrees of economic independence. Thus, while the central city tends to retain an element of dominance in the urbanized region, the functional complexity typical of the conurbation is greater than that of the city region. In Britain, the increasing functional linkages of London with towns throughout the south-east of England, as far afield as Southend-on-Sea, Luton, Reading, Southampton, Portsmouth and Brighton, have stimulated a number of regional planning proposals. The strategy of the early 1960s considered the south-east of England, with a population of upwards of 17 million, as a conurbation or metropolitan complex for practical planning purposes (HMSO, 1970). Similar units with populations of greater than 10 million have been discussed in the context of Paris, Moscow and Buenos Aires, as well as Bombay and Calcutta in the developing world context (Gottmann, 1976).

Metropolitan growth in the economic centre of the Netherlands has resulted in an interesting variant of the conurbation form, termed Randstad Holland (Hall, 1977). This has a population of approximately 4.5 million and differs significantly from the other metropolitan complexes discussed above in that it incorporates a much stronger element of polycentrism. It comprises the three major cities of Amsterdam, Rotterdam and the Hague with populations of between 500,000 and 1 million, Utrecht of approximately 250,000 and Haarlem and Leiden, both larger than 100,000 population. In addition, a number of smaller towns and suburban developments are so located as to create a significant element of urban continuity among the larger cities. The conurbation has a pseudocircular shape of approximately 176 km (110 miles) in length, open towards the south-east with a relatively undeveloped centre—hence the term Randstad (ring city) or the alternative 'greenheart metropolis' (Burke, 1966).

This particular urban form is the result of a combination of physical geographical, historical and economic factors, all of which have tended to promote urban dispersal. Of particular note in this respect were the early land-drainage problems associated with the central delta region. Similarly, in the latter half of the nineteenth century the developmental pressures associated with the growth of governmental administrative functions encouraged decentralization from the traditional commercial and cultural centre of Amsterdam to the Hague, while the attraction of port installations to the increasingly economically significant mouth of the Rhine established the basis for Rotterdam's growth in the last quarter of the nineteenth century. These developments created the basis of the tripartite urban form and as the process of economic development continued, the smaller towns accumulated manufacturing industries and grew on a smaller scale to establish the polycentric metropolitan unit in the twentieth century.

However, the polycentric form has more than merely physical connotations since its development has created a stronger degree of functional decentralization and specialization than is typical of most other conurbations. Amsterdam has retained a strong financial and cultural function, while the most specialized retail facilities are still to be found there, along with the strongest urban tourism function associated with its historic urban form. In contrast, the functional structure of Rotterdam is concentrated in the port and related heavy industry and wholesaling, while government and administration dominates the Hague. The smaller cities such as Utrecht, Haarlem and Leiden are concerned more with light manufacturing and processing industries. At the same time the 'greenheart' continues to perform an important agricultural function, while maintaining an extensive area of attractive open space near to all parts of the urban concentration. This spatial structure has tended to promote a considerable amount of economic and social interaction among its parts. In fact, it might be suggested that an approximation to the *dispersed city* concept exists in Randstad Holland, albeit on a different scale from that originally envisaged.

In the United States a unit similar to the conurbation has been described as the *urban field*, considered to be the basic urban territorial unit of post-industrial society in the United States (Friedmann, 1978, p. 42):

The urban field may be described as a vast multi-centred region having relatively low density, whose form evolves from a finely articulated network of social and economic linkages. Its many centres are set in large areas of green space of which much is given over to agricultural and recreational use. The core city from which the urban field evolved is beginning to lose its traditional dominance: it is becoming merely one of many specialized centres in a region.

Friedmann (1978) does not define urban fields with any precision, but they are regarded as core areas and hinterlands of at least 300,000 population, with an outer limit of two hours' driving time, which relates to an assumed limit of periodic recreational trips. The urban fields defined in this manner range in population size from half a million to as many as 20 million and cover that third of the areas of the United States in which 90 per cent of the population live (Figure 5.3). Urban fields are more spatially extensive than the European conurbations and metropolitan complexes since they are related to higher levels of personal mobility, including recreational visits, rather than being regarded as labour commuting areas. For these reasons, urban fields tend to include more extensive areas of low population density. Nevertheless, the concept of the urban field may well become increasingly relevant to an understanding of the functional realities of urbanized regions outside the

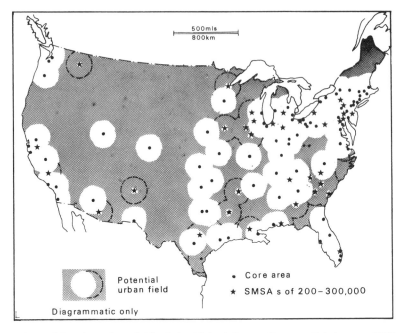

Figure 5.3 The urban field of the United States. Source: Friedmann, 1978

United States as improvements in communications and transport of a similar kind occur elsewhere.

Megalopolis

As the outer limits of the urban fields of the United States coalesce there is some suggestion of the existence of more loosely articulated urbanized regions of an even higher order. In fact, Gottmann (1961) had earlier introduced the term 'megalopolis' to describe the major unbanized areas of the north-eastern seaboard of the United States. In his encyclopaedic work, Gottmann described and analysed the development of the spatial form and functional structure of the area extending from southern New Hampshire, 800 km (500 miles) south to northern Virginia; and from the Atlantic an average of 240 km (150 miles) inland to the foothills of the Appalachian mountains (Figure 5.4). The population of this area was 38 million, orientated around the major urban concentrations centred on Boston, New York, Philadelphia, Baltimore and Washington. Based upon this initial analysis, Gottmann (1976) subsequently suggested the characteristic features of megalopolitan urban systems. He considered that the term should be reserved for very large urban units with a suggested minimum population of 25 million. Usually, it was anticipated that the emergence of such a unit would be significantly related to its potential for performing an important international exchange function for trade, technology, population and culture for the state in which it was located.

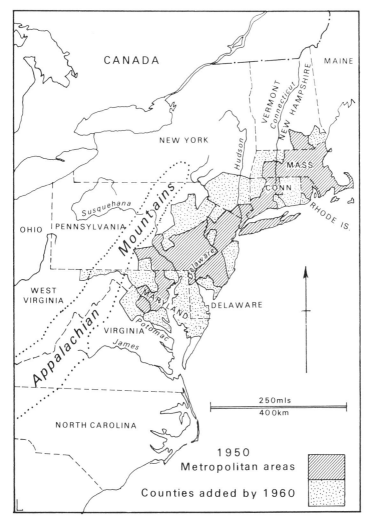

Figure 5.4   Megalopolis, United States: north-eastern seaboard, showing metropolitan areas in 1950 and counties 'urbanized' by 1960.
Source: Gottmann, 1961

Consequently, transactional activities would be a significant element of economic structure, and they would also tend to be located at major international
transportation breakpoints. In addition, because of the scale of their growth
they would typically have a distinctly polynuclear form, but with sufficient
internal physical continuity and functional interrelationships for each to
be considered a system in itself, which was distinctly separated from other
units by less urbanized areas. Complete physical continuity was *not* considered
a necessary feature of the megalopolitan system. In fact, in the archetypical
area of the north-eastern seaboard of the United States a population density

of only 250 persons per square kilometre was used to define its outer edge, while as much as 48 per cent of the urbanized region comprised commercial forest. Instead, the cohesiveness of the system was considered to depend upon, and to be best indicated by, the relative incidence of communication facilities such as highways, railways, waterways, pipelines and telephone lines, combined with transaction flows of commodities, traffic, people and messages. Also, due to the importance of communications in the efficient functioning of such units, it was anticipated that they would usually develop along major transport axes. The high levels of economic, political and social interaction typical of such areas was also considered likely to result in a strong element of self-sustaining growth with some adverse effects. The urban and social environmental problems associated with overcongestion at the centres of the major urban concentrations in developing megalopolitan systems create severe management problems for urban planning.

Defined in this manner the megalopolitan form is significantly different in both scale and function from the conurbation. As yet, it is considered by Gottmann (1976) to be restricted to six cases: comprising the type-area of the north-eastern seaboard of the United States; the Great Lakes area first described by Doxiadis (1966) as extending from Chicago east to Detroit and the southern shores of Lake Erie; the Tokaido area of Japan centred on Tokyo–Yokohama; the English megalopolis, centred on the south east and extending north-west-wards to include the West Midlands, Manchester, Merseyside and the West Riding of Yorkshire (Hall *et al.*, 1973); the megalopolis of north-western Europe considered to be emerging in the area of Amsterdam, Paris and the Ruhr; and a sixth case centred on Shanghai.

In addition, Gottmann (1976) considered that three other areas are growing fast enough to be considered as emergent megalopolitan systems. In South America rapid economic development is resulting in a corridor of development between Rio de Janeiro and São Paulo. In Europe, megalopolitan-type development centred on Milan, Turin and Genoa, extending southward to Pisa and Florence and westward to Marseilles and Avignon is suggested; while a third case is considered likely to result from developmental pressures to link the San Francisco Bay Area with the Los Angeles–San Diego complex. A possible additional case has recently been comprehensively studied by Yeates (1975). This comprises 'Main Street' Canada, a corridor of development extending along Lakes Erie and Ontario and the St Lawrence Valley, reaching from Windsor in the south 1100 km (700 miles) north-eastward to Quebec City and centred on the urban regions of Toronto, Ottawa and Montreal. This forms the economic and political centre of Canada in which approximately half of the population live, and three-quarters of manufacturing and three-fifths of Canada's total income is produced. With a population of just over 10 million in 1971, distributed over a wider area than that of the north-eastern seaboard of the United States, this area does not strictly conform to the definition of a megalopolis. Nevertheless, its degree of primacy in the Canadian context, its international functional significance and its internal functional cohesion and polynuclear urban form, combined with its physical contiguity and interrelationships with the Great Lakes megalopolis, suggests that it has the features of a megalopolis, despite its relatively small population.

Megalopolis has been designed to provide a description of the macro-scale urbanized region. It has both functional and physical connotations but has only been carefully researched in a small number of areas, including Gottmann's (1976) original work on north-eastern United States, and Hall *et al.* (1973) in the study of megalopolitan Britain. Elsewhere there are dangers of loose usage of technical terms but it is clear that interconnected urban systems at this scale are becoming more common.

Ecumenopolis

A yet more futuristic urban form, 'ecumenopolis', has been suggested by Doxiadis (1968). This is based upon speculative forecasts of world population trends which assume that a level of population, approximately ten times the current figure, will be reached towards the end of the 21st century. In these circumstances it is envisaged that a massive increase in functional linkages will occur among separate urbanized regions and there will be a related increase in the physical continuity of urban settlement. This continuous urban system which could emerge in the inhabitable world has been termed the 'universal city' or 'ecumenopolis'. Its spatial limits will be determined by the existence of reasonable flat land and climatic conditions suitable to support human settlement in the future.

Obviously, long-term forecasts of this kind involve numerous imponderables so that the population levels upon which such a structure is based must be considered highly speculative. Nevertheless, the concept of the ecumenopolis is not without value. The 'population explosion' is currently the most important facet of the demography of all third world countries, while steady population growth—though at much lower rates—is also a characteristic feature of the great majority of developed industrial countries. Thus, the increased significance of megalopolitan structures and a tendency towards the development of something resembling ecumenopolis might be anticipated. Since such eventualities are considered likely to be accompanied by an accentuation of the urban and social environmental problems associated with overcongestion, the concept of the ecumenopolis serves to underline the potential dangers of unconstrained urban growth. In fact, in North America the physical and functional divisions between the urbanized regions of the north-eastern seaboard, the Great Lakes and 'Main Street' Canada are already becoming blurred. Indeed, should the degree of functional coalescence of the urban fields of the United States illustrated by Friedmann (1978) be followed by an increased element of physical integration, the North American element of the ecumenopolis might soon be considered more than a futuristic notion. Similarly, in western Europe with the development of the European Economic Community, international developmental pressures have increased in the

Table 5.1   European 'megalopolitan' growth zones 1950–70

	Population 1950	Population 1970	Per cent change 1950–70	National rates of change 1950–70
1. Madrid	1,984,033	3,950,686	99.13	21.58
2. Basque Coast (Spain)	1,133,238	1,992,833	75.85	21.58
3. Turin	1,228,320	2,037,738	65.90	13.94
4. Lorraine	708,886	1,160,381	63.69	22.80
5. Milan	2,896,628	4,558,966	57.39	13.94
6. Rome	2,532,233	3,970,345	56.79	13.94
7. Barcelona	2,510,382	3,827,988	52.49	21.58
8. Provence–Côte d'Azur	2,788,690	4,242,828	52.14	22.80 (France) 13.94 (Italy)
9. North London fringe	3,054,552	4,578,760	49.90	10.58
10. Lyon–Grenoble	1,767,740	2,548,729	44.18	22.80
11. East Randstad–North Rhine	8,690,394	12,312,128	41.66	
(German component)	3,792,987	5,383,917	41.94	19.38
(Dutch component)	4,532,534	6,383,590	40.84	30.60
(Belgian component)	364,873	544,621	49.26	14.26
12. Geneva–Lausanne–Annecy	1,031,072	1,499,659	40.59	32.35 (Switzerland) 22.80 (France)
13. Paris	7,230,690	10,068,911	39.25	22.80
14. Upper Rhine (East Bank)– Central Switzerland	9,975,364	13,855,652	38.90	
(German component)	7,684,137	10,729,651	39.63	19.38
(Swiss component)	2,291,227	3,126,001	36.43	32.35
15. Munich	1,814,585	2,508,972	38.27	19.38
16. Stockholm	1,354,434	1,828,893	35.03	14.58
17. Valencia	1,952,185	2,585,482	32.39	21.58
Total	52,653,426	77,475,951	47.14	16.82 (Europe)

Source: Hall, P. and Hay, D. (1980), p. 155.

area encompassed by the major urban concentrations centred on London, Paris, Brussels, the Randstad and the Ruhr. At an even larger scale Hall (1974) has also already suggested the likelihood of the future emergence of a new European economic and urban heartland of the 'golden triangles' defined by Paris, Birmingham and Dortmund, or even possibly by Birmingham, Dortmund and Milan. More recently, in an extensive survey of European growth centres for the period 1950–70 Hall and Hay (1980) recognized seventeen 'megalopolitan' growth zones with a combined population of 77 million (Table 5.1). These were categorized into two types: the axial developments such as those along the Rhine and its tributaries, the Rhône–Saône corridor, and the Côte d'Azur; and the more nodal growth associated with the largest cities of southern Europe such as Rome, Turin, Milan and Madrid (Figure 5.5). Fourteen of these were considered to lie within

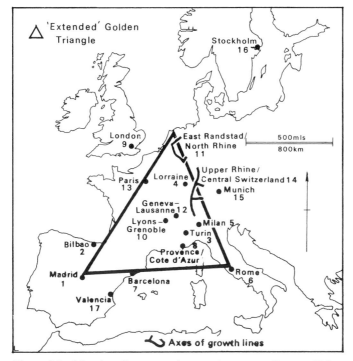

Figure 5.5   Megalopolitan growth zones in western Europe. Urban
centres are those suggested by Hall and Hay, 1980

an extended 'golden triangle' bounded by North Holland, Madrid and Rome,
while the remaining three centres of Stockholm, Valencia and the North
London fringe are located in only marginally peripheral situations.

URBANIZED REGIONS AND THEORIES OF REGIONAL
DEVELOPMENT

Regional inequalities in levels of economic development occur in virtually
all countries and are reflected in variations in the size and complexity of the
urban system. Explanations for these variations have been sought from a
variety of perspectives, and their findings provide some understanding of
spatial variations in the incidence of the different types of urbanized regions
discussed in the previous section.

Prior to the late 1950s interregional variations in levels of economic development were generally considered to be the result of temporary maladjustments
in the economic system. The assumption was that if labour and capital were
relatively mobile and reasonable information existed on the availability of
economic opportunities, then eventually movement of the factors of production
would bring about a *regional equalization* of economic development. However,
the development of such a state of *spatial equilibrium* clearly did not accord

158

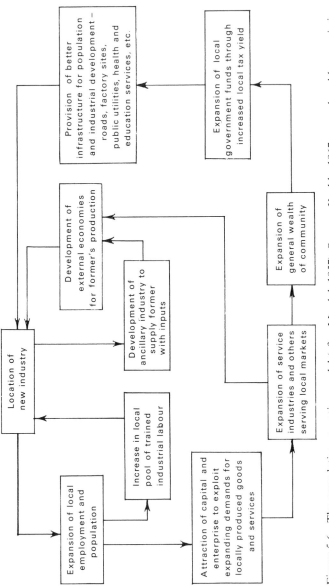

Figure 5.6 The cumulative causation model (after Myrdal, 1957). Source: Keeble, 1967; reproduced by permission of Associated Book Publishers Ltd

with the pervasiveness of regional economic inequalities in most parts of the world (Friedmann, 1966; Keeble, 1967).

The inability of the mechanisms promoting spatial equilibrium to account for the persistence of regional inequalities resulted in the formulation of new conceptual models. The most important of these is that of Myrdal (1957), initially developed in the context of underdeveloped countries. The model was based upon the process of 'cumulative causation'. During the earliest stage of economic development it was assumed that the greatest amount of economic development would occur in that region which has some initial advantage, while the remaining regions of the country would lag behind. With subsequent economic development, rather than an emergence of counter-balancing forces promoting spatial equilibrium, the initial economic advantages of the 'core' region were considered more likely to result in the accumulation of 'derived advantages' which would maintain its pre-eminent economic position. These advantages include: a concentration of skilled labour; the availability of capital and enterprise; a good economic and social infrastructure resulting from past development; access to government agencies; and the opportunity to develop ancillary and service industries. These advantages were considered by Myrdal to be interactively related in such a way (Figure 5.6) as to create *cumulative* economic growth in the core region of a country.

It is interesting to note that other authors have recognized the importance of similar factors in seeking to explain the persistence of spatial concentrations of economic and urban development. Such factors, although presented in a much more rudimentary fashion were considered by Jefferson (1939), in his study of urban primacy; by Ullman (1958), in his comments on the development of 'self-generating momentum' in the geographical concentration of economic activities; and by Isard (1960) in a discussion of 'urbanization economies'.

Myrdal's model, however, incorporates additional elements. Once economic growth has been initiated in a core region, it attracts both capital investment and the in-migration of skilled labour from the peripheral regions of a country. The concentration of the provision of goods and services in the core is also likely to stunt the development of similar economic activities in the periphery. In addition, the relative poverty of the periphery might well result in the provision of a less adequate level of public services than is offered in the core region and this would further deflate the attractions of the periphery. This combination of features, termed by Myrdal the 'backwash effect', was considered likely to accentuate significantly the economic concentration associated with the cumulative causation mechanism.

The opposite, 'spread effect', by which growth in the core area might ultimately result in the stimulation of development in the peripheral regions was also postulated by Myrdal. The core area was considered likely to stimulate demand at the periphery for such things as agricultural produce and raw materials. If the effects of this were sufficiently great, it was considered possible that this could initiate the mechanism of cumulative causation in the periphery with sufficient impetus to promote self-sustaining economic growth. However, it was considered that such a 'spread effect' was only likely to occur in the most highly developed economies, usually with the assistance of positive government policies, and even then the level of economic development was unlikely to rival that of the core. In fact, in the view of Keeble (1967) the model suggests economic divergence between core and periphery during earlier periods of growth, and convergence only during a much later period.

A similar conceptual model was independently derived by Hirschman (1958) in which 'polarization' and 'trickling-down' effects, directly analogous to the 'backwash' and 'spread' effects of Myrdal were considered fundamental to the development of interregional inequalities in economic development. However, this model is less comprehensive since it does not recognize the importance of a mechanism similar to the cumulative causation sequence within the urban concentration for which there is considerable independent support.

Empirical evidence tends to support the Myrdal model. The fundamental importance of the cumulative causation mechanism, and the backwash or polarization effects, has been widely accepted as an explanation for economic and urban concentration in the earlier stages of economic development. However, it is worthy of note that evidence for the spontaneous operation of the spread or trickling-down effects to create a measure of regional equalization in the long term is much sparser (Keeble, 1967). It may well be that forces of concentration are much stronger than was initially thought by Myrdal, and this tends to support the greater importance attached to the need for directive government influence to promote a degree of regional equalization as proposed in Hirschman's (1958) model. Nevertheless, it can be concluded that Myrdal's model provides a strong conceptual rationale for the emergence and persistence of interregional inequality in levels of economic development and associated urban concentration.

Building on these earlier models, Friedmann (1966) combined the ideas relating to the chronological stages of economic development with those concerning the development of regional inequalities to develop the more spatially explicit *centre–periphery model* as a guideline for regional development policy. The model contributes, however, to an understanding of the distribution of urbanized regions.

Friedmann's basic contention was that regional inequalities arise as a result of the spatial transformations associated with the cycle of economic growth. Four distinct stages are recognized (see discussion in Chapter 3, page 73) defined according to the percentage which industry contributes to the Gross National Product of a country:

1. Preindustrial, 0–10 per cent
2. Transitional, 10–25 per cent
3. Industrial, 25–50 per cent
4. Postindustrial, declining.

In *preindustrial* societies regional inequalities in levels of economic development were considered not to be marked. The urban system consists of small independent centres serving restricted local areas, the size of each centre reflecting the agricultural wealth of the local hinterland. The development of urban hierarchies is also limited, although it is possible that the capital city or a centre which has some distinct locational advantage could demonstrate a degree of primacy. At this stage national development policy should be concerned with the creation of the *preconditions* for economic development as regional inequalities would not yet have become evident.

During the *transitional* stage, centre–periphery contrasts begin to emerge as those places with locational advantages show the highest rates of growth. A fear of the politically disintegrative repercussions of centre–periphery contrasts may lead to policies designed to ameliorate or to redress the imbalance. A mature *industrial* stage will be reached if such policies are successful and an integrated system is maintained, though forces of centralization are likely to ensure that centre–periphery differences will remain. Again, depressed regions may occur if changing demand or technology adversely affect a particular area. Lower levels of dependence on industrial activity and more dependence on services, presages the *postindustrial* stage, likely to be accompanied by the culmination of policies aimed at greater integration and equalization and a shift towards urban and environmental planning.

Several aspects of Friedmann's concept of staged development can be questioned. Are regional policies most critical during the transitional stage, for example, when social institutions, education, literacy and mass communications are rarely well developed? Deutsch (1966) argues that at this stage most people in peripheral regions will have a low level of awareness of their relative disadvantage. It is during the industrial stage, with improved communications, that such an awareness might lead to dissent even though actual disparities between centre and periphery had diminished. British experience offers some support for this hypothesis. Again, the idea of equalization during the post-industrial phase is questionable; if such a change occurs it is most likely to be the product of policies initiated in the industrial phase. Friedmann (1966) regards the United States as the best example of a postindustrial economy, but many peripheral regions in America are clearly disadvantaged and in receipt of aid; a further clear trend at an American metropolitan scale is for centres to become disadvantaged relative to peripheries and for new major regional shifts to have effect. Despite these reservations the centre–periphery model provides a useful framework in which to view regional inequalities.

Friedmann (1966) also identified a typology of regions; the *core* region of greatest economic growth consists of one or more clusters of cities and their hinterlands; the problems are those of growth and its adverse environmental impacts; *downward transitional areas* in the periphery have moderate levels of urban development but stagnant or declining economic bases; their problems are of economic decline and the need to refurbish local infrastructures; *upward transitional areas* (Friedmann, 1973) have more potential for development and may lead to the emergence of *subsidiary core* regions with new cities; and also in the periphery there may be *resource frontier* regions of new settlement, usually associated with agriculture or mineral exploitation, and the role of regional planning in these circumstances should be concerned with developing a system of urban settlements capable of promoting a more diversified economic base to create self-sustaining growth.

Myrdal's explanation for the emergence and persistence of interregional inequalities in levels of economic development, supplemented particularly by the spatial aspects of Friedmann's work provides a useful conceptual framework within which to view the development of urban concentrations at the national scale. This is summarized for the British empirical experience in Table 5.2.

PROBLEMS OF CENTRE–PERIPHERY RELATIONSHIPS

Following the early explanations for the emergence of regional inequalities in levels of economic development, subsequent investigations of the processes involved suggest the greater likelihood over time of their persistence rather than their diminution. Pred (1966), for example, examined the process of cumulative causation in the urban-industrial growth of the United States in the nineteenth century, and suggested the importance of initial and secondary multiplier effects in the areas of early development. These are similar to the 'derived advantages' of Myrdal (1957). However, a second element promoting growth in initial concentrations was identified as the enhanced likelihood of

Table 5.2   Stages in the development of the British urban system

Urban pattern	Population	Economic development
Preindustrial stage, before 1750		
Small towns serving local rural hinterlands. *Exception*: London as a primate city; smaller port cities, such as Bristol, Liverpool	Low and fluctuating, slow growth, mostly rural	Reflects the relative prosperity of local agriculture; commercial development in London and ports
Transitional stage 1750–1850 New urban concentrations, principally in the coalfields. London continues its growth by the 'cumulative causation' mechanism—already a million city by 1801. A centre–periphery structure more evident *within* the separate regions than at a national scale	Acceleration of growth; rural-to-urban migration. In England and Wales population increased from 8.8 million in 1801 to 17.9 million in 1851—urban population from 33.8 per cent in 1801 to 54 per cent in 1851	Early industrual development based upon coal and steam: iron, steel textiles and shipbuilding become the basic industries

Table 5.2   (*continued*)

Urban pattern	Population	Economic development
Industrial stage 1850–1950 London added 5.5 million to its population 1801–1911; Birmingham, Liverpool and Manchester grew by only *ca*. 1 million each in the same period. Cities of the peripheral regions grew even more slowly. The north and west began to display downward transitional characteristics and a *national* centre–periphery structure emerged	Population growth (England and Wales) 17.9 million in 1851 to 36.0 million in 1911; 78.9 per cent of the population lived in cities by 1911. Slower growth in the interwar depression years; larger cities grew more slowly as innovations ceased to enter the urban system	Emergence of international competition Basic industries face international competition. Increasing importance of secondary manufacturing; development of cheap efficient transport; economic advantages of a centralized market location for light industrial development are emphasized. Conversely industrial decline in the north and western peripheral regions
Postindustrial stage 1950 to date As economic forces and environmental planning policies spread London's urban development, the 'Centre' gradually expands to include the south-east, the midlands and south-east Lancashire. Amelioration of urban decline in the periphery by decentralization policies	Stabilization of the population, with a tendency to grow slowly except in times of economic recession. Birthrates fluctuate at a low level	Emergence of service employment as the growth sector of the economy. The attraction of a centralized urban location re-emphasized for such development. New economic element added with the exploitation of oil and natural gas in the North Sea in the 1960s and 1970s. Marginal regions and some inner cities remain problem areas.

NB Following Friedmann (1966) a *four*-stage model is used here but transitional and industrial stages can be combined to achieve the *three*-stage model used earlier in this chapter.

invention and innovation generated by high levels of interaction among all the regions of development in centralized locations rather than elsewhere. This modification was considered sufficiently important to formulate the 'circular and cumulative causation' model of urban growth (Figure 5.7).

More recently, investigation of the diffusion of inventions and innovations through spatial systems has provided additional support for this model. Hagerstrand (1966) initially demonstrated that the process of contagious diffusion was an appropriate explanation for the spread of agricultural innovations through rural areas. The pattern of spread was considered to reflect

164

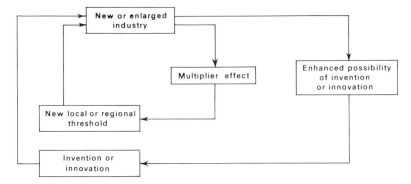

Figure 5.7   The circular and cumulative causation model (after Pred, 1965)

distance from the locations of the early adopters and, subsequently, Hager-strand (1967) suggested the applicability of Monte Carlo probability models to simulate the diffusion of innovations. However, such models depend upon the existence of a relatively uniform distribution of potential innovators and the assumption that the innovation spreads by face-to-face communication between individuals. Clearly, these assumptions are not appropriate to the adoption of innovations in systems of cities which vary in size, are spaced at varying distances and are affected by innovations which are more likely to be adopted by organizations (termed 'entrepreneurial innovations' by Pederson, 1970) than by individuals. In these circumstances, an innovation is more likely to be adopted initially in a larger rather than a smaller city, creating a 'hierarchical effect': 'The point of introduction in a new country is its primate city; sometimes some other metropolis. Then centres next in rank follow' (Hagerstrand, 1966, p. 40).

However, this tendency was considered likely to be followed quickly by the spread of the innovation into the smaller cities adjacent to the higher order initial adopters, creating a 'neighbourhood effect': 'Soon, however, this order is broken up and replaced by one when the neighbourhood effect dominates over the pure size succession' (Hagerstrand, 1966, p. 40).

Thus, the diffusion of innovation through an urban system will reflect the dual considerations of size and distance.

The pattern of innovation diffusion through an urban system might best be thought of, however, as a combination of both distance and size effects. Given a particular urban innovation, its spread within a system of towns might be expected to follow both the size hierarchy and distance spread simultaneously (Robson, 1973, p. 137).

and

The respective importance of the hierarchical and neighbourhood effect would, therefore, differ depending on the characteristics of the innovation. Those involving large economic risk or those in which technological constraints on scale economies favoured their adoption in large market areas would be determined more by hierarchical than by neighbourhood considerations (Robson, 1973, p. 140).

Robson (1973) suggests that a hierarchical diffusion occurs because of the tendency for entrepreneurs to reduce their economic risks by locating in a larger potential market. Webber (1972) discusses the element of 'uncertainty' in the location decision-making process and suggests that this results in a greater centralization of economic activity than might otherwise be expected. Uncertainty concerning the location decisions of competitors tends towards an overestimation of the advantages of agglomeration in centralized, least-risk locations. Similarly, uncertainty concerning the 'states of nature' such as the future rate of economic growth tends to accentuate the advantages of a major market location where instability is likely to be least evident. The overall effect accentuates the manner in which innovations diffuse from the most central to the least central locations in economic systems. In addition, the influence of the concentration of *inter-organization economic interaction* in central location suggested by Pred (1966) in the circular and cumulative causation model, is probably not without some explanatory value for the hierarchical diffusion effect. On the other hand, Robson argues that the neighbourhood effect probably reflects the imitation of an innovation by places adjacent to earlier adopters. Clearly, patterns of spatial inequality will be maintained rather than replaced by the equalization of development if new forms of economic activity spread through urban systems in these ways. Robson's (1973) study of the process of urban growth in England and Wales in the nineteenth century provides some empirical support for the explanatory significance of this hypothesis, although attention is also drawn to the need to appreciate the level of concentration of decision-making powers, both governmental and private, if the details of the diffusion process are to be fully understood.

A number of additional studies also provide support for the validity of the urban variant of the diffusion process. These have focused primarily upon urban service functions rather than more direct growth-inducing influences, although it is argued that the availability of such services in cities tends to enhance their attractions for further economic development. Pederson (1970), for example, investigated the spread of hospitals, fire brigades, newspapers and waterworks through the urban system of Chile in the nineteenth and twentieth centuries. The sequence of adoptions was found to be explained by the size of the centres followed by the distance from a larger centre. Similarly, Berry's (1970) study of the spread of television stations in the United States in the period 1940–68 indicated that they generally proceeded from the largest to the smallest places, while the first small towns to obtain a station were usually located close to a larger early adopter.

Clark (1974) provides information more directly relevant to the manner in which urban growth-inducing influences spread through urban systems. The development of subscriber trunk dialling (STD) telephone services, by which long-distance telephone calls can be made directly at low user cost, was traced for north-eastern England in the period 1963–71 (Figure 5.8). In the earlier years the larger centres such as Leeds, Newcastle-upon-Tyne, Sunderland and Middlesbrough obtained the service, followed by most of the remaining urban

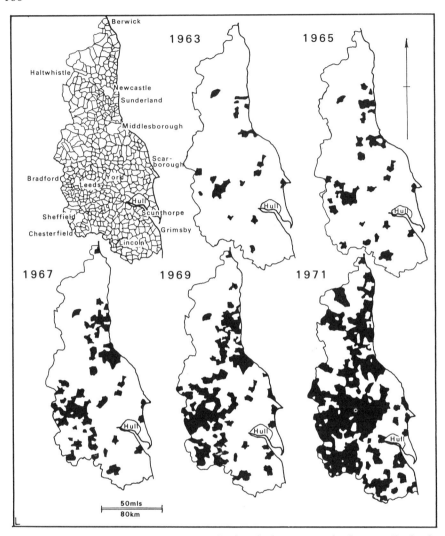

Figure 5.8 The spread of the STD system in the telephone network of eastern England.
Source: Clark, 1974; reproduced by permission of the Institute of British Geographers

centres by 1967. Clearly, a significant hierarchical effect was apparent. Subsequently, the innovation spread to adjacent suburban and rural communities in a manner analogous to the neighbourhood effect, although even by 1971 many rural areas were still without the service. The reason for this pattern of spread is that the primary aim of the Post Office is to relieve congestion on existing facilities. Thus, innovation tends to be initiated in the larger urban concentrations first.

The implications of this study for the location of economic activity are clear. All sectors of the economy depend to a significant degree upon the use of the telephone to function efficiently. Thus, new forms of economic development are more likely to locate in those areas which have efficient telephone services rather than more remote locations. Consequently, the diffusion of this particular innovation is more likely to maintain spatial inequalities in levels of economic development than to generate spatial dispersal. As Clark (1974) points out, the notion that advanced telecommunications will eliminate the frictional effects of distance to produce time–space convergence on a massive scale is probably erroneous. At the moment telecommunications technology diffuses hierarchically so that spatial differentials in its availability are likely to remain. In fact, Clark notes that direct international dialling in Britain was introduced in London in 1971, but it will not be available throughout the country until 1986. Thus in 1971 while London subscribers had direct low-cost access to North America and Europe, it still required an operator to connect a call from Woodhall Spa to Lincoln, less than 32 km (20 miles) away.

A similar sequence tends to be demonstrated in the development of transport facilities. Congestion is felt first in major urban concentrations, so that improvements are made within and between the largest centres first. Only at a later date are improvements undertaken in peripheral locations and, even then, links from centre towards the periphery tend to precede improvements within peripheral regions. Prior to 1972 there was a concentration of major motorway construction in the south-east of England, and between the south-east, the west Midlands and the north-west. This situation has not been substantially altered in the subsequent period (Figure 5.9). For example, the construction of the M4 motorway and the Severn Bridge has provided an efficient link between South Wales and London since 1972, but within industrial South Wales a vital link in the M4 still awaits completion. The result of this kind of situation tends to stimulate a backwash effect in favour of economic centres without promoting a concomitant spread effect to the periphery. Similar effects also accompany the improvement of rural and sea transportation facilities:

Other factors are also considered to contribute to the persistence of imbalances in the levels of development between centre and periphery. Pred (1973), for example, draws attention to the importance of the concentrations of *decision-making* and *information* in large urban agglomerations. The concentration of the headquarters of large organizations, both public and private, in such areas, is considered to result in a local multiplier effect which operates in favour of the increasing dominance of large cities. It is even suggested, ironically, that governmental attempts to decentralize development to peripheral regions *can* result in the growth of administrative functions in core regions.

Closely related ideas are proposed by Friedmann (1972a). He argues that earlier explanations for the concentration of urban development depend unduly on economic criteria such as the localization of natural resources, the development of transport routes, the organization of markets, and economies of scale and agglomeration. Additional to the undoubted importance of these factors, Friedmann (1972b) suggests that closer consideration should be given to the

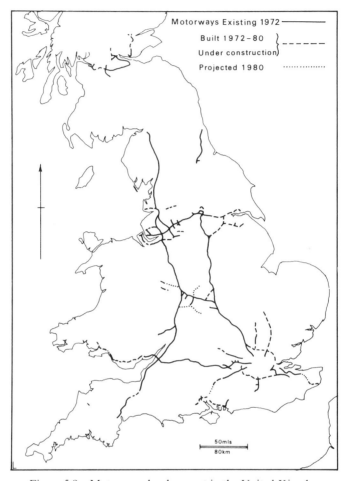

Figure 5.9   Motorway development in the United Kingdom

spatial organization of government and economic decision-making powers. During the early stages of economic development there are considered to be distinct advantages attached to a location with direct access to centres of political power. Economic enterprise is strongly dependent upon the central bureaucracy and access to channels of legislative power. In a situation of centralized political power, the national capital will normally have the best system of transport and communication and a superior economic and social infrastructure, while the importance of face-to-face relations in the conduct of business between government and entrepreneur remains. This promotes a polarized pattern of development which becomes self-perpetuating, with the result that a system of 'economic dualism' develops between the central urban industrial culture and the underdeveloped rural economy.

At a later stage, following the growth of a significant peripheral market, or with the exploitation of new natural resources outside the initial centre, some peripheral development is probable. However, the concentration of political and economic institutions at the centre maintains a centre–periphery structure because the management decisions concerning the business profits of the whole economy tend to be transferred back to the original centre. Similarly, when the industrial economy achieves maturity, Friedmann stresses that developmental advantages still accrue to the 'control centres' of initial development, despite the reduction of government influence in the economy.

Set against the strength of the array of centralization forces, evidence for the efficiency of factors promoting regional equalization is minimal. As indicated previously, there is little evidence to support the effectiveness of the spread or trickling-down effects (Keeble, 1967). In addition, Friedmann (1966) discusses the possibility of the spontaneous development of a 'spatial equilibrium' mechanism in the later stages of economic development. Attention was drawn to the possible 'diseconomies of scale' associated with large urban concentrations, particularly the potential cost of congested transport and communication facilities and the escalating price of land in locations with potential for development. However, these factors were considered insufficiently powerful to redress significantly the imbalance. It was argued that the law of diminishing returns failed to operate in the centre because of the positive attractions of a large market in conjunction with the other advantages already discussed. Also, investors were considered consistently to overestimate the profitability of a central location, while selective outmigration of the young and enterprising from the periphery deprived it of sufficient leadership to stimulate self-sustaining growth.

PLANNING POLICIES FOR NATIONAL URBAN SYSTEMS

The implication of the previous section is that if regional inequalities are to be reduced, strong government intervention is necessary. Such policies are increasingly evident and are usually implemented through the urban system. However, regional decentralization policies vary enormously among countries and a considerable literature relating to this subject now exists which it is unnecessary to review in detail. Relevant here are the major themes emerging from this work which provided additional insights into the nature of national urban systems and the ways in which these are subject to change. The four-fold classification suggested by Berry (1978), which has already been referred to, provides a useful framework within which to identify some of the current trends in urbanization and the kinds of policy-responses which are emerging. Berry's four 'types' of society are:

(1) Free-enterprise, decentralized, market-directed societies
(2) Welfare states of western Europe
(3) Socialist states
(4) Third world states.

Free-enterprise, decentralized, market-directed societies

In societies in this group, of which the United States, Canada and Australia are considered prime examples, decisions relating to the location of economic activity are made by individuals or small groups and are regulated in the market place through the free interplay of the forces of supply and demand. This creates a tradition of free-enterprise, with government intervention restricted to the maintenance of the market institutions and the alleviation of crises. Such a system encourages the centralization of economic activity in the initially advantageous locations at the expense of others, a situation which has been exacerbated by the growth of corporate and oligarchic decision-making organizations in the twentieth century. Although a limited amount of government intervention has appeared in such societies, the forces of centralization continue to dominate the location of economic activity and urban growth. Such regional decentralization policies as exist tend to be piecemeal and crisis-orientated, so that redistribution of a sufficient magnitude to solve the problems of regional inequalities does not result (Bourne, 1975; Rodwin, 1970). The 'counterurbanization' process, which is unplanned, has served to reduce regional differences (Berry, 1980) and the new 'sunbelt' regions are enjoying rising levels of prosperity.

Welfare states of western Europe

In western Europe more radical attempts have been made by governments to modify the spatial form of economic development. This has usually involved a variety of fiscal, legal and urban policies designed to reduce area inequalities in levels of living by stimulating growth in peripheral regions and curtailing development at the centre. In most cases these measures have been combined with policies designed to maintain at a minimum the diseconomies of over-congestion and urban environmental deterioration in the principal centres of economic activity.

The general principles upon which many economic decentralization policies have been based are contained in the early work of Friedmann (1966). The principle of 'comparative advantage' suggests that development should be concentrated in those locations and on those resources which are most likely to attract new development rather than be dispersed in order to alleviate local pockets of economic depression. In the short term the latter policy appeals to governments on social grounds, but it should not be the central objective since in the long term it is unlikely that such locations will develop strong economies and prove sufficiently attractive to promote self-sustaining growth. A sequel is that investment should aim at the improvement of the basic infrastructure of the areas designated for development. Particular attention should be paid to the improvement of transport and communications, the housing stock, educational, cultural and recreational facilities. Additions to the urban system could take the form of new towns or satellite communities in particularly attractive locations. Friedmann stresses the importance of the quality of the sociopolitical leadership in the peripheral regions. If such leadership is lacking as a result of a prolonged period of selective out-migration, then it should be provided through government agencies or attracted by financial incentives. Clearly, this might involve the decentralization of government decision-making powers to some new forms of political or administrative institutions. Finally, if the rural economy of the peripheral region is also in a state of decline, this should be regenerated.

Britain

Principles of this kind have been translated into practice in a variety of ways. In Britain, for example, policy has focused on the two issues of inducement and control. Industrial development subsidies in the form of building grants and tax allowances to reduce new construction costs, loans and grants for the acquisition of industrial sites, the construction of advance factories by the government, and the payment of regional employment premiums to private firms on a *per capita* basis, have all been used to encourage industrialists to locate in the relatively depressed northern and western regions of the country. These policies were initiated with the Special Areas Act of 1934 and have been varied in relative importance in a complex, but well-documented manner, in the subsequent period (Bourne, 1975; Hall, 1974). Similarly, the areas for which the inducements have been available have varied over time. Initially, subsidies were restricted to the industrial concentrations of the north-east of England, west Cumberland, South Wales and Clydeside, but following the Distribution of Industry Act of 1945, smaller areas in south Lancashire, Merseyside and north-east Lancashire, as well as a more extensive area in the Scottish Highlands, were added. These were replaced in the early 1960s by *development districts* which were much more restricted areas based upon persistently high levels of local unemployment. This reorientation of policy to areas of local disadvantage was a radical change. However, the difficulty of stimulating growth in the peripheral regions by directing investment to such areas was soon recognized (Manners, 1972). Thus, in 1965 the *economic planning regions* were created with councils to *advise* the government on appropriate development strategies. This was followed in 1966 by the designation of the much more extensive *development areas* which included the greater part of the north and west. Subsequently, in 1967, *special development areas* in which greater financial incentives were to be made available, were created to combat the most severe problems of industrial depression, while in 1970 aid was extended to *intermediate areas* to stimulate growth in potential problem areas. In addition, government finance has been available for the construction of a number of new towns to improve the attractions of the regions, as well as to alleviate local problems of high unemployment. In the late 1970s the emphasis had moved from subsidized special areas to *enterprise zones* on a smaller scale, and greater awareness of inner-city problems had led to fundamental shifts in policy. Conversely, restrictive controls have been used in the south-east. Since 1945 industrial location has been regulated by the Industrial Development Certificate, while from the early 1960s this has been supplemented by Office Development Permits (Daniels, 1975) and attempts to decentralize sections of the Civil Service (HMSO, 1973). These controls have been applied with varying degrees of restriction by successive governments, although not to such an extent that development has been severely curtailed in the south-east.

Clearly, the array of decentralization strategies applied in Britain is based upon general economic criteria and is not specifically urban in orientation. Nevertheless, in recent years regional planning councils have provided a firmer physical planning context for the economic planning strategies, albeit of advisory rather than directive significance (see, for example Northern Economic Planning Council, 1969).

France

French regional planning has forged a much stronger link between national economic policies and the urban hierarchy. The principal problem has been to redress the regional imbalances associated with the domination by Paris of French political, economic and social life. In fact, in the early 1960s the population of Paris was 8.5 million, comprising nearly 20 per cent of the total, while the next tier of Marseilles and Lyons was 750,000 and the remaining major cities less than 200,000. Nevertheless, prior to 1945 there was little support for decentralization since Paris was regarded as the centre of 'high culture' in contrast to the backwardness and parochialism of the provincial regions (Rodwin, 1970). However, increasing dissatisfaction with this pattern of development in the postwar period, epitomized in Gravier's (1947) work *Paris et le Desert Français*, has resulted in a number of innovations in regional planning policy. These sought to alleviate existing and potential problems of urban congestion in Paris and to promote overall economic development by making more effective use of peripheral resources—aims which are conceptually similar to those in Britain.

Initially, detailed strategies also paralleled those of Britain. Throughout the 1950s and early 1960s attempts were made to control the location of manufacturing and office employment, combined with incentives to stimulate decentralization. These were largely ineffective, partly because national political and economic reconstruction were more important issues at the time, and partly because the mechanisms of control were considered insufficiently strong to solve the problems at hand.

Consequently, a fundamental change of policy was introduced in the Fifth Economic Plan for 1966–69. This made the concept of the *growth centre* the basis of regional decentralization policy. This strategy was most strongly advocated by Boudeville (1966) who adapted the theoretical economic notion of the *growth pole* to the more empirical geographical concept of the growth centre. The growth pole had been introduced by Perroux (1950) to describe a sector of a national economy comprising a group of firms or industries which were strongly linked with, and tended to dominate the functioning of, other sectors of the economy. Thus, a growth pole was seen as an important *propulsive* element in an economy. However, the early economic studies of growth poles did not consider their geographical attributes, and the concept was essentially confined to abstract economic space (Darwent, 1969). The growth *centre* lacked the theoretical basis of the growth *pole* and was based on the assumption that to stimulate growth in a peripheral region potentially propulsive investment should be directed to specific, more advantageous, urban concentrations. Subsequently, it was anticipated that economic and social development would spread to adjacent areas and produce a more equitable distribution of development among regions on a national scale.

These ideas were transformed into the strategy of the *métropole d'équilibre*. Eight existing urban concentrations were designated as growth centres and it was considered that each of these could achieve a minimum population of 1 million (Figure 5.10). They already possessed a basic urban infrastructure capable of assisting further development, yet were located sufficiently distant from Paris to enable regional decentralization. The aim was to develop a central place structure for France which would maximize intraregional interdependency within the eight growth regions and also promote the interregional interdependency of Paris and its peripheral metropolitan regions (Darwent, 1969). Clearly, the policy incorporates a stronger link between national and regional economic policy and the urban hierarchy than the British case.

The French policy has achieved a reasonable measure of success. Significant growth has taken place in the *métropoles d'équilibre* and the dominance of Paris has been contained. Nevertheless, Paris continues to grow and to attract investment; a projected population of 14 million by the year 2000 is anticipated. Hall (1974) suggests that spatial inequalities in levels of development are likely to continue to be found in the rural margins beyond the spheres of influence of the major urban regions; growth centres will generate their own centre–periphery problems.

Sweden

A more comprehensive attempt to link national and regional economic development priorities with the urban system is demonstrated by Sweden (Bourne, 1975). The change from a rural society in the nineteenth century to a modern industrial state was accompanied by the concentration of population in a small number of urban centres in the south of the country. By 1965 Stockholm was pre-eminent with a population of 1,450,000, followed by Göteborg (873,000) and Malmö (661,000). The next nine-ranking cities, ranging in population from 309,000 to 78,000, are also located in the southern half of the country. In contrast, the northern region and the other rural parts of Sweden had been subject to steady depopulation and were suffering from declining municipal services and diminishing employment opportunities.

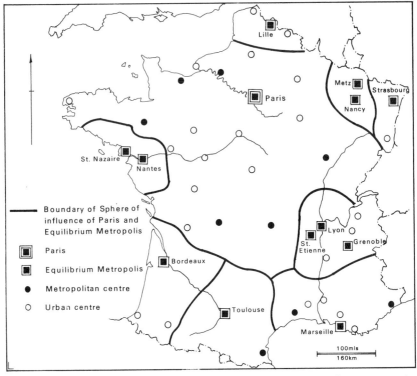

Figure 5.10   Equilibrium metropoles and metropolitan centres in France. The planning hierarchy emphasizes the supremacy of Paris and the more localized regional importance of other equilibrium metropoles (after Rodwin, 1970). Reproduced by permission of Houghton Mifflin & Co.

Attempts to redress these imbalances culminated in the Regional Structure Plan of 1972. The national urban system was divided into four hierarchical categories which were to form the framework for economic location decisions:

1. The major metropolitan centres (3)
2. Primary centres (23)
3. Regional centres (70)
4. Municipal centres or communes (150).

It was intended that growth should be restricted in the major metropolitan concentrations and redistributed through the remaining levels of the hierarchy. The primary centres were designated as urban-central regions of over 90,000 population. These were considered to have a labour force large enough to attract diverse employment opportunities and to benefit from economies of scale in the provision of public services. 'Locational consolidation' rather than large-scale expansion was the key process (Bourne, 1975). Below this level, the regional centres of approximately 30,000 population received some priority in government investment and were to act as small growth centres in areas experiencing depopulation. The lowest level of municipal centres were to provide local services.

The success of this strategy cannot yet be judged (Bourne, 1975), but the problems—both administrative/political and developmental—are considerable. Nevertheless, the Swedish experience provides an interesting example of an explicit regional decentralization strategy, using the existing urban system to implement national priorities

A final observation on the policies of the welfare states is worthy of note. A recurring theme is the dilemma in these countries between two apparently conflicting aims. On the one hand there is a desire to redress regional imbalances by promoting the periphery and controlling the largest metropolitan concentrations. On the other, governments are drawn towards a *laissez-faire* attitude on the assumption that this will maintain the steady growth of the whole economy. The latter proposition is particularly attractive during times of economic recession. On balance, governments tend to strike a balance and rarely follow decentralization policies to their limits. Physical planning to improve environmental quality and innovations to improve efficiency are frequently incorporated into policies principally designed to contain the growth of metropolitan concentrations. The structure plan for the growth of Paris is a case in point (Hall, 1974). A result is that regional imbalances tend to persist despite official commitment to the contrary.

Socialist states

The control of economic development has been taken a stage further in the socialist states with a fundamental commitment to greater uniformity in the pattern of economic development and urban concentration. This aim, which can be traced back to the ideals of Marx and Engels (Berry, 1978), is epitomized in the concept of a 'unified settlement system' which determines the growth of the urban system in the USSR:

The essence of the concept is that in the longterm, through the regional distribution of the forces of production of separate regions, the historically formed settlement pattern (both its concentrated and dispersed forms) will be transformed into integrated regional systems of settlement units which are socially and economically interlinked; their size will depend on local conditions. These units will together form the unified (economic) system of settlement (Khodzhaev and Khorev, 1973, p. 48).

Complete uniformity is not the aim but there is a far stronger commitment to spread the forces of urbanization over wider areas so that the distinctions between town and country will be blurred. Similarly, there is a firm intention to preclude the development of a significant dependence relationship between centre and periphery at a regional or national scale. Central political control of the economic system provides a stronger mechanism to achieve these aims with their outcomes of comparable work conditions and lifestyles for all parts of the national system.

As a result, the relative importance of the largest cities of the USSR has declined significantly. In 1926, for example, the seven cities with populations of greater than 1 million—Moscow, Leningrad, Kiev, Tashkent, Baku, Kharkov, and Gorki—contained 60 per cent of the population of large towns, but this had declined to just over 23 per cent by 1970. Also, the network of large towns has been extended in the postwar period by the stimulation of industrial development in provincial centres (Khodzhaev and Khorev, 1973). Although the largest centres are still growing at disproportionate rates, this is seen as a short-term problem.

Third world states

Regional equalization policies in the third world are generally the least well developed and most variable of the four groups, and this reflects the early stage of economic and political development of these countries. Economies are often dependent upon the exploitation of natural resources or the agricultural sector; there is a substantial dependence upon foreign export markets which in turn usually promotes a significant degree of urban primacy. Third world governments find such concentrations difficult to control since there is usually only a small public economic sector over which they have direct influence; promotion of development is the priority rather than its spatial distribution. Problems of physical fragmentation associated with physiographical barriers also occur frequently and these are often compounded by ethnic diversity or a growing distinction between modern urban society and traditional rural culture. The political integration of the various parts of these societies has rarely been achieved; one-party governments or military dictatorships create an additional element of potential political instability (Berry, 1978). In these circumstances, government policies are concerned more with economic expansion and political integration than with the solution of problems associated with emerging regional disparities.

Consequently, regional urbanization policies vary considerable with individual circumstances. Berry (1978) argues that in most instances this results in attempts to replicate the experiences of the welfare states, or of the command economics of eastern Europe and the USSR, while at the same time attempting to preserve elements of their distinctive cultures. However, such policies rarely reach a successful conclusion due to a poor appreciation of the functional characteristics of the necessary policies, a lack of administrative ability, or a loss of resolve related to a concern for wider economic and political issues.

This assessment might be considered unduly negative in some cases. Instances occur of the development of far more coherent urbanization policies designed to minimize spatial imbalances in levels of economic and social development. For example, in Venezuela American expertise has been used to promote the development of an integrated system of growth centres to extend modernization to significantly wider parts of the country than might otherwise have been the case (Friedmann, 1966; Rodwin, 1970). Similarly, in China, Berry (1978) notes the antiurban bias of government policy which consistently seeks to channel new industrial investment into relatively small cities in previously remote rural communes. The ultimate aim is to spread the benefits of industrialization and modernization uniformly to all areas in order to avoid the potentially destructive, dehumanizing and corrupting influences assumed to be associated with the urban concentrations of industrial capitalism. The origins of this policy are clearly related to the rural basis of the Chinese Communist Revolution.

SUMMARY

This chapter has examined some of the concepts and policies which relate to the urban systems in various parts of the world; it is concerned with relationships among cities and with cities as parts of national and regional urban systems. The concept of stages rehearses some of the arguments and classifications which were discussed above in Chapter 3 in relation to the historical development of urban systems, but the emphasis here is upon regional-scale effects. A typology of urbanized regions in some ways reflects the ideas of individual theorists but also bears a direct relationship to temporal change and the impact upon urban form of a changing technology of transport and communications and the way in which this affects different urban functions and population groups. As the compact industrial city gave way to modern metropolis, its key processes of deconcentration and decentralization can be related most clearly to technological change. The concept of urbanized *regions* accurately reflected the scale of these new 'cities'; they need both to be theorized in regional development terms and also to be tackled by regional planning policies. From this review of features of the urban system the next chapter begins to narrow the focus towards the intraurban scale and to consider some economic aspects of urban life.

Chapter 6

Movement, Employment and Services in the City: the Spatial Infrastructure

In Chapter 4 it was argued that a city may develop to perform a small range of functions but this range will increase in size and complexity with urban growth. Typically, the range consists of a combination of industrial, service and administrative activities, the absolute and relative importance of which will be associated with historical development and geographical location. However, whatever the detailed functional characteristics of a city, its internal spatial structure will be organized around concentrations of employment opportunities, service facilities and their associated land uses, and will be articulated in relation to the urban transportation network. These functional elements both influence and are themselves influenced by the process of urban growth. In addition, they have a similar interactive relationship with the spatial patterns of behaviour in the city. These include journey-to-work patterns and the complex array of service utilization behaviour such as journey-to-shop, visits to health and to leisure facilities. It follows that an appreciation of the factors determining the evolution of the spatial system of each of these elements will provide an important contribution to an understanding of the internal spatial structure and functioning of the city. For this reason this chapter will concentrate, in turn, upon the development of the urban transportation system, of the locations of employment opportunities, and of the various systems of urban service facilities. Attention will then be directed to related aspects of spatial behaviour in the urban system which increasingly have commanded the attention of urban geographers in recent years.

THE URBAN TRANSPORTATION SYSTEM

In all cities there is a close interactive relationship between the structure of the transportation network, the urban morphology and the spatial patterns of urban activities. During the process of economic development the evolving urban transportation system both *connects* the various functional elements of the urban fabric and *directs* the pattern of urban growth. A generalized evolutionary sequence can be postulated for the western city which is closely associated with innovations in transport technology.

At the preindustrial stage, urban centres emerge at particularly accessible

178

locations, frequently at important river-crossing points, to provide a surrounding hinterland with functions such as defence and marketing. For this reason the early routes *converge* on such locations, initiating a strong *radial* element in the emerging road system, which often focuses on the main market place or central square. The centripetal development forces associated with the convergence of routes, combined with a transport system based upon the pedestrian and draught animal results in a characteristically compact urban form (Figure 6.1(a)). Even in the early stages of industrialization, with the initiation of horsedrawn buses in the early decades of the nineteenth century in London, Paris and New York, the high cost of the services and their relative inefficiency served to continue to contain the pressures for urban expansion within a limited area.

The situation changed with the introduction of electric trams or streetcars during the last quarter of the nineteenth century. These provided a relatively less costly and more efficient form of public transport which allowed the growing urban population to live at lower residential densities and at greater distances from the employment concentrations in the town centres. However, their relatively substantial street-space requirements, combined with the need to maximize traffic density in order to finance the relatively high capital investment incurred in the provision of electrified rail systems, resulted in the concentration of the new services along the main radial routeways leading into the town centres. This tended to accentuate the earlier defined radial lines of urban growth along the main traffic arteries and resulted, typically, in a more *stellate* urban form (Figure 6.1(b)). Thus, the primary status of the early radial routeways was confirmed during this period. Other developments were far less significant and took the form of incremental modification to the original framework. Improvements were frequently made to the transport network within town centres to cope with the steadily increasing pressures, while river-crossings were often duplicated during this period for the same reason. Only in exceptional cases, where sufficient civic powers and foresight were available, were partial circumferential links between the radial routes developed in the growing inner suburban areas.

The next significant change was initiated in the early years of the twentieth century following the development of the internal combustion engine. This resulted in the growth in importance of, first, the motor bus and then the private car in the period prior to 1945. These developments allowed for greater flexibility in the provision of public transport routes and increased the personal mobility of the majority of the urban population. This was reflected in the steady increase in residential suburbanization both in the interstices between the earlier radial growth lines and at increasing distances from the city centres; this period also marks the beginning of a significant decentralization of urban functions from the traditional concentrations near the city centres. In terms of the transport network, the majority of these changes were accommodated by the improvement of the major arterial radial routeways, although the flexibility offered by the new modes of transport encouraged the development

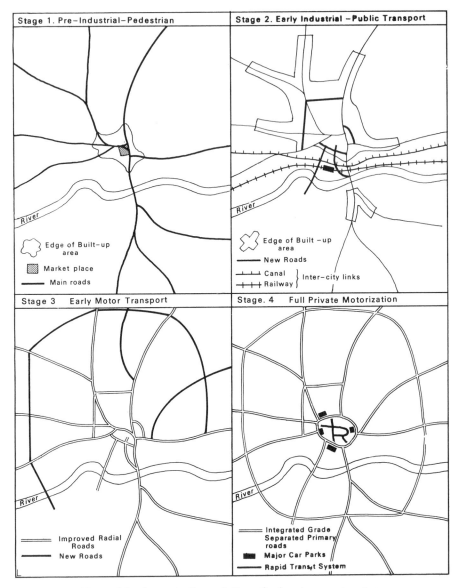

Figure 6.1 Stages in the evolution of urban transport systems

of new radial roads to service the developing residential areas and the establishment of 'ring-roads' on the peripheries of the growing urban systems (Figure 6.1(c)). However, in most cases the available powers of public control and finance failed to keep pace with the needs of the developing situation. Ringroads rarely completely circumnavigated the urban areas, and the incremental and somewhat piecemeal improvement of the transport network remained a significant facet of the evolving system.

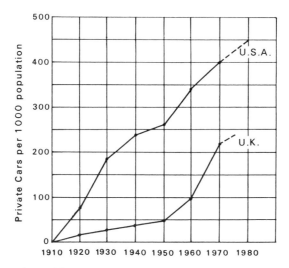

Figure 6.2   Growth of private car ownership in the
United States and the United Kingdom, 1910–1980

The post-1945 period has witnessed a rapid increase in the level of private
car ownership in most western cities (Figure 6.2). For example, between 1963
and 1971 the number of cars per 1000 population in the United Kingdom
increased from 160 to 220 with the result that 50 per cent of families owned
at least one car and 8 per cent owned two. Equivalent levels had been reached
in the United States over 30 years earlier, while it is anticipated that the current
virtual saturation level attained in the United States will be reached in Britain
after the turn of the century (Tupule, 1973). This has increased substantially
the personal mobility of a considerable section of the community and is directly
reflected in the continued suburbanization and functional decentralization of
cities. Considerable pressures have consequently been placed on road systems
which were not designed to accommodate these new traffic levels, and more
comprehensive public controls over transport planning has become essential.
In general, the initial planning response has been to attempt to accommodate
the growth in car-ownership and associated traffic levels whilst preserving,
as far as possible, the quality of the urban environment, but this has involved
various private vehicle limitation strategies in the larger conurbations and
most city centres. A typical solution involves the designation of a comprehensively upgraded road network comprising the main radial routes, an inner
ring-road surrounding the central business district and one or more suburban
ring-roads (Figure 6.1(d)). Ideally, major intersections are 'grade separated'
with flyovers, while the segregation of pedestrian and vehicular traffic with
the creation of pedestrian precincts and other traffic free 'environmental areas'
has been given some priority. The provision of car-parking facilities and their

integration with major trip destination points is also of central importance. For the central business districts various traffic limitation and management schemes in association with public transport strategies have been the usual response. Such strategies are epitomized by the Buchanan Report for British cities (HMSO, 1964). More recently, as the scale of business activities and the traffic demands on central areas have continued to increase, particularly in cities of greater than a million population, the development of inner city rapid transit systems to facilitate internal integration has been a frequent response as exemplified by Toronto, Montreal, Glasgow and Newcastle-upon-Tyne.

This evolutionary sequence is most relevant to cities in which development was initiated in the nineteenth century and has resulted in strongly centralized urban systems. However, due to the specifics of both the chronology and character of the urban development process, there are variations to be noted both within the context of the general model and with cities which have developed in different societal circumstances. A number of examples will serve to illustrate the potential variability.

Western cities: centralized systems

The most significant deviation from the ideal sequence noted above occurred in cities which demonstrated both rapid and high rates of urban development in the nineteenth century. The most marked is the case of London which had reached a population of over 6 million by 1900, although, to a lesser extent, a similar situation occurred in the smaller British conurbations. In these circumstances, the pressure for urban growth could not be accommodated by the relatively inefficient, road-based public transport system, and railways, which had been introduced initially for inter-city transportation, became a much more active agent of urban growth. Thus, from 1860 to 1914 the London Underground system and suburban railway lines were basic formative influences; they allowed extensive suburbanization and the development of commuter settlements well beyond the city centre. Access to stations was critical as the railway became a much more important element in the intraurban transportation network. The process had considerable social consequences since the higher status groups were those financially most able to benefit from the pleasant environment of the suburbs, and social polarization between the inner city and the outer suburbs was initiated during this period.

A different situation is illustrated by Paris. In this case residential densities in the inner city were extremely high due to the constraining influence of a series of successive historical fortifications, features of a relict morphology which Paris had in common with many European cities (Figure 6.3). The fortifications formed the outer limits of Paris in 1900, by which time the city was virtually completely built-up and contained a population of nearly 3 million at residential densities approaching three times those of the equivalent area of London. This high density allowed urban growth to occur without the

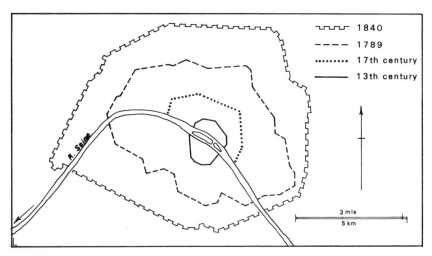

Figure 6.3   The walls of Paris: thirteenth to nineteenth centuries

necessity for an intraurban railway system. However, the growth of traffic congestions associated within the highly centralized urban structure in the last quarter of the nineteenth century provided the stimulus for the urgent construction of the *Métro* in the years after 1900. In contrast to the London underground and suburban railways, the Paris *Métro* did not direct suburban growth but was designed to integrate the existing component parts of the inner city and remains largely confined to that area to the present day (Figure 6.4). As such it has the form of a 'modern' inner city rapid transit system and the subsequent process of suburbanization in Paris is largely related to the basic radial road system.

With the growth of the Paris agglomeration to a population of 8.5 million by 1962 (Hall, 1966) and the expectation that urban growth was likely to continue into the forseeable future, the anticipated developmental pressures have necessitated a drastic re-evaluation of the transport network in recent years. Thus, in 1961 the government approved the development of a new regional *Métro* system to provide a rapid suburban rail service for the whole agglomeration (RER—*Réseau Express Régional*) (Tuppen, 1980). This was designed to complement, and to be integrated with, the inner city *Métro* and it will be largely completed by the mid-1980s (Figure 6.4). Similarly, the subsequent urban planning strategies for the Paris agglomeration, dating back to the *Schéma Directeur d'Aménagement et d'Urbanisme de la Région de Paris* of 1965, have initiated the improvement of the radial road system, the development of circumferential routes starting with the inner ring *Boulevard Périphérique* along the line of the outermost fortification, and the development of east–west routes both north and south of the Seine along the lines of the preferred axes of urban development (Thompson, 1973). Thus, despite the initial 'deviation' of the Parisian transport network evolution due to its high

184

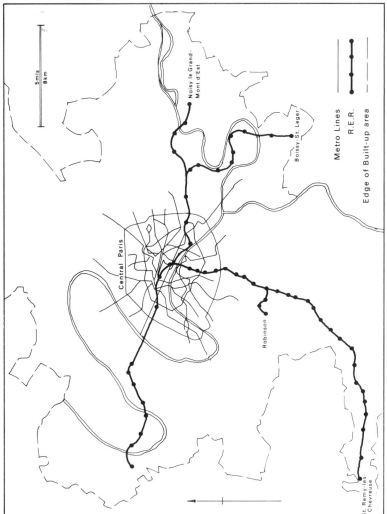

Figure 6.4 The Parisian metro system and the RER lines, 1980

185

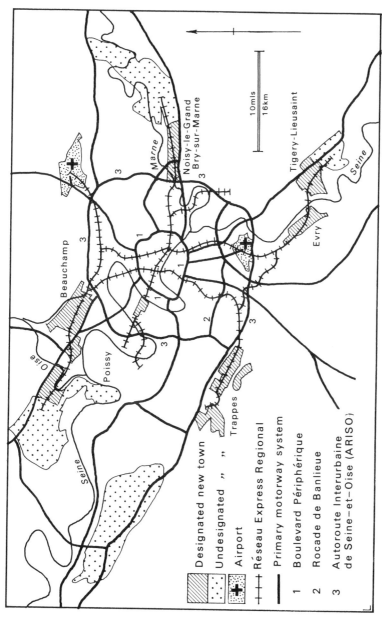

Figure 6.5 Transport systems and new town developments in Paris; reproduced from Thompson, 1973, by permission of Oxford University Press

density urban development, recent modifications have brought it closer to the suggested western model (Figure 6.5).

Developing world cities: centralized systems

Other variants on the general sequence of transport network evolution are characteristic of the rapidly growing metropolitan centres of the third world. Urban growth here is more closely related to the 'population explosion', and to strong rural–urban migration flows. Individual cities such as Calcutta with a population of 7.5 million by 1970, Mexico City with nearly 7 million in 1970 and Lagos with an estimated 1.7 million in 1972 experienced very rapid population growth and as the number of million-cities in the world almost doubled from 109 to 191 (1960–1975), nearly all those newly designated were in the third world (United Nations, 1974).

In most of these cities, where poverty is endemic, there is a lack of finance to develop adequate public controls over the structure and quality of the urban environment. High density and low quality residential developments predominate and are served by rudimentary improvements and extensions to the early radial road network. Public transport normally consists of an inadequate bus or tram system, largely confined to the radial routes which are frequently the only roads sufficiently wide for this purpose; traffic congestion of pedestrians and vehicles is usually considerable. The resulting urban structure tends to be highly centralized and inefficient, while the possibility of developing a more sophisticated transport system based on radically improved roads and railways is usually far too costly to be contemplated in anything other than a partial and piecemeal manner (Figure 6.6(a)). Such a situation has been described for Calcutta, where in 1971 the city was served by just one bridge, only 6 per cent of the land area was devoted to transport compared with 13–20 per cent in western cities, and there were as few as 500 serviceable buses (Thomson, 1977a).

Western cities: decentralized systems

A radically different transport network evolves in situations typified by the development of high levels of private-car ownership. This has been particularly widespread in more recently urbanized parts of the United States, Canada and Australia, and is epitomized by the case of Los Angeles where a metropolis of 10 million people had developed by 1970, almost entirely within the era of mass car ownerships. The combined influence of high levels of personal mobility, affluence, and the absence of significant space constraints on urban growth, encouraged low-density suburbanization. This in turn had a fundamental influence upon the functional structure of the urban system and the closely associated transport network. The dispersed population and high levels of personal mobility have positively encouraged the decentralization of employment and service activities throughout the urban system on a scale much larger than that experienced in cities more reliant upon public transportation. At the

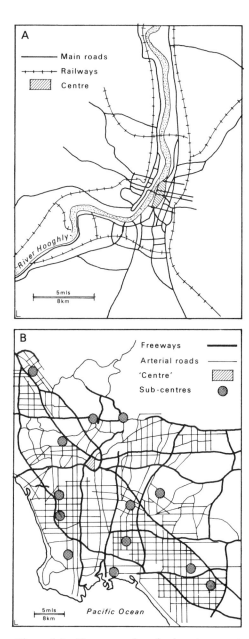

Figure 6.6 Two examples of urban transport systems: (a) The centralized system of Calcutta. (b) The decentralized system of Los Angeles

same time, the cost of providing unrestricted car access to the traditional central business districts has acted as a significant constraint upon the development of a strongly centralized urban structure. In fact, it has been suggested that whatever the scale of a metropolitan area the largest central business district can provide for a maximum of only 150,000–180,000 car commuters, and even then significant peak-hour traffic congestion is likely to result (Thomson, 1977a).

Thus, the initial centre of Los Angeles has not dominated the intraurban system of central places and a number of alternative functional nodes have emerged. This is reflected in a transport network in which the radial component of the road system centred on Los Angeles is only very weakly developed (Figure 6.6(b)). Instead, by the early 1940s the demands of a highly motorized society had necessitated the extensive development of urban motorways or freeways with their characteristic grade-separated intersections at potential points of congestion (cloverleafs). These were supplemented by the construction of a rectilinear grid system of secondary arterial roads designed to incorporate the expanding suburbs into the loosely knit urban structure. In such a system, the influence of public transport has been minimal with buses accounting for only 2 per cent of all motorized trips and 23 per cent of those to the Los Angeles downtown area (Thomson, 1977a).

Thus, urban development in the motor age is characterized by the archetypical 'suburban city' of Los Angeles. Whereas these features are particularly well marked in cities of the western United States developed in the postwar period, such as Denver and Salt Lake City, they have increasingly been superimposed upon the urban fabric of cities originally developed in earlier technological conditions.

THE URBAN TRANSPORTATION PROBLEM

Transportation problems are virtually universal facets of urban growth whatever the detailed characteristics of the transport system in specific areas. They take the form of the peak-hour congestion of public and private transport particularly in city centres and at other nodal points on the transport network; parking difficulties; adverse environmental impacts; and pedestrian and vehicular accidents. Thomson (1977a) has presented evidence from many parts of the world to suggest that road traffic congestion in city centres tends to result in a steady decline of traffic speeds over time to a common low of approximately 16 km per hour, irrespective of the size of the city, the sophistication of its transport system or levels of car ownership. At this point, motorists tend either to avoid the city centre or to transfer to other modes of transport. This situation reflects the fact that the growth of traffic demand, whether it be for public or private transport in a developed or developing world context tends to be faster than the development of either public controls or of the finance necessary to provide an efficiently functioning system.

More specifically, the number of vehicles, both public transport and private cars, can respond rapidly to the growth in demand in the absence of public controls on levels of vehicle ownership typical of most countries, and this process has been aided by the vigorous development of a car-manufacturing industry. In contrast, the provision of a system capable of accommodating the increasing traffic levels requires, in the long term, comprehensive planning and control and high levels of investment in the transport infrastructure. The

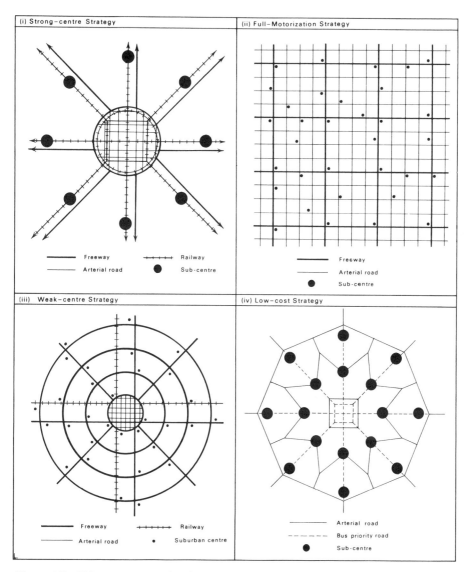

Figure 6.7 Urban transport planning strategies: (i) strong centre, (ii) full motorization, (iii) weak centre, (iv) low cost (after Thomson, 1977a). Reproduced by permission of J. M. Thomson

potential scale of this imbalance is illustrated by the fact that in the United Kingdom in 1961 investment in motor vehicles by business and private consumers reached a level of £900 million, while public authority investment in roads and lighting together reached only £100 million (HMSO, 1964).

More recently, Thomson (1977a) has stressed the economic basis of the transportation problem and the central significance of the role of 'pricing deficiences'. The essence of his argument is that the greater part of the cost of supplying transport facilities has, with the partial exception of public transport, not been directly borne by the consumer. In particular, the provision of adequate roads, parking spaces, and the minimization of environmental nuisances have traditionally been perceived as publicly provided facilities, serving the community at large rather than specific groups of transport users. Thus, the system has been funded from the general pool of central and local government expenditure, in which transport has to compete with the financing of the whole range of additional public service facilities, usually from an inadequate overall budget. As a result, insufficient investment in the transport infrastructure of cities tends to occur due to the failure to apply strict economic principles to the development and management of urban transport over a long period of time.

In these circumstances, Thomson (1977a) identifies four main strategies, each designed to improve a particular type of transport network (Figure 6.7) However, it is unlikely that any one of these strategies will provide a comprehensive solution to urban transport problems due to the complexities associated with the evolution of the transport network, although as 'ideal types' they have considerable conceptual merit. Four strategies—strong-centre, full-motorization, weak-centre, and low-cost—are considered below.

Strong-centre strategy

This strategy is seen as most appropriate to cities which developed as large-scale, highly centralized concentrations in association with public transport prior to the expansion of private transport facilities. The aim is to maintain the economic advantages of centralization, while minimizing the diseconomies of central city traffic congestion in the motor age. The main feature is the provision of an efficient public transport system to connect both the suburbs with the inner city and the component parts of the city centre with each other. At the same time, decentralization of functions is encouraged to sub-centres adequately integrated with both the public transport and road systems in order to reduce the development pressures on the centre and to spread traffic loads more evenly throughout the system.

Full-motorization strategy

At the other extreme, cities developed in the period of mass car ownership will tend to have a decentralized structure organized around urban motorway systems. Such cities tend to lack a traditional city centre and its associated problems of traffic congestion except at key nodal intersections on the network. The extension of such a system involves the continued development of urban freeways and arterial roads in association with the development of intermittent suburban centres. The principal problems resulting from this strategy are the considerable cost of the road network, the environmental impact, and the relatively long distances between the various functional nodes in the system.

Weak-centre strategy

In cities in which a significant amount of development occurred prior to 1900, followed by a subsequent decentralization phase, elements of both a centralized and decentralized urban structure respectively characterize the inner city and the outer suburbs. Ideally, such cities have the commercial and social advantages of a city centre without undue congestion, while movement by car throughout the suburbs presents few problems. To maintain this structure a strategy comprising an integrated system of radial and circumferential roads supplemented by commuter rail services is considered necessary. However, as Thomson (1977a) suggests, this strategy is inherently unstable because of the practical difficulty of maintaining a balance between the conflicting forces of centralization and decentralization to which the system is likely to be subject. If such a balance is not achieved, either a centralized system without the necessary public transport infrastructure, or a decentralized system without the necessary highway infrastructure, is likely to result.

Low-cost strategy

In the cities of the Third World the provision of costly road and public transport systems to alleviate problems of congestion are usually not financially possible. In these circumstances, low-cost 'management' strategies are the only feasible alternatives. These are likely to involve the improvement of the basic radial roads in conjuction with an improved public transport system, while at the same time encouraging a significant decentralization of urban functions from the congested city centres to a considerable number of peripheral nodal locations.

PUBLIC TRANSPORT VERSUS PRIVATE TRANSPORT

It is interesting to note that whatever the transport planning strategy adopted in a city, the steadily continuing growth in levels of private car ownership in most societies in relation to alternative modes of public transport has tended to confound solutions to the urban transportation problem. In particular, increasing road traffic levels have created pressures for more highways and this has tended to increase costs and create environmental problems.

This situation can be related to a number of factors. Of primary significance are the economic problems associated with the operation of public transport facilities. Public transport systems are usually designed to cope with peak-hour journeys to and from workplaces. In the interim periods considerable investment in capital equipment and labour is underutilized and involves costs which have to be covered by a combination of relatively high fares and cuts in offpeak services. Usually, these measures have a detrimental effect on demand, which further compounds the financial problem and frequently leads to a decline in the quality and financial viability of the services offered. In fact, a survey of urban public transport services (Thomson, 1977a) indicates their almost universal *inability* to meet costs, even though there are now few cities where public transport is not heavily subsidized. Already, the quality of public transport facilities in a city tends to reflect its degree of subsidization and it can be argued that for the purposes of transport planning it would be better to regard public transport as a publicly provided rather than a commercial service.

In contrast, apart from peak-hour journeys to city centres, particularly in the larger highly centralized cities (Table 6.1) the private car is usually a more flexible and convenient mode of transport. Also, it is often perceived as less costly since the marginal cost of a specific car journey is usually compared with the public transport fare. Thus, levels of private car

Table 6.1   Percentage of city-centre workers arriving by car

City	Number of jobs in city centre (thousands)	Percentage of car commuters	Number of car commuters (thousands)
New York (1970)	2000	7	140
Tokyo (1973)	1259	6	80 (1965)
London (1973)	1200	10.5	127
Paris (1970)	1151	19	220
Chicago (1968)	547	16.5	90
San Francisco (1965)	283	65	184
Boston (1963)	257	40	103
Toronto (1967)	231	37	85
Hamburg (1969)	230	28	64
Sydney (1966)	230	13	30
Bogota (1969)	172	11	19
Melbourne (1968)	160	31 (1964)	50
Los Angeles (1970)	157	63	99
Manchester (1965)	152	22	34
Copenhagen (1971)	150	25 (1962)	n.a.
Vienna (1971)	135	16	22
Athens (1963)	125	27	34
Stockholm (1968)	120	29	35
Brisbane (1968)	90	34	31
Detroit (1970)	80	57	40

Source: Thomson, J.M. (1977a), p. 35

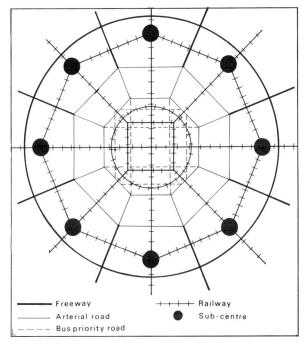

Figure 6.8 A traffic limitation strategy (after Thomson, 1977a). Reproduced by permission of J. M. Thomson

ownership have continued to increase and with them pressures for highway solutions to urban transport problems.

However, since the early 1970s a fuller realization of the economic and environmental impact of the unrestricted use of the car in cities has led to a widespread re-evaluation of the situation. Conceptually, this has resulted in increasing emphasis being given to *traffic-limitation strategies* rather than the former *car-accommodation solutions* (Figure 6.8). In centralized systems this involves the decentralization of activities to nodal locations in the suburbs, while in decentralized systems a greater degree of concentration of functions in the central city and a limited number of suburban locations is considered appropriate. In either situation, the siting of urban activities is undertaken with a view to encouraging the use of public transport, and at the same time cars are actively discouraged from situations which would give rise to heavy social costs.

As yet, no such scheme has been introduced on a scale sufficiently comprehensive to solve the urban transportation problems of a specific city. Nevertheless, examples abound of the reaction against highway dominated transport planning. For example, the heavy concentration on the provision of urban motorways in the Greater London Development Plan of 1969 (GLC, 1970) was strongly contested on financial and amenity grounds at the public enquiry of 1971–73 with the result that the proposals for Ringways 2 and 3 were rejected (Thomson, 1977b). Similarly, in San Francisco as early as 1959 the anti-highway lobby was an important element in support of the development of the Bay Area Rapid Transit System (BART), designed to avoid the financial and environmental costs of urban motorways and at the same time to maintain the advantages of a recognizable 'metropolitan centre' in a rapidly decentralizing urban structure (Open University, 1975). In the longer term it still seems likely that public transit systems must have important roles, in the shorter-term increasingly Draconian measures of traffic control are necessary to maintain a reasonable quality of life in the inner city.

MANUFACTURING AREAS IN CITIES

Manufacturing activities in cities normally comprise approximately 10 per cent of all land uses and around 33 per cent of the cities' workforce (Yeates and Garner, 1971). Consequently, manufacturing *areas* form an important element of the urban fabric and generate significant travel interaction patterns in the city. An understanding of the factors determining the distribution of the manufacturing concentrations and the characteristic activities contained within them forms an important contribution to an understanding of the spatial structure of the city. Analyses of the distribution of urban manufacturing stress the significance of a broad historical perspective on the process of urban industrial development as a basis for explaining detailed locational characteristics. This approach will be adopted here.

In the early phase of the Industrial Revolution in Britain the increasing scale of industrial establishments and the associated use of bulky raw materials and fuels asserted the locational advantages of, initially, a river transport and, later, a canal site, outside the already congested preindustrial city limits (A1 in Figure 6.9). In such locations relatively large amounts of cheap land were available which offered the considerable advantages of easy assembly of raw materials and distribution of manufactured products as well as easy access to water both for use in the production processes and for effluent disposal. This initiated the development of *linear* concentrations of industrial employment along main river valleys. The significance of these was further accentuated by the subsequent development of the railways since the early inter-city lines frequently followed the river valley and canal links. In some cases a degree of local decentralization of industries similar to those of the principal concentrations occurred, attracted by the site advantages of tributary valleys (A2 in Figure 6.9). The Lea valley in London and the Leen valley of Nottingham are both cases in point. Inner city industrial concentrations such as these are a particularly well-marked feature of the distribution of manufacturing in most major British cities, such as Manchester (Lloyd and Mason, 1978) and Clydeside (Bull, 1978), and they continue to be important, if problematic, elements of the urban industrial structure as their industries have become increasingly obsolete in recent years. In most cases they have also been responsible

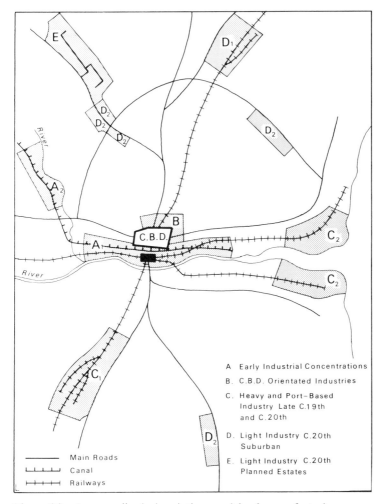

Figure 6.9 A generalized descriptive model of manufacturing areas in cities

for the creation of unattractive industrial environments over extensive parts of most inner cities and in exceptional cases, such as the lower Swansea valley, for major contemporary problems of industrial dereliction (Humphrys and Bromley, 1979).

Contemporaneous with the early period of industrialization, as the rudimentary administrative and marketing functions of the preindustrial city centres gradually grew, particularly in the largest cities, they accumulated the whole array of central business functions to serve expanding functional hinterlands. The particular locational advantages associated with a site near to the city centre initiated the development of a second concentration of manufacturing activities. Such concentrations are typically diverse in character, reflecting the operation of a great variety of often unique localization influences (B in Figure 6.9). For example, some industries reflect the availability of skills and organizations associated with the preindustrial craft industries, such as the gun and jewellery quarters of central Birmingham. Other activities have developed primarily to serve the central business district functions. In this respect, the early development of employment opportunities in wholesaling and warehousing were important and, more recently, the development of business machine servicing, while newspaper offices have often attracted printing and publishing to city centre sites. In addition, the availability of cheap, usually immigrant or itinerant, labour concentrated in the low-status 'transition zones' which developed around the expanding city centre in the early industrial period encouraged the development of small-scale manufacturing in most cities. The development of the garment trade in the lower-status districts of the central city of New York, London and Paris are all well-known examples (Murphy, 1972). More recently, the availability of small premises associated with the changing functional character of these districts over time has provided early bases for the development of new firms in such activities as electronics and other small-scale light manufacturing.

However, towards the end of the nineteenth century the combined effects of a number of technological advances associated with industrial development began fundamentally to change the locational advantages of urban sites. Of prime significance was the widespread development of larger-scale industrial units which rendered many of the early centralized sites obsolete. At the same time the expansion and improvement of rail transport in urban areas, the development of motor transport from the early years of the twentieth century, the increasing use of electrical power in industrial production and the widespread introduction of public transport all served to encourage the process of industrial decentralization.

The influence of these forces initiated two divergent locational trends. For the largest-scale *heavy and port-based* industries the importance of site constraints was fundamental (Figure 6.9). Heavy industry tended to gravitate to large railway-based sites on the peripheries of cities, the detailed location of which was frequently related to the potential availability of water supplies or considerations of environmental pollution (C1 in Figure 6.9). Alternatively, with the use of increasingly large oceangoing vessels the largest-scale port-based industries usually moved downriver from the waterfront sites to large estuarine or reclaimed coastal locations (C2 in Figure 6.9). In Britain, the decline of the London docks and the industrial development of the Thames estuary is clearly indicative of this trend (J. M. Hall, 1976), as is the development of a heavy industrial and chemical industry complex on Teesside, while the postwar development of Europoort, Rotterdam is a spectacular example of the same process (Pinder, 1978).

In contrast, most of the newly developing light industries gravitated to the less congested and environmentally more attractive sites located throughout the suburban peripheries. Initially, such developments tended to be restricted to railway sites, particularly in the United States where the railway companies frequently prepared and sold the land along with branch-line access (D1 in Figure 6.9) (Yeates and Garner, 1971). However, with the expansion of motor transport the additional flexibility offered to both industry and employees allowed a greater degree of dispersal to occur along main radial routeways and at particularly nodal locations on the highway network (D2 in Figure 6.9) (Wood, 1974). Nevertheless, the process of dispersal was not entirely unconstrained since, initially, the need for communications access and public utility services promoted a degree of centralization within the suburbs. Subsequently, to offset the environmental disadvantages of uncoordinated and unconstrained dispersal, the planning of industrial estates by public authorities in Britain and the zoning of land for industrial parks in the United States has had a similar effect.

Clearly, the location of manufacturing activities in the city has been subject to a considerable number of influences during the period of industrial development. Amongst these the contemporary importance of historical inertia is fundamental, while in most cities manufacturing industries have been responsible for the development of a multinuclear element in the urban fabric. Figure 6.9 is offered as a descriptive generalization of some of the industrial type-areas which recur in the western city. Other similar typologies are included in the work of Loewenstein (1963), Pred (1964), Hamilton (1967), and Wood (1974) and might be referred to for purposes of comparison.

However, significant deviations from the general pattern can be anticipated. For example, in cities which are largely products of the twentieth century the inner-city elements of the model are likely to be only weakly developed. In other cities a single mode of transport might dominate the industrial pattern. The influence of the railway system in Winnipeg is a case in point. Similarly, whether the industrial structure is dominated by heavy or light manufacturing is likely to have a markedly variable effect. The considerable difference between the textile towns of the East Midlands and the heavy industry centres of the North-East of England is illustrative of this point.

URBAN SERVICES

The physical expansion and increasing functional complexity of urban life in western cities in the twentieth century has resulted in a proliferation of the quantity and variety of services needed by the urban population. The resulting range of services is provided by a variety of commercial and governmental agencies so that their spatial distributions, associated functional characteristics and patterns of usage also vary significantly. Nevertheless, five centrally distinct but overlapping categories can be suggested for preliminary analysis.

Shopping activity

Numerically, the most important are the services normally associated with the shopping activity (Thomas, 1976). These comprise retail outlets; personal services such as hairdressers, dry cleaners and photographers; professional services such as banks, estate agents and solicitors; and a range of catering and entertainment facilities. Their unity derives from the fact that they are provided usually for individual customers drawn from a relatively local urban hinterland. Also, their locational patterns have resulted from the competitive decisions taken by a large number of small suppliers in an attempt to maximize the commercial advantages of accessibility in relation to the perceived distribution of consumer demand. However, in recent years the emergence of large supply organizations and the strengthening of physical planning controls have tended to complicate the latter situation significantly (Dawson, 1980).

Wholesaling and warehousing

The wholesaling function and associated warehousing activities comprise a second category which has traditionally had close functional and geographical associations with shopping. The essence of the wholesaling activity is that it sets out to serve such functions as retailing, consumer services, office activities, public utilities and industry by providing them with goods which are subsequently sold to the public, consumed by the recipient organization or used to produce a profit. The emphasis is, therefore, on the distribution function. The service is performed mainly for users who are companies and institutions of varying sizes rather than individuals. Also, in many cases the customer does not visit the point of scale. For these reasons the wholesaling function tends to be found in a greater variety of locations than are shopping centres, the locations of which are far less stringently controlled by the need for direct customer access.

Offices

Offices concerned with transactional and administrative activities associated with the collection, processing and exchange of information can be considered to comprise a third category of services. Notable amongst these are the international, national and regional headquarters of organizations involved in finance, insurance, commerce, industry and government. The 'consumers' of the services in this instance are the business organizations and administrative institutions involved in all sections of economic, social and political life rather than individual customers. Thus, the locational patterns of offices tend to demonstrate a greater degree of concentration in larger centres at both the national and intraurban scale than in the case of shopping centres. Traditionally this has been considered to reflect the stronger forces of centralization associated with the need to maintain close communication linkages between the different office functions and maximum access to a highly diversified labour market.

Medical services

A fourth category of medical services comprising general practitioners and hospitals can be suggested. These services are closely connected functionally and are significantly different from the previous groups since they are subject to a significantly stronger degree of public control. The locational decisions of general practitioners are restricted usually by a combination of professional or governmental licensing controls. In the case of hospitals, the individual units tend to be larger, relative to the scale of the system as a whole and, therefore, less responsive to changes in the nature and location of user demand, while in some countries their location policies have been subject to a greater degree of public control than shopping facilities.

Public utilities

The fifth category comprises public utilities such as local government administrative offices, schools, public libraries, recreational centres and the police and fire services. Their location policies are already subject to near-complete public control in many countries and have little dependence upon a competitive market mechanism.

In summary, it is clear that while the five categories of activities outlined above have been introduced under the general heading of 'urban services', this title subsumes considerable variability. Thus, it must be stressed at the outset that due to the differences in the nature of, and controls over, the specific categories of services, both the locational decisions—which determine their spatial patterns—and the associated user decisions—which relate to their use—exhibit considerable variation in detail both between and within the categories suggested.

THE CITY CENTRE

In the early stages of city development rudimentary versions of most of the urban services noted above emerged near to the city centre in order to serve the relatively compact urban area. With continued urban growth there was a concomitant growth in the scale, degree of specialization and range of services provided. In the context of the growing city the particular locational requirements of the various services tended to result in the emergence of a spatial segregation by function, initially in relation to an expanded central area, and subsequently throughout an extended urban area associated with the forces of decentralization accompanying suburban expansion. However, most central areas continue to contain concentrations of urban service activities, partly because the accessibility of the central area allows it to provide services performing a citywide or wider regional function, and partly because the forces of inertia have maintained elements of the original pattern. Thus, the city centre remains as a primary focus of many urban service facilities, around which the subsequently developed intraurban service systems are arranged. For this reason it will be instructive to consider the distribution of urban services in the city centre as a first stage in the development of an understanding of the spatial patterns of service facilities in the city.

THE CENTRAL BUSINESS DISTRICT (CBD)

Much of the early urban geographical interest in the city centre focused on the central business district (CBD). Initially, it was not defined in a specific manner but was recognized as a somewhat indefinite region of the city which nevertheless had certain distinctive characteristics. It was seen as the functional core of the city towards which the urban activities which required an accessible location for their economic viability or functional efficiency tended to gravitate. Typically, it comprised concentrations of retailing and associated consumer services, commercial and public office activities, wholesaling and warehousing and an array of entertainment functions such as theatres, hotels and cultural activities. It was suggested that these concentrations were arranged around the point of maximum accessibility to the surrounding hinterland and this usually coincided with the focus of the intracity transportation network. The concentrations of functions normally generated the highest vehicular and pedestrian traffic flows in the city and the highest density of daytime population. Competition for land to exploit the commercial advantages of accessibility produced the city's highest land values per unit area. Consequently, land use in this area was the most intensive in the city and this was reflected in the highest concentration of multistorey buildings.

However, it was also recognized that the CBD tended to give way rapidly to a transitional area. This was characterized by a combination of deteriorating low-status residences, reflecting the effects of ageing and the encroachment of marginal CBD functions. Typically, the latter included shops and services catering for the poorest elements of the inner city community; or wholesale and warehousing, car salesrooms, car parking and transportation termini which required reasonably central locations but could not compete for prime CBD sites. In addition, the low value of property in this area near to a supply of unskilled labour usually encouraged the development of small-scale workshop industries. The characteristics of this area were related to the fact that citywide accessibility declines dramatically with distance from the city centre, so that the commercial value of land tends to decline in a similar manner.

CBD delimitation

Following these early generalizations attempts were made to derive more precise methods of delimitation to distinguish the CBD from the transitional area. A standardized method was considered necessary if findings relating to the form, internal structure and changing character of the CBD were to be available for comparative analysis. The early attempts, however, met with the obstacle of obtaining sufficiently comprehensive and rigorously comparative data. Proudfoot (1937) and Olsson (1940) derived indices based upon volumes of retail trade in a city block, shop rentals, and the length of shopping street frontage to define the centre of the CBD. However, these measures were confined to the shopping function, and faced with the practical problems of obtaining confidential shop rental data and volumes of retail trade at a sufficiently detailed scale of analysis, presented considerable problems for comparative analysis.

Subsequently, the seminal work of Murphy and Vance (1954) provides the most comprehensive attempt to derive an objective basis for CBD delimitation. They investigated the feasibility of a number of alternative indices. The area with the lowest permanent density of population was thought indicative of the CBD, or the highest density of shop and office employment. Alternatively, the CBD was considered likely to coincide with the highest concentration of pedestrian and vehicular traffic flows, or with the area with the highest land values per unit area. The value of any one of these criteria to define the CBD of a single city was recognized but each was rejected as a sound basis for comparative analysis for reasons such as the lack of sufficient data and the limited detail available. Thus, the conclusion was reached that a detailed land-use survey was necessary, specifically for the purpose of delimitation.

The land uses which were most highly concentrated around the peak land value intersection (PLVI) were considered most definitive of CBD status. These comprised retail and consumer services, including restaurants, entertainment facilities and hotels; and commercial office activities, but also including newspaper offices since these were considered to have a closer affinity to commercial than to manufacturing activities. Other land uses were designated non-central business since their central location was not considered to be related to the commercial advantages of centrality. Wholesaling, railyards, industry, residences, parks, schools, churches and government administration were excluded on these grounds, although it was recognized that some individual establishments in these categories gained an economic advantage from a central location. Specifically, some wholesaling and manufacturing activities which were closely linked with other central business functions were in this position. However, to retain a relatively straightforward procedure, subtle distinctions of this kind were not made.

Based upon the broad division between central business and non-central business uses, a detailed land use survey, recorded in terms of the floorspace of all floors by individual ownership lots, was made for nine American city centres. The data was aggregated by city blocks and two indices were calculated for each block. These formed the basis of delimitation:

1. Central Business Height Index (CBHI)

$$= \frac{\text{Total floorspace of all central business land uses in the block}}{\text{Total ground floorspace of the Block}}$$

Values of greater than 1 were considered potentially indicative of the CBD.

2. Central Business Intensity Index (CBII)

$$= \frac{\text{Total floorspace of all central business land uses in the block}}{\text{Total floorspace of all land uses in the block}} \times \frac{100}{1}$$

Values of greater than 50 per cent were considered potentially indicative of the CBD.

To qualify for CBD status, a block had to exceed both threshold values. This indicated that there was at least a whole floor equivalent of central business land uses included in the block and the central business land uses dominated the block. Also, such a block had to be contiguous to a group surrounding the Peak Land Value Intersection, although a further set of rules allowed the inclusion of certain exceptions. For example, a non-central business block which is surrounded by CBD blocks could be included or public administrative buildings adjacent to the CBD.

The technique is schematically illustrated by Figure 6.10. After defining the nine CBDs in this way and checking the results with a subjective field assessment, it was concluded that this method was sufficiently robust to form the basis for comparative analysis.

The technique has a number of inherent limitations, most of which were appreciated by the original investigators (Murphy, 1972). The most important concern the arbitrary decisions taken at a number of stages in the regionalization procedure. The distinction between central business and non-central business land uses was provided with a rationale but, in detail, the division could not be sustained. In fact, outside the American context even the broad division could be queried. For example, in Diamond's (1962) study of Glasgow, wholesaling was designated a central business land use since in Britain it has depended to a significant degree upon centrality for customer contacts. In contrast, in American cities the concentration of wholesaling activities has been more closely related to railways and major highways than to central city accessibility. Perhaps even more significantly, it could be argued that Murphy and Vance's emphasis on commercially orientated service functions introduced an artificial distinction into studies of the central city and diverted attention away from the investigation of the complex functional interrelationships which exist between the wider range of activities usually found there.

The choice of limiting values for the indices was also assessed subjectively. In fact, in a later study of Capetown, Davies (1959) considered the values too generous so that they included many functions which were not considered to epitomize CBD centrality and were, therefore, not strictly relevant for comparative analysis. Specifically, he considered that cinemas, hotels, office headquarters, newspaper offices, government offices, and low quality retail stores should be excluded. Instead, he advocated limiting values of 4 and 80 per cent for the two indices respectively to define the 'hard core' of the CBD to represent its essential commercial character.

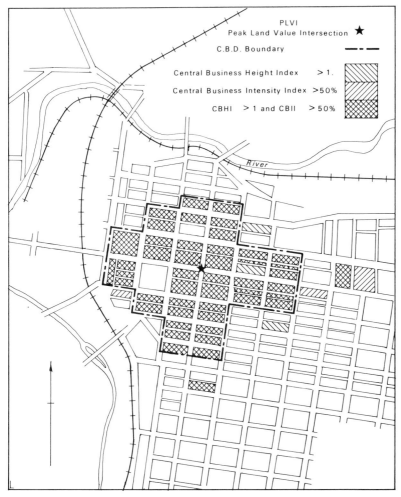

Figure 6.10 Delimiting the CBD—a conceptual representation (based on Murphy and Vance, 1954a)

Other arbitrary elements also influence the delimitation procedure. The typical block size and shape of a city can affect the precise location of the boundary. Similarly, the rules governing the status of exceptional blocks were subjectively derived, while the method is insufficiently refined to distinguish 'qualitative' variations which might have a bearing on the designation of the edge of the CBD. In retrospect, the aim of precise definition seems more an assertion of faith than a statement of fact.

The range of city-sizes for which the technique is appropriate is also limited to medium-sized cities (Murphy, 1972). The average population of the urbanized areas of the nine cities studied was 309,000 in 1960. Murphy states that the CBDs of cities of less than 100,000 are insufficiently large and distinctive for the indices to provide a meaningful basis for delimitation. Also, the method has not been used in very large cities, presumably due to the vast quantities of data necessary to apply it in its classical from. In fact, both Herbert (1972) and Carter (1972) have argued that even for medium-sized cities the technique requires too much effort to define a boundary which, at best, can only be an approximation, and by focusing attention unduly upon delimitation have diverted attention from the potentially more fruitful analysis of aspects of structure and changes within the CBD.

The pioneering work of Murphy and Vance (1954) did, however, achieve a number of significant results. The development of the CBI method drew attention to the need to define and investigate the variety of urban functions found in the city centre in a more precise manner. More specifically, the project introduced a degree of precision and comparability which was previously lacking, despite the limitations discussed. This provided additional insight into the size, shape and nature of the margins of the commercial base of the city centre.

Many subsequent studies of the CBD have used variants of the CBI method for initial definition, even though they are not primarily concerned with de-limitation in the ensuing analysis. For example, in their Cardiff study, Carter and Rowley (1966) required. . . . an efficient and general method whereby the CBD may be delimited objectively' (p. 119), though, in fact, the method used was highly subjective. The retailing of goods and services for profit were considered the essential CBD functions and a floorspace index ratio, analogous to the central business height index of Murphy and Vance, was used. This data was supplemented by maps illustrating gross rateable values per unit area and appraised land values. This information was considered to provide a sufficiently precise indication of the extent of the CBD and from this base the analysis of the urban regions of central Cardiff proceeded, although at no stage was the area precisely defined. Such a delineation was considered likely to impose an artificial constraint on the investigation of the 'central area complex'.

Although the original focus of attention of Murphy and Vance (1954) was upon delimitation, they also analysed the internal functional differentiation of the CBD.

CBD internal structure

Murphy, Vance, and Epstein (1955) considered that the spatial differentiation of business activities within the CBD was directly related to the relative *value* per unit area of sites, itself an indicator of accessibility. Thus, the extent to which an activity can profit from exploiting the advantages of accessibility will determine the price it is willing to pay—as suggested by the bid-rent model—and this will be reflected in the spatial arrangement of business activities. This contention was tested by establishing a pattern of four zones centred on the PLVI; each 90 m (100 yards) wide and of roughly concentric form but elongated along the main street to accommodate its high linear accessibility. The land use assemblage by zone for the eight CBDs was then examined and a generalized structure was suggested. Zone 1, adjacent to the PLVI was dominated by retail activities and typified by the concentration of the largest department stores and highest-status shopping activities; Zone 2 was most commonly characterized by retail services and financial activities at ground-floor level, with office activities dominating higher storeys. Here also was found the greatest concentration of multistorey buildings. Zone 3 also tended to be dominated by offices though hotels were also frequent and Zone 4 held concentrations of less commercially intensive activities such as furniture stores, automobile showrooms and supermarkets, all of which required relatively large amounts of cheap land.

However, to suggest that the internal structure of the CBD approximates to a simple concentric zonation would be to grossly overstate the case. Relative accessibility within the city centre is rarely a function merely of distance from the peak land value intersection. The morphological complexity associated with city centre development and the alteration of the process of growth by physical barriers such as canals, railways and public open space all act as modifying influences. Thus, at the outset it might be expected that relative accessibility within the city centre has strong *segregative* effects superimposed upon any tendency towards *concentric zonation*. This point is supported by Scott's (1959) study of the CBDs of the six Australian state capitals. As in the case of the American cities, the CBDs tended to be elongated in the direction of the main traffic axes and shaped by a number of barriers. In addition, Scott suggested that the internal structures were composed of three generalized but consistently recurring functional zones. These were the *inner retail* zone characterized by department stores and women's clothes shops, an *outer retail* zone which demonstrated a greater diversity of less specialized outlets such as household goods and consumer services, and a distinctive *office* zone. In each case the inner retail zone was centred upon the peak land value intersection and the geographical centre of the city. However, the outer retail zone did not always surround the first zone and the office zone frequently developed on one side of the CBD. Despite the apparent deviations from a simple geometric model of the internal structure of the CBD, Scott's study adds usefully to our understanding of CBD structure.

There are also spatial regularities within the CBD at more detailed scales of analysis. Murphy, Vance, and Epstein (1954) noted a tendency towards the clustering of *mutually dependent* elements. Department stores tended to cluster together; suppliers of stationary and office furniture were associated with concentrations of office activities; lawyers and real estate agents were grouped around courthouses; a whole array of low-status activities such as low-price theatres, pawnshops, cheap restaurants, and second-hand clothes shops competed for space at the margins of the CBD and benefited from spatial proximity to each other.

Early investigations suggested the existence of a broad concentricity of like retail types, reflecting general accessibility needs and associated land value surfaces. Garner (1966) and Scott's (1970) use of the concept of the bid-rent curve to explain a generalized spatial arrangement for the internal structure of retail nucleations, reflecting the hierarchical status of particular functions, is typical (Figure 6.11). Again it must be stressed that such a simplicity of structure is a gross overstatement of reality and there is considerable variation within the CBD reflecting both fabric effects and the detailed impacts of these upon accessibility.

This situation is perhaps not surprising when it is considered that relative accessibility, even at the *micro*-spatial scale of analysis, is not simply a function of distance from the city centre. Most retail nucleations have a linear structure, while the vagaries of the local land market and the historical process of development introduces further complexity into the spatial pattern of potential retail

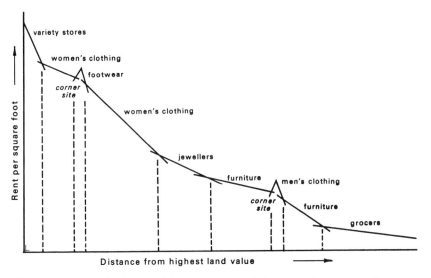

Figure 6.11 Hypothetical spatial arrangement of the internal structure of a major unplanned CBD shopping centre based upon the bid-rent curve. Source: Scott, 1970; reproduced by permission of P. Scott

sites. Again, the detailed locational decisions both of businesses and individuals are influenced by a number of principles which seem unlikely to result in a simple geometrical arrangement of shop types. The functions which serve the widest possible trade area are those most likely to be influenced by considerations of relative centrality (*trade area potential*). Functions which serve a more specific market, such as high-status or low-status groups, gravitate to sites which were particularly accessible to those subsections of the community (*growth potential*). Others serve the population working in the city centre (*business*

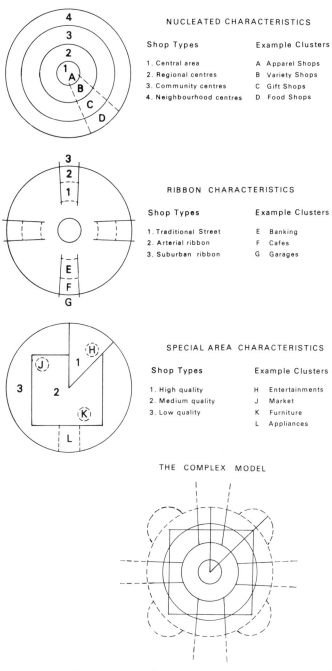

NUCLEATED CHARACTERISTICS

Shop Types	Example Clusters
1. Central area	A Apparel Shops
2. Regional centres	B Variety Shops
3. Community centres	C Gift Shops
4. Neighbourhood centres	D Food Shops

RIBBON CHARACTERISTICS

Shop Types	Example Clusters
1. Traditional Street	E Banking
2. Arterial ribbon	F Cafes
3. Suburban ribbon	G Garages

SPECIAL AREA CHARACTERISTICS

Shop Types	Example Clusters
1. High quality	H Entertainments
2. Medium quality	J Market
3. Low quality	K Furniture
	L Appliances

THE COMPLEX MODEL

Figure 6.12 A structural model of central area core retailing facilities. Source: Davies, 1972; reproduced by permission of the Institute of British Geographers

208

interception), or find locations which avoid direct competition (*minimization of competitive hazard*). In addition, a number of small specialized units might tend to cluster together to create their own centrality irrespective of their detailed location (*cumulative attraction*) (Nelson, 1958).

Despite the complexity of the real world, Davies (1972) has proposed a structural model for central area retailing facilities (Figure 6.12). This is based

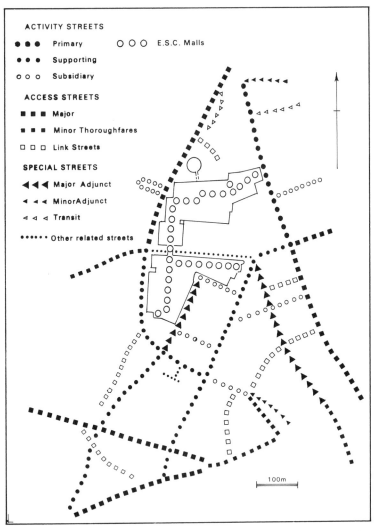

Figure 6.13   A classification of central area streets by type of activity in Newcastle-upon-Tyne's central area. Source: Davies, Bennison, 1978; reproduced by permission of KNAG

upon the assumption that the location decisions of retailers reflect three separate dimensions of accessibility rather than one. The traditional city centre shopping activities tend to locate in accordance with *general accessibility* to the distribution of consumers. These tend to be distributed in a concentric zonal pattern, reflecting their hierarchical status and associated potential profitability. Other functions, such as garages and cafés, were considered most likely to take advantage of the accessibility associated with major traffic arteries entering the city centre—*arterial accessibility*. Finally, the locations of some specialized functions, such as entertainment facilities, furniture showrooms or produce markets were considered likely to reflect the *special accessibility* attached to sites, related to particular historical circumstances or environmental conditions.

The resulting 'complex model' was found to provide a reasonable approximation of the retail structure of central Coventry and forms a useful contribution to an understanding of the underlying spatial order within shopping centres.

The search for a precise descriptive model of the micro-spatial characteristics of shopping centres is at an early stage and may well take too much account of market forces to the exclusion of others. Minimal account has been taken of the manner in which firms reach their locational decisions. This issue is taken up by Davies and Bennison (1978) who suggest that the legacy of past location decisions, recent planning constraints and the management policies imposed in newly constructed shopping malls make it unlikely that an economically optimal location decision will be possible. Instead, a range of satisficer criteria are used which are less likely to produce a simple spatial order. Thus, for practical planning purposes an intermediate scale level of analysis, focusing on the street unit rather than on individual shops, is more appropriate. Davies and Bennison applied this idea to the shopping centre of Newcastle-upon-Tyne and classified the streets according to the number and quality of the various shopping activities, patterns of consumer usage and consumer images of the different streets. The resulting categorization of the streets provides an interesting summary of the spatial structure of the shopping centre combining elements of both form and function (Figure 6.13).

CBD change over time

Interest in the CBD has not been confined entirely to delimitation and the analysis of static structures. Most of the early studies recognized the importance of dynamic changes affecting the CBD. Thus, the margins of the CBD, the location of the PVLI, and its internal functional differentiation all change over time and research has focused on the nature of these changes. Murphy, Vance, and Epstein (1955) noted a process of short-term spatial adjustment, by which the CBD was advancing in some directions, the zone of assimilation, and retreating in others, the zone of discard. The zone of assimilation was typically located in the direction of the higher status residential parts of the city and characterized by the development of new speciality shops, automobile show-rooms, office headquarters and new hotels. Conversely, the zone of discard was usually located adjacent to industrial and wholesaling activities, near the railroads and lower-status residential districts and became typified by con-centrations of pawnshops, cheap clothing stores, low-grade restaurants and transport termini. As a general process involving assimilation and discard at the margins of the CBD, this concept of change has found frequent empirical support.

Other studies have adopted a stronger historical perspective into the longer term processes of change. Ward (1966), for example, examined Boston's CBD in the context of a process of functional differentiation which was initiated in the early stages of the Industrial Revolution. In the first half of the nineteenth century an embryonic CBD emerged, associated with the early commercial growth of the city around the waterfront. The warehousing function was near the wharves, while trade in local produce was centred on the nearby market halls. Between these, State Street developed as a finance and insurance district to serve both, while the government administrative function had already moved to the less congested site adjacent to Boston Common since it did not require the centrality of the commercial functions (Figure 6.14). As available sites were limited near the emerging commercial centre, the railway terminals had to gravitate to a number of reclaimed sites to the north and south.

During the latter half of the nineteenth and early part of the twentieth centuries the central business functions of Boston expanded, but the CBD structure which emerged was fundamentally controlled by the location of the earlier functional nodes. The wholesale trade expanded southward from its earlier forms, attracted by proximity to the waterfront and the southern railway terminals. The wholesale food trade covered a much larger area just to the north but continued to be centred on the original market halls. The finance and insurance district had continued to expand, partly at the expense of the older parts of the wholesale district, while a link had also been forged with the distinct administrative district which had developed in association with the State House. In addition, a distinctive retail zone had emerged in the late nineteenth century centred on Tremont and Washington Streets. Prior to 1880 the volume of local trade for 'retail goods' had been satisfied largely by direct customer purchases from the produce markets, warehouses and small custom manufacturers established in the wholesaling district. However, the growth in the volume of such trade in the late nineteenth century resulted in many traders establishing premises specializing in direct selling to the public. These tended to gravitate to the relatively attractive area adjacent to Boston Common and the nearby high-status residential markets of Beacon Hill and Back Bay. The area also possessed the advantage of accessibility to the growing urban population to the south, while maintaining close links with the wholesale

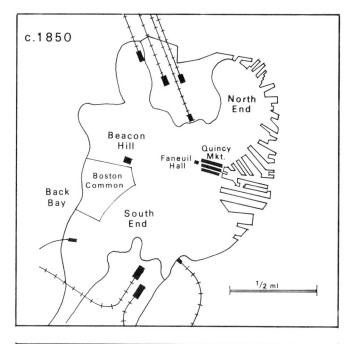

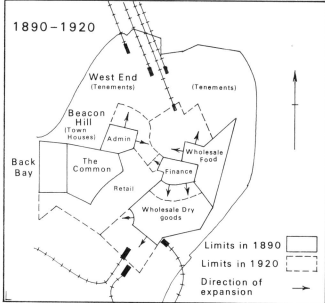

Figure 6.14 The historical development of Boston's CBD, 1850–1920. After: Ward, 1966; reproduced by permission of *Economic Geography*

district directly to the east. Thus, the attractions of this area for the emerging retail zone were strong, although the detailed form of the zone was clearly constrained by the earlier functional nodes and the barrier formed by Boston Common. The remaining part of the central area to the North and West Ends of the peninsula consisted of low-lying inaccessible land adjacent to a series of railway terminals. The lack of attraction of these areas for commercial activities or high-status residential development resulted in the development of concentrations of a mixture of small-scale industry and low-status immigrant housing. These broad functional zones continue to characterize the contemporary CBD of Boston.

Clearly, Ward's (1966) historical analysis provides the basis for an explanation for the distinct segregative tendencies which were previously noted to characterize the internal structure of CBDs. Particular functions were shown to gravitate to locations which offered some advantage for their successful operation, while the constraining influences of physical site conditions and early human geographical land-use features merely served to accentuate the segregative tendencies. Similar conclusions can be reached from an examination of Carter and Rowley's (1966) analysis of the evolution of the internal structure of the CBD of Cardiff.

Bowden (1971) investigated the CBD of San Francisco at three points in time (1850, 1906, and 1931), using evidence obtained from trade directories, photographs, newspapers and fire insurance maps, and provides a link between analyses of short and long-term change. The functional composition of the CBD is compared for the three dates and a number of influences relating to the process of change are made. Functions which were most closely related to market accessibility were those which were most likely to shift their locations in response to the changing location of their market population or to a change in the relative accessibility within the CBD. For example, clothing retailers tended to shift towards the growing higher-status parts of the town and hotels towards centres of entertainment and focal points in the transport network. Conversely, the financial district did not move significantly since its orientation to direct consumer access was slight. With these generalizations in mind Bowden suggests that three types of change influence the spatial structure of the CBD over time.

In a situation of slow population growth, change is likely to occur by *peripheral accretion*, by the addition of newly formed functional zones or the marginal expansion of established functional zones. The second type of change is the *burst* in which the CBD expands rapidly in a very short time in response to a rapid phase of urban growth. During such a phase advance tends to take place throughout the zone of assimilation and a typical sequence of functional change is suggested. Characteristically, this starts in the financial district, spreads to the clothing district which is capable of displacing most other land uses other than financial activities, and a tertiary effect may be associated with the shift of the hotel district to maintain an attractive location. The remaining CBD functions adjust to these primary changes in a sequence of reactions until a new equilibrium is achieved.

A third type of change designated *separation* occurs if a substantial rate of urban growth is sustained over a long period of time. In such a situation each major function will gravitate to areas within the central city which possess some specific advantage for its mode of operations. Market accessibility-orientated functions such as retailing may follow the changing distribution of a growing consumer market. This process leaves behind the commercial and public administrative office functions and wholesaling activities in their original locations giving greater spatial segregation of the various functional zones and an initially fragmented structure which will only regain its coherence slowly over time. In very large cities, fragmentary structure may remain as a permanent feature of the CBD as, for example, London. By the late nineteenth century the focus of retail activity had moved six times to its present centre, 4.8 km (3 miles) west of its original site. Similarly, in New York, the centre of retailing has moved from its early focus adjacent to the Lower Manhattan financial district to its present position in midtown Manhattan 6.4 km (4 miles) to the north.

A conceptual model of the CBD

Studies of the internal structure of the CBD and its changes over time have provided useful descriptive and explanatory insights into its characteristics. No comprehensive generalized structural or evolutionary model has yet been suggested as an aid to preliminary analysis, despite the fact that there is evidence to suggest recurrent patterns and a tendency for like functions to *segregate* into particular areas of the central city. Based upon an overview of this evidence a simplified conceptual model of the CBD is suggested (Figure 6.15). This comprises the specialist retail Zone I which gravitates to the most accessible location in order to serve the widest possible urban hinterland with the highest order goods and services. Here are found the concentration of department stores and large chain-stores, usually orientated along the traditional high street site. Associated with this, but usually recognizable as a distinctive unit, is a secondary retail Zone II where the less specialized durable goods and convenience goods traders concentrate. These tend to provide the lower-order goods for the more immediate inner city population rather than serving a regional function. Frequently, this zone is to be found to one side of the central retail concentration, although in some instances it will be represented in a more fragmentary form surrounding Zone I. Also found in a relatively central site is a distinct commercial office district—Zone III—often dominated by financial and insurance functions. Its central location can usually be historically related to the need for accessibility to the most diversified regional labour market, while over time it usually consolidates its position in the more environmentally attractive parts of the central city. Often associated with the retail

214

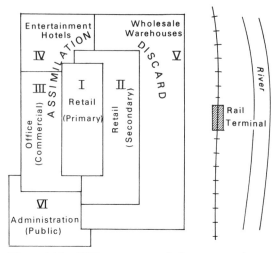

Figure 6.15   CBD structure and change over time:
a conceptual model

and office districts a distinct concentration of entertainment facilities and hotels will emerge as Zone IV, since they tend to rely to a significant extent on trade generated by proximity to these functions. In contrast, the wholesale and warehousing Zone V will usually be found in the less environmentally attractive parts of the city centre. This reflects the early gravitation of these functions to the transportation termini associated with coastal, river or canal wharves and railway yards, and the subsequent development of small-scale light manu-facturing activities in such areas. A concentration of public administrative offices—Zone VI—is also frequently found on the edge of the CBD. Often this is historically related to the location of the initial Town Hall dating back to the early stages of urban growth. Its increasingly peripheral location tends to reflect the fact that while such functions need reasonable access to the general public, they are not market-orientated and cannot usually compete with commercial activities for more central sites. In addition, the characteristic features of assimilation and discard can often be recognized in the kinds of areas predicted by Murphy, Vance, and Epstein (1955).

However, it must be stressed that this generalized model of the CBD re-presents a conceptualization of the potential relative locational characteristics of the kinds of functional zones typically found in medium-sized cities rather than a rigid geometrical expectation. Clearly, the details of the structure of the CBD of a city will reflect the peculiarities of its physical and human geo-graphical bases. Thus, while all the hypothesized zones may be present, they may be far more fragmented than is suggested here, or have a variable spatial relationship to each other. Similarly, it is anticipated that the degree of dis-tinctiveness of the various functional zones, will vary significantly between cities of different sizes. For example, for cities with hinterlands of less than

500,000 it is unlikely that the commercial office sector will be very large or that a separate entertainment–hotel zone will be easily distinguishable. However, it seems that for urban agglomerations with populations of up to 2 million the main CBD retains a relatively compact form with an internal structure broadly recognizable in terms of the suggested model and there is ample empirical evidence for this. For the very largest cities it is likely that the tendency towards functional separation noted by Bowden (1971) introduces further complexity and a more fragmentary central city.

THE CORE–FRAME AND TRANSITION-ZONE CONCEPTS

City-centre studies have focused on commercial functions and have tended to compartmentalize the CBD. Some investigators have adopted a broader perspective and have introduced ideas and information which serves to partially redress this imbalance.

Of particular note in this respect is the core–frame concept proposed by Horwood and Boyce (1959). The *core* is defined as the area exhibiting the most intensive land use characterized by the concentration of retailing, consumer services, offices, hotels and entertainment facilities. As such it approximates to the CBD defined by Murphy and Vance (1954). The *frame*, in contrast, is less intensively developed and comprises a mixture of functions with recognizable and interlinked functional nodes such as wholesaling, light manufacturing, automobile sales and service, transportation terminals and specialized professional services, all of which are considered to have important linkages with the CBD core. Over time, the accumulation of these functions around the edge of the CBD, usually by the relatively haphazard displacement or blighting of former residential areas, creates a relatively extensive area characterized by a mixture of land uses in a matrix of the poorest-quality housing conditions and car-parking lots. The outer boundary of the area is usually determined by natural barriers, heavy industrial concentrations and residential neighbourhoods.

This model was developed as a generalized description of an existing situation and has severe limitations, but it generated interest in the wider functional complex of the city centre and has conceptual links with the zone in transition concept (Griffin and Preston, 1966). Griffin and Preston initially view the zone in transition as a mixture of commercial and non-commercial land uses. This reflects the invasion of former residential areas adjacent to the CBD by functions which have extensive space demands but which, nevertheless, require a reasonably accessible central city site. These functions gravitate to the perimeter of the CBD, usually by displacing and blighting former residential areas. The intermixture of commercial activities and poor-quality housing creates a deteriorating urban environment, unattractive to those with any kind of residential choice, and typical occupants become the lowest-status groups, recent immigrants to the city and the 'socially disorganized' elements of the community. Interest in the social characteristics of this area has a long history dating back to the seminal work of Burgess (1925), from whose model the term 'zone-in-transition' can be traced.

As the transition zone develops it tends to be increasingly distinguishable from the CBD by the tendency of its commercial activities to become extensive rather than intensive space-users and to expand at the zone margins. In addition, the transition zone does not tend subsequently to evolve into a predominantly extensive commercial zone serving a different range of functions to the CBD. The early demand for central city sites is often replaced by a significant sub-urbanization of such functions as wholesaling and light manufacturing. This reflects the fact that modernizing and newly developing firms require larger sites than the city centre can offer, while improvements in transport and communications technology reduce the significance of a central city location for this type of activity. Consequently, the zone in transition tends to remain as a mixed and blighted area, presenting substantial physical and social planning problems.

However, the main concern of Griffin and Preston was not to explain the developmental processes associated with the transition zone, but to develop a precise procedure for its delimitation and representation of its internal structure. They designated transition-zone uses as public organizations, wholesale, storage, transport, light industry and retailing, and using the outer limit of the CBD as the inner limit of the transition zone, delimited its outer edge at the points where the transition-zone uses comprise less than 30 per cent of the total land use. Clearly, the method has subjective qualities in the ways in which it both designates land uses and sets the limiting value. Nevertheless, from their use of the procedure in the three cities of Richmond (Virginia), Worcester (Massachusetts); and Youngstown (Ohio) Griffin and Preston conclude that the method provides a reasonably consistent definition of the transition zone and also feel able to present a generalized model of its internal structure and change. In line with earlier CBD studies, the sector of active assimilation is located in the direction of the more attractive higher-status parts of the city, while the sector of passive assimilation (discard) typifies the least attractive margin of the city centre.

The zone-in transition concept was criticized by Bourne (1968) on the grounds that it tends to emphasize delimitation and description rather than the analysis of its functional attributes and the processes of change or stagnation operating within it. The latter were considered more important focuses of investigation in an area which was increasingly presenting problems for the urban planner. Arguably, however, the point may be made that it is often useful to have a broad descriptive knowledge of the structure of an area of the type proposed by Griffin and Preston as a prelude to analysis of processes and interactions on both a central city and wider urban scale.

PLANNING AND THE CITY CENTRE

Since 1945 town planning has had a considerable impact on the character and internal structure of city centres in both Western Europe and in North

America. A number of major modifying influences can be recognized which in combination have transformed many city centres.

Significant amounts of residential property have been removed from the transition zone and planners have encouraged the decentralization of activities such as wholesaling, warehousing and light manufacturing. In Britain, such schemes were introduced on a small scale in the 1920s, were accelerated following the 1947 Town and Country Planning Act and its Comprehensive Development Area provisions, and by 1964 Alexander (1974) notes that one-third of all urban local authorities had drawn up central area redevelopment plans. These activities have improved the environmental character of the zone-in-transition, reducing its functional complexity, and have made it more easily distinguishable from the CBD. The Urban Renewal Programmes introduced by the 1949 Housing Act had similar effects on central cities in the United States; the West End redevelopment project and the construction of the Government centre in Boston are cases in point.

Planning policies introduced to improve the environment and functional efficiency of CBDs have also had a considerable impact. In Britain a sequence of planning ideas have been proposed which have been followed in particular cities to varying degrees depending upon their timing and funding implications, which have the general effect of creating a more uniform structure. The central area redevelopment plan introduced in the early 1950s for the bomb-damaged centre of Coventry (Figure 6.16), and subsequently in the first phase of new towns around London were early examples. The kinds of redevelopment principles used in this plan were given official sanction in a government information document (HMSO, 1962) which introduced the additional suggestion that the different functions typically found in the CBD should be concentrated in specific locations wherever possible. These ideas were further developed by the Ministry of Transport following the report, *Traffic in Towns* (HMSO, 1964), which formalized the ideas of Sir Colin Buchanan on the principles of pedestrian–vehicular segregation. It was proposed that central area redevelopment should, as far as possible, accommodate the potential growth in vehicular traffic without a serious deterioration in the quality of the urban environment by the separation of vehicles from the pedestrian, often by expensive vertical segregation, with the result that the various 'environmental' areas would be strictly free of traffic.

Due to financial considerations the construction of vertical traffic segregation schemes has diminished in significance since the late 1960s, although some recurrent plan elements continue to characterize the spatial structure of the central areas of British cities. Inner ring-roads with associated car-parking facilities usually surround the CBD; pedestrianized retail concentrations, separate office districts, civic centres and possible entertainment districts are increasingly distinguishable within the CBD, while conservation areas to preserve historic city-centre land uses are frequent. In short, town planning is emphasizing the separateness of various functional elements in the central area and is producing a move towards less complexity and greater structural uniformity.

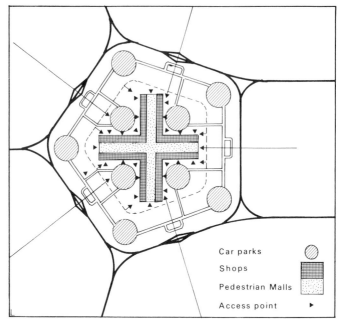

Figure 6.16   An idealized central area structure for Coventry, proposed by the City Planning Department. Source: Davies, 1976; reproduced by permission of R. L. Davies

Proposals for major shopping developments, often in the form of enclosed shopping malls, have also affected the traditional central area in British cities. Schiller and Lambert (1977) note that of the largest 155 shopping centres in Britain, 105 had initiated schemes with floorspaces of greater than 4600 m^2 (49,500 sq. feet) since 1965, usually promoted by partnerships between local authorities and private enterprise. In most cases these largely 'planned' developments have had the effect of increasing the centralization of shopping facilities into a particular section of the CBD, usually close to the existing major shopping zone. For example, Davies and Bennison (1978) show how the Eldon Square shopping development in Newcastle-upon-Tyne consolidated the principal focus of shopping activities in the area between Northumberland Street and Grainger Street (Figure 6.17). Such developments inevitably have repercussions elsewhere in the CBD. A shift in the focus of shopping trips in the direction of the new development often precipitates the decline and blighting of a significant number of small shops in the streets marginal to the CBD. This type of impact was noted in Newcastle and also in Utrecht (Netherlands), as a result of the opening of the large Hoog Catharigne Centre. Also, new precincts tend to increase the significance of the larger multiple goods shops at the expense of small independent businesses in city centres, since the former are more financially capable of renting the large units usually favoured by the letting companies. In fact, Schiller (1974) has suggested that this process has precipitated

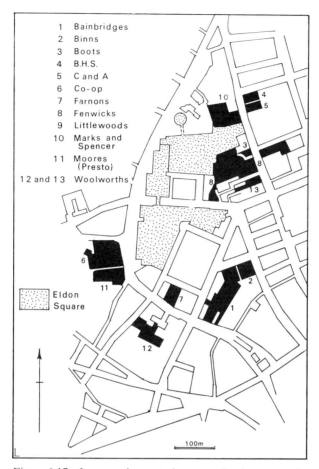

1 Bainbridges
2 Binns
3 Boots
4 B.H.S.
5 C and A
6 Co-op
7 Farnons
8 Fenwicks
9 Littlewoods
10 Marks and
    Spencer
11 Moores
    (Presto)
12 and 13 Woolworths

Eldon
Square

100m

Figure 6.17   Large-scale central area redevelopment: the
Eldon Square project, Newcastle-upon-Tyne. Source: Davies,
Bennison, 1978; reproduced by permission of KNAG

a 'Latin Quarter syndrome' by which central area redevelopment has led to
the relocation of small specialist luxury shops in small attractive centres in the
countryside near to the larger town. Windsor (Berks.) is increasingly assuming
this type of specialization. However, it is interesting to note that large-scale
central-area shopping developments in Britain have not invariably resulted
in a greater centralization of facilities, as noted in Nottingham (Giggs, 1972).
Here, two sites were available at opposite margins of the CBD core, the first as
a result of the closure of the Victoria railway station and the second following
an earlier slum clearance scheme at Broadmarsh. Both were developed with
major shopping precincts with associated car-parking facilities, giving a strong
fragmentation of shopping facilities in central Nottingham and a significant
decline in the less easily accessible former retail core. Such deviations from the
general pattern are not uncommon, and usually reflect historical constraints on

the availability of land that can be developed, and may well create significantly greater problems for the developer, planner or shopper.

In North America commercial pressures for the expansion of retailing in the CBD have often been stronger than the ability of planners to control growth. Retail development has tended to be more piecemeal and more closely associated with other commercial activities such as office development than has been the case in Britain. In Vancouver, where the Pacific Centre incorporating an Eatons department store and 17 other units in conjuction with 850 car parking spaces has been constructed virtually at the centre of the CBD, there has been an increase in centralized shopping services. More usually, however, such developments have introduced an element of fragmentation into the structure of the retail zone as, for example, with the separate development of the Place Ville Marie and the Place Bonaventure in downtown Montreal. Similarly, in Boston the development of the Prudential Centre over 1 km ($\frac{1}{2}$ mile) from the principal focus of shopping activities has created a distinct secondary commercial centre (Figure 6.18). This project covers an area of 12 hectares (31 acres) and is built above the major Massachusetts Turnpike road. It comprises the 52-storey Prudential Insurance office tower, 42 shops, eight restaurants, the 1000-room Sheraton Hotel, a major Civic Auditorium, two large apartment houses, and 3000 integral car-parking spaces.

Thus, for the most part, recent planning intervention in the city centre has served to distinguish more clearly the functional core of the city from the surrounding urban areas. At the same time, the redevelopment and increasing centralization of the internal structure of the centre has resulted in the appearance of recurring elements in many western cities and a trend towards greater structural uniformity. However, these tendencies have not been entirely unequivocal due to the varying strength and vagaries of commercial considerations in particular cities, combined with the effects of historical influences on site availability and acquisition.

More generally, the growing body of literature relating to the central city has resulted in the recognition of a number of major factors influencing land-use patterns. The primary significance of the following are fundamental:

1. The influence of *relative accessibility* in association with the *rental value* surface have combined to create an underlying *concentric zonal* tendency in the pattern of functional zones.
2. At the same time, the specific locational requirements of particular functions, often in association with 'market' considerations combine to create strong *segregative* tendencies in the land-use pattern.
3. In addition, the influence of *historical* morphological and land-use developments frequently *constrain* the operation of market forces, usually accentuating the *segregative* structure of the functional zones.
4. More recently, the *directive* influences of official *planning*, and the sometimes conflicting 'commercial' influence of major *financial institutions* have also increasingly modified the structure of the city centre.

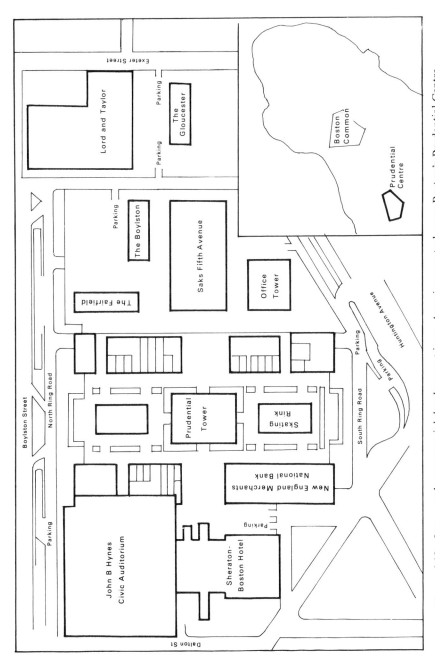

Figure 6.18 Large-scale commercial development in an American central area: Boston's Prudential Centre

THE CENTRAL AREAS OF MAJOR METROPOLITAN AREAS

Bowden (1971) observed that where an urban agglomeration exhibits sustained growth over a relatively long period the CBD functions tend to grow by separation, each major function gravitating to a location which is particularly suitable for its purposes. Only subsequently do interstitial areas accumulate CBD functions during a phase of infill, although a fragmentary quality will frequently remain. However, in those largest cities which have considerable international as well as national significance the sheer volume and range of activities which are attracted to the central area predispose it to a more complex fragmentary structure. The retailing, commercial, governmental office functions, and the ancillary activities associated with entertainment and hotels will reflect a combination of their urban, national and international functions. In addition, there are likely to be concentrations of educational, medical and cultural activities on a scale, and of a degree of specialization, not normally found in smaller cities. As a result, the typical functional zones commonly recognized in smaller cities are large enough to exhibit their own patterns of internal differentiation, or might be fragmented into spatially separate subzones in relation to their distinctive functional requirements. Comprehensive investigations of the spatial and functional structure of the central areas of such cities are uncommon, although Goddard's (1968; 1970) work on London has served to redress this deficiency.

Initially, Goddard (1968) concentrated attention on the commercial office zone in the 2.6 km² (1 square mile) administrative area of the City of London. Data was collected relating to 80 defined office types for each of the 216 city blocks and a Principal Component Analysis was used to extract meaningful dimensions which could be described in terms of four locational concentrations of particular office types (Figure 6.19). The first was a *trading offices zone*, including commodity trading, insurance and shipping offices. This was located on the eastern margin of the City near the major international insurance brokers, Lloyds. Immediately to the west, a *financial core* was recognized, comprising a concentration of the major banking houses, near the Bank of England. A *financial ring*, comprising functions associated with the capital and investment market was located further north in association with the Stock Exchange. A fourth *publishing and professional services* concentration was also noted on the western margin on the City associated with Fleet Street, although in this case the distribution was more diffuse. A fifth dimension comprising the offices of major *manufacturing and wholesaling* concerns was noted, but in this instance the spatial concentration was weakly developed.

Goddard's work was later extended to include the greater part of central London by using a similar multivariate analytical technique to extract functional nodes from taxi-flow data (Goddard, 1970). This confirmed the earlier findings for the City and also suggested a number of additional functional regions. A *legal zone* was recognized adjacent to Fleet Street, centred on the Old Bailey and extending north to include the Inns of Court. In a more eccentric location

Figure 6.19   Concentrations of office activities in the City of London. Source: Goddard, 1968

further north, the *Bloomsbury area*, characterized by a concentration of London University buildings and by less well-defined concentrations of civil engineering firms and medical facilities, was noted. The *West End* also emerged as a functional zone centred on the retailing facilities of Oxford Street, Regent Street and Bond Street, but including the entertainment district associated with Piccadilly Circus, Soho and Leicester Square in the direction of the City. Further to the south-west the government administrative area of *Whitehall–Westminster* also emerged as a distinctive functional zone.

However, Goddard (1968, 1970) stresses that while these functional regions can be broadly recognized in London, they cannot be precisely delimited. Many spatial anomalies occur both throughout the functional regions and at their margins, reflecting historical inertia and the many locational complexities which have influenced the evolutionary process. Also, the functional zones identified by the taxi-flow analysis subsume considerable internal differentiation. The West End cluster, for example, is mainly retail and entertainment but also includes a variety of other activities in the districts adjacent to Hyde Park and Kensington Gardens. A secondary high-status retail concentration associated with Harrods department store can be recognized in Knightsbridge 2.5 km ($1\frac{1}{2}$ miles) away from the major retail focus of Oxford Circus. Other clusters of activities include hotels in Mayfair, Bayswater and South Kensington, embassies in parts of Mayfair, Kensington and Belgravia, and museums in South Kensington.

Similar functional fragmentation can be observed in most major international cities, although in scale and distribution this will reflect the historical development of a particular city. New York, for example, has a distinctive financial district centred on the Wall Street area of Lower Manhattan, with a secondary centre characterized by the headquarters of insurance and manufacturing organizations in midtown Manhattan north of the Empire State Building. In Paris, the commercial office function is less well developed, reflecting its lower international status in this sphere of activities, but the traditional commercial office district is clustered around the Bourse du Commerce and the Banque de France. Large-scale planned decentralization of office facilities to the secondary node of La Defense has introduced a new element in Paris. Both New York and Paris have specialist retail concentrations, the former centred on midtown Manhattan's major department stores of Macy's, Korvette's and Gimbel's, while the latter extends in a stronger linear form from the large department stores of the Rue de Rivoli to the smaller exclusive fashion stores of the Rue St Honoré. However, in New York a second important retail concentration has been attracted to Fifth Avenue, south of Central Park, to serve the high-status population of this area, the approximate equivalent of which is seen at Knightsbridge in London. In Paris, this function remains within the general concentration, while the Champs Elysées forms a separate tourist-orientated centre characterized by a mixture of shops, cinemas, restaurants, hotels, travel offices and commercial office activities, which has no precise equivalent in either London or New York.

Both Paris and New York have well-defined entertainment districts, the former in the Montmartre area around the Place Pigalle, and the latter in the blocks adjacent to Times Square. Paris has also traditionally functioned as the administrative centre of France and a distinct government administrative zone has developed, initially associated with the Elysée Palace but subsequently, due to site constraints, expanding into a large area south of the Seine around Les Invalides. Similarly, the traditionally highly centralized French university system has resulted in a major concentration of educational establishments south of the Seine at the Sorbonne. In contrast, New York did not develop the equivalent functions for the United States so that although recognizable government administrative and educational nodes occur between lower and midtown Manhattan they do not have the significance demonstrated in the other two cities.

Clearly, there is sufficient evidence to suggest that the internal functional structures of the central areas of major international cities demonstrate extremely complex fragmented patterns. Some generalizations are possible but differences in spatial form will remain which are indicative both of more localized historical and morphological constraints and of variations in the societies in which these 'world cities' need to be viewed.

THE SUBURBS: DECENTRALIZATION OF SERVICES

The suburbanization of shopping facilities

With the physical expansion of urban areas well beyond the original city centres a point is soon reached when significant numbers of people are located too far away from the CBD to be supplied conveniently with the most frequently required goods and services. New suppliers of the most frequently required, lowest-order functions respond to this situation by establishing premises in locations accessible to the increasingly dispersed population. If dispersion of demand continues, it becomes feasible for increasingly more specialized functions to decentralize. Usually, these additional functions will gravitate to the most accessible of the original non-central locations and, in the process, create a series of second-order service centres. These centres will not normally achieve the degree of specialization found in the CBD because they will be less accessible to the citywide population necessary to support the highest-order functions. The remainder of the original non-central service locations will continue to provide lower-order functions in positions interstitial to the higher-order centres. These form a series of low-order centres.

This process ideally leads to a nested hierarchical spatial pattern of service centres in cities, similar to the central place system conceptualized by Christäller. Wild and Shaw (1979) show that such a sequence was initiated in Britain prior to 1798 and continued throughout the nineteenth century with the expansion of the central area at its margins. This resulted in the emergence of linear shopping axes along the main public transportation routes through the inner suburbs; the development of service nucleations in former villages incorporated by the urban expansion; and the emergence of small shopping clusters or corner stores at accessible points in the more densely developed parts of the urban fabric (Figure 6.20). This process was originally linked with central place theory by Berry and Garrison (1958b), and the close relationship between the hierarchy of service centres in the settlement pattern and the system of service centres in cities has since received considerable scrutiny.

The concepts developed in central place theory have been used subsequently to explain both the structure and growth of shopping centres in cities. At any one point in time the distribution of facilities is assumed to be adjusted to the nature of consumer demand, which in turn is determined by the density and distribution of the urban population, the types of goods and services required, and the transport facilities available. In addition, changes in the organizational structure of retail distribution can also create disequilibrium, which ultimately expresses itself in changes in the pattern of service centres and associated consumer behaviour.

The application of these concepts to the study of intraurban service centres was first developed in the North American literature. Berry, Simmons, and Tennant (1963) indicated that Chicago demonstrated a central commercial dominance until as late as 1910. However, by 1935, following the development of the inner suburbs, 75 per cent of business establishments were located beyond the CBD. Commercial land use extended in ribbons along most grid and arterial routeways, and at the busiest intersections outlying business centres developed which could be differentiated into neighbourhood, community and regional hierarchical orders, relative to their size and degree of centrality to the surrounding population. The essentially linear pattern was related to the dependence of the population on public transport routes in the densely populated inner suburbs.

By 1950, widespread changes in the nature of urban society created pressures which accentuated the process of service centre suburbanization and generated radical changes in the spatial pattern of shopping activities. Increases in the desire for spacious living resulted in urban residential densities decreasing from a characteristic 80,000 persons per square mile (30,880 persons per square kilometre) of the inner suburbs to 2000–10,000 per square mile (772–3860 persons per square kilometre) of the postwar suburbs. A related growth in car-ownership and the associated improvement of urban highways considerably improved intracity mobility. In addition, increases in affluence accentuated demand for specialized goods at the expense of convenience outlets. At the same time, economies of scale underlined the advantages of larger retail organizations and larger individual outlets.

These trends all favoured the development of planned car-orientated shopping facilities in the outer suburbs. Pressures to this end were accentuated by the lack of effective planning controls and the availability of suitably large, relatively cheap suburban sites with the result that the postwar period has seen the proliferation of planned suburban shopping centres, mostly at nodal locations on rapid transit routes.

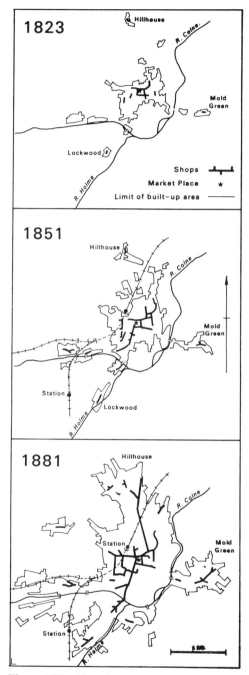

Figure 6.20 Changing patterns of retail services in nineteenth century Britain: the distribution of shops in Huddersfield, 1823, 1851, 1881. Source: Wild, Shaw, 1976; reproduced by permission of KNAG

The newly developed centres have tended to increase in size from neighbourhood to regional status and personal mobility has increased. In the process the enhanced sophistication of design and the degree of specialization of the centres has developed from parades of small shops with forecourt parking facilities providing essentially convenience items, through larger parades including superstores and junior department stores, to the enclosed regional shopping malls including superstores and department stores set in vast car parks. In many instances the more rudimentary early centres are now suffering adversely from the competition of the larger and more attractive recent developments.

The American Urban Land Institute has suggested the following hierarchical orders (Kivell, 1972):

1. Neighbourhood centres: consisting of 2750–9290 m² (30,000–100,000 square feet) of retailing space providing mostly day-to-day requirements and serving a catchment area of 5000–50,000 people.
2. Community centres: providing a greater depth of merchandising and based upon a junior department store. Typically, these offer 9290–27,500 m² (100,000–300,000 square feet) of selling space and cater for 50,000–150,000 people.
3. Regional centres: offering a full depth and variety of convenience, comparison and specialist goods and including at least one department store. In size they range from 27,500 to 92,900 m² (300,000–1,000,000 square feet), they provide up to 8000 car-parking spaces and they service a population to 150,000–500,000.

The system of shopping facilities in North American cities has also demonstrated increased *spatial* fragmentation since improved personal mobility has allowed the locational specialization of retail conformations to take place. Specialization has occurred by product, particularly for infrequently purchased goods such as automobiles and furniture, and also by social class, leading to both high-status fashion centres and low-status discount stores. In addition, highway-orientated functions such as service stations, restaurants, drive-ins and motels have accentuated the linear pattern of commercial land use.

In contrast, the CBD and the shopping facilities of the inner suburbs have often experienced 'commercial blight' (Berry, Simmons, and Tennant, 1963). CBDs have frequently failed initially to maintain their citywide accessibility and attractiveness in response to the emergence of the new suburban centres. In addition, as middle and high-income population groups have suburbanized, they have been replaced by low-income, white ethnic minorities and, particularly, black groups. This reduces both the spending power of the adjacent captive market and the commercial and environmental attractiveness of the city centre, now increasingly associated with social and racial problems. The combined influence of these factors resulted in the widespread decline of the CBD in North American cities through the 1950s and 1960s (Kottis and Kottis, 1972).

However, these adverse circumstances have not necessarily led to the inexorable decline of the CBD *everywhere*, since many city centres have retained significant advantages for the provision of specialist shopping activities. Potentially, they are still at the point of maximum accessibility to the whole city region in comparison with the sectoral accessibility of the suburban regional centres. Again, due to historical inertia, the CBD retains concentrations of functions such as office employment, governmental activities, entertainment, medical and cultural facilities which bring significant numbers of people regularly to the city centre. Many city centres have also developed an important and recently expanding tourist function. In addition, a significant demand by selective groups—the unmarried, childless, mobile sections of the higher-income categories—for middle and high-cost apartments in central locations has resulted in the residential regeneration of formerly socially declining districts in some of the environmentally more attractive city centres. This process of gentrification has the effect of enhancing the potential retail expenditure of the inner city population.

During the 1970s the formerly declining centres of a significant number of North American cities have witnessed a partial revival which has reasserted their place in the intraurban hierarchy. Other substantial investments have occurred in new shopping malls, often in conjunction with office and apartment developments in cities such as Hartford and Baltimore (Davies, 1976). This has also been a common feature in Canadian cities, less afflicted by the racial dimension of the inner city problem.

However, the partial arrest of the commercial blight of the CBD is less evident in the inner suburban retail ribbons. Here, decline has been substantial and prolonged. Retailers of the higher-order goods and the least efficient of the excess convenience goods traders have gone out of business. Vacancy rates of a third to a half are not uncommon as the residential activities have diminished status in areas of deteriorating quality.

The outcome of this overall process of change, unmitigated by planning intervention, is what Berry, Simmons, and Tennant (1963) have termed 'spatial anarchy'. In situations of this kind, while accepting the fact that some system of order can often still be recognized (Figure 6.21), the appropriateness of the concepts derived from central place theory as a basis for the analysis of the system of shopping centres in cities has become increasingly questionable.

Whereas commercial structure described for Chicago has been widely accepted as a model for the North American situation, its application in other western industrial societies is less evident. Elsewhere, suburbanization, personal mobility and retail change have not proceeded as quickly and the pattern is more akin to the North American situation in the 1950s. A four-level hierarchy was demonstrated for both Coventry (Davies, 1974) and Christchurch, New Zealand (Clark, 1967), broadly commensurate with the convenience, neighbourhood, community and CBD categories of Chicago.

European and Australasian intraurban systems are, however, in the process of change. Johnston and Rimmer (1969) identified a process of adjustment in Melbourne similar to that demonstrated in the United States; since the late 1950s a number of unplanned and planned centres at all hierarchical levels

230

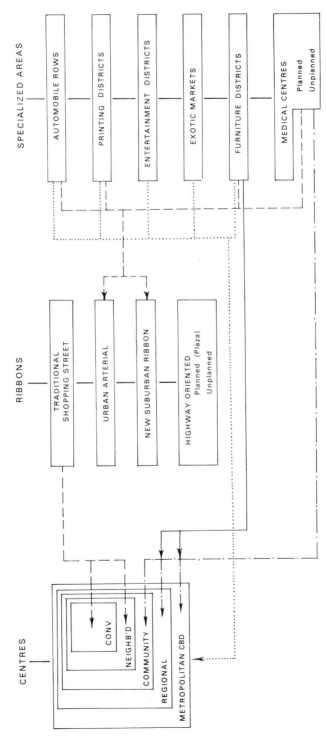

Figure 6.21   The commercial structure of the North American City: based upon Chicago. Source: Berry *et al.*, 1963; reproduced by permission of the Department of Geography, University of Chicago

have been developed in the Melbourne suburbs, and by 1965 there were six large planned centres, one of which was of regional significance. In addition, the initiation of the process of commercial blight was demonstrated for those inner suburban areas in which recent southern European immigrants were concentrated. Alexander and Dawson (1979) similarly demonstrate the familiar North American pattern of central area decline for the six Australian state capitals. Similar tendencies have emerged throughout western Europe since the mid-1960s and have involved the widespread development of car-orientated superstores or hypermarkets (ranging in size from 2325–18,400 m^2 (25,000–200,000 square feet) gross floorspace) particularly in France and Germany, as well as planned centres of community and regional significance (Dawson, 1974); 212 hypermarkets and four regional centres had been completed in France by 1972 (B. A. Smith, 1973).

In part, international variations in the process of adjustment to the new forces can be related to detailed variations in the suburbanization process, but probably of more fundamental significance is the variable influence of urban planning controls. In North America, despite the fact that individual centres are planned, comprehensive controls over the evolving retail system have been lacking. The locations of unplanned and planned developments have only been marginally influenced by land-use zoning, and this has resulted in the present complex and often irrational structure.

Stronger planning direction is likely in European countries. In France, planning at the city level has so far been relatively neglected, though in Paris growth pressures have made firm planning controls essential. As early as 1968, under the Schéma Directeur d'Aménagement et d'Urbanisme de la Région de Paris, locations for fifteen new regional shopping centres were designated in conjunction with a strategy for planned suburban growth which included five new towns (Smith, 1973), in part designed to provide strong secondary shopping, employment and social focuses for suburban Paris (Figure 6.22 and Table 6.2).

In Britain the greater formalization of planning powers has served to distinguish the experience of retail suburbanization. Both central and local government planners expressed initial opposition to the unrestrained development of new suburban facilities. Therefore, planning authorities have tended to use their powers to protect existing retailing interests by restricting the development of large new suburban facilities of the freestanding type. In fact, a cautious attitude to such developments was institutionalized in 1972 by the decision of the Department of the Environment to scrutinize individually any proposal for greater than 4650 m^2 (50,000 square feet) gross floorspace (DOE, 1972). Subsequently, official attitudes to retail planning have been clarified further, and there are four main arguments for planning controls contained in most retail planning strategies (Thorpe, 1974):

1. *The retail case*: the quantity of new retail development should be restrained to avoid excess capacity and to ensure an optimum mix of retail opportunities.

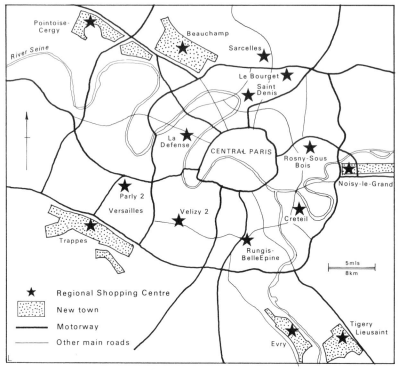

Figure 6.22   The system of regional shopping centres planned for Paris. Source:
Smith, 1973; reproduced by permission of *Town Planning Review*

2. *The urban case*: considerable care should be taken with the arrangement
   and location of shopping facilities since they exert a strong influence on urban
   morphology.
3. *The social planning case*: since most new retail facilities are designed to serve
   the car-orientated shopper, planning should ensure that all sectors of the
   community are adequately served.
4. *The environmental case*: careful site planning should attempt to separate
   retailing from 'non-conforming' land uses and minimize the environmental
   impact of new developments.

In practical terms, these considerations have resulted in retail planning
proposals which have been applied consistently to British cities. There has
been a central government commitment to the maintenance of the CBD as the
commercial and social focus of urban life. Consequently, as indicated in a
previous section, the greatest concentration of investment in retail facilities
since the mid-1960s has been directed towards the improvement of the central
area shopping facilities.

Outside the city centre, policy has promoted the ideal of an integrated system
of centres, each designed to serve a significantly more *localized* shopping

Table 6.2 Paris: regional shopping centres, 1968–85 (after Smith, 1973)

Centre	Date open	(m²)	Gross retail floor space (sq. ft.)
Le Chesnay-Parly 2	1969	55,184	594,000
Rungis-Belle Épine	1971	97,083	1,045,000
Velizy 2	1972	89,929	968,000
Sarcelles	1972	40,877	440,000
Rosny-sous-Bois	1972–73	91,973	990,000
Cergy-Pontoise	1973	40,877	440,000
Crétail	1974–75	91,973	990,000
Evry	1974–75	71,535	770,000
Defense	1974–75	143,069	1,540,000
Noisy-le-Grand	1974–75	91,973	990,000
Trappes	1976–86	81,754	880,000
Saint Denis	1976–86	—	—
Beauchamp	1976–86	—	—
Post-1985 development			
Le Bourget	1985 +	—	—
Tigéry-Lieusaint	1985 +	—	—
Melun-Sénart	Possible	—	—

function, complementary to, rather than competitive with, the CBD. This has involved the improvement of the detailed shopping, traffic, and parking environment of the unplanned, usually ribbon, centres of district status which had developed prior to 1960, the development of a limited number of planned district centres to ensure an equitable level of access to such facilities throughout a city region, such as the planned centres of Seacroft in Leeds and Cowley in Oxford, and below this level a series of neighbourhood or corner store facilities offering convenience goods for the less mobile sections of the community and serving a supplementary day-to-day convenience function for the population at large.

Similar policies of *adaptation* have been adopted in the conurbations with the renovation of unplanned centres, to constitute the secondary hierarchical level. The shopping centre strategy of the Greater London Development Plan 1969 (Greater London Council, 1970) was based upon the redesign of the existing major centres and allowed for only one new regional centre at Brent Cross in North London which remains the only example of its type in Britain (Shepherd and Newby, 1978).

However, both superstores and hypermarkets have been developed gradually in new suburban or edge-of-town sites, the incremental effect of which has resulted in a significant modification of the system of shopping facilities and associated consumer behaviour.

Discussion of superstores and hypermarkets tend to be somewhat confused by the lack of a universally accepted definition of these terms. Thus, general working definitions are proposed which are broadly applicable to the current British situation:

Superstore: Freestanding single stores of more than 2325 m^2 (25,000 square feet) (gross) but less than 4650 m^2 (50,000 square feet). The ratio of sales floorspace to storage and warehousing is typically of the order of two thirds: one third. They are usually set in extensive car parks with spaces provided at a ratio of 1:9.2–18.5 m^2 (100–200 square feet) (gross). More than 50 per cent of the sales floorspace is given to grocery retailing (more typically the ratio of food to non-food sales floorspace is of the order of two thirds: one third. The Leo's stores operated by CRS are characteristic of this type of development (Thomas, 1977).

Hypermarket: Freestanding stores of greater than 4650 m^2 (50,000 square feet) (gross). Few in Britain are currently larger than 9300 m^2 (100,000 square feet), reflecting official caution, although many continental examples are more than twice this size. The ratio of sales to storage is again of the order of two thirds: one third. However, in some instances a greater proportion is given to warehousing since the handling of bulk deliveries to achieve economies of sale in purchasing is a central feature of these retail operations. Similarly, the stores are set in extensive car parks with spaces provided at a ratio of 1:9.2–18.5 m^2 (100–200 square feet) (gross). Usually more than 50 per cent of the sales area is given over to non-food retailing and, more typically, the ratio of food to non-food floorspace is the reverse of that for the superstores, in other words of the order of one third: two thirds. The Carrefour Store at Caerphilly is characteristic of this type of development.

The basic difference between superstores and hypermarkets is the bias towards grocery retailing in the superstore and towards non-food goods in the hypermarket. However, due to the small scale of the British hypermarkets, this difference tends not to be reflected in precisely equivalent differences in their functioning. In both cases, it seems that the great preponderance of trade is in the bulk purchase of groceries (Thomas, 1978). It is also interesting to note that they do not fit conveniently into the normal hierarchy of shopping centres as they serve wider areas than traditional neighbourhood and district centres, albeit with a lower level of market penetration. They have by and large, however, been developed as components of planned district centres rather than as free-standing operations. Acceptance of this form of location by major developers such as Tesco and Woolco is evidence of the impact of planning control.

Thus, in Britain, commercial pressures for retail suburbanization have resulted in the maintenance of a more clearly identifiable hierarchical structure than has been evident elsewhere. However, whether the resulting strategies will continue to control the pressures for change, allow the business community to operate economically and efficiently, and provide a spatially and socially equitable retail system for the population at large is yet to be seen.

The spatial decentralization associated with suburbanization has also influenced the other categories of urban services, but not necessarily in the ways illustrated for shopping facilities. This adds to the complexity of the pattern of service activities in urban areas.

Wholesaling and warehousing

The essence of wholesaling and warehousing functions is that they provide a distribution and supply service for other business and industrial functions and thus gravitate towards these 'primary' activities. With the increasing demand for larger modern premises on extensive sites, the improvement in intraurban communication networks and the decentralization of the activities which wholesaling and warehousing serve since 1945, pressures for decentralization have also affected these functions. There has been little geographical analysis of the distribution of wholesaling and warehousing. Vance (1970) discussed wholesaling and warehousing, mainly in the city centres of North American urban areas and offers an instructive, but essentially exploratory, synopsis.

Vance proposed a 'Wholesaling Taxonomy' which consists of: *Traditional wholesaling districts*. Characteristically, these are sited initially near city centres to *supply* the surrounding hinterland and are usually associated with the focal points of the original transportation facilities. *Districts of customer access* are subsequent, more specialized developments which emerge either within the original concentration or at its edge. *Produce districts* are the most common of these and are initially located on the periphery of the central area in order to serve small-scale customers such as restaurants, hotels and produce retailers. *Product comparison districts* also respond to access needs of customers, particularly in the furniture and clothing trades. *Will-call delivery districts* exist to supply undercapitalized retailers in products such as auto parts and plumbing supplies, and retailers of products liable to rapid changes in taste, such as records. *Manufacturing stocks districts* supply standardized items for diversified small-scale manufacturers, such as wholesalers of paper for the printing trades, while *office wholesaling districts* supply a variety of specialized office equipment.

Changes in transport technology, particularly associated with the increased importance of road haulage, have prompted general wholesaling functions to migrate to a variety of peripheral urban locations which offer convenient road access. Again, the general increase in central city traffic congestion and site costs, with associated growth in both the scale of operations and the service areas has produced major difficulties in central city sites. Consequently, planners frequently encourage the relocation of such activities to suburban sites, both to allow them to function more efficiently and to release valuable central city locations. The relocation of the Covent Garden market from central London to Nine Elms, and the Les Halles produce market to Rungis in suburban Paris are two striking examples of this tendency.

More recently, in the British context Davies (1977) has developed ideas on these functions a little further. He suggests that the spatial planning of commercial services has been overdominated by the development of shopping centre structure plans. A comprehensive spatial framework is considered necessary for the integrated planning of 'commercial' activities as a whole and, to complement the systems of shopping centres, three additional types of development might be:

(1) *Service plazas* to be built near to city centres for functions with an affinity to retailing, to replace pressures for the creation of highway commercial strips;
(2) *Trading marts* on city peripheries to serve general wholesaling functions; and
(3) *Commercial estates* for the larger-scale wholesaling and warehousing activities, possibly linked to concentrations of industrial activities.

OFFICES IN THE SUBURBS

Offices are concerned primarily with transactional and administrative activities serving business organizations and administrative institutions involved in all sections of the life of a country or region. Consequently, office location patterns reflect the need for access to, and intercommunications between, the broad economic, social and political forces central to the life of a country. This expresses itself in a greater degree of concentrations of office activities into a relatively small number of the largest cities in the centrally significant or rapidly growing regions of developed countries than occurs for the services previously considered. In the United Kingdom the South-East region contained 43 per cent of the office jobs in 1971, compared with a 33 per cent share of all jobs (Alexander, 1979), while London dominated the distribution of the headquarters of the top 500 industrial companies in 1971–72 with 60 per cent compared with the 5 per cent of its nearest rival, the West Midlands conurbation (Evans, 1973). Paris, with 90 per cent of the headquarters of major national companies and nearly half of the civil service jobs, dominates the French pattern, and the only exception noted by Alexander (1979) was the United States where the scale of the space economy combined with the location of areas of rapid economic growth has enabled secondary nodes in Chicago, the industrial cities of the Midwest and Great Lakes, Los Angeles and San Francisco, although none rivals the concentration on New York and the associated cities of the north-east seaboard (Figure 6.23).

Similarly, at the intraurban scale there has until recently been a characteristic dominance of clusters in the CBD and its periphery. This reflects the pervasive influence of an impressive variety of centralization forces operating within the city. Generally recognized as being of permanent importance is the operational need for ease of access, for direct contact between decision-makers in related business interests, to the investment and money markets, to government agencies, and to expert consultation in the professions and higher educational establishments—the so-called external economies of a city centre

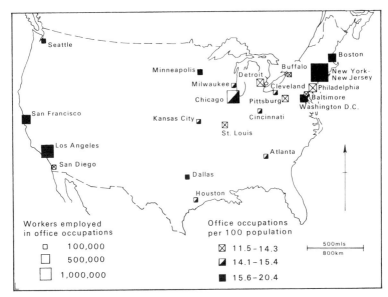

Figure 6.23 Major centres of office employment in the United States.
Source: Alexander, 1978; reproduced by permission of Regional Plan
Association

location. Also of significance is the relative ease of accessibility of the city centre
to a highly diversified labour market, since office activities employ low-grade
cleaning and ancillary staff as well as the routine clerical grades and higher level
professionals. Similarly, the advantage of a 'prestige' city centre address is frequently quoted as a factor promoting centralization, while proximity to city
centre recreational facilities for the entertainment of prospective business
contacts and to specialized shopping facilities for possible use by office employees are also considered relevant.

The combined influence of these forces is directly reflected in the postwar
office building booms in the centres of the largest western cities. Manners (1974)
notes that between 1960 and 1972 the gross office floorspace in Manhattan
increased from 9.5 million m^2 (104 million square feet) to 22 million (244 million
square feet), while the second largest concentration in Chicago expanded by
50 per cent to 6.7 million m^2 (73 million square feet), situations which had
approximate parallels in many of the other larger American cities. Similarly,
in central London the 7.2 million m^2 (78 million square feet) of 1945 (Goddard,
1975) had expanded to approximately 16.6 million m^2 (180 million square
feet), employing 750,000 people by the early 1970s (Daniels, 1976).

However, the growth in the importance of the proportion of office jobs in
western economies in the postwar period has been prodigious. Manners (1974)
indicated that in the United States the proportion increased from 36 per cent
in 1950 to 48 per cent in 1970. Elsewhere, Alexander (1979) estimates that for
seven western industrial countries 'office-type' jobs accounted for between 25

and 40 per cent of the total workforces by 1970, and that in each case the proportion had increased significantly during the 1960s. The scale of this economic shift, as well as finding expression in the central city office-building booms, has also resulted in location diseconomies within the city centre as the familiar problems of traffic congestion and rising site costs take effect. This has resulted in the reappraisal of city centre locations particularly as advances in telecommunications technology have tended to decrease some of their external economies.

Suburban locations offer lower site costs, estimated by Daniels (1974) to be on average 50 per cent of the cost of land in the CBD, giving lower rents, the opportunity to develop more car-parking facilities and the flexibility to allow incremental increases in office floorspace. Also, suburban locations tend to offer shorter journeys to work and easier access for middle and higher-grade employees, and in turn provide access to relatively highly educated part-time female labour (Manners, 1974). In addition, the more qualitative advantages of an attractive suburban environment may result in higher productivity, greater practicality, less absenteeism and labour turnover.

The factors promoting office decentralization are not, however, as strong as those operating in the retail system and there exist counter-pressures. Alexander (1979) notes that, while the external economies associated with a concentration in the city centre have declined as a 'necessary condition' for a successful office operation dispersal has been less than expected due to a combination of risk and inertia factors. Similarly, Manners (1974) suggests that in the United States the cost advantages of a suburban location tend to reduce to a 10–15 per cent rent differential which is not critical since rent comprises only 6–8 per cent of total office costs. By far the largest operating cost is labour, accounting for between 84 and 86 per cent of expenditure, and for this there is little spatial variation in most metropolitan areas. The assumed journey-to-work advantage also may well be illusory. In a survey of suburban office relocation in Greater London, Daniels (1974) indicated that the journey-to-work of 25 per cent of employees increased as a result of the change, and that whereas 90 per cent of office workers in the central city arrived by public transport, 44 per cent of workers in suburban offices used a car. There are unresolved planning implications of shifts of this kind. In addition, while a suburban location has advantages for middle-class employees in one sector of the city, there is a reduction of accessibility to the more diversified wider metropolitan labour market. Usually, a suburban location will also tend to lack the immediate availability of business services, entertainment facilities and specialist shopping opportunities which remain a strength of the CBD.

Current evidence suggests that office dispersal in the United States occurred earlier as inner city problems and suburban advantages assumed exaggerated forms. Thus, in New York by 1960 as much as 49 per cent of office floorspace was located in the suburbs, and by 1972 similar trends were apparent in most of the other large metropolitan areas. The suburban share of office space ranged from 17 per cent in Chicago to 59 per cent in Atlanta (Manners, 1974) (Table 6.3).

Although the outcomes of the dispersal process have been diffuse, clustering does occur in the inner suburban service centres of the larger metropolitan areas, in the regional shopping centres of the outer suburbs, at nodal parts on the interstate highway network, and near to airports. Although in practice American metropolitan areas still lack the political structure and planning powers necessary to control office development and to coordinate the suburbanization of services, attempts have been made to control office decentralization. In New York the Regional Plan Association (1968) suggested that office decentralization pressures which were expected to increase the number of office workers from 1.6 to 3 million in the period 1965–2000 should be channelled into fifteen suburban locations employing 20,000–100,000 persons and a further twelve locations employing 5000–20,000 persons (Daniels, 1974).

Table 6.3 Estimated growth in central-city and suburban office space in several metropolitan areas, 1960–72 (million gross square feet) (after Manners, 1974; reproduced by permission of *Economic Geography*)

SMSA	Zone	1960 (%)	1972 (%)	Increase 1960–72 (%)	SMSA population 1970
New York–	Total	275	483	208	16,178,700
north-east	central city CBDs	140 (51)	244 (51)	104 (50)	
New Jersey	rest of SMSA	135 (49)	239 (49)	104 (50)	
Chicago	Total	49	88	39	6,978,900
	central city CBD	48 (98)	73 (83)	25 (64)	
	rest of SMSA	1 (2)	15 (17)	14 (36)	
San Francisco	Total	22	52	30	3,109,500
	central city CBD	19 (86)	34 (65)	15 (50)	
	rest of SMSA	3 (14)	18 (35)	15 (50)	
Atlanta	Total	23	49	26	1,390,200
	central city CBD	11 (48)	20 (41)	9 (35)	
	rest of SMSA	12 (52)	29 (59)	17 (65)	
Minneapolis–	Total	11	45	34	1,813,600
St Paul	central city CBD	10 (91)	20 (44)	10 (29)	
	rest of SMSA	1 (9)	25 (56)	24 (71)	
Houston	Total	15	42	27	1,985,000
	central city CBD	11 (73)	22 (52)	11 (41)	
	rest of SMSA	4 (27)	20 (48)	16 (59)	
Boston	Total	19	39	20	2,753,700
	central city CBD	18 (97)	29 (75)	11 (55)	
	rest of SMSA	1 (3)	10 (25)	9 (45)	
Dallas	Total	13	29	16	1,556,000
	central city CBD	10 (77)	16 (55)	6 (38)	
	rest of SMSA	3 (23)	13 (45)	10 (62)	
Cleveland	Total	8	19	11	2,064,200
	central city CBD	8 (97)	15 (79)	7 (64)	
	rest of SMSA	(3)	4 (21)	4 (36)	

Elsewhere, the concept of the more nodal office park at accessible points on the urban periphery has been proposed, and many examples now occur.

In the western European cities the office decentralization pressures have been weaker and more fundamentally affected by central and local government controls. In the United Kingdom, by the late 1950s and early 1960s London was the only city where a limited dispersal had occurred spontaneously and had taken the form of an uncoordinated speculative scatter, with more organized exceptions in Croydon, Ealing and Wembley (Daniels, 1975). By 1963, central government concern still centred on the potential congestion likely to result from the office development pressures in Central London and the Location of Offices Bureau was established. The function of the Bureau was advisory and designed to divert offices from Central London, although there existed no clear strategy as to where they were to be directed.

In 1964 the new Labour Government introduced Office Development Permits in London for schemes over 270 m^2 (2900 square feet). These were only to be issued where the developer could convince the Government that the prospective occupier could not operate efficiently outside London. The aims of this device were three-fold:

1. to relieve congestion and to curb speculative development in Central London;
2. to limit development in suburban and urban peripheral locations to firms with an operational necessity for such locations;
3. to encourage the redirection of excess office development pressure to locations outside the South-East of England in order to redress the office employment imbalance which was considered to be adversely affecting the economic growth of the peripheral regions.

The fulfilment of these aims has varied with the strength of resolve of successive governments and the degree of efficiency of policy instruments. Proof of necessity for a London location has always been problematic and no direct financial incentives for decentralization were offered prior to 1976. Office decentralization has occurred but the contribution of government policy towards this is not easy to disentangle from 'natural' forces. Alexander (1979) estimates that between 170,000 and 250,000 jobs (the equivalent of one-third to one-quarter of its office employment) were decentralized from Central London in the period 1963–77, during which time 30 per cent of the central area floor space applied for was refused. Nevertheless, in the period 1965–77 Office Development Permits authorizing 7 million m^2 (75 million square feet) of new office floor space were issued for Central London and a further 8 million m^2 (86 million square feet) was authorized for the suburban and outer areas of the London Metropolitan Region (Alexander, 1979). Again, only 13,000 jobs diverted from London moved to areas outside the South-East, confirming the Location of Offices Bureau evidence in 1971 to the effect that 58 per cent of the offices and 45 per cent of the jobs diverted from Central

London moved less than 32 km (20 miles) and 77 per cent of firms seeking relocation information in 1970–71 stated a preference for similar locations (Daniels, 1974). More recently the Hardman Report (1973) recommended that 31,000 civil service jobs should be dispersed from London, and the government responded with a substantial increase in financial inducements in 1976, but the regional imbalances persist (Alexander, 1979; Goddard, 1975).

The Greater London Development Plan (1969) responded to problems arising from uncoordinated office development by proposing that the majority of future suburban office development should be confined to 24 of the 28 'strategic' shopping centres (Daniels, 1976). Additionally, in the six 'major strategic' centres of Croydon, Ealing, Ilford, Kingston, Lewisham and Wood Green development would be particularly encouraged so that the potential problems of traffic congestion and service coordination could be minimized and external economies of concentration and public transport provision maximized.

In general, this strategy has controlled the location of subsequent development, although in 1975, following public enquiries, Lewisham and Wood Green were dropped from the list of major strategic centres in the finally approved plan. In addition, the relative autonomy of the London Boroughs within the GLC has led to local deviations from the overall strategy as they seek to attract development in their own areas.

In the late 1970s, increased awareness of the economic and social problems of the inner city, added a new policy dimension as the Location of Offices Bureau began to seek office jobs for certain inner-city locations in order to contribute to the process of urban rehabilitation in blighted areas (Damesick, 1979). This policy is at odds with the overall strategy which now seems beset by ambiguity of its objectives and spatial outcomes.

Elsewhere in western Europe there are similar trends and policies. In central Paris planning policy has rigidly discouraged major new office development since 1960. Instead, office developments have been diverted to nodal suburban locations. Of these, the most significant and spectacular scheme initiated in 1958 is being developed at La Défense in the inner suburbs only 3.2 km (2 miles) north-west of the Arc de Triomphe. The site of 300 ha. (750 acres) offers excellent access with its own railway station, bus terminus, extensive car-parking facilities, a direct link to central Paris via the new express underground route (RER) and the urban motorway network. The first offices were let in 1964 and it currently offers approximately 10 per cent of the office floorspace of central Paris, with the eventual target of $1\frac{1}{2}$ million m^2 (16 million square feet) of floorspace accommodating 100,000 jobs in an integrated complex with retail, leisure and residential facilities. Alternative locations have also been designated in association with the system of regional shopping centres and new towns proposed as part of the restructuring of suburban Paris.

The suburban decentralization of offices is now a well-established feature of most major western cities and in most cases urban planners are attempting to control the process of relocation. The most favoured solution has been to concentrate the dispersal at a limited number of nodal locations on the urban transport system, while integrating office employment with the suburban provision of shopping facilities, leisure activities and housing. The rationale behind this policy has been the need to avoid the diseconomies of central area congestion, while at the same time maximizing the attractions of the external economies of concentration in non-central locations.

However, in detail a number of questions remain unresolved. How far, for example, can a policy of central area constraint be taken without adversely affecting the efficient functioning of commercial office activities? Apart from the observation that offices performing mechanical clerical transactions, branch offices, medium-sized firms requiring larger sites, and some government administrative activities are most likely to move to a suburban location, this question has still to be answered with any degree of precision (Alexander, 1979). Planners tend to favour caution with the almost inevitable result that the diseconomies of central area congestion are maintained at near crisis levels. Daniels (1975, 1976) considers it important to establish an optimal size for suburban office concentrations, sufficiently large to attract office development but not large enough to create diseconomies of suburban congestion. Alexander (1979) considers that such an optimum will vary with the particular characteristics of the metropolitan area under consideration and particularly with the level of investment available for transport facilities and the type and scale of suburban office centre required.

THE MEDICAL SERVICES SYSTEM

The medical services system in cities consists largely of general medical practitioners, more specialist physicians, and hospital services. Like shopping centres, the system has been viewed by geographers broadly within the conceptual framework of central place theory. The upper hierarchical levels are characterized by large specialized medical centres and teaching hospitals, while at the lowest levels a more ubiquitous distribution of partnerships of general practitioners, individual physicians or paramedical personnel located in health centres or home-based situations provides a less specialized entry to the system. Similarly, the number of levels in the hierarchy are considered to reflect a combination of the density of population, levels of personal mobility, the varying degrees of specialization and frequency of treatment required, and the finance available to provide the service (Shannon and Dever, 1974).

However, the 'commercial' central place analogy cannot be taken too far. In most societies the locational decisions of general practitioners are not market-orientated to the same degree as retailers', but are restricted by professional codes—which, for example, discourage advertizing—or government licensing controls—which frequently attempt to promote a socially equitable spatial distribution of surgeries. Similarly, in the case of hospitals the individual units tend to be larger and more costly and specialized in relation to the scale of the system as a whole compared with an individual retail outlet and, therefore, are less responsive to changes in the nature and location of demand, while in many countries hospital location policies are increasingly becoming subject to direct governmental control.

Nevertheless, in the United States the commercial basis of the health care delivery system is sufficiently strong for central place theory and the methodology of retail studies to be used as a framework for analysis (Earickson, 1970). With a fee-for-service basis, the *market* considerations of profitability and the ability of the patient to pay have strongly influenced the structure of the resulting systems and is reflected in the locational behaviour of physicians. However, a code of conduct which prevents advertizing directs physicians to shopping centres, visited by their potential patients, as best locations. In Chicago 83 per cent of physicians are located in commercial centres (Earickson, 1970), and the level of specialization of the physician is related to the hierarchical status of the centre in which he is established. Similarly, changes in the location of physicians over time closely follow the changing pattern of demand of their middle and high-status patients in a process closely analogous to that of commercial blight. de Vise (1971) illustrates the catastrophic decline in the number of physicians in selected inner suburbs of Chicago, 1950–70, from 475 to 76 associated with a transition from middle-class white to low-status negro communities, and the associated imbalance in the distribution of physicians in favour of the middle and high-status suburbs. For the less mobile, low-status communities of the inner cities which tend to exhibit the highest rates of morbidity and early mortality, there are fewer available physicians.

The locational determinants of hospitals are even more complex. Hospitals vary with respect to the type of care and the degree of specialization offered and, generally, the larger hospitals will offer the most specialized services. There may also be variations in hospital type according to their religious affiliation and to the degree to which they will accept negro and charity patients and this is paralleled by variations in demand for their services. The relationship between the supply and demand criteria results in the hierarchy of hospitals, conceptually similar to the hierarchy of shopping centres (Figure 6.24). In general, the largest, most specialized hospitals are found in the central city, while the lower order district and community hospitals are more frequently located in suburban and urban peripheral sites.

However, the shopping centre analogy has to be viewed with caution since hospitals are rarely located in shopping centres, principally because their access needs and environmental requirements differ. Nevertheless, they often occur in the general vicinity of commercial centres to share public transport facilities and the highway network. In addition, as general hospitals are extremely expensive and relatively large indivisible units they have less flexibility and there is a time-lag of approximately five years between a newly developed residential area reaching a threshold population and the construction of even a modest community hospital (Earickson, 1970). Locational inertia is even more marked in the cases of the highly specialized hospitals in city centres. Imbalances in the location of supply and demand are overcome in the short term by suburban patients undertaking relatively long journeys but this situation need not

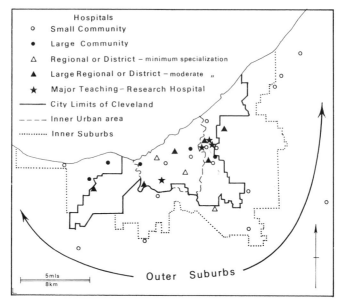

Figure 6.24   The hierarchy of hospitals within an American urban area: Cleveland, Ohio (based upon Shannon *et al.*, 1975). Reproduced by permission of the Association of American Geographers

necessarily operate in favour of the inner city concentrations of low-status communities. Their point of entry to the system of hospital services still has to be effected via a physician, frequently in a suburban practice, and in any event is restricted to the relatively small number of hospitals admitting charity patients wherever they are located.

The organization of medical services in the United States falls into four major categories, most of which have divided responsibilities between federal, state and county administrative levels. The most important are the non-profit organizations comprising hospitals responsible for 70 per cent of general hospital beds, medical societies and health planning coordination councils. Private practitioners constitute a second group, while a third comprises a complex amalgam of commercial enterprises such as health insurance interests, nursing homes and drug companies. Finally, in recent years government agencies have been increasingly significant. The relative importance of these bodies can be roughly gauged by existing methods of payment for health care: 50 per cent direct private payments, 25 per cent (and growing) health insurance, 23 per cent government assistance, 2 per cent philanthropic (Ardell, 1970). This complexity of control resulting from its free enterprise basis may well accentuate the lack of responsiveness of the system to patient needs.

Policy-related research has concentrated upon two closely related themes. The first considers policies to produce *social equality of access* to medical services by reducing existing income and racial barriers (de Vise, 1971). The Federal Medicare and Medicaid programmes initiated in 1966 to assist the aged and poor respectively represent a step in this direction. The second considers the need to promote a comprehensive health services planning system which can be effectively coordinated with urban planning agencies to create *spatial equality of access* to health facilities (Ardell, 1970). A first step was taken in this direction in 1966 with the provision of government funds to encourage the development of 'Areawide' health planning. Entrenched interests and a complex delivery system has resulted in subsequent progress in both these policy directions being slow (Shannon and Dever, 1974).

British medical services are largely financed and controlled by the government under the National Health Service (NHS) and are available with minimal direct charge. The Ministry of Health introduced a tripartite organizational structure in 1948 to replace the variety of private and voluntary general hospitals and private medical practitioners, reminiscent of the system in the United States. Hospital Authorities were created to administer general hospital and specialist medical services, Executive Councils to coordinate the services of general practitioners and related services, and Local Health Authorities to administer public health services such as domiciliary care and preventive medicine. These organizations functioned largely as autonomous entities and created considerable problems of coordination. Nevertheless, a much less complex organizational structure resulted with a strongly hierarchical ordering of services.

England was divided into fourteen areas each controlled by a Regional Hospital Board, the regions in turn being subdivided into districts of 100,000–200,000 population, controlled by Management Committees responsible for 1000 hospital beds. Initially, there was a variety of small single-purpose hospitals and clinics, but the hospital plan of 1962 proposed the General District Hospital as a means of integrating all existing hospital services into single units of 1500–2000 beds to serve populations of 200,000–300,000 (Ministry of Health, 1962).

Below this level, primary medical care was provided by general practitioners, each serving approximately 2000–2500 persons, although significant and persistent imbalances have been apparent in the peripheral regions of the country and in the less attractive parts of the major cities. In addition, the Ministry of Health encouraged general practitioners to create larger group practices to serve 10,000–15,000 people. Ideally, these were to be operated from health centres, providing a wider range of more specialized diagnostic and therapeutic out-patient facilities than the smaller practices and were designed to allow the hospitals to concentrate on more serious ailments.

The early 1970s saw a considerable increase in the development of health centres and by 1976, prior to the more recent cutbacks in health expenditure, approximately 800 had been completed (Abel-Smith, 1978). However, perhaps of greater significance was the continued and rapid increase in the number of group practices, irrespective of whether they were operated from health centres. In 1961, only 17 per cent of general practitioners were in group practices of four or more, but this had increased to 40 per cent by 1977, comprising a total of 8262 practices in England alone (Table 6.4) (Department of Health and Social Security, 1980).

Table 6.4   General medical practitioners in England

Type of practitioner (unrestricted principals)	1961	Per cent	1977	Per cent
one doctor	5337	28.3	3419	16.4
two doctors	6384	33.8	4198	20.2
three doctors	4008	21.2	4917	23.6
four doctors	1984	10.5	3872	18.6
five doctors	715	3.8	2420	11.6
six or more doctors	450	2.4	1970	9.5
Total	18878	100	20796	100

Source: Department of Health and Social Security (1980), Table 3.24

With administrative reorganization in 1974 (Office of Health Economics, 1974) a reformed system was designed to promote greater efficiency in the health care delivery system by defining more clearly the hierarchical allocation of responsibilities. *The Department of Health and Social Security* is responsible for overall resource allocation. In England the coordination of planning proposals at the regional level is administered via fourteen *regional health authorities*, and full operational and considerable planning responsibility has been devolved to the 90 *area health authorities*. The latter are the key units in the new structure since they employ the majority of the National Health Service staff. Spatially, they coincide with the recently reorganized metropolitan district and county units of local government. This was designed to promote coordination of the medical services with the social welfare, school health and environmental health services of the local authorities. Below this level a system of *district management teams* is responsible for the provision of hospital, general practitioner and community health services for populations of approximately 250,000. Where possible, these units were based upon the service areas of the *general district hospitals*.

The problems of administrative efficiency, and social and spatial inequalities of access associated with the health care system of the United States appear to have been substantially resolved in Britain. Nevertheless, the NHS has been criticized on all these issues. In particular, there is a major funding problem and cutbacks (1980) are likely to affect the administrative structure in general and the area health authority level specifically.

Also, standards of efficiency are gauged essentially from the bureaucratic or managerial viewpoint (Buttimer, 1971) and the needs of the patient or consumer of the service were assumed until 1974 to be represented by the lay members of the various administrative committees, who in practice have divided loyalties and roles. The decisions to develop general district hospitals, and to amalgamate general practitioners into health centres and group practices were decisions which did not necessarily represent the best interests of the consumers. Both decisions significantly reduced the accessibility of medical services to the patient, with scant attention given to the social implications of these actions. Clearly, professional medical criteria, managerial decisions and financial limitations still have to be accommodated but a socially optimal spatial allocation of medical services must account for the needs of both the supply system and the users.

To overcome this problem, in 1974 the control of service provision was devolved to the most local level, so that the requirements of the population could be judged more accurately. In addition, *community health councils* were created to represent public opinion, but these were still largely made up of representatives nominated by local authorities, health group interests and medics, and as currently constituted have very limited real power.

Also, despite considerable progress since 1948 there remains at regional, intra-urban and inter-social group levels considerable evidence that traditional health imbalances remain (Thomas and Phillips, 1978). Hart (1971) asserts that an 'inverse care law' characterized the availability of services, in other words the availability of good medical care tends to vary inversely with the needs of the population served; this occurs regionally, with better provision in southern England, by social class, and at an intraurban scale.

Whatever the detailed nature of the health care delivery system of a country, it might be suggested from this preceding review that there are a number of lines of investigation to which urban geographical research could direct attention. Of particular interest might be the spatial structure of the *systems of supply* of hospital facilities, primary medical care and associated pharmaceutical services. Investigation could focus on the possibility of *spatial imbalances* of accessibility to the various services enjoyed by the different communities of an urban region.

Alternatively, the *demand* side of the system could be investigated in an analogous manner to the consumer behaviour studies of retail geography. A considerable amount of research has in fact already been undertaken under the general heading of *health care utilization behaviour*. However, research lacks coordination and whereas the major reviews of this work by McKinlay (1972) and Veeder (1975) identify the four main determinants of health care utilization behaviour as: economic, social, psychological, and organizational features associated with the system; each draws attention to the lack of a significant attempt to develop an integrated understanding of this form of consumer behaviour. Also, while oblique references are made to the importance of accessibility to the utilization of health care facilities in these reviews spatial considerations are not comprehensively incorporated into the existing approaches and there is scope for the urban geographer. The importance of accessibility as a determinant of health care utilization behaviour can be investigated more directly by adopting social survey methods to investigate ways in which consumers use and relate to the various medical services.

Public utility services

By definition, the locational and operating policies of the public utility services are subject to direct public control, usually via a local government organization and its associated planning powers. As an increasing proportion of the population of developed countries is becoming concentrated into urban centres such services, particularly in the spheres of education, welfare, recreation and the provision of emergency facilities, are becoming increasingly important facets of urban life. The emerging urban geographical interest in these services centres around the following three major themes.

1. Of primary interest is the scale of units, their relative spatial locations and the sizes and dispositions of the areas they serve. Choices have to be made between a relatively small number of large units located far apart and a larger number of smaller units spaced closer together. These alternative strategies have direct implications in terms of accessibility and the nature of the services offered, since the larger units can usually offer more specialized facilities. Hillman and Whalley (1977), in a study of sports and informal recreational facilities in urban areas, argued against the development of a small number of large leisure centres because these disadvantaged the 'low mobility' younger age-groups and those without a private car. The development of large specialized recreational complexes in central locations led to potential conflicts of the policy alternatives which should be resolved on their merits in relation to the perceived needs and circumstances of particular areas.

2. A second line of interest centres on the operational implications of the alternative strategies in terms of the 'efficiency' with which the service is provided. Firefighting services, for example, need locations which allow them to reach the outer limits of their service areas within acceptable time limits (Massam, 1975).

3. Again, the social implications of alternative strategies are worthy of investigation. This might involve the investigation of patterns of consumer usage and degrees of satisfaction with such services as recreational facilities, in relation to both accessibility and specialization. Alternatively, in the case of educational facilities interest might focus upon the social implications of alternative catchment-area strategies. Herbert (1976), for example, draws attention to the adverse social repercussions felt by America's black urban communities of defining neighbourhood catchment areas for secondary schools. The general conditions of underprivilege associated with life in the Negro ghettos is compounded by the *de facto* segregated status of the school system. Ultimately, this has given rise to policies designed to assist educational integration, such as redrawing catchment-area boundaries and bussing, as well as more general policies of compensatory education to reduce the educational imbalances in the cities. Similar misgivings relating to socially rather than ethnically based disadvantage have given rise to the definition of Educational Priority Areas in British cities (Herbert, 1976).

Although much of the literature is still essentially exploratory and policy statements tend to lack precision, there are indications that research into the geography of public utility services is proceeding on sounder foundations. Massam (1975) draws upon a wide literature in the social sciences relating to the provision and evaluation of public utility services and offers a comprehensive review of the theoretical concepts and methodologies which are likely to prove valuable to the future refinement of geographical investigation in this context.

CONSUMER BEHAVIOUR

In the introduction to this chapter it was indicated that an interactive relationship exists between systems of consumer-orientated services and the spatial patterns of utilization behaviour of the urban population. Such a general statement might be taken to imply a close and predictable relationship but as systems of service facilities respond to a wide range of formative influences, patterns of spatial behaviour are similarly complex. There is no comprehensive theory of consumer behaviour at the intraurban scale and in order to develop a better understanding of the functional characteristics of the systems of consumer services in the city, this section will focus directly upon studies of consumer behaviour.

The normative models

Studies based upon central place theory and spatial interaction theory assumed a simple interactive relationship between spatial structure and spatial behaviour, and *deduced* norms from *a priori* reasoning rather than from empirical data.

Central place theory

As indicated in Chapter 4 the majority of the literature on central place theory has been concerned with the derivation of a deductive theoretical basis for the development of hierarchical systems of service centres. A consumer is expected to use the nearest centre offering the goods or service required. From this expectation 'the nearest centre assumption' is derived as the basic behavioural tenet of central place theory (otherwise, 'the movement-minimization hypothesis') (Day, 1973).

A considerable amount of information now exists which demonstrates that this axiom is a serious overstatement of behavioural realities. Clark's (1968) study of Christchurch shoppers indicated that only 50–60 per cent of convenience shopping trips conformed to the nearest centre assumption. Similarly, Day's (1973) study in a London new town indicated that, while nearly all the interviewees lived closer to a neighbourhood centre than to the town centre, only 37 per cent of food purchases were local, and only 36 per cent of clothing purchases were made in the town centre, the remainder going to higher-order centres further afield.

This situation is perhaps not too surprising since Christäller's original work recognized at least two sources of behavioural deviations (Pred, 1967):

(1) The *multipurpose trip*, whereby a consumer may obtain both low and high-order goods at a high-order centre which is more distant than the closest low-order centre—or alternatively, travel to a more distant centre if sales price savings exceed additional transport cost.

(2) The tendency for consumer behaviour to be *satisficer* rather than optimal. An individual is unlikely to have a complete knowledge of the overall characteristics of the service system, and will for many social reasons be satisfied by undertaking journeys which will not necessarily result in an economic optimization of potential opportunities.

Because of the difficulty of accommodating such behavioural variations, central place theory has been virtually abandoned as a source of behavioural explanation in recent research though some research continues to show systematic behavioural variations associated with age, car-ownership and income characteristics of consumers.

Similar findings have been reported for the use of medical services in the United States (Morrill, Earickson, and Rees, 1970). In the inner city of Chicago only 55 per cent of patients visited the nearest physician and this fell to 35 per cent in the outer suburbs. The situation was similar for hospital visits. Only 55 per cent of inner-city patients, and 30 per cent of suburban patients, travelled to the nearest hospital. The hospital case reflects the nature of the two-stage trip via a physician referral and the fact that only 45 per cent of inner-city and 25 per cent of suburban physicians are affiliated to the nearest hospital. However, also of fundamental significance in explaining these patterns were the *preferences* of patients for particular physicians or hospitals. More recently, the inadequacy of the nearest centre assumption has been demonstrated in a British study of patterns of attendance at general medical practitioner surgeries (Phillips, 1978). In a survey of four residential sites in Greater Swansea, attendance at the nearest surgery ranged from 21–57 per cent.

Thus, at best, central place theory provides only a partial explanation of service utilization behaviour in the intraurban context, while the development of refinements necessary to rectify this situation is likely to prove extremely difficult. Consequently, it might be suggested that the value of central place theory to the study of consumer behaviour in cities is most relevant to an understanding of the spatial structure of service systems. Also, it provides a useful introduction to the study of consumer behaviour, since the partial explanatory value of the nearest centre assumption attests to the continuing significance of the friction of distance for spatial behaviour in the city. However, the detailed limitations and constraints on its behavioural assumption suggests that further investigation of consumer behaviour is likely to progress through an alternative research framework.

Spatial interaction theory

Spatial interaction theory in which behaviour is assumed to be determined by a complex tradeoff of the advantages or attractions of centre size against the disadvantage or disincentives of distance offers an alternative model.

At the intraurban scale, the wider range of shopping opportunities within relatively short distances renders the two-centre interaction situation of the original formulation of Reilly's (1931) 'law of retail gravitation' inappropriately deterministic. Huff (1963) considered it more likely that more than one centre would be used by the residents of an area with varying degrees of probability—varying in direct proportion to the relative attraction of the centre; in inverse proportion to some function of distance between the centre and the residential area; and in inverse proportion to the competition exerted upon the earlier relationships by all other centres in the system. These behavioural assumptions were independently incorporated into a probabilistic reformulation of the gravity model by Lakshmanan and Hansen (1965), which was designed to estimate the shopping expenditure flows between any residential area (i) and shopping centre (j) in a system:

$$S_{ij} = C_i \cdot \frac{\dfrac{A_j}{D_{ij}{}^b}}{\displaystyle\sum_{j=i}^{n} \dfrac{A_j}{D_{ij}{}^b}}$$

where

S_{ij} = the shopping expenditure of residents in area i spent in centre j

A_j = the size (or index of shopping attraction) of centre j

D_{ij} = the distance from area i to centre j

b = an exponent empirically calibrated using known origin-destination data to express the distance disincentive function operating in the system under investigation.

C_i = the total shopping expenditure of residents in area i.

The model was applied to existing shopping trips to higher-order centres in metropolitan Baltimore and it was found to provide a reasonable description of behavioural interaction. It was then rerun incorporating possible future residential areas and service centre structures in an attempt to evaluate the planning potential and problems which might be associated with alternative strategies. The model has some advantages. It has flexibility and it can be disaggregated with respect to important variations in the behavioural dynamics of shopping interaction.

However, a number of fundamental criticisms of the gravity model approach to the analysis and prediction of service utilization behaviour have been made. Jensen-Butler (1972) considers that, like central place theory, it proposes a theory of aggregate consumer behaviour without a firm basis in behavioural investigation. The normative assumptions may be important determinants of behaviour but they are intuitively derived and may, therefore, be associated with behavioural interaction in a non-explanatory manner. Consequently, additional investigation of the behavioural dynamics of trips is necessary before the model can be considered to provide a comprehensive explanation of behaviour.

In retrospect, Jensen-Butler's point might be considered unduly pessimistic and failed to take account of the large amount of available empirical information concerning shopping trips. The three assumed determinants of intraurban shopping behaviour patterns—the attraction of centres, the disincentive of distance, and the competition of alternative centres—all appear to exert a strong influence on shopping behaviour (Thomas, 1976) and no significant additional factor has yet been consistently identified. In fact, it is interesting to note that over 78 per cent of the variance in shopping behaviour patterns on Tayside were associated with an index of centre attraction in conjunction with distance travelled (Pacione, 1974). Similarly, in a study of choices of bowling alleys used in Buffalo, 81 per cent of the behavioural variation was explained by size of centre (37 per cent) and distance travelled (44 per cent) (Lieber, 1977).

The predictive use of the model is, however, fraught with difficulties because it essentially provides an allocative description of an existing situation, established using data describing the existing or a recent past situation. The extrapolation of the parameters of the model forward to predict consumer responses into a possibly quite different behavioural context is problematic and should only be undertaken with extreme caution. Again, there are unresolved technical issues associated with this type of model (Shepherd and Thomas, 1980).

Clearly, there remain problems associated with the gravity model, but none of these seems totally insurmountable and already versions exist which approximately describe the complex patterns of behaviour between residential areas and service facilities. The potential practical value of the model remains high and the recent neglect by researchers probably reflects the alternative interests and a focus of attention on the technical refinement of the models rather than on practical issues. The range of entropy-maximizing models (Wilson, 1970; 1974) has achieved greater technical sophistication but still awaits rigorous behavioural validation.

THE BEHAVIOURAL APPROACHES

The normative models do not provide a comprehensive description or explanation of consumer behaviour within the city. Thus, alternative approaches have been generated through the analysis of survey data obtained from individual respondents. Here the emphasis is upon the inductive research method and an individual scale of analysis.

In practice, a diffuse range of studies has been undertaken under the behavioural heading and they have not yet been synthesised into a comprehensive alternative theoretical formulation. Nevertheless, they provide a considerable amount of information relevant to the evaluation and improvement of the existing theories of consumer behaviour, as well as providing material which has shorter-term practical value for planning purposes. A number of research foci can be recognized, although it should be stressed that there are strong interrelationships between the categories.

Trade area studies

This approach derives from the work of Applebaum (1965; 1968) in the United States and focuses on the analysis of the functioning and commercial viability of a store or a shopping centre, using information obtained by interviewing shoppers within centres, or from information concerning the origins of customers. The aim has been to provide answers to questions of commercial planning rather than to develop behavioural generalizations. Thus, while a rich body of detailed survey material has emerged, it has been used only in limited ways to derive theories of behaviour.

Nevertheless, a number of recurrent behavioural generalizations have emerged. There is a strong tendency, due to the friction of distance, for shopping centres of all hierarchical levels to draw the greatest proportion of their customers from nearby areas, although the higher the hierarchical level of the centre the wider will this area be. There is also a significant tendency for trade-areas to overlap both within and between hierarchical levels. These findings tend to suggest behaviour consistent with the intraurban version of the gravity model. A similar situation has been indicated for the use of medical facilities in the United States (Morrill and Earickson, 1969), while Knox (1978) illustrates an equivalent distance–decay effect for the registration patterns of patients with general medical practitioners in Scottish cities.

Recent studies of planned suburban shopping centres have indicated the manner in which these behavioural generalizations are adjusting to changes in the system of centres. Johnston and Rimmer (1969) demonstrated that two new regional centres in the Melbourne suburbs had significantly wider spheres of influence than the older unplanned centres of similar status. Both planned centres drew approximately 70 per cent of their customers from a distinct suburban sector within $6\frac{1}{2}$ km (4 miles), compared with a figure of $4\frac{1}{2}$ km (3 miles) for most of the older unplanned centres. Also, the planned centres were developing at the expense of the older intermediate level centres within their trade areas, while also beginning to function as partial CBD substitutes. The new consumer behavioural tendencies were for local neighbourhood and corner-shop facilities to be used for convenience goods; the planned regional centres for most normal requirements; and the CBD for the highest-order speciality goods. Research elsewhere in Australia (Dawson and Murray, 1973) in Europe (Gantvoort, 1971) and Britain (Thorpe and Kivell, 1971) tends to confirm these statements. The impact of the new facilities including hypermarkets was felt by the smaller intermediate level centres, while the effect on CBD trading was substantially less. Clearly, the consistent conclusions emerging from these studies could result in the formulation of valuable general principles.

Aggregate consumer-behaviour studies

A second type of study tends to concentrate on surveys of shopping behaviour with random samples of consumers drawn from residential areas. In citywide surveys of this kind behavioural variations which emerge might be related either to socioeconomic characteristics of consumers, to available shopping opportunities or indeed to a complex combination of both these factors. Results of such surveys are largely descriptive, with some useful insights, and are not normally able to isolate the independent effects of specific factors as determinants of behaviour.

Davies (1973) organized a behavioural survey using a shopping diary for a single week, in which was recorded the origin and destination of trips, mode of travel, major purpose, items purchased and shops visited for a random 1 per cent sample of Coventry households. Journeys for convenience and durable goods suggested recognizable patterns. The central area appeared to serve the whole city for durable goods and also attracted a significant proportion of convenience-goods trips. Most of the convenience-goods trips were concentrated on the various lower-order centres, and there was evidence to suggest a significant number of durable-goods trips to the district centres. This information indicated the continued importance of a strong residential location effect upon behaviour, particularly for convenience goods and journeys to shops fell into ordered patterns: 'Consumers shop either within their immediate surroundings or alternatively go to the nearest largest centre to them'. This led Davies (1973) to support the applicability of the modified behavioural postulates of central place theory rather than those suggested by spatial interaction theory. Similar work has been undertaken by the Building Research Establishment in Watford (Daws and Bruce, 1971) and includes a useful review of the shopping diary approach to the investigation of spatial behaviour.

Similar work in North America provides evidence to suggest that despite widespread decentralization of service facilities and high levels of car ownership and use, a degree of orderliness in shopping behaviour remains (Brush and Gauthier, 1968; Holly and Wheeler, 1972). Despite a strong tendency towards overlapping hinterlands at a variety of hierarchical levels, shopping facilities were found not to have lost a local identity and a significant distance constraint upon behaviour persisted. Such evidence provides some support for the applicability of the behavioural norms of spatial interaction theory in North America.

Factors influencing consumer behaviour

To overcome the problems of analysis associated with the aggregate studies to advance understanding an increasing emphasis in British studies is placed upon the clarification of the influence of particular factors on behaviour. Most research has focused on the combined influence of variations in income, social status and personal mobility. A research design has usually been adopted whereby survey areas are designated which have similar access to equivalent shopping opportunities. R. L. Davies's (1969) study on Leeds and Thomas's

(1974) in Greater Swansea produced broadly similar results. In both cases for convenience-goods shopping significantly higher percentages of the higher-status groups tended to travel to a number of middle-order centres outside their immediate residential areas than their lower-status counterparts, although the effect did not extend as far as the CBD. This reflected the higher levels of car availability and usage demonstrated by the higher-status groups (Figure 6.25). In contrast, the lower-status groups were significantly more dependent upon the lower-order neighbourhood facilities, except for a small percentage of trips to the CBD by public transport (NB: the low-status behaviour approximates to the 'dual assignment rule' noted for low mobility consumers in the case of interurban food shopping behaviour by Lentnek, Lieber, and Sheskin (1975) in Chapter 4). Similar findings have been noted by Potter (1977) in

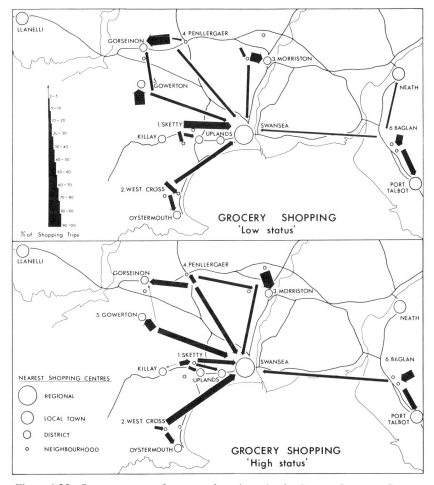

Figure 6.25 Some patterns of grocery shopping trips in Greater Swansea. Source: Thomas, 1974; reproduced by permission of Business Manager, Cambria

Stockport and they suggest that an increasingly mobile population is likely to require a wider choice of convenience goods than is normally available at the neighbourhood level, but falling short of the specialization offered by a CBD. However, for higher-order durable-goods shopping the CBDs dominated shopping trips irrespective of variations in socioeconomic status and mode of transport used.

The only other factor which has been significantly investigated to date is the effect of age-structure. Thomas (1974) suggested that an imbalance of families of preschool age is partly responsible for unexpectedly high allegiances to local facilities for convenience goods. Similarly, Potter (1977) notes the constraining influence of preschool children and also suggests a similar tendency for those over 60 years old. It may well be that the effects of age-structure are of limited importance but the evidence is both sparse and inconclusive.

Investigations of the factors affecting usage patterns of other urban services are relatively sparse, although interest is developing particularly in the sphere of medical services. Knox (1978), for example, in an introductory review indicates that while proximity is an important determinant of the choice and utilization of family doctors in Britain, there are major deviations from the nearest centre assumption. An array of factors is considered likely to contribute to this situation, such as the convenience of using surgeries near to workplaces and shopping centres, or surgeries with convenient consultation times. Alternatively, social barriers, such as perceived 'hostile territories' *en route* to a surgery, or psychological barriers such as a limited knowledge of the transport network or of the location of potential alternatives might be important. Finally, a range of other factors such as the personal attributes of the doctor or the inertial effect of a patient's former place of residence might be of some significance. However, the relative importance of the contribution of each of these factors to an understanding of either patterns of behavioural variation or to the efficiency and effectiveness of service provision is not clear.

Nevertheless, Phillips (1978, 1981) provides some explanatory evidence on these issues with reference to patterns of surgery attendance in West Glamorgan, using a methodology similar to the studies of shopping behaviour. Three survey areas were selected, each comprising two socially contrasted sites, in order to investigate the behavioural effect of variations in socioeconomic status and personal mobility. In detail, the patterns of behaviour which emerged were as complex as those demonstrated by convenience-shopping trips, despite the supposedly invariant quality of the public service offered.

However, a number of generalizations could be made, some of which closely parallel the shopping situation, though it should be remembered that each consumer could only 'enrol' with one practice. Where several practices were accessible, the high-status groups used local surgeries, but not necessarily the nearest (Figure 6.26). These were termed '*local variable*' attendance patterns and they reflected the personal choices of the patients in combination with high levels of personal mobility which allowed spatial flexibility, albeit in a relatively local area. In contrast, the low-status respondents conformed much

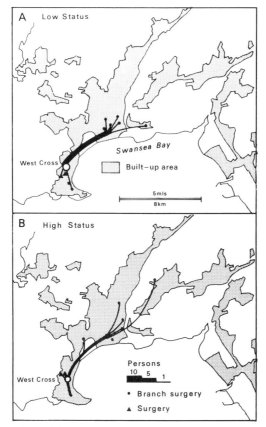

Figure 6.26 Consumer behaviour in medical services: surgeries visited by patients living in West Cross, Swansea. Source: Phillips, 1978; reproduced by permission of D. R. Phillips

more strongly to a '*dual attachment*' pattern. Either they used the nearest surgery, or, if a convenient public transport route existed, they travelled to a practice in the city centre (see 'dual assignment rule'). The latter effect was highly significant since it accounted for between 35 per cent and 57 per cent of the attendance patterns of the low-status respondents. However, unlike the shopping situation, the long-distance journey did not reflect only the availability of public transport, but was also strongly related to previous residence in the inner city prior to residential relocation to a peripheral local authority housing estate; in other words, it was in part a 'relict pattern'.

In addition, one survey area was located in the vicinity of a large health centre in an area in which no alternative practice was available. Not unexpectedly, the great majority of these respondents used this centre irrespective of their social characteristics. This illustrates the 'spatial monopoly' effect associated with the centralization of practices into larger centres, and it is interesting to note that it was the large health centres which were least favoured by the respondents (Phillips, 1978).

These studies demonstrate the influence of the socioeconomic status of consumers, their personal mobility and, to a lesser extent, their age characteristics upon the spatial behaviour. This strongly suggests that advances in the understanding of consumer behaviour in the city is likely to require the disaggregation of behaviour patterns to account for levels of social differentiation.

Constraints of spatial behaviour—'the disadvantaged consumer'

The behavioural variations associated with particular social characteristics of groups of people have in recent years given rise to increased interest in the existence of constraints. The general perspective is that particular subgroups, such as the lowest social classes or ethnic minorities, are restricted to whatever local services exist due to a combination of low income and restrictions on personal mobility. Policies affecting service distributions have, at best, ignored the needs of these groups and may even have exacerbated their adverse situation.

One area of deprivation involves personal mobility. Currently in Britain approximately 50 per cent of households have access to a private car. However, this figure obscures considerable variation. Many middle and upper-status residential neighbourhoods have ownership levels of 85 per cent, while lowstatus housing areas rarely exceed 40 per cent. This index of mobility has often been used in studies of consumer behaviour, but it still obscures much more extreme variations. Age and sex differentials are strongly related to vehicle licence holding rates (Hillman and Whalley, 1977). The younger and older age groups are potentially far less mobile than the middle age-ranges and this is particularly so for women:

	vehicle licence holders by age and sex (per cent)				
	17–20	*21–29*	*30–64*	*65 +*	all
Men	34	71	72	30	61
Women	6	32	25	4	21

(National Travel Survey 1972–73, quoted by Hillman and Whalley, 1977).

In fact, restrictions on the spatial activity patterns of women with young children have been explored in detail within the context of the 'gender role' constraint by Tivers (1977).

In addition, potential car use is further deflated for most of the day during the week due to its use in the journey to work for approximately 75 per cent of car-owning households. Hillman and Whalley (1977) suggest that this restriction is not necessarily redressed by public transport since, although 84 per cent of the population lives less than five minutes' walk from a bus stop, bus services are considered poor by at least a third of users due to unreliability, and a third of both mothers with young children and the aged reported significant difficulties with using the services. Also, the alternative of walking more than a quarter of a mile to a service poses considerable problems, particularly if the trip involves the purchase of bulky goods.

Hillman and Whalley's (1977) work was primarily concerned with travel to recreational facilities but a number of their conclusions are of wider interest. They suggest that future studies of spatial behaviour should be far more directly concerned with the potential mobility of consumers rather than the cruder indicator of car-ownership rates. Again, the policy implication that the development of a small number of large service facilities creates elements of disadvantage for these 'low-mobility' groups, so that in certain circumstances the alternative of more smaller but spatially dispersed facilities should be considered (see Shepherd and Thomas, 1980).

A second category of studies concerned with constraints focuses upon the spatial behaviour of ethnic minority groups. These groups also have low income and mobility but also have some culture-specific consumer demands and preferences, particularly for convenience goods and services. The structure of shopping facilities in such areas soon tends, like the other parts of the city, to reflect the nature of consumer demand and a particular subsystem of shopping facilities can be identified. A familiar pattern of small inefficient shops, high prices, low-quality goods, fewer services, upwards of 25 per cent of outlets catering for culture-specific products and a general air of dilapidation characterize the black neighbourhoods of North America and British cities (Davies, 1973; Rose, 1970; and Wallin, Schmidt and Lee, 1975).

Research into this theme is limited but some descriptions of behaviour in such areas exist. Caplovitz's (1960) study of the urban poor in New York indicated that the majority of shopping for convenience goods and services was restricted to the ghetto, although the younger, higher-income respondents and the long-time residents had wider patterns of behaviour. Similar findings were reported by Sturdivant (1969) for the Watts district of Los Angeles, although it was tentatively suggested that this reflected limited income and mobility rather than colour *per se*. Information for Britain is even more restricted but Davies (1973) suggests the dependence of the low-mobility coloured immigrants of Coventry upon local low-order shopping facilities for most of their purchases.

The use of other service facilities by ethnic minorities has not been investigated to a significant degree. However, the study of the health-care utilization behaviour of the negro and other low-status groups in the United States, already introduced in an earlier section, is worthy of reiteration at this point due to the central significance of constraints on the behaviour of these groups.

Also relevant to the study of constraints on behaviour is the increasing attention being given to a *cognitive* aspect of spatial behaviour. The underlying assumption of this approach (Thomas, 1976) is that an important stimulus to consumer decision-making is the respondent's perception of available opportunities. Thus, attention has focused on the measurement of 'spatial information fields', or the range of service facilities which are best known to the consumer, on the assumption that there may be a direct relationship between the spatial information field and the facility visited.

Early work by Horton and Reynolds (1971) attempted to measure the part of the urban environment which was most familiar to spatially defined subgroups (their 'action space'). This was considered likely to encompass the majority of their recurrent spatial behaviour ('activity space'). An individual's action space was conceptualized as being formed by the interaction of the social, economic and psychological characteristics of the individual with the objective spatial characteristics of the urban environment. Residential location was still found to be a dominant influence so that familiarity with the urban area was likely to decline with distance from home, while social interaction at the residential site tended to reinforce this spatial familiarity bias. Individual action spaces are to a large extent shared by persons in close geographical and social propinquity. This finding was supported for two socially contrasting areas in Cedar Rapids, Iowa. Action spaces tended to be sectoral, centring on the home area and focusing on the central business district, while the overall familiarity levels of the middle-income group were significantly higher than those of the lower-income group.

Similar findings were noted in Stockport by Potter (1976, 1977). Again, the action spaces were sectoral, centring on the residence of the respondent and including the central business district, while the same status differential recurred. In addition, a directional bias was demonstrated whereby a significantly higher degree of familiarity occurred with centres located in a *downtown direction* from the consumer's home, a feature which was earlier noted by Lee (1970) as 'Brennan's Law'. Hanson's (1977) concepts of 'cognitive opportunity set' and 'cognitive level' developed for Uppsala, Sweden are closely analogous to the action space and activity space ideas.

None of these studies attempts to distinguish whether consumer behaviour is determined by space perception or whether behaviour creates the images noted. Nevertheless, their relevance is clear. A knowledge of individual or group spatial information fields provides an indication of the area in which consumer search behaviour is likely to be constrained. Thus, the definition of such fields is likely to be relevant to the analysis and modelling of consumer spatial behaviour in general.

Consumer behaviour within shopping centres

The investigation of patterns of shopping behaviour within centres has been generated because the detailed manner in which shoppers use a centre can have a considerable influence upon the commercial viability of particular sites. The lack of integration of pedestrian flows, transport termini and shop locations in either old centres or comprehensive redevelopment schemes can result in 'dead space' and virtually unlettable shop units. Such a result has a highly detrimental effect on commercial or public investment, while at the same time

261

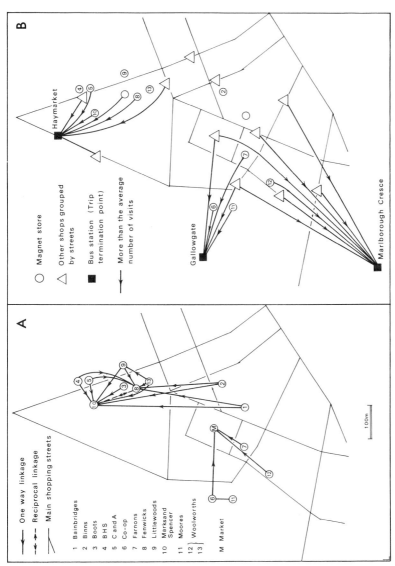

Figure 6.27 Factors affecting shopping behaviour patterns within a central area: Newcastle-upon-Tyne. (a) Shopper linkages between 'Magnet' stores. (b) Shopper linkages with selected Trip Termination Points. Source: Bennison, Davies, 1977; reproduced by permission of Department of Geography, University of Newcastle-upon-Tyne

creating adverse environmental problems. Attention has focused on the identification of the determinants or recurrent patterns of behaviour, the attitudes of shoppers to varying spatial arrangements of facilities and the definition of principles which might result in the most efficient and satisfying spatial organization of functions.

Early examples of such studies, which were partial elements in much wider investigations, are provided by Boal and Johnson (1965) in Canada, and Davies (1973) in Britain. However, a more comprehensive example has been provided recently by Bennison and Davies (1977) for Newcastle-upon-Tyne (Figure 6.27). Pedestrian flows were analysed and these were complemented by a questionnaire survey of shoppers interviewed in a variety of locations. The functional linkages between stores and shopping streets were illustrated to determine the main influences upon shopper behaviour. These suggested the primary importance of large 'magnet' stores on recurrent behaviour patterns and the secondary, but significant, importance of trip termination points at bus stops or car parks. This represents a productive line of research which promises interesting results.

Other relevant research has tended to concentrate upon more specific aspects of behaviour. Bishop (1975), for example, examines the attitudes of the public, business interests, the public transport authorities and various other organizations in Portsmouth to the pedestrianization of a main shopping street. He suggested that beneficial commercial and environmental effects resulted, which were positively received by a substantial majority of shoppers. This was related to the fact that the scheme was well integrated with natural pedestrian routes, shopping nodes and transport termini. A related study was undertaken by Schiller (1975) in eight small historic towns, half of which had undergone central area redevelopment. Attention focused on the effects of redevelopment on the commercial viability of historic shopping streets, marginal to the shopping centres, and no significantly adverse effect was demonstrated. Clearly, these sorts of findings could form a base from which general principles for the improvement of circulation patterns in city centres could be developed.

A more specifically cognitive orientation was adopted in Erlangen, West Germany (Meyer, 1977). An investigation was made of the perceptions of shoppers of distances within shopping centres. It appeared that distance was consistently underestimated in the part of the central area nearest to the respondent's home and in the parts which were most used. Elsewhere, they were significantly overestimated. These findings were directly related to variations in familiarity associated with habitual shopping behaviour patterns. The conclusion that the images noted were likely to stabilize shopping patterns rather than promote experimental variation is a contention which might be worthy of closer examination.

Clearly, some interesting findings are emerging from the study of shopping behaviour within centres and it seems that further work might provide information relevant to the planning and design of shopping centres likely to influence developers' and planners' decisions on pedestrianization, layout of malls and balance of selling space and associated facilities.

Chapter 7

The Changing Social Geography of the City: Residential Patterns

THE CITY IN TRANSITION: NINETEENTH-CENTURY URBANIZATION IN BRITAIN AND AMERICA

Processes of change

For much of the nineteenth century the city in western societies was in a stage of transition, the initiation and pace of which varied from one society to another and between larger and smaller urban areas. This transition had innumerable impacts upon the internal structure of the city, affecting its population size and density, its areal extent, morphology, economic functions, and a range of social and political characteristics, but it was underlain by far-reaching changes which were transforming the overall nature of societal organization. Economic change prompted by the forces for industrialization provided one dominant trend; a change from a traditional 'feudal' society to one dominated by the capitalist ethic was another. The changing social geography of the nineteenth-century city must first be viewed against the contexts of these adjustments in the macro-structure of society. Beyond that it is essential to identify the 'enabling mechanisms' which allowed the adjustments to find spatial expressions. In some instances, the needs of the new economies and sets of relationships brought immediate and specific changes, more usually—and especially in terms of residential structure—the traditional forms of urban life responded more slowly to new circumstances. Whereas the wealthy could initiate change and provide the means to achieve it, the large mass of urban population was governed by constraints rather than by choices, and they could only respond to possible alternatives when presented.

Most writers would agree that the transition represented in the nineteenth century is one between the city in *traditional* to the city in *modern* societies. Many make use of ideas of stage models as represented by Schnore (1965) or Timms (1971) which can usually be related to the transition from the type of spatial generalization proposed by Sjoberg (1960), in which high-status areas were located at the city centre and lowest-status areas on the periphery, to that associated with Burgess (1925) in which a reverse arrangement existed. At the broadest level of generalization both these sets of ideas, of stages and of 'model' spatial generalizations, retain some usefulness; it is increasingly clear, however, that neither are adequate either to describe the complex processes of change or their expressions in urban form and sociospatial organization. Whereas it is convenient to work within a framework of stages and models, it is also necessary to demonstrate that the details of process and pattern are at least as significant as the generalizations.

For Vance (1971) the terminology of change from preindustrial to industrial city is less appropriate than that of precapitalist to capitalist. It is this latter labelling which more adequately describes the changing relationship between employer and worker and the new interpretations which were put upon land and housing as they became 'commodities' in the new capitalist order. Industrialization and the emergence of capitalism had many expressions in nineteenth-century society; for the study of emerging residential patterns the most significant were the increases in specialization, differentiations, and stratifications which were eventually to form the bases of residential separation and segregation in the modern city. Allied to these, another key change involved the relationship between workplace and home. During the long age of the city in traditional societies, separation of workplace and home had been extremely limited; as increasing scale of enterprise prompted some levels of social stratification within the 'workshop' economy, it was contained within different floors of buildings rather than expressed in terms of different residences. As Vance (1971) suggests, floor-by-floor juxtaposition was very much the rule; the very poor occupied cellars or garrets and, otherwise, apart from the fact that the ground floor was often used for business, the status of occupants declined with increasing altitude within the building.

Before the increasing social differentiation between employer and employees and among the labour force could become spatial segregation, there had to occur a much more general separation of workplace and home than hitherto existed. This did occur during the nineteenth century and is the central process in understanding the changing social geography during this transitional period. Essential adjuncts of this process were the development of efficient enabling mechanisms, principally the ability of an emerging housing market to supply accommodation, and the evolution of a transport system which allowed this to be linked with workplace in a daily rhythm. The availability of these facilities and of other resources which allowed choice was typically limited initially to those very small sections of society which controlled wealth and power. In many ways the long duration of the transitional 'stage' and its variability from city to city was related to the variable way in which these facilities became available to other sections of the population. None of these various forces were independent; their cumulative effect during the nineteenth century was to change both the spatial generalization typical of the city in traditional societies and to establish new and more compartmentalized bases upon which the residential geography of the city was ordered.

Much of the available geographical research on the nineteenth century city has focused upon the task of providing snapshot pictures of residential structure at one or more precise points in time. This research is valuable and has been most successful in identifying patterns and their changes over time and in revealing the local processes of residential mobility which accompany those changes. It has been less successful to date, however, either in relating these patterns and processes to more general forces of societal transformation or in revealing the roles of the agencies which provide the conditions under which change can occur. Some of the detailed geographical research on pattern change will be discussed but some of the available insights on the broader processes can be summarized.

For Marxist geographers, the broad forces behind the city in transition can be squarely ascribed to the process of capital development which began, in the early nineteenth century, to force rapid urbanization, new patterns of production and new divisions of social life (Walker, 1978); the choice of urban solution is sharply defined by the structural imperatives of the capitalist mode of production. Using a more broadly based perspective, Vance (1971) argues that the changes were engendered as the growth of the industrial city prescribed new forms of land use and made new demands upon labour. The capitalist ethic, given dramatic stimulus by the forces of economic change, transformed the nature of social relationships and established both land and housing as commodities to be owned rather than simply held. In the context of housing, in particular, a number of new characteristics had emerged. Whereas in the past the offer of employment had often carried the obligation to house, this became a decreasing feature; ability to pay rent became a criterion affecting both quality and location of residence. Significant changes in attitudes and interpersonal relationships were occurring. Attitudes towards rent, property and profit, which would have been misplaced in medieval society, became acceptable.

Urban morphology began, slowly, to respond to these changing circumstances. If an individual had wished to enlarge his premises in the medieval city, he did so by building upwards, which created the tall house in northern Europe, and by extending backwards to infill the burgage plot (Conzen, 1960). Such infilling was not normally for profit in a direct sense but to extend the family business unit or occupational group. Containment of the extended family under one roof was more typical of the better-off but under the workshop principle, master, workers and apprentices all lived under one roof (Figure 7.1 (a)). Under an emerging factory system, the processes which led to separation were initiated. Vance (1966) has traced the development of 'mill villages' in both Rhode Island (Figure 7.1 (b)) and Nottinghamshire as an early clear example of the new form of workplace/residence organization. Under these first expressions of the factory system, the separate place of work became the focal point, and around this a landscape of small cellular units emerged involving short daily journeys by workmen. In these situations, the industrialist was still the provider of housing—which was an adjunct of productive activity—but an initial stage of separation had been achieved. For the labour force of these early factories, the employment link was small, direct, and highly specific.

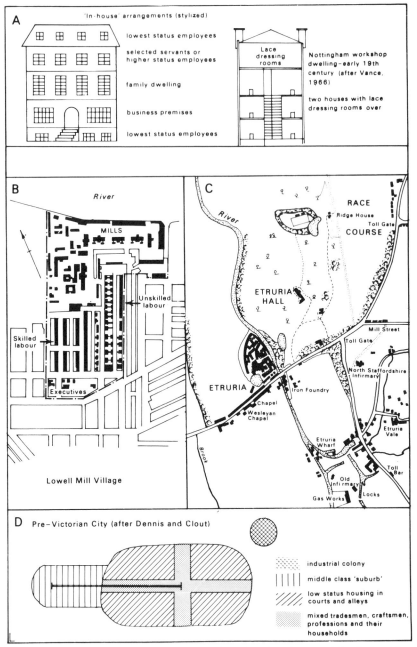

Figure 7.1 Work and residence in the city: the changing spatial relationship. (a) Work and residence within one building: social stratification by floors (derived in part from Vance, 1966). (b) Lowell mill village with separation of works and residence and 'social areas' (after Vance, 1966). (c) Etruria, Stoke-on-Trent. Wedgwood's move from Burslem to Etruria Hall, separate works on the canal and workers' cottages. (d) A schematic representation of the emerging early Victorian city (after Dennis and Clout, 1980; reproduced by permission of *Economic Geography*)

Within the context of pre-existing urban areas there were parallel developments but the spatial outcomes were less simple. Existing urban fabric did not present such unfettered possibilities; urban space was already in possession of a morphology and a set of values. As the workshop/domestic activity was replaced by the factory system, increasing scale of activity generated a demand for new labour. These workers had to be accommodated in cottages and tenements which were constructed in the alleys and courts behind the main street façades. Infill now became a more direct source of profit, and as space was used congestion began to appear in the inner city (Figure 7.1(d)). The merchants who occupied main-street housing now began to be faced with alternatives. Depending on the profitability of infill, the availability of new peripheral land and transport, there were possibilities of releasing ground-floor or first-floor space to business expansion, and managers rather than owners became the inner-city dwellers. As the attractiveness of the central city began to wane, higher-income groups began to accept short journeys to work in order to displace themselves from the workplace.

It would be wrong to locate the origins of these trends in the nineteenth-century city; in twelfth-century London there were high-status residences around the city periphery. These, however, the isolated mansions of the powerful, provide an early example of a continued preference for the rural retreat rather than any real beginnings of suburbanization. Similarly, well before the nineteenth century, early 'industrialists' had left the towns in which they had established their production processes; Wedgwood, for example, had left the Pottery town of Burslem to find a more rural setting for Etruria Hall (Figure 7.1(c)). It was during the nineteenth century, however, that the trickle became a stream and newly emerging professional men and businessmen sought to emulate the new residential examples of the élite. For Vance (1971) the significant change was in the nature of housing; from being a specific contract between employer and employee, it became generalized and by 1850 a true urban proletariat had been formed. Housing supply had now to be extensive, so a housing market—distinct from any workplace contractual agreement—was necessary to administer it. This may have had deleterious effects: 'housing generalization led to the creation of slums ... it grew out of the abandonment of the self-correcting mechanism of enlightened self-interest that had existed in factory-tied housing' (Vance, 1966, p. 324).

The acceptability of this last sentiment is questionable. That there were new attitudes to housing provision is clear; whether prior attitudes were necessarily good and subsequent ones bad is less obvious. More recently, the appropriateness of the appellation 'slum' has been questioned as a generalization upon Victorian low-cost housing (Ward, 1975). Whatever the quality of housing, however, a sequence of home/workplace relationships can be recognized from occupational district to mill village to proletariate residential quarter.

For the new professionals and businessmen, the separation of housing from area of economic effort brought new attitudes. High-income residential *areas* gave exclusion, a need arose to create symbols of affluence and power distinct from those of aristocracy and gild-leader. Whereas (Ward, 1975) the traditional system of social differentiation did not require reinforcement by an appropriate address, the new uncertain bases of status encouraged residence in socially more homogeneous areas. The emerging high-income groups acted concertively to develop particular kinds of residential districts and imbued them with lifestyles and social flavours which set them apart (Cowlard, 1979). Several writers have argued that these changes affected family lifestyle as well (Shaw, 1977; Ward, 1975). As employers loosened bonds with the workplace, they were able to choose where to live with the *nuclear* family; it was among the low-income areas that the *extended* family in close proximity was to be found by the end of the nineteenth century. As the higher-income and later the white-collar groups acted on a preference for 'rural' settings, an aversion to place of production and crowded living areas, and a desire to avoid the rising taxes of the central city, the advantages were clear to many others. For the working classes, the mid-nineteenth century was a time when it would have been desirable to secure less crowded and un-healthy quarters but their exodus had to await the development of trolleybuses in the late 1880s. The railroads had brought transport possibilities to the white-collar groups in the 1830s but as Ward (1964) suggested, innovation and expansion of the streetcar system was achieved more rapidly in the United States than in Britain. Walker summarized the trends as they affected American cities: as a concentration of production and circulation in the central city, interwoven with workers' homes; an outward residential thrust of the bour-geoisie; and a dramatic increase in the economic and social differentiation of urban space.

In addition to the general societal forces for change and their expression as urban processes, the essential mechanisms needed besides a transport system included a building and construction industry and a set of new agencies to administer the housing market. Whereas geographers have made limited contribution to the study of such agencies social historians have, properly, ascribed to them a significant role.

The character of the place and its different neighbourhoods, was determined by the builders themselves, or more strictly by the developers—those large builders ... who took large leases of building land and organized its disposition, saw to the laying out of the lesser residential roads, the making of sewers and the provision of water supply, and who generally arranged sub-leases with smaller builders for individual houses or small groups of houses (Thompson, 1977, pp. 108–9; quoted in Shaw, 1979, p. 195).

The roles of the 'managers' of the housing market were in existence and warrant closer attention.

Residential patterns in the nineteenth century

For a number of North American and British cities, detailed studies are now available which depict residential patterns at the mid-nineteenth century.

For British studies the basic data sets are provided by census enumerators' returns which, after a lapse of a century, become available in their original detailed form. This is a rich and productive data source, though it has presented some problems. Some of the manuscript entries pose difficulties of interpretation, the detail given to street addresses is variable, and the problem of interpreting and classifying descriptions—particularly those concerned with occupation—has required a great deal of detailed research in its own right. Within the *caveats* of the data, however, a range of sound and detailed studies, mainly for the census dates of 1851 and 1871, have emerged. For North American studies, data sources are more diverse but have generally allowed analyses of comparable detail.

Most empirical studies have the objectives of identifying the 'dimensions' or 'bases' of residential differentiation and the extent to which these find expression in spatial forms. Many have used factor analysis methods although there is no marked consistency in the particular technical procedures which have been adopted. Shaw (1977, 1979) studied Wolverhampton at two points in time; 1851, when it had a population of 49,985 and 1871 when it had reached 68,291. His interpretation was that by the earlier date it was well into the transition from preindustrial to modern industrial city. A principal components analysis showed that, in 1851, social status was the main dimension though this was strongly linked with family status and with domestically organized trading. An ethnic dimension, specifically Irish, was evident. The social geographical divide was between areas of relatively high social status where servants were common, dealing a principal occupation, and many household members were not related to the head, and the coalmining districts within the urban area in which social class was low, servants were rare and there were many children in employment. By 1871 some measure of change could be identified. The leading dimension was now more clearly related to family status with a range from low scores in the central, dealing district to high in wholly residential areas. In the central district, business households were run by a manager and contained many single adults; the proprietor and his family had moved to the suburbs. A separate social status dimension had emerged which located the high-status groups in the western part of the town.

Lewis's (1979) study of Cardiff used three sources of data—rate-books, census records, and health reports—to identify residential patterns at 1851 and 1871. At the earlier date, vestiges of the preindustrial city were discerned with high-status groups living mainly centrally in the main business streets and the rest of the population crowded into limited space between canal and railway. By the early 1870s, there were modifications to this pattern but the study concluded that modern conditions of segregation had not fully emerged. Other British studies have found similar blurred patterns; Gordon (1979) could identify neither preindustrial nor modern spatial generalizations in his study of mid-Victorian Edinburgh.

The major British study concerned with the reconstruction of residential patterns in the nineteenth-century city has been based upon Liverpool (Lawton

and Pooley, 1975). Here the transition towards the modern industrial city
was found to be advanced at mid-century:

the rapidly growing city of the mid-Victorian period exhibited a high degree of residential
differentiation: the main social dimensions of city structure had clear spatial expression
and were reflected in distinctive social areas (Pooley, 1977, p. 364).

The bases of separation were demographic, economic and social—reminiscent of 'modern' patterns; the central area had long since ceased to be residential
and trends towards suburbanization were evident. These apparently clear
trends away from preindustrial patterns and the less convincing evidence of
other studies, may well reflect the position of Lancashire as an early industrializ-
ing region and Liverpool as its most rapidly growing city. At the head of the
'new' urban hierarchy, movement through transition was well advanced
by mid-century; elsewhere the process probably began later and took longer
to complete. It is also unfortunate that many British studies have been of
smaller towns rather than major cities.

Goheen (1970) has provided one of the most detailed studies of a North
American city with his analysis of evolving residential patterns in Toronto
between 1850 and 1900. At the beginning of this period the wealthy were able
to segregate in their quarters but remained at the centre where they could
both take advantage of urban amenities and exercise influence on urban
affairs. At the opposite social status extreme, the unskilled were segregated
into pockets at the urban periphery with maximum disadvantages of environments and locations. Between these extremes, and accounting for a large
part of the urban population was considerable heterogeneity of functions,
classes, and residences. By 1870, there had been significant change; economic
status, family status and ethnic (Roman Catholic) segregation were distinctive
and independent dimensions, even though they found only limited territorial
expression. By the turn of the century, both the scale and texture of urban
life had become transformed; the bases of social differentiation and the distribution of groups essentially corresponded with those of the modern city.

A study of Pittsburgh (Swauger, 1978) was able, through the use of a contemporary directory, to establish the pattern of residential areas in 1815.
By that year the population of the town had reached 8000, having grown
from a 1784 figure of 376. This rapid growth had the effect of increasing
densities in the urban area with subdivision of lots and infilling of spaces
behind older properties. The great majority of workers were independent
craftsmen working at home. In 1815 a distinction could be made between a
largely high-status core and a low-status periphery, confirming the preindustrial
model. Swauger, however, regarded the peripheral residences of a small group
with private means as significant. Where higher-status residents were freed
from the necessity of daily work journeys, their preference was for peripheral
locations; even at this early date, therefore, poor transport rather than choice
dictated the need for the better-off to live centrally. In another study Radford

(1976) looked at the development of Charleston, South Carolina, as a 'slave city' in 1860 and 1880. Detailed patterns of segregation were emerging but a central feature was the pushing of the free blacks to the urban periphery, a pattern which persisted after the civil war. His detailed studies of Charleston in mid-nineteenth century have enabled him to recognize the main outlines of the preindustrial spatial model although, as might be expected, there are deviations (Radford, 1979).

Several recent writers (Ward, 1975; Muller and Grove, 1979) have stressed the relatively low levels of residential differentiation which existed in American cities throughout much of the nineteenth century. While the outward expansion of affluence can be traced to early dates, its generality was very limited. Ward's argument is that workshop districts persisted, as the only clear segregations occurred at the extremes of the socioeconomic spectrum affecting relatively small groups.

The dominant change in the social geography of nineteenth century cities was not the separation of the tiny minority of the affluent and socially prominent from the vast majority of urban residents, but rather a complex, internal residential differentiation of the less affluent majority .... Although there were undoubtedly concentrations of extremely destitute people ... far larger areas housed a mixture of lesser professionals, petty proprietors, master craftsmen, journeymen, laborers, and domestic outworkers (Ward, 1976, pp. 330–1).

If spatial segregation existed it was on a micro-scale of street or alley which nevertheless involved close and frequent contact among a heterogeneous population.

Conclusions

If the neat patterns of residential separations which typify the modern city were only slowly finding expression in physical form and social geography through much of the nineteenth century, the forces and processes which were eventually to produce them were nevertheless well under way. Walker (1978) described Southwark as Philadelphia's first suburb in the eighteenth century, and in the earlier part of the nineteenth century it began to be commonplace for the fastest-growing areas to lie outside political boundaries; the annexation process had begun. As suburbanization developed, it was related to capitalist development, new patterns of production, new divisions of social life and an evolving preference for residence on the urban periphery which an expanding urban infrastructure made increasingly possible. Ward (1975) rightly attaches significance to the increasing levels of residential differentiation among the large group of less affluent which, by the late nineteenth century, began to result in the emergence of more homogeneous social areas. These cities were truly in transition. They contained vestiges of the old patterns and portents of the new, always modified by local conditions and particular urban characteristics; but virtually ubiquitous were the processes of change which were affecting all qualities of urban life.

THE BASES OF URBAN RESIDENTIAL SEGREGATION

While some segregation of residential areas can be recognized in the city in traditional societies and—in varying degrees and forms—as the western city passed through its stage of transition, it is in the twentieth century that patterns of residential differentiation have become most clearly established. The bases of residential segregation in these cities are reasonably well-known and have been most commonly identified as socioeconomic status, family status or stage-in-life cycle, minority group membership or ethnic status, and, in many cases, migrant status (Figure 7.2). These 'dimensions' emerge most clearly in North American cities where housing is allocated on market principles in a capitalist economy. All three, therefore, have a common link with an economic basis of differentiation and the ability to buy or rent a dwelling unit which matches a household's position in social space. An orderly social geography relates both to the fact that similar households are exercising similar choices and also to the roles of the agencies of the housing market in providing a variety of types of dwellings as uniform clusters in specific spatial locations.

The notion of choice along any of the dimensions, however, requires considerable modification; constraints of some kind are always present and decisions are rarely entirely in the hands of individual consumers. Similarly, a view that economic bases produce the mosaic is seductive but only partial. Both individual dwellings and residential areas are imbued with social and symbolic values in addition to the economic rent they may command on the housing market. From that time when an urban housing market began to emerge and place of residence became separate from place of work, 'home' began to acquire special meaning. A further qualifying factor is provided by the manner in which the internal structure of the city *develops* over time. At any one point in time the city presents a 'time-layered' mosaic; its different parts have different ages, histories and morphologies, it is a multi-stranded

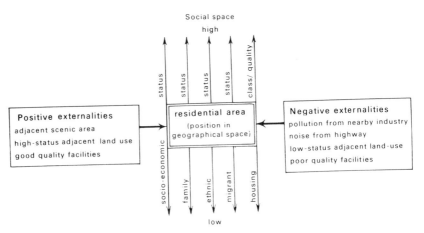

Figure 7.2 Bases of residential segregation and associated externalities

rather than a single-stranded surface. During the 1960s, much work in urban geography focused upon the task of using available objective data, mainly from national censuses, to identify the patterns of residential areas. This research will be reviewed but first some of the qualities of residential separation in western cities will be discussed.

The extent of residential separation

Attempts to establish the actual extent of residential separation have focused on the clearest ways in which social distinctions have found spatial expression; ethnicity is therefore a dominant theme. Such studies work within limits imposed by the quality of available data and the levels of spatial disaggregation for which they are available. Most commonly a number of indices of segregation are used of which the Index of Dissimilarity is the best known; this is stated

$$I_d = \frac{1}{2} \sum_{i=1}^{k} |x_i - y_i|$$

or one-half the sum of differences between two population groups, x and y, for each of i spatial units in a given city. The two population groups may be minorities, such as blacks compared with Hispanics, or may comprise one minority group compared with the total population. Indices of dissimilarity fall within a range of 0 to 100 and form measures of displacement—the proportion of the total population of one specified group required to move residence in order for no segregation to exist. A score of 100 indicates complete segregation.

Generally, results of these analyses, particularly of ethnic groups, for western cities reveal high levels of segregation. In the United States, for example, a study of cities in 1960 (Taeuber and Taeuber, 1965) obtained a median index of dissimilarity between blacks and whites of 87.8 at the city-block level of spatial disaggregation, and of 79.3 at the census tract level; Rees (1979) calculated a segregation index for blacks in twelve American urban areas of 76.2. British analyses of New Commonwealth immigrants suggest that levels of residential segregation are increasing in the 1970s, and indices based upon 1971 census data range from 38 for Indians to 51 for Caribbeans; but in Coventry the Pakistanis with an index score of 70 proved the most segregated (Jones, 1979). A study of Belfast in the late 1960s (Poole and Boal, 1973) produced an index score of 70.9 for street-by-street segregation between Catholics and Protestants, a figure certainly exceeded by the late 1970s after a decade of urban violence. Immigrant groups have been found to retain residential separation even after several decades in Australian and American cities (Timms, 1978).

Ethnic minorities have been intensively researched both because of their obvious segregation and because of the relative ease and accuracy with which ethnic variables can be identified in censuses. Accurate measures of social class or socioeconomic status are more difficult to obtain. In a study of census tract data for eight American cities using occupational groups, Fine, Glenn, and Monts (1971) found indices of 27 between professional and clerical workers, 50 between professional and unskilled manuals, and 36 between unskilled manuals and clerical workers; findings which seem, rationally, to indicate greater residential separation with increasing social distance. In a replicative study based on Australian data, Timms (1978) produced indices of 35, 46, and 32 respectively for the same groups. Duncan and Duncan (1955) brought together a large number of American studies and concluded that socioeconomic status segregation was most marked at extremes of the hierarchy; in other words, the very rich and very poor were most segregated but there was less clear differentiation by residential areas in the broad middle band. This finding has some intuitive appeal but the problems of occupational definition, upon which status divisions are based, are greatest in this middle band. Studies of British cities (Morgan, 1975) reveal similar results but tend to show less marked segregation at the lower end of the socioeconomic status scale. They also suggested that socioeconomic status segregation is higher in larger cities, particularly those in which there are high proportions of professionals and managers in the labour force.

Analyses of segregation based upon demographic characteristics have obtained modest results. Most of these have focused on segregation of the elderly, a group for which age-segregation is thought to be increasing. Golant (1980) reports a study in which indices of dissimilarity ranging between 10.8 and 37.7 were calculated between population aged 65 years and over and the rest of the population for 72 American cities. For this subgroup studied over the 241 American SMSAs, Cowgill (1978) obtained an index range from 15.2 to 44.4. The elderly possess a level of residential segregation but this is not as high as that identified either for ethnic minorities or for socioeconomic status groups. Of more general interest are the levels of lifecycle stage segregation and here the problem of data and measurement make calculation difficult. A lifecycle stage has no necessary close correlation with chronological age and is also affected by time-lags which may blur the link between change of stage and its expression in residential mobility.

The meanings of residential area: values and externalities

Studies based on indices of dissimilarity provide objective support for hypotheses that residential separation is a feature of western cities. Whereas the 'facts' of segregation may not always be convincing, either because of problems of data or measurement or because heterogeneity within some areas exists, it is nevertheless true, as Timms (1978) argues, that the notion of the city as a mosaic of social worlds has become part of the general intellectual imagery of the city. The validity of this image may become difficult to disentangle from its acceptance as part of the 'taken-for-granted' world. Similarly, Suttles (1972) argues that attempts to use cognitive mapping techniques to explore the subjective view of the city can merely provide sell-fulfilling prophecies which 'tailor' the urban landscape into discrete forms.

For many cities at late stages of the nineteenth century, the residential mosaic was still some distance away both as image and as reality. Its emergence and consolidation during the twentieth century can best be explained as a maturation of those trends and processes already identified. Place of residence acquired both a use and an exchange value. Qualities relevant to its use included design, size, access and status; its exchange value was dependent on these but found direct expression as the price it could command for sale or rent as a commodity on the housing market. In an increasingly specialized and stratified society, the economic and social roles held by an individual had to be matched by style of house and residential area. As Beshers (1962) has argued, if social structure exists as an aggregate, its effects must be revealed in residential areas and because residence is such an important item in lifestyle, residential area must act as a symbol of social position. Residential area has many meanings which will be explored; for the moment however the contention is merely that it is *one* of the significant reference points for behaviour. As Williams (1971) and Sennett (1973) have pointed out, residential area or 'sociospatial unit' provides an example of a *coalition of interests* for individuals and households who occupy a certain ecological niche within the urban residential pattern.

As residential area may provide unifying bonds for its occupants, it may also place them in conflict with occupants of other residential areas. *Externalities* are a frequent cause of such conflict (see Figure 7.2). These may be defined as goods which households consume but do not produce themselves (Cox, 1973). Positive externalities are benefits produced by the activities of others, nearby residents or owners of adjacent properties; an example would be the rezoning of a piece of land which causes neighbouring properties to appreciate in value. Negative externalities are the opposite, costs or disadvantages induced by the actions of others, such as pollution from a nearby factory. There are, broadly, three types of externality which may lead to conflict and which 'cement' the significant roles of residential areas.

The first is that the public behaviour of their neighbours should be consonant with their own, thereby assisting the household to maintain its position in society; this neighbourhood consonance is frequently seen as particularly important for the socialization and upbringing of children, who are restricted in their spatial range, particularly when young, to their immediate home environs. There, models of how to behave are provided in the home, by their immediate family, in the neighbourhood school, and in the neighbourhood itself. The first are under direct parental control; the nature of the other two reflects the area in which their home is situated, for most children attend a nearby, if not the nearest school. Thus the sort of area in which they live is crucial for most parents concerned with the nature of their children's upbringing. If neighbours do not provide the desired environment, or if neighbours change (as with the black 'invasions' with ghetto expansion in American cities: Rapkin and Grigsby, 1960), then the locality produces a negative externality.

The second externality for which people compete is status and social advancement, which may be sought through interaction with people who can assist, perhaps unknowingly, in the achievement of social aspirations. Many parents, for example, hope that their children will 'improve' their position by marrying into a group with more wealth, status and power, and believe that by living among such groups they give their children a better chance of such advancement (Beshers, 1962). Such a belief is based on an assumption that social networks are spatially constrained, that social contact is a function of spatial propinquity. Whether this is indeed so has been widely debated by social scientists from a variety of backgrounds. There is no consistent evidence, for example, that brides and grooms from the same city are more likely to live near to each other prior to their marriage than would happen with a random mate selection process (Ramsøy, 1966), or that people have more contact with their nearest neighbours than with those living a few doors away (Johnston, 1974b; Stutz, 1974). Again, many suburbs comprise a wide range of informal social groupings of neighbours (Whyte, 1960). Proof of the real influence of propinquity is less significant than the fact that people believe it to be important, so that to live in some areas is to enjoy, from their point of view, a positive externality whereas in others it necessitates suffering a negative one.

The final externality for which households compete concerns property values. Capitalist society is founded on the ownership of land and the dwellings built on it, and a major capitalist motive is to ensure that property values appreciate. Given that wealth, status and power are generally associated, then the status of an area is, not surprisingly, reflected in its property values. Because of this, the owners of property in an area will act to protect their investments, taking whatever steps are necessary to prevent the relative, let alone absolute, devaluation of their prized possessions. Thus positive externalities are sought for the area which will enhance values and, perhaps more significantly, potential negative externalities are countered whenever possible. Again, it is the richest and the most powerful who are best able to prevent the incursion of negative externalities to an area, and to ensure the most desirable situations for themselves. New intraurban motorways, for example, tend to depress property values in their paths and environs, so they are resisted by the residents of threatened areas (Wolpert, Mumphrey, and Seley, 1972). Again, it is the rich and the powerful who are most likely to win in the political battles over such locational strategies (Harvey, 1973); indeed, the techniques of cost-benefit analysis used to evaluate alternative policies are biased towards those who have most to lose in absolute rather than relative terms (Adams, 1970).

Conclusions

The residential mosaic of the city is brought about by the intersection of a large number of vested interests, most of them selfish and to do with the social and economic welfare of the individual, as he and the groups to which he belongs perceive it, rather than with society's overall welfare. To achieve their aims, many of these groups aspire to live apart from other groups, producing the demand for social areas. This aspiration is advanced by the operation of the land and property markets, in which spatial externalities are traded and constrained so as to fulfil the requirements of those with the wealth and power to manipulate the markets to their own ends. The consequence is a series of spatially separate (sometimes discrete, sometimes overlapping) housing submarkets which form the mosaic of residential areas.

THE DEFINITION OF RESIDENTIAL AREAS

The objective of delimiting different types of residential area has been pursued vigorously in social geography. In some ways it has its origins in earlier morphological studies which sought to identify urban subregions and to relate these to historical phases of growth. More properly, however, the early precursor of the line of research, referred to as *residential differentiation*, can be nominated as the natural area concept which was a product of Chicago school ecology in the 1920s and 1930s. It was at this time that the emphasis on people rather than on the physical characteristics of the environments in which they lived first emerged. Residential differentiation studies since have had a number of consistent themes. Firstly, they seek to identify distinctive residential subareas within cities and to delimit their boundaries; secondly, they seek to characterize these residential areas in terms of their key features and qualities; and, thirdly, they test and examine the bases upon which residential separation is predicated and the persistence of these over time. As the methodology to achieve these objectives has developed, it has revealed a number of trends. Whereas early studies were largely intuitive and subjective, later studies are increasingly objective. Whereas early studies were qualitative, later studies have become much more quantitatively based. As systematic quantitative approaches evolved, the progression was from single-stranded techniques, involving diagnostic variables, to multivariate statistical procedures in which wide-ranging inputs of data can be analysed. The progressions in objectives and approaches will now be examined.

Natural areas

The natural area concept was developed by Robert Park and his associates in the Chicago school of social ecology. Although this school is better known for the concentric zonal model of Burgess, its main *spatial* generalization, the natural area concept probably generated the most inspired empirical urban studies. The natural area was conceived as a geographical unit, distinguished both by its physical individuality and by the social, economic and cultural characteristics of its population. In contrast to the studies of urban subregions developed by urban morphologists, with their 'unpeopled' townscapes, the natural area was envisaged as an area of social as well as physical uniformity. The view of a total urban habitat in which particular relationships existed between the environment and population was part of the more general ecological theory of the Chicago school, and Park argued these relationships explicitly in his theoretical statements. It was in the monographs, mainly on Chicago, in which these broader theoretical statements on symbiosis were largely incidental, that the natural area concept found its clearest expression. Of these the best known were the *Gold Coast and the Slum* (Zorbaugh, 1929) and *The Ghetto* (Wirth, 1928).

The natural areas identified by Zorbaugh were delimited by the *de facto* boundaries of the urban environment: roads, railways, parks, lakes and rivers. The physical individuality of the natural area was accurately reflected by land values and rent, but Zorbaugh was at pains to stress that the natural area was not necessarily coterminous with community, as it was the result of economic rather than cultural processes. The attractiveness of Zorbaugh's study, however, lies less in any attempted justification of ecological theory than in his vivid portrayal of life in Chicago's Near North Side, a district of some 90,000 people close to the city centre. The Near North Side was an area of diversity, the main contrast being between the high-prestige district of the Gold Coast along Lake Shore Drive and the low-status district west of State Street (Figure 7.3) The latter district was itself a mosaic, containing the rooming-house district, hobohemia, Little Sicily and other ethnic quarters, and the Slum. The personalities of these sections of the city were partly derived from the physical structure of which they were composed, but much more from their distinctive populations and ways of life. Zorbaugh emphasized the dynamic qualities which these districts possessed and described the territorial shifts as the invasion–succession process took place. Always regarded as less bounded by ecological theory, Wirth's attitude was reflected in his preface to *The Ghetto* (1928): 'Having started with the study of a geographical area, I found myself, quite unwittingly, examining the natural history of an institution and the psychology of a people.

In his study, Wirth examined the evolution of Jewish ghettos in many European cities and described them as communities of interest, motivated by the need to preserve a religion and based upon the inner solidarity of strong family ties. His identification of the Chicago ghetto as a physical entity approached the concept of the natural area as closely as his ecological contemporaries. He identified the Chicago ghetto as a territory demarcated from adjacent parts of the city by environmental barriers such as streetcar lines and railway tracks. Within this territory, the natural area was a socially cohesive community with a distinctive personality. The natural areas which Zorbaugh and Wirth described were identified and defined intuitively from an intimate knowledge of the city, rather than by the use of statistical procedures. Zorbaugh, however, did make extensive use of simple indicators to characterize his natural areas, such as persons listed in prestigious directories and those receiving welfare payments. This procedure initiated a useful technique which has continued utility. Some natural areas, particularly the ethnic districts, Zorbaugh

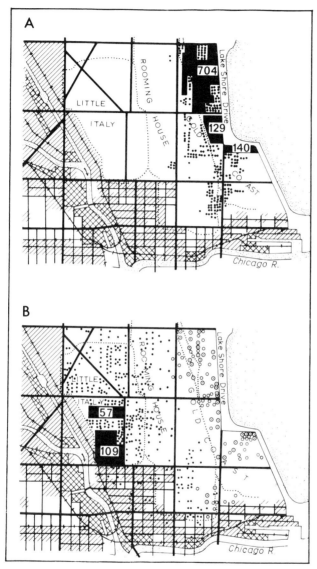

Figure 7.3   The Gold Coast and the Slum. (a) Each dot shows
a person on the high-status social register, with some block
totals. (b) Each dot is a recipient of welfare, each open
circle a donator. Shaded areas show non-residential land use
(after Zorbaugh, 1929)

described as closeknit communities whereas others were scarcely communities
at all, and a feature of the Gold Coast was that 'one does not know one's
neighbours'.

The original concept of the natural area was questioned along with other
aspects of urban ecology in the 1930s and an explicit reformulation was offered

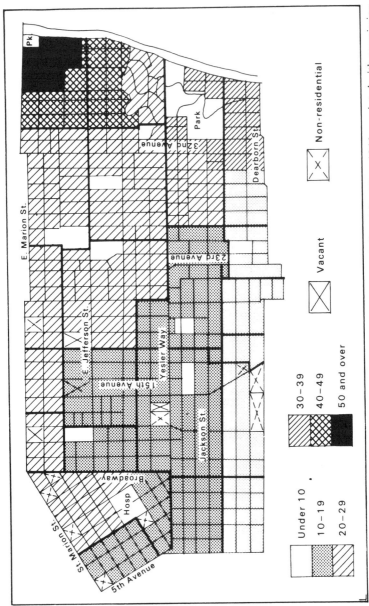

Figure 7.4   Natural areas in Seattle: based upon mean rental value in dollars (after Hatt, 1946; reprinted with permission of the American Sociological Association)

by Hatt (1946) in his study of Seattle. Hatt suggested that the natural area concept as developed by the ecologists had two interpretations: on the one hand the natural area could be regarded as a spatial unit, limited by natural boundaries and enclosing a homogeneous population with a characteristic moral order; on the other it was regarded as spatially united on the basis of a set of relationships analogous to the biological world. Hatt concluded that this latter interpretation should be rejected but that natural areas could be accepted as logical statistical constructs offering an excellent framework for further analysis. The eventual map of natural areas in Seattle was based upon a diagnostic variable, that of rental values, rather than upon the intuitive approach of ecologists (see Figure 7.4). Though Zorbaugh and others had certainly been aware of their possibilities, Hatt explicitly used rental values as delimiting criteria for the first time, suggesting that one variable could be used to characterize different parts of the city.

The potentialities of such diagnostic variables of urban structure are now well recognized and their use has extended over a considerable range of problems. In a wider context there are studies using land values, notably by Hurd (1903) and Hoyt (1939) which predate Hatt's study of Seattle, while more recently statistical analyses of the determinants and correlates of land values have been completed. In the context of defining urban subareas, a number of more straightforward British studies have adopted measures of monetary value as diagnostic variables. One problem in studying British cities has been the fact that land values and rental values are difficult to obtain in a consistent form. Therefore rateable values (a form of local taxation), based on the physical characteristics of a property and its general location, have been used instead of land values or rents. A study of Newcastle-under-Lyme (Herbert and Williams, 1964) is typical of the adaptation of this approach to define residential areas in a British town. Four categories of rateable value were mapped with the initial hypothesis that these would reflect differences in urban social structure (Figure 7.5). These assumptions were tested in a number of ways. First, a field survey of house types showed a close correspondence between morphology and the subareas: the lowest valued category corresponded with the terraced-row districts, the highest-valued category with the large private detached houses. Other tests included the mapping of other variables, such as the locations of homes of professional workers, private telephone subscribers and users of welfare services, and measurement of their degree of correspondence with the pattern of subareas. In Newcastle-under-Lyme, therefore, the utility of rateable values as a diagnostic variable could be demonstrated. Similar uses of this particular criterion have been made by Robson (1966) in Sunderland, and by Jones (1960) (who used Poor Law Valuations) in Belfast. Robson showed the incidence of cholera in low-valued, substandard parts of the town in the mid-nineteenth century, but found that rateable values in the modern city had lost much of their usefulness because of the considerable amount of municipal housing, which could not be reliably correlated to a particular level of rateable

282

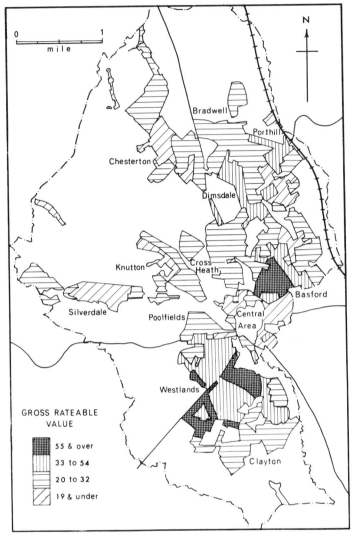

Figure 7.5   Natural areas in Newcastle-under-Lyme: based on gross
rateable values in 1963

value. His conclusion that municipal housing had seriously detracted from the use of rateable values as a diagnostic variable has considerable validity.

There exists, therefore, a wide range of diagnostic variables which can be used to identify and characterize urban subareas. Subareas defined by one variable are often assumed to have more general homogeneity, and such assumptions can be tested, as in the Newcastle-under-Lyme study. The necessity of such testing was demonstrated in a study of Lansing, Michigan (Form *et al.*, 1954), where three approaches, termed ecological, demographic and social, were used to define comparative subareas. The ecological areas were based upon traditional criteria of natural barriers, land use, land values and racial segregation; the demographic areas were based upon measures of population structure; the social areas upon measures of neighbourhood cohesion derived from field survey data. The study revealed that there was no clear relationship between areas identified from the three different criteria, and that every kind of ecological barrier was violated when demographic and social indices were used to locate boundaries. This analysis clearly warns against the use of diagnostic variables consistent only in terms of the initial delimiting criterion; any assumptions made, whether they concern related morphological structures or patterns of social behaviour, must be tested before they can be incorporated into the analysis.

The range of approaches to the definition of subareas in urban residential structure has been widened considerably by the availability of better census data for cities, both in the range of recorded information and their publication for small territorial units, census tracts in North America, enumeration districts in the United Kingdom, with equivalents in many other parts of the world. Small census areas of this type must be sufficiently small for a high level of internal consistency to be assumed, so that when scores are allocated they are the equivalents of point distributions which may be aggregated to form areal patterns. To a considerable extent, small census areas possess these qualities, but there are qualifications. The population size can vary considerably within one city; the range of census tracts in North American cities is from under 1000 to over 10,000, and of enumeration districts in British cities (which are smaller) from under 100 to over 1500. The areas are correspondingly divergent in size, although this is related to density, and the question of weighting procedures (Robson, 1969) is relevant. More fundamental questions concern the real internal consistency of small census units. Some censuses have defined boundaries only with reference to the needs of census-taking: in the British census, for example, the enumeration district is arbitrarily defined on mainly topographic criteria. The Canadian census states that census tracts are designed to be relatively uniform in area and population, and such that each is fairly homogeneous with respect to economic status and living conditions, qualities which fulfil the *desiderata* of small area statistics. This uniformity is inevitably less than perfect, however, and some research has developed techniques to accommodate heterogeneity in census districts (Newton and Johnston, 1976). More general issues concerned with the qualities of aggregate statistics are now well-known (Alker, 1969).

Census data for enumeration districts have been used extensively in Britain, more usually to analyse individual variables than to form composite subareas. Jones (1960) in his Belfast study, however, used enumeration district data to delineate social regions on the basis of population density, social status and religious affiliations; the resultant map was judged to provide meaningful subareas of the city from which the main social regions of Belfast were easily recognizable and compact and summed up features both of the landscape and human geography. The approach had self-imposed limitations, but it provides a useful link between the natural area concept and subsequent procedures which have made increasing use of census data.

Social area analysis

The main statement on the methodology of social area analysis (Shevky and Bell, 1955) followed earlier empirical work in Los Angeles and San Francisco (Shevky and Williams, 1949) in which census tract differences were examined using three indices of social rank, urbanization, and segregation. The methodology was important in its attempt to develop multivariate indices of residential differentiation to classify census tracts and, also, in its attempt to relate these indices to a more general theory of urban development. In the former of these objectives, the methodology attained considerable success, in the latter far less. Although the *theory*, as opposed to the *typology* of social area analysis, proved contentious (and, as Bell and Moskos (1964) seem to have admitted, was an *ex post facto* rationalization of earlier empirical work), the principle of establishing a theory of social differentiation and of initially recognizing variations in social rather than in geographical space, set social area analysis apart from social ecology which had sought initially to identify natural areas as geographical territories and to study them in terms of their social characteristics.

Shevky and Bell viewed the city as a part of society as a whole and suggested that change over time would be mirrored in the city. They suggested that such change had three main expressions which could be described collectively as *increasing scale*, implying a continuum of change from a traditional primitive to a more modern civilized style of life (Figure 7.6). The three expressions of this *increasing scale* they summarized as constructs, each of which was a dominant temporal trend in social organization. *Social rank* (economic status) described the tendency for society to become more precisely ordered into strata based on specialization and social prestige. *Urbanization* (family status) described a weakening of the traditional organization of the family as the society became more urbanized. *Segregation* (ethnic status) suggested that over time the population group would tend to form distinctive clusters based primarily upon ethnicity. The alternative names for the constructs were proposed and used by Bell (1955), the only difference in computational procedure being that high scores on urbanization were the equivalents of low scores on family status. Having derived these constructs, regarded as being diagnostic of change, Shevky and Bell sought to measure them from the available census data. *Social rank* was measured by ratios of *occupation*, described as the total number of operatives, craftsmen and labourers per 1000 employed persons, and of *education*, described as the number of persons who had completed no more than grade school (eight years or less of schooling) per 1000 persons aged 25 years and over. *Urbanization* was based upon three ratios: *fertility* measured by the number of children aged 0 to 4 years per 1000 women aged 15 to 44; *women at work* measured by the number of females employed in relation to the total number of females aged 15 years and over; and *single-*

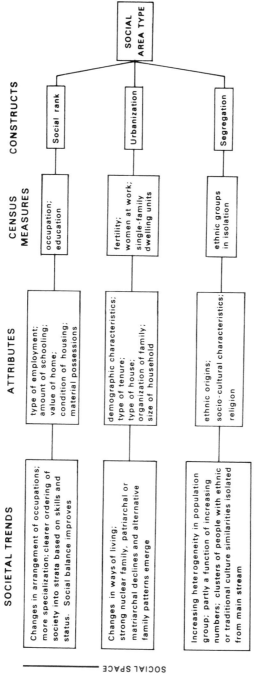

Figure 7.6 Social area analysis: derivation of constructs

family detached dwelling units, measured by the number of single-family homes (a term which has a specific meaning in North American censuses) as a proportion of all dwelling units. Social rank and urbanization were the main constructs of social area analysis and a large part of the computational procedure was concerned with their derivation. The third construct, *segregation*, was obtained as a simple percentage of the numbers in specified alien groups (mainly coloureds and all those of ethnic origins outside north-west Europe) as a proportion of the total population.

These constructs and their component ratios were thus identified from social space but were obtained as statistical expressions from the available census data and combined in stipulated ways to form criteria for the definition of urban subareas. The operational procedure which leads to the eventual social areas can be briefly summarized:

1. The scores on the individual ratios are initially simple proportions, but Shevky and Bell specify the additional step of transforming the ratios into standardized scores so that for each ratio there is a value of zero and a value of 100. The main purpose of this standardization procedure was to make comparisons more valid.
2. The construct scores are obtained by finding the average of the ratio scores.
3. The social rank and urbanization scores are each given a four-fold division which in combination provides sixteen possible social area types.
4. Segregation is added to this framework where the proportion of a census tract's total population which is in specified alien groups is above the average for the city as a whole.

The first applications of social area analysis, in Los Angeles and San Francisco, both provided some confirmation of the utility of the approach. It has become customary to ragard a social area as a contiguous territorial unit, though its initial usage was to describe a cluster of scores in social rather than in geographical space. A typical set of results from an application of social area analysis to a North American city can be described from a study of Winnipeg, Canada (Herbert, 1972).

The metropolitan area of Winninpeg had a population in 1961 of 475,989 and was divided into 86 census tracts with an average population of 5500; over half the census tracts were between 3000 and 6000, with only three with less than 1000 and five with more than 10,000. The social space diagram for Winnipeg (Figure 7.7, inset) illustrates the classification of census tracts which was obtained. Each point on the diagram represents a census tract, the position of which is determined by its scores on social rank and urbanization, with a separate symbol for segregated tracts. In this diagram, therefore, the position of each census tract is affected by its scores on the six component variables of the typology: occupation, education, fertility, women at work, single-family dwellings and ethnicity. The census tract in 4D, for example, has high social rank, with few people employed in manual occupations and few without advanced education. It is also high scoring in terms of urbanization, with

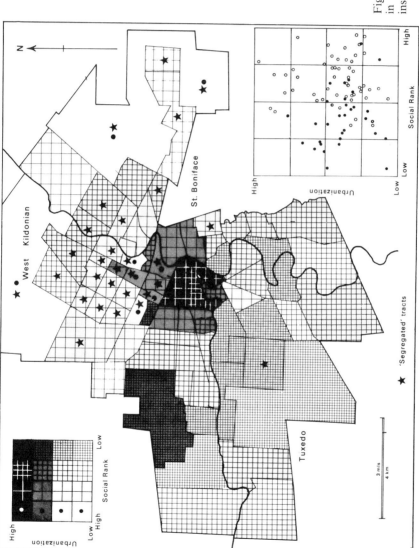

Figure 7.7 Social areas in Winnipeg 1960: with inset showing the social space diagram

few children, high numbers of women in employment and a comparative absence of single-family homes. The census tract contains few members of specified ethnic groups and is in fact part of a fairly high prestige residential district, predominantly of rented apartments, in a central city location. Besides allowing the interpretation of individual tracts, this diagram also provides an overall impression of the social structure of the city: 63 per cent of the census tracts are within the two higher social rank categories and 25 per cent are in the two higher urbanization categories; of the 31 tracts which are classed as segregated, only eight qualify as higher social rank. The analysis has so far allowed an insight into the social structure of Winnipeg by classifying the census tracts in social space.

Social area analysis, as a theory, specifies a set of relationships among its constructs and ratios which must exist if the procedure is to be valid in any case study. The theoretical rationale of these relationships has been questioned but the actual measurements can be tested by statistical techniques, the most straightforward of which is Spearman's rank order correlation coefficient. The results of these tests in Winnipeg are shown in Table 7.1 together with the set of relationships which the theory postulates.

The specified set of relationships shown overleaf requires that the ratios which make up the respective constructs should be independent. This requires high correlations between occupation and education and also among the three ratios which comprise urbanization. The women-at-work ratio is held to have an inverse relationship with both fertility and single-family homes. The results for Winnipeg confirm the existence of the specified set of relationships in a way which has been typical of North American studies. An exception in the Winnipeg results, not without precedent in North America, is that the occupation and fertility ratios have a much higher correlation and the constructs are thus less independent than the hypotheses of social area analysis suggest. The analysis of ten American cities by Van Arsdol, Camilleri, and Schmid (1958) showed a similar lack of disassociation among the constructs.

Table 7.1   Correlation scores for Winnipeg

Ratios	Occupation	Education	Fertility	Women at work
Education	+ 0.84*			
Fertility	+ 0.53*	+ 0.34		
Women at work	+ 0.03	+ 0.23	− 0.53*	
Single-family dwellings	− 0.07	− 0.33	+ 0.45*	− 0.68*

*Significant at the 0.1 per cent level

| | Specified set | | | |
	Occupation	Education	Fertility	Women at work
Education	+			
Fertility	0	0		
Women at work	0	0	−	
Single-family dwellings	0	0	+	−

In general terms, however, the correlational testing confirms the usefulness of the analysis in Winnipeg.

The social space classification forms the basis for the derivation of social areas in geographical space. Contiguous census tracts with scores in the same categories may be aggregated to form social areas in the sixteen-class typology, with the additional segregation categorization. Figure 7.7 shows the geographical patterns which can be interpreted in terms of the six component variables. Generalized patterns are most easily identified from the separate constructs and the high social rank scores: for example, the southern and western part of the city indicate the high-prestige residential areas. The more central parts of the city and the northern and eastern districts, which include the central slums and tenements and low-cost suburbs, are characterized by low scores. Urbanization scores distinguish between the central city districts of low family status and the outer suburbs of strong family life; segregation indices demarcate the Ukrainian districts extending north along Main Street.

Applications of social area analysis outside North America have been less successful in establishing the validity of the approach either as a theory or as a classificatory procedure. Herbert (1967) found that whereas the social rank construct could be identified and its constituent variables held the hypothesized relationships, the urbanization or family status construct could not. Fertility and women-at-work indices did not hold the expected inverse relationship (a finding confirmed in other British studies), and although rational explanations for this could be formed, the overall validity of the methodology could not be sustained. McElrath's (1962) study of Rome did identify the hypothesized relationships of variables within constructs but found that the constructs themselves were not independent. McElrath (1968) has also applied a social area analysis approach to Accra, Ghana, and here found it necessary to add a fourth construct, migrant status, a suggestion which has found support elsewhere (Davies, 1978a).

Of the four constructs in this model, two were defined as products of the industrialization process and two of the urbanization process. Under the heading of the former, increasing satisfaction emanating from changing distributions of skills formed the basis of the social rank dimension, whereas changes in the organization of production, involving greater female participation on the workforce and choice in family lifestyles, underpinned family status. In the latter subgroup, redistribution of population towards urbanizing centres gave migrant status, whereas the maintenance of cultural distinctiveness by some minority groups gave ethnic status. The empirical test of this model in Accra showed that the expected relationships appeared, with the exception of the family status construct which was inconsistent, dependent and weak. Fertility and women at work not only failed to relate to each other in the expected way, but actually related in the opposite way and were each more related to migrant status. Again the 'deviant' results could be explained—in this instance by the child-caring role of the extended family—but the results did invalidate the model.

For North American results only, it has been possible to form spatial generalizations from the results of social area analysis. Anderson and Egeland (1961) used analysis of variance techniques to test the existence of zonal patterns of family status scores and of sectors for economic status scores. Their studies in four American cities were able to confirm these spatial models and a similar confirmation was obtained for Winnipeg.

Although social area analysis has been eclipsed in recent years by the development of multivariate procedures, the theory and its application have stimulated a good deal of academic discussion. The concept of increasing scale, always controversial, has been questioned on several grounds. In a well-known review, Hawley and Duncan (1957) suggested that the theory was a rationalization for the choice of indices; F. L. Jones (1969) saw the use of societal scale as derivative and largely descriptive; Udry (1964) made empirical tests and found that trends suggested were not consistent over time. Urbanization is a suspect construct, and Bell (see Bell and Moskos, 1964) has suggested that Shevky's original concept was not adequately measured by the ratios employed. Bell, who always preferred family status as a description, also accepted the interpretation of Anderson and Bean (1961) that there were two distinct elements which should be known as familism and urbanism. The related point that the relationship between fertility and women at work could not be assumed but was in fact highly variable was substantiated by most studies. Other points of criticism on the theory relate to the social rank construct, which, though empirically viable, had not been rigorously tested as a theory of social stratification. Critics such as Hawley and Duncan would see little justification for social area analysis except as a classificatory device. More sympathetic writers, of whom Beshers (1962) is a representative, although admitting no theoretical basis for urbanization, regard social rank and segregation as well-established indices of social stratification. This assessment, which finds some support (Morris, 1968; Reissman, 1964), suggests that the constructs are significant as measures of social change, though they are not fully adequate in themselves.

The other key issue concerning the relationship between a theory of increasing scale and a typology of urban residential areas has been debated (Bell and Moskos, 1964; Timms, 1971) but no convincing case has emerged. In summary, social area analysis, despite its weakly developed theory, provided an important stage in the evolution of residential differentiation studies. Its typology, consistently verified in North America, accurately identified the key bases of residential separation in cities of a particular technological stage and in societies of specific characteristics.

Factorial ecology

The term factorial ecology has been used to describe those studies of urban residential areas which employ factor analysis as a technique. Social area analysis as used originally by Shevky and Bell has now been virtually replaced by this approach which allows more flexibility, no necessary adherence to a preformed theory, and potentially at least a high level of objectivity. Factor analysis is not one technique but a collective term which covers a set of alternatives. Davies (1978a) suggests that one broad distinction is between a components model which describes the maximum amount of variability in a data set and a common factor model which enables the adequacy of previous theories to be examined. Most geographers have tended to use a components model which retains, in a statistical sense at least, the independence of the successive dimensions, and have also typically used standard varimax and oblique rotations to specify those dimensions more closely. A first point to note, therefore, is that the results obtained from a study in factorial ecology may vary according to the particular procedure adopted and Davies (1978a) has emphasized the need to establish the invariant quality of results across a range of factoring techniques. A second consideration is the form of input to factorial ecology as this again will strongly influence results. Input usually comprises a set of variables, commonly derived from census sources and covering social, economic, and demographic characteristics, measured for a set of observations or small areas (Figure 7.8). The aim in selection of variables is to choose a sufficient range so that the main features of urban residential structure are represented and to obtain a balance so that the number of variables in any one set does not distort results. Observations are normally provided by census divisions, that is, census tracts or enumeration districts. Scale of units will affect results; the analysis is aggregate so ecological fallacy questions do arise; and there is usually no attempt to measure heterogeneity within observations even though they are known to exist (Newton and Johnston, 1976). There is a number of other technical problems associated with factorial ecology which include autocorrelation and standardization (Johnston, 1979b) and normality, but Davies (1978b) argues that if these problems are recognized and a data set is well-structured, then the validity of a factorial ecology study need not be in doubt.

As it has been most generally used by geographers, factor analysis can be described as a summarizing device which operates in terms of the interrelationships among the set of input variables and identifies, in the order of their significance, a series of factors which are diagnostic of the input and which account for measurable amounts of the initial variance. These qualities can perhaps be made clearer by drawing an analogy with social area analysis which, through deductive reasoning, identifies changes in society, transforms these into constructs and selects census variables or ratios with which to characterize them. Factor analysis, by contrast, derives factors which can be regarded as equivalents of constructs, by an objective statistical procedure. Three forms of output—eigen values, loadings, and scores—provide the means of interpreting the results obtained. The *eigen values* indicate the relative strengths of the factors and can be expressed as proportions of the total variance or variability in the initial input; the size of eigen value represents the ability of factor analysis to summarize a high proportion of this variability in a smaller number of factors or dimensions. A *loading* is calculated for each original variable against each factor or component and allows the 'nature' of the factor to be interpreted.

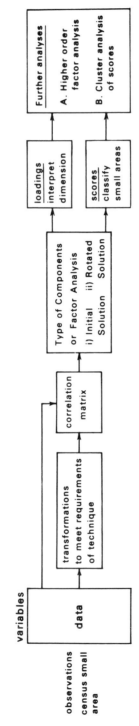

Figure 7.8   Stages in factorial ecology

Loadings range in value from + 1.0 to − 1.0. *Scores* are calculated for each observation on every factor and enable the spatial distribution of the characteristics of each dimension to be shown. The general qualities of factor analysis and its application to the study of urban residential areas as factorial ecology can be illustrated with reference to Winnipeg.

North American cities

From the 1961 Canadian census, 34 variables were calculated for each of the 86 census tracts in the urban area; this particular study used a components model with a varimax rotation. The results (Table 7.2(a)) are useful in that they

Table 7.2   Factorial ecology

(A) Winnipeg (1961): nature of factors

Factor 1 (housing style) (32.2 per cent)

Variables	Loadings
single family dwellings	+ 0.91
single person households	− 0.89
owner-occupied households	+ 0.89
tenant-occupied households	− 0.87

Factor 2 (social status) (23.8 per cent)

Variables	Loadings
high school or university	+ 0.93
males in managerial, professional, technical employment	+ 0.92
males primary, craftsmen, labourers	− 0.91
males salaries 6,000 or more	+ 0.88

Factor 3 (ethnicity) (8.6 per cent)

Variables	Loadings
French origins	+ 0.98
English language only	− 0.97
Roman Catholic	+ 0.89

(B) Winnipeg (1971)*

Component 1 (family status) (21.5 per cent)

Variables	Loadings
small households	+ 0.90
apartments	+ 0.80
children	− 0.98
family size	− 0.97

Component 2 (socioeconomic status) (13.4 per cent)

Variables	Loadings
construction/transport workers	+ 0.86
manufacturing workers	+ 0.76
graduates	− 0.91
white-collar ratio	− 0.88

Component 3 (migrant status) (10.6 per cent)

Variables	Loadings
middle-aged	+ 0.86
low intermunicipal movers	+ 0.84
non-migrants	+ 0.80
new housing	− 0.82
mature adults	− 0.66

*1971 results obtained by Dr W.K.D. Davies

294

closely resemble a large number of studies of North American cities completed in the later 1960s and early 1970s. From the eigen values it is clear that the leading dimension accounts for almost one-third of the initial variance (32.2 per cent), and the leading three dimensions for almost two-thirds. A few leading loadings are shown for each of the main dimensions in order to characterize the factors. Factor 1 is described as a measure of housing style indicative of family status or stage-in-lifecycle: Factor 2 as a measure of socioeconomic status, and Factors 3 and 6 of ethnicity. These dimensions are clearly reminiscent of the constructs of social area analysis and most North American studies show very similar results. Table 7.2(b) shows similar—though different—results from a 1971 analysis of Winnipeg; migrant status has replaced ethnic status and a family-status dimension is more clearly defined.

The last output from the analysis is that of scores, which are recorded for each factor for each census tract and allow patterns to be identified in geographical space. The spatial patterns of scores are shown in Figure 7.9. Factor 1 scores (7.9(a)) distinguish between the central city and the family suburbs; Factor 2 scores (7.9(b)) between the high-prestige districts of south and west and the low-prestige districts of north and east; Factor 3 (7.9(c)) identifies the French district of St Boniface, and scores from Factor 4 which are also included in this map identify ethnic districts which are principally Ukrainian in origin. Spatial generalizations of these scores could be described as zonal for Factor 1, sectoral for Factor 2 and clusters for Factor 3; these patterns conform with those identified by analysis of variance for social area scores and with the model suggested by Murdie (1969) for Toronto. A further expression of the spatial patterning of scores was obtained by a grouping procedure (see Figure 7.9(d)) which classifies census tracts on the basis of their similarity of scores for the

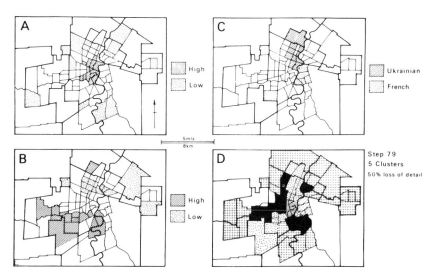

Figure 7.9   Factorial ecology of Winnipeg (1961). (a) Family status. (b) Socioeconomic status. (c) Ethnic status. (d) A cluster analysis composite areas

first six factors. Potentially this last procedure has the capability of classifying census tracts into 'objective communities' of multiple similarities, though the reality of this outcome needs to be tested by other criteria.

The Winnipeg case-study provides an example of the use of factor analytical procedures and produces a set of results which are typical of North American applications. Both those studies which have been designed as direct tests of the Shevky–Bell hypotheses, and those which evolved as independent investigations of the dimensions of urban–social space, have tended to confirm the existence of the three main constructs of economic, family and ethnic status.

During the 1970s a continuing series of applications of factorial ecology to North American cities has both refined the methodology and qualified some of the significant empirical results. Davies (1978a, 1978b) has succeeded in establishing the invariance of dimensions over a range of factorial techniques for Canadian cities. In a study of Calgary, 60 variables selected to represent nine categories were systematically reduced to fourteen indicator variables. The clearest main dimensions were labelled *age and family*, associated positively with old age and negatively with children; *socioeconomic status* associated negatively with large dwellings and positively with manufacturing occupations; *migrant status*, associated positively with non-migrants and negatively with recent housing; and *young adult participation*, which had positive links with young adults and females in the labour force. Ethnic dimensions were less highly placed but when the seven leading factors were used as input to a higher-order factor analysis, family status, economic status, migrant status, and ethnic status dimensions emerged. An analysis of Edmonton using 60 variables produced family status, socioeconomic status and migrant status as the leading three dimensions with ethnic minorities loading onto the fourth and seventh components. Figure 7.10 shows the spatial patterns of scores for components 1, 2, 3, and 7 of the Edmonton study. Although there are modifications in detail, the concentric zonal generalization still applies to family status while clear socioeconomic status sectors emerge from scores on component 2. High migrant status scores typify the inner city areas affected by redevelopment and recent suburban housing developments; the ethnic minorities were not sharply differentiated but clusters did appear.

The emergence of migrant status rather than ethnicity as a leading component suggests the increasing significance of mobility in a situation of continuing urban growth and typically increasing frequencies of residential change. The diminution in significance of a specifically ethnic dimension is possibly an indication of the greater ease of assimilation in Canadian cities of the types of minorities which they receive. There is no evidence from the United States that a black ethnic dimension has in any way blurred in the latter part of the twentieth century (see Rees, 1979).

West European cities

European cities which have been studied through factor analysis have produced results broadly similar to those in North America, but usually with some

296

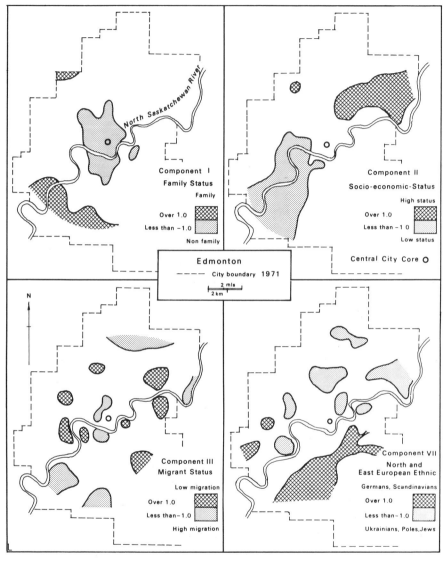

Figure 7.10   Factorial ecology of Edmonton (1971), showing family status, socio-econo-mic status, migration status and ethnic status (after Davies, 1978b; with the author's permission)

significant differences of detail. Pederson (1967) used fourteen socioeconomic variables for 76 urban zones of Copenhagen, and identified both in 1950 and 1960 three main factors which he named family status, socioeconomic status and population change. The first two displayed zonal and sectoral characteristics respectively, in accordance with North American experience, though the central city of Copenhagen was of uniformly low status. Sweetser (1965) attempted a comparative study of Helsinki, Finland, and Boston, using twenty common variables for 441 census tracts in Boston and 70 statistical areas in Helsinki. Part of Sweetser's objective was to test the value of factor analysis in the differentiation of residential areas and he considered the value proven from his results. His main factors for Helsinki were socioeconomic status, family status (progeniture) and urbanism. These studies of Copenhagen and Helsinki both reproduce the two main North American dimensions of socioeconomic status and familism/urbanism, but not the ethnic dimension. Whereas many European cities do not possess significant ethnic minorities with high levels of segregation, there have been immigrant trends likely to produce such situations during the 1960s and 1970s. In addition to the British case which is to be described below, Netherlands cities, for example, have received immigrants from former colonies in both East and West Indies, and major west European countries, principally France and West Germany, now house sizeable numbers of migrant workers from south Europe and North Africa. A factorial ecology of Leuven (Louvain), Belgium was limited to the central urban area but did identify the two main dimensions of socioeconomic and family status. A third dimension was, interestingly, linked with North African migrant workers and also with the substantial student population which dominates similar residential districts (see Table 7.3).

Factorial ecologies of British cities in the 1960s showed less conformity to the North American model. These differences may be related to available data but also seem to reflect societal differences and in particular the effect of public intervention in the housing market. A number of these earlier studies, using principal components analysis, revealed a considerable degree of

Table 7.3 Nature of components in Leuven (Louvain), Belgium

Component 1 (socioeconomic status)	
Variables	Loadings
small dwellings	$+0.93$
labourers	$+0.78$
businessmen	-0.85
large dwellings	-0.83

Component 2 (minority group)	
Variables	Loadings
students	$+0.93$
foreign-born	$+0.85$
substandardness	$+0.61$

Component 3 (family status)	
Variables	Loadings
single-person household	$+0.93$
no children	$+0.91$
two-person household	-0.94
children	-0.82

Table 7.4   Nature of components in Cardiff and Swansea

Principal component 1 (27.4 per cent) (housing tenure)

Cardiff		Swansea	
Variables	Loadings	Variables	Loadings
persons per room	+ 0.91	persons per room	+ 0.56
aged 0–14 years	+ 0.87	aged 65 years and over	− 0.85
renting municipal housing	+ 0.86	aged 0–14 years	+ 0.80
aged 65 years and over	− 0.85	renting municipal housing	+ 0.79

Principal component 2 (23.5 per cent) (substandardness)

Cardiff		Swansea	
Variables	Loadings	Variables	Loadings
foreign-born	+ 0.70	without exclusive use of WC	− 0.75
without exclusive use of WC	+ 0.69	renting private unfurnished	− 0.74
at over $1\frac{1}{2}$ persons per room	+ 0.67	shared dwellings	− 0.62
renting private unfurnished	+ 0.66	left school before 16 years	− 0.56

consistency in results. Measures of housing occupance, tenure, and dwelling conditions were repeatedly dominant and tended to disguise the presence of economic and family status dimensions. Analyses of Cardiff and Swansea using a common list of 26 variables exemplify these results (Table 7.4).

The two leading components, closely similar for Cardiff and Swansea, are typical of results for comparable British studies. The first component could be described as a dimension of housing occupance and tenure, while the second component identifies different conditions of housing. The contrasts which these components identify can be seen most clearly from the spatial patterns derived from the mapping of scores for enumeration districts (Figure 7.11). Component I distinguish between the public and private sectors in housing, with high positive scores delimiting municipal estates which occupy large districts such as Ely and Llanrumney in Cardiff. Other residential areas similarly categorized by this component include smaller pockets of urban redevelopment and some districts where small-size and low-price private housing possesses qualities similar to those found on municipal estates. The high negative scores on Component I identify those housing districts which are in most marked contrast to the public housing sector; these include high-prestige areas of Llandaff, Roath and Cyncoed and also some older districts of terraced housing with small families and a low density of occupance. This leading dimension illustrates the influence of the public sector in British cities; in Cardiff, for example, just below 30 per cent of all housing is owned by the municipality. Component II is a measure of substandardness and of overcrowded housing conditions, the high positive scores for Cardiff identifying the poorer housing of the central city which was the product of the second half of the nineteenth century; these are areas which lack basic facilities and are generally in need of rehabilitation and renewal. The high negative scores on this second component identify newer housing, both publicly and privately owned, which has been

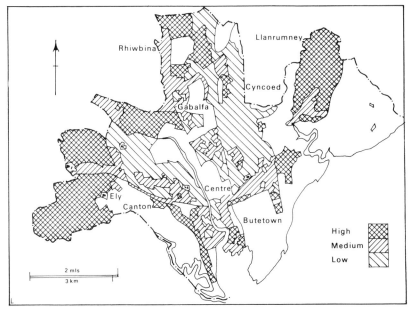

Figure 7.11   Factorial ecology of Cardiff. Component One separates public
sector (high scores) and private sector housing

constructed to modern standards of urban design, space and amenity. The
overall spatial pattern of this second component could be generalized in terms
of zones of progressively ageing urban fabric towards the centre of the city.

These results suggest that although socioeconomic and family status may be
inferred, contrasts in the types and quality of housing provision are the explicit
dimensions. A later study (Davies and Lewis, 1973) of Leicester used 56 variables from the 1966 census and employed a variety of factoring techniques.
The dimensions identified in Leicester (Table 7.5) were more closely similar to
those found in North American studies. A clear socioeconomic status dimension emerged on the first-order solution. The public sector/private sector
dichotomy of earlier studies was subsumed into a stage in lifecycle dimension
and a separate substandardness factor was identified. It can be noted from the
few loadings shown in Table 7.4 that lifecycle variables are highly associated
with Component I in both Cardiff and Swansea; the difference with Leicester
results may be more a function of the label given to the dimension than of its
nature. When higher-order analysis was applied in Leicester the dimensions
became the familiar Shevky–Bell triad; Leicester is one of those British cities
which has been a reception area for large numbers of New Commonwealth
immigrants since the later 1950s. An analysis of the spatial patterns of scores in
Leicester (Lewis, 1972) found evidence of sectors, zones and clusters and was
inclined to regard public sector housing as having a limited distorting effect.
The 'limits', however, will clearly depend on the dimensions of public sector
intervention in any one city.

Table 7.5 Urban dimensions of Leicester (association between the dimensions of Leicester)

Second-order title	Loadings	Successive levels of generalization First-order title (Communality)	First-order variance (%)	Examples of important variables
2. Social status	− 0.61	4. Sub-standardness (0.51)	8.1	+ Overcrowding; substandard housing − Rooms per person (L)
	+ 0.76	8. Urban fringe (0.61)	4.7	+ Cross-commuters; agricultural workers − None
	+ 0.69 + 0.54	1. Socio-economic status (0.72)	17.6	+ Two-car households; employers and managers − Low social class; personal service workers
3. Family status	+ 0.74	3. Life cycle (0.56)	9.9	+ Middle age; old age − Children; large households
	− 0.64	7. Economic participation (0.49)	6.1	+ Employed persons − Old age (L)
	+ 0.50	5. Mobile young adults (0.34)	5.9	+ Owner-occupiers (L) − Non-residents: young adults
1. Ethnicity-migrants	+ 0.87	6. Ethnic origins (0.74)	6.4	+ Local movers; council tenants (M) − Born overseas
	+ 0.66	2. Mobility (0.45)	8.2	+ None − Migrants

Loadings are greater than 0.7 unless shown by: (M) 0.5 to 0.69
(L) 0.3 to 0.49

⟵ First-ranking correlation

⟶ Second-ranking correlation
(0.51) The communalities of the first-order dimensions in the second-order analysis

Higher-order principal components solution

Components	1	2	3	4	5
% variance	21.86	15.93	13.03	10.95	9.74
Commulative variance	21.86	37.82	50.84	61.79	71.53

Second-order correlations matrix: biquartimin solution

	1	2	3
1. Ethnic migrant	1.00		
2. Social status	0.10	1.00	
3. Family status	− 0.15	− 0.07	1.00

Source: Davies and Lewis (1973) Table V, p. 83; reproduced by permission of the Institute of British Geographers

Socialist cities

There have been very few factorial ecologies of cities in socialist societies but Weclawowicz (1979) provides us with a useful study of Warsaw. An initial analysis of 1930 data—at which time Poland was not a socialist society—identified results closely reminiscent of the western model. Leading factors were labelled social class or housing quality, ethnicity (Jewish), and demographic or lifecycle. For 1970 (see Table 7.6) a different set of results was obtained. Some residential separation by occupational groups did remain and could be identified spatially but this was limited to the specialized artist/intellectual group provided with special quarters in the central city and a small group of managers who appeared to have achieved some privilege in housing. The main feature, however, as revealed by the composition of Factor 2 was the lack of residential segregation amongst main occupational groups resulting from the policy of equalizing housing opportunities. Apart from the central location of artists there were clear difficulties in generalizing upon the spatial form of component scores, and Weclawowicz's phrase 'mosaic spatial structure' reflects these.

Non-western cities

It is in non-western societies with considerable problems of data bases that factorial ecologies have been least developed. Two better-known early studies, of Cairo and Calcutta (Abu-Lughod, 1969; Berry and Rees, 1969) were affected by these problems revealed in the latter case by the large size of areas and in the former by paucity of variables. The leading Calcutta dimensions were labelled land use and familism, Muslim, and literacy. The first of these simply distinguishes between areas exclusively used for residential development from

Table 7.6   Nature of factors in Warsaw (1970)

Factor 1 (specialized-occupational) (55.1 per cent)	
Variables	Loadings
journalists, artists, writers	+ 0.94
higher education	+ 0.83
office workers	− 0.87
children	− 0.84
Factor 2 (housing) (18.8 per cent)	
Variables	Loadings
manual workers	+ 0.82
contracted workers	+ 0.81
white-collar workers	+ 0.79
scientists	+ 0.77
Factor 3 (socioeconomic) (8.8 per cent)	
Variables	Loadings
managers	+ 0.89

(Source: Weclawowicz, 1979)

Table 7.7 Variables used in the Colombo study

A. Age	1. Under 5 years
	2. 6–17 years
	3. 18–54 years
	4. Over 55 years
B. Ethnicity	5. Sinhalese (x^2)
	6. Tamils ($\log^{10}$)
	7. Moors/Malays ($\log^{10}$)
	8. Indian Tamils ($\log^{10}$)
	9. Burghers
C. Religion	10. Buddhists ($\log^{10}$)
	11. Hindus ($\log^{10}$)
	12. Christians ($\log^{10}$)
	13. Muslims ($\log^{10}$)
D. Size of household	14. Less than two members
	15. Three to five members
	16. Six to eight members
	17. Nine to eleven members
	18. Over twelve members
E. Shanty population	19. Shanty population ($\log^{10}$)
F. Annual value of residential unit	20. Less than Rs. 100
	21. Rs. 101 to 500 (x^2)
	22. Rs. 501 to 1000
	23. Rs. 1001 to 2000 ($\log^{10}$)
	24. Over Rs. 2001 ($\log^{10}$)
G. Access to services (water and sanitation)	25. Individual services ($\log^{10}$)
	26. Common services
	27. No services
H. Residential density	28. Persons per 100 m^2 of residential floor area
I. Size of residential unit	29. Less than 15 m^2
	30. 15–74 m^2
	31. 75–149 m^2
	32. 150–199 m^2 ($\log^{10}$)
	33. 200–299 m^2 ($\log^{10}$)
	34. Over 300 m^2 ($\log^{10}$)
J. Types of buildings	35. Shanties ($\log^{10}$)
	36. Tenements (x^2)
	37. Houses ($\log^{10}$)
	38. Non-residential ($\log^{10}$)
K. Sex ratio	39. Sex ratio (x^2)
L. Fertility ratio	40. Fertility ratio (x^2)

NB Variables were tested for normality and appropriate transformations were applied as indicated for each variable.

x^2 ... square; $\log^{10}$ ... log to base 10

commerical or institutional land; the spatial pattern of scores on this dimension was concentric zonal with an increasing trend towards functional specialization. Literacy measures in some ways related to socioeconomic status and a sectoral form while the Muslim dimension was effectively ethnic. Literacy was similarly interpreted as an indicator of socioeconomic status in the Cairo study.

A factorial ecology of Colombo, Sri Lanka (Herbert and de Silva, 1974) will be used as an example for a non-Western Asian city. For the 47 wards 40 variables were obtained (Table 7.7) within the Colombo urban area and the analysis was conducted in stages through the use of a principal components model followed by varimax and promax rotations. Component 1 could be identified as a *social status* dimension, though mainly through indices of the quality, value and size of dwelling space (Table 7.8). Some elements of familism were also linked with the dimension, especially through the association of high-fertility ratios and more children with the low-status groups. Component 2 was a measure of *land-use* and distinguished non-residential buildings from more purely residential space. Component 3 measures different types of *substandardness* from tenements at one end of the dimension to shanties at the other, and reflects the ubiquity of low housing quality. With both components 4 and 6 *ethnic groups* are recognized, showing the plural composition of society and its separate expression in residential space. These dimensions bear limited resemblance to those in western cities and reflect the different bases of both

Table 7.8   Nature of factorial dimensions (Colombo)

Component 1 (social status)			
Variables	Loadings	Variables	Loadings
residential density	+ 0.74	individual services	− 0.69
low annual value	+ 0.72	houses	− 0.69
fertility ratio	+ 0.64	high floor space	− 0.69
low floor space	+ 0.64	high annual value	− 0.56
common services	+ 0.45	burghers	− 0.43
Component 2 (land-use differentiation)			
Variables	Loadings	Variables	Loadings
Six to eight member households	+ 0.88	aged 18–54 years	− 0.83
percentage aged 6–17 years	+ 0.82	non-residential use	− 0.79
houses	+ 0.38		
residential units	+ 0.37		
Component 3 (substandardness)			
Variables	Loadings	Variables	Loadings
low floor space	+ 0.46	shanty dwellers	− 0.82
over twelve member households	+ 0.45	low floor space	− 0.58
tenements	+ 0.39	no services	− 0.54
common services	+ 0.34		
Component 4 and 6 (ethnicity)			
Variables	Loadings	Variables	Loadings
Tamils (4)	+ 0.90	Buddhists	− 0.58
Hindus	+ 0.89	Sinhalese	− 0.41
Christians	+ 0.73		
Muslims (6)	+ 0.69	Sinhalese	− 0.62
Moors	+ 0.68	Buddhists	− 0.35

societies as a whole and their urban segments upon which residential space is ordered. Figure 7.12 shows some of the spatial patterning of these dimensions in Colombo.

Generalizations from factorial ecology

The large number of factorial ecologies completed during the late 1960s and early 1970s, and the rather fewer number since, allow some generalizations to be made upon their findings. Firstly it should be stated that greater awareness of technical problems and attempts to develop sounder research strategies have typified later studies (Davies, 1978a); the early wave of analyses may well have been influenced by arbitrariness of data inputs and variability in technique as much as by anything else. There is a general confirmation, however, of the three main dimensions of economic, family and ethnic status in all North American studies. The ethnic minority may vary in type and dimensions and may be superseded by more general migrant status measures, but the 'triad' remains remarkably consistent. Abu-Lughod (1969) stipulated the conditions under which the two most stable dimensions—economic and family status— would emerge. Her reasoning was that an independent socioeconomic status dimension would occur where there was an effective ranking system in the society, distinguishing population groups according to their status or prestige, and where that ranking system was matched by corresponding subdivisions of the housing market (each prestige group lived in a particular type of residential area). Similarly, a familism dimension would occur where family types could be linked to specific stages of the lifecycle and where each stage was paralleled by available residential subareas. Socioeconomic status and familism dimensions might be associated in social space but could still appear as geographically separate where a comprehensive housing market could cater for all lifecycle stages within each socioeconomic status level. The necessary conditions for the two leading dimensions are, therefore, ranking by socioeconomic status, clear stages of the lifecycle, a housing market structured to cater for each possible combination of these characteristics in distinctive subareas, and a population consisting of independent households mobile enough to use the possibilities. A factorial ecology in which the two dimensions failed to emerge could be explained in terms of the absence or limited expression of these necessary conditions. Abu-Lughod did not include ethnic status in her interpretation, but Rees (1979) views the dimension in the American context as a limited microcosm of the city as a whole. His argument was that there are constraints which limit minority groups, such as negroes, to particular sections of the city and that within these sections the relevant range of socioeconomic status levels and lifecycle stages had to be incorporated. With reference to his Chicago study, Rees was able to identify this range within ethnic districts but owing to constraints of other kinds, mainly misallocation of resources between white and coloured people, it was never fully represented. The general milieu in which

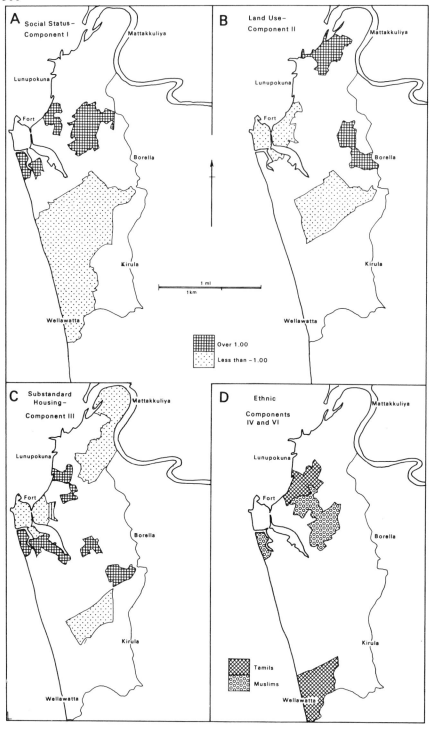

A Social Status –
   Component I

Mattakkuliya

Lunupokuna

Fort

Borella

Kirula

Wellawatta

B Land Use –
   Component II

Mattakkuliya

Lunupokuna

Fort

Borella

Kirula

Wellawatta

1 mi
1 km

Over 1.00
Less than –1.00

C Substandard
   Housing –
   Component III

Mattakkuliya

Lunupokuna

Fort

Borella

Kirula

Wellawatta

D Ethnic
   Components
   IV and VI

Mattakkuliya

Lunupokuna

Fort

Borella

Kirula

Wellawatta

Tamils
Muslims

these conditions exist might be described as a free enterprise, pre-welfare state stage of capitalism, with the additional attributes of an advanced economic and technological development, and what might be crudely summarized as a non-traditional cultural context in which economic and functional forces dominate.

This rationalization on conditions under which the key dimensions have emerged as bases of residential separation in North America, provides some guidelines for the interpretation of factorial ecologies in other parts of the world. The analogy must be handled with care as superficial similarities may result from sharply contrasted societal forces but some comparisons are possible. The clarity of an ethnic or migrant dimension will relate to the extent to which a significant minority group exists within society or to the contemporary levels of residential mobility. On a broader front, stratification may be real enough in social terms but may not find clear spatial expression either through the inadequacies of the housing market or from the preferences of those able to exercise choice. In Third World societies we are considering situations in which in addition to the non-economic bases of many preference patterns, concepts such as residential area and housing market have different meaning. Cities are often non-urban in character, infrastructures are grossly inadequate, and basic needs of shelter precede any other considerations. Though studies of Third World countries suggest cities in transition as 'modernization' diffuses through the urban and social system, there is great diversity between larger and smaller urban areas, between one part of the Third World and another. Again, in Europe, there are differing levels of public sector intervention which have sharp effects on the social geography of the city. In Britain it can be summarized as a 'distorting' effect in which the general spatial generalizations remain but in heavily modified forms; in socialist societies as key bases of separation are removed, so the utility of any western model is diminished.

From the available evidence a couple of broad generalizations may be offered. Firstly, there is some support for a type of stage-model in terms of which cities can be seen to possess particular social geographies at particular 'stages' in their development (Timms, 1971). Secondly, there is what might be termed a 'social formation' model which suggests that different types of societies will be typified by contrasted urban factorial ecologies. Free-market capitalism is one type of 'social formation', socialist societies form another, welfare states a third, and, less appropriately, the Third World countries can be placed in a very broad fourth category. Generalizations of this kind are clearly sweeping and vulnerable to detailed analyses. Factorial ecologies, however, have pro-

---

Figure 7.12 Factorial ecology of Colombo, Sri Lanka. (a) Social status is not a clear dimension but one can distinguish between low status areas around Fort and some higher status areas. (b) Land-use differentiation: the greatest admixture occurs around Fort. (c) Substandardness occurs in large parts of the city and includes both shanties (negative scores) and tenements (positive scores). (d) Ethnic areas showing two of the minority groups in an essentially plural society (after de Silva, 1973; with the author's permission)

duced evidence which gives them some level of credibility; their findings have given insights both into the nature of social stratification and its expression as residential segregation in cities.

ETHNIC AREAS

Ethnic residential segregation is often the most pronounced form of segregation within urban areas; it possesses a high level of ubiquity across contrasted types of society and can often be detected in an incipient form in the very early stages of city growth. Boal (1978), in a review of the concept of ethnicity and its manifestations in urban social geography has provided useful definitions and guidelines. The bases for ethnic categorization can be racial, religious, or national; its recognition may rest on distinguishing physical characteristics, on cultural traits such as language or custom, or on a group identity obtaining from common origins or traditions. Greeley (1969) summarized this last characteristic as a 'human collectivity' based on an assumption of common origin, real or imaginary. Most research on ethnic groups has focused upon minorities in any given society. Ethnic minority groups have varying levels of residential segregation which appear related to two key features. The first of these relates to the migrant status of the group. Virtually all ethnic minorities are initially immigrants both to urban areas and also to the wider society; the recency of migration and their migration history are clearly important considerations. The second feature is the 'social' distance which separates the ethnic minority from the 'charter group' or host society which forms the dominant matrix into which it is inserted. For those immigrants whose differences with the charter group are small, separate identity may be of only temporary duration; for those whose differences—either real or perceived—are great, separation in both society and space is likely to persist. These two factors clearly interact. New migrants, regardless of ethnic status, will be distinctive at least in social characteristics; long-term migrants, however distinctive they have remained, will have acquired some of the characteristics of the new society.

Assimilation: choice and constraint

The maintenance of the ethnic minority group as a distinctive social and spatial entity will depend on the degree to which assimilation occurs. A distinction is normally made between *behavioural* and *structural* assimilation. The former describes the process whereby members of a group acquire the attitudes, values and mores of the charter group and are 'acculturated' into the new society. Structural assimilation refers to the ability of migrant ethnics to compete successfully in the system of stratification within that society—principally its occupational, educational, and housing markets. Both types of assimilation have to be seen in a temporal context but whereas behavioural assimilation is normally attainable by all types of immigrants, structural assimilation is typically much more difficult to achieve. The rate at which behavioural assimilation takes place can vary from one ethnic minority group to another—some groups may purposely seek to retain their distinctive characteristics and thereby delay assimilation—but a common estimate is that by the third generation a migrant group has substantially acquired the behavioural traits and values of the host society. Time taken to achieve structural assimilation will vary and the type of ethnic minority is again significant; the key factor, however, is the attitude of the charter group. Whereas West European immigrants to the United States, for example, will normally achieve almost immediate structural assimilation, i.e. they will fit into existing systems at a level appropriate to their skills and qualifications, black minorities in American cities continue to occupy lower-paid jobs and low-cost housing after well over a century of in-movement. Most research in the social sciences has been concerned with those ethnic minorities for whom the constraints upon assimilation and levels of discrimination are greatest.

It is for these latter groups that membership of an ethnic minority is most likely to be accompanied in the longer term by residential segregation. The ethnic areas typical of many cities at many points in time have often been initiated and maintained by attitudes of a charter group which continues to discriminate and restrict and has the effect of creating both separation and disadvantage. Not all of the forces which promote ethnic segregation, however, emanate from the charter group. There is strong evidence that choice operates in the maintenance of ethnic group segregation; for minorities who wish to retain some level of group cohesion, the ethnic area offers an obvious instrument to that end. Boal (1978) has nominated a number of functions which the ethnically segregated area fulfils. The *defensive* function enables the isolation of members of an ethnic minority to be reduced and an organized defence to be developed within a clearly defined area. As the term 'ghetto' (from the island of Geto in Venice) was first applied to Jewish compounds in European cities, it had this kind of meaning. In that situation locked gates kept one group in and other groups out, circumstances which have subsequently been replicated in principle if not in practice. An *avoidance* function emphasized the self-supportive roles of ethnic residential segregations. Avoidance is more clearly seen in the context of recent arrivals to an established ethnic area. The area serves as a place of initiation and familiarization in which retention of traditional values and customs makes these processes easier to accomplish. Ethnic minority areas often have institutions, such as those of religion or welfare, which may be in part designed to provide sustenance at earlier stages of contact with a new society. Chain migration has frequently been recognized by which earlier migrants maintain flows of information and aid to those who follow; social networks developed in this way form part of the avoidance function. *Preservation* functions offer the most positive choice bases of ethnic segregation. Here the aim is to preserve and promote at least central features of the ethnic group's cultural heritage such as language, religion, and marriage customs. Wirth (1928), in his classic study of the ghetto, suggested that for Jews the geographically separated and socially isolated community seemed to offer the best means of preserving the traditional facets of their lifestyle. There is considerable evidence (see Dahya, 1974) that Asian communities in Britain hold the preservation function very high on their list of priorities. Finally the *resistance* function involves the use by an ethnic group of a particular territory as its power-base for action against the wider society. At times during the late 1960s and 1970s the Black Power movement in the United States aspired to use the ghettos for such purposes; the Catholic 'no-go' areas in Northern Ireland had this fairly explicit function, and in many parts of the world urban guerillas have used parts of the city in this way.

These four functions of ethnic areas could in some ways be classified as choice mechanisms but they could also be regarded as responses to constraint. Whereas both choice and constraint operate to produce ethnically segregated areas, they are invariably interwoven and explanations are rarely single-stranded. Whatever the mechanisms which produce ethnic areas, high levels of segregation—as already illustrated—typify many minority groups in western cities. In studying these segregations a number of issues need resolution. Firstly, the scale of analysis needs to be stated as different levels of spatial resolution will produce different results. These *caveats* are well known and researchers have experimented with a variety of scales. Peach (1979) has shown that high levels of segregation can occur even where the minority is numerically very small. In that group of American cities with small proportions of non-white population, ranging from 2.1 per cent to 7.0 per cent, indices of dissimilarity of 60.4 to 98.0 were still obtained. A second issue involves the extent of dominance by one group within an ethnic area. Immigrant areas were being defined in British cities, for example, when it was still rare for immigrants to form more than 20 per cent of the population in any one area; Ford and Griffin (1979) report that white Americans may regard an area as ethnic if it is 25 per cent black, whereas black Americans would regard it as integrated if it was 25 per cent white. A third issue, arising directly from this, concerns the drawing of boundaries to delimit an ethnic area. Most researchers have adopted arbitrary thresholds; Ford and Griffin (1979), for example, defined ghettos as areas with at least 50 per cent black or 70 per cent minority group (blacks, Hispanics, Asians). A problem with the second part of this definition is that each minority group may segregate within the ethnic area and there is ample avidence (Jones, 1979; Suttles, 1967) to show that this does occur. Again, it is well to remember that as ethnic areas are often dynamic with fluid boundaries, notions of core and periphery may be appropriate.

A typology of ethnic areas

Boal (1978) suggests ways of classifying ethnic areas which provide a useful conceptual typology although the 'form' may not vary significantly. He uses the term *colony* to describe an ethnic area which is temporary in character.

Its main functions are to provide a foothold in new societies for groups who are likely to have little difficulty in achieving either behavioural or structural assimilation and are motivated towards both those ends. An *enclave* is an ethnic area which is likely to persist over time but is primarily based on choice and a preservation function in particular. The term *ghetto* is reserved for ethnic areas which persist and are based largely upon constraints and the discriminatory action of the charter group. Figure 7.13 suggests some ways in which these three spatial forms might emerge and are based upon Boal's (1978) examples. Colony provides an initial cluster which disappears over time as the minority group participates successfully in assimilation processes; an example of this is the Dutch immigration into Kalamazoo (Jakle and Wheeler, 1969). Enclave need not differ significantly in spatial expression from ghetto, the indicators are found in the ways in which it functions as a

Types of ethnic area

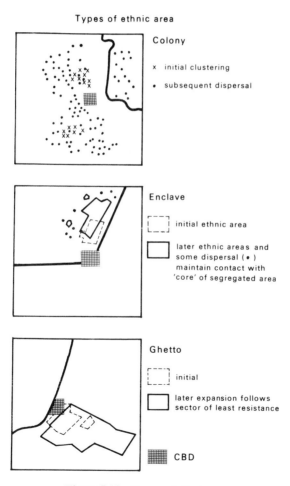

Figure 7.13   Types of ethnic area

social organization. As Jewish groups in Winnipeg (Driedger and Church, 1974) adjusted their spatial positions and in part moved to another district of the city, they remained clustered together and moved their cultural institutions to the new locations. Ghettos in American cities are best exemplified for black populations. Their typical relegation to the most substandard and lowest cost inner-city districts is a reflection of their inability to achieve structural assimilation; their subsequent restriction to limited sectors of cities for expansion indicates the barriers presented by charter group attitudes and discriminatory practice in the housing market in addition to the obstacle of cost. It is possible that different spatial generalizations can be made about the ways in which enclave and ghetto expand, though the arguments are not convincing. There is some credibility to the suggestion that the ghetto typically expands in a sectoral form, so formed by constraints which eliminate large proportions of urban space and force ghetto expansion in specified directions. Others, however (Rose, 1969), have argued that ghettos may take on a concentric form if a new ethnic cluster is established in another low-cost sector. Again there is some evidence that Asians in British cities (Jones, 1979; Kearsley and Srivastava, 1974) are forming discontinuous concentric zones in response to a 'fabric effect', that is, the location and availability of the type of housing to which they aspire. These spatial generalizations have some merit but they are less significant than the sociospatial processes which work to maintain and enlarge ethnic areas.

Ethnic areas in American cities

The subject of ethnic minorities in the United States, and especially of black ethnic groups, has attracted a great deal of research attention (see Ernst and Hugg, 1976, for a review). Studies have focused on the early development of immigrant areas (Ward, 1971), on the spatial ecology of slave cities (Radford, 1976), as well as on modern processes of ghetto formation. Ford and Griffin (1979) offer a useful typology of black ghettos in the United States (see Figure 7.14). In the *early southern* ghetto, as found for example in antebellum Charleston and New Orleans, blacks typically lived close within white neighbourhoods—for which they served domestic roles as servants or gardeners—but occupied alleys and backstreets in small dwellings. In the *classic southern* ghetto the newly free blacks were placed in purpose-built housing on unwanted land, such as near railway tracks or on badly drained areas. As southern states experienced considerable outmigration of blacks, neither of these types of ghetto had potential for growth and tended to stagnate or disappear.

The *early northern* ghetto was the product of intense competition for space in the early twentieth century. Its tenements and row-houses, especially in large north-eastern cities, are occupied at high density with chronic shortage of space and high levels of poverty and substandardness. *Classic northern* ghettos are more recent and much more extensive in scale. As the 'white-flight' from the central city gathered force, so large areas of land and housing were

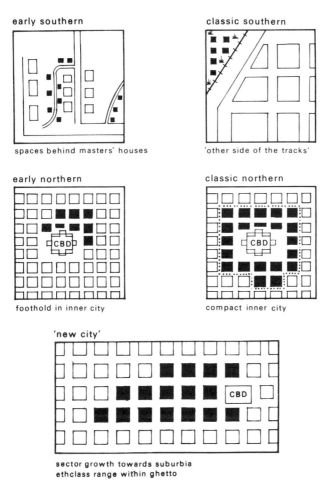

early southern

spaces behind masters' houses

classic southern

'other side of the tracks'

early northern

foothold in inner city

classic northern

compact inner city

'new city'

sector growth towards suburbia
ethclass range within ghetto

Figure 7.14   A typology of black ghettos in the United States
(derived from information in Ford and Griffin, 1979)

left to an expanding black population. This type of ghetto is also found on the west coast in its 'older' large cities. Black south-central Los Angeles, for example, extends 40 km (25 miles) from near Beverly Hills to Long Beach. Within these vast areas of this type of ghetto are enormous tracts of vacant land, dereliction and abandoned properties. Ford and Griffin (1979) argue that although this is the dominate image of the black ghetto, the reality is being modified by the emergence of a 'new city' type of ghetto in those parts of the United States which are currently experiencing significant urban growth.

As typified by San Diego and other cities like Denver and Phoenix these ghettos extend from the inner city to rural–suburban fringes. The gradient from poverty and poor environment at the inner city end of the sector to affluence and good environments on the fringe is contained within the black community. 'Ethclasses' or social stratifications within the ethnic group find

314

separate spatial expressions within the ethnic sector; there are segregated socioeconomic status groups within the black community. Although the emergence of this fifth type of ghetto suggests structural assimilation amongst some sections at least of the black population of the United States, there are no signs that the ghetto is dispersing. Fears and prejudices rooted in generations of segregated residential areas will take many years to dissipate.

Immigrants and ethnic areas in British cities

Although there were ethnic minorities in the United Kingdom before the 1950s, they were—apart from the Irish who occupied the nineteenth-century 'ghettos'—insignificant in numerical terms. The influx of immigrants from the New Commonwealth during the 1950s and 1960s gave substantial ethnic minorities, and their behaviour in residential space has been closely monitored (Jones, 1970, 1979; Peach, 1966, 1975). The main immigrant groups, from the West Indies, India and Pakistan, have followed classical patterns of immigration. They arrived with many disadvantages associated with lack of employment skills and education, and have found these exacerbated by the early discriminatory practices of the host society which has made structural assimilation a very difficult process. As a generalization the *replacement* theory is most relevant to understanding the niche which they occupy in both social and geographical space. They found employment in those types of job which either through low pay or unpleasant conditions the native British worker did not want; they obtained housing in those substandard parts of the inner city which had experienced population decline through outmigrations over a long period of time. Certainly in the earlier years, choice mechanisms did function in the initiation of segregated areas. Avoidance and preservation have been powerful roles which persist.

Studies based on 1961 census data showed that some segregation did exist but that the new ethnic minorities were relatively small elements of population in poor environments which they shared with the low-income British population and often the long-established Irish communities. Evidence from successive later censuses is that levels of segregation tend to increase, that ethnic minorities tend to become the majority group within some areas, and that the various minorities are occupying different ethnic areas. Whereas part of the segregation, of an order 10 to 15 per cent, can be explained by socioeconomic characteristics (Peach, Winchester, and Woods, 1975), it is clearly an *ethnic* basis of separation which is occurring.

Detailed case studies have been conducted in the city of Birmingham (Jones, 1970; 1979), where in 1971 the coloured minority of 92,632 comprised 9.3 per cent of the total population. By 1961 a distribution of ethnic minorities had emerged which broadly conformed to a concentric zone at 1 to 1.5 kilometres outside the city centre. Within this zone densities of immigrants were low but they were locating in response to a *fabric effect*—these were the pre-1919 terraced-row, low-cost housing districts—and to a *replacement model* in that these were also districts from which local people were moving out. By 1971 the continuing combination of demographic circumstances—out-migration of whites, inmigration and natural increase of immigrants—had consolidated this zonal concentration at much higher densities. Levels of immigrant representation within the clusters in 1971 had reached 38 to 51 per cent (Jones, 1979); for smaller areas the levels were higher and processes likely to produce ethnic areas of American dimensions were ongoing. A feature of the 1970s has been the tendency for different ethnic groups to cluster separately in different part of the zone, with Pakistanis, for example, centred on parts of south Birmingham, such as Saltley and Small Heath. Similarly, Peach, Winchester, and Woods (1975) have shown that in Coventry and Birmingham the West Indians are residentially separate from the other immigrant groups.

A significant factor in British cities is the role of the public sector in the housing market. Although this sector has a traditionally strong welfare role, there was evidence in the 1960s (Burney, 1967) that municipalities were exercising discrimination in their allocation policies against immigrant households of a kind which was also evident in the private housing market. The recency of most immigrant residence in a city was counted heavily against them; where they had to be rehoused, a series of expedients, such as deferred renewal areas, improved terraces, or old inner-city estates, was used. By 1971, however, aided by national legislation, the situation had improved; the percentage of black households—mainly West Indian—living in public sector housing had risen to 19 per cent compared to a 32 per cent figure for the total population. Municipalities were now adopting positive rehousing policies in relation to the black population occupying the most substandard sections of the urban housing market, though those policies have been sources of conflict in some cities. Public sector housing has also been a factor in increasing the degree of residential separation and 'social' position among the various ethnic minorities. West Indians are most amenable to rehousing and there is some limited evidence that their levels of segregation are decreasing; for other immigrant groups, however, these trends are far less obvious.

Asians have progressed through a number of housing situations with stages which Robinson (1979) has summarized as early pioneer, lodging-house era and family-reunion with more recent evidence for trends towards suburbanization and municipalization. Whereas some basic points have to be acknowledged, such as the fact that the Asian 'community' comprises a considerable number of ethnically different groups and that there is evidence of change over time, recent research suggests the strong influence of a 'myth of return' or the belief that their British residence is temporary. Because of this myth of return, Asians may reveal an unwillingness to assimilate or to assume ties or commitments with British society. Choice forms a strong factor, therefore, in their segregation and even where moves to private suburbs or council estates occur, they tend to remain relatively close to the 'enclave' which houses the majority of the ethnic group and in which its cultural traditions and institutions are maintained.

Whereas no British coloured ethnic minority shows clear signs for dispersal, there are variations from one group to another and the social processes underpinning the contemporary situation may vary significantly. The overall balance of evidence remains such as to suggest that in British cities ethnic areas have emerged and are consolidating. Whereas severe constraints have an instrumental role in this process, it is clear now that the choice mechanisms are also there and public policies, traditionally set towards integrationist goals, are now being modified. The city of Birmingham eventually adopted a rigid dispersal policy in its public sector housing allocations, intended to maintain an immigrant element on any one estate at a low level, but this had to be relaxed owing largely to West Indian opposition in favour of higher levels of clustering. Cullingworth (1969), in a government-sponsored report, stressed the positive effects of ethnic concentration, and public policy since has developed a much stronger regard for the choices and preferences of the minority groups. Such a policy which would allow the continuity of ethnic areas and outmovement based only on choice has a number of critical qualifications. First, as a longer-term goal, the disadvantages which ethnic minorities suffer through the inequalities present in society and its mechanisms must be eliminated. Structural assimilation must be a clear and real possibility. Second, in the short-term, it should be recognized that ethnic areas are frequently disadvantaged now in terms of quality of environment, resources and facilities; the positive discrimination and area-enrichment policies already initiated must be developed. Third, where a preference exists to live outside an ethnic area, it should be made possible and on this point there is some reassurance from the lack of problems which Asian professionals experience in residing in white middle-class areas. These qualifications are not yet realized and the fact of ethnic areas remains a policy issue which research has to monitor and comprehend.

Conclusions

The focus of attention in this section has been upon ethnic minority groups in western societies and the residential segregation which they typically reveal. Throughout many Third World countries where plural societies are much more common, the issues are more diverse and complex. Residential segregations on ethnic grounds have strong religious and language connotations and are often reinforced by extensive kinship networks and internally organized social systems. The nature of these segregations will differ within the Third World and will reflect both the societal organizations of the various countries and the stage of urbanization which they have reached. In south Asian cities, such as Colombo, the traditional societal divisions drawn on ethnic lines are strongly represented in segregated ethnic areas in cities which are only slowly being modified by modernization and westernization; in West African cities (Brand, 1972) tribal bases for segregation may exist but are subsumed within migrant status; ethnic divisions in Caribbean cities (Clarke, 1971) reflect the plural complexity of their societies. There is an absence in San Fernando

(Trinidad) of marked residential segregation except for the white minority; other ethnic groups reveal mixing but groups with high antipathy—such as Hindus and Muslims—avoid contiguity. Ethnic divisions and ethnic areas, in their diversity of forms, typify cities in many parts of the world and are likely to maintain their distinctive imprint upon urban life.

RESIDENTIAL MOBILITY

The facts of residential mobility suggest that it is a pervasive and continuing process within the city; evidence for a generally high frequency of change is available for both nineteenth-century and modern cities. Lawton (1979) reports that intercensal persistence rates (that is, no change) in English cities in the later nineteenth century may have been of the order of 40 to 60 per cent and appeared to vary with factors such as lifecycle stage, income and social mobility. A study of Liverpool revealed low levels of persistence amongst low-income inner city areas—especially of recent migrants—but high levels in high-status areas. Many of the new residential suburbs had high turnover rates and there was a general propensity towards short-distance moves. In modern times, moves within American metropolitan areas have been put at nearly 25 per cent per annum. The overall figure may exaggerate the general pattern as some households move very frequently and inflate the average rate; mobility rates in inner-city rooming house districts, for example, approximate 70 per cent while older established suburbs may have turnover rates as low as 5 per cent (Moore, 1972). An overall estimate is that 50 per cent of the entire population moves within a five-year period (Simmons, 1968). In Europe, residential mobility rates are lower but everywhere moves at the intraurban scale appear to dominate the overall pattern of migration.

Housing markets and residential change

A number of initially divergent approaches have been employed to study the housing market and the process of residential mobility; it is only in comparatively recent years that these various strands have been recognized as parts of the same overall framework. The main components of these various approaches may be summarized:

1. Attempts to model the urban housing market using a small number of basic variables and the principles of neoclassical economics.
2. Studies of the factors and agencies involved in the supply of housing and urban development in general; these studies had a more explicit concern with the decision-makers in the supply side of the urban housing markets and with the allocative systems which are involved.
3. Analyses of the residential mobility process *per se* with a focus upon the consumers in the housing market who, within recognized constraints, are making decisions on where to live. Much of this research has focused upon

individual movers as decision-makers, but its earlier content was more concerned with aggregate data and with generalizations upon the movements of groups of areas.

Discussion on each of these research areas is developed below but initially two further contextual statements need to be made. Firstly, several significant attempts have now been made to see the development of the urban housing market in western cities against a framework of broader societal change. Vance (1978) has examined the emerging housing market as western cities moved from precapitalist to capitalist to postcapitalist stages; his argument also emphasizes the contrasted attitudes of American and west European governments to the provision of low-cost housing in the twentieth century and the effects which this difference has had. Both Walker (1978) in a historical context, and Roweis and Scott (1978) with closer reference to the modern urban housing market, relate outcomes to the structural imperatives of the capitalist system. Secondly, many geographers were drawn to an analysis of the housing market as a consequence of their preoccupation with residential patterns in the 1960s and in a thrust to understand the processes which produced those patterns. An early dominant feature of this thrust was the study of movers themselves, the consumers whose decisions on where to live were the underpinnings of the urban mosaic. This research was typically overconcerned with those limited sections of society which possessed the ability to move and who exercised choice and preference. More recently the balance has been redressed and emphases have shifted from the study of the overt processes of residential change to the forces and mechanisms within society which strongly influence them.

Micro-economic models

Micro-economic models of the housing market (Bourne, 1976) are in a sense a product of their time which rest upon simplifying assumptions and attempts to generalize upon the distribution of house prices, housing supply, and densities over urban areas. The approach has long heritage and can be identified, for example, in Hurd's (1903) study of urban land values; many studies were completed in the 1960s (Alonso, 1963; Muth, 1969) as the regional science school of urban studies developed. The working bases of these models are found in the economics of supply and location and the neoclassical theories of household behaviour merged into a general equilibrium framework. The model typically makes a number of limiting assumptions such as perfect competition, a unidimensional product, invariant tastes and a single-centred city; the market process is a mechanistic one in which individual households, maximizing satisfaction, distribute themselves according to income, accessibility needs and space preferences, Suppliers seek to maximize profits in the manner in which they develop new units for the housing market.

Outputs from micro-economic models are typically a set of relatively simple generalizations (see Bourne, 1976). Population density, for example, decreases from centre to periphery, housing-lot size tends to increase as does income of householder and house-buying ability. Although these models can be refined, it has become fairly clear that their limitations are considerable and that there are many aspects of reality which either they cannot measure or which can be analysed in different and much more satisfactory ways. Palm (1979), for example, applied a micro-economic model to the study of house-price variations in the San Francisco area. There were associations with access, income and the percentage non-white but the levels of explanation afforded by the model were very small and alternative approaches were preferred.

Similar limitations apply to urban development models which are large-scale modelling strategies, incorporating housing submodels, aimed at conceptualizing the overall process of urban growth and operationalized in such ways as to enable them to have predictive functions. Again, these models have strong assumptive and simplifying bases and rely upon estimation and extrapolation techniques to provide forecasts of demography, accessibility, and other change parameters. Both these larger models and related attempts (Batty, 1973) to develop accounting systems for residential change have been widely criticized for their failure to examine the diverse nature of housing submarkets and the varying adaptability of inherited housing stock in the city. This set of approaches, then, has some value at a broad level of generalization and has added considerable technical ability to urban analysis; its scope is severely limited, however, by the restrictive assumptions upon which it is typically based.

Agencies in the housing market

The suppliers

Bourne (1976, p. 146) well summarizes the alternative framework within which the supply side of the housing market needs to be studied; it is not, he argues,

as assumed in most micro-economic models, characterized by optimal decision-making within a uniform and unconstrained environment. The housing industry itself, and the various private and public agents responsible for the provision of housing, are not homogeneous in character or behaviour.

It is in this complexity of a hierarchy of decision-makers operating within the framework of a particular society and interacting with broad market trends of supply and demand, that some of the main determinants of the changing residential geography of urban areas are to be found.

A first set of agencies is that concerned with the development of land and with the provision of new housing. Land has special features in the housing market through a number of special characteristics which it possesses. General features include its permanence, it is a resource which cannot be depleted, and the fact that its cost and scarcity in an urban setting is likely to leave

320

its control in the hands of institutions rather than individuals. A special feature of land in an urban context is that it has both a use value and an exchange value. Whereas the former relates to the use to which it is currently put and may be reflected in a form of rent; the latter refers to its value when next it enters the market as a commodity, perhaps with a potentially different use. One of the salutary experiences of western cities in recent decades is' that the land market, and through it the housing market, can be manipulated to create a shortage having short-term drastic effects upon value, price and availability of housing. Such speculation involving the buying up and 'holding' of land for future resale is guided by exchange values rather than use values. In those societies where planning powers and public intervention in urban affairs have been strengthened, much of their energies have been directed to exactly this problem.

Figure 7.15 summarizes the main stages involved in the land-development decision; this decision most typically involves the development of new housing upon virgin land but may also include the clearance of old buildings and their replacement by new constructions and the modification of existing stock. The model moves through an *interest* stage in which, for example, agricultural land on the urban fringe is recognized as having development potential in the light of current rates of urban growth; a *consideration* stage at which the developer begins negotiation with the land-owner on costs and also consolidates his assessment of its future exchange value as residential land; if favourably concluded this stage will end in the transference of the land to the developer. Prior to the *programming stage*, the developer will have researched the likelihood of any constraints upon his future use of the land, but in this stage formal planning permissions, made in the context of zoning ordinances and development control, are obtained. There is some evidence that developers are prepared to buy and hold land in the belief that presently

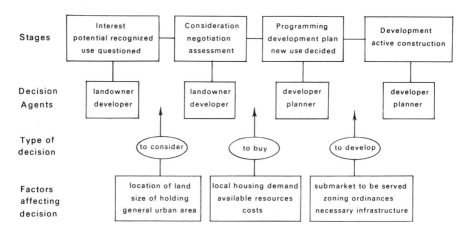

Figure 7.15   Stages in the land-development process: decision-makers involved and factors which influence them

unfavourable zoning classifications will be changed, but more typically the initial purchase is made with knowledge of favourable development circumstances. Also in the programming stage, the developer has to decide what type of housing and in which price range he intends to build, a decision most likely to be made by an assessment of the demand market. In the *development* stage actual construction takes place in which a developer may subcontract part of his holding and may phase construction to match the rate at which sales absorb the units which become available. This model has been described in terms of a private developer, but where the public sector, for example a municipality, directly intervenes in the housing market as a developer, it will behave in broadly similar ways. Differences emerge with the possible power of the public sector to acquire land by compulsory purchase and by its likely commitment to build low-cost units to rent.

The *powers* of the various decision-makers in Figure 7.16 will vary significantly over time and place and it is important to restate that the social formation within which their activities are placed has significant conditioning effects. For *landowners* the steady growth of planning controls, welfare considerations and state intervention in virtually all societies has meant an accompanying diminution of their powers. At past times landowners have held and used the power to delay urban development, as in the well-documented case of Nottingham (United Kingdom), in the early nineteenth century, or at least to mould the directions of urban growth. In most European countries these powers have been considerably reduced. Municipal authorities may stipulate the uses to which land cannot be put without changing its ownership or may use legislative authority to acquire land for its own purposes. Zoning regulations have often adversely affected a landowner's potential for profit and in general his freedom to act as a free agent in the land and housing market has been severely restricted. *Developers* have the active roles of injecting new

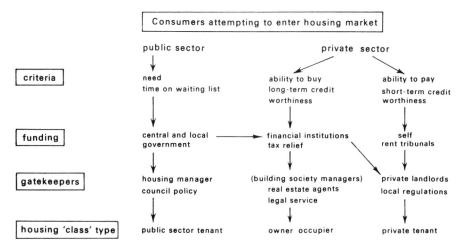

Figure 7.16 Consumers in the housing market: choices, constraints, and urban managers

housing into the system and will normally respond to the way in which they perceive the market at any one time and to their current ability to attract or use resources. In this last respect they are vulnerable to prevailing financing conditions, including interest rates and the willingness of banks to lend. Most development is speculative, that is, houses are built to be sold so that return on invested capital is not assured until transactions are completed; risk is therefore involved. A generally high demand for housing has minimized risk however over the longer term and it is only small-scale enterprises that have proved really vulnerable. Private developers have a primary interest in building new houses for middle to high-income groups; their shortcoming has been an unwillingness to provide for the higher risk, lower-profit, cheap housing market. In the United States, for example, the operative assumption for much of the twentieth century has been that the *filtering* process, by which housing passes down from higher-income to lower-income occupants, as it deteriorates and becomes less attractive (Vance, 1978), is a sufficient provider for the lower end of the market. Elsewhere—and now more so in the United States—the public sector has found it necessary to intervene directly in the housing market in the roles of both developer and landlord in order to safeguard levels of provision.

Planners have key interventionist roles in the housing market; their powers will vary considerably from one society to another and they have much more legislative power in the United Kingdom, for example, than in the United States. There is some credibility to the argument that planners are not primarily initiators of development nor do they achieve major redirections in urban growth, rather they modify market forces and effect control over its main expressions. At the broadest urban level, strategy plans seek to lay down the general allocations of land-use and the main directions for future growth; within these general and often 'blurred' blueprints, the details of zoning and development control assume considerable significance. Planners, in association with other local government departments, have key roles in the provision of basic utilities and in the stipulation of standards and quality control.

The gatekeepers

Once housing is constructed and becomes available for sale or rent on the housing market, new agents or 'gatekeepers' are involved. Figure 7.16 summarizes some of the options and constraints which the potential consumer of housing now faces and the other decision-making agencies which are involved. In the private sector, the capital held by the consumer and his creditworthiness as perceived by the gatekeepers is critical. Easiest routes to accommodation in the private sector are through rented properties. Here the demands on available capital and credit are both limited and short-term; the only real agent involved is the landlord who, along with the tenant, is controlled to varying degrees by codes of practice and local regulations. In the United Kingdom, with a rapidly shrinking private-rented sector and its increasing confinement to least-desirable properties, the members of this 'housing class'

(Rex and Moore, 1967) are among the least competitive in the housing market. They have least security, poorest living conditions and the lowest chance of real accumulation of capital. For the consumer with both the ability to buy and recognized creditworthiness, the options are more real and this group forms the most privileged housing class. Choice is possible, good living environments are likely and ownership of property carries advantages such as the appreciating value of the asset. Public sector tenants are judged in terms of need, most British local authorities operate some form of 'points system'—although some municipalities retain date-order systems—and whereas rents may be subsidized the opportunities to accumulate capital are again limited.

The key issue now is the way in which the 'gatekeepers' mediate in the housing market and some examples of their activities will be discussed. Firstly, however, some general points need to be reiterated. Managers or gatekeepers function as individuals within the frameworks of the larger organizations which they serve. In many respects they merely conform to policies laid down elsewhere or work to a few simple rules—such as maximizing profits or lending money with least risk. There is also evidence, however, that they interpret rules in an individualistic way and that judgements are tempered by local considerations and issues. The evidence for the independence of gatekeepers is ambiguous, but their roles are real enough. A key problem in using the concept of managerialism is that of theorizing their roles and defining the rationalities upon which they are based.

Managers of financial institutions are key figures in the private housing market as their decisions on the lending of housing finance—'to whom' and 'where'—have profound effects. Harvey's (1977) study of Baltimore (Figure 7.17) showed that prospects of house-ownership in different parts of the city were strongly influenced by the varying willingness of different agencies to lend money. Within Baltimore submarkets could be distinguished within which the prospects of housing finance and the availability of alternative institutions varied considerably. In the inner city, for example, what little financing existed was obtained through private sources; the ethnic areas depended upon small-scale, community-based savings and loans societies or, in the middle-income black district, on federal sources. It was in the affluent white suburbs that greatest choice of financing was available. Harvey's main concern was to relate the outcomes in the Baltimore housing market to the macro-structures of society through which financing flowed, but he also recognizes the significance of 'taps and regulators' in the allocative system.

A study of Sacramento (Dingemans, 1979) utilizes the material assembled by financing companies in response to the US Home Mortgage Disclosure Act of 1975 in order to examine patterns of mortgage lending in the city. Dingemans was especially concerned with the issue of *red-lining* as the practice of defining areas in the city within which lending is regarded as high risk; occupants of such areas are therefore discriminated against. A number of alternative hypotheses was examined—for example, that red-lined districts are declining anyway and have a low demand for mortgages—but the statistical analysis

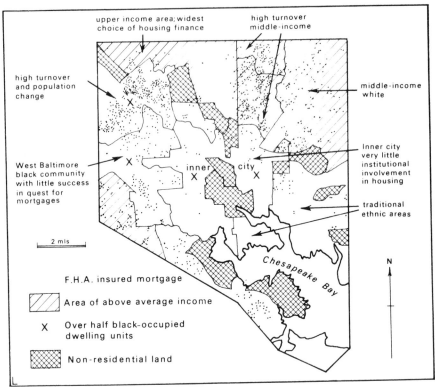

Figure 7.17 Institutional funding and the Baltimore housing market (after Harvey, 1977; reproduced by permision of John Wiley and Sons Ltd.)

showed a strong positive association of mortgage lending with socioeconomic status and a negative association with non-white residents and ages of property—even when influence of new housing units was eliminated. Of the sample neighbourhoods examined, the upper middle-income white suburb received far more loans than any other, though the direct evidence for red-lining policy in ethnic minority areas was not convincing. Other evidence, however (Stone, 1977), more emphatically asserts the reality of the practice of red-lining ethnic areas.

British studies of mortgage-lending behaviour (Boddy, 1976; Williams, 1976) have identified similar features. In Newcastle-upon-Tyne, mortgage lending within the inner parts of the city was minimal, even from the municipal authority. Consideration of risk appeared dominant amongst building societies and profiles of successful mortgage borrowers revealed a strong bias towards professional and managerial groups with above-average incomes. Loans from the local authority were clustered in those parts of the inner city in which improvement was likely to increase the stability of the area and to enable property value appreciation; the least-advantaged inner-city areas remained starved of funds. Similarly, a study of Saltley, Birmingham (Community

Development Project, 1974) revealed that only 7 per cent of owner-occupiers held a mortgage at normal interest rates. These examples show how discriminatory lending practices appear to depress housing areas and inhibit home ownership within them; the Islington study (Williams, 1976) showed how building societies responded to a 'gentrification' process by progressively increasing their investment levels in that part of inner London. Whereas in 1950 virtually all major building societies were not lending money in Islington because of its perceived lack of stability and high risk clientèle, by 1972 all but one of the major societies were lending in a rapidly appreciating residential district shifting from low-income private renters to high-income owners.

Real estate agents (realtors) form another group of managers or gatekeepers in the urban housing market. In some ways they provide a better example of managerialism in that most realtors are local businesses rather than elements of national or regional organizations. The real estate agent is the intermediary in the housing market between the buyer and the seller; as housing markets have developed there are increasing ties between the realtor and the financing, legal, and other professional services—typically the realtor acts as 'broker' for all of these. Rising house prices favour the realtor as his income normally rests on a percentage ratio of sale price; a high level of transactions in the housing market is clearly also in his interests. A number of studies of American cities suggest that realtors have very positive roles and in some ways seek to push residential area change in specific directions. A study of New England in 1953 showed that realtors were using principally ethnic criteria to direct clients away from some areas and towards others. A New Haven study in 1968, after civil rights legislation, showed that the same pattern existed and was rationalized by realtors on the grounds that it fitted in with the preferences of both black and white clients and also with the investment policies of financial institutions. The overt tactics of 'blockbusting' and 'lily-whiting' (Osofsky, 1966) have been used by realtors to direct and control the growth of black areas. *Blockbusting* involved the use of scare tactics to increase white turnover— such as advertising a house for five dollars—and bringing hordes of blacks onto the street (Ford and Griffin, 1979); *lily-whiting* involved realtors steering white buyers away from any area that had even a few blacks, thereby ensuring ghettoization.

Palm (1979) used a set of four hypothetical household profiles, sent to a sample of realtors in San Francisco, to examine the way in which realtors organized the housing market. There were territorial subdivisions within the housing market within which realtors specialized and generally there was an attempt to make a judgement on the purchasing power of the client and to fit this to the appropriate type of residential area. Some advice patterns were not contained within this general logic, however, and led to the belief that realtors were actively attempting to change the pattern of the housing market in some areas. The high-income household was often directed to neighbourhoods rather below its price expectations, the low-income households to neighbourhoods rather above. The interpretation was that both recommendations would lead to higher turnover and more buoyant housing markets as the former neighbourhood upgraded and attracted more high-income occupants whereas the latter downgraded and prompted present incumbents to move out. Williams (1976) in his study of gentrification in Islington, London, saw realtors as holding key roles in the process of upgrading; they were the 'agents' of change who by actively promoting the improvement possibilities of this part of Georgian London created higher levels of transactions and residential change. In her study of immigrant housing, Burney (1967) recognized realtors as key professionals in the housing market whose activities affected the form and location of the emerging ethnic areas.

In the public housing sector the key managers are those in municipal housing departments who supervise the allocation of tenancies to applicants. Their decisions concern who gets a tenancy at what time, and in which estate the family is to be located. The important factor is that virtually all cities in Britain, for example, have 'good' and 'bad' public sector estates, perceived with different levels of desirability both by the population at large and by prospective tenants. In earlier days it is clear that housing managers directed low-graded tenants—those with poor records as assessed by inspection procedures—to 'bad' estates, thereby compounding their problems. Whole slum clearance populations were transferred to new estates, taking their social problems with them. These are not simple issues and will be discussed further elsewhere but they do illustrate the existence of gatekeepers in the public sector whose decisions affect the pattern of urban residential areas.

The managerial thesis, even in the housing market, has not been sufficiently researched in either conceptual or empirical terms. It has its critics (Duncan, 1976), some of whom have come to negative views after empirical research. The urban gatekeepers exist however and fulfil critical roles in the housing market. Even as mere interpreters of societal rules their activities deserve close scrutiny and it is likely that within the varying limits of discretion available to them, the 'gatekeepers' interpose some independent effects.

The residential mobility process

Aggregate studies

There are two scales at which geographers have studied residential change within cities, aggregate and individual, and of these the former has the longer tradition. Aggregate analyses focus on movement of groups or areas over time or seek to establish trends and relationships from area statistics. Hoyt (1939) established the study of high-status residential areas and their typical processes of temporal change as part of the development of his sector theory of neighbourhood growth. His basic proposal—that high-status areas originate near the centre of the incipient city and migrate along specified sectors to the peripheries in alignment with urban growth—has been tested and verified in many places. Hoyt also suggested a number of laws governing the direction

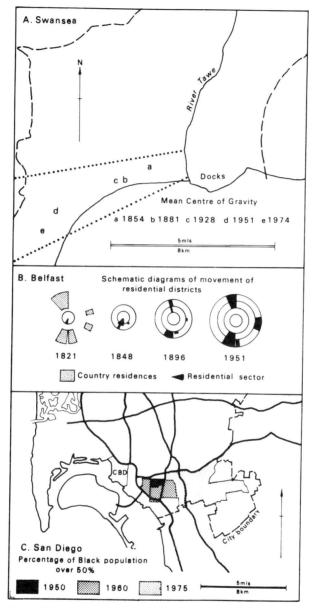

Figure 7.18 Movements of residential areas over time.
(a) Shifts of high-status residences in Swansea, 1854–1974
(after Victor, 1975). (b) Changing high-status residential
areas in Belfast 1821–1951 (after Jones, 1960). (c) Movement
of the black ghetto in San Diego, 1950–1975 (after Ford and
Griffin, 1979)

in which such movements occur and although the concepts are dated they retain some general validity. Figure 7.18 shows some patterns of movement identified by empirical studies; the sectors are often not unambiguous because of the variegated nature of landscape over which movement occurs, but can be recognized. Jones (1960) emphasized the significance of social values attached to space in interpreting the sector pattern in Belfast; an emphasis given increased credibility in later studies. The Swansea example shows a progressive migration of the core area of high-status residence from the inner city out west towards the scenic coastal and industry-free periphery over a century of urban growth. Similarly conceived studies of ethnic area change have already been discussed and Figure 7.18 (c) shows the gradual expansion of San Diego's black ghetto over the period 1950–75.

Studies of neighbourhood change provide further examples of aggregate analyses of the residential mobility process. The literature is replete with examples of this process, dating perhaps from Burgess's (1925) original statement of the invasion–succession process and consequent Chicago monographs depicting community character and change (Zorbaugh, 1929). Firey's (1947) analysis of land-use in central Boston provided graphic examples of neighbourhoods reacting to pressures for change in different ways. Whereas some Boston residential districts showed gradual declining status over the years as higher-income groups moved out, one or two districts, principally Beacon Hill, showed greater persistence—explained by Firey in terms of the sentiments and symbolism attached to place—and remained a dominantly higher social status in composition of its population. Guest (1974) found evidence that neighbourhoods in American cities did pass through a 'lifecycle' in terms of changing social status, but also had difficulties in generalizing upon this as a major metropolitan feature and problem. Whereas measurement of neighbourhood change over time may pose difficulties, the general feature of change is an important part of the filtering process whereby the gradual decreasing status of districts or the adaptation of its housing stock through subdivisions serve to create housing opportunities for different types of social groups, perhaps of contrasted household characteristics.

Gentrification is a significant form of neighbourhood change in many cities. It involves the improvement and upgrading of older property, the movement out of low-income tenants, and the inflow of high-income owner-occupiers. Washington's Georgetown is a well-known example of this phenomenon, and the case of Islington in inner London has already been described (page 326). Cybriwsky (1978) describes the example of Fairmount, a low-income Philadelphia neighbourhood, which having successfully withstood infringement from the black community, has subsequently been affected by a gentrification process. This process, which began in 1970, has typically involved young couples or single people, usually well educated and professional with 'cosmopolitan' attitudes, who constitute up to 20 per cent of the neighbourhood population. This change has raised new sources of conflict and has weakened the stability and cohesiveness of the community.

Aggregate census statistics for small areas have been used to describe patterns of change. Johnston (1969) showed an overall pattern of centre-to-periphery movement in part of London; other studies have both confirmed this expected trend and have identified other cross-city and return-to-central-city flows. Ecological analyses which demonstrate statistical association between mobility rates and other social-demographic variables provide some indications of the nature of the mobility process, but serve limited purposes (Herbert, 1973; see Moore, 1971). Simple mapping of rates of residential changes in different parts of the city (Herbert, 1972; Moore, 1972) have been of value in identifying sample neighbourhoods for more detailed investigation.

Individual studies

The shift in intraurban mobility studies to behavioural approaches and the individual scale was highly significant. Wolpert's (1965) conceptual statement had considerable influence on later work and Brown and Moore's (1970) framework for research aided this shift in perspective. Central to this approach to the study of mobility is the focus on the individual household as a decision-making unit, on the way in which the decision itself is made and becomes operative, and on the behaviour in space of individual households which leads to the emergence of orderly social areas. As suggested earlier, this research was essentially concerned with how those with choices behaved and the existence of constraints was severely understated, but it did add an important new dimension to residential change studies.

Figure 7.19 summarizes the steps in the decision-making process which leads to a residential move; several of these steps have provided research themes in their own right. The concept of *place utility* summarizes the level of satisfaction which a household experiences with its present residence—a satisfaction which is affected both by the internal characteristics of the household and by the features of the external environment in which the residence is placed. It is change in either internal or external factors which may lessen place utility, generate stress and lead the household into the mobility process. An extra child, for example, may render a house too small, an influx of black neighbours may render the neighbourhood undesirable. Key issues for geographers have been this central decision—why families move—and the ways in which search behaviour and mobility itself find expression in space.

Rossi's (1955) study of Philadelphia provided early guidelines which have not been significantly modified in subsequent research. He distinguished involuntary moves, such as urban renewal outcomes or tenant evictions, as a separate category, but it is the larger category of voluntary moves which can be related to Figure 7.19. Rossi's basic finding on reasons for intraurban moves was that a stage in lifecycle was the main cause. As family size and space requirements change at various stages of household lifecycle, so moves are made to find the appropriate qualities of dwelling design and space. A typology of lifecycle stages might be marriage, pre-child, child-bearing, child-rearing,

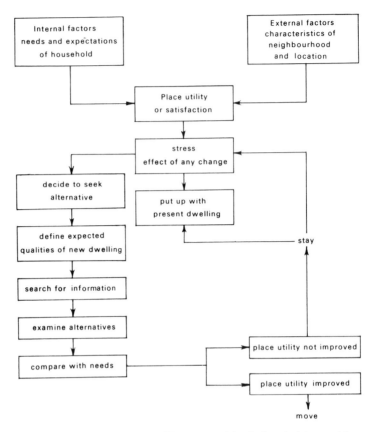

Figure 7.19   Residential mobility: a model of the decision-making
process

child-launching, post-child, and widowhood (Sabagh, Van Arsdol, and Butler,
1969) and some stages, such as child-bearing and post-child, are likely to
correspond with residential moves. A good deal of subsequent research
(Herbert, 1973; Short, 1979) has confirmed the importance of lifecycle stage
and Table 7.9 summarizes some response patterns on reasons for moves; some
research, however (Morgan, 1973), has questioned the interpretation of
changing space needs as a lifecycle factor. The point has some qualifying value
in relation to the lifecycle argument; other factors such as career advancement
may lead to an aspiration for a larger dwelling. It should also be recognized,
however, that although space-need moves may not match lifecycle changes
in chronological time, there are good reasons for time-lags which do not weaken
the significance of the lifecycle factor.

Rossi did not rate social mobility highly as a reason for mobility, arguing
that it was a minority characteristic in terms of the total volume of residential
change. It may, however, hold rather more significance than Rossi suggests.
Changes across broad social classes may be comparatively rare but career

Table 7.9   Reasons for residential moves

(A) Nationwide	per cent citing as a main reason
lifecycle (marriage, family size, space needs)	53.5
design of dwelling	9.8
access or neighbourhood quality	11.1
changing personal status	14.5
other reasons	11.1
(B) Philadelphia	per cent citing as a main reason
dwelling space	51
dwelling design	50
other dwelling features	16
costs	19
access or neighbourhood quality	41
other reasons	23

Source: Rossi (1980), Table 9.1 p. 203.

mobility within a socioeconomic status group produces very real social changes which may often be matched by residential change. The problem of measuring social class in sufficient detail is a likely factor in understating its importance. 'Complaints' are often a source of stress which may lead to residential mobility and in addition to dwelling-unit space, Rossi included dwelling facilities, accessibility, physical and social environment, and costs as the key elements of a 'complaints index'.

At the point at which a decision to move is made, several activities or stages of behaviour are stimulated and those of search and actual move have received most attention. Study of both these stages of mobility have invoked consideration of other behavioural concepts and more particularly those concerned with spatial cognition and spatial preferences. The contention here is that as households engage in activities designed to meet their desire to move, they are strongly influenced by the spatial images or mental maps which they hold of the urban environments (Lee, 1976). *Awareness space* is one such image of the city, defined by the 'experience', direct or otherwise, which the household possesses; this awareness space may be very imperfect in extent and quality of coverage but it is the reference framework within which decisions are made. Awareness space may be flexible (Boyle and Robinson, 1979) but it does have a central role in the decision-making process (Figure 7.20). Within awareness space, *preference space* is identified by a household expressing its preferences for certain types of locations or areas; this space must meet their accessibility needs to work or school, contain favourable neighbourhood qualities, and have the type of design or space features presently deficient in their residence. *Search space* is a further subset which defines the territory or territories within which alternatives are actively sought. There is now a good deal of evidence to suggest that search behaviour is neither exhaustive nor systematic. Many households appear to rely only upon casual and informal

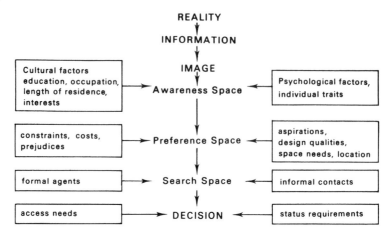

Figure 7.20   Urban images and decision-making: types of intervening space

sources of information to instruct on the number and locations of existing vacancies and conduct an active search of very few alternatives within limited areas of the city. Rossi (1980) summarizes the results of his analyses of search behaviour. His general finding supports the existence of a haphazard process with only limited use of professional and formal sources of information such as estate agents or newspaper advertisements; there is a variation by socio-economic status (Herbert, 1973) and movers in low-cost housing areas appear to consider very few alternatives before arriving at a decision.

Several generalizations are possible on the spatial forms which the individual moves take. Firstly, movers clearly operate within closely defined *submarkets* the limits of which are strongly influenced by general factors of cost and location. Secondly, there is a strong *neighbourhood factor* which has some generality but which may be especially relevant at the lower end of the market. This factor suggests that moves will be made which keep as many elements as possible constant while enabling the household to achieve the difference in dwelling characteristics which prompted the move in the first place. By moving to a larger house in the same neighbourhood, for example, a family may obtain its extra rooms but will retain established access facilities, such as use of the same schools, and social networks of neighbourhood friends, with which it has no dissatisfaction. Thirdly, there is a *sectoral bias* to moves (Adams, 1969) which again may be general but available evidence suggests that it is typical of the upper end of the housing market. The suggestion here, which conforms with the rationale of spatial generalizations on patterns of residential areas already described, is that households will move within specified status sectors and typically these follow a centre to periphery direction. Figure 7.21 contains some evidence of both the neighbourhood and sectoral factor influences on directional traits.

As public sector housing has been developed in British cities, it has become clear that although far less choice exists for consumers as they are allocated to

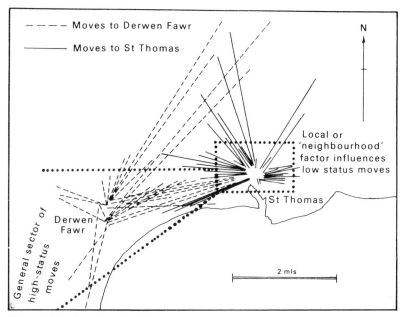

Figure 7.21   Residential moves to two areas in Swansea: corresponding to high
status sectoral movement and low-status neighbourhood factors

tenancies, there are some statements which can be made on residential moves
in this sector both in the initial and in subsequent stages of the mobility processes. Firstly, prospective tenants are offered some initial choice on which particular estate they wish to take up residence. The evidence here is that applicants
hold a ranking of estates in their preferences space which closely matches the
more general social geography of the city. In order to obtain a tenancy on a
highly desirable estate, the 'cost' is a much longer period of time spent on a
housing waiting list. Once within the public sector, there is no strong evidence
of moves to get back into the private market, but much more on application
for transfer to other estates (Bird, 1976). Here the motives for transfer request
are diverse and consist of complaints against dwelling or present estate and the
requested direction of moves reflects a more general pattern of preferences.
The public sector of the housing market, despite the greater constraints it
holds for the consumer, does contain some elements of choice and this sub-
market is likely to become more complex as, for example, British council
house sales begin to add to the heterogeneity already evident within this type
of housing stock.

Conclusions

Studies of residential mobility and the housing market have proved particularly
relevant to changing emphases in urban geographical research. As residential
differentiation studies established the basic *patterns* within western cities so the

thrust towards the study of *processes* led to the focus on movement *per se*. As these process studies were seen to rest too heavily on choice, so the criticism (Gray, 1975) which predicated the need to recognize constraint and the 'hidden mechanism' in the housing market was most clearly stated. As a series of levels of analysis (Herbert, 1979) presents itself, within each of which geographers may further their research, residential mobility and the housing market is one theme which lends itself to study at all levels.

Chapter 8

The City as a Social World

INTRODUCTION

As the industrial city developed in the nineteenth century, the focus of interest was upon the economic activities with which it was associated and the industries which were its driving force. Manufacturing activities dominated the industrial city at this time both in terms of its essential functional features and land use. Large industries often occupied large tracts of central city space, emerging patterns of social geography were closely linked to the location of places of employment, power structures were aligned to industrial interests and the city was most sharply differentiated from rural areas because it was the concentration of industry and commerce. As the postindustrial city has emerged in western societies, the character of the economic institutions has undoubtedly changed—from manufacturing to service dominance—but there is also evidence that the social dimension has become the most significant feature of urban life. Urban economic activities are now more dispersed and variegated. They remain important but the simple view of the city as an economic entity is no longer valid. The social dimension to urban life is complex and difficult to specify; older ideas of urbanism and urban/rural differences have proved difficult to maintain and are indeed hardly relevant. More important perhaps is the fact that as large cities have developed they have become the encapsulations of 'modern trends' which have profound effects upon lifestyle, quality of living, and levels of deviance in contemporary society. Over the next two chapters some of these issues will be explored. For this present chapter the emphasis will be upon social institutions and social behaviour in the city, topics for which recent work on behaviouralism and humanistic perspectives have particular relevance. The next chapter looks more generally at urban problems but emphasizes the social issues which have become most acute in the latter part of the twentieth century.

The social institutions of the city are multifarious. They include easily defined institutions such as family but also less clear concepts such as 'neighbourhood' and 'community'. Informal social behaviour such as visiting friends and neighbours has to be seen in context with more formal and regulated forms such as the voting process in political elections. These types of behaviour are different, though not necessarily discrete, from those described in Chapter 6;

they are more voluntary than involuntary and they are affected by the personalities and preferences of those involved. As a starting point, concepts of environment and behaviour are introduced. One of the city's distinguishing features is that it actually creates an environment on a scale unprecedented in other forms of settlement. Built environments are the dominant environments for city dwellers; they become the reference points for behaviour and the extent to which they act as independent sources of influence upon attitudes and activities needs to be considered (for fuller reviews, see Mercer, 1975 Michelson, 1970.)

ENVIRONMENT AND BEHAVIOUR

Geographical interest in the theme of environment and behaviour has its roots in a period during which the subject was dominated by that concept of 'environmentalism' which specifically referred to the physical setting for human activities. As the parameters concerned—climate, physiography, and pedology—were macro in scale, most generalizations were made in at least regional terms. In urban areas, however, it is not the physical or natural environments, but the 'built' and the 'social' which are important. The microscale becomes more relevant and whereas 'regional' variations have little significance, intraurban and even intraneighbourhood diversity can be meaningful.

The built environment comprises the morphological framework of streets, buildings, and open spaces which is the setting for urban behaviour. Values are attached to the elements of this framework, social as well as economic. These social values—the meanings attached to space and place—which were recognized in earlier writings (Firey, 1947; Jones, 1960), may have special significance. With the focus upon 'built' rather than 'natural' environments, none of the well-known conceptual problems disappears. Questions on the independence of the environmental variable and its definition remain along with issues such as the generality of people–environmental relationships and the nature of intervening variables. A major difference associated with studies of environment and behaviour in cities is that built environments are constructed and therefore modifiable. If environmental effects exist they have been created by architects and planners, sometimes intentionally. Of the two architectural approaches to urban design, one emphasizes *visible form* and is aesthetic and abstract in its language; the other is concerned with *social usage* and with the behavioural experience of people in different types of designed environment. Both approaches are relevant to an understanding of the interaction between people and environment, though the latter has a more direct role.

In its simplest form the urban environment is the *built environment* with its buildings, structures, design features and plan, spaces and alignments of streets and paths. This environment is visible and poses some of the main questions. Do high-rise apartment blocks engender particular types of attitude and behaviour? Is population or building density a critical variable in social pathology? These questions are typical of those framed in early stages of the debate but subsequent research has revealed the significance of intervening variables and also of the need to recognize the 'social' meanings attached to environment. Herbert (1975b) suggested a further distinction between *impersonal* and *personal environments*: the former are 'objective' and can be measured by indicators such as demographic characteristics and social class, the latter are 'subjective' and relate to prevalent attitudes and sets of values. This distinction between *objective* and *subjective* environments has become a central thrust of much geographical research, though it has been interpreted in various ways. Kirk (1963), for example, used the total or objective environment as the real world in which behaviour is contexted; individuals, however, perceive and react in much smaller sections of that totality in what might be termed a behavioural environment. Whatever the form and condition of the total environment, individuals will react to it in ways which are related to their individual differences and the diversities of their past experience. Any attempt to postulate simple associations of behaviour with environment is confounded by this diversity among the population.

Michelson (1970) makes a useful distinction between mental and experiential congruence between people and environment. Mental congruence exists if an individual *thinks* that particular spatial patterns will successfully accommodate his personal characteristics, values, and lifestyle; experiential congruence deals with how well the environment actually accommodates him. The extent to which people adapt to new environments and achieve place utility is therefore related to the extent to which mental is equivalent to experiential congruence. A further distinction in terms of environments came from Stokols (1978) who suggested the need to distinguish between *primary* and *secondary* environments. The former are those in which the individual spends most time and congruence is therefore critical; for secondary environments, however, which are only used in a transitory way, it is less important. This brief discussion is perhaps sufficient both to indicate the complexity of the concept of urban

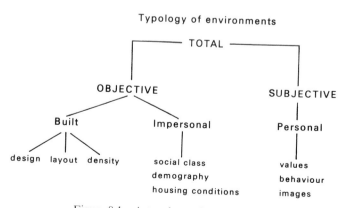

Figure 8.1   A typology of environments

environment *per se* and also to indicate some of the *caveats* in attempting to isolate an environmental influence. Figure 8.1 offers a simple typology of environments. The total environment is composed of elements which relate in different ways to different people—there is a variety of scales as well as of types. The built environment, which is the focus of the next section, has to be seen in context with the social environments formed by the people and activities which occupy space. Whatever the objective qualities of these two facets of environment—built and social—they have to be seen through the filters of people's subjective awareness, understanding and appreciation of the space they occupy. Objective conditions such as overcrowding or un-attractiveness have meaning only in terms of the cognition of the population involved.

Built environment as a conditioner of human activity

There is a strong mythology on the relationship between built environment and behaviour, most of which postulates a strong and positive effect. Many of the problems of inner-city slums in the early part of this century, for example, were attributed to the physical conditions under which people lived. Whereas some of these myths have been exposed, others persist and there is still an absence of sufficient controlled research experiments to allow firm statements on causes and effects. A number of propositions are relevant to any examination of environment and behaviour, and prominent among these are the suggested effects of design, of distance, and of density. Research has been unable to establish that any one of these effects has independent status but they continue to show superficial resemblance to some facets of human behaviour.

The best-known starting point for an analysis of built environment and behaviour is the study by Festinger, Schachter, and Back (1950) of two housing projects at the Massachusetts Institute of Technology, called Westgate and Westgate West. The former consisted of small, prefabricated single-family and detached homes, grouped around courtyards and facing away from access roads, and the latter of two-storey apartment blocks with five apartments in each storey. Festinger examined the extent to which environmental influences affected friendship patterns and attitudes. In Westgate, the strongest influence appeared to be the physical distance between the front doors of the housing units; most friendships were formed within courts and among near neighbours of courts. The localized friendship networks also seemed to foster attitudinal stances and commonly held views. Isolates from the Westgate friendship net-works were typically the occupants of end-houses facing access roads rather than interior courts, or were households where working wives did not partici-pate in the local interaction patterns. Physical distance appeared, therefore, to be a key ingredient in the Westgate friendship network. For Westgate West the critical factors seemed to be the lines of movement from dwelling-unit to exit—functional rather than physical distance. From this study it seemed possible to argue that the physical matrix within which the occupants of the project lived—through both residential proximity and channels of contact—exerted heavy influence on the way in which friendships were formed and attitudes developed. Mercer (1975) suggests that two assertions arise from this classic study. Firstly, that friendships can be determined by physical proximity and, secondly, that groups however established exert influence over members through friendships. For Mercer, the latter is the more significant finding.

An acknowledged shortcoming of the Festinger study was the fact that the study-group possessed an artificially high level of uniformity. They were all students and had similar backgrounds and ages. Other studies of institutional populations suffer similar shortcomings but have provided support for the hypothesized influence of design factors. Caplow and Forman (1955) examined a student housing project in Minnesota and observed influential effects of common points of access and orientation; interaction was high and reflected the spatial organization of the community. Case (1967) studied two dormitories at Princeton and concluded that in each case over 70 per cent of relationships were influenced by architectural features. Blake *et al.* (1956) studied social interaction among occupants of a military barracks which contained some closed and some open-cubicle living arrangements. Walls had the logical effect of intensifying social interaction within enclosed areas and decreasing contact with men outside the enclosure.

Not all studies of environmental effects have been based on institutions. Kuper (1953) studied residential districts in Coventry in which the dominant house-type was a semidetached dwelling unit with paths between each set of houses. The placement of doors was found to bring people together and enable neighbourly contact to turn into more meaningful relationships. Kuper did, however, stress that although proximity and functional distance could bring about contact and interaction, this could have both positive and negative outcomes. Whyte (1957) also studied housing estates and recorded social activity patterns in the Park Forest area at two points in time with an intervening period of three years. Proximity seemed to affect interaction markedly, and although residential change occurred over the three-year period, the same 'homes' were grouped in activity sets. Whyte made a number of observations.

1. Children had key roles in establishing contacts.
2. People in corner plots were most likely to be isolated.
3. People in central locations had the highest levels of involvement.

Whyte's sample population was not a controlled institutional group but did contain relatively high levels of uniformity. A new housing development tends to attract people of similar social status, aspirations, and lifecycle characteristics. The significance of uniformity is recognized:

We emphasize ... that where the community is heterogeneous one would expect the ecological factors to have considerably less weight than they do in communities where there is a high degree of homogeneity and common interests among the residents (Festinger, Schachter, and Back 1950, p.163).

The significance of this qualification, often ignored by critics of this type of study, is stressed by Mercer (1975) as an essential footnote to the earlier quotation which is often taken as a clear statement of architectural determinism:

The architect who builds a house or who designs a site plan, who decides where roads will and will not go, and who decides which directions the houses will face and how close together they will be, also is, to a large extent, deciding the pattern of social life among the people who live in these houses (Festinger, Schachter, and Back 1950, p. 160).

Most criticisms of environment and behaviour research have suggested a neglect of social factors. Carey and Mapes (1972) examined social activity on new housing estates and argued that common characteristics of age and lifecycle stage were far more significant than physical factors of proximity. Gans (1967) in his study of the Levittowners repudiates any notion of strict spatial determinism of friendship patterns, particularly that based on the positioning of front doors. Elsewhere, Gans (1972) argues that planners overestimate the influence of design; buildings—he argues—are of secondary importance in comparison with economic, cultural and social factors and although bad design can hinder relationships and good design can aid them, design *per se* does not shape human behaviour significantly. There are counter-arguments. Lee (1971) argues that although built environment may well influence behaviour, it 'moulds' in an manner which provides choices and possibilities. Clearly, there is a middle ground between the extremes of architectural determinism and design irrelevance; the polarities may indeed be a convenient figment of the critics' imaginations rather than the intentions of the practitioners. Built environment is a context but intervening factors are invariably acknowledged:

In short, spatial proximity often based on the position and outlook of doors may determine interaction patterns, but this normally only occurs under conditions of real or perceived homogeneity in the population and where there is a need for mutual aid (Michelson, 1970, p. 190).

Design factors have consistently been introduced into new projects as attempts at social engineering. The *neighbourhood unit*, first introduced as a planning device in Radburn, New Jersey in 1929, was an explicit attempt to create 'communities' through physical design. A set of principles involved in these neighbourhoods included size, boundaries, services, and traffic layout intended to create a physical identity and a social sense of belonging. The 1944 Dudley Report, for England and Wales, adopted the neighbourhood unit principle though with some modifications in detail. Mumford (1954) was a staunch supporter of neighbourhood planning, which he viewed as a means of recovering the sense of intimacy and locality which had been disrupted by the scale of urban growth. The evidence for the utility of neighbourhood planning is not unambiguous, however, and some research suggests that the neighbourhood unit is at best neutral and at worst antipathetic to the development of an integrated community life. Some versions of neighbourhoods continue to appear in recent city plans, basically because residential areas have to be arranged in 'unit' form with some local facilities. The thrust is now, however, towards flexibility in planning design, as exemplified in the plan for Columbia in Maryland (Hoppenfeld, 1966). Basic needs and contacts are available in localities but lines of movement are designed to maximize choice and enable interaction over a range of distances.

A further example of social engineering through design mechanisms is provided by policies to develop 'socially integrated' housing schemes. Early attempts in British new towns (Mann, 1958) proved unsuccessful as mixtures of social classes led to local fragmentation and crystallization of groups rather than integration. Deutsch and Collins (1951) studied integrated housing projects in New York and compared these with non-integrated areas in Newark. They discovered that in the integrated areas, black–white relationships were better and social networks were more strongly developed. Findings of this kind are exceptional and probably misleading. Most recent research on progress towards racially integrated housing in the United States (Berry, 1979) suggests very limited achievement and continued resistance.

Instances occur of the introduction of particular types of design into estates in attempts to influence behaviour. It can be argued that curvilinear streets and culs-de-sac promote primary interaction; the latter in particular are often thought to create conditions of privacy, sense of belonging and ease of identification. Johnston (1974b) studied culs-de-sac in Christchurch, New Zealand and found that some significant proximity effects could be specified. Whereas the general feature of research into culs-de-sac is that they do provide favour-

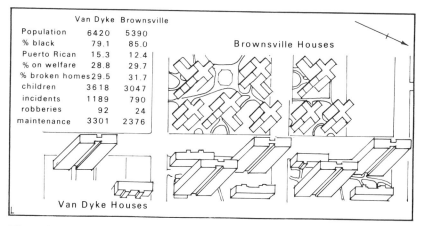

Figure 8.2 Defensible space: a comparison of the Van Dyke and Brownsville public housing projects in New York (redrawn from Newman, 1972)

able situations for social interaction, observations on curvilinear streets are more diverse.

Much research into design influences on behaviour has been stimulated by the apparent vulnerability of some types of built environment to urban problems. Newman (1972) was interested in the high crime rates typical of particular high-rise public sector housing projects in New York and developed the idea of *defensible space* as a set of primarily design principles aimed at the reduction if these rates. Newman compared projects of contrasted crime rates and found them to have different design features (Figure 8.2). Features which seemed to heighten vulnerability included upper storeys of high-rise buildings, corridors and stairways which were not well observed, and open spaces which served only to separate buildings. An extreme American example was the St Louis development of Pruitt-Igoe which became so badly affected by crime and accelerating vacancy rates that it was eventually demolished. Newman argued that design principles could be introduced which would help make such environments more liveable, and therefore reconstituted as 'defensible space'.

1. Territories must be defined and delineated. Barriers should be used to identify open spaces as extensions of the living block; amenities for a project should be located within the defined territory.
2. Windows and doors in particular should be so designed that they enable surveillance by residents, who could overlook public spaces and detect strangers.
3. Quality of built environment should be improved with progress away from featureless walkways and tiled walls.

Newman's defensible space concept provoked much criticism, principally on the grounds that it understated social factors but its broad aim was to create a local sense of identity, to increase safety and the quality of life; it sought to place 'greater control within the hands of the community and coincidentally, but just as importantly, allowed the underlying cohesiveness of the community to be articulated' (Mercer, 1975, p. 55).

High-rise buildings and flats or apartments continue to attract research interest but there are few firm conclusions which can be drawn on their relationship with behaviour. Fanning (1967) compared service families in self-contained houses with those in three to four storey apartments and found morbidity rates to be 57 per cent greater in the latter. Findings of this kind are common but can rarely be isolated as an independent effect of high-rise buildings. There are some types, indeed groups, of people for whom high-rise apartments pose problems—mothers wishing to supervise young children, old people finding difficulty with stairs or lifts. Again, it could be argued that many apartment blocks preclude or limit opportunities for casual interaction as might occur in gardens. Research is generally not supportive of any direct causal link between high-rise living and social problems, but recognizes their unsuitability for some types of household unit and the frequent poor quality of public sector projects. A related hypothesis is that levels of crowding and residential density affect human behaviour (Boots, 1979). The general supposition is that overcrowding creates stress affecting behavioural and physiological functions but research has not provided the proof: 'those who draw firm conclusions about density and behaviour are either speculating or making astounding inferences from flimsy evidence' (Fischer, Baldassare, and Oske, 1975, p. 415).

The point is made that whereas population density is a measurable, objective state, overcrowding is an experiential condition relevant to a particular time and place. These relationships are clearly complex, privacy may appear a 'good' goal but isolation may not; how individuals react may vary widely. As Boots (1979) suggests, crowding should be considered as a multivariate phenomenon resulting from the interaction of physical, social, and personal characteristics; the main reactions, where they occur at all, are likely to be psychological rather than physiological.

Summary

Research such as that discussed in this section does not produce conclusive proof that built environment through its content of quality and design features affects human behaviour in predictable ways. There are far too many other sources of variation at work for such a finding to emerge. Neither, however, does it dismiss the built environment as irrelevant. The built environment has basic functions to perform such as shelter, safety, and access which are sources of satisfaction among its occupants. Built environments can be engineered in such ways as to improve the probabilities of social interaction, safety, or access, but design is no guarantee of such outcomes. Whereas local physical arrangements are not irrelevant to ways in which individuals or groups behave, they are rarely the *main* determinants. Statements on the extent to which urban environments affect people need to be partial and prudent if they are to have any lasting value and credibility.

LOCAL SOCIAL INTERACTION

Whereas geographers have an established tradition of research in many types of interaction such as shopping trips and journey to work, social interaction has not figured at all prominently in the literature (Irving, 1978). One hindrance to the analysis of social interaction is the fact that terms and definitions and even the concept itself provides innumerable difficulties of classification. The notion of 'friendship' poses significant measurement problems, issues of kin and non-kin relationships remain unresolved, and there are several *caveats* concerning the assessment of the quality of relationships and the validity of currently favoured ideas such as that of a social network. A further problem for those geographers interested in a spatial analysis is that some of the central assumptions of many spatial interaction studies do not apply. Unless analysis is narrowed to use of a key 'social' institution, for example, such as community centre or church hall, there is no point of conflux, no single destination to which people are drawn. A study of social interaction must consider large numbers of origins and destinations, flows which are not necessarily reciprocal, and a highly fragmented and compartmentalized web of relationships albeit with overlaps and subsets. Any attempt to demonstrate a simple spatial effect such as distance–decay will have very limited value—even if proven—and traditional concerns with space and distance need to be wedded more firmly within a complex of social factors.

Allan (1979) defines a sociable relationship as one which an individual enters into purposefully and voluntarily for primarily *non-instrumental* reasons. This type of relationship excludes any kind of business or contractual arrangements, and focuses upon systems of exchange and upon emotional and affectional ties. Exchange and transactional relationships are often prominent in the literature but studies now emphasize the need to view sociable relationships in the context of the social environments and broader frameworks within which they are placed. Allan (1979) emphasizes the temporal context and subjective as well as objective qualities of relationships; social network analysis has consistently emphasized the need to view individual patterns of interaction in wider contexts. As Boissevain (1974) argues, social network analysis is one example of the reactions against the imprint of structural-functionalism on sociological analysis; it seeks to depict a framework but not necessarily one which is founded on consensus and prevailing social order.

Boissevain's empirical studies are of somewhat specialized groups, such as Sicilian and Maltese, whose social relationships have an untypical 'conspiratorial' quality but he does highlight several concepts of greater generality. Firstly, his research uses social network analysis and as such is representative of a methodology which has received considerable support over the past two decades. Secondly, he devotes explicit attention to the different *roles* which invoke varying levels of social interaction (see Figure 8.3). Some of these roles are separate from each other, others overlap and each contributes to the 'multiplexity' of social relationships which the individual holds which form bases for interaction. Thirdly, within the key roles of kinship and friendship, he offers a typology of relationships which has some general utility (see Figure 8.4). It is in the personal and the intimate cells of this typology that Allan's non-instrumental relationships are most clearly contained. These issues are important but there are several other conceptual questions which tend to bedevil the literature.

The issue of whether to contain kin and non-kin relationships within a single study is near solution. A majority view now seems to be that although kin and non-kin may fulfil very similar roles in some forms of social interaction, they are more generally different in kind and warrant separate analysis. Among non-kin relationships in particular the values and meanings attached to the term 'friend' have proved elusive to measure and define. Allan (1979) argues that research should acknowledge the distinction between those human

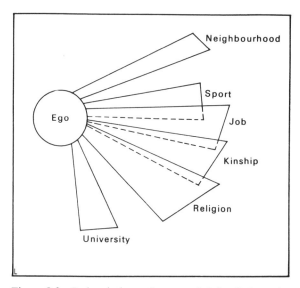

Figure 8.3   Role relations of a network (after Boissevain,
1974)

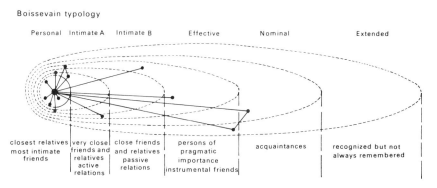

Figure 8.4   A typology of informal relationships (after Boissevain, 1974)

bonds which can be made and unmade at will and those which cannot. The
voluntaristic dimension which is contained within Allan's own definition of
sociable relationships and is commonly acknowledged in most other studies
does in fact add to the complexities of analysis. There is a wide variation
in the sociable lives led by different people: some people are highly active
and are involved with numerous contacts in a diversity of settings; others are,
through choice or circumstance, extremely isolated. The extreme contrast is
between what Irving (1978) terms the social 'lions' and the social 'recluses'.
Within this wide range of levels of involvement and activity, patterns of
sociability reflect more general leisure proclivities.

Faced with problems of definition and conceptual accuracy, there has been a variety of responses to the problem of studying social interaction. Allan's (1979) solution is subjective. Working within a framework of symbolic-interactionism, he adopts the definitions of social relationships which are held by the participants themselves, governed only by some imprecise 'rules of relevance'. Clearly there is some justification for this type of approach (see also Buttimer, 1972), as friendship is a personal and subjective form of relationship, but most studies have attempted to form objective indices. Carey and Mapes (1972) studied the number of contacts made within a particular set of residential areas over a specified time-period but neglected both the intensity and content of relationships. Irving and Davidson (1973) combined frequency and duration of contacts to form a matrix of types of interaction, but this again was a surrogate for quality of relationship. Raine (1976) considered the various attributes and concluded that it was probably impossible to incorporate all or even most of these into a single index. Irving (1975a, 1977, 1978) has devoted a considerable amount of attention to the development of indices of social interaction. Following the work of Chapple (1942), who carefully defined the basic units of the interaction process and suggested methods of measurement, Irving has isolated a number of key indices. *Intensity* indices are designed to measure the value and meaning of social interactions and tackle the central conceptual problem. Frequency and duration of contact can be measured and scaled in a variety of ways but in themselves are partial indicators of a multidimensional feature. Irving (1977) added a measure of *spread* to indicate the extent to which relationships were centred upon a small number of key interactors. A classification of four interaction types (see Figure 8.5(a)) is designed to combine the basic characteristics of duration and frequency to give a simple working typology. A similar classification by Raine (1979), which does attempt to add an indication of the content of the interaction, is also shown (Figure 8.5(b)).

Irving needed to accommodate the fact that kin and non-kin relationships were different from each other yet are not necessarily exclusive. His *kin-orientation* index was an expression of the proportion of total social interaction which involved kin. In a discussion in which the significance of space and environment was assessed, he also developed a *localization* index designed to demonstrate the extent to which social interaction is contained within a home area or neighbourhood. This particular index has relevance to studies of 'community' (Figure 8.5 (c)). Finally, Irving's *network* index was intended to characterize the overall form of the pattern of social interaction of which each respondent was part. Its measurement was concerned with degrees of connectedness within networks which could range from looseknit, where the contacts of individuals were not known to each other, to closeknit, where such reciprocity exists in an integrated system. This index is one example of a methodology which has become strongly influential.

Barnes (1954) introduced the idea of a network in his study of a Norwegian island parish in which he found that links among community members took

A Irving

Interaction types	Durational features	Frequency features
1. Low intensity	Half-day or less	Less often than once a week
2. Long frequent	Whole day or more	Less often than once a week
3. Middle range	One hour or more	Once or twice a week
4. Short, frequent	Half-day or less	More often than twice a week

B Raine

1. Acquaintance	Pass time of day if we meet but never been in house
2. Quite friendly	Chat in street if we meet, but rarely, if ever, go in house
3. Friendly	Always chat when we meet, only occasionally go in house (1/month)
4. Very friendly	Chat regularly in street, frequently visit home (1 or 2/week)
5. Very close friend	Chat daily, regularly visit home (4/week)

C Irving

Index of Localization

Local	More than two named interactors were local
	if 2 to 4 named, then two local,
	if one named, one local
Middle	Two interactors named as local
	if 2 to 4 named, 1 local
Non-Local	No named interactors local

N.B. Local if residence within half mile of each other (but this may vary with context)
Each respondent limited to 5 named interactors

Figure 8.5   Classification of measures of social interaction (after Irving, 1978; Raine, 1976; reproduced by permission of the authors and John Wiley and Sons Ltd.)

a 'network' form. Bott (1957) developed the concept in her study of conjugal roles and family relationships in London. Central to the social network approach is the notion that it is possible to view the social relations in which every individual is embedded, at one level of abstraction, as a scattering of points connected by lines (see Boissevain, 1974). The points are persons and the lines represent social relationships, so that each person can be viewed as a *star* from which lines radiate to other points, some of which are connected to each other. In this personal network, persons in direct contact are in the primary zone (see Figure 8.6) but these persons are also in contact with others whom the initial 'star' individual may not know but could come into contact with via others—these are the 'friends of friends' within the secondary zone and the network can be developed sequentially in a similar way. This concept of a personal network provides a way of viewing social relationships; it has channels of communication along which messages flow and transactions are conducted. With its topological qualities, network analysis lends itself to mathematical procedures and a range of measurement techniques from graph theory can be used. Although possessing some descriptive value, these suffer the drawbacks associated with most attempts to quantify a social system.

A number of problematic issues has affected the application of social network

348

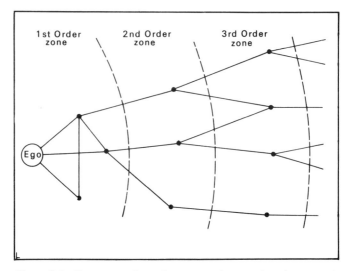

Figure 8.6 Representation of a personal network. The example is constrained to three zones but is open-ended

analysis in research terms. The question of defining the limits of the network or its 'boundedness' is central. Barnes in his original study was constrained to a small island, effectively eliminating the problem, Bott restricted her analysis to kin and held an average of thirteen interviews with each of the families in the original sample. Unless analysis is limited to the primary zone of each individual, data accumulation becomes immense and most studies have accepted some degree of partialness. This has been accomplished by taking a set number of interactors, by limiting numbers of contacts per person, or by looking only at the primary zone. The measurement of links has led to issues—there is obviously considerable variation in the value of links, some are stronger, others weaker, some dormant, others active. This issue returns again to the *content* of relationships within a network and some means of weighting links seem essential. In Bott's (1957) original argument, the network as a whole was judged to affect behaviour, irrespective of the exchange content of individual relationships, so notions of size and shape of network were thus dominant. Subsequent critics (see Allan, 1979) have argued that structure and content must be considered together and this qualification of the originally stated network effect cannot be refuted. Allan argues that the early potential of social network analysis has not been fulfilled and that its actual contribution is limited. Irving (1977) acknowledges a general inability to make network analysis operational. One general criticism is that the procedure is most effective at summarizing complex empirical structures and less so at providing *analysis per se*.

Despite reservations of this kind, social network analysis has valid research roles. It offers an organizing framework in which to study social interaction, ensures that individual relationships are seen within the broader context of a social environment and an overall system of connections, and allows detailed studies to proceed from a common, objective base. Criticisms of the past decade, such as the need to separate spouse's networks and to attach more significance to the content of relationships can be accommodated and research shows how effective networks can be.

Coalitions, groups, classes and institutions are formed of people who, in different ways are bound to each other. Together they form the constantly shifting networks of social relations that we call society (Boissevain, 1974, p. 232).

In a less exceptional example, Cubitt (1973) studied the social networks of 35 couples in Edinburgh. Links included were those with anyone whom the respondent had had contact at least once in a month or else claimed a close relationship. Husband and wife were treated as a single unit and network densities were calculated. The sample contained both middle-class and working-class couples and low network density seemed to be general. Within the overall network, however, there were closer-knit networks focused around particular roles, often involving kin and neighbours. Irving's (1977) study limited respondents to five contacts and these included both kin and non-kin. Network density was measured by actual links as a proportion of the total number named in the network. The overall conclusion from this comparative study was to suggest that social networks remain close-knit in a surprising variety of urban situations, and they continue, even in a mobile society like the United States to remain substantially rooted to the residential locality. Raine (1976) studied six survey sites in Cardiff and limited his network to relationships among 30 respondents on each site. The whole sample consisted of middle-class housewives, and one conclusion was that respondents tended to have few really strong and regular relationships. Raine also used a number of techniques derived from graph theory to provide summary measures on the nature of networks on his sites.

Social network analysis, therefore, has proved a useful means of depicting an overall pattern of relationships. For researchers such as Boissevain (1974) the larger network offered a means of explaining behaviour in particular situations, and even remote connections beyond the secondary zone were sometimes elevated to significant roles. For others such as Cubitt (1973) the larger network has identified key 'sectors' in which density of relationship is particularly high and which are worthy of closer analysis. Most of the questions raised concern ways in which networks are used and the links which have greatest meaning. These questions direct attention towards the conditions under which sociable relationships acquire greatest meaning.

Several writers have recognized wider structural influences upon levels of social interaction. Irving (1978) suggests a cultural effect by which sociability norms have their roots in the philosophical and religious value systems that underpin any society. More interest, however, has focused on particular indicators of levels of interaction. Social class has consistently been found to be a strong influence. Working-class people are thought to rely more heavily upon kin relationships and upon interaction in 'local' areas than their middle-class counterparts. More recent research confirms a set of differences in social class terms but suggests that they are less simple than was previously thought. Irving, for example, suggests that class is a telling but complex influence. Whereas his middle-class respondents tended to have less localized patterns of relationships, they attached more significance to duration of contact. They had less dependence on kin but it was argued that the independence of the nuclear family was greatest in classes which could afford it. Raine (1976) suggested that middle-class relationships were sustained by regular if not very frequent exchange visits. Allan (1979) acknowledges critical class differences but argues that comparisons of middle-class and working-class are blurred by conventional definition of sociability and the roles of kin and non-kin. Although working-class sociability is often kin-orientated, the significance of non-kin relationships may be underrated because they are limited to specific contexts. Working-class friendships may be very strong but are typically tied to specific situations such as workplace or club and may lapse if those situations are changed. Middle-class friendships have greater ability to 'broaden' and are less tied to 'contexts'. Among working-class people, kin has a strong pervasive influence and is often tied up in their everyday lives; the fact of geographical dispersion makes the roles of kin for middle-class people less active but nonetheless important. Many comparative studies of working-class and middle-class sociability may have proven fallible because of the definitions used of interaction. Herbert (1975b) compared visiting behaviour on social class bases and found this to be much higher among middle-class people. Proportions of respondents recording no visits with spouses to homes of friends, for example, were 24 per cent among middle-class groups and 72 per cent in the lowest working-class group. Visiting, however, may be a particularly middle-class form of sociability and other approaches might have shown different patterns.

Age, or more particularly stage in lifecycle, has consistently been shown to be an influence upon levels of social interaction. Stages containing most constraints are generally thought to be those of child-rearing and retirement. Young children present constraints in the sense that they tie parents to the house but they can also facilitate social interaction by drawing parents together. Among working-class people, young children can cement the bonds of kinship as they are normally involved in family sociability. Irving recognizes the influences of age but argues that it is not consistent; Raine views children mainly as catalysts in the generation of friendship among his working-class housewives; Hodges and Smith (1954) argue that dependence on neighbourhood as a source of friends tends to increase with the birth of children. Age or stage-in-lifecycle clearly has relevance but needs to be considered in conjunction with other factors. If people are geographically mobile at particular stages of their lives, for example, this has an effect upon social interaction. Friendships, even among the middle-classes, rarely survive residential change in contrast to kin relationships. Movement to a new housing estate in the

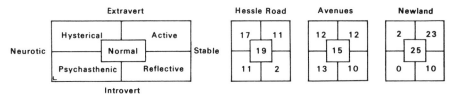

Figure 8.7 Classification of personality. The model is shown along with empirical results from three housing areas in Hull (after Irving, 1975b; reproduced with the author's permission)

early child-rearing stage may correspond with strong impetus for sociability as a new community establishes itself and its members find common issues to pursue with developer or local authority. Old people who move on retirement are strongly attracted to areas where they have kin or else are sure to find other members of their peer groups; many who age *in situ* are attracted by the social networks they may have developed over long periods of time.

In considering variation by factors such as social class and age, Irving (1975b) argues that there has been a consistent failure to examine the effects of personality—some people are by nature more sociable than others. Using a simple measure of personality based on the axes of introversion–extraversion and stability–neuroticism (see Figure 8.7), he classified a number of sample populations into personality types, and discovered that these underlay significant variations in levels of social interaction. Raine (1976) used a regression analysis to identify other influential variables and his nominations included length of residence, household size and the employment status of the housewife. Clearly a 'working' wife has significantly less time to participate in the neighbourhood social round.

Allan (1979) placed particular emphasis upon the gender differences affecting social interaction and the distinctive qualities of women's roles in a male-dominated society. One result of this is that a range of leisure pursuits is more readily available to males, many settings for sociability are male preserves, and female sociability tends therefore to be more constrained. Peterson, Wekerle, and Morley (1978) argue that male dominance is over the 'larger'-scale components of society (see Figure 8.8) whereas women's 'dominance' is typically restricted to neighbourhood and home. Neighbourhood may be an arena of action for women, but because of their limited personal mobility and the demands of a child-centred family existence their home range may be no greater than that of a small child. Palm and Pred (1976) show that women's ascribed roles create both spatial and temporal limitations on their leisure-time activities.

Although Allan (1979) is dismissive of the roles of location and spatial structure—which he labels as the ecological stance—there is much in his account which either implicitly or explicitly accepts their significance. He acknowledges, for example, that:

352

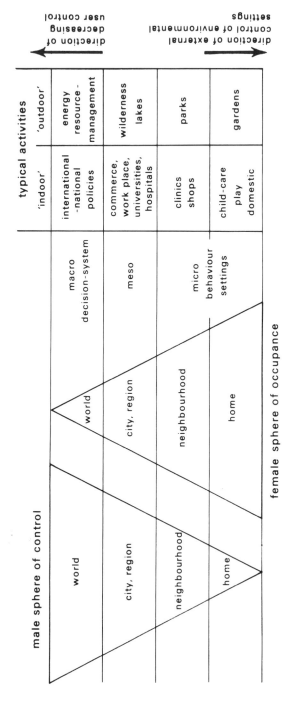

Figure 8.8 Male/female relationships in geographical space (after Peterson, *et al.*, 1978)

Table 8.1 Local interaction in Hull

Area (a) Interaction type	Low intensity	Long and infrequent	Middle rage	Short and frequent	Bimodal	Total
Hessle Road	14 (20)	3 (0)	8 (12)	15 (20)	20 (7)	60 (59)
Avenues	19 (14)	19 (6)	10 (11)	5 (23)	8 (7)	61 (61)

(b) Localization index	non-local	middle	local			Total
Hessle Road	14 (10)	12 (10)	34 (40)			60 (60)
Avenues	46 (27)	8 (17)	7 (17)			61 (61)

index scores for: kin (non-kin)

Source: data extracted from Irving (1978), Table 6.2, p. 258 and Table 6.4, p. 262.

only a minority of middle-class friendships survive actively for long after one side moves any distance away, . . . gradually but inevitably the relationships developed in the old locality get replaced by relationships created in the new one (p. 123).

The roles of location and space have been discussed in the context of environment and behaviour but the general argument is that although all other factors

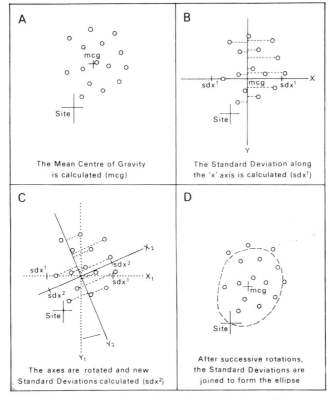

Figure 8.9 Deriving the standard deviational ellipse

need to be considered, variation in distributions can be seen as one of the major influences underlying variations in patterns of social interaction. As Irving (1978, p. 267) suggests:

Chance encounters, and here, space, position, and distance must be accorded some role, do very often lead to interaction, which in turn leads to exchange of views and accommodation of views.

Several geographers such as Irving and Raine have adopted an area-sampling framework, usually with reference to social areas or a classification of small statistical areas, and have focused on area differences in levels of social interaction. Irving's studies of Hull are particularly useful in showing how his indices of social interaction were strikingly different from one type of residential area to another, and these area differences appeared independent of the influence of social class, family, or personal characteristics. Network density, localization and intensity all seemed part of a 'neighbourhood package' of social interaction profiles. Table 8.1 shows variations on two indices—interaction types and localization—between two of his Hull districts. The Avenues, a high-status area with some transitional qualities shows an over-representation, for kin, of long, infrequent types of interaction; non-kin relationships are typically short and frequent. Hessle Road, a stable working-class area, has more short, frequent interactions typical of both kin and non-kin: family and friends were

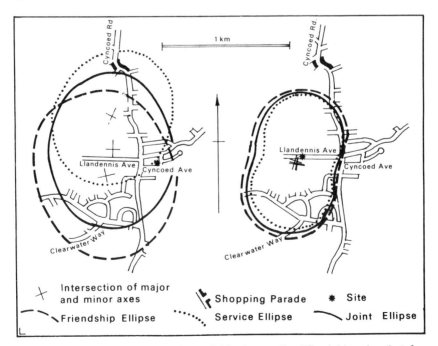

Figure 8.10 Friendship and service activities in two Cardiff neighbourhoods (after Raine, 1976)

tightly meshed in an extremely localized social network. Localization indices showed few local ties in the Avenues but more non-local friends; the high local quality of relationships in Hessle Road extended to both kin and non-kin.

Raine (1979) restricted his analysis to middle-class areas—losing a significant basis for variation—and attempted to summarize the spatial form of interaction for each area with the Standard Deviational Ellipse technique. This technique belongs to a group of centrographic measures which seek to identify the centre of the distribution of 'contacts' and the form of dispersion (see Figure 8.9). Given a pattern of points representing the interactions, a set of coordinates is centred around the mean and standard deviations are calculated. By successively rotating the axes and recalculating the standard deviations, the path of an ellipse which summarizes the form of the distribution can be plotted. From the size and shape of the ellipse and the relationship which it holds with the mean centre, generalizations upon interaction patterns for each area are possible. Figure 8.10 shows two residential areas. Ellipse A covers an area of about 1 km² (0.43 square miles) and is almost circular; ellipse B covers just under 1 km² (0.29 square miles) and has a more elongated shape. Influence of natural barriers, such as the north–south road in B can be shown and whereas the three ellipses—friendship, service, and joint—are

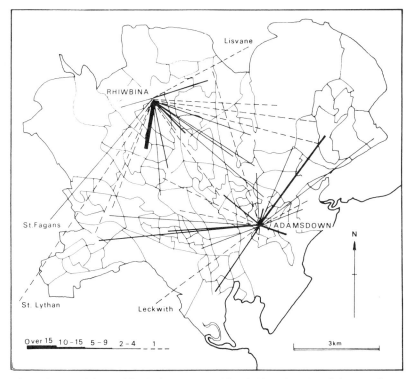

Figure 8.11   Visits to friends in two Cardiff neighbourhoods. Links are shown to non-neighbourhood friends

congruent in B, suggesting a common geographical territory, they are significantly less so in A, with the joint ellipse seeking a median position, suggesting a lack of congruence between social interaction space and service-usage.

Area differences exist in terms of social interaction. These are most marked where sampling frameworks identify contrasted types of areas—in terms of social-class composition or demographic structure—but also exist where some of these variables are held constant. Whereas the multiplexity of social interaction is acknowledged, the phenomenon of a neighbourhood effect finds some support. 'Age' of neighbourhood may itself be a factor, new estates engender high levels of interaction, albeit temporary, old-established districts tend to have their own imprint upon sociability. This and other 'spatial' qualities remain relevant to the study of social interaction. Space, distance, location all exert some influence and there is a directional component to this as to other forms of interaction (see Figure 8.11). Herbert (1975b) compared two areas—one middle-class, one working-class—in terms of friendship links outside immediate neighbourhood. For the working-class area, friends typically came from similar adjacent inner-city districts but in a minority of cases, 17 per cent, from peripheral public sector estates. For middle-class people, friends were more dispersed but nearby suburbs of similar status figured prominently in the pattern.

POLITICAL CONTROL IN THE CITY

Neighbourhoods are, for the most part, informal entities in the sense that they have emerged from the process of urban growth and have no preordained form of organization. There are many divisions of space, however, including those which occur within the city, which are parts of a formal organization for purposes of administration or representation. The most significant examples of organized space are those which are designed to administer government and represent the population at large. Government is most frequently typified by a hierarchical form of organization as the national government operates in a 'diffusive' way downwards through regional levels to reach increasingly smaller and more local units. Within this general framework there is very considerable variation both in terms of the details of the hierarchy and in the delegation of powers available to various levels. The United States, for example, with its federal system, progresses through a hierarchy of states, counties, municipalities, and townships with a considerable amount of autonomy vested at some levels such as the state. In addition to these levels of government, there is a large number of special districts for particular functions and over half of these are school districts (Johnston, 1979). The United Kingdom is now, after a tortuous and often contentious period of reorganization in the late 1960s and early 1970s, composed of six metropolitan boroughs, with subdivisions into a smaller number of districts; 39 counties subdivided into 296 district councils and a special category for the Greater London Council and its 32 boroughs. In the United Kingdom, the power at the centre is clearly far greater than exists in a federal system such as the United States but is less than would occur in the command economies of eastern Europe. This generalization, however, needs to be handled with care; Boaden (1970) concluded that central control was less apparent in British policy outcomes than might be supposed.

Many major issues have affected the organization of urban government in recent years. Excessive fragmentation, for example, often inherited from a growing mismatch of *de jure* and *de facto* urban limits over time, has seriously hindered the successful fulfilment of many urban services. A main thrust of United Kingdom reorganization has been the creation of fewer and larger administrative units. In Greater London, for example, some 80 or more former boroughs were reduced to 32 by a process of amalgamation with an overall tier of metropolitan government provided by the Greater London Council. Reducing fragmentation is one issue, the need to redraw boundaries to produce a better fit with functional realities is another. Means of identifying 'functional' regions are now well established (Bourne and Simmons, 1978) but the task of adapting these to governmental units is confounded by political and socio-economic considerations. British reorganization is strongly debated but is ultimately imposed upon the country as a whole by its central government; in the United States the tradition of privatism continues and local government is an issue to be fought over by local interest groups. Moves towards metropolitan integration in the United States have met with considerable resistance from suburban municipalities, and although metropolitan areas exist the amount of real power which they hold and exercise is very limited. Fragmentation and the need for larger units of urban government are two major issues, and a third concerns the variable level of spending which occurs among local government areas and the subsequent unequal distribution of services and welfare which results. Many researchers (Johnston, 1979) have suggested that levels of government spending are related to the needs of an area, to the resources it possesses, the dispositions of the political group in power at any one time and to the amount of pressure exerted from below. This complex of factors may often mean that 'territorial justice' (Pinch, 1979) is not always achieved and that provision does not necessarily match need. An individual's life-chances may therefore be much affected by the jurisdiction within which he or she lives; jurisdiction may refer in this context to units of local government and also to special districts such as school catchment areas, assisted areas and inner-city priority areas.

Sharpe (1976) recognizes three major functions of local government—liberty, participation, and the efficient provision of services—and regards the last of these as the most important. As services should be organized close to the point of delivery, local government is well placed to promote local demands and provide what is necessary. As local government is accountable at elections, it can respond to changes in demand and be judged both in terms of provision of services and with regard to the cost (local taxes) it charges for them. Local government also has some protective or promotional roles. As a territorial authority with some autonomy, it can be used to advance a particular cause. American experience of municipalities in the present century has often been one of conflict of an inter-municipality or state-municipality nature. Urbanization or the outward spread of metropolitan areas has meant many new units of urban government. *Incorporation* of county areas for municipal government and *annexation* of areas to larger municipalities are the two most common processes. For a long period of time it was relatively easy for small suburban communities to incorporate and establish municipal government; central cities have become surrounded by a ring of suburban municipalities. Prior to 1900 annexation was not difficult but following that date state legislation typically favoured incorporation. Recently attitudes have again changed in a belated attempt to help the central cities. Several states now have anti-incorporation laws which create a belt of land around municipalities in which incorporation cannot occur unless an existing municipality agrees to incorporate or refuses to annex.

The municipality ring which surrounds many central cities leads to competition for resources and externalities (Cox, 1973) and makes nonsense of functional government. Central cities in 150 out of the 212 metropolitan areas in the United States achieved some level of annexation in the 1950s, mostly in the South and West. A major benefit of separate municipalities is that it gives residents the power to control landuse and types of development through zoning procedures. Exclusionary zoning takes many procedural forms but the general objective is to keep out minority ethnic groups, low-income residents, and high-density developments. Several legal battles have been fought on the 14th Amendment 'No State shall make or enforce any law which shall abridge the privileges or immunities of citizens of the United States'. Devices have varied. In Cuyahoga County, which surrounds Cleveland, two-thirds of the undeveloped land zoned for single-family residences in the late 1960s had a designated minimum lot size of half an acre (0.2 ha); in an adjacent county the standard was 1 acre (0.4 ha). Also common are zoning regulations which preclude high-rise, multifamily residences.

This independence of units of urban government in the United States has served to emphasize basic segregations and the central city/suburbs dichotomy. A related facet over which residents have less control is that whereas urban government has no need to provide services for non-resident groups, it has no power to stop them using other types of facility. Neenan (1973) and others have examined the extent of suburban exploitation of the central city by commuters who use transit systems, recreational facilities, etc., and find that suburban dwellers receive more than they contribute in costs. The notion of 'free-riding' or exploitation is widely held and is supported by most though not all of the evidence.

VOTING BEHAVIOUR

Voting is a special form of behaviour in the sense that it occurs at irregular long intervals and has, in some societies at least, some degree of compulsion.

There is also an increasing number of occasions on which people are called upon to exercise their vote. In the United Kingdom each level of government—parliamentary, county, and district—has major elections and in recent years there have been referenda on issues such as the European Common Market and Devolution. Other European countries, such as France, make much more extensive use of the referendum, and in the United States there has been a significant increase in state-level polls to settle issues such as local tax levels. Although largely a product of the twentieth century, the principle of one person/one vote is now virtually universal and individuals will undertake considerable hardship to cast their vote on issues which they regard as important. There are different types of voting system and the issue of which to use remains contentious. In the widely used *plurality* system, the candidate or candidates who polls most votes in a given constituency, regardless of the form of the majority, is elected. *Proportional representation*, in which voters rank-order the candidates, has the general aim of allowing the overall distribution of votes for each party to have some effect. Dail Eirean, for example, the Irish parliament, has 144 deputies drawn from multi-member constituencies by a proportional representation system of single transferable votes. Whereas the plurality system often produces a majority government with a minority of the overall vote, proportional representation often leads to fragmentation and the lack of a clear winner.

The most explicit geographical input to voting behaviour is the spatial framework of areas for which representatives are elected. All facets of these areas, including their size, shape, composition, and stability are clearly critical determinants of the outcomes of voting behaviour. The possibilities of using these criteria as determinants have been understood since at least 1812 when Governor Gerry of Massachusetts earned himself a place in history by authorizing a rearrangement of constituency boundaries designed to produce a particular electoral result. The process of 'gerrymandering' has since been widely used and Cox (1973) describes the forms which it takes. One strategy, for example, is to seek out *districts of strength*, for instance, place all white middle-class voters in one constituency; another is the *excess vote* strategy which concentrates as much of the opposition vote as possible in a small number of areas where massive majorities produce only a few successful candidates; a *wasted vote* strategy disperses opposition votes over a large number of constituencies so that they always remain insufficient to achieve a majority; and the *silent* gerrymander involves not changing electoral districts to coincide with population change. The silent gerrymander in particular has led to an over-representation of rural and an under-representation of urban areas, a situation which reapportionment and the redrawing of boundaries has tackled in the 1960s (Morrill, 1973). For British parliamentary constituencies, reports of a Boundary Commission recommending substantial changes are emerging in the early 1980s. A result will be a decline in inner-city and an increase in suburban representation as boundaries seek to match redistribution of population. Main guidelines in the British case are equality of electoral size (set at around 63,000 for England), compactness and avoidance of irregular shape, conformity with major local government units, and awareness of the issues concerned with uniformity or heterogeneity within areas.

The constituency spatial framework is a highly influential factor in determining the outcomes of the electoral process. Although redistricting by an overall body, such as the British Boundaries Commission, strives to be impartial and objective, this is very difficult to achieve in practice and there are inevitably tradeoffs which have some partiality. Political parties and individual candidates are faced with an imperfect set of constituencies at any one point in time, the exact form of which is critical especially in plurality electoral systems. In terms of party competition, votes for some people in some places are more important than others. Parties may concentrate 'vote-buying' in some constituencies whereby large funds are spent on promoting a particular candidate or issue. Johnston (1979a, p. 137) suggests that the 'allocation of political money . . . is spatially biased by the electoral geography of the relevant territory'. The vote-buying model as an explanation of voting behaviour has some support, in other words, the more spent on a campaign, the more votes a party receives. The forms of 'vote-buying' are various. Patronage may involve the allocation of public funds into specific areas or causes.

There are other considerations which affect voting behaviour. A general assumption in western societies is that political activity in the form of beliefs, values, and actual voting behaviour is class-based. As classes tend to be spatially segregated, there is a geography of elections which reflects these biases. In the United Kingdom, working-class districts like the Rhondda produce Labour representation, whereas professional and 'county' areas produce Conservatives. In the United States, the most likely sources of Republican support are in rural conservative districts and suburban municipalities, whereas Democratic allegiance is traditionally higher in industrial regions and inner cities. Johnston (1976) has demonstrated this kind of class-vote effect and also the existence of other interest-group allegiances such as the Jewish and Italian support for specific candidates in Toronto. In addition to the actual way in which people vote, there is some suggestion that high socioeconomic status produces high turnout and therefore greater support for 'non-working-class' parties. In the United Kingdom, where voting is not compulsory, a major objective of parties is less to convert marginal voters than to get their own vote out. Canvassing is a major factor here and is normally concentrated in areas in which known support exists. The 'party-effect' or class allegiance is general but there are other factors and specific issues at times of election may become highly influential.

Ways in which information or recommendations on a particular issue reach individual voters are thought to influence voting responses. Pieces of information which are partisan to the extent that they represent advocacy of a particular issue or person are sometimes termed 'cues'. Cues originate from the parties themselves, from trade unions or pressure groups, from the media and from the whole network of acquaintances which an individual may possess.

Cox (1969) argues that a voting response is conditional upon receiving cues from politically relevant sources. The extent to which a cue is accepted is in part a function of the credibility of its sources, the force of the argument, and the predisposition of the recipient. The significance of cues is affected by several kinds of bias which include geographical distance, general acquaintance circles and more intimate social networks.

Several 'effects' have been identified in an attempt to understand the extent to which cues are accepted. A *relocation* effect occurs where an elector moves into an area of marked partisan bias and eventually, through the influence of aspirations and attitudes, accepts the majority point of view. A *neighbourhood* effect is used to explain the fact that the consensus view in a particular area may influence the voting behaviour of all residents, even though some of them may be otherwise aligned in terms of class, race, religion, or some other criteria. Individuals may be affected by informal arguments and greater flows of information of a particular type and—particularly where their formal party commitment is not strong—a neighbourhood or contagion effect affects the way they vote (Johnston, 1974a).

A *'friends and neighbours'* effect describes the situation in which the candidate receives higher than average support in a district in which he or she is very well known, such as birthplace, school, home or place of work. Attempts to attach a quantitative measure to this effect have not shown it to be very significant. In the 1968 Christchurch City Council elections (Johnston, 1979), it was found that 85 per cent of the spatial variation in a candidate's support could be accounted for by a 'party effect', 12 per cent by a random element, and only 3 per cent by a friends and neighbours effect. A *territorial protection* effect is suggested where residents of an area perceive an imminent threat to their interests and vote for a party most likely to protect them. An uncharacteristic swing towards the right and the Conservative party in the 1964 election in selected West Midlands constituencies, at a time when the national swing was 3 per cent in the opposite direction, reflects a fear of the growth of immigration and coloured communities. In local elections, issues relating to externalities, which party will produce a new school or block a new highway, are common.

The right to vote concerns a special form of behaviour, often achieved in embattled circumstances, but at the present time frequently typified by apathy and low electoral turnouts. A recent trend which promises to reverse this, although only on localized and diverse bases, is the growth of pressure groups outside the party system designed to campaign on specific issues which may eventually enter the political arena. At a neighbourhood level, Christensen (1982) has documented the emergence of pressure groups to protect the Covent Garden district of London and other residents' associations have performed similar roles. Ecological and environmental lobbies have become of increasing significance and there are specific instances, such as the Swansea District Council elections of 1976, in which reactions to corruption and misuse of power by prominent politicians had a major effect. In this example (although other relevant factors must be acknowledged), the former Labour-dominant group

362

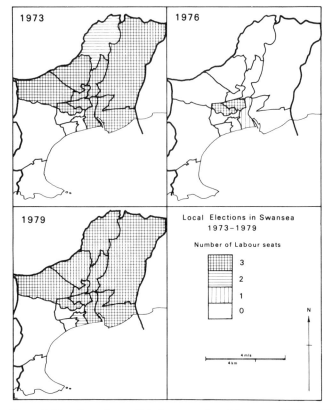

Figure 8.12   Changing political geography of Swansea, 1973–1979

was reduced to a small minority (Figure 8.12). Notions of community action (Bell and Newby, 1978) are becoming widespread and United Kingdom reform of local government now provides for community councils at a neighbourhood scale within cities. This under-participation in government and grass root demands for greater accountability may prove to be one of the more significant factors affecting ways in which cities are governed in the last part of the twentieth century.

PEOPLE AND SPACE: ACTIVITY PATTERNS IN URBAN SETTINGS

Mobility *per se* has received a great deal of attention in the geographical literature (Daniels and Warnes, 1980). The purpose of this section is to summarize some of the recent issues concerning the analysis of activity patterns in cities. These are varied and complex:

Each individual has a moving pattern of his own, with turning points at his home, his place of work and his shopping centre during the week and his recreation gounds on a holiday or a Sunday (Hagerstrand, 1971, p. 144).

Kofoed (1970) classified the various elements of mobility in what he termed 'person-movement' research, a study consisting of fields of contact, patterns of activity, and processes of movement. For any individual, the field of contact will be related to personal potential for mobility, preferences for particular types of activity, and spatial location relative to the distribution of activities. The range of activities has strong effects upon actual patterns of movement. Some activities, such as work and school, are fixed in place and time and evoke regular patterns of movement at constant frequencies; others, such as shopping and recreation, may involve a great deal of variability. Kofoed describes travel patterns as responses to activities; they are affected by the characteristics of the urban system and the quality of physical channels of movement.

Many earlier studies are concerned with aggregate forms of movement such as migration and journey to work, and generalizations upon such well-defined 'rhythms' remain relevant. Regular flows of workers along particular channels at particular times and similar flows of children to schools tend to impose order upon movement within the city. Beyond generalizations of this kind which are relevant to 'prescribed' movements, it is diversity rather than order which is typical. As the variety of 'voluntary' movements and activities has become more obvious, geographers have turned increasingly to aspects of the behavioural sciences both for descriptive tools and explanations.

Classifications of types of spaces have been one outcome and follow the behavioural rationale that the total urban environment contains subsets within which interaction occurs (see also Figure 7.20). *Awareness space* is that portion of total reality which is known to the individual, either through direct experience or by communication from others. In one sense awareness space has the quality of a mental map, it is the imperfect image of the city which the individual holds. Awareness space can be enlarged by a spatial learning process for either general purposes—to know one's city better—or for a particular need such as the desire to change residence or to use a new recreational area. *Action space* summarizes an individual's total interaction with and response to environment:

The collection of all urban locations about which the individual has information and the subjective utility or preference he associates with these locations (Horton and Reynolds, 1971, p. 37).

Action space is a subset of awareness space in the sense that the latter is held as an image, sometimes in a vague way, but elements of the former are capable of being ascribed values, preferences, and place utilities. Action space comprises all those places in which we potentially operate and thus provides a framework within which to view an individual's or group's spatial interaction. *Activity space*, or all urban locations with which the individual has direct contact as a result of day-to-day activities, is that part of action space which involves direct contact between individuals and their social and geographical environments. Jakle, Brunn, and Roseman (1976) differentiate between activity space and action space by limiting the former to actual movement and enlarging the latter to include communication.

The activity space of an individual will vary with roles. Each role promotes different scales and frequencies of activities with separate spatial qualities. Of the attempts to represent a typology of activity spaces, that by Hall (1966) though widely quoted has been little used and is discussed in a later context. Other classifications focus less on the nature of person-to-person contact than upon variations in *types* of roles and spatial implications of these. The roles of family member, neighbour, worker, student, club member and holiday-maker, all involve different forms of movement. Roles of family member and neighbour in particular involve small spatial orbits and frequent contact; the activity spaces associated with these roles are circumscribed but intensively used. Jakle, Brunn, and Roseman (1976) suggest that activity space for the typical individual is dominated by:

1. Movement within and near the home.
2. Movement within and near the sites of regular activities such as work, school and shops.
3. Movement between these places and home.
4. Movement involving the use of specialized services which are used on an irregular basis such as holiday sites and conference centres.

Individual characteristics will influence roles and also the distribution of activities over the various types of spaces. Housewives with young children, the elderly and the immobile are all likely to have highly localized activity spaces. The more roles an individual adopts, then the more diverse are the activity spaces used. Spatial generalizations in terms of activity spaces are of limited value but an inverse relationship is generally thought to be held between frequency of participation in an activity and distance travelled to it, and Adams (1969) suggested a directional bias in relation to residential mobility which may have more general application in the sense that people tend to restrict many of their voluntary activities to particular parts of the city.

Research into relationships between time and geographical space has added a new dimension to the study of activity and movement. Time has always been an implicit component of activities research and urban planners, such as Chapin (1968), have been investigating the time-budget qualities of urban living patterns for some time. The Lund school of geography, led by Hagerstrand, has strongly influenced time–geographical studies and much of this literature has been summarized by Carlstein, Parkes, and Thrift (1978). The broad aim of these studies is to add a temporal dimension to the spatial analysis of activities and to portray the temporal structuring of space. Hagerstrand's general theme is that human behaviour needs to be considered from a biographical perspective in order to study the interwoven distribution of states and events in coherent blocks of space–time. Parkes and Thrift (1978) define 'realized place' as *place* in the *temporal* structuring of space. The activity

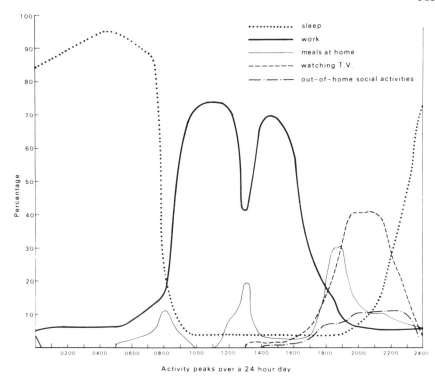

Figure 8.13   Time-rhythms of activities over a 24-hour day

patterns of individuals result from a matching of temporal and experiential environments to locational environments; both objective and subjective 'maps' and 'clocks' are relevant. *Biological* time will make certain places, such as restaurants, obligatory; *socioecological* time defines the norms that society expects in roles such as work and education; *psychological* time defines the adequacy of allocations to the individual.

Most researchers seem to agree that analysis must begin at the individual scale with *routines*. Once regularities in behaviour are understood at the micro-level, horizons can be expanded to all individuals in the community and generalizations attempted in a wider social context. Figure 8.13 shows the displaced peaks of sleep, work-trips and social trips with the former involving movement in morning and early evening, the latter occurring at midday and in late evening. Shapcott and Steadman (1978) emphasize the constraints which lead to the generalizing of time and space, movement and activity. Figure 8.14 demonstrates this with some activities set in particular locations, many of which are fixed, but also constrained by the times during which facilities are available. Shops have flexibility within fixed hours of opening, social interaction has greater flexibility within the convention of 'reasonable' hours of visiting. The rhythmic pattern of availability of facilities or opportunities are not all independent of each other, they in fact form a highly

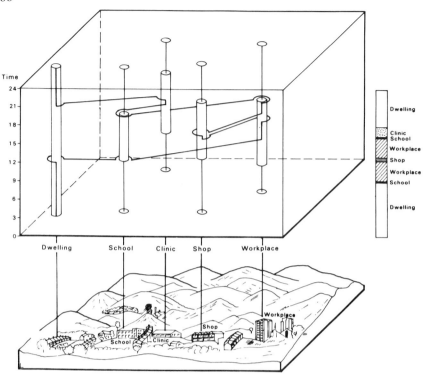

Figure 8.14   Time and space: a schematic representation of a working housewife's spatial activities in a temporal setting

integrated and coordinated structure within which individual life-patterns must be contained. There is a simultaneous timing of many people's hours of work—imposed by the needs of industry, commerce, and administration— which has strong effects on those not directly involved such as retired people and housewives. Despite recent attempts to produce variations, such as flexi-time, most work movements continue to be placed within narrow time bands (see Carlstein, Parkes, and Thrift, 1978).

Some research has focused on the particular problems of women, especially those with out-of-home employment, in allocating time to a range of domestic roles. Palm and Pred (1976) argue that women's activities in the city are inhibited by difficulties of arranging work schedules to conform with domestic 'duties' and access to public service facilities Shapcott and Steadman (1978), in their Reading study, devoted considerable attention to housewife time-budgets and the variety of constraints upon their time; cooking and food preparation controlled and dominated a large part of the day and care of young children could consume large amounts of time. Households with young children allocated three to four hours each day to basic child care whereas the demands of older children, involving for example the need to convey them to and from activities, were not inconsiderable. Sex roles discriminate against women, there is a 'gender role constraint'. In the Reading flexihours scheme, all of the men, but only 50 per cent of the women, had access to a car. Palm and Pred (1977) noted the findings of a San Francisco survey in which 42.5 per cent of all females aged 19 years or over lacked personal access to a car compared to 18.7 per cent of males. It is clear that the macro-structure of social-economic time-rhythms is set on traditional male/female roles; many of the difficulties of the working wife arise from the dissonance between the demands of the job, family commitments and this macro-structure. Societal rhythms of time allocated for sleep, work, and school have changed more slowly than female availability for paid work; there are societal differences with, for example, greater female involvement over a wider range of occupations in the United States. Working wives have to use early evenings and weekends, what might 'normally' be regarded as leisure time, for household chores.

Time–geographical studies have some way to go before they present either a clear set of testable concepts or a synthesized methodology. That time is a critical ingredient for studies of movement and activity and uses of space is undeniable and analyses on these lines provide valuable prespectives relevant to the location of facilities and their availability. A number of firm guidelines on research frameworks are emerging. Firstly, there is a 'structure' of traditional routines and practices which effectively pose constraints; secondly, there is a physical framework of facilities which needs to be synchronized in both time and space; thirdly, the basic building blocks for further research must be individual households and the daily and weekly routinized rhythms around which their activities are patterned. Incorporation of a time dimension promises to add to our understanding of human behaviour in geographical space.

SPATIAL LEARNING: CHILDREN AND URBAN ENVIRONMENTS

Studies of urban imagery have followed several paths and have used a variety of scales from the general idea of city landscapes (Lynch, 1960) to specific components of urban areas (Herbert and Raine, 1976). The essence of these studies is their attempt to understand the subjective ways in which people relate to urban environments, but measurement problems have proved considerable and basic conceptual frameworks within which to work have yet to be generally agreed (Boyle and Robinson, 1979). This debate has ranged widely and this necessarily selective review will centre upon those aspects of particular relevance to an understanding of spatial behaviour and notions of 'territory' in the city.

Much spatial learning research is concerned with the child's development of spatial awareness and is generally related to the pioneering work of Piaget and Inhelder (1956). Their developmental framework consists of four phases:

1. The *sensorimotor* stage (up to 2 years of age) is that during which the child defines his place in the world in terms of actions operative through tactile senses and the manipulation of objects.

2. In the *preoperational* stage (between the ages of 2 and 7 years) children may acquire awareness of a few topological properties of space such as proximity, separation, enclosure, surrounding and order; recognize home as a special place with strong emotional attachment and develop elementary notions of territoriality. This phase represents the transition between the stage of intuitive thought and behaviour and later stages which contain clearer evidence of organization.

3. The *concrete operational* stage (between ages of 7 and 11 years) is marked by a maturing of the abilities to represent environment and to recognize interrelationships of the topological properties in an integrated system.

4. The *formal operations* stage (from 11 years of age) is marked by an increasing ability to use abstract spatial hypotheses which involve the use of symbols and transformations. Topological transformations, for example, involve rules of proximity, separation and sequence, geometrical transformations involve metric relationships which coordinate space with respect to a system of outside reference points.

Piaget and Inhelder's approach has been labelled as 'constructivist' in the sense that it argues that children construct a means of understanding environment by their own 'transformations'. These are not necessarily images of reality but are derived from interacting with environment. An opposite point of view is that of the 'incrementalists' who assume that children have an innate ability to generate knowledge which simply unfolds through experience or interaction, they are capable of a perceptual copying of environment. Practical research has drawn upon both perspectives but most geographers have found the constructivist notion of experience-based spatial learning more attractive:

I . . . fundamentally accept the idea that learning about an external environment results from primarily interacting with it, and that more complex cognitive representations of physical environments are built up over time . . . . Knowledge about places and their perceived significance can accrue from continued interaction (as with a place of work or residence), or because of social, historical, economic, ethnic, aesthetic or other criteria of importance. Consequently, any individual's cognitive representation of, say, a city probably consists of points, lines, and areas which are connected to a greater or lesser extent depending on experience with the environment; these points, lines and areas together form the 'psychological mapping' that individuals compile of their environment (Golledge, 1978, p. 78).

This is a more general argument than that of children in urban environments but much of the research literature is more specific. Stea and Taphanel (1974) are aligned to incrementalism and argue that children have an innate ability to develop sophisticated spatial learning at a very early age. Using survey data from the United States, the Caribbean and Latin America, they were led to the proposition that the genesis of spatial learning may lie in the crib. Similarly, Blant, McCleary, and Blant (1970) observed that a 3 year old could model an urban landscape and was already a mapmaker. Piaget from his constructivist viewpoint would see these characteristics as play—models and maps which bear no relationship to reality.

Piché (1977) analyses the geographical understanding of children between intuitive and systematic approaches to spatial learning. Her findings were broadly in accord with Piaget's scheme of development and the view that the child progresses from an egocentric confusion of self and environment, with space defined entirely in terms of personal actions, to a practical apprehension of Euclidian space in which objects, including self, have positions. Piché's experiments with children show how they begin to analyse routes into segments and imagine directions at the intuitive stage. The children did, however, refer to landmarks and displacements within their own intuitive representations and could not construct overall cognitive schemes with flexibility or reversibility. Older children in the sample often failed to close the network but were able to represent it and to predict shorter routes. Other research on routes has points of interest. Stea asked children to draw routes from home to school and found that the youngest children drew straight lines whereas older children children show changes in direction (Downs and Stea, 1977). Jakle, Brunn, and Roseman (1976) recount the ability of a child of find the way home but only by orientating along a familiar route. Shemyakin (1962) argues that 6 to 8 year-olds define routes without reference to other roads, 8 to 12 year-olds depict other roads as offshoots, but after that age the interconnectivity of routes begins to be shown.

Piché (1977, 1981) examined the ability of her sample to construct 'models' of places; these she found to be circular and interconnected in the form of a network. Younger children had circular modes with arbitrary placements of landmarks, older children produced good topological representations. Piché explained some apparent regressive tendencies in the transition between intuitive and early concrete operational stages in terms of a setting aside of partly developed abilities in favour of a conceptual view of the world. Hart and Moore (1973) try to relate Piaget's four stages to three geometrical models.

1. The *egocentric* system is based entirely on the child's own actions and person and leads to representations in the form of disconnected route maps. There is no *gestalt*; links and places are fixed only in terms of these routes.
2. The *fixed frame of reference* allows the child to relate his position and movements to fixed 'places' which are disjointed areas centred around home.
3. The *coordinated framework* is equivalent to a surveyed map in which an organized whole emerges with places coordinated by a variety of routes.

The changes from the spatial learning of the child to that of the adult is a complex continuum but adult skills will also vary considerably. Boyle and Robinson (1979) compare the maps of Sunderland constructed by correspondents with sharply contrasted cartographic experiences. Whereas one drew a conventional map with places and routes in relative positions, the other could only construct a long transect route from home to city centre.

370

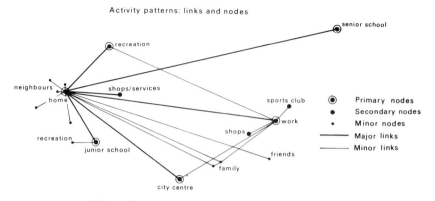

Figure 8.15   Activity patterns: linkages and nodes

Golledge (1978) hypothesizes a buildup of spatially learned environment around key nodes such as home and workplace. These, along with school and shopping centre, may become primary nodes and routes between them acquire special significance. Neighbourly contacts develop around home and other contacts are related to workplace, shopping centre and school with extra links developing to other intermediate locations. Figure 8.15 demonstrates development of this network with its nodes and connections.

COGNITIVE MAPPING

Spatial learning processes form a basic means of understanding spatial behaviour but have not yet been adequately researched by geographers. Much behavioural geography has focused on notions of urban imagery and cognitive mapping and refers to the earlier writings by Boulding (1956) who argued that human behaviour depends upon images or the pictures of the world which we carry around in our heads. Boyle and Robinson (1979) are critical of this over-reliance on Boulding and the tendency to conceive the image as synonymous with subjective knowledge. The older psychological tradition has its roots in the nineteenth century when there was already a prevalent view that humans had an innate sense of spatial orientation, comparable to their senses of smell and taste. Trowbridge (1913) used the term 'imaginary maps', Lewin's (1951) concept of life space had subjective qualities and the ideas of social space developed by de Lauwe (1952) involved consideration of space as perceived by members of particular groups. Buttimer (1969) summarized the primary value of de Lauwe's work as the connection postulated between the internal subjective order (attitudes, traditions, and aspirations) and the external spatial order within an urban milieu.

Although the possibilities of identifying cognitive maps which depict an individual's subjective view of environment rather than total reality has a great deal of appeal to geographers, the concept, as Boyle and Robinson

(1979) point out, is difficult and ambiguous. Hart and Moore (1973) use the term cognitive map to imply a visual image which has some of the properties of the conventional cartographic map—'the internalized reconstruction of space in thought'. This narrow view, analogous to Tuan's (1975) 'mental map' and Canter's (1977) cognitive cartography is also preferred by others: 'It is an internalized, predominantly visual structure, and it is dissociated conceptually from any affective connotations' (Boyle and Robinson, 1979, p. 63).

This view of the cognitive map can be related to Down's (1970) threefold typology of approaches to the study of geographical space perception. Of his 'evaluative', 'preference' and 'structural' approaches it is the last, concerned with the identity of space perceptions and the mental adjustments of space users, which most resembles the Boyle and Robinson interpretation of the cognitive map:

We accept that cognitive maps play only a minor and intermittent role in effective thinking and that it is misleading to impute to them any great significance in the co-ordination of our spatial activities (Boyle and Robinson, 1979, p. 64).

The argument suggests that mental maps have little place in routine activities, which dominate normal patterns of urban living and when special activities, such as a visit to a new shopping centre or search for a new home, arise, they prompt particular responses which may include consulting maps or some formal information-seeking. Subjective images of the city which are generally held may be influential but are not likely to be relied upon in a detailed way. Given this line of argument, mental maps have some intrinsic interest but are of limited use in explaining behaviour; much of the geographical literature on cognitive mapping has to be regarded in this qualified way.

The task of identifying the cognitive maps which people hold, especially in some conventional graphical form, has raised a number of measurement problems. Measurement can be based upon verbal responses and some success has been achieved by this method; more generally, however, researchers have aimed at 'graphic' responses and people's ability to draw their images of the city. Lynch (1960) demonstrated the potential of sketch maps which gave some insight into the form which spatial awareness of Boston took. Other ways of identifying cognitive maps have involved completion tests in which respondents are presented with an incomplete cartographic stimulus and are requested to add detail. Lee (1963) presented Cambridge housewives with a standard 1:10,560 map and asked them to draw a line around their neighbourhood. *Cloze* procedure involves the superimposition of a grid upon a map from which some cells are subsequently deleted. Respondents are then asked to add detail to the blank cells. Size of grid cells and density of detail on the original map are clearly critical factors and these procedures, which require people to use maps, do introduce new sources of error. Sketches in part reflect an ability to draw and to represent things in graphical form, cloze procedures involve ability to 'read' maps and use the information which they contain. Individuals have these abilities to varying degrees and it is noticeable that many experiments have used groups, particularly students, with 'controlled' levels of ability.

Other procedures rely less upon abilities to draw or interpret maps. Herbert (1975b) presented each of his respondents with a list of sites and asked if they were or were not parts of their neighbourhood. This involved some control in that sites were preselected but did allow aggregate cognitive maps to be derived. Similarly, Klein (1967) presented respondents in Karlsruhe with a total of 24 cards bearing the names of well-known streets and landmarks with a request that they select those which were part of the city centre. Other researchers have used photographs in place of named sites but here the quality and content of the photograph became critical variables. Ranking or scoring places in terms of desirability has been a common approach (Gould and White, 1974). Such exercises can be conducted at an intraurban scale—preferences among residential neighbourhoods or shopping centres—or national scale—preferences among regions of a country. Such exercises have some interest but are of limited value. There are typically local preferences, which affirm the preference for present place of residence, and a general tendency to opt for aesthetically more attractive places with amenable climates or unspoiled environments. Preferences or choices made in an unfettered way without necessity to account for costs or other practical constraints, are unlikely to reveal more than fairly obvious idealistic attitudes.

Urban images

Lynch's (1960) seminal work on Boston provided some systematic ways of approaching the measurement of urban images and his typology of paths, landmarks, nodes, edges, and districts has been widely adopted. More generally the attempts to identify images of the city has received many replications. De Jonge (1962) compared the images of Rotterdam, Amsterdam and The Hague, using small groups of residents from each city. Amsterdam proved the most 'legible' city with its distinctive morphology oriented around the concentric canals and well-known landmarks such as the Royal Palace and the Dam Square. Francescato and Mebane (1973) investigated the images of Milan and Rome and found them both to be highly legible but in different ways. The Milanese emphasized work, activity, dynamism, active recreation and sport; the Romans saw their city in terms of its art, culture and history and most frequently metioned its monuments, buildings, and museums.

At the neighbourhood scale, urban imagery has some well-established lineage (Lee, 1976). Sweetser (1942) studied residents at Bloomington, Indiana and used their information on forms of neighbourly interaction to identify 'personal neighbourhoods' which emerged as compositionally unique and spatially discontinuous. Lee's (1968) Cambridge study involved the delimiting of neighbourhoods and although 80 per cent of his respondents were able to delineate a neighbourhood, these emerged as highly idiosyncratic and

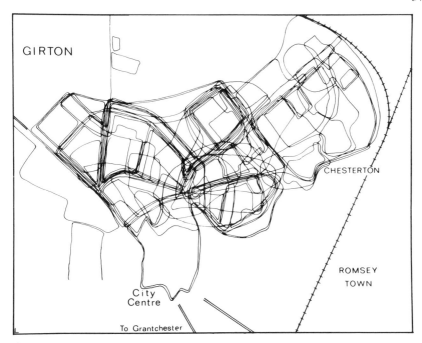

Figure 8.16   Housewives' neighbourhood images in Cambridge. (This is a modified version of a diagram which first appeared in T. R. Lee: *The Study of Urban Neighbourhood* Unpublished Ph.D. dissertation, University of Cambridge, 1954. and is reprinted with the author's permission)

personal (see Figure 8.16). In an attempt to extract some meaning from the maps and relate cognitive mapping to the concept of neighbourhood, Lee was attracted by the notion of *consentaneity* implying agreement and interdependence though not necessarily in reciprocal systems. The survey evidence was regarded as sufficient:

to indicate clearly that people must form 'inner representations' of the external environment. We must not presume that these are pictorial in form and it is clear that there are large individual differences in the clarity of the images as well as in particular ways which people structure their environment (Lee, 1968, p. 276).

As a final empirical example, Herbert and Raine (1976) developed a number of procedures whereby 'subjective' or 'personal' neighbourhoods could be identified in Cardiff. Procedures were designed to produce aggregate 'images' and in that sense hide the considerable individual diversity shown in Lee's survey which undoubtedly exists. Respondents in six different parts of the city were asked to categorize a list of sites in relation to their neighbourhood and also to name the locations at which their neighbourhood ended. Marked differences were apparent among types of residential district. A high-status area (see Figure 8.17) was defined in an extensive way, with little more than

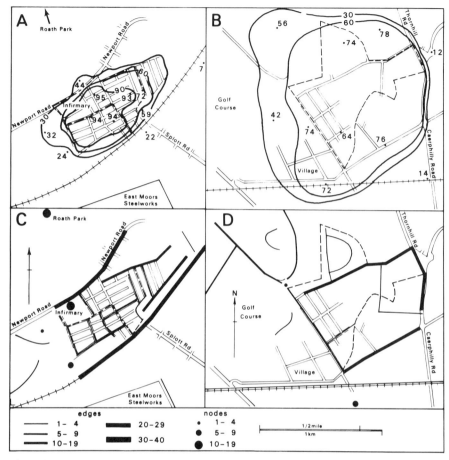

Figure 8.17   Images of neighbourhood in Cardiff: (a) Low-status area isopleths (surface); (b) High-status area isopleths (surface); (c) Low status area edges; (d) High status area edges

60 per cent consensus at any one point, a low-status area was intensively defined with a much higher level of consensus, often over 90 per cent. Boundaries were often formed by environmental features such as railway lines or main roads but key landmarks, such as parks and hospitals, were frequently nominated. Large local authority estates, sometimes designed as neighbourhood units were in fact segmented into smaller, more manageable units in the images of their inhabitants. As another aggregate device to define neighbourhood, the standard deviational ellipse was used and although this produced idealized shapes it did indicate the compactness and directional biases of subjective neighbourhoods. Urban imagery has stimulated a good deal of interesting empirical work in urban geography. The concepts, however, remain weakly defined and as such hinder the attempt to place detailed meaning and understanding upon the evidence which this research is producing.

TERRITORY, LOCALITY AND NEIGHBOURHOOD

Attachment to place and its associated sense of belonging is a concept which can be applied at several scales. National affiliation, regional identity, and city pride are all expressions of place-attachment but social geographers have focused most of their systematic research on more local place-attachments at community or neighbourhood scales. The associated concept of territory has its roots in the environmentalist paradigm and has strong symbiotic connotations. In Ardrey's (1967) study of the territorial imperative, territory was defined as an area which a single animal or a group defined as its exclusive preserve and within which security, stimulation, and a sense of identity were available. Social geographers have built upon this type of definition:

the space which may be continuous or discontinuous, used by an individual or group for most interactions and which, because of this, goes a long way towards satisfying the needs of identity, stimulation and security (Eyles, 1970, p. 2).

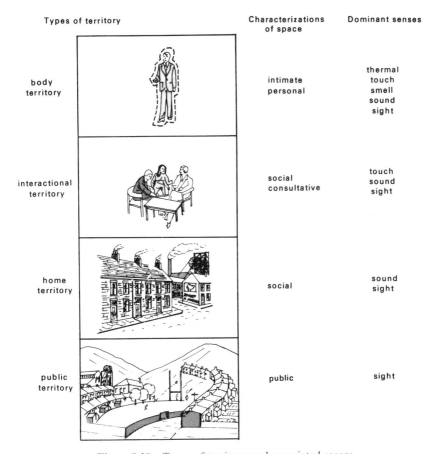

Figure 8.18   Types of territory and associated senses

Several writers concerned with the meanings of space and distance relationships have devised classifications of the types of territories. Hall (1966) takes the five senses of touch, 'thermal', smell, sight and sound and considers the distance zones within which contact by senses are meaningful and correspond to various forms of relationship (see Figure 8.18) Lyman and Scott (1967) developed a less person-to-person based classification in which activity spaces and varying forms of spatial interaction could be accommodated. *Body territory* is likened to a 'bubble' or protective envelope which individuals 'carry' around them and is violated only in close emotional relationships or else involuntarily, such as in crowded places. *Interactive territory* resembles Hall's social or consultative space in which two or more individuals come together for some common purpose such as a transaction, work, conference or social gathering. Relationships within this type of space may be functional or social. *Home territory* is probably closest to the concept of locality or neighbourhood and provides the daily framework for social ties outside home. *Public territory* contains space to which the individual has no special sense of belonging yet has general familiarity. It may include recreational space occasionally used or routes regularly traversed between home, work and services, the city centre and other public facilities. Of the elements in this four-fold typology, social geography has focused most firmly on home territory, with excursions into both interactive and public territories as locales for activities, but has shown little interest in body territory.

Suttles (1968) showed in his study of the Addams area of Chicago, how a relatively small segment of urban space of less than a square kilometre (half a square mile) in area, was subdivided among a variety of ethnic groups into well-recognized territories. Each territory could further be associated with distinctive social orders which had a very localized frame of reference and behaviour. Teenage groups have often been shown to possess particularly strong territorial associations and 'turfs' which are resolutely defended from outsiders. Ley and Cybriwsky (1974a) demonstrated how such gangs in inner Philadelphia occupied territories which were sharply demarcated by graffiti which had the additional quality of representing the 'imprints' of specific groups. With greater proximity to the edges of a group's territory, the graffiti becomes more strident and abrasive in its assertions. Boal (1969) studied territoriality in Belfast and used a number of approaches to demonstrate the relatively sharp divisions between Protestant and Catholic communities. Clonard and Shankill, 99 per cent Catholic and Protestant respectively, had separate patterns of spatial interaction with very little overlap. Since the late 1960s the continuing situation of conflict in Belfast has given territories an even sharper distinctiveness and a more intense meaning. Constraints and the heightened need for group cohesiveness or security often exaggerate the need for territory considerably; the greater these constraints, the more completely contained within territories the group activities will be.

The notion of territoriality has often been linked with the central but elusive concept of *community*. Hillery (1955) identified 94 definitions of community and no fewer than 70 of these included a territorial point of reference, only marginally less than the citations of common ties and social interaction. Bell and Newby (1971) stress that territorial location of people and activities has only a partial determinance of the emergence of community. This is obvious enough but the thrust in social geographical research has been to examine the territorial basis of local community and to analyse its implications in a variety of circumstances. Neighbourhood is the term which most clearly represents this idea of local community associated with a particular place within a city. It suggests not only an identifiable territory to which individuals feel some attachment but also some sense of cohesion as a group. Queen and Carpenter (1953) defined a neighbourhood as an area in which there is the habit of visiting one another, of exchanging articles and services and, in general of doing things together. Others have arrived at similar definitions of neighbourhood: 'a territorial group the members of which meet on common ground within their own area for primary school activities and for spontaneous and organized social contacts' (Glass, 1948, p. 124).

Usage of the term 'neighbourhood' has frequently not been confined to situations which satisfy definitions of this kind. A difficulty is provided by the gap between the task of identifying distinctive segments of the city which might be classed as neighbourhoods and have often been designed as such, and the task of demonstrating that they actually function as 'communities'. One result of this difficulty has been the tendency to resort to typologies which make different claims on the concept of neighbourhood. Morris and Mogey (1965) distinguish between *physical units* in which territory alone provides the neighbourhood cement, and *neighbourhoods* in which regular interaction occurs and *residential groups* where homogeneity rather than interaction was

Types of Neighbourhood

Neighbourhood type	Qualities	How defined
Recognized area	spatial identity legibility	images of city mental maps
Morphological unit	physical definition common design features recognizable limits	observation morphological mapping
Social area	social homogeneity demographic unity	social area analysis census indicators
Local activity system	local social interaction local nodes or points of conflux	activity studies trip patterns
True community	sense of belonging social cohesion identify with place	cognitive maps social interaction common bonds 'communion'

Figure 8.19   Types of neighbourhood

evident. Blowers (1973) envisaged a continuum from 'arbitrary' to 'community' neighbourhoods along similar lines. Figure 8.19 is a synthesis of this type of classificatory approach. In order to qualify as a *recognized area* the demands are very limited, districts within the city need only to be known, to possess some legibility; *morphological unity* is the product—planned or otherwise—of a particular phase of urban development; *social areas* emerge from the sifting out of social groups in space; *local activity systems* incorporate both social interaction and use of essential local services. Classifications go some way to clarifying the ways in which neighbourhood can be defined, but as one moves towards the most demanding classification of neighbourhood as *true community*, problems of measurement and validation increase. Although it runs some risk of treating a middle-class model of sociability as standard, Bell and Newby's (1978) distinction between community and communion offers a key perspective. Community, it is argued, involves an implicit sense of belonging in a taken-for-granted situation, any social area with recognizable boundaries can thus constitute a community. Communion rests upon a form of human association which refers to affective bonds, it implies an active and involved group rather than one which is passive and apathetic. Community can at any time be transformed into communion by an event such as an issue which affects the neighbourhood as a whole or by an 'activist' who launches an innovative idea or activity.

Defining neighbourhood boundaries is an issue which has stimulated a large literature and a range of possibilities. Ecological barriers are commonly used, small area statistics involved in social area analysis provide predetermined building blocks which set the detail of boundaries, activities can often be used as links between nodes and residences, and images of neighbourhood, as discussed above, give some pointers towards the existence of limits and edges. A larger question of definition concerns the characterization of identified units—How real is the concept of neighbourhood in empirical terms? Where in the typology of neighbourhoods does a particular district lie? Sociologists have tended in general to be dismissive of neighbourhood as a concept but social geographers continue to recognize its validity and contemporary signi-ficance as shown by: 'the emergence of the community or neighbourhood associations; groups striving for varying degrees of political decentralization, for discretion over use of neighbourhood space' (Ley, 1974, p. 7).

This rebirth of localism and the decentralization of problem-solving, decision-making, and provision of services manifests itself in many ways. In the United States, the development of neighbourhood associations has been a striking recent development; in the United Kingdom community councils are being created within cities as part of the framework of local government. Several positions have crystallized around the issue of community. The 'community lost' argument is that ties to localities have been so badly eroded that city living no longer provides any real community feeling (Fischer, 1976). It was this type of argument which Webber (1963) launched in the 1960s with his notions of **cosmopolites** and **urban realm** in opposition to those of localities and urban place. 'Community saved' is the other polarity in the argument in which a strong sense of community and local attachment is still thought to exist in many well-defined city neighbourhoods. Examples of this view are found in Gans's (1962) exposition on the urban villagers of Boston's North End, and Jacobs's (1961) somewhat nostalgic essay on the neighbourhood as a source of vitality and a good quality of life in American cities. The roots of the 'community saved' school can be traced to the early part of the twentieth century and the still extant neighbourhood unit principle. Advocates of planned neighbourhoods claim to replicate one of the better elements of natural or 'organic' city growth. Mumford (1954) found ample evidence of neighbourhoods in the European cities of Paris, Venice and Florence, 'quarters' typically formed around focal points such as church or square and possessing some level of local organization. Following its precursors, the Garden City movement, social settlement schemes, and garden suburbs, the planned neighbourhood unit principle found its clearest expression with the work of Perry (1939) and the working example of Radburn, New Jersey. Radburn as a planned neighbourhood incorporated ideas on population size, boundaries, provision and location of open space, local stores, institutions and an internal street system. At the centre of the neighbourhood unit was an elementary school intended to act also as a community centre, shops were peripherally located and population size, 7500 to 10,000, was related to the catchment of an elementary school. With modifications on design, size and internal organization, the basic principle of neighbourhood planning was incorporated in many urban developments in several parts of the world including the British new towns.

Much time and effort has been spent in establishing the details of design for neighbourhood units, but perhaps of greater importance are the purposes and underlying assumptions of neighbourhood planning. There was clearly an idealism among some early writers who viewed neighbourhood as a device to improve the quality of life and obtain some return to rural standards. The aim was to introduce physical order, to encourage face-to-face relationships, to promote local togetherness and feelings of identity, security and stability. Any measurement of the success or failure of neighbourhood units has proved an impossible task. Judged by the criteria of 'true community' they have no significant claims to success, but measured by their success in creating acceptable urban environments in which to live which provide opportunities for local interaction, their case is much stronger. Sociologists continue to dismiss neighbourhood planning:

> The problem with the neighbourhood unit idea is not, therefore, that it cannot be shown to coincide with the existence of a local social system, but that it misinterprets the nature of this system (Bell and Newby, 1978, p. 288).

In Bell and Newby's judgement, the role of a local basis of human relationships is overstressed, it confuses a sufficient with a necessary condition. Territory

Roles of Neighbourhood

Type of neighbourhood role	Environment qualities	Dominant emotions	Personal roles and needs
Humanistic	home, haven, refuge	sense of belonging, affective ties	participation, involvement, close identity
Locational	address, residence, identity	social status, reference group	access to formal services, housing, recreation, education, library, information
Structural	built environment, urban design, social environment, type of people	quality of life, satisfaction with environment	access to informal services family and friendship network, caring community, neighbourhood 'effects'

Figure 8.20 Roles of neighbourhood (after Smith, 1980)

often leads to close human bonds but is not an essential ingredient for 'community' to develop.

Between the extremes of 'community lost' and 'community saved', some middle ground is both possible and desirable. 'Community transformed' (Wellman, 1978) represents this third group who view urban communities as moving through a phase of adjustment rather than one gradual decline; local place continues to provide the context for some, occasionally new, forms of activity, community action and identity. With the passage of time and the advent of more mobile, intercommunicative societies, the 'tyranny of space' has obviously been reduced. As C. J. Smith (1980) argues, whereas 'true' communities may have only existed in the imaginations of a few people who witnessed exceptional neighbourhoods, such as Boston's North End and London's Bethnal Green, it is reasonable to observe that even in very large cities, people are not 'placeless'. People certainly have more choice about where to interact; many will have almost 'aspatial' behaviour but for a large majority locality will remain a significant context for social interaction. The notion of incorporating choice and flexibility into urban design while retaining 'locality' is evident, for example, in the American new town at Columbia, Maryland. Here housing cluster, neighbourhood and village are elements within the city available for local interaction in an overall structure which allows movement and accessibility. Smith (1980) offers a simple though useful typology of the roles which a neighbourhood possesses (see Figure 8.20).

Neighbourhood as a *humanistic element* has subjective qualities such as home, place to which one belongs, and centre of personal meaning (Relph, 1976). As humanistic geography develops, the social values attached to space and place acquire increased significance in research endeavours:

How mere space becomes an intensely human place is a task for the humanistic geographer; it appeals to such distinctively humanistic interest as the nature of experience, the quality of the emotional bond to physical objects, and the role of concepts and symbols in the creation of place identity (Tuan, 1976, p. 269).

For the humanistic geographer, place is a shared feeling and a concept as much as it is a location and a physical environment. Similarly, Buttimer (1976) writes of the affective and symbolic foundations of identification with space; place provides an anchoring point in human experience. A significant role of neighbourhood in this context is as a refuge or haven (Sennett, 1973); within a sometimes hostile and occasionally dangerous urban world, neighbourhood serves as a place in which safety and familiarity are at a premium. Neighbourhood as a *location* provides a range of household activities. These may be formal with foci provided by institutions such as clubs or associations, or informal, revolving around kinship or friendship linkages. Living in a neighbourhood also provides an individual with a spatial identity, a smaller-scale niche within the city as a whole. Neighbourhood as a set of *structural characteristics* describes its nature as an aggregate of a particular set of 'built' or social environmental features. These range from types of housing, layouts and open spaces to levels of social organization and subcultural characteristics.

If these are the roles of neighbourhood, the remaining question is whether they can be used in constructive and positive ways. At a general level, Tuan (1976) suggests ways—measurable by the sense of place which has been achieved—in which the humanistic neighbourhood can contribute to human welfare. Neighbourhood planners have for decades used neighbourhoods in attempts to achieve a better quality of urban life. Smith (1980) is concerned more narrowly with neighbourhoods as providers of care. His concern is particularly with mental health in which a number of deinstitutionalization policies, prompted both by fears of rapidly rising demands for hospital beds and by genuine doubts on the value of prolonged institutional care, has the effect of returning mentally ill people to residential neighbourhoods. Community-based services require resources and organization, but as important may be the informal set of relationships which neighbourhood provides. It is this which may provide the individual with a protective envelope against the stresses of personal and civic life.

CONCLUSIONS

The themes which have been discussed in this chapter all relate to the 'social dynamic' in urban life and also, in various ways, to the influence of behavioural-ism in human geography. One can find examples of both behaviourist tenden-cies with, for example, the spatial learning processes of children, and of more subjective humanistic interpretations of space, place and urban territories. Some of these research strands, such as that concerned with urban neighbour-hood, have practical relevance and will be returned to in Chapter 10. Firstly, however, the continuing need for urban geography to develop its applied qualities and relate to public policy can be exemplified by those recent studies which have become centrally concerned with identifying and understanding the problems of the modern city.

Chapter 9

Urban Problems

INTRODUCTION

For most societies the emergence of problems and problem areas has been especially associated with urbanization and the growth of cities. It can be argued that this association is an inevitable consequence of the scale and dimensions of the urban phenomenon, and therefore that society's problems are *merely manifested* in intense form within the city, but there is also an argument that some problems are *particularly urban*, there are differences of kind as well as of degree. At least to a large extent, however, the city is the mirror-image of the societal context of which it forms part. If a social formation engenders gross inequalities, these will find sharp expression in urban areas; if the technological base of an economy produces hazardous byproducts, these may well accumulate in urban areas; and if rising material and social aspirations are not being matched by essential forms of change and broadening opportunities, the diverse forms of evidence for these 'failures' will occur in cities. The focus in this chapter is upon some of the problems manifested in cities which can be taken as evidence of inequality, disadvantage and the hazards of urban life. Some of these problems are as old as cities themselves, others are of recent emphasis if not of origin. The issues of inner cities and the crises of city government have long roots but it is only in the 1970s that they have become regarded as critical. As with most phenomena, therefore, urban problems have to be viewed in a time–place–social context continuum.

The selection of a problem-focus for analysis of the city does pose issues in itself (Lee, 1979). A focus on problems, it can be argued, diverts attention from society itself and the means of social reproduction; the focus may appear to be on the surface manifestation and not upon the root cause (see also Thrift, 1979). Questions of *definition* are also critical. The 'problems' most commonly studied are those which are defined as such by official agencies and the statistical returns which they generate. There is a growing literature in the social sciences (Hindess, 1973) which questions the existing assumptions, traditions and biases upon which agencies and their official statistics work. Data from which social problems may be defined are neither neutral nor absolute facts, they have been defined by the data compilers and involve subjective judgements which have no theoretical bases. More pragmatically, data bases are often incomplete

383

and may be so composed as to generate doubts on their representativeness. The proportion of actual crime which is known to the police and therefore enters official statistical returns, for example, is of a consistently low order.

A further criticism of a problems-approach is that it has a strong tendency to be reformist and ameliorative in its prescriptions; the most common focus is upon the remedying of visible effects rather than upon addressing the deeper sources of inequity. If a continuum can be envisaged in a social critique which ranges from being 'radical' at one extreme to 'welfare' at the other, then problems-oriented research has generally led to welfare solutions. This poses a genuine dilemma for most social scientists, including geographers. Representatives from both 'poles' of the critique can be identified and the gulf between them is often considerable. Compromises run dangers of eclecticism but the approach followed in this chapter is one which accepts the need to place problems within the context of societal structures and to ask real questions of data and problem definition, but which still focuses most attention upon ways in which problems find expression within cities. Despite the conceptual inadequacies of definition and origin, these are *real* problems which affect the lives of many people in significant ways. We should be more concerned with the *fact* that people are dying and suffering rather than with getting the concepts straightened out. Similarly, ameliorative reform may do little to change, perhaps something to enable, the persistence of basic sources of inequality, but in the short term at least, as part of a wider strategy, it can help those in need. Some problems, such as the living conditions of old people, are more susceptible to short-term measures, others, such as inner-city unemployment, require more radical change. A focus on problems has value as a basic inventory, as a portrayal of the extent of human misery, and as one stage in a broader strategy for change.

From the range of urban problems, a selection is made to represent its diversity. The chapter begins with a discussion of the current crises of the inner city—crises which clearly find their origin in wider contexts. The associated issue of urban government is related to inherited patterns of fragmentation and political interaction in large metropolitan areas. Most urban problems are economic, social, and political but the hazards of environment—both natural and manmade—are assuming larger significance. A thrust towards social indicators and analysis of the quality of life has provided much recent research interest and this is discussed. Finally, some specific problems—ill-health, crime and the disadvantages attached to old age—will be isolated to demonstrate ways in which geographical research has focused upon contemporary issues.

DEFINING THE INNER CITY AND ITS PROBLEMS

Through the many centuries when cities took a 'preindustrial' form, and even during the nineteenth and early twentieth centuries when urbanized areas were compact and of limited spatial dimensions, there was no real sense of the division between 'inner' and 'outer' cities which has come to typify many modern metropolitan areas. Clearly there were divisions within these older forms of urban area, as previous discussion has shown, but their scale and organization was such as to function as one city, at least in a *de jure* sense. The notion of an inner city in these terms is a function of the modern western metropolis and often has some kind of legalistic definition such as the separate municipalities in the United States, metropolitan boroughs in London and *départments* in Paris. Research which begins with the need to define the inner city usually adopts these legalistic definitions or else constructs an amalgam of administrative units on an *ad hoc* basis. For example, Berry (1980) suggests that a good definition of the American inner city is that part constructed before the Great Depression. Inner cities have a number of common characteristics. They are the oldest parts of the urban fabric and hence contain the historic buildings in addition to the most outmoded morphology. They typically accommodate the main institutions of government and culture in addition to the central business district; within their confines are both traditional forms of economic activity and the residual areas of high-density residential districts built to house workers in the industrial city.

There is nothing new about inner-city problems; they have been features of the industrial city over several stages of its evolution. A consistent problem, which may even predate the industrial city is that of the congestion and overcrowding of people and activities into a limited amount of central space. As transportation routes focused in a radical manner on a central location so the conditions for convergence were set; as industries demanded easy access to cheap labour, the need for high-density housing was created. A technology which only permitted a basic infrastructure of services and facilities in the nineteenth century, promoted the compact city. These basic problems of central overcrowding were not restricted to large industrial cities in the western world. As the 'metropoles' (McGee, 1967) of the Third World have struggled to cope with the sheer weight of urban populations, so their levels of inner-city congestion have reached new dimensions which show few signs of abatement. Industrial cities of the western world have adapted to this basic problem in a number of ways. The processes of concentration and centralization which dominated earlier stages of industrial city growth, were replaced by deconcentration and decentralization as people and functions began a long process of dispersal towards the periphery and thus initiated the transformation of the compact city.

These processes were tied to an evolving transport technology which enabled the process of urban growth to occur, albeit in a selective way; to the availability of space on the urban periphery—though initially in limited amounts in some cities; and to the space preferences of the owners and managers in the new urban society. The ongoing dispersal process, filtering downwards through society, has been a dominant trend during the twentieth century and has allowed some measure of control over problems of congestion in the inner city. Many cities continue to experience considerable problems of traffic congestion, shortage of car-parking space and pressures on public transit systems; the 'new' twentieth-century cities of the United States are conspicuous for their alternative urban forms with less reliance upon highly centralizing radial transport systems. The dispersal process has affected retailing, manu-facturing, and office functions as well as population; in some ways the conges-tion of the inner industrial city has been replaced by vacua in modern metropolis. Decreasing population densities are reflected in the changing gradients from centre to periphery (Figure 9.1) but for non-western cities the change has a

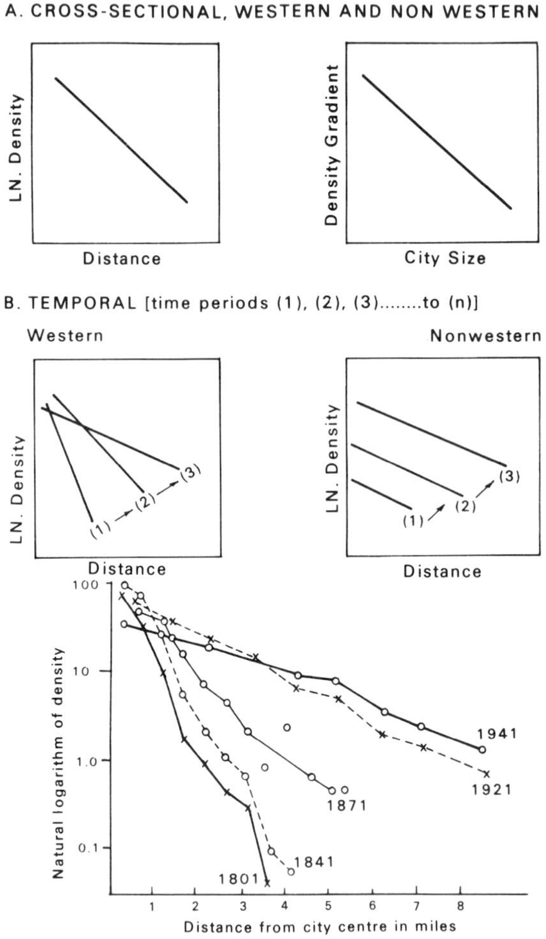

Figure 9.1   Changing urban population densities over time.   (a)   Cross-sectional—Western/non-Western. (b)   Temporal   change—Western/non-Western.   (c) Changes in urban density curve of London 1801–1841. (Reprinted (adapted) from Berry, Simmons, and Tennant, *Geographical Review*, Vol. 53, 1963, pp. 389–405, with the permission of the American Geographical Society)

different character. Here overall densities are high and population congestion in the crowded inner-city tenements continues to be a feature, even though it may be paralleled by high densities in peripheral areas.

A second problem of the inner city over time has been its role as a locale for the concentration of poverty and deprivation. Initially, in its preindustrial form, the central city was the focus of wealth, affluence and power in prestigious buildings and the vestiges of this system may persist in residual quarters or morphological heritages. As the wealthy progressively use their prerogative to divorce workplace and residence, the inner city began to acquire more uniform characteristics of a different kind. The industrial proletariat became the occupants of inner-city residential space, tied to workplace and living in crowded, often polluted environments. The homogeneity of this condition— the Victorian slum—must not be overstated (see Ward, 1975) but notions of poverty and substandardness in the inner cities of western Europe were marked by the mid-nineteenth century. Added to these features were social problems such as ill-health and crime and an emergence of ethnic minority districts which sometimes created their own forms of tension. There are many graphic accounts of the inner-area problems of nineteenth-century cities ranging from the contemporary observations of Mayhew (1862) and Booth (1891) to the retrospective analyses of Stedman-Jones (1971). The early problems of the inner city revolved around congestion and overcrowding on the one hand and poverty and deprivation on the other, both set in ageing and progressively inadequate urban environments.

Different societies responded to these problems in different ways. West European countries such as Britain inherited extra difficulties created by morphological barriers and a reluctance of landowners to release peripheral building land; there were in fact some modest attempts at inner-city building projects and 15,000 dwellings were completed in central London between 1889 and 1912. As land became available and urban infrastructure improved, the attraction of easily prepared peripheral sites and of the 'return to the countryside' ethic became dominant (see Chapter 7). During the interwar period, some 2.25 million private houses were constructed in the United Kingdom. The United States also continued a suburbanization process (Walker, 1978) which had its origins in Philadelphia in 1830 as the 'bourgeoisie' began to place distance between themselves and industrial activities; preferences for space and for the rural ideal were strong. The adequacy of funding institutions was a critical element to suburbanization in both countries, though by the end of the nineteenth century the available capital was estimated in the United States to be twice that of the United Kingdom. This suburbanization process was selective and was in part at least a reaction to the kinds of urban environment which the inner city was presenting. The relatively disadvantaged became more and more the dominant element in inner-city populations as those who were able migrated outwards. As selective outmigration began to filter downwards to affect the working classes, subgroups such as the elderly and recent immigrants became the typical populations; in the United States, the poorest sections of white populations—often recent rural migrants—shared inner-city areas with a diverse ethnic group with the black ghettos gradually becoming the most significant element. Modern accounts of socialist cities (Weclawowicz, 1979) suggest that the inner city has in the past had problems, elements of which persist, but the 'special' groups which occupy inner-city areas now are there by preference rather than constraint.

Recent trends in the inner city

The inner city is therefore no stranger to problems, and the processes of social separation towards the suburbs in western cities—in many ways a reaction against those problems—have been ongoing for long periods of time. During the 1970s, however, awareness of inner-city problems in western urban areas has increased dramatically. It is unlikely that any emergence of new problems underlies this change, but a number of precipitating conditions can be classified. Firstly, there has been a continuing *decline of population* in inner-city areas. Between 1966 and 1976, Liverpool lost 22 per cent of its population, Manchester 18 per cent, and Hall (1973) showed that in the 1960s the 'cores' of British urban areas were decentralizing in absolute as well as in relative terms, and similar trends are observed in European cities (Drewett, 1980). Evidence for American urban areas in the 1970s (Berry, 1980) suggests unprecedented population losses from central cities with 30 out of 50 larger cities showing losses since 1970. As Table 9.1 shows, the most affected cities are those in the manufacturing belt. The image of the American city has changed from one of a high-density and congested but vital centre in which face-to-face relationships could still exist, to that of an ageing, polluted, crime-ridden vacuum typified by declining services and employment bases and escalating taxes (Berry, 1980). In both European and American cities there have been compensating population flows but these have added to the changing character of the inner city. Foreign immigrants from less developed countries—often former colonies—have moved into inner cities in Britain and in Europe; these some-times started as seasonal labour migrations but they have tended to acquire permanence. In the United States the black population has gradually moved to numerical dominance over large areas of the central city. Mayor Koch of New York estimates that the large majority of the million people who left his city in the 1960s were middle-class and white, while the large majority of those who moved in were black, Hispanic, and poor (*Firing Line*, 1979). This accelerating ethnic distinctiveness of inner-city populations, particularly in American but also in British cities, was at the roots of civil disorder in the later 1960s and early 1970s and forms one powerful reason for a heightened awareness of inner-city problems. It became clear that the disadvantage under which inner-city residents lived—with its discriminatory connotations—required at least am-eliorative action. One other compensating flow into central cities warrants mention. Gentrification of selected neighbourhoods in particular cities has allowed the localized return of middle-class population and some evidence—such as at Capitol Hill, Washington and parts of London—suggests that it

Table 9.1   America's largest central cities showing population
losses > 5 per cent 1970–75

	1975 population	
New York	7,481,613	− 5.2
Chicago	3,099,391	− 8.0
Philadelphia	1,815,808	− 6.9
Detroit	1,335,085	−11.8
Baltimore	851,698	− 6.0
Washington	711,518	− 6.0
Milwaukee	665,796	− 7.2
San Francisco	664,520	− 7.1
Cleveland	638,793	−14.9
New Orleans	559,770	− 5.7
St Louis	524,964	−15.6
Seattle	487,091	− 8.2
Denver	484,531	− 5.9
Pittsburgh	458,651	−11.8
Atlanta	436,057	−11.9
Cincinnati	412,564	− 9.0
Buffalo	407,160	−12.0
Minneapolis	378,112	−13.0
Fort Worth	358,364	− 8.9
Portland	356,732	− 6.7

Source: US Bureau of Census (extracted from Berry (1980), Table VII)

is increasing. Gentrification, however, is selective both of the conditions under which it can occur and of the population it can attract; there is no evidence that it has affected the residential preference patterns of the majority of urban populations, nor indeed is it likely to do so.

Population decline, therefore, is one recognized inner-city problem of the 1970s; the second which has received increasing attention is that of *declining employment opportunities* particularly in manufacturing industry. Again the problem is not new as industries and businesses have been migrating out to peripheral highway-based locations for some decades, but closure rather than transfer and the attendant total losses of jobs has become a feature since the later 1960s. A series of studies of the British inner city has pinpointed the nature and dimensions of these job losses. Lomas (1975) showed that between 1966 and 1973 there was an overall loss of 200,000 jobs from inner London, 140,000 of these in manufacturing and the rest in services. Gripaios (1977) in a more detailed study of south-east London suggested that 69 per cent of closures resulted from 'deaths' of firms rather than transfer; a Manchester study (Lloyd and Mason, 1978) discovered that 85 per cent of the total employment decline 1966 to 1972 was due to deaths and transfers and most of these were actual closures. Districts within inner cities with an above-average reliance on traditional industries were particularly affected; Canning Town in London and

Saltley, Birmingham suffered job losses of 24 and 14 per cent respectively between 1966 and 1972. Closures of single-plant firms were a major contribution to this decline, but Cameron (1973) argued that lack of firm births rather than deaths was significant. Type of city seems also to be a factor (Thrift, 1979); Liverpool with its 'top-heavy' industrial structure relying on a few firms susceptible to world trade fluctuations is particularly vulnerable to decline. From these British studies a number of generalizations are possible.

1. The inner-city manufacturing sector is sharing a downturn in fortunes and viability with the total urban and national economy.
2. Inner-city firms of a traditional kind are proving particularly vulnerable because of their small size and high costs.
3. Some transfers from inner city to outer city (and within the inner city) are occurring, but most losses are associated with total closures.
4. Urban redevelopment schemes have had adverse effects on small firms through displacement and higher costs.

The direct result of this decline in the inner-city job market is rising unemployment. Thrift (1979) estimates that the unemployment rate in the inner city may be 3 to 5 percentage points above the city average and perhaps of the order of 15 per cent. These levels are viewed seriously from more than one perspective and in particular because they exhibit disproportionate effects on youth and minority ethnic groups. Schemes initiated during the 1950s and 1960s have had few lasting effects and the structural bases of inner-city unemployment remain. These economic downturns and their adverse effects on inner-city employment are also evident in American metropolitan areas (Berry, 1980). Growth industries are increasingly being dispersed towards the peripheries of the manufacturing belt cities, older slow-growth industries remain as the former core. From 1969 to 1977 the manufacturing belt in the United States on a whole lost 1.7 million industrial jobs; New York City is estimated to have lost 600,000 jobs between 1968 and 1978. Although there were compensating flows in other sectors, of the 500 large industrial corporations surveyed by *Fortune Magazine* in 1965, 128 had New York headquarters, but 1975 only 90 retained them.

The third aspect of the inner-city problem as it emerged during the 1970s can be summarized as the *low quality of life* which it appeared to present to the vast majority of its permanent residents. These conditions, as discussed earlier, have long records but in some ways have worsened in the 1970s despite formidable planning machinery in western societies. Physical environments in the inner city remain substandard with residual low-quality tenements and other urban fabric elements, high densities and overcrowding and an increasing amount of derelict land. Berry (1980) argues that with the expansionist activities of construction industries on the edges of American cities, 27 million new dwelling units were added between 1963 and 1976 at a time when household expansion was only 17 million. As 'filtering' occurred and older housing was passed down the line, 'abandonment' began to occur in the inner city and

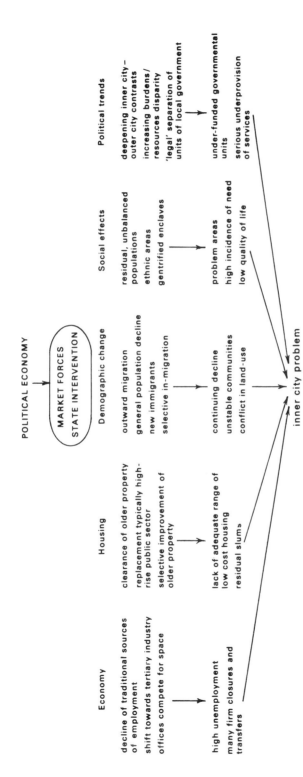

Figure 9.2   Sources of the inner city problem

dereliction spread. Redevelopment, often of high-rise blocks has lacked both functional and design qualities and built environments, aesthetically unattractive and poorly endowed with services, become typical. The social disadvantages of the inner city also continue. Poverty, disadvantage and their attendant characteristics are concentrated within central-city districts which are often composed of ethnic minorities. Levels of crime and violence, ill-health and mental instability, educational disadvantage and low employment skills are disproportionately high, and the type of community cohesion which has often been advocated as a redeeming feature of inner-city neighbourhoods seems to be conspicuously absent. Figure 9.2 attempts to draw together some of the contributory factors to the inner-city problem and its main contemporary features.

Inner-city problems are real enough and seem to have a high level of generality in western societies, but their nature and intensity vary from place to place and over time. Some bases of these variations can be suggested:

1. The size of the urbanized area is clearly a factor; the larger the city, the more acute its inner-area problems are likely to be (see Holtermann, 1975). Within their respective societies, for example, London, New York, and Paris appear to have the greatest problems.
2. The age of the city has relevance though probably as an indicator of other qualities such as overall design and economic base. Within the United States, cities like New York and Chicago have inherited economic bases, including traditional industries, and transportation systems which ex-aggerate their problems. Long histories of immigration have modern con-tinuity and extensive tenement areas are part of the housing stock. Newer cities like Denver, Dallas and San Diego, the last showing an 11 per cent increase in population 1970–75, have inner-city problems of a lesser kind and degree.
3. Urban tradition is related to age but has some status as a separate variable. Some cities have maintained the prestigious qualities of parts of their inner areas; the thrust towards detached dwellings and garden space has been less ubiquitous in some European countries. Policies of equity and the allied strong redistributive powers of planners in socialist societies have apparently led to an avoidance of inner-city concentrations of poverty and deprivation. Individual cities such as Glasgow (Holtermann, 1975), can be identified which have more than their share of inner-area problems and in American cities, where much of the inner city can be labelled as an ethnic ghetto, new dimensions are added.

Something of the variety of inner-city problems has been revealed by the re-search studies of the 1970s in the United Kingdom. Three government-sponsor-ed studies of London, Birmingham and Liverpool (Department of the Environ-ment, 1977) revealed strong common strands but also significant variations in quality and emphasis. Whereas the loss of manufacturing jobs in inner London was causing several problems for the 'traditional' labour force, there were also significant issues arising from the pressures for growth. Demand for office space—often speculative—remained high and construction in areas such as Southwark play active roles in reducing the amount of space available for low-cost housing. Offices generated a demand for labour but this was met by sub-urban commuters rather than by the indigenous labour force with its more traditional skills. Similar service-sector pressures are discernible in New York where foreign concerns leased 43,500 square metres of office space in 1975 to 1977 and 6000 new hotel rooms were under construction in 1979. Gentrification was another pressure evident in parts of inner London, such as Islington, which effectively was reducing the available low-cost housing. Birmingham's tradi-tional role as a base for traditional industries on a small scale of enterprise was sharply affected by the economic decline of the 1970s, and the city's role as a reception area for immigrants had led to profound changes in the social geo-graphy of the inner city. Liverpool's industrial structure was generally vulner-

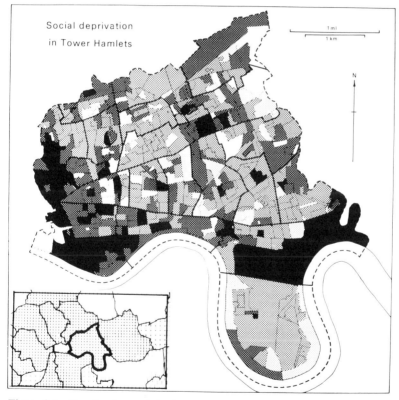

Figure 9.3 Deprivation and the inner city. Inset shows: Tower Hamlets as a deprived borough within London; main map shows: Variations of deprivation within Tower Hamlets. In both cases, most intense shading shows highest rates of deprivation on a composite index (after Smith, 1979; this modified version is produced with the author's permission)

able but the inner city was a 'waste-land' still suffering the consequences of overzealous clearance schemes and unimaginative redevelopment remains a powerful image. Liverpool's traditional Catholic component makes it, along with Glasgow, one of the few mainland cities in which religious conflict has any meaning. For these British cities and others, the early studies tended to classify central districts as concentrations of multiple deprivation. This view has some credibility but as D. M. Smith (1979) and others have shown, finer-grained analyses reveal significant variations in deprivation within inner-city areas (Figure 9.3). Despite these variations, the common characteristics evident in Britain and America remain pervasive, and inner cities have become the weak links of the urban system which are proving the most vulnerable to macro-scale fluctuations in economic wellbeing.

European cities have less publicized inner-area problems though some trends are discernible. Drewett (1980) has identified those European cities which have experienced decentralization from the core and the trends are often reminiscent of American experience. The 'city' of Paris, at the centre of the metropolitan area, has been losing population since the 1950s through decline in household size and reduction of housing stock. During the 1970s, the city and its inner suburbs lost manufacturing jobs at a rate of about 40,000 per year with closures and intraregional dispersal responsible in roughly equal degrees. Of new industrial building 70 per cent is now in the outer suburbs with offices concentrating in the inner ring of Hauts de Seine; at a time when manufacturing employment declined by 3 per cent, service employment grew by 16 per cent in Île de France. The features are reminiscent of British and American cities, but in Paris the suburbanization of manual workers has allowed them to escape the consequences of decline in the inner-city employment market. There are inner-city housing problems in Paris but they are restricted to certain sectors and communes and are associated with foreign immigrants. Interestingly, most of the new housing currently under construction in Paris is destined for the higher-income groups. Clearly, there are variations over time and place and some contrary trends can be discerned, but the generalization that inner cities have become problem areas has some credibility.

Inner city–outer city and the issues of urban government

The continuing decline of the inner city in much of the United States has had the effect of widening the gap between the quality of life which it offers in comparison with that available in many suburban areas. As Vance (1978) has shown, the United States during the twentieth century relied upon the free market economy to solve the problem of housing the poor; this is in contrast with the interventionist social welfare solutions preferred in many European countries including Britain. Americans built upon available cheap land, developed good transportation facilities and responded to a preference for the single-family house on its own plot for those who could compete in the housing market and who had access to the necessary funds. At a time when British local authorities were constructing peripheral estates of 'council' housing, there were no real American equivalents. A result was the clearer inner-city outer-city separation of socioeconomic (and ethnic) groups in American cities. Residential segregation was as typical in most British and European cities but it had rather more complexity than was evident in the United States. During the 1970s the American situation has been changing, not yet uniformly nor in clear directions, but the undiluted 'market' solution seems unlikely to survive.

For American cities, the geographical sorting of population groups and employment opportunities has been reinforced by jurisdictional frameworks of local government. Fragmentation, generally a feature of the western metropolitan area, takes a variety of forms with a multiplicity of municipalities, school districts, special districts, counties and precincts, most of which have separate roles in the allocation of services and revenue-raising powers. Cox (1973) recorded the fact that Chicago was fragmented into over 1000 different district authorities and the average number of authorities per metropolitan area in the United States was 87. It is in terms of jurisdictions with elective systems and 'governmental' status that inner-city/outer-city separations become acute. In a typical American metropolitan area, there is a central-city jurisdiction surrounded by a ring of separate suburban municipalities. For most of the twentieth century, state legislation favoured the process of suburban municipalization, often extending the privilege to very small communities, and resisted central-city annexation of peripheral land. This rural/ suburban dominance of state legislature persisted until the 1970s at which time a number of moves began to protect the interests of the central city and to enable its legitimate expansionery needs.

For the central cities, bounded by suburban jurisdictions and suffering an exodus of middle-income householders and enterprises, extra burdens developed as they were increasingly called upon to support a rising proportion of the nation's poor. The problems of sustaining a workable form of urban government on sound fiscal bases have become critical in the 1970s. The components of the inner-city government problem are several-fold:

1. The outward-movements of people and activities have deprived inner-city jurisdictions of the tax revenues upon which they depend.
2. The compensating inflows of poorer people have not made up the tax loss from outgoing middle-income households.
3. As the central city population becomes more uniformly low income and often unemployed, the welfare burden increases.
4. Many public services, such as schools, police departments, firefighters and street cleansing units, are disproportionately expensive to run in the inner city. There are many more educationally deprived children, for example, higher rates of crime and more arson.
5. The inner city often supports services which are used by metropolitan populations as a whole, such as transit systems and cultural institutions; there is 'suburban exploitation' of the central city.

Cox (1973) and others have documented the disparities which exist between inner cities and suburban areas both in terms of the 'burdens' which they have to bear and the levels of provision which they manage to achieve. In older industrial cities such as New York, Newark, Cleveland and St Louis, particularly, the disproportionate burden resting upon the inner-city government has become intolerable.

New York has had the most publicized inner-city government crisis and by the early 1970s was experiencing income shortfalls of a kind which meant basic services could not be supported. In 1975, Congress gave short-term loans to meet the immediate crises and in 1978 Federal guarantees allowed long-term loans to be negotiated with the aim of regaining financial stability. There were costs to be met, 60,000 jobs were cut from the municipal payroll, subway fares were raised 42 per cent and free tuition at City College was ended. Some residents faced a fifth local tax and New York remained the highest taxed city in the nation; out of a total annual welfare bill of 4 billion dollars, 1 billion had to come from city taxes. Other inner-city governments in the United States have faced similar problems to New York though not yet of such intensity. Problems of maintaining services have become more acute in states attempting to reduce local taxation in the wake of California's Proposition 13. In the early 1970s (Cox, 1973) there was already evidence of the effects of growing burden disparities between inner city and suburbs. Services such as street-lighting, provision of sidewalks and paved streets were deficient in inner-city areas. The district of Watts held 17 per cent of the population of Los Angeles, but 65 per cent of its tuberculosis and 46 per cent of its venereal disease yet on a *pro-rata* basis had only one-third of health provision services of suburban areas.

Inner-city/outer-city differences exist and the evidence demonstrates the fact that the established jurisdictional framework in the United States and the way in which it operates serves to perpetuate them. Discriminatory zoning by suburban municipalities which aims to retain their present character and to resist infiltration by other population groups is common. Similar attitudes prevail to prevent public housing projects being constructed in suburbs, and within the private housing market discriminatory practice is well-established. During the 1970s Federal action against each of these procedures has led to some bases from which integration of city and suburb populations may proceed but this progress is extremely slow.

It is clear that inner-city populations consistently come off worse in the conflict over externalities in urban areas. The most powerful lobbies of the business élites and middle-class householders consistently work to divert negative externalities away from the suburbs and to attract the positive externalities towards them. Suburban areas tend to attract modern facilities, inner-city areas have to accommodate freeway schemes which cause disruption and displacement. It is only when special interests come together that potentially negative effects can be diverted from the inner city (Wolpert, Mumphrey, and Seley, 1972). Most American metropolitan areas now acknowledge the need to equalize funding and opportunities over the whole urban complex but major obstacles towards this end remain. Principal among these are the entrenched nature of existing structures of urban government and continued opposition to overt use of the welfare principle in deciding the allocation of resources. Proposals for integrated metropolitan government with overall strategic power in key decision-making areas have been in existence for a considerable time but little actual progress has been made towards making these a reality. Central cities continue to rely on their own revenue-raising resources—albeit with standard sources of federal aid—which are inadequate with respect to the burdens which they carry. Suburban municipalities retain their independence and through a combination of their own fund-raising capacity and superior advocacy in resource conflicts are able to at least maintain the *status quo*.

Besides the metropolitan-integration solution, other proposals (see Cox, 1973) have included community control over limited issues within a wider strategic framework, and a range of fiscal policies to promote equity and open up the suburbs. These include ideas on more federal and less local tax, federal insurance against property value losses, progressive taxation and greater use of federal powers in public housing projects. Much of this involves issues of federal/local roles and although, in the case of New York, federal participation may become essential, the notion of local autonomy is not easily changed and there is very little evidence of either moves towards or desire for, more government.

Although the inner-city/outer-city dichotomy is clearest in large American cities, it exists elsewhere. For large British cities the general contrast in levels of living is evident and many studies have shown the disparities in burden which exist. A range of area policies have been designed to tackle the problems of the worse-off inner-city areas (see Thrift, 1979); the accumulated burdens posed by unemployed youth, by the educationally disadvantaged and the elderly all fall most heavily on inner-city areas. British cities have some organizational advantages over their American counterparts. Firstly, the jurisdictional distinction is much less valid and the local costs of funding disadvantaged individuals and groups are spread much more widely over the whole urban area. This principle was consolidated by local government reorganization in 1974 which created large county and metropolitan-level authorities with overall powers in key areas such as planning and social service provision. The districts and community councils within this framework have powers in separate categories—such as housing—but administratively inner cities are not separated off as independent entities. London's local government reorganization along these lines in fact predated the rest of the United Kingdom and the original independent municipalities numbering nearly 100 were finally reduced to 32 metropolitan boroughs in 1961, with a single Greater London Council as the overall tier of local government. Secondly, for British cities there are strong flows of central government funds and policies into the urban system (see Bennett, 1981). These may take the form of varying levels of rate-support grant and other grants in aid and also specific urban policies such as housing action

398

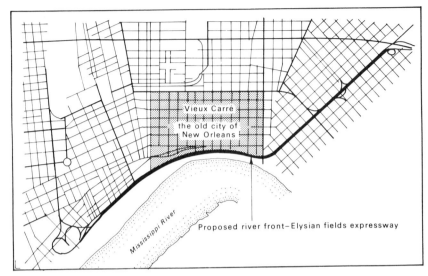

Figure 9.4 Inner-city redevelopment and community action: the New Orleans expressway project (redrawn from Wolpert, Mumphrey and Seley, 1972)

areas. The forms and activities of central and local government, therefore, are such as to provide mechanisms for the reduction—though certainly not the elimination—of inner-city/outer-city differences. Elsewhere the differences are less marked, suburbs may not have their own jurisdictions but they do have different political complexions and power-groups with varying ability to argue in the externality debate. Whereas there is evidence of increased community action among inner-city groups to protect and promote their interests, some of the success stories, such as the contest over Covent Garden (see Christensen, 1981), are reminiscent of the special interests evident in some American cities such as activities of preservation groups in parts of inner New Orleans (Wolpert, Mumphrey, and Seley, 1972), in which objectors organized against detrimental effects upon the historic core of the city successfully stopped a proposed riverfront expressway scheme (Figure 9.4).

Both the form of urban government and its powers to combat problems of the inner city clearly varies considerably from one society to another. Hall (1977), in his survey of problems and policies in a selection of major metropolitan areas in the world, provides some valuable insight into the nature of this variation. Many European countries have achieved some measure of metropolitan government which allows disparities to be reduced. Urbanized Paris, for example, is organized into eight *départements* which comprise the overall planning region of Île de France. Policies for suburban growth poles and new towns are bound to affect the inner city; British new towns were originally conceived as a response to inner-city congestion and substandard housing. Socialist societies pursue policies designed to bring uniformity and equity over the whole area of the urban agglomeration and inner-city/outer-city comparisons have different meaning. Planning emphases are often centred on the efficiency of transport systems and on the links between workplace and dwelling-place rather than upon the quality of housing and environment. The central city which continues to hold the administrative functions and the institutions of government remains a strong focus.

For the closely studied metropolitan areas of North America and Europe, the reality of inner-city problems is self-evident. To a large extent ameliorative measures can be focused within the inner city itself, the internal resources of the inner city can be more efficiently organized, and the positive qualities which inner-city locations offer can be more vigorously promoted. Longer-term solutions, however, are likely to be found in broader contexts. The economic frailty which is apparent within the inner city, the accumulation of poverty and disadvantage, the badly maintained environments and poorly serviced communities, all find their origins in the structural framework of society and it is from this macro-level that more effective change must come.

URBAN ECOLOGICAL CRISES

During the 1960s and 1970s there has been a strong surge towards greater environmental awareness and the need to monitor and protect the ecological habitat. Although many of these habitats are in non-urban locations, they primarily serve urban populations and many country parks and reserves have been 'developed' with urban needs in mind. The city itself, however, despite its predominantly manmade qualities, is also an 'ecological habitat' and its condition in these terms has become a matter of increased—though by no means new—public concern. Historically, concern was with the squalid conditions of streets, services, and houses at particular stages of urban development, such as the industrial cities of nineteenth-century Europe. Contemporaneously in modern cities of Europe and North America, this concern focuses on the quality of goods and services emanating from cities and on the ways in which urban areas threaten natural environmental qualities.

There are perhaps three main headings under which the ecological issues posed by and within cities can be grouped. Firstly, there is the role of the city as a *generator of waste*. Urban populations by the fact of their concentration in space are typified by concentrations of the byproducts of human activity from the throwaway garbage of households to the smoke emissions of industrial plants. Secondly, there are the roles of cities in *modifying the local environments* in which they are placed, and both climatic and hydrological conditions can be affected in highly significant ways. The growth of urban–industrial societies has been coincident with the types of hazard termed 'quasi-natural' in which the 'urban effect' added to the natural phenomenon produces a malevolent output such as 'smog'. The third group contains the roles of cities in relation to more purely *natural hazards*. Here it is the built form of the city and the intensity with which it occupies space which places its population at high risk to natural phenomena such as floods, hurricanes, tornadoes and earthquakes. A natural

Type of problem	Pollutants/ sources	Nature of damage	Indicators	Treatment	Recent trends
Man-made					
Air pollution	sulphur oxides nitrogen oxides carbon oxides hydrocarbons	health hazard loss of amenity	indices show concentrations of pollutants	ban on fuels emission control	sources decline with more control on fuels and emission increase in small particulates
Water pollution	industrial commercial waste: sewage	health hazard polluted waterways aesthetic problems	biological oxygen demand P.D.I. index	emission control water processing	increasing sources stricter controls several irredeemable outcomes
Solid waste	industrial domestic building rubble packaging	fire risk health hazard aesthetic deterioration disrupted ecosystem	visible environment weight collected	collection disposal recycling	increasing problem technology available re-cycling
Noise and heat	highways industries airports	physical and mental property value	decibels noise exposure index	noise shield land-use planning	increasing problem more attempted control
Natural					
Fogs	particulates urban climates	traffic hazard safety, stress health	visibility		
Floods	drainage condition flood plain	threat to life and property	water level frequency	channels flood control	greater control higher losses
Special events: earthquake hurricane drought	geological or climatic conditions	life, property urban system	frequency vulnerability	basic precautions warning systems	greater disasters increased vulnerability

Figure 9.5 Ecological hazards and cities

hazard has been defined (Burton and Kates, 1964a) as an element in the physical environment, harmful to man, which is caused by forces extraneous to him. Such hazards become meaningful in their effects and it is in urbanized areas, with their concentrations of large numbers of people and properties in a limited space, that the effect is likely to reach disaster proportions.

With these groupings in mind, Figure 9.5 has been constructed to list some

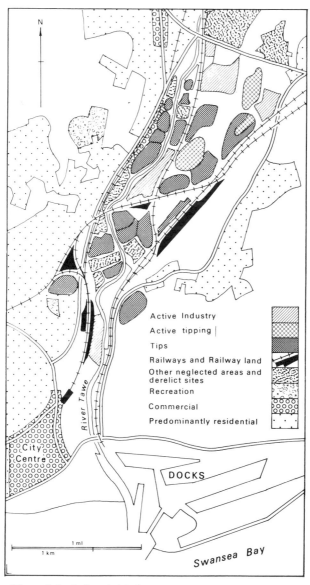

Figure 9.6   Industrial dereliction in urban areas: the Lower Swansea valley

of the main sources of ecological hazards related to cities. Some of these hazards are entirely manmade, such as traffic noise, others are purely natural, such as tornadoes, but most draw some influence from both sets of agents. The emissions which constitute air pollution are manmade but a set of natural conditions—presence of temperature inversions, lack of ventilation— are necessary before they constitute a major hazard. Similarly, periods of torrential rainfall may produce flood conditions but the high runoff rates of urbanized surfaces and interventions into natural drainage conditions produce large-scale flood hazards. The list is by no means complete, but it does provide a set of major categories with which to assess the reality of urban ecological crises.

Comparisons in terms of environmental quality can be made at an interurban scale and here the generalizations are largely predictable. Firstly, the dimensions of ecological hazard will show a propensity to increase with size of urban area, larger cities entail greater interventions into nature, generate most waste, and place more people at risk in a single location. Secondly, some types of city are more likely to have low-quality environments, in both general and specific terms, than others. Older cities which contain large-scale industries functioning in more traditional ways are likely to generate contaminants on a greater scale; many older industrial areas contain the scars on landscape and vegetation of years of industrial–urban contamination (see Figure 9.6). More specifically, cities in particular regions—such as Nevada with its high level of radioactive elements in the atmosphere (Mason, 1973)—or which contain particular industrial activities, such as coalmining or petrochemicals, may possess high vulnerability to particular hazards. Los Angeles, with its combination of local climatic conditions and intense motor vehicle usage, may qualify for this category. Thirdly, cities in particular geographical locations may be placed at highrisk in relation to natural hazards. Cities on floodplains, or near coasts with subsidence or inundation problems (such as Venice), on regular hurricane or tornado tracks, or in earthquake zones, all provide examples of this group of urban areas at risk. How much risk such urban areas face must be a function of probabilities of hazard occurrence, likely severity, and the measures which have been taken to mitigate the effects.

Those attempts which have been made to classify cities according to their overall environmental quality are based upon a series of indicators. In the main American classification (Liu, 1975), indicators covered topics such as air and water pollution (see Figure 9.7), solid waste, climatic factors, automobile registrations, and availability of recreational space. The composite index extends beyond strict measures of ecological hazard but gives some general indication of inter-city variations. As a generalization, the most favourable urban environments in the United States are found in newer cities and in the western part of the country; the worse are in the older industrial–commercial regions of north-east and mid-west. Highest concentrations of both air and water pollutants correspond with older centres of heavy industry such as Pittsburgh, Cleveland and Baltimore.

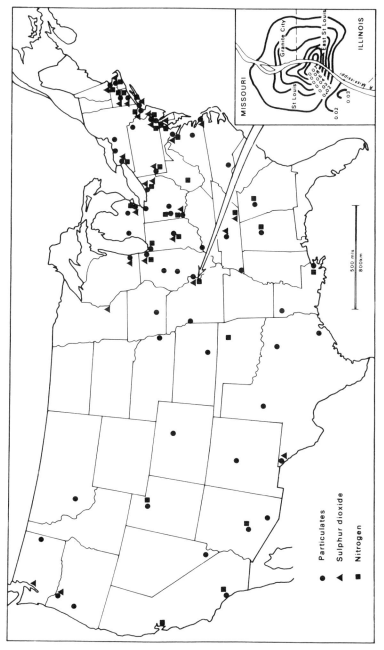

Figure 9.7   Pollution and American cities. The map shows the worst cities on indicators of air pollution with an inset which shows sulphur dioxide levels at the intra-urban scale. (Based upon information derived from Liu, 1975, and Northam, 1979)

At the intraurban scale, some fairly obvious generalizations are again possible on overall pollution levels. A basic distance–decay effect has been observed. Pollution levels tend to be highest at the central parts of cities, corresponding with highest concentrations of buildings, people, traffic, and activities, and decline towards urban peripheries. Wood *et al.* (1974) demonstrated this effect by mapping a composite pollution index in the Greater Manchester area; in American cities one effect of this pattern is that low-income neighbourhoods, and especially urban black populations, are placed at highest risk. A variety of hazards, such as winter smoke and 'heat island' effects have adverse influences on the health of central-city occupants; these promote chest infections, for example, and affect the elderly and disabled in particular (see Giggs, 1979). Local wind conditions may modify the urban 'dust dome' into a 'dust plume' effect spreading over adjacent rural areas (Bryson and Kutzbach, 1968); Terjung (1974) suggests that megalopolitan areas may already have begun to function as vast pollution 'sheds' and to show effects on a regional scale.

Air pollution has been one of the most closely monitored of urban hazards, partly through the notoriety attached to events such as the 1952 London smog and also because of its close links with analyses of local climatic conditions. Figures cannot be precise but one estimate (Northam, 1979) suggests that in the United States, 173 million tonnes of contaminants are released into the atmosphere annually (see Table 9.2) Leighton, (1966) reports that photochemical air pollution has been observed in over half the states of the United States having strong effects on the quality of the air. He categorized the three main progressive effects as impairment of visibility, effect on plants, and damage to eyes. Of the populated areas of California, 97 per cent had recorded incidence of impaired visibility, 80 per cent suffered plant damage, and 70 per cent eye irritation. The automobile constituted the greatest single source of emissions by contributing 60 per cent of the state's nitrogen oxides and 80 per cent of its reactive hydrocarbons. Chicago is estimated to experience air pollution on half the days of an average summer along a narrow zone adjacent to Lake Michigan.

Local climatic conditions have a strong link with air pollution and Terjung

Table 9.2 Major sources of air contaminants in United States

Contaminant	Annual volume (millions of tonnes)	Proportion of total volume
Carbon monoxide	87	50.3
Hydrocarbons	23	13.3
Nitrogen oxides	18	10.4
Particulate matter	15	8.7
Sulphur oxides	30	17.3
Totals	173	100.0

Source: American Society of Engineering Education (extracted from Northam (1979), Table 5.2, p. 97).

(1974) argues that of the climatic changes effected by man, those emanating from urbanization have been the most radical. A city's compact mass of buildings constitutes a strong intervention into local climate affecting exchange of energy, levels of conductivity and the well-known 'heat island' effect. This last feature in particular, associated with the artificial heat generated by traffic, industry, and domestic buildings, shows marked temporal variations on daily, weekly, and seasonal cycles. Precipitation tends to be higher in urban areas: Bremen has a rainfall 16 per cent higher than its port 1.5 kilometres away, central Moscow records 11 per cent more rainfall than its peripheries (Lakshmanan and Chatterjee, 1977). Emitted particulates in the air serve as nuclei in fogs which occur with a frequency twice to five times that typical of rural areas. Urban haze can reduce visibility by 80 to 90 per cent and some of the major ecological 'disasters' in cities have resulted from smog formation. These occur in weather conditions which promote multiple elevated temperature inversions, trap ground air, and prohibit natural ventilation processes in the atmosphere. At Donora, Pennsylvania in October 1948, the weather situation was such that contaminated air accumulated in the valley in which the city is located, twenty people died and several thousand became ill; some estimates put the deaths related to London smogs in 1952 at 3000 to 4000; in New York in 1963, 405 deaths may have resulted from similar conditions. Overall disadvantages of urban over rural areas in percentage terms have been put at 1000 for contaminants, 26 for visibility, and 60 for fogs.

Water pollution has particular significance because of its critical roles in urban life; polluted streams cause loss of amenity and pose threats to life. The roles include supply of clean drinking water or water for industrial purposes, maintenance of recreational and biotic waterways, and 'channels' for the disposal of waste. Unfortunately these roles are often in conflict; discharge of heated power station water, for example, may have bad effects on the biotic life of a stream. Supply of drinking water in western cities is now carefully monitored but accidental contamination does occur and poor resource management renders cities vulnerable to shortages during periods of moderate to severe drought conditions. Despite the place of clean drinking water as a basic necessity, *adequate* supply has often been a slow and piecemeal process, water supply for western cities in the nineteenth century was often a response to calls for control of disease and fire rather than to meet a basic need. Lakshmanan and Chatterjee (1977) estimate that between 40 and 70 per cent of the urban population of less-developed countries live in districts without safe water or sanitation. Main sources of water pollutants in urban areas are sewered municipal waste and industrial discharges—the problems are well-known but largely because of the prohibitive costs, methods of dealing with them remain primitive. Much waste water and raw sewage is discharged into rivers and seas from European cities and sewage 'lagoons' are still found in modern American cities. The devastating effects of industrial pollution on lakes and rivers have reached disaster proportions and have prompted significant legislative measures and controls.

The amount of *solid waste* generated by cities bears a close relationship with urban population size; there is also a correspondence with affluence and the material conditions of urban life. For Washington between 1914 and 1956, paper as a proportion of total waste increased from 45 to 64 per cent; for São Paulo, 1927 to 1969, paper waste increased from 13 to 25 per cent, while organic material declined from 83 to 52 per cent. The marked increase in glass, metals, and plastic waste in advanced societies seems associated with increases in prepackaging and decreases in recycling. Western societies have been slow to respond to the problem of solid-waste disposal and as late as the mid-nineteenth century, New Yorkers permitted vast quantities of refuse and excrement to accumulate in streets, with severe repercussions on public health. Methods of solid-waste disposal remain primitive with landfill and dumping the most common methods although the advantages of recycling and alternative technologies are well known. De Bell (1970) suggests that many cities have reached a point of 'solid-waste crisis'; New York must dispose of 4.3 million tonnes of waste each year. Although many Third World cities may be approaching similarly desperate straits, more of their waste is organic, and Haynes and Hakim (1979) describe the situation in Cairo where a programme of maximum recovery is operated. Some types of solid waste are dumped but much is used for fertilizer or else 'digested' within the city. Itinerant dealers, the *rubabikya*, collect bulk waste for resale, the *zabaline* collect and sort domestic waste and have an allied pig-raising activity, the *wahiya* are the brokers of the waste enterprise. This is a massive, labour-intensive, recycling operation providing livelihoods for several ethnic groups. There is a cost, however. Rates of infant deaths before the age of one year run at 60 per cent among the *zabaline*, a cost unacceptable to western societies.

Noise is typically an urban and manmade environmental hazard. To most faced with infrequent contact with high noise levels, it is a minimal problem, to those living or working in close proximity to highways, airports, or industrial machinery it is a major urban hazard. People may become accustomed to such high noise levels but this fact does not render them harmless or acceptable. Most urban noise comes from transportation systems. Decibels, which measure the intensity of sound on a logarithmic scale are most commonly used in noise comparisons. Readings between 85 and 145 decibels are rated as typical discomfort levels (Northam, 1979) whereas 145 is recognized as a level at which physical pain is normally experienced. Within the discomfort range of 85 to 145 decibels, normal urban experiences such as busy streets and road construction work can be fitted. Local circumstances in which noise occurs—enclosed or open space, duration and frequency—are clearly critical in assessing the impact of this hazard on the quality of urban life.

Shifts in public policy towards more control over urban pollution levels have been progressive but slow. Most direct action has been reactive to publicity surrounding specific hazard events. Realization of the accumulating effect of motor vehicle emissions, for example, led to new specification on design of exhaust systems and related car components. Similarly, policies towards smokeless fuels in domestic heating and control over industrial smoke emission have allowed significant progress towards clean air. Solutions to other major problems, such as solid waste disposal, are known but high costs prohibit progress. Lakshmanan and Chatterjee (1977) suggest that although evidence on the relationship between urban form and waste disposal systems is somewhat ambiguous, *compact* high-density urban areas may favour disposal and recovery systems. Energy savings would also be high in such cities but there would be costs in noise, air pollution and other sources of stress.

In terms of *natural hazards*, the relevance of 'urban' is the fact that cities place a large number of people at risk in a minimal amount of space. Urban impacts on natural environment also have some relevance, however. Air pollutants may exaggerate a natural propensity towards fog and create smog; builtup areas may interrupt natural drainage conditions and increase flood liability; building morphology may accentuate wind movements. As cities have been built over floodplains awareness of flood risk amongst administrators if not the general population has increased. The epitome of a 'bad' location is perhaps the appropriately named town of Hazard, Kentucky, located on a narrow floodplain with difficult access on the north fork of the Kentucky river. Between 1960 and 1970 its population declined from 5958 to 5459; it was in fact inundated with flood water in March 1963. Within large urban areas houses continue to be constructed and people continue to live on flood-plains, even when they are known to have high flood probabilities. As runoff rates are much higher in urban areas—60 per cent compared with 15 per cent in rural—storm flows are intensified. Perception studies (Burton and Kates, 1964a) show people's unwillingness to respond to hazard, limited awareness and a typical 'stoicism' in acceptance of periodic disruption. Many floodplain users assume that floods are preventable through controls, though technical experts accept the virtual impossibility of controlling larger floods. Expenditure on controls has increased in recent years but so have flood losses to life and property, a reflection of greater use of floodplains.

Coastal cities are highly vulnerable to floods and related hazards and most rapid urbanization has tended to occur on seaboards (Burton and Kates, 1964b) London has a high level of vulnerability to exceptional tidal conditions on the river Thames, but it is only in the last quarter of the twentieth century that effective control measures are being taken. Most coastal cities have some form of protection—centuries-old in the Netherlands—and can cope with all but extreme events. Abnormal weather conditions can produce disaster, however, as witnessed in the hurricane-prone areas of America's Gulf coast and the tornado-track cities of Texas and Oklahoma. Earthquakes pose a significant threat to urban areas in many parts of the world. Generally the regions at risk are well known, but there is a limited amount which technology can achieve and monitoring rather than controlling is the realistic objective. Japanese cities have specialized construction forms to minimize earthquake effects, and rehearsed procedures can be initiated in response to early tremors. San Francisco's position on the San Andreas fault makes it a well-known city at risk, but legislation to warn against building and occupance in most vulnerable areas appears to have had little effect. There is some evidence that human activity can exacerbate problems; the disposal of liquid waste into deep strata at 3600 m (12,000 feet) near Denver in the 1960s coincided with a striking increase in earthquake activity.

Management approaches can reduce the risks and effects of natural hazards, but in many cases there is little control over the hazard itself. Flood control systems can be constructed but there is no control over the movement of hurricanes and tornadoes. A consistent research finding has been that people do not respond to awareness of hazards, there are examples of objections to flood control schemes because of their impact on aesthetic features. The pace and nature of urban growth contains its own priorities for those involved and environmental stress may be relegated in relation to other perceived goals and difficulties. Responsibilities lie with those professionals whose jobs are to administer cities and to make decisions in the allocation of funds and resources. They should respond not merely to disaster but also to the more general task of ensuring the liveability of urban environments and a good quality of life for the people who inhabit them.

SOCIAL PROBLEMS AND THE CITY

Cities clearly face ecological problems stemming either from natural hazards or from outputs of the urban system which interact with the environment in such ways as to endanger health or the quality of life in more general terms. The most widely recognized of urban problems however are not those which could be termed ecological in this sense. They are social and economic problems which find expression both as problems *in* the city, implying that they are found throughout society but surface more dramatically in urban areas with their concentrations of both people and activities, and as problems *of* the city, implying that the particular form they take is a product of the urban environment *per se*. The economic and social problems associated with cities are manifold and can be classified under numerous headings; several of the most significant issues have been discussed in the context of the inner city. One significant role of urban geography during the past decade has been that of presenting an accurate portrayal of the extent of these problems, both singly and in association with each other, and of demonstrating the intensity within which they occur in particular urban areas. Rates of unemployment, of substandard housing, of ill-health, deviance and many other persistent urban problems can be shown to be highly clustered in specific parts of the city which often show features of multiple deprivation. Having made this point, it is as well to note that large cities have no monopoly of such problems; unemployment and poverty are just as likely to occur in rural areas or small towns—it is the size and density of the city which principally sets it apart. The further qualification is that economic and social problems are both culturally and historically specific, the significant frame of reference is constructed from the type of society, its stage of development, and the ways in which people perceive the conditions under which they live. 'Deprivation' in its various forms is everywhere a relative rather than an absolute concept.

Territorial social indicators

Social indicators research has provided a significant thrust towards the analysis and monitoring of the quality of urban life in both general and specific terms. As developed by geographers in the guise of territorial social indicators, there have been attempts to measure both interurban and intraurban variations, but the research field at large has much broader bases. During the early stages of the movement, some impetus came from dissatisfaction with the quality of available data on social conditions from official sources. By comparison with the way in which national economic accounts were kept, the recording of the social state of the nation was unsophisticated in the extreme. The objectives of the movement pioneered by social scientists such as Bauer (1966) were to improve the quality of social statistics, to impose some order and systematic organization on the ways in which these were collected and reported upon and, later, to improve the analytical procedures with which such data could be used. Successful outcomes of these pressures are evidenced by the appearance of new journals, such as *Social Indicators Research* in 1974, and by the willingness of governments to produce new statistical series aimed at filling those gaps which had been identified. In the United States, a new official series titled *Social Indicators* appeared and *Social Trends* became the British equivalent. Similar responses at an international level can be found in OECD publications and in ongoing United Nations projects.

The phase during which interest by geographers in social indicators grew, was paralleled by the emergence of the relevance issue; the shift from studies of residential differentiation to the use of the same methodologies to identify 'problem' residential areas was a simple and logical step. As geographers developed their research, they focused upon the particularly spatial implications of social indicators research. D. M. Smith (1973) defined territorial social indicators as quantitative measures of the incidence of given types of social problems in each of a number of spatial subdivisions. Successive emphases in geographical analyses were on the provision of better spatial recording units for spatial statistics, greater disaggregation to give a finer mesh, and upon more consistency of spatial units over time and place to allow comparability; the issues of ecological fallacy, sample-size, definition of population at risk, spatial autocorrelation and other *caveats* involved in using aggregate data for spatial units, received varying degrees of attention. With active interest from geographers, a new and significant dimension was added to the study of social indicators (Knox, 1975; Smith, 1973, 1979).

Social indicators may be used to classify cities according to what are variously termed levels of living, social wellbeing, or quality of urban life. There are different origins to these concepts, Knox (1975) argues that the level of living approach has a better conceptual heritage than the others, but distinctions among the approaches are rarely made in empirical research. Smith (1979) identifies two important problems which arise from any attempt to derive

Table 9.3 Alternative criteria of human wellbeing

---

(1) *UN components of level of living*
Health, including demographic conditions
Food and nutrition
Education, including literacy and skills
Conditions of work
Employment situation
Aggregate consumption and savings
Transportation
Housing, including household facilities
Clothing
Recreation and entertainment
Social security
Human freedom

(2) *Composition of Drewnowkski's level-of-living index*
Nutrition
Clothing
Shelter
Health
Education
Leisure
Security
Social environment
Physical environment

(3) *O. E. C. D. areas of social concern*
Health
Individual development through learning
Employment and the quality of working life
Time and leisure
Personal economic situation
Physical environment
The social environment
Personal safety and the administration of justice
Social opportunity and participation
Accessibility

(4) *Criteria of social well-being in the United States*
Income, wealth, and employment
The living environment
Health
Education
Social order
Social belonging
Recreation and leisure

Extracted from Herbert and Smith (1979), Table 2.3, p. 21, reproduced by permission of authors and Oxford University Press.

composite territorial social indicators; these are choice of conditions to be included and the relative weights to be allocated to them. The wide range of variables used in different studies reflects the diverse guidelines adopted as well as the vagaries of local data sources and availability. It is frequently noted that there is no general theory to provide a 'correct' set of conditions, along with their relative importance which could be regarded as analogous to the situation of national economic indicators in which prices supposedly reflect consumer preference as to various goods and services offered in the marketplace. The several major attempts which have been made to choose conditions which reflect levels of human wellbeing in advanced industrial countries, however, reveal broad levels of consensus. Table 9.3 lists four proposed sets of criteria and reveals a high degree of overlap amongst them. These sets identify 'conditions' and can be related to more general theories and concepts; the further step is to select variables or indicators in order to measure these conditions, and it is at this stage that the kind of diversity in practice which has become typical makes comparability difficult.

Comparisons among cities

At an interurban scale there have now been several attempts to classify American cities according to the quality of urban life. D. M. Smith (1973) used a form of factor analysis to classify metropolitan areas according to a range of social indicators; Table 9.3 shows the criteria of social wellbeing which he employed. Liu (1975) used five broad classes of social indicator—economic, political, environmental, health/education, and social. Variously sized sets of indicators were used to measure each class. The economic component, for example, comprised eighteen variables measuring individual and community wellbeing with indices of income, wealth, employment and availability of capital; a health and education component was based on indices such as infant mortality, numbers of physicians, school enrolment and educational attainment; and the social component had an input of 54 variables. Figure 9.8 shows Liu's classification of American cities on the economic and social components. Larger metropolitan areas generally tend to score highly on the economic component with Dallas, Houston and Portland in the south and west, a cluster of manufacturing metros in the mid-west, and emerging clusters of smaller cities in 'sunbelt' states such as Texas. On the social component, the high-scoring metropolitan areas are found in the Rocky Mountain states and on the west coast, together with the 'newer' urban areas of the plains and broad west. By contrast, the low-scoring metropolitan areas are found east of the Mississippi and in older urban America. Although regional generalizations can be made, they always need to be modified by individual cities. Similar, though less comprehensive, exercises in assessing regional variations have been made in England and Wales showing broad patterns of low scores in remote rural and old industrial towns (Knox, 1975) and others have examined inter-area comparisons at subnational scales.

412

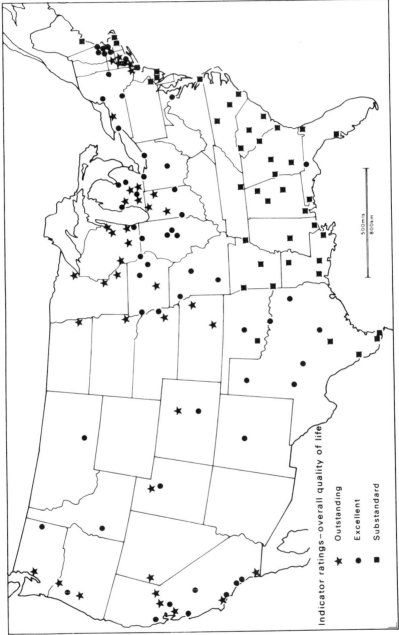

Figure 9.8   Overall quality of life in American cities. (Based upon information derived from Liu, 1975 and Northam, 1979)

Indicator ratings–overall quality of life

★ Outstanding
● Excellent
■ Substandard

Studies at this scale have some value though their limitations are evident. They are as effective as the data and analytical techniques upon which they are based and are particularly vulnerable to the problems of interpretation and overgeneralization because of the large aggregate spatial units upon which they are normally based. Again, as suggested earlier, the construction of indicators and weights is critical as an eccentric score on one indicator can distort the overall classification. All of the studies so far described have employed *objective* indicators based on official statistics; the argument for *subjective* indicators rests on the proposition that it is the way in which people feel which matters. Objective conditions such as jobs, housing quality, income, and services can affect people's level of satisfaction or happiness but it is the way in which people react to these objective conditions which is significant. The subjective approach relies largely on attitudinal survey instruments designed to find out how people view their own life quality and its contributory 'domains' such as work, neighbourhood and social services. There are attempts to survey these qualities at national and regional scales (see Bohland and Davis, 1979; Knox, 1975) but data collection is both expensive and time-consuming. A basic exercise of this type was conducted by Gould and White (1974) but their sample populations had no necessary knowledge or experience of the regions they were asked to grade and the value of the results is questionable. The general increase in attention paid to subjective indicators raises new questions of measurability and also of the gap between the subjective and objective qualities of life. Dalkey and Rourke (1973) examined the elements of life quality as rated by college students and produced a leading component composed of attributes such as love, caring and affection—all very real qualities but extremely difficult to measure and nowhere approached by current sets of indices. Similarly, the essentially conceptual essay by Campbell, Converse, and Rodgers (1976) on the quality of American life, for example, finds limited expression in empirical research.

Patterns within cities and the theories of poverty

At an intraurban scale, territorial social indicators have most commonly been used to identify problem areas, to monitor change over time, and to compare the spatial incidence of various types of problem. The possibilities and limitations of research at this scale are more closely researched though problems of data and selection of indicators remain. The standard ecological approach is superficially simple. Data are compiled for small areas and calculated scores are mapped to reveal patterns, or else are subjected to an ecological correlation exercise or some form of causal modelling in order to examine cause and effect. Individual territorial social indicators can be used to identify distributions of particular problems, specific criteria may be judged to serve as diagnostic indicators identifying a more general malaise, or more typically, several criteria may be combined into a composite indicator which measures multiple deprivation. In all of these approaches, however, research into territorial social

Theory	Source of problem	Characteristics of problem	Perpetuating features	Main outcome
Structural class-conflict	Social formation	unequal distribution of power maintenance of disparities	organization of labour class distinctions	inequality
Institutional management	allocative system	uneven distribution of resources inefficient bureaucracies weak communications/awareness	maintenance of elitism low welfare inputs non-sharing of opportunities	disadvantage underprivilege
Cycle of deprivation	social group residential area	few opportunities limited access to social mobility transmission of poor attitudes disadvantaged environment	sub-cultural norms lack of positive interventions	deprivations low aspirations low achievement
Culture of poverty	individual inadequacies family background	group apathy inherited deficiencies	fatalism failure of welfare services	retardation poverty

Figure 9.9   Theories of poverty and deprivation

indicators is vulnerable to the criticism that it is focused upon the spatial manifestation of problems—even in its correlative studies—and has little to offer in terms of explaining the origins of problems which may well have their roots in the broader structure of society. Some consideration of the concepts of deprivation and poverty *per se* and of the 'theories' which have been developed to explain them throws some light on this issue.

Both deprivation and poverty pose definitional problems. Many societies define poverty levels, usually in terms of income, below which households are recognized as poor or deprived. The 'levels', however, will vary from one society to another according to some *internal* standard of assessment and point to the relative nature of the concept. Perceptions of poverty are similarly internalized. The poor American may appear affluent in comparison to the Bangladeshi peasant, but his points of reference are not in the Third World but in middle-income America. With this qualification of the relative nature of poverty and deprivation in mind, some theories can be discussed and Figure 9.9 summarizes these.

Theories of poverty and deprivation exist for different scales of analysis. *Structural class conflict* theories, for example, suggest that poverty and deprivation arise out of particular social formations and the capacities for inequality which they promote and perpetuate. Capitalism may, it is argued, invariably produces inequality as it allocates differential rewards in a competitive society; whereas inequality need not imply the existence of poverty in absolute terms the critical relative conditions are established. In this sense poverty exists because it has so many positive functions for an affluent society as argued, for example, in the Marxist concept of an industrial reserve army as a natural outcome of the capitalist social formation. If this source of deprivation is recognized, it clearly requires a considerable change in societal structure and attitudes. *Institutional* sources of deprivation develop from the inability of the allocative systems of government and of private institutions to channel goods and services in ways effective enough to reduce or eliminate disadvantage. On some counts, allocative systems can only behave in ways prescribed by the social formation, but there is also evidence that the failure of bureaucracies to promote awareness of welfare, for example, can lead to unnecessary incidence of deprivation. Administrative or investment policy failure may also divert resources and reduce the ability of the system to eliminate poverty. The old people, the educationally disadvantaged, and the transients may suffer disproportionately from this type of mismanagement and the problem requires more efficiency in the application of welfare provision. Although the *cycle of deprivation* thesis has received detailed scrutiny (Rutter and Madge, 1976) the evidence remains inconclusive. The thesis suggests that children born into deprived households and (typically) into deprived areas may consistently be faced with less opportunities to advance because of their limited access to alternative paths and possibilities. A 'cycle' is perpetuated as children go from deprived homes to schools which they share with similar children, acquire few qualifications, usable skills, or different sets of values, and in adulthood

416

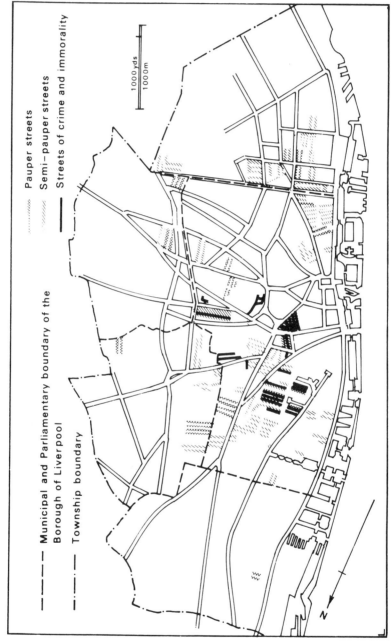

Figure 9.10 Social problem areas in Liverpool, 1858. (Redrawn from Lawton, 1972, which is based upon an original map by the Rev. A. Hume.) Reprinted with the permission of Professor Lawton and *Town Planning Review*

find themselves as uncompetitive in employment or housing markets as their parents were. This concept calls for positive intervention into home, school, and neighbourhood in order to compensate for inadequate aspirations, attitudes, and behavioural norms. Finally, the *culture of poverty* thesis provides a more individually based theory with some genetic connotations. It also, however, suggests a general group attitude in which low-key aspirations and fatalistic assessments of low achievement and norms are typical. Again this theory calls for more individual treatment and for positive intervention through educational and social work systems.

There are therefore a set of different theories against which research into territorial social indicators can be put into context. The consistent failure of much of this research however has been to proceed without reference to theory and to practise empiricism rather than careful empirical examination of key hypotheses. As territorial social indicators have been developed, their first objective has been that of identifying areas within the city which warrant scrutiny. This type of analysis has roots in the nineteenth century (see Figure 9.10) and Davies (1978c) has recently reanalysed data from Booth's classic studies. The well-known Liverpool 'malaise' study (Amos, 1970) used multivariate analyses to reduce a large input of variables to more manageable dimensions of deprivation. Other analyses have, sensibly, reduced inputs and exercised discrimination in the use of both indicators and procedures (Boal, Doherty, and Pringle, 1978). Results from these studies were unexceptional with concentrations of deprivation in the inner city emerging as the most striking feature. Levels of spatial disaggregation have been shown to be critical as D. M. Smith (1979) demonstrates for London. If boroughs form the observational units, the whole of inner London emerges as deprived; if, however, enumeration district data are used, significant variations within boroughs emerge (see Figure 9.3).

The principle of maintaining some consistency in the selection of variables and of relating these to theory can be illustrated by reference to a study of Cardiff (Herbert, 1975). Some of the ideas are drawn from conceptual frame-

Competitive markets and social indicators

	Employment	Housing	Education
Problem	Failure to find work Failure to find job with good rewards or high satisfaction	Inability to obtain mortgage or to own house Inability to qualify for good local authority house	Failure to obtain good educational qualifications Inability to obtain access to educational opportunities
Outcome	unemployment low-skill job low-paid job	substandard housing overcrowding lack of privacy	no educational qualifications few usable skills poor attitudes to schooling
Indicators	percent unemployed percent low-skill workers	percent without household facilities percent overcrowded or sharing percent private rented furnished	percent leaving school without O levels percent leaving school at minimum school-leaving age

Figure 9.11   Competitive markets and social indicators

418

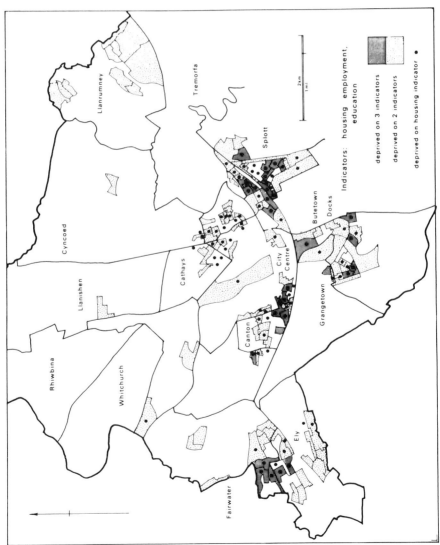

Figure 9.12 Deprived areas in Cardiff, 1971

Table 9.4　Social deprivation in Belfast

	urban area	households	unemployment	Percentage share of: children in care	delinquents	illegitimacy	infant mortality	bronchitis
10 worse areas	3.60	9.88	18.76	26.62	18.70	19.02	13.88	21.72
20 worse areas	7.79	19.84	32.64	47.75	32.40	33.43	25.98	37.94
30 worse areas	13.57	31.61	51.28	64.65	52.85	48.99	43.06	51.34

Source: Pringle (1979). Reproduced by permission of D. Pringle.

works developed during the Home Office's Urban Programme (Edwards, 1975) in which it was argued that deprivation could be measured by a failure to compete in the main societal 'markets'. These were nominated as employment, housing, and education and for each indicators were selected which would identify an inability to compete successfully (see Figure 9.11). Figure 9.12 shows the distribution of deprived enumeration districts in Cardiff based on each of the indicators and also upon a composite index. Several observations may be made. Firstly, the uniformity of the inner city is disrupted by the disaggregated analysis which reveals significant variation within the zone of nineteenth-century terraced-row housing. Secondly, the housing indicator reveals a strong concentration of substandardness in the inner city, though the Ely cluster represents a public sector estate built in the interwar period and already substandard. Thirdly, whereas public policy has had some impact in reducing the deprivation suffered in terms of the *built* environment through its rehousing programme, inequalities in the *social* environment remain and the tenants of modern projects remain disadvantaged in terms of occupational and educational achievement. Ameliorative public policy has apparently some way to go before persistent deprivation is removed. Whereas the sources of such inequality are structural, the Cardiff study did identify some evidence of local effects influencing the form and incidence of deprivation. To this extent, although the case cannot be argued in detail, theories relating to the local environment, principally the cycle of deprivation, could be given some support.

Studies involving the use of territorial social indicators of the type described here have been widely used as policy instruments, particularly in the development of positive discrimination and area policies. This link is contentious, as will be discussed later, but has found some support in many analyses. Holtermann (1975) argued that in order to give priority treatment to 61 per cent of Britain's deprived households, positive area policies would need to be allocated to 15 per cent of the enumeration districts. Boal, Doherty, and Pringle (1978) showed that in Belfast the ten worst-off areas contained 10 per cent of the households, 19 per cent of the unemployment, 27 per cent of the children in care; the twenty worst areas contained 33 per cent of the unemployed and 48 per cent of the children in care (see Table 9.4). Statistics of this kind are frequently used as criticisms of area policy (Hamnett, 1979), but do show an ability of territorial social indicators to isolate a relatively small number of areas in which a relatively large number of social problems are accumulated. Area policies miss some dependent households and are not sufficient in themselves but matched with individual policies, such as family benefits and housing subsidies, they offer an effective planning tool (see Chapter 10).

Use of subjective indicators at an intraurban scale remains largely exploratory (see Knox and Maclaran, 1978). Some research in Detroit (see D. M. Smith, 1979) has attached significance to the availability of interpersonal relationships at a neighbourhood level. A study of Fresno, California, (see D. M. Smith 1979) showed some social 'class' bases for variation in subjective assessments of life quality. Over the six survey districts and 2500 residents in the sample, there was some general consensus on the significance of health-care cost and drug addiction levels to their personal wellbeing, but whereas flood hazards and the number of people on welfare became issues from residents in the affluent north, it was access to health care and jobs which dominated priorities in the low income areas. As Smith (1979, p. 18) argues, 'what constitutes a social problem in a city depends, then, on who you are and where you live, at least to some extent'. Besides the practical problems, there are conceptual difficulties with subjective indicators revolving around the interpersonal utility comparison on which welfare economics has already foundered.

Some specific social problems

Studies of deprivation have covered a wide range of circumstances and conditions under which urban problems occur. Each 'condition', though, may constitute an issue in its own right and a sample of these may be selected for detailed analyses. Discussion will be structured under a number of headings: firstly, ill-health as an example of physical deprivation, secondly, crime and delinquency as examples of behavioural deviance, and, thirdly, the elderly as an example of a subgroup under stress.

Ill-health

The association of ill-health with particular types of urban environment and with specific districts within cities has been studied over long periods of time. There are significant global and regional variations of illness and disease (Howe, 1977) which have generated a considerable literature, but published work at the intraurban scale is sparse. One of the best-known early examples of the spatial ecology of disease in a western city was provided by Snow's study of cholera in mid-nineteenth-century London. In establishing a link between a contaminated water supply and the residences of cholera victims, Snow established a basic procedure which has endured over time. In this instance the causal link between environment and illness was clear, and studies of other cities at this time were able to demonstrate that districts of substandard housing, water, and sanitation services were breeding places for disease. Rowntree's (1901) survey showing a relationship between poor physique, poverty, and malnutrition in the inner city was of a similar *genre*. The overall effect was to give distinctive spatial concentrations of ill-health where disease and high infant mortality accompanied bad living conditions. As improvements in medical science and basic living conditions have taken place in western cities, so absolute standards have been raised.

Relative concentrations of ill-health remain however. Coates and Silburn (1970) described children in the St Ann's district of Nottingham in the early 1960s as generally being in a poor state of physical development, noticeably smaller and less well developed than children from suburbia. The Belfast study (Boal, Doherty, and Pringle, 1978) showed a disproportionately high concentration of infant mortality in the most deprived areas of the city. Outside western societies, close correlations are postulated between ill-health and those living areas which are badly served in terms of water supply and sanitation. Lakshmanan and Chatterjee (1977) have estimated that nearly 250 million urban dwellers occupy districts without safe water or sanitation in unserviced 'settlements' and these are growing by 12 million persons each year. This type of problem appears to be reaching crisis proportions in less-developed countries and in Calcutta 79 per cent of households occupy a single room, 1.8 million live in slums in which latrines are shared among 30 to 50 people and 62 per cent have no regular water supply. De (1961) described cholera as endemic in the bustees or squatter settlements—life is often brief and brutal. As already noted, infant mortality rates among Cairo's *zabeline* population have been put as high as 60 per cent.

More recent studies of physical ill-health in western cities have confined the existence of distinctive spatial concentrations. Shannon and Spurlock (1976) hypothesized 'environmental risk cells' within cities in which urban inhabitants are exposed to above average health hazards. They argue that both 'structural' health hazards and communicable diseases are distributed differentially across urban landscapes, and individuals are at risk both by area of residence and activity patterns which may involve contact with such environmental risk cells. Those ecological hazards—air pollution and contaminated open water—already discussed are major factors and numerous epidemiological studies suggest links between atmospheric pollution and several types of morbidity and mortality. Gastro-intestinal and respiratory complaints are common in most cities and often assume debilitating forms.

Epidemiological studies based upon the social characteristics of population groups have also produced significant results (see Giggs, 1979). There are clear demographic correlates. Propensity to most diseases increases with age but for particular diseases there are specific age-groups, lifecycle stages, and sexes which have above-average vulnerability. When demographic variables are controlled, socioeconomic status consistently appears to have a strong inverse relationship with ill-health. Pyle and Lashof (1969) factor-analysed nineteen health indices from 75 communities in Chicago and produced a 'poverty syndrome' which accounted for almost 40 per cent of the variance. Pyle and Rees (1971) used a similar analysis to identify three ill-health dimensions which they labelled 'poverty', 'density', and 'respiratory'; these showed correlations with low income, overcrowding, and adjacency to open water surfaces respectively. Each dimension had a specific spatial form with the main poverty syndrome revealing the strongest central-city concentration.

Many contagious diseases have temporal as well as spatial dimensions and diffusion techniques have proved useful exploratory tools. Pyle (1973) examined measles epidemics in Akron, Ohio, for four periods of outbreak between 1965 and 1970. The clusters of high rates were consistently in central and south-eastern parts of the city despite the fact that numbers of children at risk were greater elsewhere. A diffusion process could be traced from the poverty area in the south-east to the inner-city transitional districts, to some suburbs and eventually back to an area near its point of origin. There was some evidence that in the low-income areas, where most of the outbreak was contained, preventive measures were not fully adopted. It appears, therefore, that despite the general improvements in living conditions during the past few decades, vulnerability to some kinds of disease remains high in specific urban districts.

Mental illness

Mental illness as an urban problem bridges a gap between physical disabilities and forms of behaviour which might be categorized as deviant. Geographers' interests in mental illness research have broadened considerably in recent years from earlier emphases on epidemiology and spatial ecology. Faris and Dunham (1939) provided one of the best-known early studies with data collected for the city of Chicago. Using 120 community areas within the city as data-recording units, incidence rates of new cases occurring within a given population group over a specified period were calculated and spatial distribution patterns derived. The schizophrenic sample of 7253 cases revealed a regular gradient from incidence rates of 1195 per 100,000 near the city centre to 111 at the urban periphery. Other disorders such as senile and alcoholic psychoses showed similar patterns but others—notably manic depression—did not. Manic depression was randomly distributed and drug addiction had peripheral as well as inner-city concentrations. Over a majority of types of mental disorder, some districts of the inner city—rooming house areas, transient quarters, and some low-income ethnic communities—had marked spatial concentrations. More recent studies (Mintz and Schwarz, 1964) have produced similar patterns, but Levy and Rowitz (1973) suggested that significant changes have occurred since the early ecological analyses of the 1930s.

Studies outside the United States have produced inconsistent evidence for the spatial 'model'. The several Liverpool surveys conducted during a 40-year period, showed a clear centre–periphery gradient in 1931 and 1954 but a more diffuse pattern in 1973 (see Giggs, 1979). Bagley, Jacobson, and Palmer's (1973) study of Brighton calculated prevalence rates—calculated as the total number of cases occurring within a defined population over a given period—and again showed a centralized cluster of high rates for most types of disorder. Giggs (1973) had a similar result for schizophrenics in Nottingham, but Timms (1965) and others have shown that several neuroses seem to cluster in peripherally located public-sector housing projects.

Correlative exercises with mental illness variables show association with low-income deprived neighbourhoods, whether in the inner city or in the 'replacement' public-sector housing. Overcrowding and density have often been proposed as significant correlates of mental disorder but evidence is inconclusive; Freedman (1975) argues that crowding in cities has brought benefits and that people are able to adapt effectively to high-density living— for some neuroses, low density and isolation may be important precipitating factors. Age, lifecycle stage and marital status are correlates of mental illness but are modified by socioeconomic status and by the complex of attributes of which they are part. Mental subnormality among children and psychoses of the elderly tend to be higher in low-income areas. Bastide (1972) suggested that although mental disorders were more typical of single than married people this might relate to the vulnerability to single events and the lack of a support system.

Aggregate statistical associations of this kind offer guidelines on the ecology of mental disorder, but do not offer causal explanations. Causality in this field is clearly a complex feature and needs to account for individual and genetic as well as environmental precipitating conditions. Some forms of mental illness are clearly inherited and the role of 'environment' as home, community and neighbourhood is to cushion the individual against both its manifestations and implications. In this sense, ecological studies are identifying the environments which are least successful in those roles. Other mental disorders emanate directly from environmental 'stresses' which either accumulate or are related to a specific traumatic event. In this category, studies may seek to identify the environments in which stress is most likely to occur. Ongoing research is concerned with both genetic and environmental sources of mental illness— such as the tracing of cohorts through their life-history and detailed analyses of the place of the mentally ill within communities—but recent shifts towards analysis of provision of services to deal with the problem are now evident. (see Giggs, 1979)

Urban crime and delinquency

One of the most consistent findings of analyses of official crime statistics has been the association of crime rates with urbanization and the growth of cities. Crime rates over a range of offences seem to increase with urbanization and, despite the fact that some societies are well-known for 'rural crime', within any country rates tend to be higher for urban than for rural areas. Evidence to support this contention has been available from the early nineteenth century with the statistical mapping exercises of the cartographic school in France (see Phillips, 1972) and of social reformers such as Mayhew (1862), and continues to receive confirmation from a variety of contemporary sources (Connor, 1970). In addition to this link with cities *per se*, there are striking regional variations in crime rates and the most comprehensive recent work of this kind has demonstrated this fact in the United States (Harries, 1974). Perhaps the best-known American pattern is that which depicts the 'violent south' with high rates of crimes of violence in the southern states. In 1975, the southern region had 42 per cent of the nation's homicides and 75 per cent of its prisoners under sentence of death, both statistics suggestive of distinctive regional characteristics. Harries and Brunn (1978) discussed some of these characteristics and summarized them as a 'traditionalistic political culture' which in some undefined way 'nurtures' both violence itself and a set of attitudes related to it.

Although there can be little doubt that associations of crime with cities and with particular regions are real enough, most criminologists stress the need for caution in the use of official statistics (see Hindess, 1973). There are problems of the completeness of data, of the extent to which they may contain biases, and of the ways in which 'definitions' of offences are arrived at and interpreted. Crime and delinquency are defined as such by the societies in which they occur—or at least by the lawmakers—and reflect their particular traditions and value-systems.

Most western societies have experienced increases in crime in general over recent years, a fact which has aroused both concern and a closer scrutiny of effective policies of policing and sanctions. There are marked differences among societies. From 1957 to 1976 the crime rate in the United Kingdom quadrupled and between 1972 and 1976 there was a 50 per cent increase in crimes of violence. These are dramatic relative rates of increase but United Kingdom rates remain undramatic in comparison with those from the United States. In 1975 there were 493 recorded homicides in the United Kingdom but in the same year the American total was 18,780 and New York alone had 1622 homicides, followed by Chicago with 814, Detroit with 663, and Los Angeles with 501. In 1979, Oklahoma City's homicide score neared 100 and it was described in the local press as entering the 'big league'. Why American crime rates are so high is a very large question which cannot be considered here—different laws as they affect gun ownership may be one factor, as is the relative disadvantage under which many inner-city populations live—but the issues are complex and not easily summarized. Of interest is Clinard's (1978) recent attempt to characterize a society in which crime rates are very low.

There are many theories which seek to explain crime but none of these has achieved anything like universal acceptance (see Herbert, 1977a). The range of theories is considerable and extends from *structural* theories, which find the roots of criminal behaviour in the inequalities that have been created by the capitalist system, to *ecological* theories which attach more importance to group and area characteristics. Social disorganization, delinquent sub-culture, and alienation, for example, all consider the place of the individual in local social networks and frames of reference albeit in the context of the wider social system. A traditional division in theories of causation has been between those which focus on individual or genetic characteristics (Glueck and Glueck, 1950; Lombroso, 1968) and those which refer to the social environment (see Mannheim, 1965). The former point to factors which are internal to the individual—the 'criminal type'—the latter to the conditioning circumstances of the local environment in which individuals are placed and the acquired characteristics of the group *per se*. Most sociological theories relating to crime and delinquency, such as anomie and social disorganization, have only an indirect reference to local environment and relate an individual's disposition towards criminal or delinquent behaviour to the nature of the encompassing social system and the individual's place within it. More recent sociological theories of *deviance* focus on social controls and definitions and upon criminal law and the judicial system rather than upon offenders.

426

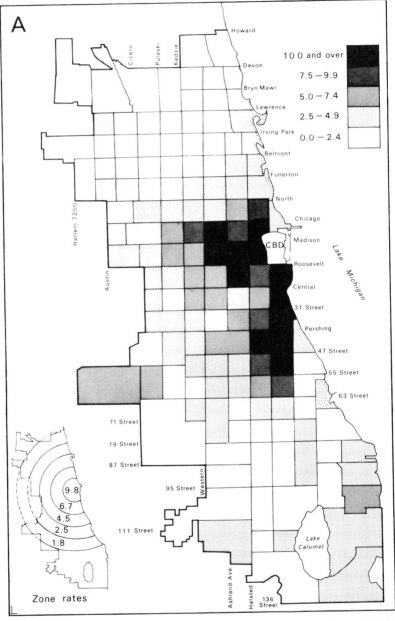

Figure 9.13   Delinquency areas in Chicago. (a) Delinquency rates for 1927/1933 per 100 males aged 10–16. (b) Delinquency rates for 1963/1966 expressed in terms of a grand mean of 1.00 (Reprinted from *Juvenile Delinquency and Urban*

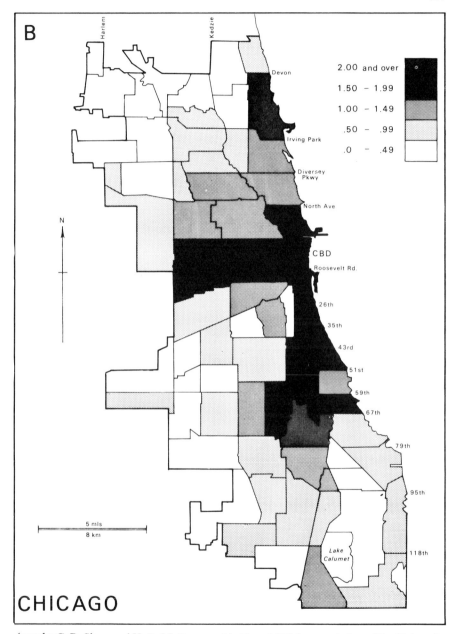

Areas by C. R. Shaw and H. D. McKay, pp. 54, 69, and 355, by permission of the University of Chicago Press; © 1942 University of Chicago Press)

Evidence for the spatial concentration of crime and delinquency within particular districts of cities has again been available for some time. Tobias (1976) has reconstructed the salient features of a nineteenth-century crime area, Booth (1891) and others have characterized parts of contemporary London in similar terms. The 'areal' hypotheses which emerged from the substantive works of Shaw and McKay (1942) in Chicago were few and simple. They observed that both offence and offender rates were highest among population groups in central zones of the city and decreased progressively towards peripheral zones (see Figure 9.13); the gradient principle replicated the zonal generalization. More recent American studies (Schmid, 1960) have tended to confirm these patterns as a generalization but studies elsewhere in the world have provided less empirical support. In this sense, crime rates may be viewed as one type of social indicator. Official statistics characterize typical offenders as low income and unskilled and incidence rates appear to be high where these population groups live. As the social geography of the American city has a broadly zonal character, a similar form typifies crime rates; in a welfare state such as Britain where interventionist housing policies redistribute low-income groups to peripheral estates, the zonal pattern of crime rates is distorted; in Third World countries where there is intermixing of servants' quarters and shanties with high-income enclaves, no simple spatial pattern of crime is evident (de Fleur, 1967). Use of crime rate as an indicator should acknowledge the existence of white-collar crime as an underrecorded and under-researched topic (D. M. Smith, 1974).

The areal hypotheses have some value, at their traditional scale of analysis, but it has always been recognized that even within high-rate zones there will be large numbers of non-offenders; the ecological fallacy has to be recognized. This is a *caveat* which typifies both the areal hypotheses which relate to spatial pattern and the ecological hypotheses which examine relationships between crime rates for areas and scores on other environmental variables.

While the areal hypotheses were derived mechanically by mapping crime statistics and generalizing upon the observed patterns, the ecological hypotheses were more directly concerned with the question of the relationship between crime rates and the urban environment in which they occurred. In a series of analyses using crime and census variables derived for small areas, the ecologists employed a variety of statistical techniques to measure this relationship. Shaw and McKay (1942) suggested that the main correlates of delinquency rates in Chicago were substandard housing, poverty, foreign-born population, and levels of mobility; some studies before this and a great many since have identified statistical groupings of a similar kind. Schmid (1960) used a multivariate analysis based upon a large number of variables, and listed low social cohesion, weak family life, low socioeconomic status, physical deterioration, mobility, and personal disorganization as the social characteristics of crime areas in Seattle. Wallis and Maliphant (1967) relied upon the simpler procedure of examining pairwise correlations, but suggested links between delinquency rates and overcrowding, substandardness, population decline, non-white residents, and low socioeconomic status in London. Most of these analyses of aggregate data would acknowledge that a statistical association is not necessarily a causal one and have looked at more general hypotheses to provide explanations. For Shaw and McKay, for example, social disorganization theory provided the key, and although criticized (Mays, 1963) it did find recent support in the work by Baldwin and Bottoms (1976). For purposes of discussion, three ecological hypotheses will be identified and two of these tested with empirical data.

The first hypothesis, for which no further empirical evidence will be offered here, is that proposed by Lander (1954) as a result of his study of Baltimore. Lander used a number of correlational and regression techniques to analyse associations between delinquency rates and seven social variables (education, rent, overcrowding, non-white, substandardness, foreign-born, and owner-occupance). His hypothesis, from the results of this analysis, was that the concept of anomie was a valid explanatory basis for the incidence of delinquency in Baltimore. Lander based this hypothesis upon the observed links between high delinquency rates and percentage of non-white (positive) and level of owner-occupance (negative) and, also, from observation of the nature of an area's ethnic mix. Some debate has been generated by Lander's findings and methodology (Chilton, 1964; Gordon, 1967), but whether a complex sociological theory such as that of anomie can be proven or otherwise by ecological analysis is doubtful, and this particular hypothesis has not been explicitly supported in replicative research.

A second hypothesis, and one which has found most general support in ecological analyses, is that of the effect of 'poor environment'. Statistical studies using indicators of built environmental disadvantage such as sub-standard housing, and social problems such as unemployment and poverty have demonstrated their correspondence with high rates of delinquency. There is ample evidence that simplistic interpretations of links between bad housing and crime are misplaced but correlates with measures of bad social environment are more persistent. Table 9.5 provides an example of evidence supportive of the poor environment hypothesis. These figures are drawn from a detailed statistical analysis of Cardiff data (Herbert, 1977a) in which, for the regression part of the study which is reported here, delinquency rate formed the dependent variable and sixteen independent variables were derived from census data. Before the regression analysis was applied, the sixteen independent variables were subjected to a varimax rotation in factor analysis and the derived factor scores formed the input to regression. This procedure has the advantage of ensuring the statistical independence of the 'independent' variables. As Table 9.5 shows, step one, identifying the most closely linked independent variable, designated a factor positively associated with owner-occupance and high social status. From the evidence in this table, high delinquency rates occur in those parts of the city that suffer poor built environments, as indicated by lack of amenities and fixed baths, and poor social environments, as indicated by high levels of unemployment, shared dwellings and overcrowding. As the

Table 9.5 Delinquency rates and social variables: a regression analysis (Cardiff, 1971)

Regression step	Factor	High loadings	Standard error	Cumulative R^2	Regression coefficient	Standard error
1	3	+ overcrowding unemployed males − owner-occupiers − social class 1 + 2	1.72	0.15	0.71	0.16
2	5	+ unemployed males foreign-born	1.60	0.27	0.71 0.64	0.15 0.15
3	2	+ no amenities no fixed bath shared dwellings − social class 1 + 2	1.51	0.36	0.71 0.64 0.54	0.14 0.14 0.14

NB The independent variables are varimax scores from factor analysis of the sixteen socioeconomic–demographic measures derived from the Census. Source: Herbert (1979).

Table 9.6 Offender rates* by housing (tenure) class in Cardiff

1966	council	rented	owner-occupied	mixed	all districts	overall SD**
Number of EDs	28	6	74	11	119	
Male 10–19	29	45	18	33	23	20
Female 10–19	5	50	5	12	8	24
Male 15–19	46	60	27	34	34	37
1971						
Number of EDs	28	14	64	13	119	
Male 10–19	40	59	24	39	33	29
Female 10–19	11	13	6	12	9	11
Male 15–19	63	90	35	66	51	47

*Offender rates = number of known juvenile offenders per 1000 population at risk.
**SD = standard deviation.
Source: Herbert (1979)

ordering of factors in Table 9.5 suggests, deficiencies in the social environment are of greatest significance and these findings, generally supportive of the poor environment hypothesis, are typical of many research findings.

The third hypothesis is of more recent origin, though some of the earlier evidence can be discerned in Lander's (1954) study of Baltimore. Baldwin and Bottoms (1976), with some reference to an earlier concept developed by Rex and Moore (1967) proposed a 'housing class' hypothesis on the basis of their empirical study of Sheffield. This hypothesis suggests that crime rates are lower in owner-occupier tenure groups than in rented tenure groups. On examining the proposition that this variation was simply a reflection of social class differences, Baldwin and Bottoms found that, for adult male offenders, the link between tenure group and offender rates remained even when socio-economic status differences were controlled. They concluded that in considering the pattern of adult male offender rates, 'It is essential to bear in mind type of tenure area in addition to social class' (Baldwin and Bottoms, 1976, p. 111).

It was possible to test this hypothesis using data for Cardiff in 1966 and 1971. Using the procedure adopted by Baldwin and Bottoms (1976), enumeration districts in Cardiff were classified as owner-occupied, local authority-rented, private-rented, or mixed. This procedure involved, for designation of the first three categories, the requirement that over one-half of households should fall into the particular tenure group. Table 9.6 shows the distribution of mean offender rates for three subgroups by the four classes of tenure type in Cardiff. In each case it is clear that offender rates in the owner-occupier group are well below city averages and are substantially below those recorded for other tenure groups. Highest offender rates occur in the private-rented sector (though it should be noted that the number of enumeration districts in this group is small) and are also relatively high on local authority estates.

On the straightforward comparison of mean offender rates, therefore, the Cardiff evidence is supportive of that reported for Sheffield, but it remains, however, to test the independence of the relationship from socioeconomic status. The calculation of partial correlation coefficients among five variables, three of which described tenure groups and two the social class composition of the enumeration districts reveals some limited support for the 'housing class' hypothesis, though still at a descriptive level. A low-order correlation −0.2 remains between delinquency rate and owner-occupance even when social class differences are controlled. This is true of three of the offender rates, and the limited-housing class hypothesis which can be supported is that owner-occupiership appears to have *some* influence upon offender rates regardless of social-class variations. This influence, by implication, is one which deters criminal behaviour, but although plausible reasons could be formulated for this—ownership of property places the interests of people on the side of maintenance of law and order, and such areas are more benevolently viewed by law enforcers—these can only be conjectural from evidence at this scale of analysis.

Ecological analysis, though possessing a useful role in identifying the contextual circumstances in which crime and delinquency are likely to occur and therefore suggesting ameliorative measures, does suffer severe problems in the extension of statistically measured associations into theoretical constructs. Taylor (1973) was critical of ways in which ecologists had yielded to the temptation to progress from observations on characteristics of urban life to theories, which view offenders as products of particular local environmental features. What is not understood is how these environments look to the offenders themselves. The Chicago ecologists saw dereliction, diversity, and transience as underpinnings of delinquency, Fyvel (1961) suggested that modernity, uniformity, and stability had similar effects. Both were objective analyses of local environments, but more significant may have been the subjective images of youths themselves. Again, it is critically important to remember that while local environment may provide clues or pointers, it is in itself merely one expression of the encompassing societal structure which provides the broader frame of reference.

Empirical research into the spatial ecology of crime statistics has shown the importance of making a number of distinctions. Firstly, the distinction between the spatial ecology of offences, where the criminal act is committed, and of offenders, where the criminals live. Secondly, between crime and delinquency with the latter confined to juvenile offenders, usually between the ages of ten and nineteen years, though the classification of their offences is common. Thirdly, there is a need to distinguish among the many types of offence on official lists; the 'geography' of shoplifting is clearly very different from that of homicide, for instance.

When Shaw and McKay (1942) conducted their original research in Chicago they focused on delinquency data for offenders, and their 'delinquency areas' were those in which disproportionately large numbers of juvenile offenders lived. With their objective indicators such as unemployment, poverty, and mobility they characterized these delinquency areas and the theories, such as social organization, were a product of their empirical research. Using similar methodologies, delinquency areas can in relative terms be identified and characterized in most cities; the comparative use of the concept has to be handled with care; a delinquency area in Glasgow or Detroit, for example, is likely to be of different dimensions from a delinquency area in Swansea or San Diego. Such delinquency areas are no longer confined to old inner-city districts; the problem estate has for some time been a feature of British cities. More recent research has sought to identify the subjective environments of such areas. Herbert (1976, 1979) described a study of Cardiff in which six districts were selected for detailed investigation in a controlled area-sampling framework. Areas were controlled for objective characteristics, such as demographic structure, socioeconomic status, and tenure type, and also in terms of delinquency rates. Two districts for example, were low income, inner city but one of these had a much higher delinquency rate; three public sector housing projects were included but two had high and one low rates of delinquency. Within this framework, the objective was to investigate variations in the subjective environments of the selected districts. Evidence was found to be

434

supportive of the hypothesis that deficiencies in the subjective environments of some districts were associated with above-average delinquency rates. In the 'delinquency areas', parents made more use of physical punishment, were less dedicated to the educational prowess of their children, and had 'weak' or blurred definitions of the differences between right and wrong. This set of characteristics typified both the inner-city delinquency areas and the peripherally located 'problem estates'.

Identification of individual offenders in this study allowed some insights into patterns and processes at a micro-scale. Data were not complete but did allow homes of individual offenders to be plotted and, from knowledge of other individuals with whom they associated in commission of a specific offence, links could be made (see Figure 9.14). Several comments can be made on this exercise. Firstly, notwithstanding the fact that the data comprise only a one-year sample and that 'hidden' delinquency must be acknowledged, the fact that delinquent households form a minority within a high-rate area is demonstrated. Secondly, the links among offenders cannot be explained in any simple terms of distance–decay. The 'neighbourhood' as a whole seems a relevant frame of reference (there were very few links outside the immediate

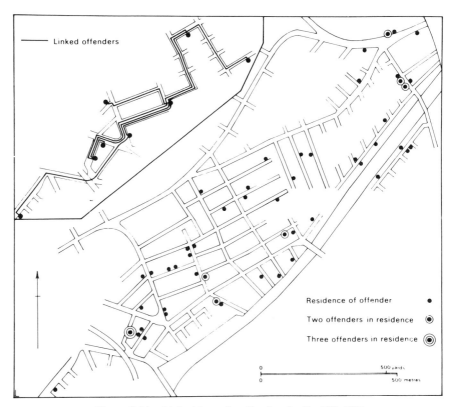

Figure 9.14   Linked juvenile offenders in Cardiff, 1971

locality) rather than adjacent houses or even streets. It should be noted that apart from a 100 per cent house-to house survey, there is no way of ascertaining which households contain juveniles in the relevant age range. Other points of conflux such as school, club or workplace are probably significant and there was a strong 'cohort effect', in other words, most members of one group were of the same age. Thirdly, the links suggest that there are delinquent networks at a neighbourhood scale which may add to the more general 'contagion' effect (Johnston, 1974), hypothesized for residential areas.

Studies of this kind qualify the traditional areal and ecological hypotheses. They show both the need to experiment with different scales of analysis and with new forms of data. Delinquency areas exist but the variations and nuances within them may also be of significance (see also Morris, 1957). Evidence indicates that hidden delinquency is of considerable proportions but would probably have the effect of confirming currently held generalizations on the incidence of high rates. The most ominous hypothesis concerning delinquency areas is that the chances of an individual becoming an offender is greater if he or she lives in such a district. Questions of why and how such problem areas emerge and persist become relevant. The nineteenth-century 'rookeries' are more comprehensible than their equivalents, albeit in a diluted form, in modern cities. British research on this question has focused on those local authority estates which have acquired reputations as foci of offenders, vandalism, and other expressions of social malaise.

Baldwin (1975) suggests that in Sheffield the continuing problem of criminality remains, for the most part, on those local authority estates built in the 1930s or earlier; these are the 'problem estates' and are so regarded by local population, local agencies, social workers and police alike. Several significant studies (Damer, 1974; Gill, 1977) have examined such problem areas in detail and suggest that the characteristics of the initial occupants of the estate and subsequent labelling are key features. In both of these study-areas, the original occupations came from slum-clearance schemes with adverse reputations and which were located in other parts of the city. A similar situation could be detected in Cardiff's Ely estate (Herbert, 1979) which was occupied by slum-clearance tenants from a district called Grangetown near the docks who were also distinguished by the fact that they were both Irish and Catholic. The estate kept its reputation even though the actual record was no worse than other districts; single incidents appear to have been exaggerated disproportionately.

Most studies have attributed considerable significance to the attitudes held by official agencies, by the housing managers, rent collectors, welfare services and in particular the police who may patrol the area intensively and thus enable more offences to enter official records. Figure 9.15 summarizes these factors and adds the extra dimension suggested by Wilson (1963) as a result of a Bristol survey. This argues that once an estate is established with a particular type of reputation, it tends to be reinforced by a self-selection process among applicants for tenancies. Families on the waiting list with higher social aspirations are prepared to wait longer for a 'better' estate, whereas those with low

436

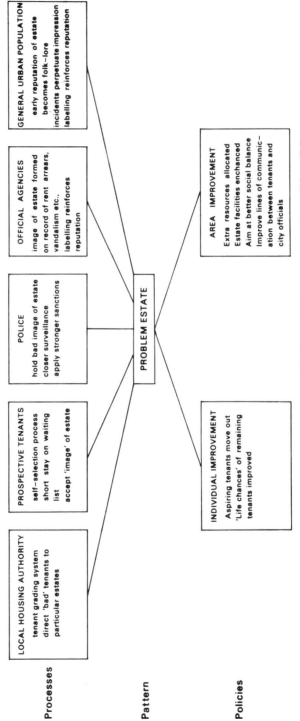

Figure 9.15   Problem estates: factors contributing to their emergence and possible policies

aspirations accept vacancies on less-attractive estates and tend to perpetuate existing attitudes and forms of behaviour.

Much recent 'explanation' for the incidence of high offender rates in inner-city districts and public-sector estates has been couched in structural terms (Peet, 1975; Taylor, Walton, and Young, 1973). Accumulated disadvantage is seen as the general source of frustrations of which crime is but one expression. Structural effects do not, however, provide a total picture. Not all poor areas have high offender rates, not all households in delinquency areas contain offenders. There are local effects to be considered which may help to explain variations with reference to the different environmental stimuli—objective and subjective—to which the individual is exposed.

One of the more promising avenues for research in crime lies in the detailed analysis of offences rather than of offenders. Newman's (1972) ideas on defensible space focusing on the possibilities of prevention through design (see also Chapter 8) have at least stimulated research, and the experiences of projects such as Pruitt Igoe in St Louis and Bijlmermeer in Amsterdam have sharpened the interest of planners. Newman's empirical evidence from surveys on New York public-housing projects suggests that an area would be well 'defended' if it was visible, if a community spirit develops to control neutral space, and if private territory is clearly demarcated physically or symbolically. Key features are thus observability, surveillance and the meanings attached to space. Some of these ideas have been paralleled in work by social geographers on the occurrence patterns of some offences (Ley and Cybriwsky, 1974b) and also more generally in the framework of humanistic geography. The thesis here revolves around the meanings attached to place and space and the existence of local control systems. A Philadelphia study on 'stripped cars' showed that it was in the vacua of local control systems that offences were likely to occur. Some preliminary work in Swansea also finds some support for the 'meaning-of-place' hypothesis. Within what at an aggregate level appears to be a general zone of high burglary rates, the one district which could be described as a cohesive community with low levels of transience, was also the least burgled.

Several studies have examined the offence environment at a micro-scale. Pablant and Baxter (1975) tested and found support for three main hypotheses related to school vandalism: low rates will typify well-maintained, attractive schools, those located in active neighbourhoods, and those placed at visible sites. These findings are supportive of Newman's thesis but Mawby's (1977a, 1977b) more critical arguments are derived from an empirical study of Sheffield. Using data for four estates, labelled council housing (CH) and council flats (CF) with high (H) or low (L) *offender* rates, it was found that when rates per 1000 for residential *offences* were calculated, a contrasted pattern (CHH 85.1; CHL 23.7; CFH 29.9; CFL 20.2) appeared. The fact that the highest offence rate was recorded for low-rise housing contradicted one of Newman's central ideas. More importantly, Mawby noted that Newman had failed to clarify some of his concepts; individual components of the built environment could, for example, have more than one role, dependent upon the ways in which they

438

were perceived by offenders. A garden could in itself present opportunities for theft, but it could also act as a barrier to the house or even diminish the visibility factor for the burglar. In another reported investigation, Mawby (1977b) obtained data on 27 telephone kiosks in Sheffield which had above-average vandalism rates. His evidence suggested that a number of available hypotheses for high rates of vandalism, such as adjacency to high-rise flats could be discarded, but that when levels of usage were controlled for, a relationship did exist between visibility and vandalism. Mawby, therefore, supported one of the defensible-space concepts, but again commented upon its ambiguity. Greater use of public space provides more 'witnesses' and increases its visibility, but it also provides more potential offenders. Visibility may have protected kiosks in Sheffield, but those which were most publicly sited had higher vandalism rates simply through greater usage.

Mayhew *et al.* (1979) have also tested aspects of defensible space in a series of studies. An analysis of vandalism of telephone kiosks was not supportive of some of Mawby's findings on the same theme, but neither could much importance be attached to the casual surveillance aspect of the defensible space concept. Results showed most vandalism affected kiosks on council estates, in areas of high unemployment and low socioeconomic status, and in districts with large numbers of youths. The significant correlates were at the standard ecological scale and classified prone *areas* rather than individual *site* characteristics. This finding was judged to be consistent with Newman's (1976) later work on the social makeup of the surrounding area. Another study

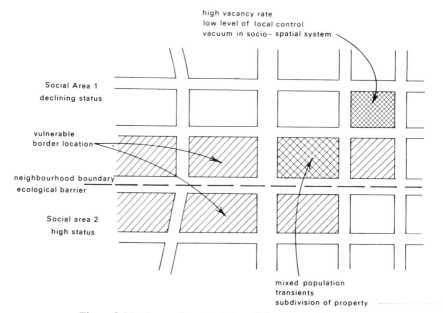

Figure 9.16   Some characteristics of the vulnerable area

of housing projects in London (Clarke, 1978) found child density and numbers of children to be key variables in vandalism rather than qualities of design. It did suggest, however, that in the future design of housing estates principles of defensible space should be incorporated.

Research by Brantingham and Brantingham (1975) has identified some useful features at a neighbourhood scale for the analysis of patterns of burglary. The study involved the classification of the city into neighbourhoods as a framework against which to study burglary rates. A principal conclusion was that border blocks between neighbourhoods proved the most vulnerable and explanation was couched in terms of the anonymity which such blocks offered and the unwillingness of offenders to venture too far from familiar territory (see Figure 9.16). In some ways this study adds an extra dimension to defensible space—in other words, the further within a neighbourhood a block is located the less vulnerable it will be—and accords with some of Sennett's (1973) ideas of neighbourhood as refuge or haven in which intruders are easily recognized. Yet this type of study is limited because it seeks to interpret the behaviour of the offender in terms of an offence pattern which serves as an indicator of his activities. There is research which attempts to understand offence behaviour by direct surveys of offenders. Scarr (1972) studied a sample of burglars and suggested that there were perceived opportunity areas; Repetto (1974) also questioned burglars and identified key factors such as identified affluence, low levels of policing, ease of access and isolation as *desiderata* of a 'target'; and R. L. Carter (1974) produced empirical evidence to show that criminals discriminated among areas of the city according to familiarity and excitement. In this last study, samples of both black and white criminals were matched with non-criminals in Oklahoma City. White offenders were found to have a greater range of perceived favourable alternatives than blacks who were spatially restricted. For both groups, upper and middle-income areas were attractive but unfamiliar and were regarded as having strong police protection, and targets were selected in nearer, more familiar districts.

Several aspects of the geographical study of crime and delinquency may lead to public policy-related conclusions. In terms of offenders and problem areas the finding of local effects prompts ameliorative measures in terms of welfare services, inputs of social justice and local organizations. The need to reach parents and to improve the subjective environments in which children are placed is clear. In terms of offence patterns the priority may be that of providing guidelines to crime prevention, with ideas on design, land use and space and ways in which social awareness of place may be increased. Spatial analysis with its roles in planning of services is one policy input, community-based studies on attitudes towards offences, offenders, safety and security is another. Recent work on differential attitudes and practices by police and courts may have roles in reducing spatial injustice. Harries and Brunn (1978) have shown for the United States that there are wide regional variations in sentencing levels, court procedures and use of prosecuting discretion. They advanced a number of specific proposals to increase efficiency and equity in court administrations from the basis of an essentially geographical perspective on laws and justice.

Old people in cities

Within most societies there are minority groups, unified on the basis of one or more characteristics, which suffer from disadvantage. Best-known and most closely studied of these are those minority groups which can be distinguished on ethnic grounds and some of their problems have already been discussed; other groups are made distinctive by their religious beliefs and cultural backgrounds. Demographic characteristics have played some role in residential segregation—as witnessed by the significance of the stage in lifecycle or familism dimension in factorial ecologies—and there is some evidence that one demographically defined group, the elderly, is currently typified by above-average levels of deprivation and disadvantage. For the large majority this is an inevitable consequence of growing old. Retirement from employment means a significant loss of income and retirement migration to amenable environments is a minority prerogative. Old age often involves increasing disability, loss of mobility, and greater dependency on others.

There are clear reasons why life-expectancy should continue to rise in western societies and equally clear indications that this is happening. In the United States in 1900, 4.1 per cent of the population was over 65 years of age, and by 1970 it was 9.9 per cent. Many states exceeded this figure by a wide margin, with Florida heading the list with 16.4 per cent, followed by Arkansas with 13.2 per cent and Iowa with 12.8 per cent. California's 2.1 million old people formed 9.9 per cent of the state population. Florida's position is in large part a reflection of its attractiveness to retirement migrants moving to the 'sunbelt' and most countries have similar 'retirement areas'. British retirees show some migration flows to coastal districts such as North Wales and the south coast of England (Law and Warnes, 1980) and, in Canada, west coast cities such as Victoria fill similar roles. Such migration flows are of interest and are increasing but for the large majority of old people such choices are not available and they are likely to spend their old age in the cities where they have spent the latter part of their working lives. The constraints which lead to this decision may be reinforced by a preference to remain within an established network of neighbours, friends and relatives. This may pose its own problems. Eckert (1979) estimates that many of the 6.8 million elderly who live in American inner cities occupy single rooms in cheap hotels and rooming-houses in areas that are often scheduled for renewal or redevelopment; they rely upon local services and people but are in fact living in areas of rapid change. Golant (1980) estimates that in 1970, 55 per cent of America's elderly lived in urbanized areas; 34 per cent occupied central cities where they formed 11 per cent of the total population as against 21 per cent in suburbs representing 7 per cent of that population group. Golant (1975, 1980) predicts increasing clustering of old people into a range of 'nodes' dispersed throughout the urbanized area, perhaps reinforced by planned or semi-planned components which include retirement residences and hotels, trailer villages, low-rent public housing projects and intermediate (sheltered) housing.

One qualification which needs to be made consistently with reference to the elderly is that they do not constitute a uniform group. Normally an age-limit, typically over 65 years, is taken as a definition but one product of increasing longevity is that as the age-span beyond 65 years increases, there is a significant range within the age-group labelled as elderly. There are large numbers of over 75 year-olds and some studies already distinguish between the 'young-old' and the 'old-old'. Again, chronological age is a crude indicator. Variables such as health and morale are involved (Herbert and Peace, 1980) and ageing is a multidimensional process, the product of social contexts as well as of biological and psychological conditions. These characteristics affect the individual in different ways and are central to the achievement of 'successful' ageing; hazards of old age such as chronic illness—mental or physical—and increasing disability are strongly inhibiting factors. Most theories stress the need to measure these individual characteristics before attempting to incorporate the effects of exogenous or environmental influences.

The more competent the organism in terms of health, intelligence, ego-strength, role-performance, or cultural evolution, the less will be the proportion of variance in behaviour attributable to physical objects or conditions around him (Lawton and Simon, 1968, p. 108).

Whereas the accuracy of this statement can be recognized, it is also clear that considerable problems of measurement are posed in any attempt to evaluate competence. Rosow and Breslau (1966) adopted a functional scale of health based on ability to climb stairs and other measures; Herbert and Peace (1980) used attitudinal questions on state of health and mobility to grade their survey respondents. There have been several attempts to measure the morale of the elderly. Lawton's (1970) 22-item scale is the best known of these and incorporated indices of stress, boredom, and satisfaction; Neugarten (1968) also developed what he termed a 'life satisfaction index'.

These attempts to recognize significant subgroups within the elderly population are an important part of any research strategy. As important, however, is the need to evaluate the increasing environmental constraints which are imposed upon the elderly. As Rowles (1978, p. 22) has argued:

The elderly gradually become prisoners of space. Certainly some individuals remain active and mobile into their advanced old age . . . for many older persons physiological decline, economic deprivation and traumatizing effects of rapid societal change, herald physical, social and psychological withdrawal. This withdrawal, it is implied, is accompanied by progressive construction of the individual's geographical life-span and associated intensification of attachment to the proximate environmental context.

Although the diversity within the elderly population must be acknowledged, there are common bonds which help to distinguish them as a subgroup. The fact that they have generally finished their active working lives is a key feature; the elderly have a considerable amount of time to occupy in recreational and leisure activities, the large majority are 'dependent' in some way upon others. Increasing age may often mean decreasing mobility and the dependence upon locality becomes greater, the local environments assume greater significance not only as a provider of services but also as a 'caring' community. Personal mobility clearly decreases among old people. In Florida, 89 per cent of the adult population is licensed to drive, but only 52 per cent of the 65 to 75-year-olds and only 39 per cent of those over 75 years of age. Societies with low rates of car ownership show similar relative differences at much lower absolute levels. Again, as Birren (1970, pp. 37–8) points out.

the old become discouraged by environmental obstacles which would not inhibit the young—high bus steps, the need to cross wide busy streets, to catch a bus, fast-changing traffic lights, high curbs, and inadequate building labels. The aged may do without banks, doctors, repair services, dentists, shops, lawyers and parks because of the energy it takes to get to them.

This vulnerability to environmental obstacles affects the normal activity patterns of the elderly and the capacity for social interaction and also their access to key services which the community offers at specific locations.

The principal theories of ageing reflect some of these constricting attitudes to life-space, though they are largely founded in terms of social rather than spatial relationships. *Disengagement theory* postulates that old people will tend to turn inwards psychologically, a process which may be closely linked with key events such as retirement or loss of spouse. This kind of psychological disengagement is followed by social disengagement in which the old person moves into new and qualitatively different relationships with society which 'withdraws' from the old person. An extreme stage in terms of this theory would be a 'subculture of the elderly'. *Activity theory* suggests that old people will attempt to prolong the pattern of middle-age for as long as possible despite the process of chronological ageing. Roles will be maintained even though substitutes may be found for those which are lost. Palmore (1979) found some support for activity theory with the suggestion that men and women who are most active in organizations and who engage in more physical activity are more likely to age successfully. *Continuity theory*, unlike disengagement or activity theory, does not have a developmental basis. Its principal statement is that a person will generally wish to maintain familiar roles but will adapt and substitute these as need be, giving the individual a neverending capacity to change. None of these theories has achieved universal acceptance, and clearly there are compromise positions to be explored and the dimension of individual differences to be considered.

How can the elderly be studied in their urban environments? One task is to identify the elements of environment which are relevant, and Yeates (1979) categorized these as personal space or room geography, design space/neighbourhood, small cities, large cities/metropolitan areas and rural areas. Michelson's (1970) more generalized 'systems' approach was composed of social, cultural, psychological, behavioural and environmental variables. Whereas Yeates focuses upon different 'scales', Michelson's emphasis is upon functional roles; the two are clearly interrelated and time is an extra dimension. Both Yeates and Michelson concentrate upon the objective qualities of environment, but Rowles (1978) examines subjective qualities which he categorizes as action, orientation, feeling, and fantasy. This initial task in itself therefore identifies a multivariate and complex context. Successive tasks are to relate different subgroups of old people to these environments in order to understand their activities and reactions. There have been specific attempts to conceptualize the age–environment relationship. Pastalan and Carson's (1970) idea of an age–loss continuum has evolved in a concept of changing 'life-space' during the ageing process. The *environmental-docility* theory in its original form postulated declining competence to deal with environmental problems; the more prescriptive environmental congruence idea seeks to match individuals to suitable environmental circumstances. All of these conceptual positions are based on the assumption that ageing involves a decreasing ability to cope with 'normal' urban environments; old people therefore face diminishing life-space, limited activity patterns, and 'stresses' in environment which do not concern other demographic groups. This is an assumption which has found the expected high level of support from empirical research; the Swansea study (Herbert and Peace, 1980) confirmed that increasing age usually involves greater limits of movement and interest, though it did also show that an individual's state of health and morale provide important sources of information.

A number of recent studies have investigated the place of old people in urban environments with emphases on levels of satisfaction, patterns of activity, and imagery. Bohland and Davis (1979) show that old people structure neighbourhood satisfaction in ways similar to younger persons, the greatest observed contrast being, in fact, with the 55 to 64-year-old group. Spirit of 'neighbourliness' and physical appearance of neighbourhood was judged important but safety had a surprisingly low rating. This last point should be qualified by the fact that the sample areas were not inner city. Conner, Powers, and Bultena (1979) found that quality rather than quantity of relationships was the key feature of adjustment and satisfaction with living area. The content of social networks, especially siblings and other close family, was diagnostic together with the extent to which social interaction was centred around key individuals with close family bonds. The elderly may be heavily constrained within urban environments but given key ingredients, such as intense relationships and care, their levels of satisfaction may be high; as Rowles (1978 p. 216) argues: 'the old may be prisoners of space but it can also be a jail without walls'.

The activity patterns of old people are limited, trip frequencies are lower, and total distances travelled are less than those of other age-groups. Declining ability to drive cars leads to an increasing reliance on public transport and an American survey calculated thresholds at which dissatisfaction with services became dominant. For a bus-stop the threshold was placed at three blocks from home, for a grocery a quarter-mile, for a restaurant a halfmile, and for a

444

drugstore one mile (1.6 km) In Swansea, Herbert and Peace (1980) found distance to be a major constraint and few respondents claimed an ability to walk more than quarter of a mile in each direction. Community facilities were used in inverse proportions to the distances that individuals were removed from them, and any organized activities needed to provide transport. Studies of the images which the elderly hold of the environments in which they live suggest congnitive maps which are constricted in both content and dimensions, though Rowles's ideas on the role of fantasy are important. Regnier (1974) shows that old people have a strong sense of neighbourhood and delineate its 'core' to produce an image over which a high level of consensus is evident. More active old people with high socioeconomic status tend to have more extensive images and other contributory variables are good health, long residence and participation in specialized activity interests. In Swansea, elderly

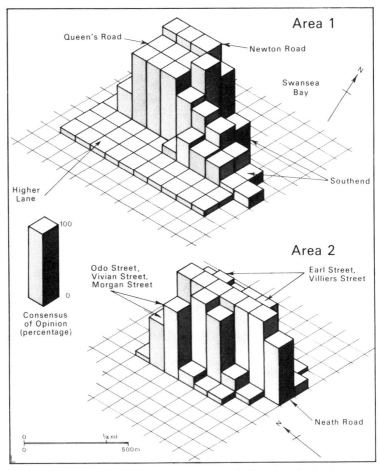

Figure 9.17 Images of elderly people: neighbourhoods in Swansea. (after Herbert and Peace, 1980)

respondents in two areas were asked to delineate their 'neighbourhood' graphically and identified 'core' areas which were commonly perceived (see Figure 9.17); results pointed to a strong sense of place and well-defined images of locality. The critical point from the study by Rowles (1978) is that physical activity amongst the elderly has to be considered in relation to their mental activity; the pleasure which they derive from observing the activities of others, and the ability to draw upon reservoirs of memories and life experiences are highly significant facets of their wellbeing. Surveillance zones are thus important and residential design should accept this as a priority.

Studies have been able to demonstrate spatial clustering of the elderly at regional and local scales but do not support the idea of a 'geriatric ghetto'. Many who are able to change residence on retirement do so, but the large majority have to spend old age in the same environments in which they have lived for many years. The problems they face are therefore those of the population at large but these assume greater proportions and meaning for old people. In this context the increasing numbers of old people occupying inner-city areas is a cause for concern. A range of special services is being developed and this may help the elderly to cope. Examples are reduced bus fares, better design of buses, careful location of services, mobile facilities such as meals-on-wheels, in addition to the increasing range of types of residential accomodation. Present policies favour deinstitutionalization and a greater reliance on community services, trends probably in line with preferences held by the elderly. One estimate suggests that 5 per cent of old people live permanently in institutions but 20 per cent spend *some* time there during their postretirement years. As the emphasis shifts away from institutions the need to provide community services and attitudes which ensure the right environment for 'successful' ageing becomes an imperative.

SUMMARY

This chapter has discussed a number of urban problems, some of which are a consequence of the wider and ongoing process of urbanization, others are directly or indirectly manifestations of societal conditions which find expression, often in exaggerated form, within urban environments. As the urbanization process continues and as individual cities grow larger, so the visible evidence of urban problems will become more apparent. Urban geographers have for many years been concerned with research which is 'relevant' to real problems but during the 1970s this concern has become more sharply focused. The emphasis in this chapter has been upon research which seeks to enhance our *understanding* of urban problems; in the chapter which follows this emphasis will shift to the search for solutions and attempts to bridge the gap between academic research and public policy.

Chapter 10

Urban Trends and Urban Policies

URBANIZATION AND URBAN GEOGRAPHY

The global trend towards increased levels of urbanization, which has characterized virtually the whole of the twentieth century, continues to dominate processes of human settlement over its last two decades. Whereas this is by no means an even process over time and space, its most general outcome remains the large city. The dynamism inherent in urbanization, however, affects the form which these cities take and, more critically, there are functional changes which modify the organization of the urban system. Advanced countries have, through the urbanization process, been transformed into closely interconnected urban systems in which distinctions between town and country have become blurred. As Third World societies, generations later, experience broadly comparable 'stages' of the urbanization process, they meet the challenges of large cities in completely different circumstances. They lack the capital, the technology and the organization to cope with the enormous pressures of urban population growth and the demand for basic facilities which these create. The 'planned' or 'command' societies of the USSR, eastern Europe and China occupy some broad intermediate bands in which pressures of urbanization probably exist but are controlled by absence of free movement between rural districts and cities.

A rapidly increasing awareness of the extent to which the process of urbanization and the cities which it produces are shaped by the macro-features of the societies within which they occur, has been a significant feature of urban geography in the past decade. Vance (1978) argues that cities are shaped by institutions of many kinds and his categorization of these includes social, economic, governmental, religious and cultural groupings. Major differences between twentieth-century urbanization in Britain and the United States, for example, can be related to the contrasted attitudes of governmental and financial institutions. Explicable in such terms is the twentieth-century divergence in attitudes to low-cost housing provision with a social welfare mechanism being adopted in Britain and a market principle in the United States. Dicken and Lloyd (1981) argue that modern industrial society is becoming increasingly characterized by very large organizations, in both private and public sectors. For people living in such societies, much of their day-to-day lives is conducted by, or for, large impersonal bureaucratic institutions; values held and decisions made in these institutions permeate downwards through society and have considerable influence. Institutional influences of this kind are macro enough but even wider societal forces can be suggested. Walker (1978), for example, sees modern urbanization within the United States as part and parcel of a larger process of capitalist development in which the choice of urban solution is sharply circumscribed by the structural imperatives of the capitalist mode of production. For Walker, a distinctive twentieth-century form of urban growth and suburbanization corresponds to the stage of modern corporate capitalism; the imperatives of a market society will be revealed in the continual struggle to accumulate and create a built environment in harmony with the needs of capital rather than labour.

A general feature of contemporary urban geography, therefore, is some recognition at least of the need to understand the interplay between 'structural' and local effects, to relate spatial outcomes to the macro-societal levels at which they originate. This 'macro' level can be interpreted in various ways. For Walker (1978) it is clearly the political economy, for Dicken and Lloyd (1981) it is the organization of big business and the multinational company, and for Vance (1978) it is the 'institution' in more diverse forms. All of the *integrating* themes have virtue. Whereas there is an inescapable logic in tracing inequalities in urban environments back to the political economy, there is also merit in tracing the impacts of decisions made in the boardrooms of multinational companies or agencies of the state on local housing markets. If this kind of analysis can be seen as a unifying general thrust, there is far less evidence of uniformity in terms of methodology. The range of methodological perspectives is formidable, is novel in the geographical literature, and has provided indications of divergence and contradiction in recent years. This present eclecticism of epistemologies can be identified as a source of strength rather than of weakness. It demonstrates a vigour in geographical research and a new willingness to explore in depth the philosophical bases upon which the discipline is practised. For eclecticism of this kind, which offers a range of methodological perspectives including Marxism, phenomenology, and logical positivism, to remain a source of strength there are some essential conditions. Firstly, differences in approach should be accommodated within a disciplinary framework such as that suggested by a 'branching' model (Herbert and Johnston, 1978) or by different 'levels of analysis' (Herbert, 1979). Secondly, advocates of different positions should recognize the possibilities at least of flexibility at some junctures and the need for 'openings' which enable constructive dialogue between apparently alternative perspectives.

A further outcome of the shift to studies which seek to integrate structural and local effects has been the adding of a new dimension to the long-established tradition of comparative studies. Such comparative studies in cross-cultural contexts which preferably involve contrasted political economies, should attempt to relate basic differences, at a macro-societal scale to forms of output at the consumption level. Comparative studies of socialist and capitalist states, for example, are still rare and could relate particular forms of urban environment to the policy-circumstances which produced them. Pahl has argued this *desideratum* for some time:

A systematic sociology of the *system of rational redistribution* to compare with more *price regulating systems* is urgently needed (Pahl, 1977, p. 55)

Again, different epistemologies could be applied to the same empirical issue, or, rather more narrowly, comparative research might focus on specific institutions, such as housing finance, and relate national policies and organizational characteristics to outcomes in local housing markets. Other comparative themes might be drawn from the geography of welfare (D.M. Smith, 1977). Analyses of health-care systems and social services provision, for example, could be related to the varying forms of organization in different societies. Whereas much urban geography has been concerned with the developed world and very largely with the first world of advanced capitalist economies, there is a quickening of research interest in other types of societies and a recognition of the fact that over-restricted approaches have typified much of the existing literature. Abu-Lughod and Hay (1979) emphasize the need to break away from an analysis of Third World urbanization which: (a) is too narrow in terms of both time and space; (b) views the city as a self-contained entity within the larger society, and (c) places too much credence on the competitive and impersonal qualities of socioeconomic processes.

Much of the thrust towards a better theoretical conceptualization of the urbanization process as a whole is emerging from analyses in various parts of the Third World. There has been a strong theory-development in relation to Third World urbanization and even though some of the deficiencies of evolutionary theory, modernization theory and dependency theory are now being recognized, the outcome of current debate may be a more dynamic and potentially incisive conceptual framework (Burgess, 1982; Portes and Browning, 1976). These theories are of central relevance to urban geographers as is the need to extend their own research priorities of 'integration' and comparative studies into Third World situations. Although the Third World is moving towards urbanization, there are parts of Africa, especially south of the Sahara and on its eastern coast, which remain relatively unurbanized, and here the possibilities of understanding potential outcomes before the process has matured remain a feasibility. Such studies should pay greater regard to the role of history and to the antecedent and often inertial forces which may continue to mould the form of cities here and elsewhere in the third world. As recent commentators on the nature of Latin American urbanization have suggested:

The economic and social evolution of Latin American cities never deviated markedly from the general directions set in colonial days. It is this inertial force of early events that permitted the natural acceptance of subsequent chains of events, an almost imperceptible evolution that led by gradual steps, to present patterns of massive poverty and structural polarization (Portes and Browning, 1976, p. 25).

URBAN OUTCOMES

Although this statement on contemporary urban trends and the response of urban geography has focused upon processes and the structural conditions from which they emanate, it has to be recognized that the weight of research in urban geography and certainly the bulk of the literature is concerned with spatial outcomes and with the form of the cities and urban systems. A terminology designed to classify various forms of urban area has become closely associated with geographical study which has progressively linked morphology more 'dependently' with the functional organization of the urban system. Conurbation, metropolis, megalopolis, and urban region are all attempts to describe the physical expressions of the urbanization process. Recent major studies in Britain and the United States indicate a continuing evolution in the morphology of the urban systems in those countries which may have more general application in advanced societies. Hall *et al.* (1973) identify two main features of British urbanization as, firstly, a *regional effect* which reflects the dynamism of midland and southern England and the relatively slow growth or even stagnation and decline in other parts of the United Kingdom. The urban outcome of this effect is 'megalopolitan Britain' which has evolved from the long-recognized 'axial belt' between Birmingham and London. Perhaps more significant are the strong *local decentralization* trends which involve decline at the centres of large metropolitan areas and high rates of peripheral growth:

we should expect both decentralization trends in population and in employment, to re-inforce each other and to intensify . . . a number of larger metropolitan areas may follow in the path of London; their growth may reach a point where both people and jobs decentralize altogether out of the metropolitan area, into peripheral complexes of living and working, based on smaller employment centres. This would represent an advanced stage in a process which can be traced back to the nineteenth century at least—the suburbanization of the English people (Hall *et al.*, 1973, p. 253).

This scenario is in some ways reminiscent of the American 'counter-urbanization' movement identified by Berry (1980) and others, though it does not have all of its features. In the United States there is a significant regional shift which involves a decline in the dominance of the urbanized north-east seaboard—the initial megalopolis—and the rise of the 'sunbelt' cities. This latter trend is effectively creating new metropolitan areas. The common feature of recent British and American urbanization is the process of decentralization and its effects in both widening the range of peripheral urban growth and emphasizing the depth of inner-city/outer-city divisions. American urban systems in particular are assuming dispersed forms on a new scale, the future trends in which are dependent upon a number of increasingly imponderable factors. If energy crises, problems of governance and fiscal issues make the future form of American urban systems hazardous to predict, forecasts for the future form of Third World urbanization are at least as difficult. Clearly there will be continuing urbanization, more and larger cities which will continue to warrant titles such as 'pseudo-cities' as they emerge without an accompanying functional base or ability to cope with the inflow of rural migrants and their own population increases. Friedmann's (1973) notion of dominant 'cores' and dominated peripheries, with associated spread and diffusion effects, may be a useful model for change in some parts of the Third World but its generality is questionable. Levels of urbanization vary considerably, from under 10 per cent in East Africa to over 60 per cent in Argentina, societal conditions in which the process occurs are equally variable; the diminutive sizes, peripherality and 'fewness' of Tanzanian towns, for example, can only as yet be explained in the context of colonialism rather than of modern circumstances.

URBANIZATION, PLANNING AND POLICIES

Introduction

As urbanization has progressed in the western world, so the interventionist roles of the state, at various levels, have become more evident. In some respects the two trends may be unconnected. More planning, increased organization and greater central control may reflect a particular form of political economy rather than a response to urban growth. In 'command' economies, such as USSR, Cuba, and China, planning and state interventionism and control become more imperative. The growth of cities both exaggerates existing problems and creates new ones. There are associated increases in crime rates, pollution levels, and traffic congestion which arise from the new density and size of population concentrations; there are issues arising from the conflict over land and space. Many of these are management problems and the organizing of an urban society becomes a necessity. Large cities exaggerate some of society's malaise and portray its gross inequalities in stark form. Urban policies are needed to cope with inequalities and their local environmental expressions, to manage land and the uses to which it is put, to organize flows of traffic and to impose standards and controls on urban development. In a more fiscal and administrative sense, large cities have problems of government which often require centralized direction. The experience of western societies is such as to suggest that planning is a necessary activity and particularly so if any kind of welfare criteria is accepted.

Geography and urban policy

Urban geography has a long history of association with the practice of planning and the formulation of urban policies. This association has been pursued over a narrow front, and as Hall (1974a) suggests, has assumed *descriptive* and *positive* roles—providing factual surveys and manipulating models under specified ideal conditions—rather than a *normative* role which advocates the kind of action needed to produce the best results. Geographers in their descriptive roles were closely involved in physical planning programmes concerned with issues such as urban reconstruction, development control, and land-use arrangements within cities. The land-use survey methods devised by geographers, notably Stamp and Platt, in the 1930s, were ideally suited to the perceived tasks of planning. These involved the mapping of existing land uses, the evaluation of land capability, and the design of zoning schemes which separated non-conforming land uses. This type of physical planning, aimed at creating a better environment which, it was believed, would in turn create a better society, had great demands for personnel in the heady days of the immediate postwar years, and many human geographers found important careers in this expanding profession. This type of involvement with urban planning was especially marked in Britain following the 1947 Town and Country Planning Act and has continued to be a feature of urban geography. There are parallels elsewhere and the concept of the geographer/planner has become established in several parts of the world.

In the 1950s and 1960s, planning became increasingly concerned with movement patterns, a concern made necessary by the rapid growth of vehicle ownership and the accompanying traffic congestion within urban areas. A new emphasis on flows and their relationships with land-use arrangements and urban structure, occurred contemporaneously with the growth of spatial analysis in geography, with its twin foci on spatial patterns and interactions. Again, therefore, it seemed that urban geographers could play an important role in the development of models of urban systems which linked movement and land use and allowed prediction of the impact of changes in the latter on the former (Batty, 1978). These efforts cast urban geographers in their *positive* roles as contributors to the planning process and involved a much greater degree of sophistication of mathematical modelling than had previously been general in geographical work. Work on large urban models continues but has a diminishing influence on policy-making as experience reveals the task of matching models to the realities of urban situations to be virtually intractable; their value is likely to be that of a guideline rather than a detailed planning specification.

Also in the 1950s and 1960s, the long-established geographical concern with natural resources and environmental quality provided a bridge with the process of planning. Cities and urban plans had clear ecological consequences and issues such as air pollution and flood hazard became of central significance. Gilbert White initiated the very active research field concerned with environmental hazards and with the management of flood plains; others were concerned with coastal areas, with drought liability and a host of other ecological circumstances (Berry et al., 1974). Of more recent origin is the broad field of environmental impact assessment which has strong links with the earlier resource management tradition. As the ecological lobby grows and legislation is framed to protect the environment, geographers, trained in both natural and social sciences, will have important roles in assessing the environmental impacts of

452

both new projects and the expansion or continuation of existing facilities.
Spatial analysis techniques developed in the 1960s were key features of
geographers' involvement in macro-models of urban structure. They also found
a wide range of applications at more localized and specialized scales. Urban
geographers have developed techniques which allow them to monitor change
and also to predict its spatial outcomes in different parts of the city. Outcomes
of a specific kind may have more general effects upon locational decisions
involving other land uses. Urban models can be of many kinds and include
partial and general models, static or dynamic models, individual or aggregate
models (Batty, 1978). There are two issues which have stimulated a great deal
of research by urban geographers concerned with the development of models
and spatial algorithms. The first issue is that of *optimal location*, the identification of 'ideal' sites for new urban facilities. The second of the issues concerns
optimal regionalization, the identification of territories or subregions within
the city which best serve a specific administrative or social welfare purpose.

Spatial analysis and urban policy

Problems of urban education have provided subject matter for policy-orientated
research on both these issues. F. L. Hall (1973), for example, developed a
programming model for the location of high schools in Chicago. The terms of
reference for the model were to provide locations for new schools and to allocate
students in such a way that the cost of transporting all students to schools was
minimized. A number of constraints was accepted. Each school was allocated
a maximum capacity, with strict upper and lower limits of black and white

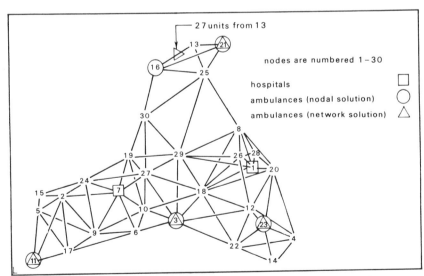

Figure 10.1 An optimal location model for medical services (after Church and
Meadows, 1979)

students, and a specified number of new schools was to be constructed. One question inevitably linked with location algorithms of this kind relates to the fact that they can be programmed to satisfy various criteria and are heavily conditioned by these initial assumptions or priorities. Centrographic models may seek the 'minimum' point or centre of gravity in a given distribution; other types of models seek locations which involve the smallest number of links between nodes on a network. Added constraints may ensure that no individual is more than a specified distance from any one facility (Rushton, 1979). Optimal location models of this kind have been widely used by urban geographers in the context of allocation problems such as the siting of new stores, schools, recreational centres and police facilities (See Figure 10.1).

The regionalization concept has a long heritage in human geography and the central objectives of defining the most meaningful divisions of space and identifying their boundaries, remain the same. Technically, the concept has been developed from the point at which it relied heavily upon an intuitive approach, with its accompanying imprecision and inconsistency, to a set of procedures which have claims to be objective, scientific, and testable. Urban education issues again provide examples of the application of systematic regionalization techniques. Jenkins and Shepherd (1972) examined alternative strategies for decentralizing high school administration in Detroit following state legislation in 1969. Given an initial set of 21 areas, a target of between seven and eleven school-boards, and a desired size-range of between 25,000 and 50,000 students, 7330 possible amalgamations were identified. By applying further constraints, which included contiguity, shape and level of ethnic mix with each school-board, the range could be narrowed to a small number of alternative solutions but these did not closely resemble the eventual outcome in Detroit which was largely a political decision. By and large the *desiderata*— with accompanying judgements—for the regions have become far more significant than the technical procedures used. Regionalization procedures which employ basically spatial criteria to minimize distance travelled will typically produce compact 'neighbourhood' catchment areas (Figure 10.2(a)). As the school population will than mirror residential segregation, this outcome is at odds with policies designed to 'integrate' children along either ethnic or social class lines. Regionalization procedures have also been widely used in the designation of administrative areas (Figure 10.2(b)) and voting districts. For the latter case, in which vested interests are clearly heavily involved, the arguments for adopting some 'objective' or 'neutral' allocative procedure are strong. Johnston and Rossiter (1981) have devised a procedure to identify local government and parliamentary electoral districts on the bases of population-size, shape and administrative organization, which also takes account of past voting behaviour.

Optimal location, regionalization, and spatial analysis procedures provide examples of ways in which geographers can contribute to the formulation of urban policies. Although many policy-decisions of this kind emanate from government and other agencies, they have in the past often been made without

454

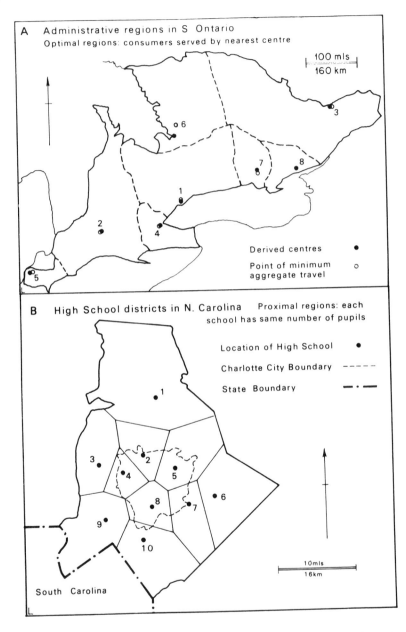

Figure 10.2 Regionalization procedures. (a) Administrative regions in South Ontario (after Massam, 1972, p. 14, Figure 8). (b) High school districts in North Carolina (after Lord, 1977, p. 8, Figure 15). (Reprinted by permission of the Association of American Geographers)

reference to the specialized expertise which urban geographers can offer. More recent evidence suggests however that levels of consultation are increasing, and the practical advice of urban geographers is becoming more widely used (see, for example, Davies, 1977). For geographers, however, there is also the need to accept that their advisory roles are partial and contributory, and there may be good reasons why the 'ideal' or optimal *spatial* solutions which they offer may not be those which are eventually adopted. As experience during British local government reorganization in the early 1970s showed, factors to which geographers give particular weight, such as distance, access, and uniformity, may in the final analysis be regarded less highly than others such as considerations of revenue-raising capacity, traditional allegiances and even political expediency. A further point about which urban geographers as spatial analysts are becoming increasingly aware is the critique that the type of research which geographers are qualified to carry out may idealize and optimize locations and areas and, further, may not be independent of the desires of planners and politicians and their concepts of efficiency. To this extent geographers may be describing those optimal locations which are permissible under the present system of society and as such may be providing input for political or establishment manoeuvres. This criticism has some meaning but cannot easily be avoided as values will permeate any selection of assumptions, ranking of objectives or attempts to define optimal. One way forward may be the common practice of providing more than one answer to a locational or territorial problem by examining the variety of options which emerge when assumptions and objectives are changed.

Area policies

As the general interest of urban geographers in residential differentiation, deriving its technical procedures from spatial analysis, became more focused upon the identification of local concentrations of deprivation, other paradigms—behaviouralism and relevance—began to influence research. A parallel literature on social indicators and levels of living brought cross-fertilization of ideas and territorial social indicators were developed which could be used to identify *areas* which warranted special policies and resource allocations. Area policies and the related concept of positive discrimination are closely related to this type of research development. The content of area policies varies considerably from environmental improvement to social and economic development. In the United States, the Ford Foundation was, during the 1950s, especially concerned with the problem of metropolitan government and inner-city research. The 'grey areas' programme funded experiments in parts of selected cities such as Oakland and Boston; federal programmes as part of the War on Poverty legislation similarly focused on inner-city districts; the Housing and Urban Development Office (HUD) has sponsored Urban Initiatives in the 1970s.

In the United Kingdom, housing programmes involving both clearance and improvement provide the most established links with area policies. These links were perpetuated with the Housing Acts of 1969 and 1974 which introduced the policies of General Improvement Areas (GIAs) and Housing Action Areas (HAAs). GIAs were intended to *concentrate* the improvement effort, though grants to householders under the 1969 Act were available on the same terms to those not resident in designated areas. Within GIAs the local authorities were empowered to spend up to £200 per dwelling on general environmental improvements such as pedestrianization and landscaping. As HAAs were defined in the 1974 Act, the emphasis was on social stress, measured by indices such as overcrowding, and the aim was to upgrade both the physical qualities of urban environments and related social conditions. Householders within HAAs were given preferential access to grants for improvement and these were more generous than previous legislation had allowed. Up to 1976, 195 HAAs and 1085 GIAs had been declared in England and Wales and these provide major examples of the pursuance of area policies.

Urban education provides another example of the use of area policies in Britain. The 1967 Plowden Report was basically concerned with primary schools, but its examination of the relationship between urban deprivation and educational disadvantage had far-reaching effects. A relationship between social class and educational attainment had been well understood for some time (Douglas, 1964) but the Plowden report pointed to deprived *areas* in which inadequate schooling facilities combined with poor home background to produce disadvantage. The recommended policy was that of positive discrimination towards Educational Priority Areas (EPAs), the research task became one of identifying where the *areas* were and the form which positive discrimination should take. Of the attempts to use territorial social indicators, the ten-point index used in the Inner London Education Authority (ILEA) was the most widely cited. This index included measures of home environment and school quality but was not generally adopted and approaches used in the definition of EPAs were various. Eventually a total of 150 schools in 51 education districts shared a £16 million grant and became the recipients of positive discrimination.

The whole notion of the EPA as an area policy has been consistently criticized (Barnes, 1975) on the grounds that many disadvantaged children may live outside designated areas and therefore not benefit from the extra resources. Barnes shows that resources going to EPA schools in inner London reach 13.6 per cent of all children but only 20.2 per cent of the most disadvantaged children in the ILEA. This type of criticism is real but not conclusive, the empirical analysis of the effects of area policy in London was limited to an inner-city area which lacked the range of absolute standards necessary for adequate comparisons. Again, the EPA is a means to an end rather than the sole form of policy:

The district as a means of identifying problems and allocating resources is held by us to be no more than a convenient framework within which closer and more detailed work has to be done with schools, school classes, individuals and families in order to realize a fully effective policy of positive discrimination (Halsey, 1972, p. 181).

There are other examples of area policies in Britain in the 1970s. In 1968, the Urban Aid Programme was one component of a more general examination of levels of social provision. Positive discrimination projects were especially designed to provide for localized areas which bore the marks of multiple deprivation. These schemes were funded from the Rate Support Grant and local authorities were invited to bid for funds. Batley and Edwards (1974) estimated that up to 1973, some 2300 projects worth £32 million had been allocated. In 1974 the Home Office Deprivation Unit developed the idea of Comprehensive Community Programmes (CCPs) which were again aimed at areas of intensive deprivation. This concept was overtaken by the Inner Areas Bill of 1977 through which central government could establish special partnerships with a limited number of major cities, including London, Manchester, Liverpool and Birmingham, with a view to regenerating the problematic inner cities. These are all major attempts at area policy at a variety of scales from local neighbourhoods to inner cities. There have been consistent problems of funding, of clear designation of power and responsibility, and of a lack of management and organization principles, but *some* redistribution of resources and initiatives to places where these are most needed has been achieved.

The Community Development Projects (CDPs) deserve separate mention. These were funded by the Home Office as experiments for the concentration of research on small pockets of deprivation in which surveys could be conducted, services coordinated and public participation encouraged. Twelve CDPs were established at a cost of £5 million, mostly in inner-city areas. The outcomes of the CDP research were very different from those anticipated by central government. Established to find ways of achieving local improvements through evolutionary change, the projects began to see poverty as the outcome of fundamental inequalities in the capitalist politicoeconomic system, their policy recommendations were far more radical than any government could countenance. At a more local government level, the municipalities began to see the CDP workers as political agitators and the original 'self-help' and citizen participation evolved into conflicts between residents and institutional sources of power. CDPs had most impact upon the academic research community and the reports were influential in the reaction against 'cosmetic' local planning. Their effect on policy-makers was limited and the projects were terminated in the late 1970s.

Examples of area policies could be replicated for many parts of the world in both urban and rural settings. Such policies can be closely related to the research methodology of urban geography in its traditional roles of defining regions, identifying boundaries and characterizing internal structure. The limitations of such a perspective, such as the imprecision which boundaries often possess and the aggregate quality of the region, are well known. Criticisms of area policies are often along these lines. Holtermann (1975) argued that the degree of spatial concentration for individual aspects of deprivation is low and that priority treatment of 15 per cent of census enumeration districts would be needed to account for 61 per cent of the overcrowded households in Britain. A study of deprivation in Dundee led to the conclusion that:

> The only type of area-based policy which is likely to be cost-effective would be one of discrimination against the privileged who are concentrated geographically to a greater extent than the deprived (Maclaran, 1981, p. 65).

The persistence of this type of criticism (see also Townsend, 1976) raises doubts on the value as well as on the sufficiency of area policies. Many of the critiques, however, rest on questionable empirical bases. The untypicality of the ILEA study area has been mentioned; Hamnett (1979) notes that Holtermann needs to qualify her observations on local concentration when she extends her analysis beyond three overcrowding indicators. It could anyway be argued that if 15 per cent of EDs account for 61 per cent of overcrowding, that is good evidence for the *value* of an area policy. In summary, it can be accepted that *area* policies are insufficient in themselves and need to be supplemented by policies aimed at *individuals* or *households*, but not that they have no value. Many forms of deprivation are locally concentrated, and in common with other problems which possess spatial manifestation, require spatially based study and policy.

In addition to this pragmatic kind of criticism of area policies is the 'CDP-type' of critique which suggests that 'tinkering' with the local environment misses the fact that social problems have their roots in the political economy and may divert attention from the points upon which it ought to be focused. Spatial reformism, it is argued, suggests distributional solutions to structural conditions and class divisions, academic research should be more concerned with policies of radical reform at this structural level. The logic of this critique has not been lost by the academic community and there are signs that research which may lead to constructive policy alternatives at this level may emerge. What the radical critique may miss, however, is the fact that while this kind of research goes on, people continue to suffer deprivation in localized areas of cities; ameliorative reform does help people in need even if it cannot provide long-term solutions. There is a thin line between action which serves the needs of deprived people and those activities which bolster up a system in need of more radical change. Clifford Shaw recognized this when assessing his own Chicago Area projects in the 1930s:

> In an ironic way, the projects protected the property and equipment of the very concerns which were the root causes of disorganization and delinquency (Shaw, quoted in Snodgrass, 1976, p. 17).

Although these *caveats* are real, urban policies need to be developed along several fronts and at various scales in order to protect the present needs of the deprived as well as to promote a future, more just society.

Community action and community care

Area policies can be related to community involvement and public participation. The 1969 Skeffington Report in the United Kingdom was specifically concerned with public participation in planning and its recommendations have affected local procedures. Wolpert, Mumphrey, and Seley (1972) and Christensen (1982) have documented ways in which community action has been organized to combat what residents have seen as negative changes. Geographical research into urban community and neighbourhood can therefore be assessed as a contribution to possible urban policies and there is evidence of new insight into these. Several geographers see a re-emergence of neighbourhoods as bases for community action in the United States:

the emergence of the community or neighbourhood association; groups striving for varying degrees of political decentralization, for discretion over the use of neighbourhood space (Ley, 1974, p. 7).

C. J. Smith (1980) argues that behind this rebirth of localism and the decentralization of problem-solving and service-provision is an implicit belief that localism and smallness are associated with a higher quality of life. There is less evidence for this type of 'community found' movement in Britain but community councils, established as part of local government reform in the 1970s, at least provide a framework within which a reassertion of localism can occur.

Neighbourhood definition, in subjective as well as in objective terms, provides one avenue for policy-related research. Another emerges from the concept of the 'caring community' particularly as it is being developed in relation to the mentally ill and the elderly. The importance of community care is increasing, partly because of a growing belief that local community has a real role, and partly in response to a process of deinstitutionalization. Patients are being discharged from hospitals both in an attempt to cope with the bottomless pit of medical care and also to restrict the long-term use of hospital beds to priority needs. *Normalization* describes the attempt to integrate the mentally ill into situations, including communities, in which people live normal day-to-day lives. Mental health poses particular problems in so far as people who fully approve the principle of the caring community are nonetheless usually unwilling to accommodate the mentally ill in their own neighbourhoods. A central research issue is to identify the types of neighbourhood into which the mentally ill can and cannot be discharged. Smith (1980) suggests that the optimum community setting is one which involves living with a close and supportive family; if, however, the family is not supportive the mentally ill are better off away from its influence. Trute and Segal (1976) argue that discharged patients can integrate most effectively in communities which are neither highly socially cohesive not completely socially disorganized; the optimum setting is a neighbourhood with a substantial proportion of 'socially detached' non-family-oriented residents. These are crude approximations of the types of neighbour-

460

Form of care	Place of care	Agents
Informal	Home	kinship network neighbours care home visitor general practitioner
Formal-community	Neighbourhood	day centre sheltered home outpatient clinic
Formal-Institutional	Hospital	full-time care

Figure 10.3   Sources of care: formal and informal. Care or treatment has its most direct relevance for the ill but is also of central importance to 'dependent' populations such as the elderly

hood capable of providing community care and there is need for much more research into the policy implications related to deinstitutionalization. Similarly, the ways in which local communities react to a locational role for some facilities, such as day centres, for the mentally ill requires careful investigation. Dear and Wittman (1980) have provided some guidelines for research with their attempts to classify treatment settings along a range which includes volunteer aid, informal community-based services such as home visits, formal facilities, such as outpatient centres, and fully-fledged institutional care (Figure 10.3). They summarize the key issues under headings of *assignment*, matching client to treatment setting, and *siting*, fitting facilities into their community contexts.

Community-based facilities are also, and perhaps more obviously, of critical importance to the elderly. Here the stigma attached to the mentally ill is absent but the elderly person becomes increasingly dependent on others and may move through a range of treatment settings to institutional care. Most evidence suggests that old people want to stay independent as long as possible, so the development of the *range* of community care options is an important policy priority. In seeking to identify those neighbourhood characteristics which are most amenable to the elderly, stability and a significant presence of groups to whom they can relate, either kin or friends of a similar age, must be key components. The idea of the caring community is not new but there are innovative features, including the revival of community action and the role of community-based facilities, which warrant continued urban geographical study.

Social justice and welfare

Area policies, optimal locations and regions, and notions of community-based action are elements of a broad strategy for urban geographical research which has the general aim of working towards a more equitable distribution of resources in space. There have been attempts to mould these strands into a general theory and the concept of territorial social justice, which links with Davies (1968) and his study of social needs and services, is important. Pinch (1979), in a study of Greater London, examined the extent to which a mismatch between need and provision amounted to spatial injustice. Empirically both need and provision are measurable, at least through objective and aggregate indices, conceptually a 'just distribution' is more difficult to articulate. Harvey (1973) has tackled the conceptual problem with both 'liberal' and 'socialistic' formulations. Harvey suggested need, contribution to the common good, and merit as the components of social justice. *Need* is a relative concept which has to be defined in relation to specific categories such as food, housing, medical care and education. Territorial social indicators have been used to measure its incidence in space.

Contribution to the common good is concerned with ways in which the allocation of resources to one territory affects conditions in another. Cox's (1973) idea of externalities is an important concept as Pahl's (1975) description of a socio-spatial system in which residential locations can determine access to both 'goods' and 'bads'. Similarly, Jones and Eyles (1977) refer to opportunity structures and the relevance of location in space to an individual's life chances. *Merit* is a criterion designed to meet the needs of areas of special difficulty. Particularly adverse conditions of the natural environment or special circumstances associated with the accumulation of social deprivation may, at specific points in time, justify positive discrimination towards specific groups in particular places.

Territorial social justice emerges as a policy for resource-distribution which meets the needs of people in areas, accommodates externalities and other inter-area effects, and responds disproportionately to areas of special disadvantage. In his 'liberal formulation', Harvey (1973) stresses the importance of *efficiency*, to which territorial social justice is *not* an alternative. In his later 'socialist formulation', however, he comes to the proposition that efficiency is equity and that production is distribution:

The collapse of the distinction between production and distribution, between efficiency and social justice, is part of that general collapse of all dualisms of this sort accomplished through accepting Marx's approach and technique of analysis...move from a pre-disposition to regard social justice as a matter of eternal justice and morality to regard it as something contingent upon the social processes operating in society as a whole (Harvey, 1973, p. 15).

Smith's (1977) ideas on the development of a geography of human welfare run parallel with concepts such as social justice and the just distribution of resources. His attempt to redefine human geography as the study of 'who gets what, where, and how' rests on the premise that welfare themes permeate the whole of human geography. For Smith, the scope of human geography can be summarized as: *description* or the empirical identification of territorial levels of wellbeing; *explanation* or the study of cause and effect, the origins of patterns; *evaluation* or judgement on the desirability of alternative geographical states, the form of desired distributions; *prescription* or the statement of policies needed to achieve change; and *implementation* or the assuming of roles needed to carry through policies for change.

It is questionable whether a geography of welfare has yet been adequately theorized. Welfare economics, which is used extensively by Smith, has limitations and the key explanation stage of the strategy remains not fully specified. The objectives of welfare geography—greater involvement with social issues, collective management of space, reveal the spatial malfunctions of society, and contribute to the design of a spatial form of society in which people are free to fulfil themselves—are all fully acceptable and are indeed common strands to much urban–social geography practised in the 1970s and 1980s. Utopia remains some distance away, however, and both understanding the present and prescribing the future remain many-faceted problems facing urban geographers as much as any other social scientist. The signal service which welfare geography and other perspectives of the 1970s offer is one of widening the horizons of urban geography, of indicating the need to context local environments, to integrate themes, to compare alternative states and to adopt positive stances towards the 'state'—present and future—of the societies which we analyse.

SUMMARY AND CONCLUSIONS

Urban geography, and indeed human geography, has by the 1980s assumed a state in which, superficially at least, eclecticism appears to be one of its more obvious features. Practitioners pursue different methodologies towards diverse ends, there is variability in the practice of urban geography of a kind which has not been previously experienced. In a major sense this is a product of success, the demonstrated ability to mount new paradigms, to break away from the narrow confines of analyses of land use and morphology and to add new dimensions without necessarily discarding the old. In another sense, however, eclecticism creates problems and it is these which urban geography needs to resolve.

1. There is the central issue of whether an urban geography remains a recognizable and viable field of study following, in particular, the spatial analysis paradigm and its focus on thematic interactions over space. Is urban geography a kind of regional geography at the urban scale with its quest for the elusive synthesis and its overwhelming *breadth* of interests? On the first of these questions the answer must be that urban geography is a reassertion of the value and meaning of *place*. There is support for that focus from other paradigms of the 1970s; relevance with its acceptance that contemporary and economic problems find local spatial manifestations and nowhere more

than in the city, humanistic geography with its return to the finer qualities of regionalism and the social values attached to place and territory. On the second of these questions there is the fact that broad though urban contexts may be, the great bulk of urban geography is concerned with a smaller number of themes which it analyses at considerable depth.

2. A second issue revolves around the ability of urban geography to identify a framework within which the variety of contemporary perspectives is both unrealistic and undesirable but it should be possible to see how various approaches relate to each other, how they might seek 'openings' for constructive dialogue, and how they continue to *belong* to some integrating framework. Branching models and levels of analysis are suggested frameworks, Ley's recognition of the attractions of Marxism—'holistic not piecemeal, synthetic not atomistic, concerned with questions which matter'—while asserting the humanistic stance that no social study which ignores biography and history is sufficient, offers evidence of one such 'opening'. Bennett and Wrigley's (1981) efforts to demonstrate the value of spatial analysis offer another.

3. The final issue involves the kind of role which urban geographers can fill in the fields of policy and decision-making in the last part of the twentieth century. The spectrum of possibilities is wide and includes traditional descriptive roles, classifications of land use, portrayal through indicators of the extent of man's inhumanity to man; prescription of ameliorative policies which 'positively discriminate' under a general umbrella of socio-spatial justice or welfare; or advocacy of radical reform from a belief that inequality will continue and this is a proper course. There is room for the descriptive fact-finding and the evaluative model-building. There is also room, and must be, for a range of beliefs among urban geographers which leads them towards analysis of social problems from different assumptions and towards different views of what a better society might be. Some may criticize society from a fundamental belief that the whole order is wrong, others may criticize but will have a far different view of the extent of the malaise or of the scale of necessary change. Evidence so far suggests that if the choice is between evolutionary change within the framework of existing institutions or revolutionary change which overthrows existing orders, most urban geographers by sentiment are very firmly committed to the former of these paths.

In attempting to develop urban geography as a policy-oriented discipline there are positive qualities from the past record, notably the long record of applied geography and the links with planning, but there are negative qualities in that the research has tended (Hall, 1974) to be descriptive and evaluative (positive) rather than normative. Hall argues that geography has neither an implicit nor an explicit normative base except in terms of spatial efficiency and environmental quality. These two themes, very significant in themselves, can be added to as urban geography develops a professional expertise applicable to all levels of urban policy-making. A final and cautionery consideration is that voiced by Hare (1974) who argues that in the major policy issues there are no real experts, things are too complex and interconnected for expertise to flourish. Academic disciplines and public policy-making, Hare argues, are separate and distinctive domains, geography as a discipline is largely irrelevant and effective individual commitment by geographers is more important than the general application of geography itself. Urban geography must properly seek to extend its contribution to the study of problems and the formulation of policies, but in the end it is likely to be one contribution among others and rarely a specific solution in itself. As a field of study, however, urban geography remains both definable and dynamic and capable of producing students well grounded in the understanding of urban patterns, processes and problems.

References

Abel-Smith, B. (1978) *National Health Service. The First Thirty Years*, DHSS, HMSO, London.

Abrams, C. (1964) *Man's Struggle for Shelter in an Urbanizing World*, MIT Press, Cambridge, Mass.

Abu-Lughod, J. L. (1961) Migrant adjustment to city life: the Egyptian case, *American Journal of Sociology*, **67**, 22–32.

Abu-Lughod, J. L. (1969) Testing the theory of social area analysis: the ecology of Cairo, Egypt, *American Sociological Review*, **34**, 198–212.

Abu-Lughod, J. L., and Hay, R. (1979) *Third World Urbanization*, Methuen, New York.

Ackerman, E. A. (1945) Geographic training, wartime research and immediate professional objectives, *Annals, Association of American Geographers*, **35**, 121–143.

Ackerman, E. A. (1958) *Geography as a Fundamental Research Discipline*, Research Paper No. 53. Department of Geography, University of Chicago, Chicago.

Adams, J. S. (1969) Directional bias in intra-urban migration, *Economic Geography*, **45**, 302–323.

Adams, J. S. (1970) Residential structure of mid-western cities, *Annals, Association of American Geographers*, **60**, 37–62.

Adams, R. McC. (1966) *The Evolution of Urban Society*, Weidenfeld and Nicolson, London.

Adams, R. N. (1970) Brokers and career mobility systems in the structure of complex societies, *Southwestern Journal of Anthropology*, **26**, 315–327.

Ahmad, Q. (1965) *Indian Cities: Characteristics and Correlates*, Research Paper No. 102, Department of Geography, University of Chicago, Chicago.

Alexander, I. (1974) *City Centre Redevelopment. An Evaluation of Alternative Approaches*, Pergamon, Oxford.

Alexander, I. (1979) *Office Location and Public Policy*, Longman, London.

Alexander, I., and Dawson, J. A. (1979) Suburbanization of retailing sales and employment in Australian cities, *Australian Geographical Studies*, 76–83.

Alexander, J. W. (1954) The basic-nonbasic concept of urban economic functions, *Economic Geography*, **30**, 246–261.

Alexandersson, G. (1956) *The Industrial Structure of American Cities*, University of Nebraska Press.

Alihan, M. (1938) *Social Ecology*, Columbia University Press, New York.

Alker, H. R. (1969) A typology of ecological fallacies, in M. Dogan and S. Rokkan (eds.), *Quantitative Ecological Analysis in the Social Sciences*, MIT Press, Cambridge, Mass., pp. 69–86.

Allan, G. A. (1979) *A Sociology of Friendship and Kinship*, George Allen and Unwin, London.

Alonso, W. (1963) *Location and Land-use*, Harvard University Press, Cambridge, Mass.

Althusser, L. (1969) *For Marx*, Penguin, Harmondsworth.

Amos, F. C. (1970) *Social Malaise in Liverpool*, City Planning Office, Liverpool.

465

466

Anderson, T. R., and Bean, L. L. (1961) The Shevky–Bell social areas: confirmation of results and a re-interpretation, *Social Forces*, **40**, 119–124.

Anderson, T. R., and Egeland, J. A. (1961) Spatial aspects of social area analysis, *American Sociological Review*, **26**, 392–399.

Applebaum, W. (1965) Measuring retail market penetration for a discount food supermarket: a case study, *Journal of Retailing*, **41**, 1–15.

Applebaum, W. (1968) Store characteristics and operating performance, Ch. 10; Advanced methods for measuring store trade areas and market penetration, Ch. 24; The analogue method of estimating potential store sales, Ch. 27, in C. Kornblau (ed.), *Guide to Store Location Research*, Supermarket Institute, Chicago.

Araud C., Boon, C. K., Garcia, R. A., Rincon, S., Strassman, W. P., and Urquidi, V. L. (1975) *La construction de vivienda y el empleo en Mexico*, Colegio de Mexico, Mexico City.

Ardell, D. B. (1970) Public regional councils and comprehensive health planning: a partnership? *Journal of the American Institute of Planners*, **36**, 393–404.

Ardrey, R. (1966) *The Territorial Imperative*, Atheneum Press, New York.

Aurousseau, M. (1921) The distribution of population: a constructive problem, *Geographical Review*, **11**, 563–592.

Bagley, C., Jacobson, S., and Palmer, C. (1973) Social structure and the ecological distribution of mental illness, suicide and delinquency, *Psychological Medicine*, **3**, 177–87.

Baldwin, J. (1975) Urban criminality and the problem estate, *Local Government Studies*, **1**, 12–20.

Baldwin, J., and Bottoms, A. E. (1976) *The Urban Criminal*, Tavistock, London.

Barnes, J. A. (1954) Class and committees in a Norwegian island parish, *Human Relations*, **7**, 39–58.

Barnes, J. A. (1975) *Educational Priority*, Vol. 3, HMSO, London.

Barnum, H. G. (1966) *Market Centers and Hinterlands in Baden-Wurttemberg*, Research Paper No. 103, Department of Geography, University of Chicago, Chicago.

Barrows, H. H. (1923) Geography as human ecology, *Annals, Association of American Geographers*, **13**, 1–14.

Baskin, C. W. (1966) *Central Places in Southern Germany* (translation of Christäller). Prentice-Hall, Englewood Cliffs, New Jersey.

Bastide, R. (1972) *The Sociology of Mental Disorder*, Routledge and Kegan Paul, London.

Batley, R., and Edwards, J. (1974) The urban programme, *British Journal of Social Work*, **4**, 305–31.

Batty, M. (1973) A probability model of the housing market based on quasi-classical considerations, *Socio-economic Planning Sciences*, **7**, 593–598.

Batty, M. (1978) Urban models in the planning process, in D. T. Herbert and R. J. Johnston (eds.), *Geography and the Urban Environment*, Vol. 1, Wiley, London, pp. 63–134.

Bauer, R. A. (ed.) (1966) *Social Indicators*, MIT Press, Cambridge, Mass.

Beavon, K. S. O. (1977) *Central Place Theory: A Reinterpretation*, Longman, London.

Beavon, K. S. O. and Mabin, A. S. (1975) The Lösch system of market areas—derivation and extensions, *Geographical Analysis*, **7**, 131–151.

Becker, J. F. (1976) *Marxian Political Economy: An Outline*, Cambridge University Press, London.

Bell, C. R. and Newby, H. (1971) *Community Studies*, George Allen and Unwin, London.

Bell, C. R. and Newby, H. (1978) Community, communion, class and community action: the social sources of the new urban politics, in D. T. Herbert and R. J. Johnston (eds.), *Social Areas in Cities*, Wiley, London, pp. 283–301.

Bell, D. (1974) *The Coming of Post-Industrial Society*, Heinemann, London.

de Bell, G. (1970). *The Environmental Handbook*, Ballantine, New York.

Bell, W. (1955) Economic, family and ethnic status: an empirical test, *American Sociological Review*, **20**, 45–52.

Bell, W. and Moskos, C. (1964) A comment on Udry's increasing scale and spatial differentiation, *Social Forces*, **42**, 414–417.

Bennett, R. J. (1981) The rate support grant in England and Wales, 1967–68 to 1980–81:
a review, in D. T. Herbert and R. J. Johnston (eds.), *Geography and the Urban Environment*, Vol. 4, Wiley, London, pp. 139–191.

Bennett, R. J. and Wrigley, N. (1981) *Quantitative Geography in Britain*, Routledge and
Kegan Paul, London.

Bennison, D. J. and Davies, R. L. (1977) *The Movement of Shoppers within the Central
Area of Newcastle upon-Tyne*, Summer Paper 34, Department of Geography, University
of Newcastle-upon-Tyne.

Berry, B. J. L. (1959) Recent studies concerning the role of transportation in the space
economy, *Annals, Association of American Geographers*, **49**, 328–342.

Berry, B. J. L. (1961) City size distributions and economic development, *Economic Development and Cultural Change*, **9**, 573–587.

Berry, B. J. L. (1967a) Cities as systems within systems of cities, *Papers and Proceedings
of the Regional Science Association*, **13**, 147–163.

Berry, B. J. L. (1967b) *Geography of Market Centres and Retail Distribution*, Prentice-Hall,
Englewood Cliffs, New Jersey.

Berry, B. J. L. (1970) The Geography of the United States in the year 2000, *Transactions,
Institute of British Geographers*, **51**, 21–54.

Berry, B. J. L. (1973a) *The Human Consequences of Urbanisation*, Macmillan, London.

Berry, B. J. L. (1973b) *Growth Centers in the American Urban System*, 2 Volumes, Ballinger,
Cambridge, Mass.

Berry, B. J. L. (1976) Introduction: on urbanization and counterurbanization, in B. J. L.
Berry (ed.), *Urbanization and Counterurbanization*, Urban Affairs Annual Reviews, **11**,
Sage Publications, Beverly Hills, 7–14.

Berry, B. J. L. (1978) Comparative urbanization strategies, in L. S. Bourne, and J. W.
Simmons, (eds.), *Systems of Cities, Readings on Structure, Growth and policy*, Oxford
University Press, New York, 502–510.

Berry, B. J. L. (1979) *The Open Housing Question*, Ballinger, Cambridge, Mass.

Berry, B. J. L. (1980) Inner city futures: an American dilemma revisited. *Transactions,
Institute of British Geographers*, **NS5**, 1–28.

Berry, B. J. L. *et al.* (1974) *Land-use, Urban Form, and Environmental Quality*, Geography
Research Paper, University of Chicago, No. 155.

Berry, B. J. L., Barnum, H. G., and Tennant, R. J. (1962) Retail location and consumer
behaviour, *Papers and Proceedings of the Regional Science Association*, **9**, 65–106.

Berry, B. J. L., and Garrison, W. L. (1958) Recent developments of central place theory,
Papers and Proceedings of the Regional Science Association, **4**, 107–120.

Berry, B. J. L., and Garrison, W. L. (1958a) The functional bases of the central place
hierarchy, *Economic Geography*, **34**, 145–154.

Berry, B. J. L., and Garrison, W. L. (1958b) A note on central place theory and the range
of a good, *Economic Geography*, **34**, 304–311.

Berry, B. J. L., and Garrison, W. L. (1958c) Alternate explanations of urban rank-size
relationships, *Annals, Association of American Geographers*, **48**, 83–91.

Berry, B. J. L., Goheen, P. G., and Goldstein, H. (1968) *Metropolitan Area Definition:
Re-evaluation of Concept and Statistical Practice*, Working Paper 28, US Bureau of
Census, Washington.

Berry, B. J. L., and Horton, F. E. (eds.) (1970) *Geographic Perspectives on Urban Systems*,
Prentice Hall, Englewood Cliffs, New Jersey.

Berry, B. J. L. and Rees, P. H. (1969) The factorial ecology of Calcutta, *American Journal
of Sociology*, **74**, 445–491.

Berry, B. J. L., Simmons, J. W., and Tennant, R. J. (1963) Urban population density:
structure and change, *Geographical Review*, **53**, 389–405.

468

Berry, B. J. L., assisted by Tennant, R. J., Garner, B. J., and Simmons, J. W. (1963). *Commercial Structure and Commercial Blight*, Research Paper No. 85, Department of Geography, University of Chicago, Chicago.

Beshers, J. M. (1962) *Urban Social Structure*, Free Press, Glencoe, Ill.

Bird, H. (1976) Residential mobility and preference patterns in the public sector of the housing market, *Transactions, Institute of British Geographers*, NS1, 20–33.

Birren, J. E. (1970) The abuse of the urban aged, *Psychology Today*, 3, 37–38.

Bishop, D. (1975) User response to a foot street, *Town Planning Review*, 46, 31–46.

Blake, R. R. *et al.* (1956) Housing, architecture and social interaction, *Sociometry*, 19, 133–39.

Blant, J. M., McCleary, G. S., and Blant, A. S. (1970) Environmental mapping in young children, *Environment and Behaviour*, 2, 335–50.

Blowers, A. T. (1973) The neighbourhood: exploration of a concept. Open University, *Urban Development*, Unit 17, 29–50.

Boaden, N. T. (1970) Central departments and local authorities: the relationship examined, *Political Studies*, 18, 175–86.

Boal, F. W. (1969) Territoriality on the Shankill/Falls divide, *Irish Geography*, 6, 30–50.

Boal, F. W. (1978) Ethnic residential segregation, in D. T. Herbert and R. J. Johnston (eds.), *Social Areas in Cities*, Wiley, London, pp. 57–95.

Boal, F. W., Doherty, P., and Pringle, D. G. (1978) *Social Problems in the Belfast Urban Area: an Exploratory Analysis*, Occasional Paper, No. 12, Department of Geography, Queen Mary College, London.

Boal, F. W., and Johnson, D. B. (1965). The functions of retail and service establishments on commercial ribbons, *Canadian Geographer*, 9, (3), 154–169.

Boddy, M. J. (1976) The structure of mortgage finance: building societies and the British social formation, *Transactions, Institute of British Geographers*, NS1, 58–71.

Bohland, J. R. and Davis, L. (1979) Sources of residential satisfaction amongst the elderly: an age comparative analysis, in S. Golant (ed.), *Location and Environment of the Elderly Population*, John Wiley, New York, pp, 95–109.

Boissevain, J. (1974) *Friends of Friends: Networks, Manipulators, and Coalitions*, Blackwell, London.

Booth, C. (1891) *Life and Labour of the People*, Williams and Margate, London.

Boots, B. N. (1979) Population density, crowding and human behaviour, *Progress in Human Geography*, 3, 13–63.

Bose, A. (1971) The urbanization process in south and southeast Asia, in L. Jakobson and V. Prakash (eds.), *Urbanization and National Development*, Sage, Beverly Hills, pp. 81–109.

Bott, E. (1957) *Family and Social Network*, Tavistock, London.

Boulding, K. (1956) *The Image: Knowledge in Life and Society*, University of Michigan, Ann Arbor.

Boudeville, J. R. (1966) *Problems of Regional Economic Planning*, Edinburgh University Press, Edinburgh.

Bourne, L. S. (1967) *Private Redevelopment of the Central City*. University of Chicago, Department of Geography Research Paper No. 112, Chicago.

Bourne, L. S. (1968) Comments on the transition zone concept, *Professional Geographer*, 20, 313–316.

Bourne, L. S. (1975) *Urban Systems: Strategies for Regulation*, Clarendon Press, Oxford.

Bourne, L. S. (1976) Housing supply and housing market behaviour in residential development, in D. T. Herbert and R. J. Johnston (eds.), *Spatial Processes and Form*, Wiley, London.

Bourne, L. S., and Simmons, J. W. (eds.) (1978) *Systems of Cities: Readings on Structure, Growth and Policy*, Oxford University Press, New York.

Bowden, M. J. (1971) Downtown through time: delimitation, expansion and internal growth, *Economic Geography*, 47, 121–135.

Boyle, M. J., and Robinson, M. E. (1979) Cognitive mapping and understanding, in D. T. Herbert and R. J. Johnston (eds.), *Geography and the Urban Environment*, Vol. 2, Wiley, London, pp. 59–82.

Bracey, H. E. (1953) Towns as rural service centres, *Transactions of the Institute of British Geographers*, **19**, 95–105.

Braidwood, R. J., and Willey, G. R. (eds.) (1962) *Courses towards Urban Life. Archaeological Considerations of Some Cultural Alternates*, Aldine, Chicago.

Brand, R. R. (1972) The spatial organization of residential areas in Accra, Ghana, with particular reference to aspects of modernization, *Economic Geography*, **48**, 284–298.

Brantingham, P. L., and Brantingham, P. J. (1975) Residential burglary and urban form, *Urban Studies*, **12**, 273–84.

Bromley, R. D. F. (1979) The function and development of colonial towns: urban change in the Central Highlands of Ecuador, 1698–1940, *Transactions, Institute of British Geographers*, **4**, 1, 30–43.

Bromley, R. J. (1980) Trader mobility in systems of periodic and daily markets, in D. T. Herbert and R. J. Johnston (eds.), *Geography and the Urban Environment*, Vol. 3, Wiley, London, pp. 133–174.

Bromley, R. J., Symanski, R., and Good, C. M. (1975). The rationale of periodic markets, *Annals, Association of American Geographers*, **65**, 530–537.

Brown, L. A., and Moore, E. G. (1970) The intra-urban migration process: a perspective, *Geografiska Annaler B*, **52**, 1–13.

Brush, J. E. (1953) The hierarchy of central places in Southwestern Wisconsin, *Geographical Review*, **43**, 380–402.

Brush, J. E., and Bracey, H. E. (1955) Rural service centres in Southwestern Wisconsin and Southern England, *Geographical Review*, **45**, 559–569.

Brush, J. E., and Gauthier, H. L. (1968) *Studies on the Philadelphia Metropolitan Fringe*, Research Paper No. 113, Department of Geography, University of Chicago, Chicago.

Bryson, R. A., and Kutzbach, J. E. (1968) *Air Pollution*, Association of American Geographers, Commission on College Geography, No. 2, Washington.

Bull, P. J. (1978) The spatial components of intra-urban manufacturing change: suburbanization in Clydeside 1958–68, *Transactions of the Institute of British Geographers*, **3**, 1, 91–100.

Bunge, W. (1962) *Theoretical Geography*. Lund Studies in Geography, Series C. No. 1, Gleerup, Lund.

Burgess, E. W. (1925) The growth of the city, in R. E. Park, E. W. Burgess, and R. D. McKenzie (eds.), *The City*, University of Chicago Press, Chicago.

Burgess, R. (1976) *Marxism and Geography*, Occasional Paper No. 30, Department of Geography, University College, London.

Burgess, R. (1982) Ideology and urban residential theory in Latin America, in D. T. Herbert and R. J. Johnston (eds.), *Geography and the Urban Environment*, Vol. 4, Wiley, London.

Burke, G. L. (1966) *Greenheart Metropolis*, Macmillan, London.

Burke, J. (1975) Some reflections on the pre-industrial city, *Urban History Yearbook*, pp. 13–21.

Burney, E. (1967) *Housing on Trial: A Study of Housing and Local Government*, Oxford University Press, London.

Burton, I. (1963) A restatement of the dispersed city hypothesis, *Annals of the Association of American Geographers*, **53**, 285–289.

Burton, I. and Kates, R. W. (1964a) The perception of natural hazards in resource management, *Natural Resources Journal*, **3**, 412–41.

Burton, I. and Kates, R. W. (1964b) The flood plain and the seashore: a comparative analysis of hazard-zone occupance. *Geographical* Review, **54**, 366, 85.

Buttimer, A. (1968). Social geography, in D. L. Sills (ed.), *International Encyclopaedia of the Social Sciences*, Collier-Macmillan, New York.

Buttimer, A. (1969) Social space in interdisciplinary perspective, *Geographical Review*, **59**, 417–26.

Buttimer, A. (1971) Health and welfare: whose responsibility? *Antipode*, **3**, (1) 31–45.

Buttimer, A. (1972) Social space and the planning of residential areas, *Environment and Behaviour*, **4**, 279–318.

Buttimer, A. (1976). Grasping the dynamism of the life-world, *Annals, Association of American Geographers*, **66**, 277–92.

Butzer, K. (ed.) (1978) *Dimensions of Human Geography*, University of Chicago, Geography Research Paper 186, pp. 166–184.

Buursink, J. (1975) Hierarchy: A concept between theoretical and applied geography, *Tijdschrift voor Economische en Sociale Geografie*, **66**, 194–203.

Cameron, G. (1973) Intra-urban location and the new plant, *Papers of the Regional Science Association*, **31**, 125–143.

Campbell, A., Converse, P. E., and Rodgers, W. L. (1976) *The Quality Of American Life*, Russell Sage Foundation, New York, 1976.

Canter, D. (1977) *The Psychology of Place*, Architectural Press, London.

Caplovitz, D. (1960) *The Poor Pay More*, The Free Press, New York.

Caplow, T., and Forman, R. (1955) Neighbourhood interaction in a homogeneous community, *American Sociological Review*, **15**, 357–66.

Carey, L., and Mapes, R. E. A. (1972) *The Sociology of Planning*, Batsford, London.

Carlstein, T., Parkes, D., and Thrift, N. (eds.) (1978) *Timing Space and Spacing Time*, 3 volumes, Edward Arnold, London.

Carruthers, W. I. (1962) Service centres in Greater London. *Town Planning Review*, **33**, 5–31.

Carter, H. (1965) *The Towns of Wales*, University of Wales Press, Cardiff.

Carter, H. (1969) *The Growth of the Welsh City System*, University of Wales Press, Cardiff.

Carter, H. (1972) *The Study of Urban Geography*, Edward Arnold, London.

Carter, H. (1977) Urban origins; a review, *Progress in Human Geography*, **1**, 12–32.

Carter, H., and Rowley, G. (1966) The morphology of the central business district of Cardiff, *Transactions of the Institute of British Geographers*, **38**, 119–134.

Carter, R. L. (1974) *The Criminals' Image of the City*, unpublished PhD thesis, University of Oklahoma, Norman.

Case, D. F. (1967) The influence of architecture on patterns of social life, unpublished m/s, Princeton University, cited in W. A. Michelson (1970) *Man and his Urban Environment*, Addison-Wesley, Reading, Mass.

Chance, J. K. (1975) The colonial Latin American city: pre-industrial or Capitalist? *Urban Anthropology*, **4**, 211–228.

Chandler, T. and Fox, G. (1974) *3000 years of Urban Growth*, Academic Press, New York.

Chapin, J. S. (1968) Activity systems and urban structure: a working scheme, *Journal, American Institute of Planners*, **34**, 11–18.

Chapple, E. D. (1942) The measurement of inter-personal behaviour, *Transactions, New York Academy of Sciences*, **4**, 222–232.

Childe, V. A. (1950) The urban revolution, *Town Planning Review*, **21**, 3–17.

Chilton, R. J. (1964) Continuity in delinquency area research: a comparison of studies for Baltimore, Detroit, and Indianapolis, *American Sociological Review*, **29**, 71–83.

Chisholm, M. (1975) *Human Geography: Evolution or Revolution*, Penguin, Harmondsworth.

Chorley, R. J., and Haggett, P. (1967) *Models in Geography*, Methuen, London.

Christäller, W. (1933) *Central Places in Southern Germany*, Gustav Fischer, Jena.

Christäller, W. (1966) *Central Places in Southern Germany*, translated by C. W. Baskin Prentice-Hall, New Jersey.

Christensen, T. (1982) The politics of redevelopment: Covent Garden, in D. T. Herbert and R. J. Johnston (eds.), *Geography and the Urban Environment*, Vol. 4, Wiley, London.

471

Church, R. L. and Meadows, M. E. (1979) Locational modelling utilising maximum service distance criteria, *Geographical Analysis*, **11**, 4, 358–378.

Clark, D. (1974) Technology, diffusion, and time-space convergence: the example of STD telephone, *Area*, **6**, 181–184.

Clark, W. A. V. (1967) The spatial structure of retail functions in a New Zealand city, *New Zealand Geographer*, **22**, 23–34.

Clarke, C. G. (1971) Residential segregation and inter-marriage in San Fernando, Trinidad, *Geographical Review*, **61**, 1971, 198–218.

Clarke, R. V. G. (ed.) (1978) *Tackling Vandalism*, Home Office Research Unit Research Study No. 47, HMSO, London.

Clements, D. W. (1977) The dispersed city: myth or reality. *Professional Geographer*, **29**, 26–31.

Clinard, M. (1978) *Cities without Crime: The Case of Switzerland*, Cambridge University Press, Cambridge.

Coates, B. E., and Rawstron, E. M. (1971) *Regional Variations in Britain*, Batsford, London.

Coates, K. and Silburn, R. (1970) *Poverty: the Forgotten Englishman*, Penguin, Harmondsworth.

Collingwood, R. G. (1956), *The Idea of History*, Oxford University Press, New York.

Community Development Project (1974) *Inter-project Report*, HMSO, London.

Conner, K. A., Powers, E. A., and Bultena, G. L. (1979) Social interaction and life satisfaction: an empirical assessment of late life patterns, *Journal of Gerontology*, **34**, 116–121.

Connor, W. D. (1970) Juvenile delinquency in the USSR: some quantitative and qualitative indicators, *American Sociological Review*, **35**, 283–97.

Conzen, M. P. (1978) Analytical approaches to urban landscape, in K. Butzer (ed.), *Dimensions of Human Geography*, University of Chicago, Geography Research paper 186, pp. 128–165.

Conzen, M. R. G. (1960) *Alnwick, Northumberland: A Study in Town Plan Analysis*, IBG Monograph No. 27, London.

Conzen, M. R. G. (1962) The plan analysis of an English city centre, in K. Norborg (ed.), *Proceedings of the IGU Symposium in Urban Geography, CWK Gleerup, Lund*.

Cooley, C. H. (1894) The theory of transportation, *Publication of the American Economic Association*, **9**, 5–7.

Cowgill, D. O. (1978) Residential segregation by age in American metropolitan areas, *Journal of Gerontology*, **33**, 446–453.

Cowlard, K. A. (1979) The identification of social (class) areas and their place in nineteenth-century urban development, *Transactions, Institute of British Geographers*, **NS4**, 239–257.

Cox, K. R. (1973) *Conflict, Power and Politics in the City: A Geographic View*, McGraw-Hill, New York.

Crowe, P. R. (1938) On progress in geography, *Scottish Geographical Magazine*, **54**, 1–19.

Cubitt, T. (1973) Network density among urban families, in J. Boissevain and J. C. Mitchell (eds.), *Network Analysis: Studies in Human Interaction*, Mouton, Hague, pp. 67–82.

Cullingworth, J. B. (1969) *Council Housing: Purposes, Procedures, and Priorities*, HMSO, London.

Cybriwsky, R. (1978) Social aspects of neighbourhood change, *Annals, Association of American Geographers*, **68**, 17–33.

Dacey, M. F. (1962) Analysis of central place and point patterns by a nearest neighbour method, in K. Norborg (ed.), *Proceedings of IGU Symposium in Urban Geography*, Gleerup, Lund.

Dahya, B. (1974) The nature of Pakistani ethnicity in British cities, in A. Cohen (ed.), *Urban Ethnicity*, Tavistock, London, pp. 77–118.

Dalkey, N. C. and Rourke, D. L. (1973) *The Delphi Procedure and Rating Quality of Life Factors. The Quality of Life Concept*, Environmental Protection Agency, Washington, DC, ii, 209–21.

472

Damer, S. (1974) Wine alley: the sociology of a dreadful enclosure, *Sociological Review*, **22**, 221–248.

Damesick, P. (1979) Offices and inner-urban regeneration, *Area*, **11**, 1, 41–47.

Daniels, P. W. (1974) New offices in the suburbs, in J. H. Johnson (ed.), *Suburban Growth*, Ch. 9, 177–200.

Daniels, P. W. (1975) *Office Location. An Urban and Regional Study*, G. Bell & Son Ltd., London.

Daniels, P. W. (1976) *Office Location Policy in Greater London: A Review*, Paper presented at Institute of British Geographers Urban Studies Group, University of Keele.

Daniels, P. W., and Warnes, A. M. (1980) *Movement in Cities. Spatial Perspectives on Urban Transport and Travel*, Methuen, London.

Darwent, D. F. (1969) Growth poles and growth centers in regional planning: a review, *Environment and Planning*, **1**, 5–32.

Davies, B. P. (1968) *Social Needs and Resources in Local Services*, Michael Joseph, London.

Davies, B. P. (1977) Social service studies and the explanation of policy outcomes, *Policy and Politics*, **5**, 41–59.

Davies, D. H. (1959) Boundary study as a tool in CBD analysis: an interpretation of certain aspects of the boundary of Cape Town's Central Business District, *Economic Geography*, **35**, 322–345.

Davies, R. L. (1969) Effects of consumer income differences on shopping movement behaviour, *Tijdschrift voor Economische en Sociale Geografie*, **60**, 111–121.

Davies, R. L. (1970) Variable relationships in central place and retail potential models, *Regional Studies*, **4**, 49–61.

Davies, R. L. (1972) Structural models of retail distribution: analysis with settlement and land-use theories, *Transactions, Institute of British Geographers*, **57**, 59–82.

Davies, R. L. (1973) *Patterns and Profiles of Consumer Behaviour*, Research Series No. 10, Department of Geography, University of Newcastle-upon-Tyne, Northumberland.

Davies, R. L. (1974) Nucleated and ribbon components of the urban retail system in Britain, *Town Planning Review*, **45**, 91–111.

Davies, R. L. (1976) *Marketing Geography—with Special Reference to Retailing*, Retailing and Planning Associates, Corbridge, Northumberland; and (1977) Methuen, London.

Davies, R. L. (1977) A framework for commercial planning policies, *Town Planning Review*, **48**, 42–58.

Davies, R. L., and Bennison, D. J. (1978) Retailing in the city centre: the character of shopping streets. *Tijdschrift voor Economische en Sociale Geografie*, **69**, 5, 270–285.

Davies, W. K. D. (1967) Centrality and the central place hierarchy, *Urban Studies*, **4**, 61–79.

Davies, W. K. D. (1968) The morphology of central places: a case study, *Annals, Association of American Geographers*, **58**, 91–110.

Davies, W. K. D. (1972) Conurbation and city region in an administrative borderland: a case study of the greater Swansea area, *Regional Studies*, **6**, 217–236.

Davies, W. K. D. (1978a) Alternative factorial solutions and urban-social structure: a data analysis exploration of Calgary in 1971, *Canadian Geographer*, **22**, 273–297.

Davies, W. K. D. (1978b) A social taxonomy of Edmonton's community areas in 1971, in P. J. Smith (ed.), *Edmonton: the Emerging Metropolitan Pattern*, Western Geographical Series 15, Victoria, Canada, pp. 161–197.

Davies, W. K. D. (1978c) Charles Booth and the measurement of urban social character, *Area*, **10**, 290–296.

Davies, W. K. D., and Lewis, C. R. (1970) Regional structures in Wales: two studies of connectivity, in H. Carter, and W. K. D. Davies (eds.), *Urban Essays: Studies in the Geography of Wales*, Chap. 2, 22–48, Longmans, London.

Davies, W. K. D, and Lewis, G. J. (1973) The urban dimensions of Leicester, England, Institute of British Geographers, Special Publication No. 5, *Social Patterns Cities*, 71–86.

473

Davies, W. K. D., and Robinson, G. W. S. (1968) The nodal structure of the Solent region, *Journal of the Town Planning Institute*, **54**, 18–22.

Davis, K. (1974) Colonial expansion and urban diffusion in the Americas, in D. J. Dwyer (ed.), *The City in the Third World*, Macmillan, London, pp. 34–48.

Daws, L. F., and Bruce, A. J. (1971) *Shopping in Watford*, Department of the Environment, Building Research Establishment.

Dawson, J. A. (1974) The suburbanization of retail activity, in J. H. Johnson (ed.), *Suburban Growth*, Ch. 8, John Wiley and Sons, London, 155–176.

Dawson, J. A. (ed.) (1980) *Retail Geography*, Croom Helm, London.

Dawson, J. A., and Murray, I. D. (1973) *Aspects of the Impact of Karrinyup Shopping Centre, Western Australia*, Geowest Working Paper No. 1, Department of Geography, University of Western Australia, Perth.

Day, R. A. (1973) Consumer shopping behaviour in a planned urban environment, *Tijdschrift voor Economische en Sociale Geografie*, **64**, 77–85.

De, S. N. (1961) Cholera in Calcutta, in *Cholera: its Pathology and Pathogenesis*, Oliver and Boyd.

Dear, M. J., and Wittman, I. (1980) Conflict over the location of mental health facilities, in D. T. Herbert and R. J. Johnston (eds.), *Geography and the urban Environment*, Vol. 4, Wiley, London.

Dennis, R., and Clout, H. (1980) *A Social Geography of England and Wales*, Pergamon Press, Oxford.

Department of the Environment (1972) *Development Control Policy Note 13*, HMSO, London.

Department of the Environment (1977) *Policy for the Inner Cities*, Cmnd. 6845, HMSO, London.

Department of Health and Social Security (1980) *Health and Personal Social Services. Statistics for England 1978*, HMSO, London.

Deutsch, K. W. (1966) *Nationalism and Social Communication*. MIT, Press, Cambridge, Mass.

Deutsch, M. and Collins, M. E. (1951) *Inter-racial Housing*, University of Minnesota, Minneapolis.

Diamond, D. R. (1962) *The Central Business District of Glasgow*, Proceedings of the Lund Symposium on Urban Geography, 1960, University of Lund, Sweden.

Dicken, P., and Lloyd, P. E. (1981) *Work, Home and Well-being*, Harper and Row, London.

Dickinson, R. E. (1947) *City, Region and Regionalism*, Kegan Paul, Trench and Trubner, London.

Dickinson, R. E. (1964) *City and Region*, Routledge and Kegan Paul, London.

Dingemans, D. (1979) Red-lining and mortgage lending in Sacramento, *Annals, Association of American Geographers*, **69**, 225–239.

Doherty, J. M. (1969) *Developments in Behavioural Geography*, Department of Geography Discussion Paper No. 35, London School of Economics and Political Science.

Douglas, J. W. B. (1964) *The Home and the School*, MacGibbon and Kee, London.

Downs, R. M. (1970) Geographic space perception: past approaches and future prospects, in C. Board *et al.* (eds.), *Progress in Geography*, 2, pp. 65–108.

Downs, R. M., and Stea, D. (1977) *Maps in Minds*, Harper Row, New York.

Doxiadis, C. A. (1966) The great Lakes megalopolis, *Ekistics*, **22**, 13–31.

Doxiadis, C. A. (1968) *Ekistics. An introduction to the Science of Human Settlement*, Hutchinson, London.

Drewett, R. (1980) Changing urban structures in Europe. *Annals of the American Association of Political and Social Science*, 451, 52–75.

Drewett, R., Goddard, J., and Spence, N. (1974) *Urban Change in Britain: 1966–1971*. Working Paper No. 1, Department of Geography, LSE London.

Driedger, L., and Church, G. (1974) Residential segregation and institutional completeness: a comparison of ethnic minorities, *Canadian Review of Sociology and Anthropology*, 11, 30–52.

Duncan, O. D., and Duncan, B. (1955) Residential distribution and occupational stratification, *American Journal of Sociology*, **60**, 493–503.

Duncan, S. (1976) Self-help: The allocation of mortgages and the formation of housing sub-markets, *Area*, **8**, 307–315.

Dwyer, D. J. (ed.) (1974) *The City in the Third World*, Macmillan, London.

Earickson, R. (1970) *The Spatial Behaviour of Hospital Patients*, Research Paper No. 124, Department of Geography, University of Chicago, Chicago.

Eckert, J. K. (1979) Urban renewal and redevelopment: high risk for the marginally subsistent elderly, in S. M. Golant (ed.), *Location and Environment of Elderly Population*, John Wiley, New York, pp. 496–508.

Edwards, J. (1975) Social indicators, urban deprivation and positive discrimination. *Journal of Social Policy*, **5**, 275–87.

Eisenstadt, S. N., and Curelaru, M. (1976) *The Form of Sociology: Paradigms and Crises*, Wiley, London.

Entrikin, J. N. (1977) Contemporary humanism in geography, *Annals, Association of American Geographers*, **66**, 615–32.

Ernst, R. T., and Hugg, L. (eds.) (1976) *Black America: Geographic Perspectives*, Anchor Books, New York.

Evans, A. (1973) The location of headquarters of industrial companies. *Urban Studies*, **10**, 387–395.

Eyles, J. D. (1970) *Space, Territory and Conflict*, University of Reading, Geographical Paper No. 1.

Eyles, J. D. (1971) Putting new sentiments into old theories: how else can we look at behavioural patterns? *Area*, **3**, 242–250.

Eyles, J. D., and Smith, D. M. (1979) Social geography, *American Behavioral Scientist*, **22**.

Fanning, D. M. (1967) Families in flats, *British Medical Journal*, **18**, 382–386.

Faris, R. E. and Dunham, H. W. (1939) *Mental Disorders in Urban Areas*, University of Chicago Press, Chicago.

Festinger, L., Schachter, S., and Back, K. (1950) *Social Pressures in Informal Groups*, Stanford University Press, Stanford.

Fine, J., Glenn, N. D., and Monts, J. K. (1971) The residential segregation of occupational groups in central cities and suburbs, *Demography*, **8**, 91–102.

Firey, W. E. (1947) *Land use in Central Boston*, Harvard University Press, Cambridge, Mass.

Firing Line (1979) Interview with Mayor Koch of New York City.

Fischer, C. S. (1976) *The Urban Experience*, H. B. Ivon, New York.

Fischer, C. S., Baldassare, M., and Oske, R. J. (1975) Crowding studies and urban life, a critical review, *Journal, American Institute of Planners*, **31**, 406–18.

de Fleur, L. B. (1967) Ecological variables in the cross-cultural study of delinquency, *Social Forces*, **45**, 556–570.

Ford, L., and Griffin, E. (1979) The ghettoization of paradise, *Geographical Review*, **69**, 140–158.

Form, W. H., Smith, J., Stone, G. P., and Cowling, J. (1954) The compatibility of alternative approaches to the delimitation of urban and sub-areas, *American Sociological Review*, **19**, 434–440.

Forster, C. A. (1968) The development of by-law housing in Kingston-upon-Hull, *Proceedings IBG Urban Study Group*, Salford, 115–131.

Fourastié, J. (1963) *Le Grand Espoir Du XX Siècle*, Gallimard, Paris.

Francescato, D., and Mebane, W. (1973) How citizens view two great cities; Milan and Rome, in R. M. Downs and D. Stea (eds.), *Image and Environment*, Aldine, Chicago, pp. 131–47.

Freedman, J. L. (1975) *Crowding and Behavior*, Viking Press, New York.

Frey, A. (1973) The teaching of regional geography, *Geography*, **58** 119–128.

Friedmann, J. R. (1966) *Regional Development Policy: A Case Study of Venezuela*, MIT Press, Cambridge, Mass.

Friedmann, J. R. (1972a) A generalized theory of polarized development, in N. Hansen, (ed.), *Growth Centres in Regional Economic Development*, Free Press, New York.

Friedmann, J. R. (1972b) The spatial organisation of power in the development of urban systems, *Comparative Urban Research*, **1**.

Friedmann, J. R. (1973) *Urbanization, Planning and National Development*, Sage, Beverly Hills.

Friedmann, J. R. (1978) The urban field as a human habitat, in L. S. Bourne, and J. W. Simmons (eds.), *Systems of Cities. Readings on Structure, Growth and Policy*, Oxford University Press, New York, pp. 42–52.

Friedmann, J., and Wulff, R. (1976) *The Urban Transition, Comparative Studies of Newly Industrialising Societies*, Edward Arnold, London.

Fyvel, T. R. (1961) *The Insecure Offenders*, Penguin, Harmondsworth.

Gans, H. J. (1962) *The Urban Villagers*, Free Press, New York.

Gans, H. J. (1967) *The Levittowners*, Pantheon, New York.

Gans, H. J. (1972) *People and Plans*, Basic Books, New York.

Gantvoort, J. T. (1971) Shopping centre versus town centre, *Town Planning Review*, **42**, 61–70.

Garner, B. J. (1966) *The Internal Structure of Shopping Centres*, Northwestern University, Studies in Geography, 12.

Garrison, W. L. (1956) Applicability of statistical inference to geographical research. *Geographical Review*, **46**, 427–428.

Garrison, W. L. (1959, 1960) The spatial structure of the economy, I, II, and III. *Annals, Association of American Geographers*, **49**, 232–239 and 471–482; **50**, 357–373.

Garrison, W. L. (1962) Discussion. *Proceedings of I.G.U. in Urban Geography*, Lund Series, B. No. 24, 463.

Garrison, W. L., and Marble, D. F. (1967) *Quantitative Geography*, Parts 1 and 2. Northwestern University Studies in Geography, Nos. 13 and 14, Evanston, Ill.

Geddes, P. (1915) *Cities in Evolution*, Williams and Norgate, London.

Giggs, J. A. (1972) Retail change and decentralisation in the Nottingham Metropolitan Community, *Geographia Polonica*, **24**, 173–188.

Giggs, J. A. (1973) The distribution of schizophrenics in Nottingham, *Transactions, Institute of British Geographers*, **59**, 55–76.

Giggs, J. A. (1979) Human health problems in urban areas, in D.T. Herbert and D. M. Smith (eds.), *Social Problems and the City: Geographical Perspectives*, Oxford University Press, Oxford, pp. 84–116.

Gill, O. (1977) *Luke Street*, Macmillan, London.

Glass, R. (1948) *The Social Background to a Plan: the Study of Middlesbrough*, Routledge and Kegan Paul, London.

Glueck, S. and Glueck E. (1950) *Unravelling Juvenile Delinquency*, Commonwealth Fund New York.

Goddard, J. B. (1968) Multivariate analysis of office location patterns in the city centre: a London example, *Regional Studies*, **2**, 69–85.

Goddard, J. B. (1970) Functional regions within the city centre: a study by factor analysis of taxi flows in central London, *Transactions of Institute of British Geographers*, **49**, 161–182.

Goddard, J. B. (1975) *Office Location in Urban and Regional Development*, Oxford University Press.

Goheen, P. G. (1970) *Victorian Toronto 1850–1900: Patterns and Processes of Growth*, University of Chicago, Geography Research Paper 127.

Golant, S. M. (1975) Residential concentrations of the future elderly, *The Gerontologist*, **15**, 16–23.

Golant, S. M. (1980) Locational–environmental perspectives on old-age segregated areas in the United States, in D. T. Herbert and R. J. Johnston (eds.), *Geography and the Urban Environment*, Vol. 3, Wiley, London, pp. 257–294.

Golledge, R. G. (1978) Learning about human environments, in T. Carlstein, D. Parkes and N. Thrift (eds.), *Making Sense of Time*, Arnold, London, pp. 76–98.

Golledge, R. G., Rushton, G., and Clark, W. A. V. (1966). Some spatial characteristics of Iowa's dispersed farm population and their implications for the grouping of central place functions, *Economic Geography*, **42**, 261–272.

Gordon, G. (1979) The status area of early to mid-Victorian Edinburgh, *Transactions, Institute of British Geographers*, **NS4**, 168–191.

Gordon, R. A. (1967) Issues in the ecological study of delinquency, *American Sociological Review*, **32**, 927–944.

Gottmann, J. (1961) *Megalopolis: The Urbanized Northeastern Seaboard of the United States*, MIT Press, Cambridge, Mass.

Gottmann, J. (1976). Megalopolitan systems around the world, *Ekistics*, **243**, 109–113.

Gould, P., and White, R. (1974) *Mental Maps*, Penguin, Harmondsworth.

Gravier, J. F. (1947) *Paris et le Desert Français*, Flammarion, Paris.

Gray, F. (1975) Non-explanation in urban geography, *Area*, **7**, 228–235.

Greater London Council, (1970) *Greater London Development Plan*, Statement, GLC, London.

Greeley, A. (1969) *Why Can't They Be Like Us?* Institute of Human Relations Press, New York.

Gregory, D. (1978) *Ideology, Science and Human Geography*, Hutchinson, London.

Gregory, S. (1976) On geographical myths and statistical fables. *Transactions, Institute of British Geographers*, **NS**, 385–400.

Griffin, D. W., and Preston, R. E. (1966) A restatement of the 'Transition Zone' concept. *Annals, Association of American Geographers*, **56**, 339–350.

Gripaios, P. (1977) The closure of firms in the inner city: the south-east London case 1970–75, *Regional Studies*, **11**, 1–6.

Guelke, L. (1974) An idealist alternative in human geography, *Annals, Association of American Geographers*, **64**, 193–202.

Guelke. L. (1978) Geography and logical positivism, in D. T. Herbert and R. J. Johnston (eds.), *Geography and the Urban Environment*, Vol. 1, Wiley, London, pp. 35–61.

Guest, A. M. (1974) Neighbourhood life cycles and social status, *Economic Geography*, **50**, 228–243.

Habermas, J. (1972) *Knowledge and Human Interests*, Heinemann, London.

Hagerstrand, T. (1957) Migration and area, *Lund Studies in Geography*, **B, 13**, 27–158.

Hagerstrand, T. (1966) Aspects of the spatial structure of social communications and the diffusion of innovations, *Papers and Proceedings of the Regional Science Association*, **16**, 27–42.

Hagerstrand, T. (1967) On Monte Carlo simulation of diffusion, in W. L. Garrison, and D. F. Marble, (eds.), *Quantitative Geography, Part I*, Economic and Cultural Topics, Northwestern University Studies in Geography, No. 13, 1–32.

Haggett, P. (1965) *Locational Analysis in Human Geography*, Edward Arnold, London.

Haggett, P. (1979) *Geography: A Modern Synthesis*, Harper and Row, New York.

Haig, R. M. (1926) Towards an understanding of the metropolis, *Quarterly Journal of Economics*, **40**, 421.

Hall, E. T. (1966) *The Hidden Dimension*, Bodley Head, London.

Hall, F. L. (1973) *Location Criteria for High Schools*, Geography Research Paper, University of Chicago, No. 150.

Hall, J. M. (1976) *London: Metropolis and Region*, Oxford University Press, Oxford.

Hall, P. (1966) *The World Cities*, Weidenfeld and Nicolson, London.

Hall. P. (1974a) The new political geography, *Transactions, Institute of British Geographers*, **63**, 48–52.

Hall, P. (1974b) *Urban and Regional Planning*, Penguin, London.
Hall, P. (1977) *The World Cities*, 2nd edition Weidenfeld and Nicholson, London.
Hall, P., and Hay, D. (1980) *Growth Centres in the European Urban System*, Heinemann, London.
Hall, P., Thomas, R., Gracey, H., and Drewett, R. (1973) *The Containment of Urban England Vol. 1. Urban and Metropolitan Growth Processes*. Vol. 2. *The Planning System. Objectives, Operations and Impacts*, Allen and Unwin, London.
Halsey, A. H. (ed.) (1972) *Educational Priority*, HMSO, London.
Hamilton, F. E. I. (1967) *Models of industrial location*, Ch. 10, in R. J. Chorley and P. Haggett (eds.), *Socio-economic Models in Geography*, Methuen, London, pp. 361–424.
Hamnett, C. (1979) Area-based explanations: a critical appraisal, in D. T. Herbert and D. M. Smith (eds.), *Social Problems and the City: Geographical Perspectives*, Oxford University Press, Oxford, pp. 244–260.
Hanson, S. (1977) Measuring the cognitive levels of urban residents, *Geografiska Annaler*, **59B**, 67–81.
Hare, F. K. (1974) Geography and public policy: a Canadian view, *Transactions, Institute of British Geographers*, **63**, 25–28.
Harloe, M. (ed.) (1974) *Captive Cities*, Wiley, London.
Harries, K. D. (1974) *The Geography of Crime and Justice*, McGraw-Hill, New York.
Harries, K. D., and Brunn, S. (1978) The *Geography of Laws and Justice*, Praeger, New York.
Harris, C. D. (1943) A functional classification of American cities. *Geographical Review*, **33**, 86–99.
Harris, C. D., and Ullman, E. L. (1945) The nature of cities, *Annals, American Academy of Political and Social Science*, **242**, 7–17.
Harrison, R. T., and Livingstone, D. N. (1979) There and back again—towards a critique of idealist human geography, *Area*, **11**, 75–79.
Hart, J. T. (1971) The inverse care law, *Lancet*, 405–412.
Hart, R. A., and Moore, G. T. (1973) The development of spatial cognition: a review, in R. M. Downs and D. Stea (eds.), *Image and Environment*, Aldine, Chicago, pp. 246–88.
Hartshorne, R. (1939) *The Nature of Geography*, Association of American Geographers, Lancaster, Pennsylvania.
Hartshorne, R. (1955) Exceptionalism in geography re-examined, *Annals, Association of American Geographers*, **45**, 205–244.
Harvey, D. (1969) *Explanation in Geography*, Edward Arnold, London.
Harvey, D. (1973) *Social Justice and the City*, Arnold, London.
Harvey, D. (1977) Government policies, financial institutions and neighbourhood change in United States cities, in M. Harloe (ed.), *Captive Cities*, Wiley, London. pp. 123–139.
Harvey, D. (1978) Labor, capital and class struggle around the built environment in advanced capitalist countries, in K. R. Cox (ed.), *Urbanization and Conflict in Market Societies*, Maaroufa Press, Chicago, pp. 9–37.
Hassan, R. (1972) Islam and urbanization in the medieval Middle-East, *Ekistics* **33**, 108–109.
Hatt, P. K. (1946) The concept of natural area, *American Sociological Review*, **11**, 423–427.
Hauser, P. M. (ed.) (1957) *Urbanisation in Asia and the Far East*, UNESCO, Calcutta.
Hawley, A. H., and Duncan, O. D. (1957) Social area analysis: a critical appraisal, *Land Economics*, **33**, 227–245.
Hay, A. M. (1979) Positivism in human geography: Response to critics, in D. T. Herbert and R. J. Johnston (eds.), *Geography and the Urban Environment*, Vol. 2, Wiley, London, pp. 1–26.
Haynes, K. E., and Hakim, S. M. el (1979) Technology and public policy: the urban waste management system in Cairo, *Geographical Review*, **69**, 101–108.
Herbert, D. T. (1967) Diagnostic variables in the analysis of urban-social structure, *Tijdschrift voor Economische en Sociale Geografie*, **58**, 5–10.

478

Herbert, D. T. (1972) *Urban Geography: A Social Perspective*, David and Charles, Newton Abbot.

Herbert, D. T. (1973) Residential mobility and preference: a study of Swansea, *IBG Special Publication*, 5, 103–121.

Herbert, D. T. (1975a) Urban deprivation: definition, measurement, and spatial qualities, *Geographical Journal*, **141**, 362–372.

Herbert, D. T. (1975b) Urban neighbourhoods and social geographical research, in A. D. M. Phillips and B. J. Turton (eds.), *Environment, Man, and Economic Change*, Longman, London, pp. 459–478.

Herbert, D. T. (1976) Urban education: problems and policies, Ch 3, in D. T. Herbert and R. J. Johnston (eds.), *Social Areas in Cities*, Vol. 2, *Spatial Perspectives on Problems and Policies*, John Wiley, London.

Herbert, D. T. (1977a) Crime, delinquency and the urban environment, *Progress in Human Geography*, **1**, 208–239.

Herbert, D. T. (1977b) An areal and ecological analysis of delinquency residence: Cardiff 1966 and 1971, *Tijdschrift voor Economische en Sociale Geografie*, **68**, 83–99.

Herbert D. T. (1979) Introduction: geographical perspectives and urban problems, in D. T. Herbert and D. M. Smith (eds.), *Social Problems and the City: Geographical Perspectives*, Oxford University Press, London, pp. 1–9.

Herbert, D. T., and Johnston, R. J. (1978) *Geography and the Urban Environment*, Vol. 1, John Wiley, London, pp. 1–33.

Herbert, D. T., and Peace, Sheila M. (1980) The elderly in an urban environment: a study of Swansea, in D. T. Herbert and R. J. Johnston (eds.), *Geography and the Urban Environment*, Vol. 3, Wiley, London, pp. 223–255.

Herbert, D. T., and Raine, J. W. (1976) Defining communities within urban areas, *Town Planning Review*, **47**, 325–38.

Herbert, D. T. and Williams, W. M. (1964) Some new techniques for studying urban subdivisions, *Applied Geography 2, Geographica Polonica*, 3, 93–117.

Herbert D. T. and de Silva, S. K. (1974) Social dimensions of a non-western city: a factorial ecology of Colombo, *Cambria*, 1, 139–158.

Herbert, D. T. and Smith, D. M. (eds.) (1979) *Social Problems and the City: Geographical Perspectives*, Oxford University Press, Oxford.

Her Majesty's Stationery Office (1962) *Town Centres: Approach to Renewal*, Ministry of Housing and Local Government and Ministry of Transport.

Her Majesty's Stationery Office (1964) *Traffic in Towns*, The specially shortened edition of the Buchanan Report, Penguin, London.

Her Majesty's Stationery Office (1970) *Strategic Plan for the South East*, London.

Her Majesty's Stationery Office (1973) *The Dispersal of Government Work from London* (The Hardman Report), Cmnd. 5322.

Hillery, G. A. (1955) Definition of community; areas of agreement, *Rural Sociology*, **20**, 111–23.

Hillman, M., and Whalley, A. (1977) Fair play for all: a study of access for sport and informal recreation, *PEP Broadsheet* No. 57.

Hindess, B. (1973) *The Use of Official Statistics in Sociology*, Macmillan, London.

Hirschman, A. O. (1958) *The Strategy of Economic Development*, Yale University Press, New Haven.

Hodder, B. W. (1961) Rural periodic day markets in part of Yorubaland, *Transactions of the Institute of British Geographers*, **29**, 149–151.

Hodge, G. (1965) The prediction of trade center viability in the Great Plains, *Papers and Proceedings of the Regional Science Association*, **15**, 87–115.

Hodges, M. W., and Smith, C. S. (1954) The Sheffield estate, in T. Simey (ed.), *Neighbourhood and Community*, Liverpool University Press, London.

Holly, B. P., and Wheeler, J. O. (1972) Patterns of retail location and the shopping trips of low-income households, *Urban Studies*, **9**, 215–220.

Holtermann, S. (1975) Areas of urban deprivation in Great Britain: an analysis of 1971 census data, *Social Trends*, **6**, 33–47.

Hoppenfeld, M. (1966) A sketch of the planning-building process for Columbia, Maryland, *Journal, American Institute of Planners*, **33**, 398–409.

Horton, F. E., and Reynolds, D. R. (1971) Effects of urban spatial structure on individual behaviour, *Economic Geography*, **47**, 36–46.

Horvath, R. J. (1969) In search of a theory of urbanisation: notes on the colonial city, *East Lakes Geographer*, **5**, 69–82.

Horwood, E. M., and Boyce, R. R. (1959) *Studies of the Central Business District and Urban Freeway Development*, University of Washington Press, Seattle.

Hoselitz, B. F. (1960) *Sociological Aspects of Economic Growth*, Free Press, Glencoe, Ill.

House, J. W. (1973) *The UK Space. Resources, Environment and the Future*, Weidenfeld and Nicolson, London.

Howe, G. M. (ed.) (1977) *A World Geography of Human Disease*, Academic Press, London.

Hoyt, H. (1939) *The Structure and Growth of Residential Neighbourhoods in American Cities*, Federal Housing Administration, Washington.

Hoyt, H. (1954) Homer Hoyt on development of economic base concept, *Land Economics*, **30**, 182–186.

Huff, D. L. (1963) A probablistic analysis of shopping centre trade areas, *Land Economics*, **39**, 81–90.

Humphrys, G., and Bromley R. D. F. (1979) *Dealing with Dereliction. The Redevelopment of the Lower Swansea Valley*, University College of Swansea, Swansea.

Hurd, R. (1903) *Principles of City Land Values*, New York Record and Guide, 19–21.

Husserl, E. (1970) *The Crisis of European Sciences and Transcendental Phenomenology*, Northwestern University Press, Evanston, Ill.

Irving, H. (1975a) Distance, intensity, kinship: key dimensions of social interaction, *Sociology and Social Research*, **60**, 77–86.

Irving, H. (1975b) A geographer looks at personality, *Area*, **7**, 207–12.

Irving, H. (1977) Social networks in the modern city, *Social Forces*, 867–880.

Irving, H. (1978) Space and environment in interpersonal relations, in D. T. Herbert and R. J. Johnston (eds.), *Geography and the Urban Environment*, Vol. 1, pp. 249–284.

Irving, H. and Davidson, R. N. (1973) A working note on the measurement of social interaction, *Transactions of the Bartlett Society*, **9**, 1–15.

Isard, W. (1960) *Methods of Regional Analysis: An Introduction to Regional Science*, MIT Press, Cambridge, Mass.

Jacobs, J. (1961) *Death and Life of Great American Cities*, Random House, New York.

Jacobs, J. (1969) *The Economy of Cities*, Random House, New York.

Jakle, J. A., Brunn, S., and Roseman, C. C. (1976) *Human Spatial Behaviour: a Social Geography*, Duxbury, New York.

Jakle, J. A., and Wheeler, J. O. (1969) The changing residential structure of the Dutch population of Kalamazoo, Michigan, *Annals, Association of American Geographers*, **59**, 441–460.

Jakobson, L., and Prakash, V. (eds.) (1971) *Urbanization and National Development*, Sage, Beverly Hills.

James, P. (1972) *All Possible Worlds: A History of Geographical Ideas*, The Odyssey Press, New York.

Jefferson, M. (1939) The law of the primate city. *Geographical Review*, **29**, 226–232.

Jenkins, M. A., and Shepherd, J. W. (1972) Decentralizing high school administration in Detroit, *Economic Geography*, **48**, 95–106.

Jensen–Butler, C. (1972) Gravity models as planning tools: a review of theoretical and operational problems, *Geografiska Annaler*, **54B**, 68–78.

Jessop, B. (1972) *Social Order, Reform, and Revolution*, Macmillan, London.

Johnston, R. J. (1969) Population movements and metropolitan expansion, *Transactions, Institute of British Geographers*, **46**, 69–91.

Johnston, R. J. (1971a) *Urban Residential Patterns*, Bell, London.

Johnston, R. J. (1971b) On the progression from primacy to rank-size in an urban system: the deviant case of New Zealand, *Area*, **3**, 180–184.

Johnston, R. J. (1972) Towards a general model of intra-urban residential patterns: some cross-cultural comparisons, *Progress in Geography*, **4**, 83–124.

Johnston, R. J. (1974a) Local effects in voting at a local election, *Annals, Association of American Geographers*, **64**, 418–29.

Johnston, R. J. (1974b) Social distance, proximity and social contact, *Geografiska Annaler*, **56B**, 57–67.

Johnston, R. J. (1976) Political behaviour and the residential mosaic, in D. T. Herbert and R. J. Johnston (eds.), *Spatial Perspectives on Problems and Policies*, Wiley, London, pp. 65–88.

Johnston, R. J. (1979b) On the characterization of urban social areas, *Tijdschrift voor Economische en Sociale Geografie*, **70**, 232–238.

Johnston, R. J. (1979a) *Political, Electoral and Spatial Systems*, Clarendon Press, Oxford.

Johnston, R. J. (1980) *City and Society: an Outline for Urban Geography*, Penguin, Harmondsworth.

Johnston R. J., and Rimmer, P. J. (1969) *Retailing in Melbourne*, Research School of Pacific Studies Publication HG/3, Department of Human Geography, Australian National University, Canberra.

Johnston, R. J. and Rossiter, D. (1981) An approach to the delimitation of planning regions, *Applied Geography*, **1**, 55–69.

Jones, E. (1960) *The Social Geography of Belfast*, Oxford University Press, Oxford.

Jones, E. (1966) *Towns and Cities*, Oxford University Press, London.

Jones, E. (ed.) (1975) *Readings in Social Geography*, Oxford University Press, London.

Jones, E., and Eyles, J. (1977) *An Introduction to Social Geography*, Oxford University Press, Oxford.

Jones, F. L. (1969) *Dimensions of Urban Social Structure*, Australian National University Press, Canberra.

Jones, P. N. (1970) Some aspects of the changing distribution of coloured immigrants in Birmingham, 1961–1966, *Transactions, Institute of British Geographers*, **50**, 199–219.

Jones, P. N. (1979) Ethnic areas in British cities, in D. T. Herbert and D. M. Smith (eds.), *Social Problems and the City: Geographical perspectives*, Oxford University Press, Oxford, pp. 158–185.

Jones, R. (ed.) (1975) *Essays on World Urbanization*, G. Philip, London.

de Jonge, D. (1962) Images of urban areas, *Journal, American Institute of Planners*, **28**, 266–76.

Kearsley, G. W., and Srivastava, S. R. (1974) The spatial evolution of Glasgow's Asian community, *Scottish Geographical Magazine*, **90**, 110–124.

Keeble, D. E. (1967) Models of economic development, in R. J. Chorley, and P. Haggett, (eds.), *Models in Geography*, Methuen, London.

Kerr, D., and Spelt, J. (1965) *The Changing Face of Toronto—A Study in Urban Geography*, Queen's Printers, Ottawa.

Khodzhaev, D. G., and Khorev, B. S. (1973) The concept of a unified settlement system and planned control of the growth of towns in the USSR, *Geographia Polonica*, **27**, 43–51.

King, L. J. (1966) Cross-sectional analysis of Canadian urban dimensions: 1951 and 1961. *Canadian Geographer*, **10**, 205–224.

Kirk, W. (1951) Historical geography and the concept of the behavioural environment, *Indian Geographical Journal*, Silver Jubilee Volume, pp. 152–160.

Kirk, W. (1963) Problems of geography, *Geography*, **48**, 357–371.

Kivell, P. T. (1972) Retailing in non-central locations, *Institute of British Geographers*, Occasional Population No. 1, **1972**, 49–58.

Klein, H. J. (1967) The delimitation of the town centre in the image of its citizens, in W. F. Heinemeijes *et. al.* (eds.), *Urban Core and Inner City*, Brill, Leiden, pp. 286–306.

481

Knos, D. (1962) *Distribution of Land Values in Topeka*, Lawrence, Kansas.

Knox, P. L. (1975) *Social Well-being: a Spatial Perspective*, Oxford University Press, Oxford.

Knox, P. L. (1978) The intra-urban ecology of primary medical care: patterns of accessibility and their policy implications. *Environment and Planning*, A, **10**, 415–435.

Knox, P. L., and Maclaran, A. (1978) Values and perceptions in descriptive approaches to urban-social geography, in D. T. Herbert and R. J. Johnston (eds.), *Geography and the Urban Environment*, Vol. 1, John Wiley, London, pp. 197–247.

Kofoed, J. (1970) Personal movement research: a discussion of concepts, *Papers, Regional Science Association*, **24**, 141–55.

Kottis, G. C., and Kottis, A. (1972) A statistical exploration of some factors responsible for decline of the Central Business District, *Land Economics*, **48**, 2, 169–173.

Kuhn, T. S. (1962) *The Structure of Scientific Revolutions*, University of Chicago Press, Chicago.

Kuper, L. (1953) *Living in Towns*, Cresset Press, London.

Lakshmanan, T. R. and Chatterjee, L. R. (1977) *Urbanization and Environmental Quality*, AAG Resource Paper, 77–1, Washington.

Lakshmanan, T. R., and Hansen, W. G. (1965) A retail market potential model, *Journal of the American Institute of Planners*, **31**, 134–144.

Lampard, E. E. (1965) Historical aspects of urbanisation, in P. M. Hauser and L. P. Schnore (eds.), *The Study of Urbanisation*, Wiley, New York, pp. 519–554.

Lander, B. (1954) *Towards an Understanding of Juvenile Delinquency*, Columbia University Press, New York.

Langton, J. (1975) Residential patterns in pre-industrial cities: some case studies of the seventeenth century, *Transactions of the Institute of British Geographers*, **65**, 1–27.

Langton, J. (1978) Industry and towns, 1500 to 1730, in R. A. Dodgson, and R. A. Butlin (eds.), *A Historical Geography of England and Wales*, Academic Press, London, pp. 173–198.

Laquian, A. A. (1971) Slums and squatters in South and South-east Asia, in L. Jakobson and V. Prakash (eds.), *Urbanization and National Development*, Sage, Beverly Hills, pp. 183–203.

de Lauwe, P. C. (1952) *Paris et L'Agglomeration Parisiennes*, Paris.

Law, C., and Warnes, A. M. (1980) The characteristics of retired migrants, in D. T. Herbert and R. J. Johnston (eds.), *Geography and the Urban Environment*, Vol. 3, John Wiley, London, pp. 175–222.

Lawton, M. P. (1970) Ecology and ageing, in L. A. Pastalan and D. H. Carson (eds.), *Spatial Behavior of Older People*, University of Michigan, pp. 40–67.

Lawton, M. P., and Simon, B. (1968) The ecology of social relationships in housing for the elderly, *The Gerontologist*, **8**, 108–115.

Lawton, R. (1972) An age of great cities, *Town Planning Review*, **43**, 199–224.

Lawton, R. (1979) Mobility in nineteenth-century British cities, *Geographical Journal*, **145**, 206–224.

Lawton, R. and Pooley, C. G. (1975) *The Urban Dimensions of Nineteenth Century Liverpool*, Department of Geography Project Working Paper 4, Liverpool University.

Lazarsfeld, P. F., Berelson, B., and Gaudet, H. (1944) *The People's Choice*, Columbia University Press, New York.

Lee, R. (1979) The economic basis of social problems in the city. In D. T. Herbert and D. M. Smith (eds.), *Social Problems and the City: Geographical Perspectives*, Oxford University Press, Oxford, pp. 45–62.

Lee, T. R. (1963) Psychology and living space, *Transactions, Bartlett Society*, **2**, 9–36.

Lee, T. R. (1968) Urban neighbourhood as a socio-spatial schema, *Human Relations*, **21**, 241–268.

Lee, T. R. (1970) Perceived distance as a function of direction in a city, *Environment and Behaviour*, **2**, 40–51.

482

Lee, T. R. (1971) Psychology and architectural determinism, *Architect's Journal*, **154**, 253–62.

Lee, T. R. (1976) Cities in the mind, in D. T. Herbert and R. J. Johnston (eds.), *Spatial Perspectives on Problems and Policies*, Wiley, London.

Leighton, P. A. (1966) Geographical aspects of air pollution, *Geographical Review*, **61**, 151–174.

Lentnek, B., Lieber, S. R., and Sheskin, I. (1975) Consumer behaviour in different areas, *Annals, Association of American Geographers*, **65**, 538–545.

Leonard, S. (1979) Managerialism, manager and self-management, *Area*, **11**, 87–88.

Levy, L., and Rowitz, L. (1973) *The Ecology of Mental Disorder*, Behavioral Publications, New York.

Lewin, K. (1951) *The Conceptual Representation and Measurement of Psychological Forces*, Duke University Press, Durham, North Carolina.

Lewis, C. R. (1975) The analysis of changes in urban status: a case study in Mid-Wales and the middle Welsh Borderland. *Transactions, Institute of British Geographers*, **64**, 49–65.

Lewis, C. R., (1979) A stage in the development of the industrial town: a case study of Cardiff, 1845–1875, *Transactions, Institute of British Geographers*, **NS, 4**, 129–152.

Lewis, G. J. (1972) Leicester-urban structure and regional relationships, in N. Pye (ed.), *Leicester and its Region*, Leicester.

Lewis, O. (1966) The culture of poverty, *Scientific American*, **215**, 19–25.

Ley, D. (1974a) *Community Participation and the Spatial Order of the City*, Tantalus Research Ltd., Vancouver.

Ley, D. (1974b) *The Black Inner City as Frontier Outpost: Images and Behavior of a Philadelphia Neighbourhood*, Association of American Geographers, Monograph No. 7. Washington.

Ley, D. (1977) Social geography and the taken-for-granted world, *Transactions, Institute of British Geographers*, **NS2**, 498–512.

Ley, D., and Cybriwsky, R. (1974a) Urban graffiti as territorial markers, *Annals, Association of American Geographers*, **64**, 491–505.

Ley, D., and Cybriwsky, R. (1974b) The spatial ecology of stripped cars, *Environment and Behavior*, **6**, 53–67.

Lieber, S. R. (1977) Attitudes and revealed behaviour: a case study. *Professional Geographer*, **29**, 53–58.

Linsky, A. S. (1965) Some generalisations concerning primate cities, *Annals, Association of American Geographers*, **55**, 506–513.

Liu, B. C. (1975) *Quality of Life Indicators in United States Metropolitan Areas, 1970*, US Environmental Protection Agency, Washington.

Lloyd, P. E., and Mason, C. M. (1978) Manufacturing industry in the inner city: a case study of Greater Manchester. *Transactions, Institute of British Geographers*, **NS3**, 66–90.

Loewenstein, L. K. (1963) The location of urban land uses, *Land Economics*, **39**, 406–420.

Lomas, G. M. (1964). Retail trading centres in the Midlands. *Journal of the Town Planning Institute*, 50, 104–119.

Lomas, G. M. (1975) *The Inner City: A Preliminary Investigation*, London Council of Social Services, London.

Lombroso, C. (1968) *Crime: Its Causes and Remedies*, Patterson, Smith, Montclair, New York (first published in 1911).

Lord, J. D. (1977) *Spatial Perspectives on School Segregation and Bussing*, Association of American Geographers, Research Paper 77–3, Washington.

Lösch, A. (1954) *The Economics of Location* (translated from 1940 version by W. H. Woglom, and W. F. Stolper), Yale University Press, New Haven.

Lowenthal, D. (1961) Geography, experience, and imagination: towards a geographical epistemology, *Annals, Association of American Geographers*, **51**, 241–260.

Luxemburg, R. (1913) *The Accumulation of Capital*, London.

Lyman, S. M., and Scott, M. B. (1967) Territoriality: a neglected sociological dimension, *Social Problems*, **15**, 236–49.

Lynch, K. (1960) *The Image of the City*, MIT Press, Cambridge, Mass.

Mabogunje, A. L. (1974) The pre-colonial development of Yoruba towns, in D. J. Dwyer (ed.), *The City in the Third World*, Macmillan, London, pp. 26–33.

McCarty, H. H., Hook, J. C., and Knos, D. C. (1956) *The Measurement of Association in Industrial Geography*, Department of Geography, University of Iowa.

McElrath, D. C. (1962) The social areas of Rome: a comparative analysis, *American Sociological Review*, **27**, 376–391.

McElrath, D. C. (1968) Societal scale and social differentiation: Accra, Ghana, in S. Greer, D. C. McElrath, D. W. Minor, P. Orleans (eds.), *The New Urbanization*, St Martin's Press, New York, pp. 33–52.

McGee, T. G. (1967) *The South-east Asian City*, Bell, London.

McGee, T. G. (1971a) *The Urbanization Process in the Third World: Explorations in Search of a Theory*, Bell, London.

McGee, T. G. (1971b) Catalysts or cancers? The role of cities in Asian society, in L. Jakobson and V. Prakash (eds.), *Urbanization and National Development*, Sage, Beverly Hills, pp. 157–181.

MacKinder, H. J. (1902) *Britain and the British Seas*, Heinemann, London.

McKinlay, J. B. (1972) Some approaches and problems in the study of the use of services, *Journal of Health and Social Behaviour*, **13**, **2**, 115–152.

Maclaran, A. (1981) Area-based positive discrimination and the distribution of well-being, *Transactions, Institute of British Geographers*, **6**, 53–67.

Mann, P. (1958) The socially balanced neighbourhood unit, *Town Planning Review*, **29**, 91–8.

Manners, G. (ed.) (1972) *Regional Development in Britain*, Wiley, New York.

Manners, G. (1974) The office in metropolis: an opportunity for shaping metropolitan America, *Economic Geography*, **50**, 93–110.

Mannheim, H. (1965) *Comparative Criminology*, Routledge and Kegan Paul, London.

Mason, P. F. (1973) Spatial variability of atmospheric radioactivity in the United States, in M. Albaum (ed.), *Geography and Contemporary Issues*, John Wiley, New York, pp. 357–363.

Massam, B. (1972) *The Spatial Structure of Administrative Systems*, Association of American Geographers, Research Paper No. 12, Washington.

Massam, B. (1975) *Location and Space in Social Administration*, Edward Arnold, London.

Mauss, M. (1970) *The Gift: Forms and Functions of Exchange in Archaic Societies*, Routledge and Kegan Paul, London.

Mawby, R. I. (1977a) Defensible space: a theoretical and empirical approach, *Urban Studies*, **14**, 169–179.

Mawby, R. I. (1977b) Kiosk vandalism: a Sheffield study, *British Journal of Criminology*, **17**, 30–46.

Mayer, H. (1954) Urban geography, in P. James and C. F. Jones (eds.), *American Geography: Inventory and Prospectus*, Syracuse, New York.

Mayer, H., and Kohn, C. F. (eds.) (1959) *Readings in Urban Geography*, University of Chicago Press, Chicago.

Mayhew, H. (1862) *London Labour and the London Poor*, Griffin–Bohn, London.

Mayhew, P. *et al.* (1979) *Crime in Public View*, Home Office Research Study No. 49, HMSO, London.

Mays, J. B. (1963) Delinquency areas: a re-assessment, *British Journal of Criminology*, **3**, 216–230.

Mellaart, J. (1967) *Catal Huyuk: a Neolithic City in Anatolia*, Oxford University Press, London.

Mellor, J. R. (1977) *Urban Sociology in an Urbanized Society*, Routledge and Kegal Paul, London.

Mercer, C. (1975) *Living in Cities*, Penguin Books, Harmondsworth.

Meyer, G. (1977) Distance perception of consumers in shopping streets, *Tijdschrift voor Economische en Sociale Geografie*, **68**, 355–362.

Michelson, W. A. (1970) *Man and his Urban Environment*, Addison–Wesley, Reading, Mass.

Ministry of Health (1962) *A Hospital Plan for England and Wales*, HMSO, London.

Mintz, N. L., and Schwarz, D. T. (1964) Urban ecology and psychosis, *International Journal of Social Psychiatry*, **10**, 101–118.

Moore, E. G. (1971) Comments on the use of ecological models in the study of residential mobility in the city, *Economic Geography*, **47**, 73–85.

Moore, E. G. (1972) *Residential Mobility in the City*, AAG Resource Paper 13, Washington.

Morgan, B. S. (1973) Why families move: a re-examination, *Professional Geographer*, **25**, 124–129.

Morgan, B. S. (1975) The segregation of socio-economic groups in urban areas; a comparative analysis, *Urban Studies*, **12**, 47–60.

Morgan, E. (1978) *Falling Apart: the Rise and Fall of Urban Civilization*, Abacus, London.

Morrill, R. L. (1973) Ideal and reality in re-apportionment, *Annals, Association of American Geographers*, **63**, 463–72.

Morrill, R. L. and Earickson, R. J. (1969) Problems in modelling and interaction: the case of hospital care, in K. R. Cox and R. G. Golledge (eds.), *Behavioural Problems in Geography: a Symposium*, Research Studies No. 17, Department of Geography, Northwestern University, Evanston, Ill, pp. 254–276.

Morrill, R. L., Earickson, R. J., and Rees, P. (1970) Factors influencing distances travelled to hospitals, *Economic Geography*, **46**, 161–171.

Morris, R. N. (1968) *Urban Sociology*, Allen and Unwin, London.

Morris, R. N., and Mogey, J. M. (1965) *The Sociology of Housing*, Routledge and Kegan Paul, London.

Morris, T. P. (1957) *The Criminal Area: a Study in Social Ecology*, Routledge and Kegan Paul London.

Morrissett, I. (1958) The economic structure of American cities, *Papers and Proceedings of the Regional Science Association*, **4**, 239–256.

Morse, R. M. (1971) Planning, history and politics: reflections on John Friedmann's role of cities in national development, in J. Miller and R. Gakenheimer (eds.), *Latin American Urban Policies and Social Sciences*, Sage, Beverly Hills, pp. 189–200.

Moser, C. A., and Scott, W. (1961) *British towns: a Statistical Study of their Social and Economic Differences*, Centre for Urban Studies, Report No. 2, London.

Moss, R. P., and Morgan, W. B. (1967) The concept of community: some applications in geographical research, *Transactions, Institute of British Geographers*, **41**, 21–32.

Muller, E. K., and Grove, P. A. (1979) The emergence of industrial districts in mid-nineteenth century Baltimore, *Geographical Review*, **69**, 159–178.

Mumford, L. (1938) *The Culture of Cities*, Harcourt, Brace and Co. Inc., London.

Mumford, L. (1954) The neighbourhood and the neighbourhood unit, *Town Planning Review*, 256–70.

Mumford, L. (1961) *The City in History*, Secker and Warburg, London.

Murdie, R. A. (1969) *The Factorial Ecology of Metropolitan Toronto, 1951 and 1961*, University of Chicago, Geography Research Paper 116.

Murphy, R. E. (1972). *The Central Business District. A Study in Urban Geography*, Longman, London.

Murphey, R. (1974) The city as a centre of change, West Europe and China, in D. J. Dwyer (ed.), *The City in the Third World*, Macmillan, London, pp. 49–66.

Murphy, R. E. and Vance, J. E. (1954a). Delimiting the CBD. *Economic Geography*, **30**, 197–223.

Murphy, R. E. and Vance, J. E. (1954a). A comparative study of nine Central Business Districts. *Economic Geography*, **30**, 301–336.

Murphy, R. E., Vance, J. E., and Epstein, B. J. (1955) Internal structure of the C. B. D. *Economic Geography*, **31**, 24–40.

Musil, J. (1971) Town planning as a social process, *New Atlantis*, **2**, 5–29.

Muth, R. F. (1969) *Cities and Housing*, University of Chicago Press, Chicago.

Myrdal, G. M. (1957) *Economic Theory and the Under-Developed Regions*, London.

Neenan, W. B. (1973) Suburban-central city exploitation thesis: one city's tale, in K. E. Boulding, M. Pfaff and A. Pfaff (eds.), *Transfers in an Urbanized Economy*, Wadsworth, Belmont, California, pp. 10–38.

Nelson, H. J. (1955) A service classification of American cities, *Economic Geography*, **31**, 189–210.

Nelson, R. L. (1958) *The Selection of Retail Locations*, Dodge.

Nëugarten, B. L. (1968) *Middle Age and Ageing*, University of Chicago Press, Chicago.

Newman, O. (1972) *Defensible Space*, Macmillan, New York.

Newman, O. (1976) *Design Guidelines for Creating Defensible Space*, US Department of Justice, Washington, DC

Newton, P. W., and Johnston, R. J. (1976) Residential area characteristics and residential area homogeneity, *Environment and Planning*, **A8**, 543–552.

New York Regional Plan Association (1968) *The Second Regional Plan*, New York.

Norman, P. (1975) Managerialism: a review of recent work. *Centre for Environmental Studies*, **cp 14**, London.

Northam, R. (1979) *Urban Geography*, John Wiley, New York.

Northern Economic Planning Council (1969) *An Outline Strategy for the North*, HMSO, London.

Nystuen, J. D. (1963) Identification of some fundamental spatial concepts, *Papers of the Michigan Academy of Science, Arts and Letters*, **57**, 401–422.

Nystuen, J. D., and Dacey, M. F. (1961) A graph theory interpretation of nodal regions, *Papers and Proceedings of the Regional Science Association*, **7**, 29–42.

Office of Health Economics (1974) *The NHS Reorganisation*, Studies of Current Health Problems No. 48, OHE, London.

Olsson, W. W. (1940) Stockholm: its structure and development. *Geographical Review*, **30**, 420–438.

Open University (1975) *All about BART*, Media Booklet for Block 8, Course D101, Open University Press, Milton Keynes.

Osofsky, G. (1966) *Harlem: the making of a Ghetto*, Harper, New York.

Pablant, P., and Baxter, J. C. (1975) Environmental correlates of school vandalism, *Journal, American Institute of Planners*, **42**, 270–279.

Pacione, M. (1974) Measures of the attraction factor: a possible alternative, *Area*, **6**, 279–282.

Pahl, R. E. (1965) Trends in social geography, in R. J. Chorley and P. Haggett (eds.), Frontiers in Geographical Teaching, Methuen, London, pp. 81–100.

Pahl, R. E. (1975) *Whose City?*, Penguin, Harmondsworth.

Pahl, R. E. (1977) Managers, technical experts and the state, in M. Harloe (ed.), *Captive Cities*, Wiley, London, pp. 49–60.

Pahl, R. E. (1979) Socio-political factors in resource allocation, in D. T. Herbert and D. M. Smith (eds.), *Social Problems and the City: Geographical Approaches*, Oxford University Press, London, pp. 33–46.

Palm, R. (1979) Financial and real estate institutions in the housing market: a study of recent house price changes in the San Francisco Bay Area, in D. T. Herbert and R. J. Johnston (eds.), *Geography and the Urban Environment*, Vol. 2, Wiley, London, pp. 83–123.

486

Palm, R., and Pred, A. (1976) A time-geographic perspective of problems of inequality for women, in K. P. Burnett (ed.), *A Social Geography of Women*, Maarouffa, Chicago.

Palmore, E. (1979) Predictors of successful ageing, *The Gerontologist*, **19**, 427–431.

Park, R. E., Burgess, E. W., and McKenzie, R. D. (eds.) (1925) *The City*, University of Chicago Press, Chicago.

Parkes, D., and Thrift, N. (1978) Putting time in its place, in T. Carlstein, D. Parkes, and N. Thrift (eds.), *Making Sense of Time*, Arnold, London, pp. 119–129.

Parr, J. B. (1978) Models of the central place system: a more general approach, *Urban Studies*, **14**, 35–49.

Pastalan, L. A., and Carson, D. H. (eds.) (1970) *Spatial Behavior of Older People*, University of Michigan.

Pattison, W. D. (1964) The four traditions of geography, *The Journal of Geography*, **63**, No. 5

Peach, G. C. K. (1966) Factors affecting the distribution of West Indians in Great Britain, *Transactions, Institution of British Geographers*, **38**, 151–163.

Peach, G. C. K. (1975) Immigrants in the inner city, *Geographical Journal*, **141**, 372–379.

Peach, G. C. K. (1979) Race and space, *Area*, **11**, 221–222.

Peach, G. C. K. Winchester, S. W. and Woods, R. I. (1975) The distribution of coloured immigrants in Britain. In G. Gappert and H. M. Rose (eds.), *The Social Economy of Cities*, Sage, New York, pp. 395–414.

Pearson, H. W. (1957) The economy has no surplus: a critique of a theory of development, in K. Polyani, C. M. Arensberg, and H. W. Pearson (eds.), *Trade and Market in Early Empires*, Free Press, New York.

Pederson, P. O. (1967) *Structure model study*, State Urban Planning Institute, Copenhagen.

Pederson, P. O. (1970) Innovation diffusion within and between urban systems, *Geographical Analysis*, **2**, 203–254.

Peet, R. (1975) The geography of crime: a political critique, *Professional Geographer*, **27**, 277–280.

Peet, R. (ed.) (1977a) *Radical Geography: Alternative Viewpoints on Contemporary Social Issues*, Methuen, London.

Peet, R. (1977b) The development of radical geography in the United States. *Progress in Human Geography*, **1**, 64–87.

Perroux, F. (1950) Economic Space, theory and applications. *Quarterly Journal of Economies*, **64**, 89–104.

Perry, C. (1939) *Housing for the Machine Age*, Russel Sage, New York.

Peterson, R., Wekerle, G. R., and Morley, D. (1978) Women and environments, *Environment and Behaviour*, **10**, 511–534.

Phillips, D. R. (1978) *The Utilisation of, and the Attitudes of the Public to, General Practitioner Services: A Geographical Study in West Glamorgan*, unpublished PhD thesis, University of Wales, (Swansea).

Phillips, D. R. (1979) Spatial variations in attendance at general practitioner services, *Social Science and Medicine*, **13D**, 169–181.

Phillips, D. R. (1981) *Contemporary Issues in the Geography of Health Care*, Geo Books, Norwich.

Phillips, P. D. (1972) A prologue to the geography of crime, *Proceedings of Association of American Geographers*, **4**, 59–64.

Piaget, J., and Inhelder, B. (1956) *The Child's Conception of Space*, Routledge and Kegan Paul, London.

Piché, D. (1977) *The Geographical Understanding of Children aged 5 to 8 years*, unpublished PhD, University of London.

Piché, D. (1981) The spontaneous geography of urban children, in D. T. Herbert and R. J. Johnston (eds.), *Geography and the Urban Environment*, Vol. 4, Wiley, London, pp. 229–256.

Pickvance, C. G. (1974) On a materialist critique of urban sociology, *Sociological Review*, **NS22**, 203–219.

Pinch, S. P. (1979) Territorial justice in the city, in D. T. Herbert and D. M. Smith (eds.), *Social Problems and the City: Geographical Perspectives*, Oxford University Press, London, pp. 201–223.

Pinder, D. (1978) *The Netherlands*, Hutchinson and Co., London.

Pirenne, H. (1925) *Medieval Cities*, Princeton University Press, Princeton.

de Planhof, X. (1959) *The World of Islam*, Cornell University Press, Ithaca, New York.

Poole, M. A., and Boal, F. W. (1973) Religious residential segregation in Belfast in mid-1969: a multi-level analysis, *Institute of British Geographers Special Publication*, **5**, 1–40.

Pooley, C. G. (1977) The residential segregation of migrant communities in mid-Victorian Liverpool, *Transactions, Institute of British Geographers*, NS2 364–382.

Popper, K. (1960) *The Poverty of Historicism*, Routledge, London.

Portes, A., and Browning, H. L. (1976) *Current Perspectives in Latin American Urban Research*, ILAS, Austin.

Potter, R. B. (1976) Directional bias within the usage and perceptual fields of urban consumers, *Psychological Reports*, **38**, 988–990.

Potter, R. B. (1977) Spatial patterns of consumer behaviour in relation to the social class variable, *Area*, **9**, 153–156.

Pownall, L. L. (1953) The functions of New Zealand towns, *Annals, Association of American Geographers*, **43**, 332–350.

Pred, A. R. (1964) The intra-metropolitan location of American manufacturing. *Annals, Association of American Geographers*, **54**, 165–180.

Pred, A. R. (1965) Industrialization, initial advantage, and American metropolitan growth, *Geographical Review*, **55**, 158–185.

Pred, A. R. (1966) *The Spatial Dynamics of US Urban-Industrial Growth 1800–1914: Interpretive and Theoretical Essays*, Cambridge, Mass.

Pred, A. R. (1967) *Behaviour and Location Part I*, Lund Studies in Geography Series B Human Geography No., 27, University of Lund, Sweden.

Pred, A. R. (1973) The growth and development of systems of cities in advanced economies, in A. R. Pred, and G. Tornqvist. *Systems of Cities and Information Flows. Two Essays.* Lund Studies in Geography, Ser. B. No. 38, Gleerup, Lund, 9–82.

Preston, R. E. (1971) The structure of central place systems, *Economic Geography*, **47**, 136–155.

Preston, R. E. (1975) A comparison of five measures of central place importance and of settlement size, *Tidjschrift voor Economische en Social Geografie*, **66**, 178–187.

Pringle, D. G. (1979). Unpublished discussion paper: The social indicators approach to the study of urban social problems. Social Science Research Council Seminar, *Social Geography and the City*.

Proudfoot, M. J. (1937) City retail structure, *Economic Geography*, **13**, 425–428.

Pyle, G. F. (1973) Measles as an urban health problem: the Akron example, *Economic Geography*, **49**, 344–356.

Pyle, G. F., and Lashof, J. (1969) The geography of disease and death in the two Chicagos, in P. de Vise (ed.), *Slum Medicine: Chicago's Apartheid Health System*, University of Chicago, Chicago.

Pyle, G. F., and Rees, P. H. (1971) Problems of modelling disease patterns in urban areas: the Chicago example, *Economic Geography* **47**, 475–488.

Queen, S. A., and Carpenter, D. B. (1953) *The American City*, New York.

Radford, J. P. (1976) Race, residence, and ideology: Charleston, South Carolina in mid-nineteenth century, *Journal of Historical Geography*, 329–346.

Radford, J. P. (1979) Testing the model of the pre-industrial city: the case of ante-bellum Charleston, South Carolina, *Transactions, Institute of British Geographers*, NS4, 392–410.

Raine, J. W. (1976) *Social Interaction and Urban Neighbourhood*, unpublished PhD, University of Wales (Swansea).

Ramsoy, N. R. (1966) Assortative mating and the structure of cities, *American Sociological Review*, **31**, 773–786.

488

Rapkin, C., and Grigsby, W. G. (1960) *The Demand for Housing in Racially Mixed Areas*, University of California Press, Berkeley.

Ratcliff, R. V. (1949) *Urban Land Economics*, McGraw-Hill, New York.

Redfield, R., and Singer, M. (1954) The cultural role of cities, *Economic Development and Cultural Charge*, **3**, 53–73.

Rees, P. H. (1979) *Residential Patterns in American Cities: 1960*, University of Chicago, Geography Research Paper 189.

Regnier, V. A. (1974) Matching old persons' cognition with their use of neighbourhood areas, in D. H. Carson (ed.), *Man–Environment Interactions*, Hutchinson and Ross, Pennsylvania.

Reilly, W. J. (1931) *The Law of Retail Gravitation*, Putman and Sons, New York.

Reissman, L. (1964) *The Urban Process: Cities in Industrial Society*, Free Press, New York.

Relph, E. (1976) *Place and Placelessness*, Pion, London.

Repetto, T. A. (1974) *Residential Crime*, Ballinger, Cambridge, Mass.

Rex, J. A., and Moore, R. (1967) *Race, Community and Conflict*, Oxford University Press, London.

Rivet, A. L. F. (1964) *Town and Country in Roman Britain*, Hutchinson, London.

Roberts, B. (1978) *Cities of Peasants*, Edward Arnold, London.

Robinson, V. (1979) *The Segregation of Asians within a British city: Theory and Practice*, Oxford School of Geography Research Paper, No. 22, Oxford University.

Robson, B. T. (1966) An ecological analysis of the evolution of residential areas in Sunderland, *Urban Studies*, **3**, 120–142.

Robson, B. T. (1969) *Urban Analysis*, Cambridge University Press, London.

Robson, B. T. (1973) *Urban Growth: An Approach*, Methuen, London.

Robson, B. T. (1976) Editorial introduction, *Transactions, Institute of British Geographers*, **NS1**, 1.

Rodwin, L. (1970) *Nations and Cities. A Comparison of Strategies for Urban Growth*, Houghton, Mifflin, Boston.

Rose, H. M. (1969) *Social Processes in the City: Race and Urban Residential Choice*, Association of American Geographers Resource Paper 6, Washington.

Rosow, I. and Breslau, N. (1966) A Guttman health scale for the aged, *Journal of Gerontology*, **21**, 556–559.

Rossi, I. (ed.) (1974) *The Unconscious in Culture: the Structuralism of Claude Lévi-Strauss in Perspective*, E. P. Dutton, New York.

Rossi, P. A. (1955) *Why Families Move*, Free Press, Glencoe, Ill.

Rossi, P. A. (1980) (reprint) *Why Families Move*, Sage, London.

Roterus, V., and Calef, W. C. (1955) Notes on the basic–nonbasic employment ratio, *Economic Geography*, **31**, 17–20.

Roweis, S. T., and Scott, A. F. (1978) The urban land question, in K. R. Cox (ed.), *Urbanization and Conflict in Market Societies*, Maaroufa Press, Chicago, pp. 38–73.

Rowles, G. (1978) *Prisoners of Space: Exploring the Geographical Experience of Older People*, Westview, Boulder, Col.

Rowntree, B. S. (1901) *Poverty, a Study of Town Life*, Macmillan, London.

Runciman, W. A. (1973) What is structuralism? in A. Ryan (ed.), *The Philosophy of Social Explanation*, Oxford University Press, Oxford, pp. 189–202.

Rushton, G. (1969) Analysis of spatial behaviour by revealed space preference, *Annals, Association of American Geographers*, **59**, 391–400.

Rushton, G. (1979) *Optimal Location of Facilities*, Compress, Hanover, New Hampshire.

Rushton, G., Golledge, R. G., and Clark, W. A. V. (1967) Formulation and testing of a normative model for the spatial allocation of grocery expenditures by a dispersed population, *Annals, Association of American Geographers*, **57**, 389–400.

Rutter, M., and Madge, N. (1976) *Cycles of Disadvantage*, Heinemann, London.

Ryan, A. (1973) *The Philosophy of Social Explanation*, Oxford University Press, Oxford.

Sabagh, G., Van Arsdol, M. D., and Butler, E. W. (1969) Some determinants of intra-urban residential mobility: conceptual considerations, *Social Forces*, **48**, 88–98.

Sack, R. D. (1972) Geography, geometry and explanation, *Annals, Association of American Geographers*, **62**, 61–78.

Sack, R. D. (1978) Geographic and other views of space, in K. Butzer (ed.), *Dimensions of Human Geography*, University of Chicago, Geography Research Paper 186, pp. 166–184.

Saey, P. (1973) Three fallacies in the literature on central place theory, *Tidjschrift voor Economische en Sociale Geografie*, **64**, 181–194.

Sauer, C. O. (1925) The morphology of landscape, *University of California, Publications in Geography*, **2**, 19–53.

Scarr, H. A. (1972) *Patterns of Burglary*, US Department of Justice, Washington.

Schaefer, F. K. (1953) Exceptionalism in geography: a methodological examination, *Annals, Association of American Geographers*, **43**, 226–249.

Schiller, R. (1974) Retailing and planning, *The Planner*, **60**, 744–749.

Schiller, R. (1975) The impact of new shopping schemes on shops in historic streets, *The Planner*, **61**, 367–369.

Schiller, R., and Lambert, S. (1977) The quantity of major shopping development in Britain since 1965, *Estate Gazette*, **242**, 359–363.

Schmid, C. F. (1960) Urban crime areas, *American Sociological Review*, **25**, 527–554.

Schnore, L. F. (1965) On the spatial structure of cities in the two Americas, in P. M. Hauser and L. F. Schnore (eds.), *The Study of Urbanization*, Wiley, New York, pp. 347–398.

Schutz, A. (1973) Problems in interpretive sociology, in A. Ryan (ed.), *The Philosophy of Social Explanation*, Oxford University Press, Oxford, pp. 203–219.

Scott, P. (1959) The Australian CBD, *Economic Geography*, **35**, 290–314.

Scott, P. (1970) *Geography and Retailing*, Hutchinson, London.

Sennett, R. (1973) *The Uses of Disorder*, Penguin, Hamondsworth.

Shannon, G. W. and Dever, G. E. A. (1974) *Health Care Delivery: Spatial Perspectives*, McGraw-Hill, New York.

Shannon, G. W., and Spurlock, C. W. (1976) Urban ecological containers, environmental risk cells and the use of medical services, *Economic Geography*, **52**, 171–180.

Shannon, G. W., Spurlock, C. W., and Gladin, S. T. (1975) A method of evaluating the geographic accessibility of Health Services, *Professional Geographer*, **27**, **1**, 30–36.

Shapcott, M., and Steadman, P. (1978) Rhythms of urban activity, in T. Carlstein, D. Parkes and N. Thrift (eds.), *Human Activity and Time Geography*, Arnold, London, pp. 49–74.

Sharpe, L. J. (1976) The role and functions of local government in modern Britain, Layfield Report, *The Relationship between Central and Local Government*, HMSO, London, pp. 203–220.

Shaw, C. R., and McKay, H. D. (1942) *Juvenile Delinquency and Urban Areas*, University of Chicago Press, Chicago (revised edition, 1969).

Shaw, M. (1977) The ecology of social change, Wolverhampton 1851–71. *Transactions, Institute of British Geographers*, **NS2**, 332–348.

Shaw, M. (1979) Reconciling social and physical space, Wolverhampton 1871, *Transactions, Institute of British Geographers*, **NS4**, 192–213.

Shemyakin, F. N. (1962) Orientation is space, in B. G. Ananyer (ed.), *Psychological Science in the USSR*, Technical Services, Washington, pp. 185–255.

Shepherd, I. D. H., and Newby, P. T. (1978) The Brent Cross regional shopping centre: characteristics and early effects, *Retailing and Planning Associates*, Corbridge, Northumberland.

Shepherd, I. D. H., and Thomas, C. J. (1980) Urban consumer behaviour, in J. A. Dawson (ed.), *Retail Geography*, Ch. 1, pp. 18–94.

Shevky, E. and Bell, W. (1955) *Social Area Analysis*, Stanford University Press, Stanford, California.

Shevky, E. and Williams, M. (1949) *The Social Areas of Los Angeles*, University of California Press, Los Angeles.

Short, J. R. (1979) Residential mobility in the private housing market of Bristol, *Transactions, Institute of British Geographers*, NS3, 533–547.

de Silva, S. K. (1973) *Socio-spatial Patterns of the City of Colombo: A Factorial Ecology*, unpublished M.Sc. thesis, University of Wales, (Swansea).

Simon, H. (1955) On a class of skew distribution functions, *Biometrika*, **42**, 425–440.

Simon, H. A. (1957) *Models of Man: Social and Rational*, Wiley, New York.

Simmons, J. W. (1968) Changing residence in the city: a review of intra-urban mobility, *Geographical Review*, **58**, 621–651.

Simmons, J. W., and Bourne, L. S. (1978) Defining urban places: differing concepts of the urban system, in L. S. Bourne and J. W. Simmons (eds.). *Systems of Cities: Readings on Structure, Growth and Policy*, Oxford University Press, New York, 28–41.

Sjoberg, A. (1960) *The Pre-Industrial City: Past and Present*, Free Press, New York.

Sjoberg, A. (1965) Cities in developing and in industrial societies, in P. M. Hauser and L. F. Schnore (eds.), *The Study of Urbanization*, Wiley, New York, pp. 213–263.

Sjoberg, A. (1973) In *Scientific American, Cities: Their Origins, Growth and Human Impact*, W. H. Freeman, San Francisco, pp. 25–39.

Skinner, G. W. (1965) Marketing and social structures in rural China. *Journal of Asian Studies*, **24**, 3–43, 195–228, 363–399.

Smailes, A. E. (1944) The urban hierarchy of England and Wales, *Geography*, **29**, 41–51.

Smailes, A. E. (1947) The analysis and delimitation of urban fields, *Geography*, **32**, 151–161.

Smailes, A. E. (1955) *The Geography of Towns*, Hutchinson University Library, London.

Smailes, A. E., and Hartley, G. (1961) Shopping centres in the greater London area. *Transactions, Institute of British Geographers*, **29**, 201–213.

Smith, B. A. (1973) Retail planning in France, *Town Planning Review*, **44**, 279–306.

Smith, C. J. (1980) Neighbourhood effects on mental health, in D. T. Herbert and D. M. Smith (eds.), *Geography and the Urban Environment*, Vol. 3, John Wiley, London, pp. 363–415

Smith, D. M. (1973) *The Geography of Social Well-being in the United States*, McGraw-Hill, New York.

Smith, D. M. (1974) *Crime Rates and Territorial Social Indicators*, Queen Mary College, Geography Occasional Paper No. 1, London.

Smith, D. M. (1977) *Human Geography: a Welfare Approach*, Edward Arnold, London.

Smith, D. M. (1979) The identification of problems in cities: applications of social indicators, in D. T. Herbert and D. M. Smith (eds.), *Social Problems and the City: Geographical Perspectives*, Oxford University Press, Oxford, pp. 13–32.

Smith, R. D. P. (1968) The changing urban hierarchy, *Regional Studies*, **2**, 1–19.

Smith, R. H. T. (1965a) Method and purpose in functional town classification, *Annals, Association of American Geographers*, **55**, 539–548.

Smith, R. H. T. (1965b) The functions of Australian towns, *Tidjschrift voor Economische en Sociale Geografie*, **56**, 81–92.

Snodgrass, J. (1976) Clifford R. Shaw and Henry D. McKay: Chicago criminologists, *British Journal of Criminology*, **16**, 1–19.

Stafford, H. A. (1963) The functional bases of small towns, *Economic Geography*, **39**, 167–175.

Stanislawski, D. (1946) The origin and spread of the grid pattern town, *Geographical Review*, **35**, 105.

Stea, D. (1973) Rats, men and spatial behavior, all revisited, *Professional Geographer*, **25**, 196–112.

Stea, D., and Taphanel, S. (1974) Theory and experiment in the relationship between environmental modelling and environmental cognition, in D. Canter and T. Lee (eds.), *Psychology and the Built Environment*, Architectural Press, London, pp. 170–178.

Stedman-Jones, G. (1971) *Outcast London: A Study in Relationships between Classes in Victorian Society*, Oxford University Press, Oxford.

Steigenga, W. (1955) A comparative analysis and a classification of Netherlands towns. *Tidjschrift voor Economische en Sociale Geografie*, **46**, 105–119.

Stewart, J. Q. (1947) Empirical mathematical rules concerning the distribution and equilibrium of population, *Geographical Review*, **37**, 461–485.

Stoddart, D. R. (1975) Kropotkin, Reclus, and 'relevant' geography, *Area*, **7**, 188–190.

Stokols, D. (1978) Environmental psychology, *Annual Review of Psychology*, **29**, 253–295.

Stone, M. E. (1977) The housing crisis, mortgage lending and class struggle, in R. Peet (ed.), *Radical Geography*, Maaroufa Press, Chicago, pp. 144–179.

Stouffer, S. A. *et al.* (1950) *Measurement and Prediction, Studies in Social Psychology in World War II*, Princeton University Press, Princeton.

Sturdivant, F. D. (1969) *The Ghetto Market Place*, The Free Press, New York.

Stutz, F. P. (1974) Interactance communities versus named communities, *Professional Geographer*, **26**, 407–411.

Suttles, G. D. (1968) *The Social Order of the Slum*, University of Chicago Press, Chicago.

Suttles, G. D. (1972) *The Social Construction of Communities*, University of Chicago Press, Chicago.

Swauger, J. (1978) Pittsburgh's residential pattern in 1815, *Annals, American Association of Geographers*, **68**, 265–277.

Sweetser, F. L. (1965) Factor structure as ecological structure in Helsinki and Boston, *Acta Sociologica*, **8**, 205–225.

Sweetser, F. W. (1942) A new emphasis for neighbourhood research, *American Sociological Review*, **7**, 525–533.

Taeuber, K. E. and Taeuber, A. F. (1965) *Negroes in Cities: Residential Segregation and Neighbourhood Change*, Aldine, Chicago.

Taylor, I., Walton, P., and Young, J. (1973) *The New Criminology*, Routledge and Kegan Paul, London.

Taylor, L. (1973) The meaning of environment, in C. Ward (ed.), *Vandalism*, Architectural Press, London.

Taylor, P. J. (1976) An interpretation of the quantification debate in British Geography, *Transactions, Institute of British Geographers*, **NS1**, 129–142.

Terjung, W. H. (1974) Climatic modifications, in I. R. Manners and M. W. Mikesell (eds.), *Perspectives on Environment*, AAG Resource Paper 13, Washington, DC.

Theodorson, G. A. (1962) *Studies in Human Ecology*, Row, Peterson, Evanston, IH.

Thomas, C. J. (1974) The effects of social class and car ownership on intra-urban shopping behaviour in Greater Swansea, *Cambria*, **2**, 98–126.

Thomas, C. J. (1976) Sociospatial differentiation and the use of services, in D. T. Herbert and R. J. Johnston (eds.), *Social Areas in Cities*, Vol. 2, Ch. 1, John Wiley, London, pp. 17–63.

Thomas, C. J. (1977) *Cooperative Society Superstores. Leo's Superstore: Pyle, Mid Glamorgan*, Retail Outlets Research Unit, Manchester Business School, Research Report No. 22, pp. 1–41.

Thomas, C. J. (1978) Retail change in South Wales—with special reference to redevelopment in small town centres, *Retailing and Planning Associates*, Corbridge, Northumberland.

Thomas, C. J., and Phillips, D. R. (1978) An ecological analysis of child medical emergency admissions to hospitals in West Glamorgan, *Social Science and Medicine*, **12D**, 183–192.

Thompson, F. M. L. (1977) Hampstead, 1830–1914, in M. A. Simpson and T. H. Lloyd (eds.), *Middle-Class Housing in Britain*, David and Charles, Newton Abbot, pp. 44–85.

Thompson, I. B. (1973) *The Paris Basin*, Oxford University Press, Oxford.

Thomson, J. M. (1977a) *Great Cities and Their Traffic*, Victor Gollancz Ltd., London.

Thomson, J. M. (1977b) The London motorway plan, in W. R. D. Sewell and J. T. Coppock (eds.), *Public Participation in Planning*, Ch. 1, Wiley, London.

Thorpe, D. (1968) The main shopping centres of Great Britain in 1961: their locations and structural characteristics, *Urban Studies*, **5**, 165–206.

492

Thorpe, D. (1974) *Research into Retailing and Distribution*, Saxon House, Farnborough, Hants.

Thorpe, D. and Kivell, P. T. (1971) *Woolco, Thornaby*, Manchester Business School, Retail Outlets Research Unit, Report No. 3.

Thorpe, D., and Rhodes, T. C. (1966) The shopping centres of the Tyneside urban region and large scale grocery retailing, *Economic Geography*, **42**, 52–74.

Thrift, N. (1979) Unemployment in the inner city: urban problem or structural imperative? A review of the British experience, in D. T. Herbert and R. J. Johnston (eds.), *Geography and the Urban Environment*, Vol. 2, Wiley, London, pp. 125–226.

Timms, D. W. G. (1965) The spatial distribution of social deviants in Luton, England, *Australia and New Zealand Journal of Sociology*, **1**, 38–52.

Timms, D. W. G. (1971) *The Urban Mosaic*, Cambridge University Press, London.

Timms, D. W. G. (1978) Social bases to social areas, in D. T. Herbert and R. J. Johnston (eds.), *Social Areas in Cities*, Wiley, London, pp. 35–55.

Tivers, J. (1977) *Constraints on Spatial Activity Patterns: Women with Young Children*, Department of Geography, King's College, London, Occasional Paper No. 6.

Tobias, J. J. (1976) A statistical study of a nineteenth century criminal area, *British Journal of Criminology*, **14**, 221–235.

Townsend, P. (1976) *The Difficulties of Policies based on the Concept of Area Deprivation*, Department of Economics, Queen Mary College, London.

Trowbridge, C. C. (1913) Fundamental methods of orientation and imaginary maps, *Science*, **38**, 888–97.

Trute, B., and Segal, S. P. (1976) Census tract predictors and the social integration of sheltered care residents, *Social Psychiatry*, **11**, 153–161.

Tuan, Y. F. (1968) A preface to Chinese cities, in R. P. Beckinsale and J. M. Houston (eds.), *Urbanisation and its Problems*, Oxford University Press, London.

Tuan, Y. F. (1975) Images and mental maps, *Annals, Association of American Geographers*, **65**, 205–13.

Tuan, Y. F. (1976) Humanistic geography, *Annals, Association of American Geographers*, **66**, 266–76.

Tunbridge, J. E. (1977) Spatial change in high-class residence: the case of Bristol, *Area*, **9**, 171–174.

Tuppen, J. (1980) Public transport in France: the development of the *Métro*, *Geography*, **287**, **65**, **2**, 127–130.

Tupule, A.H. (1973) *Forecasts of Vehicles and Traffic in Great Britain in 1972*, Transport and Road Research Laboratory Report, LR 543.

Turner, J. F. C. (1967) Barriers and channels and housing development in modernising countries, *Journal of American Institute of Planners*, **32**, 167–181.

Udry, J. R. (1964) Increasing scale and spatial differentiation: new tests of two theories from Shevky and Bell, *Social Forces*, **42**, 404–413.

Ullman, E. L. (1958) Regional development and the geography of concentration, *Papers and Proceedings of the Regional Science Association*, **4**, 179–198.

Ullman, E. L., and Dacey, M. F. (1960) The minimum requirements approach to the urban economic base, *Papers and Proceedings of the Regional Science Association*, **6**, 175–194.

United Nations (1974) *Concise Report of the World Population Situation in 1970–75 and its Long Range Implications*, UN, New York.

United States Bureau of the Budget (1964) *Standard Metropolitan Statistical Areas*, Washington DC, Government Printing Office.

Van Arsdol, M. D. Camilleri, S. F., and Schmid, C. F. (1958) The generality of urban social area indexes, *American Sociological Review*, **23**, 277–284.

Vance, J. E. (1966) Housing the worker: the employment linkage as a force in urban structure, *Economic Geography*, **42**, 294–325.

Vance, J. E. (1970) *The Merchant's World: the Geography of Wholesaling*, Prentice Hall, Englewood Cliffs, NJ.

Vance, J. E. (1971) Land assignment in pre-capitalist, capitalist, and post-capitalist cities, *Economic Geography*, **47**, 101–120.

Vance, J. E. (1977) *This Scene of Man*, Harper's College Press, New York.

Vance J. E. (1978) Institutional forces that shape the city, in D. T. Herbert and R. J. Johnston (eds.), *Social Areas in Cities*, John Wiley, London, pp. 97–125.

Veeder, N. W. (1975) Health services utilization models for human services planning. *Journal of the American Institute of Planners*, 101–109.

Victor, C. R. (1975) *The Changing Location of High Status Residential Areas on Swansea, 1854–1974*, unpublished B. A. thesis, University College of Swansea.

Vining, R. (1955) A description of certain spatial aspects of an economic system, *Economic Development and Cultural Change*, **3**, 147–195.

de Vise, P. (1971) Cook County Hospital: bulwark of Chicago's apartheid health system and prototype of the nation's public health hospitals, *Antipode*, **3**(1), 9–20.

Walker, R. A. (1978) The transformation of urban structure in the nineteenth century and the beginnings of suburbanisation, in K. R. Cox (ed.), *Urbanisation and Conflict in Market Societies*, Maaroufa Press, Chicago, pp. 165–212.

Wallin, D. R., Schmidt, C. G., and Lee, Y. (1975) A comparative analysis of black ghetto commercial structures, *Proceedings of the Association of American Geographers*, **7**, 259–263.

Wallis, C. P., and Maliphant, R. (1967) Delinquent areas in the county of London, *British Journal of Criminology*, **7**, 250–284.

Ward, D. (1964) A comparative historical geography of street-car suburbs in Boston and Leeds 1850–1920. *Annals, American Association of Geographers*, **54**, 447–489.

Ward, D. (1966) The industrial revolution and the emergence of Boston's Central Business District, *Economic Geography*, **42**, 152–171.

Ward, D. (1967) The Victorian slum: an enduring myth, *Annals, American Association of Geographers*, **66**, 323–336.

Ward, D. (1971) *Cities and Immigrants*, Oxford University Press, New York.

Ward, D. (1975). Victorian cities: how modern? *Journal of Historical Geography*, **1**, 135–151.

Watson, J. W. (1959) Relict geography in an urban community: Halifax, Nova Scotia, in R. Miller and J. W. Watson (eds.), *Geographical Essays in Memory of Alan G. Ogilvie*, Nelson, Edinburgh, pp. 110–43.

Webber, M. J. (1972) *The Impact of Uncertainty on Location*, MIT Press, Cambridge, Mass.

Webber, M. M. (1963) Order in diversity: community without propinquity, in Wingo, L. (Jr.) (ed.), *Cities and Space. The Future Use of Urban Land*, Johns Hopkins Press, Baltimore, pp. 23–54.

Weber, A. F. (1899) *The Growth of Cities in the Nineteenth Century: A Study in Statistics*, Macmillan, New York.

Weclawowicz, G. (1979) The structure of socio-economic space in Warsaw 1931 and 1970: a study in factorial ecology, in R. A. French and F. E. I. Hamilton (eds.), *The Socialist City*, Wiley, London, pp. 378–423.

Wellisz, S. H. (1971) Economic development and urbanization, in L. Jakobson and V. Prakash (eds.), *Urbanization and National Development*, Sage, Beverly Hills, pp. 39–55.

Wellman, B. (1978) *The Community Question: the Intimate Networks of East Yorkers*, University of Toronto.

Wheatley, P. (1963) What the greatness of a city is said to be: reflections on Sjoberg's pre-industrial city, *Pacific Viewpoint*, **4**, 164–188.

Wheatley, P. (1971) *The Pivot of the Four Quarters*, University of Chicago Press, Chicago.

Whitehand, J. W. R. (1967) Fringe belts: a neglected aspect of urban geography, *Transactions, Institute of British Geographers*, **41**, 223–33.

Whyte, W. H. (1957) *The Organization Man*, Anchor Books, New York.

494

Whyte, W. H. (1960) *The Organization Man*, Penguin, Harmondsworth.

Wild, M. T., and Shaw, G. (1979) Trends in urban retailing: the British experience during the nineteenth century. *Tijdschrift voor Economische en Sociale Geografie*, **70, 1**, 35–44.

Williams, O. P. (1971) *Metropolitan Political Analysis: A Social Access Approach*, Free Press, New York.

Williams, P. (1976) The role of institutions in the inner London housing market: the case of Islington, *Transactions, Institute of British Geographers* NS 1, 72–82.

Williams, P. (1978) Urban managerialism: a concept of relevance? *Area*, **10**, 236–240.

Wilson, A. G. (1970) *Entropy in Urban and Regional Modelling*, Pion, London.

Wilson, A. G. (1972) Theoretical geography: some speculations, *Transactions, Institute of British Geographers*, **57**, 31–44.

Wilson, A. G. (1974) *Urban and Regional Models in Geography and Planning*, John Wiley, London.

Wilson, R. (1963) *Difficult Housing Estates*, Tavistock London.

Wirth, L. (1928) *The Ghetto*. University of Chicago Press, Chicago.

Wirth, L. (1938) Urbanism as a way of life, *American Journal of Sociology*, **44**, 1–24.

Wirth, L. (1945) Human ecology, *American Journal of Sociology*, **50**, 483–8.

Wolpert, J. (1965) Behavioural aspects of the decision to migrate, *Paper and Proceedings of the Regional Science Association*, **15**, 159–169.

Wolpert, J., Mumphrey, A., and Seley, J. (1972) *Metropolitan Neighbourhoods: Participation and Conflict over Change*, American Association of Geographers, Resource Paper 16, Washington.

Wood, C. M., Lee, N., Lukes, J. A., and Saunders, P. W. (1974) *The Geography of Pollution: a Study of Greater Manchester*, Manchester University Press, Manchester.

Wood, P. A. (1974) Urban manufacturing: a view from the fringe, in J. H. Johnson (ed.), *Suburban Growth*, Ch. 7, John Wiley and Sons, London, pp. 129–154.

Yeates, M. (1965) Some factors affecting the spatial distribution of Chicago land values, 1910–1960, *Economic Geography*, **41**, 55–70.

Yeates, M. (1975) *Main Street: Windsor to Quebec City*, Macmillan, Toronto.

Yeates, M. (1979) The need for environmental perspectives on issues facing older people, in S. M. Golant (ed.), *Location and Environment of Elderly Population*, John Wiley, New York, pp. 71–80.

Yeates, M. H., and Garner, B. J. (1971) *The North American City*, Harper and Row, New York.

Young, M., and Willmott, P. (1957) *Family and Kinship in East London*, Routledge & Kegan Paul, London.

Zipf, G. K. (1949) *Human Behaviour and the Principle of Least Effort*, Addison-Wesley, Reading, Mass.

Zorbaugh, H. W. (1929) *The Gold Coast and the Slum*, University of Chicago Press, Chicago.

Zweig, S. (1942) *The World of Yesterday*, Vienna.

Author Index

Subject Index

508